W9-DCH-382

THE PEOPLE'S GUIDE
TO
Backpacking
Boating &

IN

MEXICO

by

Carl Franz

&

Lorena Havens

John Muir **Publications**

SANTA FE *NEW MEXICO*

Copyright © 1981 by Carl Franz
All rights reserved

Published by John Muir Publications
P.O. Box 613
Santa Fe, New Mexico 87501

Library of Congress Catalogue Card No. 80-84600

ISBN 0-912528-24-9

First Edition September 1981

Table of Contents

ILLUSTRATIONS

Cover, Illustrations and Graphics:
GABRIEL DAVALOS
México

Introduction

Discover Mexico

I balanced a fresh steaming cup of coffee on my knee, reaching out with my right hand to feed another careless fly to my favorite lizard. Toes the size of pin heads tickled across the palm of my hand as he crawled eagerly toward breakfast. The growing heat of the morning sun massaged my bare shoulders; beyond the edge of the woven reed mat, the sea curled lazily onto the sand, ruffled only by the fins of a passing school of hungry jacks. I eyed my fishing rod, propped beside the doorway of our thatched hut. As though reading my mind, Lorena's voice called from beneath the wide canopy of mosquito netting. "What are you working on today?"

I twitched guiltily, slopping coffee across the blank yellow pages of my notebook. My reptilian visitor scampered to safety in the thick palm fronds overhead.

"The Introduction," I answered, my attention suddenly drawn to a flurry of activity in the surf. A lumbering brown pelican, one of three who patrol this stretch of beach, neatly folded its long wings and plunged headlong into the face of a shimmering blue wave. I forced my attention back to the empty notebook.

"I'm thinking about 'Why Mexico?'" I called. "I'll open with a simple question. *Why camp in Mexico?*" Lorena's response was lost in the cries of excited seabirds following the pelican's example, wheeling and diving in frantic hunger. That huge awkward bird was my infallible guide; I knew the big fish had to be in close. I tossed the notebook aside and reached for my fishing rod.

"Why camp in Mexico?" is a question I've been asked hundreds of times but I have yet to come up with a snappy, one-line response. This entire book, in fact, is my detailed answer to that question. But if a picture is worth a thousand words, how many tightly packed volumes would it require to adequately describe just my mental images of Mexico's beaches? Can your imagination grapple with more than 6,000 miles of sun and wave washed coastline, the majority not only undeveloped but rarely visited by anyone but itinerant fishermen and the occasional sea turtle?

But beaches are just part of the answer. "Why Mexico?" also conjures up visions of languid tropical rivers, shrieking parrots, a cool, shaded desert canyon crowded with strange cacti, the eerie cry of a howler monkey prowling a long forgotten and ruined temple, the creak of saddle leather, the chill clarity of desert nights and the rich smell of corn tortillas heating on mesquite coals . . . all of the sights and sensations of Mexico's vast back country.

In spite of a long common frontier with the United States, Mexico remains one of the most 'foreign' countries in the world. It is also among the largest and most varied. An early explorer, overwhelmed by the impressions of his journeys in New Spain, described this new territory as "a topographic labyrinth." The climate, from polar on the highest volcanic peaks to tropical in the southern jungles and coastal plains, is equaled in variety by the people: Spanish culture has been liberally mixed over the centuries with that of native Indians, almost one hundred distinct groups, many of whom still conserve ancient languages, traditions and colorful costumes. It is no wonder that foreign visitors to Mexico often feel as though they've travelled to another time and to another world.

"Something for everyone" is a phrase that inevitably comes to mind when I try to describe camping in Mexico. For those who want rest and relaxation there are many beautiful, well-established trailer parks and campgrounds, not to mention popular — and safe — beaches where campers, foreign and Mexican, congregate every year. Or would you prefer something more adventurous? A dugout canoe voyage in one of the vast jungle lagoon systems in the state of Tabasco? Or a guided mule trek into the rugged sierras of Durango? A mushroom hunt in Oaxaca's cloud forests? Treasure diving on the barrier reef of Quintana Roo?

If your idea of Mexico comes from Late Night movies: endless cactus-studded deserts inhabited only by rattlesnakes and wild burros, you're in for a very pleasant surprise — in fact, many pleasant surprises. On a long hike in southwestern Mexico one of our companions stopped to take in a deep breath and to enjoy the staggering view. Cloud shrouded forests of pine, oak and madrona clung to row after row of rocky peaks, the slick black granite mirroring an intensely blue sky. "I just can't believe we're in Mexico!" our friend gasped. "It's a poor man's Nepal!" I couldn't resist the temptation to throw out one of my beloved statistics: "I bet you didn't know that only two other areas in the world have permanent inhabitants at such a high altitude — Bolivia and Tibet!" He seemed adequately impressed.

Fortunately this truly amazing country is not hidden halfway around the world but lies, literally, at our side, a neighbor easily accessible by car, RV, bus, train or plane. Travel to Mexico (and within) is not only simple but inexpensive, especially in comparison to Europe or South America. Mexico welcomes this attention and ranks tourism second only to petroleum in economic importance. The future for camping in Mexico is unmatched, and in spite of inflation, travel and camping there remain a real bargain.

But what about the other side of the coin? What of bandits and health problems? Does Pancho Villa's ghost still prowl and will "Montezuma's Revenge" be exacted on innocent tourists?

Unfortunately I can't magically dispel the popular bandit myth with reassuring words alone. The image of Mexico and its people has been badly warped by the American media; bandits live mainly in the frustrated imaginations of bored television producers and armchair travel writers. As for health hazards, with reasonable precautions (given in detail in this book) and self-restraint, no traveller should have unusual problems, whether it's with the 'trots', hangovers or sunburn.

Although I've often described this book to friends as "a personal guide to safe, inexpensive and easily accessible adventures," I hope that it proves to be much more. Use the book not just for camping but as an introduction to another way of life, to another people and to their personal and unique view of the world. The people of Mexico, in fact, are one of its greatest attractions and assets. Our memories after many years in Mexico are as filled with the faces of friends there as they are with palm-lined beaches and remote canyons. The custom of treating visitors with warmth and hospitality is taken quite seriously by Mexicans; those of us who enjoy it should return the favor in full measure. "Poor Mexico, so far from God and so close to the United States!" merits more than a superficial visit. Use this book as a starting point for your explorations and you'll find that fine sunsets and good camping are only the beginning.

Have a good trip,

Carl & Lorena

Carl Franz and Lorena Havens
Playa Salsipuedes, Mexico

Unknown Mexico: A Quick Glimpse

In spite of Mexico's popularity with tourists and campers, very little has been published, particularly in English, on the country's natural attractions and out-of-the-way places. Several portions of this book entitled *Unknown Mexico* attempt to fill in some of this missing and tantalizing information. Unfortunately, it is impossible to include detailed road and trail directions. In most cases, such directions are either not available or wildly unreliable. Use these sections, then, as hints toward making your own discoveries, rather than as firm goals.

In researching Unknown Mexico I found that the country's leading geography books disagree on many vital statistics, from the heights of volcanos and the lengths of rivers to the number of hotsprings (generally agreed, however, to number over 10,000). Whenever possible I have checked my information with several sources but don't be shocked by discrepancies between what you read and reality.

Listings in Unknown Mexico are by state (in alphabetical order). Browse through these sections as you travel and you'll soon form an image in your mind of an area's geography. Look at the climate table and charts. Does your road map show a route into a region of volcanos, rivers and high forests? If so, follow a whim and your imagination; much of Mexico's most exciting country is seldom visited, mainly because travellers simply fail to look for it.

I would like to extend my deepest thanks to Harry Moller: writer, explorer and founder of *Mexico Desconocido* magazine. Without señor Moller's very generous support and assistance, this valuable information could not have been included. His magazine represents an approach to travel and camping that all of us would do well to emulate.

Last, but certainly not least, I would like to ask *you*, the readers and travellers for whom this book was written, to contribute your own information about Unknown Mexico for future editions. Details of river running, hikes, fishing, mountain climbing, caves, rock formations . . . anything that you feel should be shared for our mutual enjoyment will be appreciated. Write directly to me, in care of John Muir Publications, Box 613, Santa Fe, N.M. 87501.

Acknowledgements

It is very difficult to adequately acknowledge the many people who have helped make this book a reality. In particular I want to thank Lorena Havens and Linda Reybine. Editors have an even tougher job than writers, since they get the worst of the work and the least of the praise and rewards. At the risk of being corny I can say with complete honesty that without their help this book would never have been completed. Their work and support can be read between every line.

In no particular order but with the deepest appreciation, thanks also go to: Steve, Eve, Susan Fiksdal, Lety, Jim Jameison, Grover, Tom and Bob, Geri and Carmen, Pierre, Nancy, Don, Cam, Scott S., Felisa, Doña Cuca, Dr. Matt Kelly, Judy B., Dave F., Diana, Bob "the Mayor," Betina, Casey Bill, Sandi, the Espinoza family, Michele Moore, Rick and Jackie, Don Marcos y familia, Doña Petra y Don Pancho, John and Mary, the fine people at the San Miguel de Allende library, the Secretary of Turismo office in Mexico City, Detenal, Toby Williams, for the use of his illustrations marked T.W. and the many readers of the People's Guide and fellow campers who gave suggestions and support throughout this long project.

A special *gracias y abrazos* to Gabriel Dávalos T., who gave us more than good art: his friendship, support and steadying sips of tequila.

"Luego me dijo un arriero, que no hay que llegar primero, sino hay que saber llegar."
Then a muleskinner told me, that you don't have to arrive first, but only have to know how to arrive.

popular Mexican ballad

¡Hay que ir a llegar!
You have to go to get there!

Mexican trail saying

We dedicate this book to Eve, John, Ken and Barbara: Friends, family and so much more . . .

1. Camping

"Now this is going to be *really* exciting!" I said, rubbing my hands together in anticipation. Lorena stood beside me as I smoothed the creases from a fresh gas station map of Mexico. The light from a gooseneck lamp illuminated the vast northwestern deserts.

"Brace yourself for some good news," I raised my right hand dramatically, "because our next camping trip in Mexico starts right *here*!" The tip of my pencil bore directly into the center of a large blank spot in upper Baja California.

Lorena's long blond hair swept the edge of the desk as she bent down for a closer look. "There?" I secretly rejoiced at the note of wonder in her voice. "What's *there*?" She asked, adjusting the lamp for a better view.

"Nothing!" I crowed. "Absolutely nothing! It's a barren godforsaken desert! The perfect place to get away from it all!" I hurried to erase the growing frown on her face. "It's actually the site of some little-known rock paintings. Petroglyphs or whatever they call them." I sensed resistance; Lorena's interest in prehistoric grafitti is even less than my own. "We'll only be there for a day or two. Just long enough to sort our gear before we start walking."

"Walking? Did you say *walking*?" she was looking out the front door, toward the VW van and the small mountain of camping gear she'd been packing for the trip south.

"Don't panic, okay?" I took a deep breath. On the desk before me lay a sheet of notes I'd scribbled while poring over my reference library of old magazines, outdated guidebooks, travel brochures and tattered, annotated road maps. "Here's the new Plan!" I cleared my throat.

"We drive the van to San Diego and leave it at one of those storage places. Then we load our gear into a cab and zip across the border. The cab takes us directly to the

Tijuana airport where we charter a small plane to drop us . . ." I jabbed the map with my pencil, "Right here, near the rock paintings. Got it so far?"

Lorena breathed heavily down my neck. "Will we be free falling or wearing parachutes?"

"Very funny! We'll land on a dirt road or a dry river bed, unload the kayak and head for the coast." I slashed a route directly across the rugged Sierra San Pedro Mártir to the rich blue water of the Sea of Cortez. Saint Peter the Martyr Mountains! What adventures awaited us in those . . .

"*Carl*?" Lorena's voice had that peculiar tone of patience-strained-to-exasperation she normally uses on large dogs and small children. "You want to leave our van? We've already blown our budget getting it ready!"

I jumped to my feet and crossed the small room, waving my arms toward the scene beyond the rain spattered front windows. "Think of the skin diving out there! The unspoiled coral reefs! The red snappers just waiting to be barbecued!" My hands slashed the air as I described the untrammeled beaches, the unmapped hiking trails, the unexplored side roads. Her eyes went to the tall dripping cedars bowing in the wind, the low scud of dark clouds obscuring a feeble yellowish sun; in short, a typical Pacific Northwest afternoon.

"Can't you see it?" I cried, "In Mexico it's all the right 'Un's-': uncrowded, unspoiled, undeveloped. Up here it's just the opposite: unavailable, unliveable, un . . ."

"*Stop*!"

I took a steadying breath. "Forget the van," I urged. "Didn't Cortez burn his ships to keep his men from thinking about going home? No, no!" I brushed away her look of horror. "We won't burn it, we'll just park it at the border. Here, look at this." I moved back to the map, tracing my finger down the eastern shore of the Baja peninsula.

"We assemble the kayak and paddle down the coast until we're across from Isla Del Tiburón, The Island of the Sharks! Incredible, isn't it? The diving must be absolutely . . ." I choked up, unable to restrain the finger that urged me farther into the Sea of Cortez. "Then it's straight across. Get this! *Across* the Sea, right into Kun Kaak Bay! From here it's a hop, skip and a few hundred miles to . . ." I skewered a large coastal city with my pencil, momentarily overcome by excitement.

"Wait a second, Carl," Lorena said, pulling the pencil from my hand. "We're going to do all this in August, right?"

I hesitated for a second. Every true adventurer must endure their Devil's Advocate, the sneers of the armchair skeptic. But Lorena has an irritating habit of supporting doubts with facts. I felt a shudder of dread; surely The Plan was flawless . . .

"August in Baja? Backpacking across the mountains and desert with a seventy pound folding kayak? What about our other gear? The tent? The stove? What about your precious reference library?"

"Well . . . I . . ." Inspiration struck, ". . . We'll be going light. *Very* light. A few fishhooks, some knives, a bag of salt, goatskins . . . er, canteens of water. The kayak won't be that heavy. We'll get good hats."

"Those are just annoying details," I continued. "We'll work them out later." I took a freshly sharpened pencil and resumed the journey. "From the coast we take a second class bus up into the highlands, rent a string of pack burros and . . ." My imagination leaped ahead to some remote mountain trail. I shifted my aching hips in the saddle, savoring the unforgettable odor of well oiled leather and freshly fallen pine needles. Juan, our trusty local guide, turned to me and said, his voice thick with excitement,

". . . the kayak?"

"What? What did you say?" Lorena's finger continued to tap relentlessly on the Sea of Cortez. Had I left her that far behind? "Oh, the kayak!" I gave a patient sigh. "We'll leave it somewhere. *¡No problema!* Hahahaha!"

She responded with a peculiar snort that I chose to ignore.

"Okay, then," I continued. "So it's up and over the Sierra and right to the headwaters of this *río.*" I dropped the Spanish word in for flavor; like a hot *jalapeño chile* in a cold soup it would surely fire her enthusiasm for The Plan. There was no doubt that she was interested; in fact, she couldn't seem to take her eyes off the thick dark line I'd drawn through one of Mexico's most rugged and unexplored mountain ranges. Hidden valleys, lost canyons, mysterious ruins!

"We assemble the kayak again, pay off Manuel . . . no, Juan, and strike off downstream toward . . ."

"Hold it!" There was a cutting edge to her voice now. "Who is Juan and how did another kayak get to the river? Did it walk?"

I let the full oppressive weight of my burdens push the sigh from my lungs. Doubt and ridicule! Give me scorpions and stinging ants instead!

"Juan is just an imaginary name for our guide," I explained, "and we aren't getting another kayak. Brother!" I took a deep breath. "We'll have our kayak transported by . . . er . . . overland." *Overland*! What a fine word! Overland to India! Overland to Afghanistan! Overland to . . .

"What month is all this taking place?"

I suppressed a cry of triumph; I had her now!

"Oh, I don't know exactly. There's no point in over-planning you know." I continued. "Looks like February or maybe . . . " I did a few quick calculations on the edge of the map. "May. Yeah, that's it. Next May."

Lorena gave me the dreaded Fisheye Stare, dull and lifeless, like a cod headed bellyup for the deep fat fryer. "There probably isn't any water in that river in May." she said, continuing in a flat discouraging monotone, "as it just happens to be in a high desert. That's why the map is yellow there. Sand." She gave me no opening, no chance of an early rainy season. "What would we eat?"

I thought for a moment. "We'll forage. Live off the fat of the land." Her eyebrows shot up. "There's more to those deserts than meets the eye. Plenty of kangaroo mice. See, you take a dozen fresh mice and you boil . . ."

"No water, Carl. There's no water." Her voice chipped away at The Plan like a jackhammer. Juan faded from the mountain trail; the Island of Sharks receded on the horizon, obscured by a fog of doubts . . .

"Don't panic!" I shouted, grabbing the map and holding it close to my face. "Just calm down!" My finger raced over roads, mountain ranges and rivers.

"Got it!" I quickly smoothed out the map. "We start here!" The pencil lead snapped on Puerto Barrios, Guatemala. "We drive the van to Chetumal, in Quintana Roo, put it into storage and zip to the beach in a cab. Then we kayak down the Caribbean coast all the way to Barrios. From there it's a quick hop up the Río Dulce and Lake Izabal, portage across the jungle in the Peten, pick up the headwaters of the Usumacinta and drift down to Villahermosa. From there it's just a few hundred miles to . . ."

"It'll be raining," Lorena said, "Try again."

The pencil cracked between my fingers.

"How about *this*?" I snarled. "We take a first class champagne flight to beautiful Acapulco and spend two glorious days and nights in the El Presidente hotel and then come home and *sit in the rain until next summer*!" My voice cracked beneath the sudden increase in blood pressure.

Lorena reached calmly for the sharpened half of my pencil, shot me a "Come now!" look and jabbed the point into the edge of the Pacific Ocean. "Let's start at the beach, right here," she said. "And just leave the plans for later. Take it as it comes. Wherever you go, there you are. Remember?"

I took a closer look. There were virtually unexplored mountains rising into the clouds not far behind that beach, not to mention a large lowland lagoon fed by a slow jungle river . . . We could make a small side trip, portage the kayak . . . *overland* . . . to the headwaters . . . meet Juan and the burros near these canyons, then . . .

Camping Questionnaire

So many people have asked for advice about planning a camping trip to Mexico that I've devised a quick questionnaire to reduce the confusion and frustration such decisions often involve. Answer these questions honestly and you'll find a clue, if not the solution, to the puzzle of 'where, when and how?'

How do you feel about going to Mexico?

Let's be honest; quite a number of people find the idea of travelling and camping in Mexico to be scary. What about bandits? Rip-offs? Getting lost? Maybe we ought to poke around the Adirondacks this year instead of exploring the Isthmus of Tehuantepec?

Relax, please; your trip will probably be highly interesting, entertaining and basically uneventful. Don't listen to 'horror stories'; more than four million foreign tourists visit Mexico every year and very few of them have serious problems. Camping will be easy and safe. Once you get to Mexico and see how many others are camping, you'll soon forget your early nervousness.

What do you enjoy (and not enjoy) on a vacation?

I ask myself this one when lounging in a comfortable daydreaming chair, preferably alone, with the lights dimmed. As soon as my eyes close I'm hiking some distant trail in the high *sierra* or casting a spoon into a school of hungry roosterfish. I *am not* driving in rush hour traffic in Mexico City or wearing out my hiking boots touring museums, souvenir shops and churches. I consider a camping trip to Mexico to be a period of relaxed self-indulgence, not a marathon bout of frantic sightseeing. I leave such important decisions as backpacking versus boating for a later stage of planning. It's an important choice, but as pleasurable as choosing between strawberry or chocolate ice cream.

What are your limitations?

How much time have you got? Two weeks? Better forget a camping trip in the Yucatan unless you can afford to fly there and back.

How's your bank account? Unless it's bulging, you'll want to calculate the unavoidable costs of round-trip transportation, equipment, meals and lodging. Money can be squeezed until it screams, but some expenses are inevitable. You have to eat, even if it's just beans and bananas.

Is your health a little shaky or your nerves shot after too many months without a genuine rest? If so, postpone the potentially grueling expedition through the Great Sonoran Desert and plan something genuinely relaxing: a tranquil camp on a mountain lake or a leisurely van tour through the southeastern jungles.

Are you itching for a genuine adventure and have more time and energy than money or fancy gear? You're lucky! Reach for the map; there are more camping trips waiting for you than can be fit into this lifetime. Continue daydreaming and we'll catch up with you later.

How will you be travelling to Mexico?

Unless you're certain that you'd prefer to drive south, consider backpacking, hitching rides (including on boats) or vagabonding via public transportation. Gasoline is still a bargain in Mexico but so is the cost of buses, trains, boats, small airplanes and cabs. How you arrive at the trail head won't greatly influence the actual hike. All you really need, for example, are two strong feet (or a tall burro as our friend Monoped Fred says) and a sense of adventure.

Camping and travelling in your own vehicle has definite attractions. "The highway is my home" strikes a romantic chord that I find almost irresistible. Postpone this decision until you've finished reading the rest of the book; there are just too many factors left to cover.

Will you travel alone? With children? With friends?

Camping alone in Mexico is a lot easier for men than it is for women. I wish it weren't true but *machismo* ruins camping for single women and even groups of women. The relentless attention of Mexican men can be unnerving, irritating and potentially dangerous. (See *Machismo:* Chapter 4.)

Children, however, find camping in Mexico a true delight. I wouldn't hesitate to take a child camping or even backpacking. Mexicans are literally crazy about kids. Friends who camp with children, from toddlers to teenagers, are almost unanimous in urging others to take their kids south rather than leaving them at home. Some kids make better campers than their parents, happily ignoring minor discomforts and taking pleasure in simple camp chores.

Camping with friends, especially on a trip to Mexico, requires cooperation and mutual respect. Sharing expenses is the most commonly used rationale for travelling in groups. In my opinion, it should be the last consideration, especially if you have any doubts that your group can get along under the normal pressures of travelling and camping in a foreign country. The few bucks you'll save by sharing expenses won't seem very important when your friends refuse to wash the dishes or complain endlessly about mosquito bites.

Pick your group carefully. Discuss plans in some detail and if conflict arises, don't be afraid to resolve it by saying, "Maybe I'll meet you in Mérida." I've seen a number of groups (including some I was in) explode under pressure. Don't let a break-up become irreconcilable, even if it means gritting your teeth and saying "see 'ya later" before it's too late.

Some people think group camping requires drinking out of the same cup and pitching tents side by side. I prefer cooperative camping, where each member of the group maintains a certain independence and respects the needs of others for moments of privacy, solo side trips and so on. (See *Group Hikes:* Chapter 3.)

Where does all of this leave me?

Now that your mind is swirling with even more questions and answers, it's time to get down to details. Read through the rest of this book for a better idea of what you'll actually find while camping in Mexico. Consult the maps, look over the climate information later in this chapter, visit the local library and thumb through guidebooks and photo books on Mexico. When a daydream begins to form, you're on your way.

Trip Planning

The more flexible your approach to travelling is, the more enjoyable and relaxed your trip is likely to be. I find tight planning and scheduling to be as restrictive and uncomfortable as tight underwear. Creative travelling is a constant process of information gathering and compromise: is it too hot for you in Guaymas? By all means go up to the cooler mountains rather than suffering. Have you overheard an interesting conversation about newly discovered ruins in Zacatecas and are tired of fighting the Easter crowds in Palenque? Go ahead, hop on a bus and make a side trip; no one is going to take you to task when you get home. It's your time and money.

Like most good lessons, I've learned to stay loose the proverbial hard way. My last fling at rigid planning began several years ago, when Lorena and I decided to hike the fabled Copper Canyon in north central Mexico.

Our first step was to gather information on the area. A cheap brochure printed by the Mexican Tourism Department was all we had to go on. It contained the usual vague description of spectacular natural wonders that can be applied to any extra-grand mountain, river, lake or valley. "Four times larger than the Grand Canyon" was as specific as it went but that was more than enough to maintain our interest. Suppressing a natural instinct to just go there and see the canyon for ourselves, we set about being methodical.

Three years later we had everything totally under control. I had fairly detailed maps of the area, copies of magazine articles by reliable authors, letters from friends who had visited the Canyon and were keen observers and journal keepers, and a painstakingly compiled mini-dictionary in Tarahumara, the Indian group we expected to meet.

As a final frosting on our preparations we made two backpacking trips in the Cascade Mountains of Washington state to test and evaluate our gear.

Just before we left home for the trip south I re-checked the weather records I'd compiled. An earlier attempt at exploring the *Cañon* had been cancelled because of late summer rain and mudslides. This year would be different; our visit would fall between the end of the rainy season and the beginning of cold winter weather. The bottom of the Canyon is semi-tropical but the upper elevations, where our trip would begin, can be very cold.

The train ride from Ciudad Juarez to Chihuahua passed in a blur of excitement. By the time we pulled into the station I was in a frenzy, leaping off the train almost before it had stopped. I took half a dozen steps, hesitated, then looked at my boots. They were white with fresh snow. We got back aboard the train, disillusioned and depressed.

As we rattled southward that night, we pored over the map, formulating a slight change in plans: we would hike the lower western slopes in Nayarit, far enough south to escape the cold, but high enough in elevation to avoid excessive heat. After a chilly wet summer at home we wanted time to acclimatize to warmer weather.

At the station in Zacatecas our plans ran afoul of the local newsboy, who thrust a paper in my face that proclaimed, "Floods Isolate Mountain Communities!"

"Stay loose!" I kept telling Lorena as we trudged the sidewalks to a hotel. A backpack is never heavier than when carried in a city.

"Why don't we just hike around here?" Lorena suggested that evening, as we pored over the map once again. "If it rains we can just zip back to the hotel and ride it out." On a normal hike at home such weather would be expected and hardly noticed; in Mexico, however, my tolerance for rain drops sharply. I agreed to her plan. What else was there?

The next morning, after a refreshing night's sleep, I sprang out of bed and reached for my hiking boots. I bent down to tie the laces, screamed once and fell backwards onto the floor.

"You have separated the tendons in the lower back," the doctor said, scribbling out a prescription for heavy pain killers and handing it to Lorena. I lay in bed, immobilized, grinding teeth as best I could without cracking a filling. "Stay loose!" I thought bitterly. "Just stay loose!"

Three days later we were down at the bus depot. The driver stared at me in frank admiration as I climbed aboard the bus carrying nothing but a paperback novel. Lorena brought up the rear, staggering under the weight of two full backpacks. I didn't bother to explain this apparently monumental feat of *machismo*; the effect of the painkillers made simultaneous walking and talking impossible. I eased myself gingerly into a seat and passed out.

I came to at the beach.

Typical Camping Trips

One of the simplest ways to plan a camping trip to Mexico is to follow in the footsteps of someone who has done a trip you would enjoy, too. If a friend gives a glowing report of hiking in Oaxaca or skin diving in the Caribbean, why not imitate them? You might not be breaking virgin trails but you'll have a good time. And later, when you've picked up more experience, confidence and information, you can strike off on your own.

When pumping friends for information, don't insist on exact details of how to get there and what to take. Your trip will be more challenging without an all-inclusive blueprint of what to expect. Get general directions on how to get there, plus suggestions on special gear (extra fishing lures) or clothing.

When a friend isn't available or you don't feel too enthusiastic about visiting their favorite trailer parks, read on for descriptions of trips we and many others have made. They cover just about every extreme of gear, time and money; with minor changes and the addition of your personal fantasies, these trips will keep you busy for years to come.

Shovel-And-Run

Reach for a snow shovel, open the trunk of the family car and start filling it up with gear. When it's full, slam the trunk lid, slide behind the steering wheel and head directly for Mexico. Anything that didn't cram in or was forgotten should be erased from your mind. A friend who shovels-and-runs every winter from a depressing job in the snowy Northeast says, "I usually forget half my stuff but when I get to the beach I'm *there*, on the beach!"

The bigger and more box-like your vehicle, the easier it will be to pack and to use as a mobile camp. That doesn't mean, however, that a VW Bug or Dodge sedan can't be used for a long camping trip. You can easily convert the family car to a temporary camper by using a car top carrier and by packing small equipment in strong cardboard boxes or light wooden fruit crates.

Many family car campers restrict their travelling as much as possible once they get to Mexico. This avoids the hassle of setting up and breaking camp every day. It also saves a good deal of money and wear and tear.

Shovel-and-run camping is favored by Mexicans, few of whom can afford the outrageous price of even the most basic factory made campers. *Gringos* who take the consumer approach to camping, with expensive and specialized equipment for the simplest camping chores (yes, they now sell a portable kitchen sink), would do well to observe how well Mexicans cope with basic gear in the same situation.

Gear Trippers

On the opposite end of the spectrum from shovel-and-run camping are gear trippers. Two friends are a good example: they spent three long years planning, assembling and testing a camping outfit that fit into a custom equipped four-wheel drive vehicle. Their truck could crawl over the Andes, their kitchen feed a small army and their treasure chests of spare parts and goodies would stock a sporting goods shop. Need a folding boat for a fishing trip? It's right here, neatly stowed under the portable darkroom. They have star finders, a mini meteorological station, a lavish medical kit, battery powered hand tools and last, but definitely not least, a new can of touch-up paint to match the pinstriping on the specially reinforced front bumper.

A place for everything and everything in its place. Which is how they spend their time while camping: keeping it all in place and operating order. To those of us who consider packing up to be a necessary evil, this style of camping seems very odd. It works quite well for them, however, which is what really matters.

Surprisingly enough, their attention to detail goes entirely out the window when the time comes to plan a travel route. They rely entirely on spur-of-the-moment decisions, whims, recommendations from other campers and the weather to guide them on their somewhat erratic journeys.

RV Nomads

There is a large and expanding mobile community of campers, mainly Americans and Canadians, who flee winter weather and take refuge in Mexico. These people prefer to travel in pickup campers, large vans, schoolbuses, motorhomes and trailers. Some drive directly to a favorite campsite in Mexico, park and don't move again until springtime lures them homeward. Others move from one familiar camp to another (often trailer parks), following a circuit that begins and ends at the U.S. border.

These campers are modern nomads, following fine weather and low prices, enjoying a carefree lifestyle that most people only dream of. Many are dedicated foragers, canning and preserving their own seafoods, fresh local fruits, meat or whatever else is a current bargain.

Because RV nomads are often retired, self-employed or temporarily between jobs, they are very good at stretching their *pesos* to the limit. They tend to complain loudly

about inflation but when pressed for an accounting, most admit that it's still far cheaper to travel and camp in Mexico than in the cold North.

"I guess you could call us hopelessly middle class," one woman said to me. We stood on a grassy campsite near the edge of a rather run-down trailer park. She and her husband had been coming there for years; their van was parked to take advantage of a fine view of the Pacific Ocean. A cool breeze ruffled the tarp they'd erected over a set of folding chairs and a card table. They had hammocks, a barbecue pit and even a badminton net. This was *it*, their home for six months of the year.

I looked around their camp again, thinking of people

at home, fighting winter weather, frustrated at rising prices and decreasing incomes, struggling to enjoy their free time or retirement.

"*Hopelessly* middle class?" I took another bite of her delicious fresh mango pie. "I don't think I heard you quite right."

Another retired gringo described his life style to me like this: "I've got my little boat (a twelve-foot aluminum runabout), my outboard and my fishing poles. "I drive around Mexico, looking for good water. When I see some, I stop. I hardly ever fish the same place for more than a week. I've been doing this for years now and still haven't seen it all. Probably never will."

He had an encyclopedic knowledge of Mexican fishing spots but getting it out of him would have taken bamboo splinters and truth serum. "Down Michoacán 'way," was about as close as he'd come to divulging information.

Vagabonding

I like advance planning once in a while, mainly because it offers such rich material for daydreaming when suffering the tedium of pre-departure chores. Some of our best camping trips to Mexico, however, have been inspired by bolts out of the blue. A friend casually says, "Have you ever been to . . . ?" or a magazine article refers to " . . . an otherwise deserted coastline". Our imaginations are off and running, filling in the exciting blanks.

Very little of Mexico's camping potential has been described in guidebooks. Large areas of the country, in fact, haven't been described in detail at all. The gaps between known tourist centers are large, you may never get off the well-beaten tourist tracks if you don't submit to the temptation of following a whim. Let inspiration be your best guide; even if you don't end up where you'd expected to, the experience should be more than satisfying.

A friend was trying to leave for Mexico but couldn't make up his mind where to go. He was sipping beer in a tavern one afternoon when a fellow offered to sell him a bag of opals. Their fiery glitter against the dark mahogany of the bar was very tempting, but even more tempting, in fact, downright irresistible, was the description of the remote mine in north central Mexico where they came from.

A month later our friend was there, buying a few opals from independent miners, camping and hiking in an area he'd have otherwise never visited. "Buying opals was just the excuse I needed," he said. "I can let you have a real deal on this one . . . "

Another friend loaded a canoe on top of his small Datsun pickup and headed for Mexico with a very simple plan: stop at the first tempting river, lake or lagoon and spend two weeks floating around.

Then, in the dreaded middle-of-nowhere, just one day south of the border, his truck had a stroke and died. "A beer truck stopped and the driver offered to tow me to a village. What a place! I mean it was *desolate!*"

A mechanic appeared (out of nowhere, of course) and looked the truck over. "One week, maybe two," he said. "I will have to take a bus to the border for parts."

Our friend considered the situation: he had limited time and very little extra money. His long awaited vacation was going to be spent in the desert rather than on the water, like it or not.

"I was pretty depressed," he said, "and spent a lousy night in the back of the truck. When I got up the next morning, really early, I could see the sun just peeking over some mountains. That gave me an idea."

He spoke to the mechanic and learned that a few poor *rancheros* lived in the mountains, occasionally visiting the village for supplies. "I had a backpack in the truck so it didn't take long to get ready. I bought a bunch of cigarettes to trade and give away and took off." He came back a week later. "It was the kind of trip I'd never do on purpose," he said, "but I sure learned a lot." He waved at his canoe. "One thing I learned was the value of water."

On our first ambitious hiking trip in Mexico we found that careful advance planning was almost useless (not that I don't still plan, just to be safe). We bought maps and compasses; dried large stocks of beef, vegetables and fruit; packed nuts, seeds, vitamins and staple foods and carried sufficient water for three days. Our packs would have staggered a Sherpa.

We chose a route that gringos had probably never before followed: it left the highway at the top of a major mountain range and plunged directly into the Unknown. Would we have to bushwhack? Were the deep *barrancas* (canyons) passable? The rivers? Would there be food? Grasshoppers to munch? Bark to gnaw?

The reality of the hike was much easier than our rather paranoid fantasies: trails crisscrossed the region, the obvious means of transportation and communication for the few thousand Indians and *campesinos* (country people) who had lived there for hundreds of years. Food was scarce, but not so scarce that we couldn't eat our fill of beans and rice. Water was precious, but by careful rationing we rarely dipped into our one liter reserve bottles. As for our maps and compasses — the sun sets in the west, more or less, and you follow the trail no matter where it goes, on the simple faith that it has to go somewhere.

Although this hike was unusual by gringo standards it was typical of Mexico: depending on local people for food, water and directions; never quite knowing where we were but not wondering too much; walking slowly but steadily, timing our pace to enjoy the countryside; gossiping with strangers, sharing their hospitality and answering endless shy questions, experiencing whatever was offered.

My favorite example of quick trip planning was related to me by a fellow I nicknamed Robinson Crusoe. He was walking idly down a street in San Francisco when a notice in the window of a travel agency caught his eye. It advertised a super-cheap round-trip fare to the Pacific coast of Mexico, an offer he literally couldn't refuse. Being self-employed and accustomed to poverty, he wasn't afraid to blow most of his remaining money on the ticket. There was just one catch: the last flight available left in eight hours.

"I bought my ticket and ran like a maniac for the nearest discount store," he said. "It took about an hour to buy bug dope, a frying pan, water jugs and a cheap sleeping bag. I didn't have any spare clothes with me, either, so I took a cab to the Goodwill and got a suitcase and a whole wardrobe. I climbed on the plane wearing an Al Capone style suit. It felt kind of ridiculous, but when I got to Mexico I traded the suit to a cab driver for a ride to a beach."

That's where I met him one morning, while I was beachcombing and surfcasting for a breakfast fish. He'd been on the beach for ten days, hiking back and forth to a nearby village for food and water, conserving his money as carefully as possible. "One catch on that discount fare," he explained, "was that I had to stay three weeks."

When he left, he traded his hobo camping outfit for a ride to the airport. For what most tourists spend on a long weekend he'd had a round-trip three-week vacation on a beautiful Mexican beach.

Backpacking Trips

It can be downright embarrassing to try to explain the term 'backpacking' to a typical *campesino*, who sees walking as a natural activity for the feet, rather than a sport. The situation only gets worse when you lay out the contents of your pack and try to explain what it all is and *why you need it*.

I once hiked with a Mexican who prepared for our trip by lifting a plastic shopping bag off a nail in his one room house, stuffing in a few kilos of tortillas wrapped in a rag, a block of homemade white cheese and a *jicara* (gourd canteen) of water. He stripped a threadbare blanket off the family bed, rolled it tightly around a spare shirt and tied it up with twine. *"Listo,"* he said, heading for the door.

"Ready?" How could he be ready? "What about your family?" I asked, "Don't you have to tell them we're leaving?" He shrugged.

"How long will we be gone?"

"A week or so," I answered.

"Then let's go," he said. "When I am not here, they know that I've gone."

This type of attitude takes years to acquire, years in which it helps to hand plow and plant mountainsides, to subsist on tortillas and beans and to shrug off hunger, cold and other discomforts. I was surprised, therefore, to run into a gringo who could give the most hard core *campesino* a run for his money.

This fellow travelled the back country with a heavy wool serape, a tattered airline flight bag and nothing else. He missed his dog, he said, but it had come with him once and had eaten a few too many convenient chickens.

His mode of hiking was as simple as his gear. "I make shortcuts between towns," he explained. "Look at a map. The highways go around things like mountains. That's where the hiking is good. I just draw a line between two places and sort of follow it."

His longest 'shortcut' had taken a full month, traversing one of Mexico's wildest mountain ranges. Needless to say, he depended heavily on the hospitality of local people. "I always try to do something in return, kind of like drifters during the Depression, who chopped wood for a meal or spaded the garden for a glass of milk. It always blows the *campesinos'* minds when I pitch in but they sure love it."

When I asked if he did much camping in the States he laughed and said, "Nope. I can't afford it."

Boating Ideas

"If I'd only brought a boat!" is a commonly heard lament among campers in Mexico. The popular image of Mexico as a dry, desert-like country is very misleading. There are thousands of miles of rivers and streams, hundreds of lakes, huge lowland estuaries and lagoons, all in addition to more than six thousand miles of ocean coastline. The boating possibilities are more than good; they are downright staggering.

Unfortunately, boats are an additional expense. They also tend to be bulky. These factors, combined with an unlucky series of maritime disasters, have often left Lorena and I high and dry, without a boat. This doesn't stop us from making boat trips, however. In fact, it sometimes makes boating even easier.

Our first boat camping trip in Mexico was completely un-plannned: the bus we were on stopped at a wide river so that the *chófer* (driver) could indulge in a lunch of huge fried crayfish. While he ate, Lorena and I sipped cold Pacificos and contemplated the flow of deep brownish water. Naked children dove from the sandy bank as a few fishermen puttered over nets in the shade of a nearby *ramada*. A young boy deftly maneuvered a shallow dugout canoe to within a few yards of where we sat.

"Where does the river go?" I asked. He made a vague motion downstream. "Where does the river come from?" An even vaguer motion upstream.

"How long is it? How deep?" A shrug. "Are there big fish?" His eyebrows lifted slightly. "Do you know the river?" His face brightened. Of course he knew the river, he answered, he lived here.

I looked at his canoe closely, then over at Lorena, sprawled in the shade. I looked back at the bus: it was hot in there and smelled of cranky babies and scorched brake linings. We were headed much farther south but still, a bird in the hand . . .

"Will you take us *río arriba*, upstream?" I kept my tone of voice very serious; as the Master of an independent vessel the boy deserved our respect. His face squirmed with excitement.

"*¿Quizás . . . ?*"

His vague "perhaps" was good enough for us. We notified the somewhat mystified bus driver that we were getting off, aided his helper to excavate our backpacks from the luggage compartment and returned to the riverbank. When the boy-captain saw our gear he summoned his father from the net mending shed for advice.

It took a while to explain to the father that we were basically just sightseeing, interested in the local forests, the birds, the strange wildlife that lived along the river. "*Hay mucha naturaleza aquí*" (There is much nature here), he agreed, finally proposing a simple voyage that would have his son home before darkness fell.

Agreeing on a fair price for the trip involved quite a lot of mumbling, long silences, whispered calculations and a general review of the plan: to take us upstream, drop us off for the night and return to pick us up the following afternoon. A sum was proposed: I gave it a minute of token thought and said, "*De acuerdo, gracias*" (Agreed, thanks.). Bartering for such transportation is a delicate business; I prefer to pay a little more for the security of knowing the other person is satisfied and will definitely fulfill the bargain.

Our departure was a minor local event. There were good natured warnings from the fishermen to avoid snakes, lions and *caimanes* (alligators); the captain's mother gave us a few oranges and a bundle of tortillas, and his father reminded him not to dawdle.

Finally, we shoved out into the main current, hanging onto the smooth sides of the canoe as the boy dug deep with his crudely carved paddle. Scarcely half an hour later we were there, a narrow but well drained gravel bar with a fine view of a wide quiet pool. We dumped our packs onto the ground, shook hands with the captain and prepared to set up camp.

The following twenty-four hours were spent quietly poking into the fringes of the forest for leopards, wading the shallows for freshwater clams and crayfish and fantasizing future trips. With our own boat we could reach the very headwaters, penetrate far inland, then glide lazily back downstream toward the mouth.

All too soon we heard the boy's cheerful, "*¡Buenas tardes!*" and boarded the dugout for the return trip to the highway. In less than an hour we were loading our gear aboard another bus, on the road again. By evening our voyage seemed dream-like, almost as though we'd never interrupted our journey south.

Two friends who camped on the shore of a large lake solved the no-boat problem in an ingenious way. They bought a tiny dugout from a local family, crammed themselves inside and took off towing their gear behind them, packed into a large galvanized washtub. The washtub immediately rolled over and sank. Undaunted, they salvaged their gear, dried it all out and had another brainstorm: fit the washtub inside a truck innertube.

"It looked pretty ridiculous," they said, "but we sure had a good time. We paddled very close to the shoreline, just in case of trouble, and made it around the lake in about ten days."

By the end of their strange voyage their fame had spread; they had no trouble reselling everything, including the innertube.

"It would have been easier if the washtub had a sail. Next time I'd rig up something, maybe some broom handles and a tarp, or some pieces of cane and a sheet of plastic . . . "

Camping In Mexico: What To Expect

Camping in Mexico is different in many ways from camping in the U.S. and Canada. Many Mexicans live all of their lives on a scale that we would consider 'camping'. Chopping firewood, hauling buckets of water, hunting, fishing, foraging herbs, wild fruits and vegetables and sleeping on mats or hard cots are all part of the normal daily routine for millions of people. Most Mexicans, especially *campesinos*, find it difficult to understand why rich people, and *we are rich by their standards*, deliberately regress from luxury to 'roughing it'.

Camping is therefore an unusual activity, something to be curious about. This curiosity makes 'getting away from it all' next to impossible. The farther you venture from cities and tourist areas, the more interesting you become to the local people. Your arrival in a remote area will not go unnoticed. People — curious, questioning, staring — seem to be everywhere. You're mistaken if you think that all of those interesting natives are just going to stand there like natural rock formations while you point and take photographs. You'll find, instead, that the interest is mutual. They'll soon be outstaring you and even taking *your* picture.

How To Find A Campsite

Mexico has yet to experience the incredible crowding that is so typical of popular campgrounds and wilderness areas in the U.S. Although some trailer parks and well-known beaches do fill up in the winter months, there are still countless places to camp, most of them free of charge. Where are these campsites and how do you get to them? There's just one sure way: *explore*.

Before you reach for your compass and pith helmet, keep in mind that many fine campsites can easily be found close at hand, rather than hidden deep in the jungle. Some of these are described later in this chapter; you'll soon be able to sniff out others on your own. One of the first lessons to learn about camping in Mexico, one that is quite contrary to camping in the U.S., is that almost any place can be used as a campsite, if only for a night or two. We've camped in dumps, town squares, churchyards, cemeteries, gas stations, traffic islands, construction sites; you name it, some hardy soul has probably tried it. When someone asks "*¿Qué hacen aquí?* (What are you doing here?), the obvious answer is "*Pasando la noche. ¿Está bien?* (Spending the night. Is it okay?). Rather than being treated like a dangerous weirdo or told to get moving, you'll probably get a smile and an offhanded, "Why not?"

Yellowfin tuna   *Atun*

Campsites can be divided into two basic categories: overnight and long term. Guidebooks and campground directories tend to list trailer parks and popular areas that offer little privacy or tranquility. These places may be convenient but for camps of more than a day or two we prefer an uncrowded beach, canyon or lake shore. Here's how we go about finding them.

Every traveller has their favorite spot, their private vision of Shangri-La at the end of a long dirt road. Some campers guard their favorite places with a degree of secrecy that would delight the CIA, others freely pass information along to anyone willing to ask. Trade-offs of information between campers are one of the most useful and reliable ways I know of to simplify the search for the perfect campsite.

Problems can arise, however, in defining the word 'perfect'. I've heard some of the best (in my opinion) camping areas in Mexico described as "bug infested," "absolutely no food or water" or "really not very interesting".

When talking with another traveller about campsites, frame your questions around your particular interests. If the mosquitoes are bad, how's the fishing? I can put up with a lot of scratching and blood donations if the bass are biting, too.

Is food available? What kinds? Lorena and I often live for months on the standard Mexican staples of beans, tomatos, onions, chilies, eggs and tortillas. Other people can handle about two days of this diet before they abandon Paradise for access to a supermarket.

By giving other campers a polite version of the third degree, tempered by liberal doses of tongue-loosening refreshments, you'll soon have the information you need.

WARNING: there is a rare breed of camper who can endure anything when one major requirement is met. We talked to three young men who had just returned from what they swore was the mythical Perfect Beach. They hardly looked like they'd been in the Garden of Eden; they were emaciated, terribly sunburned and seemed to suffer some type of group delirium. They talked just like Huey, Dewey and Louie.

I started off the questioning by asking the obvious: "How was the food at this beach?"

"It was . . . "

" . . . really awful . . . "

" . . . and expensive!" they said, shaking their heads in disgust as they went on to describe the diet of greasy fried bananas and watery beans they lived on. I asked about the weather.

"Too hot to . . . "

" . . . sleep and really . . . "

" . . . humid."

They told of the lack of shade, the brackish drinking water and the scorching sun. What about insects?

"Giant mosquitoes and . . . "

" . . . clouds of no-see'ums and . . . "

" . . . huge horseflies and scorpions!"

They lifted their shirts to reveal scars, welts, sores and infected swellings. Mosquitoes bit swimmers half a mile from shore. Well then, how were the local people?

"Nobody there . . . "

" . . . except for some . . . "

" . . . really mean cops!"

"Then what the hell were you doing there for six months?" I finally yelled.

"The surfing there is . . . " For once they were simultaneously speechless, "UNBELIEVABLE!"

Good campsites are not always obvious. Lorena and I were sitting in a small open air restaurant on the Pacific coast, speculating on possible camping places nearby. Because it had been an especially tiring day, half of it spent driving in low gear on a hot, dusty road, we decided to ask the owner for advice rather than explore.

"A place to camp?" she said, staring vaguely off into the distance as if we'd just ordered Oysters Rockefeller. "Well, I'm not really sure," she muttered, "but if we move these chairs . . . and that table . . . "

Five minutes later I carefully eased the van into the space she'd cleared behind the jukebox. A few late evening diners gave us rather odd looks as we prepared for bed in the center of the restaurant, but we were otherwise ignored. Once the jukebox had been unplugged, we spent a very pleasant night.

In the morning our 'landlady' graciously refused payment and invited us to return whenever we were in the area.

Don't fall into the habit of passing up any spot that doesn't meet *all* of your requirements. Once you've stopped long enough to do some additional exploring on foot, you'll often find that there's more to a place than first meets the eye. We once spent a week camped next to a high stone wall surrounding an ancient cemetery. What we'd chosen out of desperation at the end of a hard day's travelling, turned out to be the best campsite for miles around. It was within easy walking distance (easy coffin-carrying distance) of a village, convenient to a large network of interesting mountain trails, quiet during the daytime and dead quiet at night.

Friends of ours stumbled upon a beautiful secluded campsite overlooking a small beach. There was just one minor problem: the site could only be reached by a narrow, mile long footpath and they were travelling in a van. Rather than pass the place by, however, they came up with an ingenious solution. First, they went to the nearest village and found a shade tree auto mechanic who was happy to keep their van behind his shop for a small fee. Then they tracked down a farmer who 'leased' them a pack burro to carry their gear out to the campsite. Whenever they hiked into the village for food and water the animal was waiting patiently to haul everything back for them. The cost of parking the van and using the burro was more than made up by having access to a spectacular camp that otherwise would have been impractical.

Campers, travelling by public transportation or hitching often find themselves moving from one town to the next, making little contact with the countryside. This makes finding a campsite especially difficult. The answer is to leave your luggage at a hotel, trailer park, restaurant or bus baggage room and explore on foot, by local bus or taxi. The few dollars you spend on being driven to a campsite by *coche* (cab), will be quickly saved by cooking your own meals and paying for a room.

Asking Mexicans for advice on campsites seldom pays off. Because few Mexicans camp, they find it difficult to understand what you're looking for. It's usually simpler to find a reasonable spot and then ask for permission to use it.

Don't open your conversation with the landowner by bluntly asking, "Can we camp here?" This is too abrupt and doesn't give them a reasonable opportunity to size you up. Mexicans are very hospitable to strangers, *especially gringos*, but they prefer to avoid head-on questions and answers.

Start with the customary and very necessary polite greeting (see *Stranger In A Strange Land: Polite Phrases*), comments on the weather, etc. When the ice is broken, ask, "*¿Se puede acampar aquí?*" (Can one camp here?) or better yet, "*Por favor, podemos pasar la noche aquí?*" (Please, may we pass the night here?) The word *acampar*, to camp, may be as strange to them as tap dancing. If they look startled or dubious, I add, "*Tenemos todo. Cobijas, comida y cama.*" (We have everything. Blankets, food and bed.) This clarifies that you only want a place to camp, not a bed and meals. Unless the person recognizes camping gear they might assume that you come empty-handed.

Ask for permission even if you're sure it doesn't really matter that much. How can a rancher object if you occupy a few square yards of a vast *hacienda*? That's not the point; you are asking for two reasons: to be polite (which once again, is extremely important in Mexico) and to advise people of what you are doing there. If, by any chance, you are told that you cannot camp, *don't argue*. There's nothing to be gained.

You might be sitting in the middle of someone's cattle rustling operation or on the spot their grandfather saw Pancho Villa's ghost. Thank them for their trouble and continue on your way.

In many cases, there won't be anyone around to ask permission of. Don't worry; you'll have company before too much longer. An old man once asked us why we parked in the middle of a dusty field, in the hot sun, when there were fine shade trees a short distance away.

"*La barda,*" I answered simply. "The fence."

He reached into his pocket, pulled out a pair of much used wire cutters and proceeded to snip through the barbed wire strands, pulling them aside. "*Pasa,*" (Go, ahead), he said, graciously waving us toward the trees. After I drove the van through the hole in the fence he twisted the wires back together. "Just do the same when you leave," he said, continuing on down the road.

Beauty or Comfort?

Once you find an area you like, the decision of exactly where to park the RV or pitch the tent comes up. The more people there are in your group the more difficult this final selection can be.

Everyone wants both a beautiful and a comfortable campsite. Unfortunately the most comfortable places are not always the most aesthetically pleasing. You may find your group torn between camping in a grove of trees, with lots of shade and places to hang hammocks, or on the beach with beautiful sunsets and the sound of the surf. I advise you to choose in favor of the most comfortable location. You'll be able to enjoy everything much more: sleeping, the weather, the food and the view. If you have to stake your sleeping bag down to keep from sliding over a cliff, the fabulous sunrises and sunsets will soon begin to pale in comparison to a good night's sleep.

Camping on the beach means *sand*. Sand can drive you crazy. It will soon be in your hair, food, clothes, crotch, books and toothbrush. Beaches also mean salt mist from the spray of waves and the wind blowing over the sea. This mist makes things feel damp and slightly greasy and salty. Avoid this by camping back from the beach if possible. You'll be amazed at how much easier and more enjoyable your camp life will be.

Camping away from the beach often means, however, that you lose cooling breezes that keep the temperature down and act as a barrier against insects. We've camped on a number of beaches that were unlivable unless we set up right on the edge of the water. Trees and brush, no matter how skimpy, are favorite mosquito haunts, even on cool windy days.

If insects bother you, avoiding them is the most important thing you can do for your comfort and peace of mind. This is a good example of finding the proper balance between yourself and Mother Nature.

Protection from the sun is very important, both for comfort and health. Many careless *gringo* campers have been laid low by the stunning effect of the Mexican sun. If you can't erect an effective sunshade, you'll have to seek natural protection, such as a tree or overhanging cliff. If you do find a cliff, examine the possibility that it may quit hanging one day and start falling, either in pieces or all at once. I prefer a stout tree and on the coast of Mexico this almost always means a *coco* (coconut) palm.

When I first began camping in Mexico, I spent a lot of time underneath coconut palms, loafing in the shade without a care in the world. I was oblivious to the danger until a large green coconut fell one night, narrowly missing my head but knocking some sense into it. On calm nights when there isn't the slightest breeze to disturb them, you'll hear the palms shedding their heavy nuts. The thudding impact will give you an idea of what they can do to a human skull or the roof of a car. Fronds that are brown and obviously dead also have the disturbing habit of falling unexpectedly. One missed us by inches on a quiet afternoon, splattering into the middle of our camp kitchen like Sky Lab, destroying our lunch and a great deal of pottery.

Another potentially dangerous tree, the *Manzanillo*, is found on the Pacific coast. It is quite large, offers excellent shade and bears a distinctive fruit that resembles a small green apple. The fruit and the sap of the *Manzanillo* tree are poisonous. If you break off one of these 'apples' you'll notice a milky white fluid exuding from both the stem and fruit. This fluid will raise blisters on your skin and tongue if you taste it, as I did. This tree occasionally drips its poisonous sap onto the ground. Woe to anyone underneath.

Huts, Houses and *Jacales*

On beaches where palm thatched huts and sun shelters (*palapas*, *ramadas*) are built to accomodate Christmas and Easter crowds, traditional times for Mexicans to flock

to the sea, you can often just move into an empty one during the long off-season. Depending on how energetic and business-like the owner is, you may or may not be asked to pay rent. Bartering over the price, in a polite respectful manner, is al-most expected. If the rent asked is very high (the case during holiday periods) and you don't want to pay it, just go some-where else. We've seen a dis-turbing number of gringo camp-ers who seemed to think that they had a *right* to use a palapa, rather than an obligation to pay

rent when asked to. In most cases, the owners of these huts actually have to pay taxes on them, in addition to the not inconsiderable expense of building and maintaining them. Be cooperative rather than *chocoso* (aggravating), and it will benefit those who follow you.

Abandoned huts and shacks (*choza*, *jacal*) are uncommon, but you may occasionally come across one that can be used as a camp. Farmers who tend *milpas* (cornfields) a good distance from home will erect shelters, or even small houses, in the vicinity of their fields. When not in use as a dwelling they often double as *bodegas* (storerooms) for corn, fodder or tools. If you find one, use it with respect and take great care to avoid burning it down or otherwise damaging the contents. *Campesinos* do not like to camp in the open, under the stars, and will often direct hikers to shelters such as these. If you're lucky the fleas will have hitched a ride on a passing dog.

Food & Water

A good camping place will hopefully have access to food and water. Long trips for a few tomatoes and a canteen of water tend to get longer and less enjoyable, even though the campsite itself is otherwise ideal. If water isn't readily available you may decide to dig for it (see *Camping Skills*), but few campers will have the time or energy to plant a vegetable garden (though we've seen a few who have).

Since you'll save money and eat better by living on fresh rather than canned foods, you'll want to to be able to buy the basics: eggs, tomatoes, onions, beans, rice, bananas, salt and cooking oil. What a feast! Ask local people if they can sell you fruits, vegetables and eggs from their own homes. In isolated areas, it may take a week or more to establish good contacts. Allow for this by carrying sufficient food, booze and water to avoid running out completely.

Depending on local supplies has advantages other than convenience: you visit people's homes and *ranchos*, observing how they live and work, have the opportunity to practice Spanish in real situations rather than a classroom and generally learn to relate to Mexicans as people, rather than strangers.

Casual requests for a few eggs can lead to the most interesting and unusual side trips. You notice, for example, that a farmer has a few bee hives in his backyard. "*¿Hay miel?*" (Is there honey?) you ask, and before you know it, you're following him to his brother-in-law's *rancho*, to see if his hives are producing. Along the way the farmer suddenly plunges into the bushes and emerges a few seconds later, hands filled with a strange bittersweet berry. At the relative's *rancho* there is no honey but how about some fine fresh goat's cheese? How about a bowl of beans and a few tortillas? How about going hunting tonight? How about . . . "

The more remote your campsite is, the less you'll want to depend on tedious and time-consuming side trips to town for supplies. This is especially true when camping with a vehicle. "Let's run into the store for an onion," takes half a day or more and a tank of gas. Those are expensive onions. The solution is simple to describe but often not so simple to do. It requires a change in your attitude toward your vehicle and some very careful shopping.

First of all, prepare for long periods away from stores by making detailed lists of what you eat and drink. Don't forget things like cigarettes and vermouth; when you can't have a smoke or evening martini, you'll be back behind the wheel, barreling toward town.

We have a master list that ranges from spices and potatoes to midnight snacks and matches. When we stock up we use the list (if I haven't forgotten it at camp) as a reminder, adjusting the quantities according to where we're camping and for how long. (See Chapter 7 for more.)

Your second line of defense against trips to town is to learn how to stretch what you've got to the maximum or just plain do without. This rather obvious measure can have curious side effects: I've noticed, for example, that few cigarette smokers care to face the reality of how much tobacco they really consume over a period of time. The same goes for booze drinkers, candy bar munchers and other addicts. Be honest; if you don't buy enough now you'll just have to bite the bullet or resign yourself to another supply run.

Stretching supplies teaches that you can get along quite well on a lot less than you'd have thought. A friend who spent several weeks holed up on a remote beach told me, "I didn't really appreciate onions until I found myself using every bit, including the outer skin for soup stocks." When the bananas get black and mushy you won't just toss them into the garbage; you'll dig out the flour and make a delicious loaf of banana bread.

Local people are good examples of how to live on what's readily available, rather than what you *want*. Their diet may seem monotonous, but with a good dose of imagination you can make it quite satisfying.

In many popular camping areas people get together to make communal supply trips. I also like to take a local person with me, not only to give them a ride but to take advantage of their knowledge of where to shop and how much to pay for things. A guide can save hours of searching for things like purple sewing thread, size 29 *huaraches* (sandals) and all the other odds and ends that make these trips so . . . *interesting*.

One morning a fellow gringo camper asked for a lift to town. As we passed another camp, on the way out, a voice called, "Get some *bolillos* (bread rolls)! Get lots!"

"How many is 'lots'?" our passenger cried.

There was a moment of hesitation. "All they got!"

When Lorena and I returned from a long foray into the market we found our friend sitting in the back of the van, surrounded by bulging flour sacks stuffed with *bolillos*. There weren't just a lot of *bolillos*, there were several hundred, all freshly baked, without preservatives.

"Boy, oh boy, are those folks gonna be happy!" he chortled.

He is still remembered as the Bolillo Kid and the camping area is called Bolillo Flats.

Being offered gifts of food by local people is common, especially in areas where few gringos or other campers have visited. *Campesinos* are quite generous, though they can often ill-afford to give things away. If there is any doubt in your mind that something is being offered as a gift or is for sale, quietly ask, "*¿Cuánto le debo?*" (How much do I owe you?). The standard refusal of payment is a negligent wave of the hand or a simple, "*Nada.*" (Nothing.) Don't push it; you'll offend them by insisting on paying. A sincere "thank you" is sufficient or often a small gift in return. (See *Gifts:* Chapter 4.)

Privacy

Unless you camp in trailer parks and organized campgrounds, your camping trip will turn into a 'people' trip. There are ways, fortunately, to increase your privacy without hiding inside a tent or camping on the edge of an active volcano.

Children are the worst intruders. To avoid them, camp a long way from the nearest village or ranch. This certainly won't eliminate their visiting, but it will keep the smaller and less adventurous away. Large kids are notoriously difficult to avoid and if they have to walk five hot dusty miles to see you (which they will do), they'll probably make a day of it.

Avoid camping near trails, usually the major travel routes for local people.

Don't camp near obviously popular swimming holes. Half-used bars of soap, discarded scrubbers and picnic garbage near an inviting pool of water are sure indications that weekends and evenings will find it full of people.

After you've chosen a campsite, you can expect visitors within hours. On the coast and in the lower mountain areas, people are generally more open with strangers than the Indians of the high mountains. You can expect them to stare. Silent staring can be unnerving (to say the least), especially if you're alone or don't speak Spanish.

Armadillo   *Armadillo*

Paranoia may have you packing up and heading to a city if you don't understand — and try to accept — the reasons for this mute intrusion.

Natural curiosity is obviously part of the reason that people want to stare at you. You look funny. Your hair is weird, your clothes are strange, your car and all of your possessions are wonderful to look at and you talk and act like no normal person in the village. Curiosity itself isn't difficult to understand, but the open staring, pointing and excited talking over everything you unpack or do can be infuriating, and for some, quite frightening.

Why do they do it? How can they be so blatant and unembarrassed? The answer is that they have no feeling of "each man's house being his castle" and no concept of being rude or impolite merely because they are observing what you are doing in your house, i.e., car or tent.

You will probably notice that this open curiosity doesn't normally reach the point where visitors will walk uninvited into your camp or actually handle your things. When you want someone to 'come in', you'll usually have to invite them (women are especially shy). It's as if invisible boundaries marked off the area of your camp from the general community.

This attitude can best be understood by visiting one of your curious visitor's homes. Communal activity isn't restricted to work in the fields. The same people who sat twenty feet from your car for hours on end will crowd around the house you're visiting, hanging on every word of conversation between you and your hosts.

You'll inevitably have people around camp at mealtimes. I personally find it difficult to eat in front of a staring crowd. Remember, however, that your guests do not feel embarrassed by eating in front of others. This, too, is just another aspect of village life.

When the food supply or budget is limited, a polite offer to share a meal with ten or fifteen others could lead to a food crisis in your camp. We often invite Mexican visitors to eat and they almost always politely refuse or accept only a token bite as a gesture of appreciation. It's the other tourists who eat you out of house and home.

Maintaining normal activities (eating, reading, writing, lying around in your underwear) can be difficult with a group of people looking on but it can be done. Present a rather unexciting appearance and don't do anything hilarious or unexpected. Your visitors will eventually drift away or at least relax the intensity of their stares. Keep high interest items such as radios, tape recorders, cameras, fishing and diving gear and tools out of sight. This will greatly reduce their interest once visitors have recovered from the initial shock of your presence. If you decide, however, to do a tune-up on the car, you'll undoubtedly have them on the edge of their seats, if not right in the engine compartment with you, for the entire fascinating procedure, no matter how long it may take.

Once you've accepted the fact that there are going to be people around, take advantage of their curiosity to satisfy your own curiosity about them. I've found that there's no better way to get into an area than to select some likely looking person and suggest that I'd like to do something: go fishing, hunting, exploring, collect water or gather firewood. The response is almost automatically enthusiastic. This quickly changes the relationship from frustrated curiosity about you to a desire to demonstrate something that they can do, whether it's climb a coco palm or lead you to an interesting ruin.

By doing this, you'll soon have real friends among your guests. Rather than feeling a slight sense of dread at their visits, you'll begin to look forward to them.

Relax Your Mind

Camping in Mexico is very safe but it can, and very probably will, make you slightly nervous until you've become acquainted with the country and with new night sounds and activities. You don't expect a burro train of firewood to pass by your sleeping bag at three a.m., so when it does it'll probably startle you. It's not easy to be completely relaxed when you don't fully understand what everyone else is doing and why.

A friend had the wits scared out of him on his first night in Mexico. He camped in the middle of an old cornfield, well away from the nearest highway. He woke in the middle of the night to the sound of gunshots and shouts, some quite close. Before he could gather his gear and flee, a very excited *campesino* appeared, yelling something about rabbits. Once our friend had regained his composure, he realized that he'd camped in a popular hunting area; the farmer only wanted to know if he'd be interested in buying a freshly killed *conejo* (rabbit).

There are many strange things, at least strange to the complete newcomer, that can turn a perfectly normal day into a bad experience. Learn to accept the unknown gracefully. Don't be scared off by your own imagination; once your fears have been explained you'll be glad you didn't overreact. (See *Scared? Bandits?* and *Rip-offs:* Chapter 4.)

"Carl! Stop! Hold it!" Lorena's voice held a note of panic; she braced herself against the dashboard, twisting her long legs protectively toward her chest.

"Oh, relax!" I laughed, "We can go through *anything*!" To prove my point I eased my foot off the brake and allowed the van to roll down the crumbling sand bank and into the shallow river. "Take it easy!" I mocked, pushing the gas pedal toward the floor. "Did Cortez take it easy? Did Livingstone? Sheckleton? Hell no!" I continued, fighting the steering wheel. "If they'd had VW vans their motto would have been the same as mine. Floorboard it and pray!"

"OH, NO!"

"I told you so," Lorena sighed.

The man with the team of oxen was a real godsend; I didn't bother to ask what brought him to the middle of nowhere. For the price of a few smiles and a ham sandwich, his tractor-like beasts dragged us from deep water to the edge of the road.

"Now it'll be 'way past dark before we get back to camp," Lorena predicted, adding a gloomy, "as bad as this road is we'll be lucky to make it by midnight."

I gave myself several hearty mental kicks for persuading Lorena earlier in the day not to pack everything up and load it into the van. We were camped in a very remote forest, far from the nearest village and *ranchos*. The place was about as deserted as Mexico ever gets. "It's just a quick side trip," I'd said. "Don't be so paranoid. We've been here almost a month and nobody's touched a thing." She'd finally agreed and our tent, bedding, fishing gear, kitchen, clothing and a lot of odds and ends were left under the pine trees.

"You've just got to learn to relax!" I'd urged as we drove away that morning in search of . . . in search of . . . "What is it we're looking for?" I asked, swerving around a fallen tree.

"A river," Lorena answered.

"Oh yeah, right. A river. Anyway, don't worry about our stuff; it's perfectly safe."

". . . and my shawl and the quilt Mother made me and my . . ."

"Oh, knock it off!" I moaned. "What's the difference now? It's too late to cry over sour milk!"

"Spilt milk," Lorena corrected. "And what about your precious radio?"

I didn't answer; twenty futile searches of the bare tent had failed to turn up my beloved multi-band receiver. Tension in the Middle East! Double digit inflation! Presidential hopefuls to issue statements! How could they keep the world running without me listening in, whispering solutions and consolation? My radio!

Let's try to blank this whole disaster from our minds," I suggested sadly. "There's still a couple of blankets in the hammock. I could use some sleep."

". . . blankets in the hammock . . ." I jerked up and shook Lorena awake. "Hey look," I said. "What kind of rip-off is this? Why did they take my radio, the fishing stuff and your things but not our new blankets? Or the hammock?"

"And they left the stove," Lorena added, "but it hasn't been cleaned for a month. The cups and plates are missing, though, and they weren't washed after breakfast. It doesn't make much sense."

I lay back, puzzled. Come to think of it, the tent had not only been empty; it had been suspiciously *clean,* not a trace of the dirt and pine needles Lorena and I had long ago given up on keeping out.

"Just hope they don't come back for the leftovers," I said, falling quickly toward sleep.

I woke quite early, slipped into my pants and stepped out of the tent, eyes bleary from lack of sleep.

"*¡Buenos días amigo!*"

I leaped into the air, turning toward the voice behind me. A dark, thickly mustachioed man stood a few yards away, a heavy rifle slung casually over one shoulder.

"Domingo!" I laughed with relief. "How are you?" The man was a local small-time rancher and farmer, barely able to support his family in spite of unflagging energy and devotion to work. I was surprised to see that he appeared nervous, shifting awkwardly from one foot to the other.

"We heard you return last night," he said quietly, "but did not want to call out. I hope you were not surprised . . ." His voice trailed off as he waved his hand toward our camp. "We came yesterday," he continued, "so that my wife could meet your *señora*. But you were not here." He smiled awkwardly, perhaps as amazed at the length of his spiel as I was. Like most *campesinos* he normally spoke in reluctant monosyllables.

"We waited for you until dark," he continued, "but then we thought, 'What if someone comes by while our friends are not here?'" His embarrassment increased at having obliquely accused a non-existent person of evil thoughts. "So we stayed." He took a deep breath. "Then my wife got cold and we thought . . ."

"To borrow blankets?" I suggested.

"*¡Eso es!*" Domingo cried, obviously relieved, "That's it!" He looked back toward the trees behind us. "We also borrowed a few *trastos,* dishes, to prepare the food we had brought. The children were hungry." His eyes narrowed as his 'confession' drew to a close. "I did not want to sleep in your tent so we carried your nicest things with us." He gave me a "that's it!" shrug, then stood silent, waiting for my reaction. I could hear the subdued chatter of children in the bushes, waiting for his signal. I thought of what I'd promised to do if I caught my radio thief . . .

"Lorena!" I called, "Time to get up! We've got company for breakfast!"

Where Not To Camp

Moonshine and Marijuana, Heroin and Sindicatos

Like most of the so-called Third World, Mexico receives little attention from the U.S. media, other than reports of new oil discoveries, cataclysmic earthquakes and especially violent crimes. A shoot-out between feuding farmers becomes an 'agrarian war' or 'popular uprising,' angry marijuana growers sniping at U.S. supplied helicopters that spray dangerous chemicals on their fields and villages constitute 'organized resistance' and so on, until the reader cringes at the thought of what awful things lie in wait just south of the border.

Relax. Use these reports to start the barbecue or to hang on a nail in the outhouse. Yes, there are incidents in Mexico that can be called "violent" and groups of people (most wearing government uniforms of one stripe or another) who settle sticky problems with guns, but very few tourists or campers will even be aware that anything unusual is going on, much less be involved in it.

The greatest potential hazard for a camper in Mexico is to stumble into a place or situation where any stranger, gringo or otherwise, is unwelcome. This means dope fields (marijuana or opium poppies), moonshine stills and local disputes or feuds. This latter category is difficult to define; it can be a boundary dispute between rural *ejidos* (agricultural cooperatives) or a confrontation between big landowners and landless farmers. Look for large groups of angry men waving banners. Camp somewhere else.

When travelling in the back country be receptive to discreet warnings about where and where not to camp or hike. A Mexican friend warned us repeatedly about leaving the trail in one area, insisting that, "there is nothing interesting in the bottom of these canyons." With a little persistence I learned that there was something very interesting in those shady hollows: a lucrative and very illegal series of mescal stills, cranking out tax free moonshine.

Remote fields of marijuana or opium poppies are often jealously guarded by armed farmers. These fields are quite well hidden, especially after the considerable success of the Mexican/American drug eradication programs of the past few years. If you should stumble upon a field of dope, turn around quickly and leave. It takes a real persistence and foolhardiness to find these fields and the problem will rarely arise for even the most adventurous camper.

Although drugs can be cultivated almost anywhere, the state of Sinaloa is considered the opium and heroin capital of Mexico. I know a number of gringos who have hiked in the mountains of Sinaloa without problems, but I cannot recommend it unless you travel with a local guide. This area is also frequently embroiled in disputes between farmers and *latifundistas* (big landowners, agri-business). If you camp there, keep your ear to the ground and your mouth shut on the subject of dope or politics.

The state of Guerrero is somewhat notorious in Mexico, both for dope cultivation and the traditional resistance of its people to domination by the federal government. A school teacher who protests inhumanly low wages, for example, will be branded a 'guerrilla' and hounded into the mountains. We and many friends have camped in the state of Guerrero and thoroughly enjoyed it. Once again, your own awareness and attitude will be your best protection against potential trouble.

Other potentially 'dangerous' areas are borders between the U.S. and Mexico and Mexico and Guatemala. The border patrols of all three countries will be curious about anyone camping, hiking or boating very close to the boundary line. Bureaucrats take borders seriously so you'd better humor them and observe the law carefully. With what seems to be an inevitable increase in political violence in Guatemala, that border will undoubtedly attract more attention from both Mexican and Guatemalan authorities in the future. Have your papers in order and don't stray from one country into another.

The following suggestions about places *not to camp* are included to help you sleep better and not because they involve any threat to your safety. If you camp in one of these places, as we often do, you will be quite secure.

Hills
Because of the number of large trucks and buses on the highways at night, most without mufflers, a hill is a lousy place to get any sleep. We once camped in a place even worse than a hill — a tiny valley between *two* hills. The little valley, so peaceful in the early afternoon, was just one-eighth of a mile long and represented over twenty shift points for the trucks and buses, which passed at the rate of one every thirty seconds. Each shift brought forth a great diesel blast amid awful rasping of gears.

Markets
If you find yourself forced to camp in town, don't park near the market, even if it appears to be deserted and quiet. In the very early morning all of the trucks that kept the people camped on hills awake will roar into town and head for the marketplace. If the sound doesn't ruin your sleep, exhaust fumes will.

Archaeological sites
These used to be favored campsites and for very good reasons: they are interesting to

visit, especially at the crack of dawn or during the full moon when camera-toting, children-dragging tourists are safe in their hotels. These sites are often near water or a prominent hill. Recently, however, the government has been cracking down on camping in or near ruins, not without justification. Vandalism, theft and amateur efforts to make midnight archaeological discoveries really irritate authorities and authentic archaeologists. Another reason, particularly exasperating for the cops, is having people in various states and stages of 'non-ordinary reality' tripping around, over and off of pyramids, temples and tombs. It may be groovy to get stoned and play Mayan priest at the full moon, but the caretakers and police never seem to quite appreciate what you're doing.

Camping is still allowed in some sites, but in general it is either officially prohibited or really frowned upon (which means you may or may not be run out in the middle of the night, depending on the local attitude and your behavior).

Where To Camp

Camping becomes much easier in Mexico once you've accepted that almost any place can be a campsite.

Although your mode of travel will affect your choice to a certain degree, most of the places described here will do just as well for backpackers as van nomads and motorhomers. With increased crowding and steadily higher prices for spaces in trailer parks and campgrounds, the alternatives become even more attractive for campers on a limited budget.

Note for motorists: no matter where you camp, park with the assumption that your trusty vehicle will have either (or, heaven forbid, both) a flat tire or a dead battery in the morning. Better safe than sorry, especially if it means jacking the car up in sand or pushing it backwards onto the highway. The simple precaution of turning the vehicle around, so that it points in the direction you plan to leave, can greatly simplify a push start. Flat tires in Mexico are as inevitable as hangovers after a union hall beer bust so park on level solid ground whenever you have the chance.

Wide spots

It's the end of a hot day and you have mild diarrhea. You haven't eaten enough and would like to cook a good dinner, but you've fought off hunger with a few hits of cheap *tequila*. Suddenly you feel the crushing hand of exhaustion descending on your mind and body. Your companions are getting bitchy because they spotted a good place to stop forty miles back but you casually said, "I feel like I could drive all night."

The smartest and most logical thing to do under these circumstances is to find a wide spot — any place wide enough to get safely off the highway and to forget about plugging along until something better shows up. It probably won't anyway, so you might as well stop before you're totally done in.

Side roads

These all lead to that mythical Perfect Camping Spot, or at least it seems as if they should. Of the hundreds of side roads that we've followed, most led to sand traps, mudholes, ranches and towns. Unlike secondary roads in the U.S., which seem to go everywhere and nowhere in particular, Mexican side roads almost without exception lead to a group of houses or a small town. If you park your car so that it blocks the road, even though you'll swear it's a long abandoned trail, you can almost count on being blasted out of bed by someone leaning impatiently on the horn of a bus or truck.

Schoolyards and Soccer Fields

You may be driven by desperation to stop near a town or village. The edge of a schoolyard has the advantages of being reasonably level and away from noisy *cantinas* and drunks. The big disadvantage, however, is that schoolyards, playfields and soccer fields are frequented by packs of children and there's no place to take a crap. Don't park in front of the goal posts of a soccer field or you might block (as we did) an early morning game.

Dumps

I personally rate camping in dumps over all other desperation campsites. Unlike dumps in the U.S., full of rotting food and rats, Mexican dumps are usually dry and pest-free. This is undoubtedly because few Mexicans throw away food. Dumps are often just flat areas close to the road, easily spotted by swirling heaps of discarded plastic. Not AAA approved but very convenient.

Gas stations

You can try this but it doesn't always work: buy some gas and then ask the attendant if you can park behind the station for the night. Noisy, bright and smelly but better than nothing.

Cemeteries

Don't drive right into the cemetery, but don't make yourself conspicuous by attempting to hide. Park openly near an entrance and you won't arouse suspicions of grave robbery. I enjoy an early morning tour of the graves and have never met with any resentment or hostility from caretakers or visitors. Cemeteries are quiet, peaceful places with very few curious children hanging around, especially after dark.

Police station

Some people seem to think the police (being public 'servants') should know of good camping places and they make a point of going to the station to ask where they can park. The usual answers seem to be: 1) a motel, 2) a parking lot or 3) nowhere, get out of town. But there is a sneaky way to avoid actually going to the station while still enjoying its protection. (I don't recommend this if you look very weird.) Find the police station and then park on the street, just around the corner. The logic to this is that criminals and drunks won't be lurking so close to the cops. I prefer the cemetery or a good dump.

Street

When you have to park on a city street, do it very near the *plaza* in a small town or on a side street in the business district of a larger town or city. If anyone asks what you're doing, give them a simply honest answer — *durmiendo* (sleeping). Believe it or not, even the police won't think that this is unusual.

Bridges

Most bridges are of fairly recent construction. Some replace ferries and others have been built to replace damaged or washed-out bridges. At one or both ends of many newer bridges, you should see the remains of a road leading to the old bridge or ferry landing. These roads are often quite indistinct, particularly at night. They are good camping places, especially as many lead right to the water's edge.

Quarries and dirt pits

Found along many highways, especially if they are new or recently repaired. Be very careful when driving into one of these places; some are soft, others have huge pits and trenches that you could easily fall into at night. If it has been raining, send someone ahead to check the firmness of the ground, but don't forget that a human foot may not make a dent where a heavy truck would sink.

Friends of ours almost lost their van when the wife walked ahead into an old excavation, on what looked and felt like wet grass. It turned out to be a bog, covered with a very thick layer of floating weeds. It took a passing team of oxen and a large gang of men to save the van from sinking.

The Desert

Many unfortunate travellers reach the desperation point and say, "Hell, let's just pull off into the desert!" And there they remain, stuck in sand or dust, until help comes along.

The desert is occasionally made of rocks, but more often of something softer. In winter, when rain is extremely rare, the ground dries out quite hard in some spots and quite soft and dusty in others. During the rainy season it may be surprisingly soft, even after a light sprinkle.

Always check the ground directly in line with where you're moving the vehicle before leaving the road. Once off the road, don't get carried away and race a quarter of a mile onto the desert just because the ground is solid; it may suddenly change to a sand trap.

Among the worst hazards of off-the-road driving in the desert are cactus spines and thorns. They are all over the ground and will play hell with your tires.

Dams

We rate *presas* as choice camping areas. Keep your eyes peeled for signs; many dams and reservoirs are poorly marked, even on major highways. Hundreds of dams have been built around the country and there are many more to come as the government fights a chronic shortage of surface water.

Don't pass up a sign for a *presa* just because you can't see something on the order of the Grand Coulee or an obvious lake. In the desert, for example, dams are often hidden in narrow canyons. One of our favorites is tucked away near the edge of a vast barren plain, one of the most unappetizing camping areas imaginable. But inside the foothills there's a deep stream shaded by ancient mesquite trees, draining a large artificial lake. The water is full of fat bass and attracts a wide variety of birds and wildlife.

Most dams have the added attraction of large flat spaces to park on, the result of excavations and earth-moving during their construction. (See *Unknown Mexico: Lakes & Dams* at the end of Chapter 6.)

Hotsprings and Spas

There's nothing quite like camping with natural hot water for bathing and relaxing in. Mexico has thousands of hotsprings and spas, some developed centuries ago by Spanish colonists, others just bubbling out of the earth in a completely natural state.

Look for *aguas termales*, *aguas medicinales*, *aguas calientes*, *ojo de agua* ('eye of water' also means spring or pool), *balneario* (bathing spot, not always hot water) or *atotonilco*, a Mexican word often given to villages or ranches located on or near hotsprings.

Some spas have been developed to the point where you might not want to camp near them, especially on weekends when the crowds flood in. In most cases, however, a large developed hotspring won't be the only one around. Smaller springs serve *campesinos* and their families at a fraction of the price of fancier facilities. There probably won't be an organized campground so just ask for permission to camp.

Backpackers should keep their ears open for mention of hotsprings. We've often been directed to hot water while walking in the back country. After a hard day on the trail the pleasure of a bath is indescribable. (See *Unknown Mexico: Hot Springs* at the end of Chapter 8.)

National Parks

Camping facilities within Mexican parks, reserves and national monuments are very rare. Most are closed to the public at night and camping is *prohibido*. If you are told that you can't camp, it is sometimes possible to make a 'special arrangement'. This means you pay the guard or caretaker to forget that you are there. (For a complete list of national parks, see *Unknown Mexico: National Parks* at the end of this chapter.)

Pipeline Access Roads

Mexico's booming petroleum and natural gas industry has spawned a number of pipelines, some hundreds of miles long. During their construction, access roads are bulldozed for heavy equipment and maintenance crews. These narrow dirt roads are poorly marked but you'll soon learn to recognize the coded signs and the word *PEMEX*, for *Petróleos Mexicanos*, the government oil monopoly. Some pipeline roads cross private property, but if you carefully close cattle gates you probably won't bother anyone by camping.

Microwave Stations

There are hundreds of *microondas* towers (also called *estación de microondas*, microwave station), most located on top of mountains or large hills. These are federally operated relay stations for television and communications. Since the towers and their relay transmitters are deliberately built on the highest ground, they make fine campsites. Most are reached by cobblestone roads, narrow and often quite steep. Think twice before attempting one of these roads in an extra-large or underpowered vehicle.

Microondas stations are not usually staffed, so you probably won't find anyone around to ask permission to camp. Please keep in mind, however, that they are government property. If campers are suspected of vandalism or mischief (like climbing the tower to howl at the moon), they will undoubtedly be closed to the public, in the same way that many parks and archaeological sites have been put on limited access.

Parking Lots

Public parking lots are not common but privately operated *estacionamientos* (parking lots) are found in all cities. Some accommodate half a dozen cars, others are huge. Security varies quite a bit and in many of the loosely supervised lots, a deal can be made to allow discreet camping. It may not be very scenic but it beats sleeping on the street.

If you want to get an early start, don't allow your vehicle to be blocked in by others. We once had to delay our departure for three hours because a careless client had neglected to leave his keys with the attendant. The problem was finally solved Mexican fashion: by grabbing half a dozen passing men and asking them to carry the keyless car to another spot.

Public Buildings

In small towns and villages, especially remote ones, you may be allowed or invited to sleep in the school, jail, town hall or other communal building. I've tried them all and what they lack in comfort is more than made up for in hospitality. In one case, however, we accidentally stirred up a hornet's nest by accepting a young school-teacher's offer of a bed on the classroom floor. We had just begun to lay out our sleeping bags when the teacher began apologizing profusely for embarrassing us, but the truth was, he'd overstepped his authority and had to withdraw the offer.

We had been hiking for several hours and were extremely tired. Even the bricks looked tempting. Could we sleep in front of the school? No, he said, that would offend the town elders, since it would appear that they were being inhospitable. The problem, in fact, was that the townspeople had built the school without federal assistance but the teacher was a federal employee, not a local man. Did we understand?

Sure, sure. But where could we sleep?

Four hours later, after a town meeting, we were invited by the elders to sleep on the *porch* of the school, satisfying all factions. Once this minor problem had been resolved they kept us awake half the night asking eager questions about our *tierra* (land, home country).

Hotels and Motels

Camp in a hotel? Now that prices have risen in many fancy trailer parks, campers are coming full circle and discovering that hotels can be a bargain. This is especially true if you stay in a very cheap hotel, one that qualifies as 'roughing it' even in a camping sense. Erratic water and lighting, minimal security and privacy, strange noises at night — sound like your last camp in the woods? That, in fact, is the best way to relate to a cheap hotel room, as a temporary camp until something better comes along.

Lorena and I deliberately stay in very cheap hotels when we want to do our own cooking (in the room on a back-packer's stove), our laundry (in the bathroom or out back, by the mana-

Double yellow headed Amazon Parrot

Loro

ger's chicken coop) and generally rest for a night (on our backpackers' mattresses) without paying through the nose. Fancier hotels don't approve of camping activities; in the cheaper ones they rarely even notice.

Cheap hotels are also good campgrounds for car campers. I prefer to look for a larger hotel that has fallen on hard times, one that has plenty of room in the central patio to park long-forgotten carriages and horse-drawn wagons. In one hotel of this type the desk clerk agreed that the decaying patio was even more comfortable than the decaying rooms, and let us camp for the night providing we didn't build a camp fire or hang our laundry in plain view.

Some motels now offer camping and RV hook-ups, others are open to suggestion: "May we pitch our tent near those trees?" Unfortunately, motels are still considered something of a novelty in Mexico and few of them are bargains.

Trailer Parks & Campgrounds

If you've been staring over the hood of your pickup truck for five days and have a bad case of white-line fever, the thought of another night in a dump or soccer field might not click. It's time to look for a trailer park. Have a shower, do your laundry, shoot the breeze with other travellers and start poring over the map to plan the next leg of your adventure.

Although trailer parks are relatively common on major highways and around popular tourist towns (usually right on the outskirts), they are few and far between elsewhere. Look for roadsigns that show a picture of a small house trailer or the words *Parque de Trayler, Trailer Parque, Campamento* (campground), *Remolques* (trailers) or any other combination of English and Spanish that may have struck the management as appropriate. My favorite, one that has puzzled Mexicans and gringos alike is *"Trailer Parque y Cabañas de Tio Tom de Mark Twang"*. It's hard to pass up a place like this.

Although campground directories published in the U.S. list trailer parks in Mexico, the information is often hopelessly out of date by the time you get there. (See *Appendices: Recommended Reading*.) The most reliable information will be given by other travellers. I've seen quiet, funky trailer parks transformed almost overnight into camper concentration camps, offering noise, crowding and overloaded facilities for outrageous prices. Another park, half a mile away, might be all but deserted and much more of a bargain. Some trailer parks specialize in RV campers and won't allow a mere tent camper to pitch their miserable shelter, other campgrounds are that in name only, with nothing offered but bare ground. It makes life interesting; like everything else in Mexico trailer parks are not stamped out of one mold.

People who travel in large motorhomes, with house trailers or in converted buses and large pickup trucks find that trailer parks save them untold hours of frustration when it comes time to park for the night or longer. Some Mexican trailer parks (especially near the beach) specialize in long-term visitors. Reservations are made well in advance and jealousy over prized parking spots provides rich gossip material for the afternoon cocktail crowd. Check into their special long-term rates and compare the possibilities of camping somewhere nearby for free; many of these trailer parks charge whatever the traffic will bear, plus several pesos.

Trailer parks can be very convenient for backpackers. When you're travelling by thumb or public transportation it is often difficult to break out of the highway/town/ hotel & restaurant cycle. Camping out will save you money and though a trailer park may not be much when compared to the wilderness, it offers certain advantages.

Hitching rides in a trailer park is very easy. If you're like us and don't really enjoy hurtling down the highway on the back of an overloaded banana truck when it's possible to hitch with more moderate *gringos,* you'll find trailer parks invaluable contact areas. If you speak Spanish, make it known among the other campers; many will spontaneously offer a lift in exchange for having a translator in the back seat. Your ride will probably end that night in another trailer park, giving you the option of continuing on with the same people or changing your route and travelling with others.

Women find trailer parks to be good protection against the hassles of *machismo*. It's usually easy to find someone who will make side trips with you, if only to offer the protective coloration of being with others, rather than alone.

Rip-offs are rare in trailer parks and backpackers will appreciate the convenience of being able to leave their camp and gear without too much risk. It is best, however, to

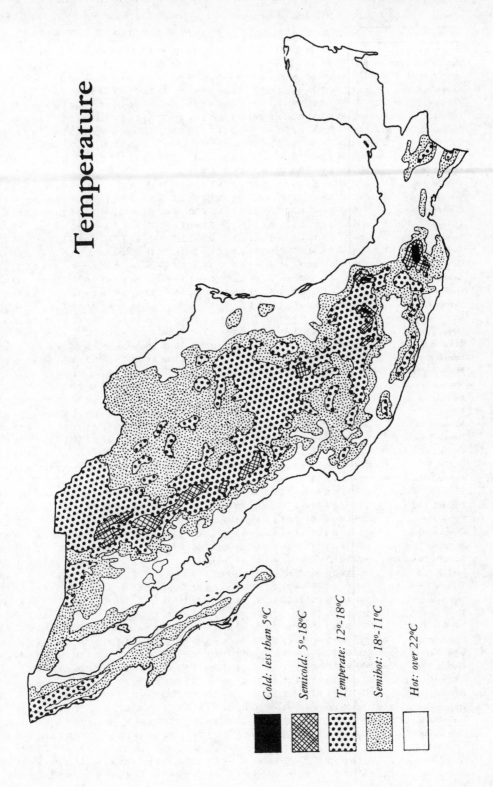

Temperature

Cold: less than 5°C

Semicold: 5°-18°C

Temperate: 12°-18°C

Semihot: 18°-11°C

Hot: over 22°C

ANNUAL AVERAGE TEMPERATURES AND RAINFALL

T* = Temperature in °F, R* = Rainfall in inches. Altitudes are in feet.

Location	Altitude	Jan T	Jan R	Feb T	Feb R	Mar T	Mar R	Apr T	Apr R	May T	May R	Jun T	Jun R	Jul T	Jul R	Aug T	Aug R	Sep T	Sep R	Oct T	Oct R	Nov T	Nov R	Dec T	Dec R
Acapulco, Gro.	23	78	0.4	78	0.0	79	0.0	80	0.0	83	12.	83	17.	83	8.6	83	9.8	82	14.	82	6.7	81	1.2	79	0.4
Aguascalientes, Ags.	6258	55	0.5	58	0.2	63	0.1	68	0.1	72	0.7	70	4.8	69	5.8	67	4.1	67	3.6	66	1.3	64	0.7	56	0.6
Apatzingán, Mich.	2237	78	.16	80	.28	84	.06	86	.04	90	.56	88	3.5	84	7.4	82	6.8	83	6.6	83	1.8	81	.32	78	.63
Campeche, Camp.	26	72	0.7	74	0.4	77	0.5	79	0.2	81	1.7	81	6.1	80	7.0	81	6.7	81	5.7	80	3.4	76	1.2	74	1.2
Chetumal, Q. Roo	13	73	3.0	75	.86	77	1.1	80	1.2	81	5.5	82	7.0	82	5.1	82	4.2	81	5.5	79	8.4	75	3.4	75	3.7
Chihuahua, Chih.	4690	49	0.1	52	0.2	59	0.3	65	0.3	74	0.4	79	1.0	77	3.1	75	3.7	72	3.7	65	1.4	56	0.3	49	0.8
Chilpancingo, Gro.	3800	66	0.1	67	0.2	70	0.1	72	0.2	73	2.8	70	6.0	70	7.8	69	6.6	69	6.2	70	3.4	69	0.9	67	0.8
Cd. Obregón, Son.	131	65	.27	68	.20	72	.06	77	.16	81	0.0	90	.07	93	.27	93	1.8	91	1.7	85	.57	75	1.7	67	.51
Cd. Victoria, Tamps.	1053	60	1.4	64	1.0	70	0.8	76	1.5	79	5.0	81	4.8	81	4.1	82	2.7	79	7.9	74	4.3	67	1.7	60	0.6
Colima, Col.	1657	72	0.5	72	0.3	74	0.0	77	0.0	79	0.3	79	5.7	78	7.7	78	7.2	77	7.7	78	3.1	76	0.9	73	1.3
Cordoba, Ver.	3049	61	1.8	63	1.5	67	1.5	62	2.2	73	4.3	72	13.	70	15.	70	16.	70	18.	68	9.1	65	3.7	63	2.1
Creel, Chih.	7724	41	1.9	41	.31	42	.59	50	.55	55	1.1	63	5.3	63	5.3	61	5.5	59	1.1	54	2.6	44	1.3	39	1.8
Cuernavaca, Mor.	5000	65	0.1	67	0.2	70	0.3	72	0.3	74	2.1	70	7.8	68	8.6	68	8.7	68	9.7	68	3.1	67	0.3	66	0.1
Culiacn, Sin.	216	67	0.4	69	0.4	71	0.2	74	0.0	79	0.1	83	1.2	83	5.8	82	6.8	82	4.6	80	1.6	73	0.4	67	2.1
Durango, Dgo.	6209	53	0.5	56	0.4	60	0.0	65	0.1	69	0.5	62	2.4	69	4.9	69	3.6	67	4.0	64	1.2	58	.06	54	0.7
Fortín, Ver.	3326	61	1.9	64	1.5	67	1.6	70	2.1	72	5.0	71	14.	71	15.	70	16.	70	18.	69	8.5	64	3.5	62	2.4
Guadalajara, Jal.	5220	58	0.7	61	0.2	65	0.1	70	0.0	72	0.7	71	7.6	69	10.	68	7.9	67	7.0	65	2.1	61	0.8	59	0.8
Guanajuato, Gto.	6835	57	0.5	60	0.3	64	0.2	68	0.2	71	1.1	68	5.4	67	6.6	66	5.5	65	6.0	63	2.0	60	0.7	59	0.6
Guaymas, Son.		64	0.3	66	0.2	69	0.2	73	0.1	73	0.1	84	0.0	87	1.8	87	3.0	86	2.1	81	0.4	72	0.4	65	1.1
Hermosillo, Son.	638	60	0.1	63	0.6	68	0.2	73	0.1	79	0.1	88	0.1	90	2.8	88	3.3	87	2.5	79	1.6	70	0.2	60	1.0
Ixtapan la Sal, Mex.	6349	84	0.6	67	0.5	70	0.3	72	1.2	75	2.3	73	6.4	68	7.3	68	11.	69	9.5	67	0.6	66	0.6	66	0.3
Jalapa, Ver.	4540	58	2.1	60	2.1	63	2.1	67	2.3	68	4.7	67	12.	66	8.5	66	8.0	65	11.	64	5.1	60	2.8	52	1.9
La Paz, B.C.	59	64	.13	68	.45	71	.03	74	0.0	81	0.0	88	.25	88	1.6	85	2.0	80	.37	72	.54	60	1.3		
León, Gto.	6180	58	0.5	61	0.2	66	0.2	70	0.1	73	0.9	71	4.3	68	6.6	68	5.5	68	5.2	66	1.5	61	0.7	60	0.5
Manzanillo, Col.		75	0.9	74	0.5	74	0.0	76	0.0	79	0.1	81	4.0	83	5.4	83	7.4	81	15.	81	5.0	79	0.7	77	2.1
Mazatlán, Sin.	3	67	0.5	67	0.4	67	0.1	70	0.0	75	0.0	79	1.1	81	6.6	81	9.6	81	10.	79	2.4	74	0.5	69	1.7
Merida, Yuc.	30	73	1.2	74	0.6	78	0.8	81	1.0	82	3.2	81	5.9	81	5.5	81	5.1	81	6.0	79	4.0	75	1.2	74	1.2
México, D.F.	7240	54	0.2	56	0.3	61	0.4	63	0.5	65	0.2	63	4.2	61	4.9	61	4.1	60	4.6	59	1.3	58	0.6	54	0.3
Monterrey, N.L.	1749	59	0.8	62	0.9	68	0.6	74	1.1	78	1.7	81	3.3	81	2.9	82	2.5	78	8.1	72	4.3	63	1.0	57	0.9
Morelia, Mich.	6234	57	0.5	60	0.3	64	0.3	67	0.3	69	1.7	67	5.2	65	6.8	64	6.4	64	6.2	63	2.3	60	0.8	58	0.2
Oaxaca, Oax.	5068	63	0.1	66	0.1	70	0.4	72	1.0	73	2.4	71	4.9	70	3.7	69	4.1	69	6.7	67	1.6	65	0.3	64	0.4
Orizaba, Ver.	4079	59	1.8	61	1.6	64	1.0	68	1.9	70	5.3	68	14.	67	15.	67	13.	67	17.	66	7.3	61	3.9	66	2.1
Pachuca, Hgo.	7999	53	0.2	55	0.5	58	0.6	61	0.7	61	1.3	60	2.8	59	2.3	59	2.1	59	3.1	56	1.9	54	0.8	55	0.2
Patzcuaro, Mich.	7180	57	0.8	56	0.5	61	0.3	64	0.2	68	1.5	68	7.9	63	9.8	63	9.5	63	8.5	61	3.1	58	1.0	55	0.9
Progreso, Yuc.	46	73	1.3	74	.67	76	.59	80	.70	79	2.1	80	2.9	80	1.8	80	1.8	80	2.1	79	2.7	76	.80	74	1.0
Puebla, Pue.	7200	54	0.2	60	0.2	62	0.5	65	0.5	66	2.9	64	6.2	63	5.4	63	5.8	62	7.4	61	2.2	58	0.8	56	0.3
Queretaro, Qro.	6160	57	0.4	60	0.1	64	0.2	68	0.5	70	1.1	69	3.7	67	4.1	67	3.4	66	4.8	63	1.3	61	0.4	59	0.5
Sn. Cristóbal L. C., Chis.	7087	54	0.3	55	0.0	57	0.4	60	1.4	60	5.1	60	10.	60	5.6	60	6.3	60	9.9	59	6.0	55	0.9	55	0.6
San Jose Purúa, Mich.	6335	57	0.7	60	0.6	63	0.3	67	0.3	70	0.2	71	6.3	70	7.1	69	6.6	68	7.0	65	2.5	64	0.8	60	2.5
San Luis Potosi, S.L.P.	6157	55	0.5	59	0.2	63	0.4	69	0.2	70	1.2	70	2.8	67	2.3	67	1.7	65	3.4	63	0.7	59	0.4	57	0.6
Tampico, Tamps.	39	65	2.1	68	0.9	71	0.5	77	0.4	80	2.0	82	7.9	82	5.8	82	5.9	81	13.	78	7.0	72	2.2	67	1.7
Tapachula, Chis.	551	77	.28	78	.24	80	1.2	81	2.9	80	12.	78	19.	78	12.	78	13.	77	18.	77	16.	77	3.4	77	.45
Taxco, Gro.	5500	66	0.0	69	0.2	72	0.4	75	0.9	76	3.0	72	10.	70	12.	70	14.	69	13.	69	3.5	68	0.2	67	0.1
Tehuacán, Pue.	5509	60	0.1	62	0.1	65	0.1	68	0.6	70	2.6	69	3.7	67	2.8	68	2.2	68	4.7	65	1.3	61	0.2	61	0.3
Tehuantepec, Oax.	328	58	1.5	66	0.2	69	0.3	72	1.4	74	3.6	72	6.5	69	4.9	71	3.2	69	8.5	68	3.6	67	1.5	66	0.6
Tepic, Nay.	3000	63	1.2	63	0.8	65	0.0	70	0.0	71	0.1	74	6.8	74	14.	74	12.	74	8.1	73	8.0	78	0.3	64	2.1
Tlaxcala, Tlax.	7500	55	0.2	57	0.1	61	0.3	63	0.7	64	2.9	63	5.0	61	5.3	61	5.9	61	5.4	60	1.9	58	0.3	57	0.2
Toluca, Mex.	8712	49	0.4	52	0.4	55	0.4	57	1.1	59	2.0	58	5.3	56	3.6	56	5.7	56	6.0	54	1.9	52	0.8	50	0.3
Torreon, Coah.	3720	54	0.5	60	0.2	65	0.0	70	0.2	81	0.5	83	1.5	80	2.1	81	0.9	80	1.4	74	0.9	62	0.5	56	0.5
Tuxpan, Ver.		67	1.6	70	1.0	72	1.0	78	1.5	81	3.4	83	8.0	82	6.9	82	6.7	81	12.	78	8.9	72	2.1	78	1.5
Tuxtla Gutierrez, Chis.	1759	71	0.0	73	0.2	77	0.4	80	.22	81	3.0	79	9.2	78	7.0	78	6.1	77	8.0	76	3.2	73	.16	70	.25
Uruapan, Mich.	5500	61	0.6	62	0.8	68	0.3	70	0.2	72	1.3	71	11.	70	14.	69	13.	69	16.	68	7.1	64	1.5	61	1.2
Valladolid, Yuc.	72	70	2.5	73	1.0	77	1.0	80	3.0	81	4.7	80	6.0	80	5.5	80	6.3	79	7.0	77	5.7	73	1.9	72	2.2
Villahermosa, Tab.	33	72	5.5	75	3.9	77	1.8	80	1.8	83	3.5	83	8.0	82	7.6	83	7.6	82	10.	80	11.	76	5.6	73	7.1
Zacatecs, Zac.	8187	49	0.4	51	0.2	54	0.1	59	0.1	62	0.9	61	2.1	57	3.5	58	2.3	57	3.0	56	0.9	52	0.6	50	0.5

* T = Temperature in °F, R = Rainfall in inches. Altitudes are in feet.

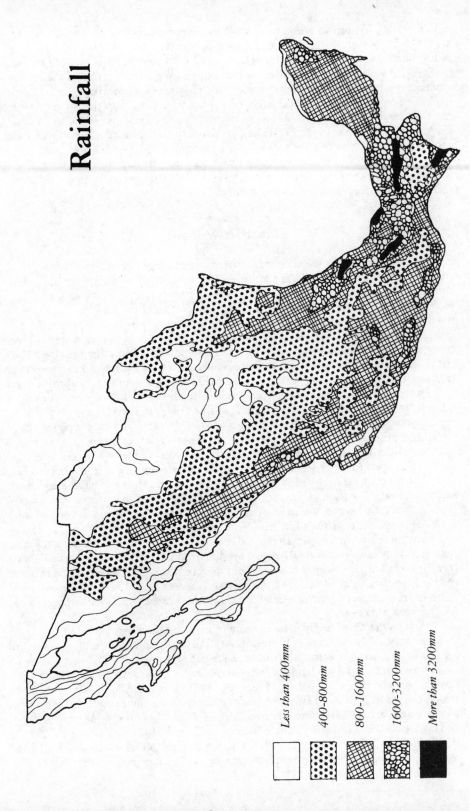

Rainfall

Less than 400mm

400-800mm

800-1600mm

1600-3200mm

More than 3200mm

ask a neighbor to keep an eye on things; our experience has been that other travellers are much more light fingered than the local people. For long side trips the manager will probably store your things for you, especially if you offer to pay for the service.

Trailer parks are centers of information about all sorts of things: local attractions, where to shop, where the fish are biting, etc. They are excellent places to find bargains on camping gear, especially polar-quality sleeping bags that have turned their owners into steamed tamales a few too many times. Every park also has its Total Camper, someone like my father who can produce the inner lock washer of an obscure model of Swedish backpacker's stove or the December 1934 issue of *National Geographic*. I believe that these campers have been put on earth to make travelling just a little bit easier for the rest of us, the poor fools who get to the beach before realizing we've forgotten our bathing suits.

Climate & Weather

Mexico's climate and weather are as varied as its topography. Campers can encounter everything from polar conditions on the highest peaks to steaming jungles and scorching, tongue swelling deserts. Abrupt changes in elevation are usually accompanied by abrupt changes in climate: a drop of three thousand feet can mean the difference between cool or hot nights, pine forests or semi-tropical jungle. Smart campers soon find themselves studying 'the lay of the land' to take advantage of the topography. If you see a mountain range ahead, logic will tell you that the air will be cooler up there and the mosquitoes perhaps less aggressive. While hiking we do our best to situate our campsites to take advantage of the sun — or to hide from it if it's quite warm. The same goes for boaters, especially those who follow rivers through canyon areas. I've camped in deep narrow canyons that rarely feel the sun's warming rays; if you prefer mornings that aren't quite so brisk, camp in a more open spot.

Because climate and weather are so varied in Mexico your best bet is to plan ahead in a general sense and then see what happens when you get there. We once spent a summer camped in the Yucatan, in spite of the sincere warnings. It was hot, to be sure, but we camped near the edge of the Caribbean, on a deserted white coral sand beach, and rarely wore anything but bathing suits. Trips to town for supplies were pure hell, mainly because we had to wear clothing. After a sweltering day of driving and shopping, the beach felt like heaven rather than a furnace.

Study the temperature/rainfall chart and maps. Remember: averages are a combination of highs and lows and 90 degrees might not sound too bad until you find that it really means 100 or more in the middle of the afternoon. Once again, if you make a mistake, just move until you find an area that is agreeable.

Here are some very general guidelines about the weather that should give you an idea of what to expect:

Pacific Coast: Absolutely ideal in the winter, with good weather often lasting through May. May is Mexico's hottest month but oddly enough it is often cooler in the lowlands during this month than in the highlands.

Summertime in the lowlands (all coasts) is hot and humid, perfect for beach lizards, sun worshippers and campers equipped with air conditioners. The hurricane season begins in June but reaches its peak (along with the temperature) in late summer and early fall. The weather usually breaks in October, becoming much drier and cooler. Fall is a favorite time for fishing, diving and boating.

Highlands (5,000' and higher): the climate at higher elevations is often described as 'Mediterranean', conjuring up pleasant images of orange groves, clear skies and

Climate

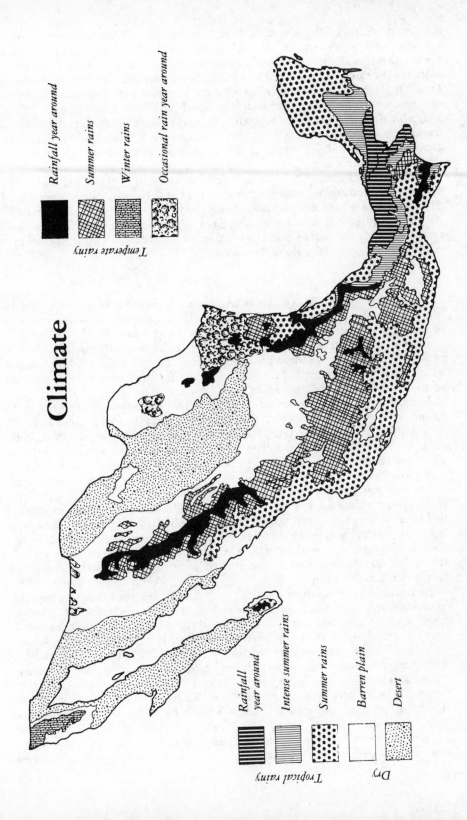

Temperate rainy
- Rainfall year around
- Summer rains
- Winter rains
- Occasional rain year around

Tropical rainy
- Rainfall year around
- Intense summer rains
- Summer rains

Dry
- Barren plain
- Desert

dry, warm weather. This is reasonably accurate but don't forget variations in annual rainfall; some higher areas are arid, others are very heavily forested. The weather in the highlands is almost always pleasant (May can be an exception) and in summertime the rains cool the air considerably. *Gringos* are often quite surprised to see forests that closely resemble those of the American west and southwest. In winter it can get quite cold at higher elevations, especially on clear nights.

Gulf Coast: The Gulf isn't as predictable as the Pacific coast, though in general the Gulf is wetter than the rest of Mexico. Summers are hot and humid and winters are cooler and humid. The entire Gulf coast is largely overlooked by campers, a situation that should change once people realize its incredible potential.

Yucatán Peninsula: The Yucatán is really two regions: the coast and the interior. The interior tends to be much warmer than the coast, especially in summertime. In the winter, mainly in December and January, *nortes* blow in (from the colder north, as the name implies) and make the weather downright miserable. A *norte* can last two or three days or longer than a week, you never know . . . Late winter and early spring are especially nice, especially along the Caribbean.

The Rainy Season

The rainy season usually occurs between May and September. When it is approaching, select a campsite that won't be inundated or made unlivable. Anticipate that a lot of rain, even for a short time, can turn a creek into a river and a pond into a lake.

If your camp centers around a car, you'll want to be especially careful where it's parked. This doesn't just mean preventing it from being washed away but parking where you won't be isolated by the first heavy rain. Be sure there is some way to get to an all-weather road once the rains begin.

In many remote areas, the arrival of the rains is the beginning of a long period of isolation, when the only contact with the rest of the world is by foot or canoe and sometimes only by radio. Food becomes scarce and the people who are too poor to stockpile ahead have to endure real hardship until the roads and bridges are repaired. In some places even the beer runs out during particularly bad rainy seasons — which should give you an idea of the seriousness and extent of the isolation that has to be endured.

The rain may begin quietly with a few weeks of occasional afternoon drizzling, telling you it's time to move on. Or it may come dramatically with an unexpected torrential downpour, cutting you off before you've had time to get away. We always question the local people closely when the rainy season approaches and establish: 1) the condition of the roads after the rains begin, 2) alternate routes out of the area, 3) the earliest date that the area has been isolated, and 4) if it was cut off temporarily or for the entire rainy season.

Fortunately, there are many places to camp during the rainy season that have year 'round access to all-weather roads. With adequate protection from the rain and a good parking place, camping in the rainy season is quite enjoyable. (In most cases, it only rains for a short time in the afternoon, even at the height of the rainy season.)

Violent rainstorms are usually preceded or accompanied by strong gusting winds. By anticipating the wind, you can avoid having your camp stirred up and blown around.

Late summer and early fall are the usual months for *ciclónes* (hurricanes). Hurricanes frequently strike very close together and large areas of the coasts are often flooded. Roads are cut, food is scarce and you may actually face the possibility of danger to yourself and your car.

Listen to the radio for hurricane warnings, but don't absolutely depend on it to warn you; they often bungle their predictions. *The News,* an English language paper printed in Mexico, gives weather forecasts, but the paper is available only in tourist areas and larger cities.

Should you be caught in the path of a hurricane, go to high ground or as far from the beach as possible. A palm hut will not survive a hurricane, so don't decide to lie in your hammock with a bottle of rum or a lid of grass and ride it out. A hurricane will uproot trees, particularly coconut palms, and flying limbs, roofs and junk will be in the air.

Unusual Weather

Have you ever made a long trip and had the weather defy logic and prediction wherever you went? "Never seen it rain in February!" a local swears, offering you the use of a leaky umbrella. The weather in Mexico is still the weather: cranky, unpredictable and likely to make a fool of anyone willing to bet money that it will or won't rain or shine on any particular campsite. There are two weather oddities, however, that are 'somewhat' predictable. The first comes in late July or early August (usually) and is called *la canícula,* loosely: dog days. This is a period of a few weeks when normal summer rains stop and are replaced by hot and dry weather. The dog days are traditionally a time to become ill and many Mexicans suffer colds, flu, grippe and headaches during the *canícula*. It is also a great time to go hiking, since trails dry out and the weather is generally more favorable for camping, especially in areas that receive heavy summer rains.

The other side of the weather coin comes in early January, when it suddenly rains in the middle of the dry season. These unseasonal rains don't last long — a few days in some places, a week or two in others — and are often gone before bewildered tourists can figure out what's happening. It all seems designed to make you pack a poncho when you'd rather carry another bottle of tequila.

Unknown Mexico

National Parks

Mexican National Parks are often a disappointment to campers who expect to find picnic tables, neatly maintained campsites, graveled trails and lectures on local flora and fauna by a highly trained ranger. In many cases the Mexican government has done little more than declare an area a Park, erect a few signs and appoint a caretaker. Litter and mindless vandalism within parks are not uncommon and camping may actually be prohibited (though erratically enforced). Why bother with National Parks? Fortunately the best parks overcome minor disadvantages by their relatively isolated settings and natural beauty. Parks are created in areas of obvious interest to those who love the outdoors and a park's greatest use may be as a departure point for side trips into the surrounding countryside.

The following list and brief description of Mexican National Parks is based on a report published by Harry Moller in his camping magazine, *México Desconocido* (Unknown Mexico, October 1979). Moller pointed out that of an original 49 *Parques Nacionales* that existed in 1969, ten short years later only 29 parks could actually be called parks in the common definition of the word. Farming, uncontrolled mining and timber cutting, urban sprawl and just plain neglect have reduced many fine parks to a sad condition. *México Desconocido* is making an admirable effort to educate Mexican campers about the problems of litter and vandalism, not only in parks but in all natural areas of the country. Tourists should be especially careful to set a good example when visiting Mexico. It just takes a few minutes a day to clean your campsite and to make a noticeable dent in the litter that others have left before you.

Parques Naturales or Natural Parks are areas of special beauty or interest that are too small to qualify as National Parks. Natural Parks sometimes include commercial tourist facilities such as spas, hotels or restaurants. We always try to check them out; some are very nice and others over-developed.

Parques Estatales, State Parks, include historical monuments, natural areas and whatever else the local government thought was special enough to warrant being declared a park. There are far too many of these parks to list here. Information on state parks tends to be very unreliable, since it often reflects what the bureaucracy would like to have in a park, rather than what you'll actually find there. By all means check them out; just don't expect too much.

Baja California Norte: *San Pedro Mártir:* 155,600 acres; runs from the desert to almost 10,000 feet above sea level. Forests, streams, rocky pinnacles, mountains. Access via km 138 on highway from Ensenada to the south. Road closed by snow in winter. *Constitución de 1857:* Reaches up to 10,100 feet, forested and undeveloped. Access by 130 km of dirt road from km 115 of Hwy 2 (Tijuana-Mexicali).

Chiapas: *Lagunas de Montebello:* The famous "Colored Lakes"; over one hundred lakes and *cenotes*; ruins, forests, wildlife, hiking, basic campsites. Access: at km 16 on the highway from Comitán to the Guatemalan border, go left for 55 km on a paved highway. Avoid straying into Guatemala if you hike in this area.

Chihuahua: *Cumbres de Majalca:* Almost 12,000 acres of forests, rivers, streams; wildlife. Access is by dirt road: 10 km before El Sauz, 50 km toward Ciudad Juárez on Hwy 45.

Distrito Federal: *Desierto de los Leónes:* Forests and basic facilities. Access by paved roads: at km 24 of Hwy 15 to Toluca. A small park and one of Mexico's oldest. *Cerro de la Estrella:* Of historical interest only. *Cumbres del Ajusco:* Views of forests, semi-alpine vegetation; a peak reaches almost 13,000 feet.

Guerrero: *Grutas de Cacahuamilpa:* See *Caves.* Very developed.

Hidalgo: *El Chico:* A very famous park. Over 3,500 acres of rock formations, escarpments, streams and waterfalls. Basic facilities. Access: by paved highway, 6 km from Pachuca on the road to Venado. *Los Marmoles:* A canyon 1,640 feet deep with a wide variety of flora and fauna; rock formations. Access: by paved road from km 230 of Hwy 85 (México-Laredo). Undeveloped.

Jalisco: *Nevado de Colima:* High mountian forests, interesting vegetation and views, undeveloped. Access: via Atenquique at km 109 of Hwy 110 (Jiquilpan-Colima).

México: *Desierto del Carmen:* Waterfalls, rock formations, canyons and forests; small and undeveloped. Access: via Tenancingo at km 115 of Hwy 55 (Toluca-Ixtapan). *Zoquiapan:* High forested mountains, canyons and streams. Access: by paved road from km 54 of Hwy 6 (México-Puebla). *Nevado de Toluca:* High mountain scenery, forests. Access: by dirt road from km 26 of Hwy 124 (Toluca-Temascaltepec).

México-Puebla: *Itza-Popo:* High mountains, alpine scenery, forests, canyons, rivers, wildlife, snow. Access: by paved road from km 61 of Hwy 160 (México-Cuautla).

México-Morelos: *Lagunas de Zempoala:* Forested mountains, very rugged and undeveloped. Access by paved road at km 51 (Tres Cumbres) of Hwy 95 (México-Cuernavaca).

Michoacán: *Pico de Tancítaro:* Densely forested mountains and canyons, rivers, waterfalls, wildlife. Large and undeveloped. Access: from Uruapan, 45 km to Tancítaro (near volcano of Parícutin). *Cerro de Garnica:* Forests, canyons and streams. Access: by dirt roads from Puerto Garnica, km 258 of Hwy 15 (México-Morelia). *Barranca de Cupatitzio:* Canyon with dense semi-tropical vegetation, streams, springs and waterfalls. In the immediate vicinity of Uruapan. *José María Morelos:* Broken forested terrain. Access: by dirt road from km 282 of Hwy 15 (México-Morelia).

. **Michoacán-México:** *Bosencheve:* High forests, two small lakes (occasionally dry). Access: by rough dirt road from km 133 of Hwy 15 (México-Morelia).

Oaxaca: *Lagunas de Chacagua:* Tropical lagoons surrounded by forests, jungle and mangroves; wildlife, boating and fishing. Access: 57 km south of Pinotepa Nacional on Hwy 200 (Acapulco-Salina Cruz). *Benito Juárez:* Forests and mountains (Sierra de San Felipe del Agua) just north of Oaxaca City. Difficult access, undeveloped.

Puebla: *Pico de Orizaba:* High mountain views and vegetation. Access: via Ciudad Serdán, 18 km from Esperanza at km 103 of Hwy 150 (Puebla-Orizaba).

San Luis Potosí: *Gogorrón:* Temperate climate; escarpment, forests, caves, wildlife, hotsprings. Access: from km 25 of the highway between San Luis Potosí and San Felipe. The park itself is undeveloped but some of the hotsprings are; see *Hotsprings*. *El Potosí:* Forests, rocks, canyons and rivers. Access: from km 98 of Hwy 70 (San Luis Potosí-Río Verde). Go toward Cañada Verde (also called Cañada Grande).

Tlaxcala: *La Malinche:* High mountain views and forests. Access: by dirt road from Tlaxco and Atotonilco.

Veracruz: *Cofre de Perote:* Varied views and vegetation, from semi-tropical to alpine. Access: by dirt roads from Perote, at km 277 of Hwy 140 to Veracruz. The best dirt road leads to the *estación de microondas*. *Cañon del Río Blanco:* Semi-tropical to cold (mountains of Acultzingo). Access: by dirt roads from Tecamalucán, 10 km east of Acultzingo or from Maltrata.

Waterfalls

Mexico's rugged topography has created innumerable *caídas de agua* (waterfall; also — *salto, cascada, catarata, chorro*). Some areas, such as El Lugar del Rayo in San Luis Potosí, have too many falls to list. The following include the most famous waterfalls and others that are relatively unknown but quite spectacular. I'm sure that you'll run across many more, especially if you travel on back roads or hike into mountainous country. It is in this spirit of adventure that I dedicate this list to the memory of Professor Emeritus Harry Rogers. "Don Enrique's" own uncompleted work, *Waterfalls I've Never Visited And Other Unnatural Wonders* inevitably comes to mind when I pass up yet another road sign for "Waterfall 47 kilometers."

Aguascalientes: *Cascada de Maravillas:* Rainy season only. *Cascada del Rodadero:* Rainy season only; in the Sierra de Laurel.

Chiapas: *El Aguacero:* Multiple cascades; west of Ocozocuautla. *Agua Azul:* One of the country's most beautiful falls; in the Palenque area, *municipio* of Chilón.

Chihuahua: *Cascada de Basaseachic:* The eleventh highest in the world and Mexico's highest: 1,020 feet (311 meters) *straight down*. I call natural attractions like this "gaspers"; even the most jaded traveller can't restrain a quick breath at the sight. By the end of the winter the falls don't have much water but it's still worth seeing. *Cascada de Cusárare:* "Place of Eagles"; near Creel. 115 feet high (35 m) and 100 feet wide (30 m).

Guerrero: *Cascada Cacalotenango:* Near Taxco. *Cascada Chontalcuatlán, Cascada Acuitlapan.*

Jalisco: *Cascada Juanacatlán:* Near Guadalajara on Río Santiago. *Chorros de Tala:* Hotsprings nearby.

México: *Salto de Chihuahua:* Near Ixtapan del Oro; 131 feet high (40 m). *Salto de Toxhi, Los Pastores — Temascalcingo,* on Río Lerma. *Salto de San Lucas:* Valle de Bravo area. *Cascada de Tixhiñú:* On Río Ñado, near Aculco. *Cascada de la Concepción:* Near Tepozan and Amealco. *Salto de Santa Ana:* Near Tenancingo.

Michoacán: *Chorros de Varal:* One of Mexico's finest; southwest of Zamora, toward Tingüidín and Los Reyes. Difficult access. *Salto de Enandio:* on Río Zitácuaro, near Presa El Bosque and Enandio; 164 feet high (50 m); difficult access includes two hour hike. *Tzaráracua:* 10 km from Uruapan in the park on the Río Cupatitzio. *Cascadas de Santa Rosa, Santa Paula, Caracho:* Near Tacámbaro. *El Salto:* Near La Piedad.

Morelos: *Salto de San Antón:* Near Cuernavaca; basalt formations.

Nayarit: *Cascada de Jumatán:* Difficult access; almost 400 feet high (120 m). *Cascada El Punto:* On Río Tepic. *Cascada El Jihuite:* Río Zapotán, west of Santa Mariá del Oro. *Salto de Volantín:* Close to Atonalisco; two other falls nearby.

Nuevo León: *Cola de Caballo:* A famous spot but the falls appear only on Sundays and fiestas, by official decree (controlled water source for factories). *Cascada El Halcón* and *El Salto:* near Monterrey.

Oaxaca: *Cascada de Río Seco:* Near Huautla; almost 500 feet high (150 m).

Puebla: *Cola de Caballo:* Close to Molcaxac. *Cascada Los Pescaditos, Cascada La Gloria:* On Apulco river.

San Luis Potosí: *Los Trampolines:* An area of waterfalls around Tamasopo; many rivers and caves. *La Catarata de Tamul:* If not the most beautiful falls in Mexico this certainly has to be the most unusual: the Río Gallinas drops almost 350 feet on top of the Río Santa Marín. Very difficult access; no vehicles. *Las Cascadas de Micos:* Northwest of Ciudad Valles; described as "unforgettable". Difficult access. *El Salto:* Near El Naranjo. Appears only in the rainy season but smaller falls nearby are permanent.

Tlaxcala: *Cascada de Atlihuetzia:* The beautiful "Waterfall In The Desert" is now polluted by industrial wastes but there are "hopes" of cleaning it up.

Veracruz: *Salto de Eyipantla:* About 150 feet high (45 m); beautiful jungle filled canyon near San Andrés Tuxtla. *Cascada Tenexamaxa:* Near Huatusco. *Cascada de Soteapan:* "Very impressive".

2.   Boating

There's nothing quite like several long months on dry land, or at least what passes for dry land in the Pacific Northwest, to inspire romantic dreams of sun-warmed jungle streams and tropical seas. Your boat glides smoothly through the salty waves, following the shimmering white line of the beach. The sun's rays massage your bare back, loosening muscles that ache with the pleasure of long hours of fishing and skin diving. A distant grove of swaying coconut palms guides you to your picturesque palm frond hut. Soon, as the sun dips toward another colorful farewell to the day, friendly natives will wave and shout greetings from the doorways of their own picturesque palm frond huts. Eager hands will drag your boat onto the smooth clean sand, excited voices offering to exchange plump, exotically-flavored papayas, sweet golden bananas and heavy refreshing coconuts for the silvery bounty of seafood you have gathered. And at night, as the moon's gentle light washes away your cares, everyone will gather to strum guitars and sing lusty folk songs.

"Anything interesting in the newspaper?" Lorena asked, shaking drops of rain from her umbrella and hanging it from a nail near the wood heater.

"Um?" I answered, struggling back to a somewhat harsher reality.

"I asked you what you're reading. It must be pretty good to take you that far away. Anything earth shaking?"

"Ads," I said. "Just some ads."

She paused halfway across the living room. "Not *Boats and Motors* perhaps?" From her tone of voice you might have thought I'd been caught drooling over a well-thumbed issue of *Hustler*. "I thought we agreed not to take a boat this time. Remember?"

"So what's the crime in just *looking*?" I countered, flapping the pages in a futile attempt to drive her into the next room. "Boat ads happen to interest me, that's all. Nothing sinister in that, is there?"

"Oh, no!" Lorena laughed. "And there was certainly nothing sinister about the Bloater, was there?"

I flinched. The Bloater was a ten foot Czechoslovakian imitation of a French version of a well-known British inflatable runabout. Because of certain minor flaws in the construction I'd picked the boat up for a song. It was tough, almost unsinkable and as maneuverable as a disabled supertanker. The maiden voyage, through a thundering Mexican surf, lasted just under two minutes. I recall a sense of acute disappointment and impending doom as a monstrous breaking wave hurled us upside-down into shallow water, then dropped onto our heads in a watery avalanche. But later, after repairs and recuperation, the Bloater carried us through fantastic jungle lagoons teeming with waterfoul, strange plants and . . . yes . . . the odd mosquito or two.

I quickly scanned the crowded columns. Thanks to a few landlubber oil sheiks in some distant parched desert, the price of overpowered gas-guzzling boats had gone straight to the bottom. Which was right where they belonged, I mused, my attention suddenly drawn to a one line ad at the bottom of the page.

"Hey, here's a paddleboard for sale. That's not really a boat. It's a . . . "

"White elephant!" Lorena interrupted. "Just like the last one."

I bit my tongue. The "last one" had been a fiberglas jewel, a sleek and slithery vessel from which to harvest untold quantities of fish and oysters. It was unsinkable, or so the previous owner had sworn with great sincerity.

"We had a lot of fun with that paddleboard," I snapped through the Classifieds. "Even you have to admit that!"

"Great fun," Lorena agreed. "I'll never forget the fun of swimming back to the beach. How far was it? Five miles?"

I felt the blood rush to my cheeks. "It wasn't even half a mile!"

"Right," she drawled, "about half a mile deep where you managed to sink it."

I retreated with a snarl; no matter what Lorena said the paddleboard had served us well. We'd explored small lakes and rivers and though we hadn't found the Seven Cities of Cibola, we'd undoubtedly come close.

And then there was the Shark, a homemade fiberglas and styrofoam diver's paddleboard with an enormous, razor sharp sheet metal keel. I shouldn't have tried to land it through the surf. The first wave sucked away my fish and diving gear. With the second wave the Shark somehow became airborne. Several children lolling in the shallows were nearly decapitated when the Shark flew between them like some monstrous scythe. No one had been injured but there'd been that annoying young mother who refused to stop screaming . . .

I cleared my throat and began reading aloud. "Twelve foot sailing dinghy in perfect condi . . ."

A wild and cynical laugh cut me off.

"*It was his own fault!*" I shouted. "I told him not to sail that close to the rocks!" My wonderful mini-yacht had been thrown onto the jagged stones, the shattered mast driven like a battering ram through the bottom of the boat, splitting it in two. A maritime disaster. My so-called friend at the helm had escaped with his life and an interesting pattern of bruises and abrasions. It hurt me much more than it did him; I'd sailed that boat many miles, rowed rivers large and small, why one time I even . . .

"Any kayaks in there?" Lorena asked, a delicious note of genuine interest creeping into her voice. I had her now! Lorena is mad for kayaks.

I scanned the ads quickly. The bait had been offered and taken; the hook was sharp. I began to reel her in ever so gently.

"Well here's one that might interest you. Owner transferred. Must sell plans and nearly complete seventeen-foot, ferrocement, Polynesian-style, decked kayak with bamboo masts and . . ."

Taking A Boat To Mexico

Selecting a boat to take to Mexico is complicated by the many different kinds of trips you can make and the varied conditions you will encounter. There is everything from white water rafting to lazy African Queen style canoeing down jungle rivers; from bass fishing in high desert lakes to diving world renowned Caribbean coral reefs; from cruising the Sea of Cortez to sailing the rugged broken shores of Oaxaca; from poling a shallow dugout in the lagoons and estuaries of the Gulf of Mexico to kayaking unmapped mountain streams.

Versatility and ease of maintenance are very important factors when choosing a boat for Mexico. This is especially true if you don't have a clear idea of what lies ahead or don't wish to tie yourself down to a rigid plan. You may not get out to the marlin fishing grounds in your twelve foot canoe, but you'll certainly find enough quieter water to explore.

There is a basic rule of boating that says "the simpler a boat is to operate and maintain, the more time it spends in the water." How many times have I stood on the beach, cursing in frustration at a balky outboard motor or a broken piece of unbreakable rigging? If parts, special tools and repair shops are scarce — and in Mexico they're downright rare — you'll probably want to trade your fancy boat for a pair of oars and a wooden skiff. A row boat may raise blisters on your hands and be slower than the Ark, but it will get you to that tantalizing island or down a tempting river when other boats are laid up on the beach for repairs.

Look over your prospective boat very carefully for signs of strain, wear and tear and likely trouble spots. What happens if those pop rivets pop or an oarlock cracks? Is that motor mount going to survive a hard grounding through the surf? If in doubt, fix it now and pack plenty of spares and repair materials. The only things you'll find in Mexico with any certainty are rope, twine, baling wire, nails, tar and the odd piece of wood or two. That's why many tourist boats that have been in hard use there look like Thor Hyerdahl's rejects.

The strain of travelling thousands of miles on a trailer or car top can play hell with new boats as well as your trusty canoe that hasn't leaked in thirty years. Throw in a few bad scrapes on the beach and you might have serious problems. A favorite small sailboat of mine seemed to fall apart before my very eyes after a few months in Mexico, though it had survived years of hard use in Puget Sound and British Columbia.

Careful handling is an obvious answer but even the fussiest boaters have to contend with Fate and Bad Luck. If the boat looks weak at home it should probably stay there. At the very least assemble a good repair kit, with tools that don't require electricity to operate.

Versatility in a boat is more important to us than such details as looks, speed and comfort. As confirmed boating maniacs, we want to get on the water — any water — with as little delay as possible. If it takes two hours to unload the boat, excavate the outboard motor from the trunk of the car and find the elusive drain plug, you'll soon be passing up a lot of opportunities to fish and explore.

The most versatile boat we've used in Mexico was a twelve-foot wooden sailboat, designed to be used as a rowboat or with a small outboard motor. We could make a quick stop on the side of the highway to row into a small stream or use the motor for longer trips against strong currents or for fishing expeditions. The sail was handy for crossing large bays and tacking back and forth on windy lakes. The boat held two people comfortably or three in a pinch; with great care we could stow our camping gear and almost keep it dry.

Small Sailboats

Sailing is not a subject for rational discussion and any true sailor who dreams of filling canvas with tropical wind might as well submit to the fantasy as soon as possible. I often try to cover up my addiction for sailing with statements like "Wind is free; gas and oil are expensive," or "With proper handling we can use our sailboat for trolling *and* diving trips." The reality is that sailboats are comparatively expensive, even small ones, and they rarely make good fishing or diving boats. Most are difficult-to-impossible to row or paddle for more than a few minutes, require skill to handle safely in unknown waters and are too much hassle to throw into the water for a noontime boat ride. When you add such factors as maintenance of the hull, the sails and rigging, and the cost of spare parts it's a wonder you see sailboats in Mexico at all. It's a wonder, that is, until you've gone sailing there. Like all true addictions, you have to be an addict to understand.

Here, then, are some suggestions based on my experiences with a number of small sailboats in Mexico, most of them boats that were basically impractical for anything but blowing around in the wind.

• Assemble a sail repair kit and make or buy spare battens.

• Rinse your sail in fresh water as often as possible, especially on long trips.

• Check all hardware and rigging that is attached to the boat and assume that it will come unattached after hard use on a remote stretch of water. What can be used for

jury-rigged repairs? Small pieces of plywood, galvanized wood screws, nuts and bolts, eyebolts and heavy gauge baling wire are all very useful. Mexican twine is the material of the future; carry a ball at all times.

• Rudders, tillers and centerboards are essential and therefore give a great deal of trouble. Be prepared to fix them all.

• Carry a good supply of quick drying caulking material, enough to patch the boat after a major disaster. Hot *chapopote* (tar) can be used in a pinch, but it's messy stuff and doesn't hold well.

• Carry oars or a good paddle. I've seen many *gringo* sailors stuck for hours when the wind shifted and a handy tow home wasn't available.

• Don't leave any easily detachable rigging on the boat when it is not in use — or on top of the car — or some curious kid will easily detach it.

Canoes and Kayaks

Dugout canoes of all sizes and shapes have been in use in Mexico for thousands of years. *Gringos* are just beginning to realize that modern lightweight canoes and kayaks make almost ideal boats for travellers who don't quite know where they're going or what to expect when they get there. The initial cost of a good quality boat is reasonable, maintenance is simple and repairs can be done with duct tape and hand tools; they are easy to transport and easy to power with paddle, sail or the smallest and most economical of outboards. Canoes and kayaks are capable of navigating all types of water, including open ocean passages with caution and careful planning. They are quiet, non-polluting, unostentatious, convenient for overnight or extended camping voyages and just plain fun to be in.

How can you possibly do without one?

The next step is to decide: canoe or kayak? Wood, aluminum, fiberglas or canvas? Open, decked, folding or rigid? One or two person? Short or long?

Our first choice, our all-time favorite, is a folding two place kayak, made by the Klepper company in Germany. They aren't cheap but they're definitely worth the price if you're in the habit of risking your necks and your gear from time to time. American and British folding kayaks cost a lot less and it shows in their performance and durability, though they're still quite suitable for all but the most arduous paddling conditions.

Sail rigs are available for folding kayaks, but you can save a lot of money by making your own or buying only those parts (such as the foot-controlled rudder assembly) that require special tools and skills to fabricate.

Skin diving from a canoe or kayak is tricky, but by practising in shallow water you'll soon learn how to get in and out without capsizing. Leapfrogging over the bow or stern is probably the safest method, though with two people, the boat can be counter-balanced effectively at the crucial moment.

Any daydreamer worth their romantic salt has fantasized buying a luxuriously outfitted sailing yacht and escaping to the South Seas. It doesn't take that much: a handful of charts, a sextant, a stout-hearted companion or two and $100,000 in the bank will do it nicely. Unfortunately, such dreams rarely become reality. Unless, of course, we are willing to settle for something different — not less, just *different*.

"Circumnavigate the Sea of Cortez in a twenty-year-old folding kayak that has only been seriously wrecked one time? Did I get that right? Just *one* serious wreck and now it floats *pretty good*? Carl? Are you still there?"

"Yeah, I'm here." I eased the phone away from my ear and reached for another handful of quarters. "That's what I call the Overall Grand Plan. We may not make it. I mean to say, we may not complete the entire trip around the Sea before the weather gets too hot. I know we'll make it otherwise, from a survival standpoint."

"Are you worried about *survival?*" My brother's voice rose sharply then faded; I realized he'd turned from the telephone to relate the latest news to my parents.

"Listen, Rob!" I added quickly, "Just forget what I said. This is a long kayak trip. Nothing more. A long camping trip on the water. Do you or don't you?"

There was a long silence, followed by heavy sighs. "Sure, why not?" Rob gave a slightly nervous laugh. "I'll have to wrap some things up first, take care of a few details." This meant: quit his job, borrow some money and perhaps sell his latest overpowered pickup truck for ready cash.

"That's great!" I cheered. "Now listen, Lorena wants you to pick up a couple of things for the trip. We'll meet you in L.A. Take care. Here she is."

Lorena took the receiver, balancing it on her left shoulder as she quickly thumbed through a thick sheaf of lists. "Rob? Got a pencil? Okay, here we go." She took a deep breath. "Forty two pounds of dried fruit but no apples. Yes forty two. FORTY TWO. No, no! FORTY two! Yeah, I know but what can I say, we gotta eat . . . Ready? . . . One hundred and seventy-five chocolate bars with almonds . . . What? . . . Yes, this connection is fine. Why don't you just take it down and then we'll go over it? . . . Great. Three pairs of cotton gloves, three pounds of bag balm, six quarts of raisins, five pounds of miso paste, three tubes of barge cement, sixteen 1-1/2 gallon water jugs with handles . . ."

Great books on exploration often include exciting descriptions of important rendezvous in exotic, faraway places. Lorena and I met Rob a week after our phone call, behind the Lil' Stinker gas station, somewhere in the suburban wilderness of Greater Los Angeles.

"This isn't a camping trip; it's an expedition!" Rob's tone was less than enthusiastic as he surveyed the mountain of loose equipment heaped in the back of his truck.

"Don't panic," I said. "It'll all fit somehow." I lifted the edge of a tarp, looking curiously through the gear he had bought. "Speaking of which, where's your kayak?"

He turned slowly, fixing his eyes on me in a disturbingly silent stare. "I was just going to ask you the same thing," he finally said. "Is this some kind of joke?"

I was momentarily stunned. Had I actually neglected to tell him to buy a kayak? It hardly seemed possible, but then again . . .

Although Los Angeles is one of the world's largest cities, it is a lousy place to buy a cheap secondhand, ocean cruising one person kayak on a Sunday afternoon. We invested a small fortune in newspapers and a larger one in a pay phone, tracking down leads from the Classifieds.

"Here's one," Lorena said, handing me another folded paper. The ad was brief and to the point: "Kayak. Cheap."

The kayak in question turned out to be less than ideal, a fifteen footer that had seen better days cruising inland lakes and ponds. I looked at its bottom and was reminded of Woody Guthrie's description of a bowl of soup, "so thin you could read a magazine through it." But as Rob was quick to point out, the price was right and time was short. We loaded the kayak onto the truck and headed south, just three days away from adventure, three days to the Big One, the first leg of the Overall Grand Plan & Sea of Cortez Circumnavigation, three days to April 1.

"April Fool's Day!" Rob laughed as we roared down the freeway, "April Fool's Day! I should have guessed."

The actual details of that voyage would require another book to describe. Although the Grand Plan to circumnavigate the Sea of Cortez was soon abandoned in favor of a more leisurely exploration of the Baja coastline, our expectations were more than fulfilled. For thirty-five days we paddled through a magical — and sometimes overwhelming world, our presence as fleeting as the ripples of our wakes. Day after day of paddling with the sun burning through our clothing, hands and arms encrusted with salt, the rhythm broken by brief periods when the wind filled our sail, pushed us recklessly along, the kayaks lashed together to form an ungainly catamaran. We lay back, seawater damp bandannas cooling our heads, waiting for the sudden tension on a handline that would mean sierra mackerel for dinner.

Food: we can't get enough of the stuff. Our moments of 'rest' are spent foraging reefs and underwater caves for snappers, grouper, cabrilla, lobster, rock scallops and whatever other edible curiosities cross our paths. For two weeks we gorge on plump two pound squid, picking them live and squirming from the beaches where they end their strange breeding cycle in self-destruction. Fried squid, baked squid, boiled squid and finally, smoked squid. We rummage our cupboards like demented Mother Hubbards, licking candy bar wrappers, scraping the noodle pot shiny, measuring out precious shares of honey like liquid gold.

Our camps are haphazard affairs, often a meager compromise between comfort and the need to escape the relentless glare of the sun. We soon learn to love arroyos for their afternoon shade, the pile of broken hardwoods trapped at every tight bend, by long-ago rushing water, the smooth sandy bottom that offers tempting side trips into the forbiddingly barren interior.

Darkness comes early and bedtime shortly after; crystalline skies, the distant laugh of a coyote, the furtive rustle of plastic as Rob raids his munchie bag for a dried fig.

Solitude, as much as food or drinking water, becomes a major preoccupation. We find ourselves setting up hidden camps on deserted islands, detouring from lonely fishermen, the almost legendary *vagabundos del mar*, sea gypsies, who take one hard disbelieving look at our kayaks, our gear and our sun scarred bodies and laugh. Desert brown faces wrinkle in amusement as they ask, over and over again, "Where is your boat? Your big *yate?*" We share hard candies and information on wells and waterholes, then slide away, drawn forward by the hypnotic rhythm of the paddles.

Whales! We hear their whooshing exhalations for days, strain our backs trying to catch a glimpse of their mighty heads, then, suddenly, the whales come to watch *us*, bearing down in stately formation like a flotilla of submarines. At the last moment, resigned to Jonah-dom, we shout in excitement and relief as the whales surface, roll their eyes at us, turn and power away with awesome tail strokes.

Late afternoon at the mouth of another nameless cove. Rob rests his paddle across his knees, tilts his head back for a slow gurgle of very weak cold tea. The water alongside his kayak darkens for an instant, then explodes upward as a giant manta ray tumbles into the sky, six feet over his head. It crashes down in a world record belly flop that sweeps a tidal wave of foam over his kayak. "Why do those things jump like that?" Rob mutters, and leans into his paddle for the final sprint to shore, watching the water nervously for more tons of flying mischief.

Fantasies within fantasies: Rob investigates a curious fold in the side of a rocky cliff. It is a cave, *the* cave of our dreams, complete with a hidden rope ladder over the cliff edge to a lookout point above. It is a cave by Walt Disney, with a clean flat floor of crushed coral, a table fashioned from an ancient hatch-cover and a landing place of soft sand hidden between pinnacles of jagged rock, protected from the sweep of the sea and pirates' eyes. Or is this the pirate cave itself? We wonder about that — and a great many other things — during the nine days and nights we are trapped there by an unexpected storm (unexpected because we hadn't fantasized it yet).

We live largely on squid and noodles and instant coffee, keeping a nervous eye on the level of our water jugs and the sky, which shows no sign of clearing up, Disney-like, into perfect escape and paddling weather. We explore the rope ladder route but it leads to blind canyons and sheer crumbling cliffs. Anyway, where could we go? This is a desert island, an island that is deserted for a good reason: there's nothing on it but rocks. We drink more brackish Nescafé and play Crazy Eights and wait.

Our luck turns with the weather. We leave the cave, almost regretfully, and make our way to the far end of the island. A group of *vagabundos* hail us from another cave; over the entrance, in phonetic English, are daubed the words, "HOM SWIT HOM." An enormous fat lady sits behind a real, if weatherbeaten, kitchen table and orders her naked husband to give us water. We take it reluctantly, embarrassed by our predicament but scared to go without. A week later Rob strikes again and locates a genuine freshwater well, bored into thirty-five feet of solid stone. Water! We bathe several times a day, wash our miserable clothes to tatters and prepare huge, watery soups and pots of weak tea and coffee. Our kidneys are working overtime, like bilge pumps on the Titanic.

And then, inevitably, it is over. The return to civilization becomes a long weary goodbye; we paddle for mile after mile, silently, with a growing awareness that it isn't just our mood but the weather itself that is oppressive and ominous. "The calm before the storm" doesn't sound like a worn out cliche when you're five miles from land in an overloaded kayak. Although Rob's kayak is light and fast, it is also fragile; he sprints ahead of us in a desperate run to shelter while Lorena and I urge each other to keep stroking against the increasing force of wind and waves. Our minds barely register our last sunset on the Sea; we are too busy with the business of survival. An hour crawls painfully by and we are reduced to robots, chanting "Row! Row! Row your boat!" to coordinate our paddling in the pitch darkness. A wave sweeps us; our fantasy trip did not include spray covers and the boat is swamped. "Think of it as ballast," I scream and plunge my paddle deep into a breaking wave.

We enter a narrow passage between the mainland and a small island but there's no safe landing, huge waves crash against the cliffs and rebound in crazy foaming patterns that make paddling almost impossible. Did Rob get through this? I force myself not to wonder and concentrate on the cramps in my legs, arms and back. My body has entered a Zen-like state of pain that will have no real meaning until we've reached safety. I am completely blinded by spray; in the bow Lorena activates some inner radar and guides us through the channel with high-pitched cries of "Left! Right! Right-Right!" The howl of the wind against the cliffs, shadowing us from the faint star-glow, the violence of the kayak's motion through the water, is almost too much for me; I feel rat-like scurryings undermining my confidence. The kayak slows, begins to wallow and turn sideways. If we broach we're done for. Lorena suddenly turns, thrusting her right hand toward me. I lean forward instinctively and she jams a candy bar into my mouth. How she found it I'll never know. I chew the foil wrapper and sweet candy greedily, expending its energy in a renewed frenzy of paddling even before it hits my stomach.

"Almost!" Lorena shouts, and we skirt a foam capped reef that would tear the guts out of a supertanker. The wind is suddenly behind us, driving us at an incredible speed toward a dark line of beach. I fumble in the darkness for my flashlight and find it jammed under my right hip. The light works, even after a long saltwater bath, and I wink it quickly up and down the length of the beach, praying for an answering signal from Rob. "Hurry!" Lorena is fighting to steady the kayak as it lunges heavily with the waves. If this isn't the right beach we're really in the soup; I spray the place with light and there, almost too good to be true, comes an answering flash . . . and another! Not one response but two, widely separated.

We go for the nearest light. With the wind and waves at our backs and the promise of safety ahead we propel the waterlogged kayak forward like a surfboard . . . and slam into the beach, the kayak rolling heavily onto its side, spilling us out on hands and knees. A light bobs across the beach, then fixes on my face.

"¿Qué diablos?" A young frightened voice cries. "What devils?" Lorena tries to stand, staggers forward, and falls flat on her face. I crawl to the bow, oblivious of the waves washing over me, and attempt to drag the kayak higher onto the sand. The voice continues to shout assorted exclamations of surprise in Spanish as Lorena and I work the boat safely out of the surf. And then, before I can allow myself to think ahead, to let the rats of paranoia out of their cage, Rob is there, hauling at the bow like a madman, shouting over the wind, "We made it! We made it!"

A folding kayak stows easily inside a car, van or pickup camper. When travelling by public transportation you'll probably be charged overweight fees, but they're more than worth it, especially after you've assembled the boat and paddled or sailed away. A folding kayak solves the painful dilemma of how to have your own boat without needing a vehicle to transport it. Your folding boat can even be carried in another boat, either to avoid long or dangerous passages or to quickly travel to a better jump-off point (see *Hitching By Boat* later in this chapter).

When not in use, a folding kayak can be kept out of sight, either in a vehicle, hotel room or baggage room, freeing you for side trips on land.

Folding boats shouldn't suffer as much from travelling as rigid boats, especially if you supervise their loading (or do it yourself) when going by bus or train. A generous tip to the baggage handler or bus driver's *ayudante* (helper) is cheap insurance against rough treatment.

The time required to assemble a folding kayak is really insignificant when compared to its advantages, though it is true that quick 'in-and-out' trips tend to be a hassle.

Our second choice is a rigid open canoe, of fiberglas or aluminum. This type of boat costs substantially less than a folding kayak, weighs less, handles better and is very easy to load and unload from a vehicle, even for one person. When carried on a roof rack (securely lashed and locked down), it has little effect on the vehicle's performance or gas consumption. A friend who travels throughout Mexico with an aluminum canoe says he can have it in the water in less time than it takes most people to put on their bathing suit. He keeps his camping gear neatly packed inside his car and can be prepared for an overnight voyage within minutes of parking. Canoes are much easier to load with camping equipment than kayaks and can be carefully over-loaded in emergencies. Sleeping inside a canoe, either afloat or ashore, is possible (and hellishly uncomfortable), and upside down they give shelter from the elements.

Inflatable Boats

Small inflatable boats offer many of the advantages described earlier for folding kayaks. Unfortunately the larger models are just too cumbersome and expensive for the average camper. Jacques Cousteau cuts a fine figure in one of these high speed inflatables, tracking down some Mystery of the Depths, but he has a nice cozy ship and a stout crew to handle details such as huge outboard motors, gas tanks, heavy rigid floorboards, repair kits and costly air pumps. The development of the inflatable motor boat has finally come full circle and most weigh as much or even more than an equivalent aluminum boat. Their prices . . . well, it's more like an investment.

Inflatable boats have the advantage over rigid boats of being full of air, at least until they're punctured, but a well made boat of any material usually has buoyancy tanks or blocks of foam to keep you above Davey Jones' Locker.

Sun and salt water take their toll on inflatables, but nothing hurts them worse than bashing into coral or cactus spines (commonly found on Mexican beaches). Carry a good patch kit and keep the boat in the shade as much as possible.

Inflatable kayaks and rowboats and two to three person economy model motor-boats are light in weight, compact when not inflated, quite durable and not outrageously expensive. They are ideal for camping from a small vehicle or for someone who doesn't want to cope with a rigid boat or larger inflatable. The smallest models can be backpacked, opening up all kinds of walking/floating trips. Friends carried two one-person inflatable kayaks in their van and used them for everything from surfing (an addictive pastime) to poking into lagoons and small lakes. If you don't pit yourself against a strong river or rough ocean, one of these boats can be quite satisfying.

Outboard Boats

There's one type of boat that is the undisputed hands-down favorite among *gringo* boaters and fishermen for Mexican waters: a twelve to fourteen foot, v-bottom, welded aluminum 'runabout' or 'fisherman's boat'. These boats are unusually wide and stable for their length, light in weight but incredibly strong, and seaworthy enough to tackle open ocean. They are shallow draft, very fast with a ten to fifteen horsepower outboard and almost maintenance free. I've tried them in all types of water, including some rough ocean conditions that I wouldn't care to repeat, and can't think of a better boat for the size and money. They will carry up to four people or two with a lot of camping gear.

These boats can be carried on top of a car or truck. It usually takes two people to load and unload, but I've seen many boaters do it alone with mechanical devices for assistance (ask a boat dealer for suggestions).

Tourists who haul huge speedboats and cabin cruisers to Mexico usually end up wishing for one of these smaller open boats. Since good skin diving can be found close to shore and blue water gamefish often come within a few miles of the beach, it doesn't take a big boat and motor to get the best sport. The economy of a smaller boat is very important, especially if you are camped in an area where gasoline is difficult to find and of dubious quality.

Boats of less than twelve feet, what I call 'lake boats', should be used with the greatest caution in the open ocean. The temptation to get just a little farther offshore for a chance at a sailfish can easily lead to disaster. The danger increases greatly if your boat isn't fast enough to run inshore at the first sign of rough water or changing weather. You don't have to risk your life to have a good time; just wait for the best conditions before going out.

Car Top or Trailer?

Driving in Mexico can pose a considerable challenge to the stamina of both you and your vehicle (see Chapter 10 and *The People's Guide to Mexico*). Trailering a boat, especially on a long camping trip that will include back road driving, may take a heavy toll. Launching facilities are limited (and permits may be required in some popular spots), insurance rates are higher for trailers and parking is a problem, especially on narrow colonial city streets. In spite of these disadvantages, many tourists do tow boats to Mexico. Most of them have no special problems, especially if they drive with extra caution and don't try to launch where conditions are not reasonable.

It is customary for Mexican fishermen to help anyone who needs to launch or retrieve a boat. Most of their own boats are far too heavy for one or two people to move. *Gringos* should pitch in, especially if they want the favor returned. Your assistance is likely to be accepted without thanks but you'll be offered help just as casually.

Boaters who stay in one place for a long period of time can make the chore of launching and retrieving much easier by buying large inflatable plastic rollers. Or here's an ingenious device suggested by a boater friend: buy three or four inexpensive inflatable balls (the size of a soccer ball) and stuff them, in a row, inside a flour sack. Tie the sack closed and use this as a roller; when you leave Mexico give the balls away to the local children. Inflatable rollers can also serve as life preservers, but should not replace basic safety equipment.

If your trailered boat won't reach the water while attached to the vehicle, just unhitch it and walk it to the water. You may have to deflate the tires quite a bit to avoid sinking into the sand. Boats and/or trailers can be retrieved across a beach by winches or by towing them very carefully with a rope tied to the bumper of a car or truck. Have someone walk with the boat and be prepared to stop instantly if it runs into an obstruction.

Give your boat trailer a complete servicing and check up before you leave home. If the tires are not standard auto or truck sizes, take at least one spare. If you're going on a long trip in hot country or expect to travel rough roads, two spares are even better. Small trailer tires are generally as scarce as hen's teeth in Mexico.

There are alternatives to hauling your boat for thousands of miles over dry land. Find a trailer park or enclosed parking lot (*estacionamiento*) and store your boat and trailer while you make side trips. It saves wear and tear, both on your equipment and nerves. The cost of storage will probably be less than maintaining an insurance policy on the boat and trailer. Many tourists do this, not only with boats but with camping trailers and even motorhomes. If you're in Mazatlán and want to do a quick trip to the Yucatán or Oaxaca it's probably cheaper (and definitely quicker) to fly or take the bus.

Although your trailer and boat will be noted on your tourist papers (see Chapter 11), it is not illegal to separate them from the car — or yourself — as long as you remain inside Mexico. Just don't forget where you left them.

When car-topping or trailering a boat, lash it down tight! Stop every hour during the first day on the road to check the boat, the roof rack and the trailer hitch. Ropes, cotton straps, rubber cords and other fasteners will stretch over a period of time, especially if they are new. The first days are the most critical, though after a few weeks in the blazing sun breakage can be expected. Rubber shock cords are especially notorious for snapping unexpectedly after long exposure to the sun.

I tie my boat down securely and then add a couple of 'paranoia ropes' for good measure and peace of mind. More than once these extra tie downs have saved a boat from slipping or serious shifting.

Boat theft is probably more of a hazard in the U.S. than in Mexico but "better safe than sorry" is my rule: chain the boat to the trailer or roof rack, or better yet, to the vehicle itself. Keep the lock well oiled or you'll soon need a hacksaw.

Boats make convenient places to store extra camping gear. The last time I did this we lost two expensive life jackets in the middle of the Sonora deserts. At fifty miles per hour the wind sucked the jackets from their 'secure' position inside the bow of a kayak and blew them away. A tightly tied-down tarp is your best bet. It will also provide protection from the elements and curious wandering fingers.

"What was that?"

"Huh? What?" Lorena's eyes opened slowly, fighting the tranquilizing effect of a hot afternoon sun and the steady rocking of the car as we headed south. Her gaze shifted lazily to the palm trees on our right. Somewhere just beyond those shimmering green *cocos* lay the blue Pacific Ocean and True Bliss.

"I felt something back there. Kind of a lurch." I glanced into the rearview mirror. "Lorena, there's . . . *OH NO!*" My foot mashed the brake pedal as I steered the overloaded station wagon onto the narrow crumbling shoulder.

"Carl, what's wrong?"

I stared at the scene in the mirror, dumb with shock. Lorena turned slowly in the seat.

"It's a wreck!" she gasped. "Oh, look!" There was a catch in her voice. "That banana truck is right on top of a little red car!"

I sagged over the steering wheel, pressing my forehead into the searing hot plastic.

"That's no car," I groaned, "That's my boat! MY BOAT!" I resisted the urge to punch holes in the windshield, settling for a series of anguished animal-like howls and shrieks.

Lorena waited until my grief had subsided and said, "Well, aren't you going to *do* something?"

I looked at the scene behind us, wondering what possible solution she could see to the tangle of crushed plywood, torn sails and splintered spars that had been cruelly ground into the hot asphalt. I slipped my foot off the brake and put the car into gear.

"Yeah, I'm going to do something," I sighed, pressing the accelerator to the floor. "I'm going to stop at the next Wide Spot, slash my wrists and throw myself into a ditch. You do whatever feels right after that." I snapped the radio on, tuning in a Mexican teenybopper station at mind numbing volume. Lorena shook her head a few times before slumping back into the seat. Dreams of skimming along some offshore coral reef, sails full and tight, a feather jig skipping the wave tops as a fat *dorado* thrashed the water nearby were now reduced to a roadside litter. Children would return home from scavenging firewood with odd bits of oak and mahogany. Stainless steel rigging would be reduced to holding up some chicken coop; fine Egyptian cotton sails cut into handkerchiefs and . . . diapers! I tried to sympathize with the startled driver of the banana truck but an evil glow in my heart wished him . . .

"So now what?" Lorena's yawn couldn't quite conceal a note of genuine concern. After all, we'd planned our entire camping trip around that wonderful little boat. Without it I was . . . lost? . . . adrift? No, *sunk* was more like it. I mentally reviewed my file of Dream Trips, pulling the index card marked "Sail Dinghy To Desert Island." So much for that one. I wrote an imaginary *Deceased* across the card. Wait a second! What about this other card under 'D'? "Dugout Canoe to South America." Why not?

Outboard Motors: Repairs, Parts and Fuel

The most common outboard motors in Mexico are Evinrude and Johnson, with Suzuki and Mercury a distant third and fourth. The best rule about outboards is: don't expect parts and servicing and you won't be disappointed. Be prepared to do it yourself. In large cities and some fishing towns you can find repair shops for *motors de afuera borda*, but if the job isn't a minor one or requires parts, you may be completely out of luck or have to wait (and wait) for parts.

The more you love to use your boat and motor, the better prepared you should be to keep it going yourself. People who are casual about routine maintenance and repairs usually find themselves sitting on the beach while fussier types are out hauling in the fish.

Give your motor a thorough check up and test before you leave home. An amazing number of people say, "It ran fine last year," and toss their outboard into the trunk without a second thought. Run it for at least an hour or two; it might save you a lot of hair pulling and teeth gnashing later on.

Carry a full tune-up kit and if your trip will last for more than a couple of weeks, carry a generous supply of spare plugs, shear pins, gaskets, gear lube, a service manual, a carburetor rebuild kit (or two) and any other small parts or servicing materials you can think of. If your motor requires special tools for normal servicing, buy them now. I also carry a spare gas tank hose and clamps; even brand new hoses can be cut accidentally.

Outboard gas cans are very expensive in Mexico, so if you can afford it take at least one extra. They are easy to sell if you find you don't need it.

Carry more oil than you'll need, especially if your motor is under warranty. Some oils are dyed; if the dealer has to work on your motor later and finds you didn't use the right oil, it could void your warranty. Never let anyone mix gas and oil for you, unless you're willing to risk your motor's health to their judgement. A fisherman proudly boasted to a friend, "My new motor is so good it ran all day without any oil in the gas."

You'll have to buy gas at a regular Pemex station; marine gas stations are only now being planned in Mexico. In out-of-the-way villages and *ranchos*, gasoline is sold from rusty barrels. Filter it carefully. Fishermen often buy gas on a cooperative basis and they'll probably sell or trade off a few gallons as a favor. Don't depend on them for regular quantities; in fact, they'll soon have you making runs to the nearest gas station with their empty barrels.

Camping By Boat

For Lorena and me, camping from a small boat is just about *it*, an irresistible combination of freedom and adventure, nicely balanced by the security and comfort of dry land under us at night. Nothing is more enjoyable than a camp on a small island or a remote cove, or a quiet night on a sandbar, cut off from the rest of the world by a deep river gorge. The anticipation of visiting a distant village is even more intense when it must be reached by boat.

Once you've tried boat camping in Mexico you'll probably be hooked for life. I can think of no other way to so completely and easily slip away than by putting a few miles of water between myself and civilization. Anyone who has dreamed of their own yacht or of voluntary exile in the South Pacific should first try it in Mexico. The fantasy can become a reality almost quicker than you could believe possible.

Trip Planning

Mexico's extensive coastlines haven't yet suffered the type of wall-to-wall development that is so typical in the United States. Tourist centers and resorts tend to be concentrated, alternating with long stretches that are all but uninhabited. This is ideal for beach camping, either by boat, backpack or vehicle. It comes as a pleasant shock that undeveloped beaches can be found within sight of crowded tourist towns. Many small villages and *ranchos* are accessible only by water or arduous treks over very rough terrain; they offer no great potential for tourist development and will hopefully remain isolated to all but the more adventurous.

Keep in mind that a successful boat camping trip in Mexico doesn't have to involve a long, arduous voyage. Once you get out of town, you're really *out there*. You don't have to travel great distances to avoid crowds and find adventure.

One of our favorite places to camp by boat in Mexico is within half a mile of a very popular Pacific coast beach. Our spot can be reached on foot, but the trail is poorly marked and the steeper sections are treacherous. The campsite itself is very small: about ten feet in diameter, a rough circle of gravel in the mouth of an arroyo, heavily overgrown with small trees and thorn bushes. It takes great caution to land a small boat on the rocky shore but it can be done. With a few gallons of drinking water and a sack of fresh food we can easily stay for four or five days. The only people we see are passing fishermen, both Mexicans and *gringos* from the nearby trailer parks. At night, roasting a fish over the campfire, we might as well be a thousand miles from the nearest city. Such a place is not at all unusual; in fact, there are at least a dozen similar campsites within another mile of ours.

On another boat camping trip, along a 150-mile stretch of deserted shoreline, we discovered a campsite so perfect we couldn't force ourselves to pass it up. It was five miles from our launching point. We used our boat for side trips, diving and fishing. There were moments when we felt guilty about not forging on ahead, but on a later trip we completed our original plan and never found a better camping spot than the first.

Ocean beach camping requires much more caution than protected lagoons and gentle rivers and lakes, but don't feel that these safer choices are less interesting or enjoyable. Such river-estuary systems as the Papaloapan (Butterfly) offer camping possibilities that stagger the imagination. Inland lakes and reservoirs are another unexploited alternative. (See *Unknown Mexico* at the end of this chapter.)

Boat Camping Suggestions

• Over-exposure to the sun and over-exertion plague eager boat campers. It's so easy to pass up a potential campsite, especially when you just *know* that the next cove or river bend hides the perfect spot. Camp earlier rather than later; any extra energy you have can be well spent on chores and cooking. Side trips and activities like fishing, skin diving or crashing through the underbrush in search of lost cities often puts you on your knees by sundown. That's fine, at least as long as you don't do anything but rest the next day.

• Treat your gear, especially your boat, with extra care. A hundred miles up an uncharted river or deserted coast is no

Man of War/Frigate Birds   *Tigeras*

place to negligently knock a hole in the bottom of your canoe. On a long trip protect your boat from the sun when not in use by covering it with a tarp, palm fronds or brush. Salt water corrosion is a real problem, especially on camping gear that is bolted, hinged or screwed together. Wipe things down with a damp rag or rinse them in fresh water. Use light non-corrosive oil liberally.

• Check your anchor and mooring lines *daily* for signs of wear and chafing. Don't maroon yourself just because you were too cheap or lazy to replace a worn line.

• When beaching your boat, especially for the night, pull it beyond the reach of the current or tide and then pull it even farther. The safest method is to sleep between the boat and the water. When a wave slaps you in the face in the middle of the night it's time to move everything to higher ground.

• If you must anchor your boat offshore, don't leave basic survival gear aboard. Should the boat disappear, you'll need food, water, matches, bug dope and a good thick novel.

• Wind squalls come by many names in Mexico and we've been struck by them everywhere: the Caribbean, high desert lakes, Baja, etc. They can hit at any time but seem to prefer moments of weakness, such as the middle of lunch or two hours after dark. There's nothing quite like leaping naked out of bed to chase down flying hats, journals and food bags that were resting quietly when you fell asleep. One squall pelted us with sticks and stones, forcing us to drag our kayaks into a wave-washed cave. We soon learned to put rocks on top of all loose gear, no matter how stable it looked.

• Of all boat camping hazards, I'd say that crabs have scared more people than tidal waves or hurricanes. Crabs come out at night to rummage in your gear for snacks. Some will even rummage in your sleeping bag. Relax, once you've gotten over the initial shock of having a hermit crab tug at your hair, you'll find that they mean no harm.

• Should you find yourself in a bind: sick, broken down or just plain exhausted, consider hiring a passing boat to tow or carry you back to civilization. Wave them down and start bartering. We watched an old man, who had been paddling his heavy dugout past our camp, load it aboard a big fiberglass *panga* for a quicker trip to town.

Gear

Gringos have been thoroughly trained to believe that new activities require new and different gear. Many people can't imagine that boat camping is no different than backpacking or even camping from a small car. Once you've got a boat, just use the same basic equipment and follow the same camping routines you've practised on land. In fact, you'll still be on land; it's just how you get from one campsite to another that has changed — by boat rather than car or foot.

Boats, like vans and backpacks, have tempting corners to overload with unnecessary gear. Unless you've camped from a boat before, you'll probably feel better by taking more equipment than you'll need and use. Live-and-learn is still the most reliable teacher, just don't let a *lack* of gear stop you from making a trip.

A more general and detailed discussion of camping gear can be found in *Preparations & Camping Gear*. The following comments are directed specifically to those planning a boat trip. If you should find yourself in Mexico without having read this earlier, please don't let it deter you. Some of our best boat camping trips were made almost without any gear at all — including a boat (see *Hitching By Boat* later in this chapter).

Waterproof cargo bags: Heavy duty inflatable cargo bags are made especially for kayaking and white water boating. We use one for our binoculars, flashlights, camera, film, medical kit and personal papers and money. On long trips into really remote areas, we stuff another bag with emergency food rations. Because these cargo bags are expensive, we carry our clothing and general gear and food inside heavy-gauge, plastic garbage bags. Three bags, one inside the other, make a fairly durable and waterproof container. Carry it inside a cotton flour sack for additional protection.

Plastic food buckets with tightly sealing lids (put some Vaseline on the lip for extra sealing) are also handy.

Tarp, Mosquito Net: Because boat camping often takes you to that rarest of places — privacy, a tarp is sufficient for sun and rain protection. Just don't forget your mosquito net for those irritating insect visitors.

Clothing: Take the bare minimum. Once you've got a good protective suntan, you'll probably live in a swim suit or loin cloth. We each carry one pair of pants, a pair of shorts or swimming suit, two long sleeved shirts, one or two pairs of socks and light shoes or sandals, depending on the terrain and our desire to make side trips on land.

I carry two hats while boating long distances to avoid the awful prospect of losing one and having to expose my head to the sun.

Sunscreen, skin conditioners & insect repellent: Wind and sun will do their best to erode your skin, especially on salt water. On a long trip by kayak in the Sea of Cortez I developed painful open sores on my arms and wrists in spite of what I considered liberal use of various lotions and liquid sunscreens. Wear clothes and lather yourself with sunscreen, several times a day.

Bag balm, fondly known as 'udder butter,' works great on paddle-weary hands.

I don't like to use chemical insect repellents but only a masochist would venture into a mangrove swamp without a full bottle in each hand. Carry enough to get you through a few bad nights. (See *Bites:* Chapter 8 for making your own repellents.)

First Aid Kit: In addition to our normal Health Kit (see Chapter 8) we carry extra salt tablets. Keep your kit dry and easily at hand; when you need a salt tablet, you won't want to have them buried under other gear.

Sunglasses: Polarized sunglasses reduce glare off the water. This helps prevent eyestrain and headaches and also makes it easier to spot sunken rocks, reefs, fish and Spanish treasure. I carry an additional pair of clip-on sunglasses to use over my regular sunglasses. When boating in the Caribbean the glare off the white coral sand bottom was so intense we had to wear two pairs of sunglasses, taped together on top of each other.

Camera filters: A polarizing filter will improve your photos by reducing water glare. It also protects the surface of the lens from scratching and water spotting. In low light conditions we replace the polarizing filter with a clear filter.

Compass: We carry a shock proof compass for security and use it for simple mapping and orientation. It's doubtful that you'll need a compass, but take one anyway.

Signal Mirror: A good survival tool. We used ours a lot while kayaking in Baja. It solved the problem of trying to communicate between two widely separated kayaks, especially while searching for the next campsite. A steady flashing meant "come here"; no signal meant "keep looking". Crude but effective.

Binoculars: We use a very cheap pair that can be lost, traded, dropped overboard or given away without breaking our hearts or pocketbooks. They are very handy for inspecting campsites and alternate routes, and for snooping on other boats, interesting villages or approaching whales.

Fishing and diving gear: We rely very heavily on foraged food while boating and our gear is simple but complete. (See Chapter 6 for details.)

Food and water: Once we've assembled our basic gear, including stocks of food and water, we use extra space — space that can be filled without jeopardizing the safety of the boat — for extra food and water. You can never have enough drinking water while boating on the ocean, so I give it priority over food. On freshwater rivers and lakes, food takes precedence. If the food isn't needed, trade it off or give it away as you travel. To people in isolated areas a few pounds of sugar or flour will be greatly appreciated.

Repair kit: What if a paddle breaks? You hit a submerged rock or log? The prop falls off? Tailor your repair kit to your worst disaster dreams and it'll probably weigh two hundred pounds. I settle for the basics: waterproof glue, wood screws, nails, twine, pieces of wood, caulking material, duct tape, wire and whatever else jumps into my hand at the hardware store. Repair kits should be replenished after you use them for idle camp projects like building a kitchen table or a *palapa*.

Trade goods and gifts: Don't go into the wilderness loaded down like a Hudson's Bay Company trader (unless, of course, you really want to play out that fantasy). I pack extra fishing gear (hooks, line and sinkers), maybe a couple of knives, candy, sewing stuff and a pair of spare pliers. On some trips I may never part with any of it, on others I'll be giving away my clothes to repay favors. Don't act like a representative of Foreign Aid; give when it feels natural.

Safety gear: I can't over emphasize that your safety on a boat camping trip depends basically on common sense and caution. Ask Mexicans you'll meet along the way for advice on weather and water conditions. It is time well spent and will improve your Spanish. (See the following pages for more details).

Safety, Seamanship and Survival

I once hired a Mexican diver to take me on an overnight trip to a particularly good spearfishing area. His boat was a narrow open *panga* powered by a very battered ten horse outboard. The throttle control had been jury-rigged with baling wire and a bent screwdriver. There were no life jackets, no spare gas cans, no paddles and no charts. A Coast Guard inspector's nightmare.

"What if we have bad weather?" I asked. "Or *problemas* with the motor?" He stared at his feet for a few minutes, then looked up at me with a bright reassuring grin. His hand dipped into the neck of his faded t-shirt and came out with a gold religious medal.

"Don't worry yourself," he said. "This *santo* is all we need."

Although Divine Intervention has saved my neck on more than one occasion, I still prefer more tangible safeguards against maritime disasters. Because safety equipment is rarely actually used, it's awfully tempting to leave it behind. Just as you're about to shove off the beach you realize that you've forgotten the flare pistol and shark repellent. Why bother? Ten minutes later a waterspout hits your boat.

I fight off such unseamanlike habits by indulging in creative paranoia, also known as the pre-launch "what-ifs?" What if we sink? Lorena, load the life jackets! What if we run out of gas? Get the spare cans! What-ifs are cheap insurance and will help guarantee that your trip is both safe and enjoyable. A friend who found himself drifting in a strong current off the coast of Yucatán in a disabled small runabout told me, "You can't even begin to imagine what I would have given for one crummy little paddle." Passing fishermen saved him from a long stretch of cutting sugarcane for a Better Cuba.

Boating conditions are so varied in Mexico that you might be overwhelmed by trying to plan for everything, from uncharted rapids to unexpected local tide rips. The most important safety gear therefore is not a Personal Flotation Device but good old common sense and caution.

When in doubt, *don't*. This doesn't mean you have to be a stick-in-the-mud. Make your plans and daily decisions carefully, as if your life and well-being depended on no one but you — which is the case, especially if you enjoy wandering far afield. Disasters and near-misses make great tales but I'd prefer to risk boring my friends with stories of trips that went without a hitch.

Most boat camping trips will be done within a relatively short distance of your car or camp. This can lead to a dangerous sense of complacency. Load your safety gear as a habit, not as an irritating hassle. If you only need it once, that's more than enough.

Safety Gear

Life jackets: The last unsinkable vessel was the Titanic. Take life jackets for everyone and if you don't have enough, either tell guests to provide their own or stay ashore. If they call you Captain Bligh take it as a compliment; he survived.

Paddles: One paddle is almost worthless in any boat but a canoe or kayak. Take two and if you're alone be sure they can be used together as oars.

Anchor and line: When things go wrong, get the anchor out. A heavy anchor (not a toy) with a long stout line and several feet of heavy chain, carefully tied to the bow of the boat, is better than any insurance policy. Mexican boaters (commercial divers and fishermen) use rocks, cement blocks or *arañas*, spider-like grappling hooks made of steel rods. In very small boats or kayaks we use a folding anchor. This is fine for fishing and rest stops but I won't trust it to hold my boat overnight.

Bailing can: Pick up a plastic bleach bottle off the beach and tie it to the boat with a piece of cord. Cut out the bottom and you've got a Mexican bilge pump.

Extra gasoline: "Let's make one more pass by that reef," inevitably leads to breaking out the spare gas can in a rough sea. Pre-mix the gas and oil on shore to avoid dangerous messes. A large plastic funnel and length of siphon hose are very handy.

Drinking water: I've been without this precious fluid for long enough periods to know that dying of thirst isn't the way to go. Carry *at least* one liter, even for short trips.

Sun protection & shoes: A few extra hours in the sun can send you to the hospital. I once had to make an emergency landing without shoes. I walked, very painfully, over several hundred yards of rocks and thorns, looking for a trail or road. I had no clothes, other than a bathing suit, and the minute I entered the scrub jungle the thorns and mosquitos nailed me. Then, just like in a bad movie, I stepped in an underground hornet's nest. I made it to safety but looked like a piece of bloody hamburger after a mad dash through the thorn bushes. Accounts of shipwrecked survivors on desert islands always seem to mention sore feet; take a pair of sandals, at least.

Waterproof matches & bug dope: Two very small items that can make an unexpected night on a deserted beach an Adventure rather than an ordeal.

Navigating

Common sense is reliable but certainly not infallible. The fact that "this river shouldn't have a waterfall," isn't much consolation when you find yourself desperately paddling air. To avoid the unexpected, ask other boaters what surprises might be in store for you and your boat. Local knowledge is especially important in Mexico, since few charts or reference books are detailed enough to aid small boaters. Many of Mexico's rivers and estuary systems are essentially unexplored. Existing maps can be considered general guidelines, not what you can expect to find when you get there.*

Unfortunately, local knowledge of boating conditions is often as obscure as an explanation of dialectical materialism. We spent two dry weeks combing a small island for a freshwater well that local fishermen swore was as obvious as our noses. Four reliable sources gave us four completely different (and incorrect) sets of directions. My brother finally stumbled upon the fabled waterhole while wandering in the bushes in search of firewood. The well was less than a hundred yards from our camp.

Asking for directions and advice is always a chancy business (see Chapter 3). In

---

* The problem of map accuracy is easily demonstrated by comparing any two Mexican highway maps. Roads that exist on one map don't show on another, and vice versa. If such things as small bays, lagoons, lakes and rivers are noted at all, they're rarely exactly where they should be. (See *Maps & Sources: Appendices*.)

the Sea of Cortez, for example, we found that people couldn't accept that we'd actually travelled for weeks in kayaks without disaster. They were unwilling to take the awful responsibility of sending us into what they considered certain death. "Impossible! Not in *that!* You're not serious!" was the inevitable response to questions about what lay ahead. Fishermen gave us distances to villages or fish camps where water and supplies might be available in terms of travel in a fast boat. Their "one hour" was likely to be days of hard paddling along a deserted shoreline that they themselves paid no attention to as they sped from one fishing ground to another. We never stopped asking for advice, but we soon learned that relying on it too heavily was a mistake.

If you intend to boat on an unknown river (which is most of them in Mexico), it is best to expect the worst and plan around it. Check rapids and gorges out on foot; a few hours of hiking and a few days of delays might be frustrating but it can prevent serious or even fatal mistakes. Unless you're highly skilled at whitewater boating, stick to calmer rivers until you can find reliable information.

It is especially important when asking for boating advice to ask the right person. The friendly lady frying fish in a beach restaurant may know the exact distance to the next village, but can she be expected to forecast sea conditions during the full moon? Or the best place to land a boat in the next bay? Ask someone who goes there regularly: a fisherman, diver or crewman on a cargo canoe. If their answers are vague, don't press for details; you've got the wrong person. Be patient. I once spent hours discussing a potential boat trip with a fellow who finally admitted — when he realized I was serious about doing the voyage — that he didn't know the area quite as well as he'd pretended at first. I controlled the urge to bounce a beer bottle off his head and asked, "Then who do you advise me to see?" It took less than an hour to locate his brother-in-law and get the information I needed.

I don't have either the energy or the experience to write a manual of "How To Explore" or "How To Go Boating In Ten E-Z Steps." The following advice can't take the place of personal experience. One day on the water is worth several thousand words of caution. Do whatever you can to prepare and practice for your trip and I'm confident it won't be wasted. Something as simple as a sailing lesson from the local Park Department can be invaluable if you find yourself up a long bay without a paddle.

An intelligently planned boat trip into unknown territory should have no fixed, rigid goal. "Push on!" is for racing, not safe adventuring. Keep your eyes peeled for alternate routes, unexpected campsites and interesting side trips. When you get home and tell your friends, "We spent six days exploring a lake," they won't care that you never made it to the opposite shore.

Wind, Tides and Surf

Unexpected and violent wind squalls are called *chubascos*. They are often preceded by a period of unnatural calm (the classic calm before the storm). Look carefully for a distant line of dark, wind-ruffled water, a hazy dust cloud or a dark patch of sky. The smell of wind-whipped water also means it's about to hit the fan.

Unless you can make a quick escape to the shore or find shelter behind a reef or rock, you'll just have to ride it out. Point the bow into the wind, drop all sails without delay or idle the motor down — and hang on. Small boats can do very well in terrible sea conditions as long as the people aboard stay calm and don't panic. *Keep the bow into the wind* and don't try to run for it until the wind has passed and the sea's calmed down. If the motor fails or you don't trust it, use paddles and oars to steady the boat against the waves and wind. Patience and a steady hand at the bailing bucket are your best tacks. It'll be all over and past before you know it.

There are four *mareas* (tides) every twenty-four hours: two low tides and two high tides, about six hours each. Slack tide lasts an hour or less and comes at the change from high to low and vice versa. Very rough seas can be created by changes in the direction of tidal currents before and after the slack periods. Watch out, especially around islands, reefs, river mouths, sandbars and headlands. Learn to use the tides to your advantage; they are literally rivers in the sea.

Surf is probably the greatest hazard you will face if you go boating in the ocean. My opinion of surf is tempered by several disasters that all support the old sailor's saying, "The most dangerous place in the sea is along the shore."

Unfortunately, surf is about as easy to avoid as mosquitoes; some day you'll have to face it. Handling a boat in the surf, especially one that is loaded with camping gear, takes good reflexes, a cool head and lots of caution. I've seen so many over-confident boaters lose their gear in the surf that it's almost funny — funny, that is, until someone is injured or drowned.

Even small waves contain great relentless power. I watched two experienced canoeists on their first venture into the ocean. Halfway through the surf line, they stopped to congratulate themselves on a successful launching. A small wave rolled them over, without physical harm to either person. The canoe, however, was twisted like a pretzel and a total loss. Several hundred dollars down the drain, not to mention a sudden end to plans for fishing, diving and exploring.

Don't launch your boat through the surf unless you're quite confident you can also make a return landing. A slight increase in the wind or a shift in the tide can turn small waves into backbreakers in a few short minutes.

Look for alternative landing and launching places. You might have to go an inconvenient distance from camp but if it saves an accident, it's more than worth the trouble. I watched several happy campers launching a large inflatable outboard boat through a medium surf. One was gashed by the propeller and another badly bruised when the boat was thrown sideways. By the time the boat capsized the entire group was in a rage. I made the mistake of asking later why they hadn't tried a much calmer spot at the end of the beach. "We didn't have time!," one of them snapped, "we had to get some fish for dinner!" They not only ate beans but lost a lot of good fishing gear. Time meant nothing to the waves; they just kept pounding in.

When launching and landing, tie everything down as securely as possible. Anything sharp, pointed or heavy can injure someone or damage the boat if there's a spill or rough movement.

Passengers should sit quietly, maintaining a proper balance in the boat. Refrain from loud cries or screams that might distract the person at the helm.

Launching: Watch the surf for several minutes until you recognize the pattern of little waves and big waves (called 'sets'). When you decide to go, go very quickly but not in a panic. Don't try to start the engine or raise the sails until the boat is well beyond the reach of the unexpected rogue wave.

Landing: Waves look smaller when viewed from the rear, your perspective when you approach the beach. Take plenty of time to study the sets. An extra five minutes here is better than two days of drying damp gear.

Mexican fishermen have two schools of thought on landing a boat through surf. The first is "*¡Adelante mis valientes!*" (Onward my valiant ones!) or better known as "Damn the torpedoes, full speed ahead!" until the boat runs aground. The second, and far safer method, is to position the bow of the boat on the back of a wave and ride it in past the breaker line. You've got to go just fast enough to stay behind the wave and maintain steering but not so fast that you begin to surf or so slow that a wave catches you from behind. This takes a cool head but once you've mastered it, you'll save a great deal of wear and tear on the boat.

Issue paddles to your passengers but impress upon them that they are not to move until you give the order. A paddle dipped at the wrong moment can throw the boat dangerously off balance.

If the boat crosses over the back of the wave and begins to surf at high speed, you've got two options to avoid broaching (turning sideways and exposing the boat to the full force of the wave). The secret in both cases is to act fast, before the boat has picked up a lot of forward speed. First, and safest, is to idle your motor down or carefully 'backwater' with oars or paddles. The wave should surge ahead again, leaving you on its safer back side. Don't lose all forward motion or the next wave will clobber you.

The second method is tricky, the sort of turn that an experienced surfer makes when hanging on the forward edge of disaster. With a motor boat the technique is to turn in whichever direction will get you back over the wave quickest. For example, if your boat begins surfing and slews to the right, goose the engine and turn harder to the right. As you cross the crest make another full turn to point the boat back toward the beach.

Most boaters will prefer, however, to keep the boat pointed back out to sea and smoother water. A quick nerve-calming rest and a reassessment of the surf conditions are probably in order anyway. Canoes and kayaks can make a similar maneuver but the timing is critical.

A friend who had been assigned to stand in the bow of a boat with a paddle told us that no matter how loud he yelled at the guy running the motor, he couldn't seem to make him turn the boat. When he finally looked back the 'captain' was swimming for shore, having decided to abandon ship. A few seconds later the uncontrolled boat and faithful crewman went "over the falls".

What if the boat is swamped in the surf? The bigger the waves are, the greater the danger is that someone will be injured or drowned. When in doubt, bail out. If you are a strong swimmer (hopefully wearing a lifejacket) and the situation doesn't look too dangerous, grab the bow of the boat and turn it into the waves. You can try to swim the boat away from the beach or, if the waves push you toward shore, guide the boat in backwards.

Keep the bow pointed into the waves, at right angles to them. Let the waves move the boat while you concentrate on keeping it properly positioned. The idea is to avoid rolling or battering the boat in the surf, to let the force of the waves break on the bow and sweep harmlessly over the submerged boat. WARNING: never get between the boat and the beach or you risk being crushed. Stay at the bow and if the boat turns, move to keep the boat between you and shore.

Once in shallow water, don't allow anyone to leap out until you're certain the boat is grounded or nearly so. In the time it takes to clamber over the side, the boat will be dangerously exposed to the next wave. This either soaks the person at the helm or worse, knocks the boat sideways into the departing passenger. I watched an elderly woman attempt to steady a fourteen-foot aluminum boat while her husband fussed with their gear in knee-deep water. It took two small waves to break her leg: the first knocked the boat slightly sideways, the second threw it over her, pinning her to the sand.

Landing a canoe or kayak through the surf is especially exciting. Our standard conservative method is to get out and swim the boat in. If you've got gear that you don't want soaked or lost by a possible spill, you're better off lightening the load before entering the surf line.

There are various ways to swim a boat in. One person can get into the water and

hang onto the stern as the second person paddles the boat in.
This slows the boat considerably and prevents it from surfing. The boat is also lighter and
the swimmer can help position
it at a ninety degree angle to the
waves. Once the swimmer
touches bottom, the boat can be
pushed into shallow water. Remember, however, that the battle with the surf isn't won until
the boat is high and dry.

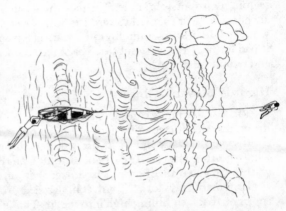

If the surf area is narrow enough (steeper beaches), try this:
one person swims into the beach with a line attached to the stern of the boat. The
other person gets into the water and hangs onto the bow. The boat is going to go in
backwards, since the bow should be lighter and higher and is designed to flare off the
waves. When the person on the beach has a good foothold, the boat is hauled in as fast
as possible, steadied by the person at the bow.

This method also works bow-first. Most outboard boats are very difficult to haul
in backwards, but you'll probably take some water over the stern if you do it bow
first.

If you are alone, position the boat outside the surf line with the bow pointed
seaward. Get into the water, grab the bow and swim the boat in backwards.

What if the surf is just too scary to attempt a landing? Reach for the anchor. It is
far better to suffer the inconvenience of anchoring well offshore than to wreck your
boat or lose your gear. I watched a couple attempt a very dangerous landing in a
beautiful new aluminum canoe. "We were afraid it would blow away or get stolen if
we anchored it out," they said later. Their canoe looked like an aluminum beer can
squeezed by an angry pro football player.

Hazards: Immovable Objects

Rocks, reefs and unexpected underwater pinnacles are common hazards, especially
in salt water. Charts are often inaccurate and small boaters should learn to 'read the
water' rather than depend on printed advice. Watch carefully — and constantly —
for changes in the color and action of the water. A sudden dark spot might be the tip
of an undersea mountain, a school of fish or a patch of drifting seaweed. Sudden steep
waves or breaking seas in an unlikely place are a good indication that something big
and hard lies beneath the surface. Give it a wide berth.

Hugging the shoreline is a temptation for small boaters, but ironically the sea is
often rougher as you get closer to the beach. Reflected waves, currents swirling over
submerged reefs and tidal surges are especially tricky in shallower water. Find a
happy medium; it's usually not very far offshore.

I was riding in a twenty-foot boat with a Mexican fisherman at the helm who
suddenly decided to show me an offshore reef at very close range. Just as the boat
reached the reef, a monster wave formed beneath us. The water was pushed up into a
fantastic bulge as it swept over the reef. We found ourselves hanging on the face of an
awesome breaking wave. Without warning the boat shot forward, surfing uncon-
trollably. As the wave's crest curved ever higher over us, the boat's stern lifted at a

seemingly impossible angle. The fisherman clung to the motor as I dodged loose anchors and gear that fell toward the bow. Over the incredible roar of the wave and wind I could hear an unintelligible stream of fervent prayer. Then, just as suddenly as it had formed, the wave subsided back into the sea, leaving us with shaking knees and pounding hearts.

Hazards: Movable Objects

Whale watching is considered a great sport and highly educational, but it makes my palms sweat to see a fifty-foot *ballena* coming to check *me* out. Whales (especially the distinctive black and white orcas, killer whales) are big enough to deserve your whole-hearted respect. The risk of intruding on their privacy might seem worthwhile until you realize how much damage they can do with a casual swat of a tailfin.

Giant manta rays love to swim at high speeds, suddenly bursting from the sea like enormous bats, tumbling high into the air. This is spectacular stuff, the sort of thing people pay money to watch at Marineland. Consider, however, the effect on you and your boat if one of these huge rays should land on top of you.

Rays are very easy to approach, even in noisy motor boats, and many people have accidently collided with them. This is dangerous and probably very painful for the ray. Keep an eye out for dark spots and the occasional fin breaking the water (usually mistaken for a shark's fin).

Watch closely for net floats and give them a wide berth. Many are homemade from scraps of wood and are difficult to spot. If you tangle with a net, please don't chop it up. A few minutes of patient work will save a fisherman hours of tedious mending and lost fishing time.

Finally, we come to the last word in disasters: boaters themselves. You've got a hot new outboard and a heavy load of passengers, beer and fishing poles and a blazing sun. What could possibly go wrong on a day like this? Let's hope the answer is *nothing,* but don't let enthusiasm overwhelm good sense.

While camping on a popular Mexican beach we joined a group of people who were rather enviously giving a send-off to a young couple in a fourteen-foot sailboat. Their boat was loaded with camping gear and fresh food; obviously they were about to embark on a long-awaited True Adventure. When several campers questioned the safety of leaving on an especially windy day, they answered with "We've been out in a lot worse." Being mere land lubbers what could we do but help them shove off and give a heartfelt "Good luck!"

Half a mile offshore they capsized. It took them hours to right the boat, bail it out, collect what they could of their gear and paddle back to shore. When they landed they were exhausted, scared and angry.

"Why the hell didn't somebody *do something?*" they yelled at us.

We beach bums just looked at each other and shrugged. What could we have done? There were no other boats available, no handy fishermen to hire for a rescue operation, no Coast Guard unit to alert for a helicopter. In short, the unlucky couple had been completely on their own the second they left the beach. It took them a couple of days to dry their gear, straighten away the boat and come to grips with a simple truth: being on your own means self-reliance is a reality rather than a romantic daydream. What you can't do yourself won't get done. When they sailed away the second time their gear was carefully stowed and lashed down, the wind was moderate and their sailing style conservative enough to insure that they'd make it, *on their own.*

"Are we there yet?"

"Very funny!" I lowered my paddle across the dugout canoe and slumped over with a low groan. I looked back; we had come at least a thousand yards. Sweat stung my eyes; my back and arms felt as though each painful yard had been a full mile. I could still see a group of teenagers loitering in the cool shade of a palm tree, watching our progress with cynical amusement.

"This is *exciting*," Lorena said, laying the paddle across the bow and probing the palm of her hand gingerly, wincing as she found another blister. A puff of wind cooled my face, taunting me with memories of my trusty red sailboat. The dugout wallowed in the sea like a drowsy whale. I gave a low sigh and raised my paddle.

The path to Adventure might raise a few blisters but that was a small price to pay indeed for the glories that would be ours when we . . . After the disastrous end of the sailboat I'd conceived a new Grand Plan: brilliant, daring, simple and inexpensive.

"Paddle a dugout canoe from Mazatlán to Guatemala? Do you feel okay?" Lorena's initial skepticism had only fired my imagination and tempered my resolve. I'd steered our station wagon to a small village south of Mazatlán and immediately begun searching for a suitable canoe. The search ended beneath a pile of sun-faded palm fronds. In a nearby *ramada* an old fisherman patiently repaired nets, finally agreeing to sell me the dugout. His fourteen-year-old grandson, a sneering kid who would surely end his days knitting sweaters in some Mexican penitentiary, had the gall to laugh when I explained the Plan.

"If we are careful with *ciclónes* and reefs and the current and can rig some kind of a *vela*, a sail, we should make it in a year. Well, perhaps one year and a half." The old man's response was a vague, "Hmmm?"

"Let's launch the *canoa*," I'd said, clearing off the fronds that protected the ancient wood from further cracking.

"It's a little *pesada*, eh?" I struggled to lift one end of the boat above the sand. The old man shrugged; of course it was heavy. It was the major portion of a very large *huanacaxtle* tree. In fishermen's terms a 'stout boat'.

The grandson, who had now fallen victim to a compulsive case of the giggles, was sent off for the paddles. I inspected them carefully, with a slight feeling of dread. Each was as thick as my arm and carved from some heavy tropical hardwood. The shafts were polished to a fine golden hue from countless hands and long forgotten voyages to . . .

"Don't get wet," the old man chuckled, tossing a rusty Pemex oil can into the bottom of the dugout. He signalled to a group of boys nearby. They came obediently, eyes filled with curiosity. "All together!"

Ten backs bent to the task, sliding the canoe into the low surf. The grandson showed a sudden burst of spirit by wading into chest-deep water to give us a final helpful push.

"It's coming in all over the place!" Lorena shouted reaching for the oil can. Water squirted through several heavily tarred cracks.

"Details! Just details!" I assured her, wrestling my paddle into position. I took a bearing on the horizon; Guatemala was almost visible. The paddle resisted for an instant, then sliced cleanly through the water.

"WATCH OUT!" Lorena gave a wild scream and grabbed for the thick sides of the canoe as it tipped wildly.

"It's a little tender," I laughed, "but we'll soon get used to it." I took another hard stroke. "Weigh 'ho and up she rises!" I chanted, taking another bearing on the horizon. Guatemala had receded.

An hour later, weary and worn, we nudged the canoe back onto the beach. Grandson and friends, all now afflicted with irritating grins, helped us drag the boat onto the sand. The old fisherman crouched at his nets, fingers flying over the broken webbing. Lorena staggered away, then suddenly flopped down onto her stomach into a very un-explorerlike posture.

"We'll have to hire paddlers," I said, brushing sand from my swollen palms. "I'll bet a couple of these kids would just jump at the chance for real adventure. They can pick up a few pesos and have one hell of a good time, too. What do you say?"

She groaned and burrowed deeper into the beach, like a ghost crab fleeing a seagull. I felt a great sadness settle onto my shoulders. It's tough to see a person you really care for cave in like that. A lack of intestinal fortitude; that's what they always yelled about in gym class.

"I'll go hire the paddlers, Lorena. Don't worry."

"*. . . una oportunidad increíble!*" The boys listened to my empassioned spiel, shifting nervously from one bare foot to another. I'd made it clear that there was room in the canoe for just two, no more than two.

The grandson tapped himself silently on the chest. I felt a sudden rush of affection for this obviously bored kid, who like so many others had grappled with inner doubts and now held his own destiny in his hands. I was tempted to tell him of my search for the trail . . . the treasure of the . . .

"*Quiero diez mil dolares, capitán. En adelante.*"

What was that? Did he say "ten thousand dollars?" In advance? Why I'd have the little beggar trussed onto the yardarm before he . . .

"*Buen viaje, capitán!*" With hoots of laughter my crew deserted into the coco plantation, condemning themselves to a life of tedium.

"Now what?" Lorena rolled onto her back, flicked her eyes toward the canoe, then looked quickly away.

"Let's go backpacking down the beach," I suggested, overwhelmed by the loneliness of command.

"All the way to Guatemala?"

"No, just a mile or two," I answered, not bothering to respond to her sarcasm. There was no point in irritating her further and besides, unless I was mistaken, those marks I'd seen earlier along the beach had been curiously familiar. They were gone now, erased by the waves. Where had I seen them before? Could this be the trail to the Lost Elephant Graveyard? Was that a distant trumpeting?

Buying A Dugout Canoe

Although authentic dugout canoes are still made in Mexico, most fishermen and divers now prefer lightweight fiberglas *pangas*. That doesn't mean traditional heavy wooden *canoas* aren't still used and appreciated — they are, in fact, used until worn out or lost. Some of the larger *cayucos* are veterans of the banana trade, when fleets of huge sailing dugouts converged on Mexican ports with cargoes of fruit to be shipped to the United States. Some of these dugouts have been converted to power, others serve ignoble retirement as decorations for tourist hotels and restaurants.

Even though the heyday of the dugout has now passed they are not necessarily cheap. Any boat that can carry a man out to fish or dive can provide a living for a family. Its value includes a potential income and may therefore be relatively high.

Also, any canoe that survives its first few years without serious splitting or cracking is presumed to be tough enough to last another forty or fifty seasons.

Carving dugouts is a risky business. A typical large dugout will be made from a tree that grows a considerable distance from the sea. After felling, the trunk is dragged and rolled to a suitable place for carving, which may be all the way to the beach. If a crack appears as the canoe is being formed or cured, the boat must be rejected. Fishermen have told me of unlucky boat builders who had to carve three canoes to end up with one good one.

Even a good dugout suffers heavily from long years of hard use. A typical veteran canoe will be caulked with *chapopote* (tar), patched with flattened tin cans and reinforced with nails, scraps of wood and even fiberglas. Be especially wary of long cracks that run below the water line. If you hit a rock too hard or run into a rough sea, these cracks may split the canoe open like a torn banana peel. Large pieces of a dugout make picturesque driftwood; lots of broken canoes are bleaching their bones on deserted beaches.

Paddling a dugout for more than a few minutes or a few miles requires real stamina, tough hands (or gloves) and a strong determination to get wherever you're going. Unless the canoe is quite large it will be difficult to balance. Dugouts do tip over and are all but impossible to right without a crane or a lot of helping hands. Stability comes with greater size, but greater size means a crew of at least four, a good sail or an outboard motor.

Discouraged? Don't be; any logical evaluation of a dugout is like comparing the advantages of a VW Rabbit over a Stutz Bearcat. The traditional dugout may not offer much in the way of comfort and speed but it appeals to entirely different senses. Fish caught from a dugout taste far better than those taken from modern boats, sunsets are far brighter and more memorable, and distant palm-covered shorelines are slower to reach but much more romantic when you finally get there.

Renting A Boat

Renting a boat in Mexico can be the solution to a lot of problems, especially if you don't have a boat already or are reluctant to take one. You can rent a boat that matches the conditions and requirements of a particular trip, whether it's fishing far offshore or taking a group of friends into an interesting lagoon to photograph birds. The cost of rental boats is almost always reasonable in Mexico, especially when you consider prices at home and the expense of owning and maintaining your own boat.

Unless you intend to rent a small boat from an established resort on one of the many bass fishing lakes in northern Mexico, you'll probably have to include a hired crew — the owner or someone he trusts. Exceptions to this are few; after all, the boat and motor represent a large investment and the owner will have justifiable doubts about your knowledge of the area and boat handling. The best way to avoid hiring a crew is to provide the motor yourself (usually the most expensive and difficult piece of equipment to replace) or to rent a boat that isn't worth much. Leaky dugout canoes, for example, or someone's homemade Queen Mary.

Regular charter fishing boats operate out of coastal tourist towns, but better bargains can be found by hiring local commercial fishermen to take you out. Ask around the waterfront or wherever you see a concentration of boats. Don't hesitate to barter and to inquire of several people for the best deal.

Going out with fishermen will be a basic trip: no seat cushions, life jackets, cold beer or fancy fishing gear. Just a hardcore fishing expedition.

When hiring a boat be sure you know what you're going to get for whatever price is agreed upon. Is it by the hour, day or trip? Charter boat owners will make this clear; others will wheel and deal.

I wanted to rent a boat to go skin diving but couldn't afford the price asked, low as it was. After long discussion with the owner we agreed on this plan: I found a few tourists who were interested in a short boat ride and a picnic on a beach near the diving area. They paid to be taken to the beach and we picked them up after I'd finished diving. The boat owner deducted what they contributed from the original price he'd asked for my trip. I also gave him half my catch and we were both quite content.

When renting a boat for longer trips, I've found it cheaper to offer to pay for the gas and oil, plus a certain amount per day for the boat. Then, if you want to change your route or extend the trip, the owner won't balk at what would be his additional expense on a 'package' deal.

Once the arrangement is made, don't be surprised if the owner invites friends along. This is quite common, especially if he wants somebody to chat with or to help handle the boat. When I don't want unexpected company I say so beforehand. I learned this the hard way — when the boat owner showed up with two very cranky children.

I've also learned not to take along enough booze or beer to get anyone aboard drunk. On one trip my innocent generosity resulted in the boat owner passing out in the bilges, leaving me to handle the boat, not to mention his foul mood when he finally came to. Sailors the world around have a reputation for over-indulgence and Mexican fishermen are no exception. Most of them drink only on the beach and after work, but some just can't resist, especially if there's a group of fun-loving tourists aboard.

Hitching By Boat

Hitching by boat in Mexico takes patience, good humor and a constant come-what-may attitude. The rewards for these Scout-like traits are many: imagine yourself lounging on a cozy bale of dried shark meat, trailing a fishing line in the brilliant deep blue water as the *panga* follows some inaccessible coastline. A bright lazy sun, warm water, green jungle behind white sandy beaches — how can you beat it? At moments like these the thought of hefting a backpack and thumbing on the highway is about as attractive as snowshoeing to a job in the salt mines.

Sea turtle   *Tortuga*

Although Mexico's rivers, lakes, lagoons and sea coasts have very few regularly scheduled passenger or cargo boats, there is frequent water traffic on them. Hitching (and by hitching I don't exclude the possibility that you'll pay something for the ride) therefore involves finding a spot to get aboard. Look at your map. Your best chance for a trip into undeveloped and really interesting areas is to find a nearby fishing village or market town. A medium-sized town on the end of a large lagoon or lake, for example, will be the commercial center for people living both on the shoreline and inland. They'll use boats to carry their goods to and from the market, and perhaps mule and burro trains for transport farther inland.

We wanted to visit a stretch of Pacific coastline that was inaccessible except by water or a hot and tedious week-long mule ride. We went to a large town bordering the area and asked various fishermen if they'd take passengers. Unfortunately they had all shifted their fishing to another region, but one helpful man suggested that we walk the beach outside town: a cargo canoe serviced villages along the coast but he wasn't sure where it left from.

A few hours later I asked a group of *campesinos* sitting around a huge pile of grain sacks, cases of soda pop, cartons of canned goods and crates of fresh vegetables if they knew of *"una panga de carga?"* (a cargo boat). They did. In fact, they were waiting for it themselves and had been all day. If the lazy bum who ran it didn't show up soon, they said, they'd have to camp overnight on the beach. Why didn't we join them?

The cargo canoe soon appeared and after a brief discussion with the first mate (a boy of about twelve), Lorena and I were ferried out to the boat in a very leaky dugout, backpacks carefully balanced across our knees. The captain, a wheezing fat man with no great love for his job, promptly put me to work unloading the dugout as the mate ferried the *campesinos'* goods out from the beach. After an hour or so of sweaty labor we raised anchor and headed off. Our ride cost one dollar each (compared to thirty dollars or more to hire a fisherman for a special trip). We also received several invitations for meals and shelter from the other passengers. We didn't really know where we were going, but what did it matter?

Once you arrive somewhere, ask for advice on further rides and side trips. When you demonstrate patience, people often become very cooperative. This is especially true when they themselves have no respect for schedules. If someone offers you a vague ride, so what if it's a day or two late? Use the time for something other than fretting and you'll enjoy the trip much more.

Trade goods can often work magic with fishermen who don't want to bother carrying passengers, free or paying. Since many of them make a relatively large amount of money fishing, the lure of something they can't get easily is more tantalizing: diving and fishing gear (I buy used diving masks at flea markets), knives, clothing, tools; just make sure the deal is firm and clear before you leave.

When you can't find a free or inexpensive ride, it often pays to do whatever is necessary to get the first stop away from civilization: hike it or pay for a shorter ride to a village or *rancho*. Once you're out in the boondocks, you'll be treated less as a rich tourist and more for what you really are — just a person in need of a ride or other favors.

Paraíso

"How can you stand it?" I asked, abandoning my careful scrutiny of the palm-fringed bay for pirates, descendants of Moby Dick or fiercely painted war canoes. Nothing in sight but a small dugout, paddled by a crew of laughing half-naked children.

"Stand what?" Lorena stretched lazily, sinking even deeper into the hot sand. Her face was red and slick from sun and coconut oil; she hadn't moved for a week.

"Lying there like an iguana. How can you stand the heat and the sweat and . . ."

"Relax," she yawned, "just lie down and relax." Her eyelids closed slowly.

"*Relax?*" I jumped to my feet, brushing the sticky sand from my hands. "How the hell can anyone relax when nobody's doing anything?" I kicked sand onto her glistening stomach.

"Lay off," she muttered.

A few yards away the only other sun junkies to have discovered El Rincón's small, commercially unimportant beach lay in similar positions of addiction, soaking up fixes of solar radiation. Earlier I had attempted to interest them in a joint expedition into the surrounding jungles. The couple's response was a torrent of French and fractured Spanish. The woman interrupted the ritual kneading of a pint of lotion into her astounding topography long enough to make me understand that they didn't want whatever I was selling: hammocks, coconuts or *refrescos*.

Now what? El Rincón offered few distractions: no *cantina*, no handicrafts, no restaurants and no hotels. There weren't even the usual sunburned tourists flogging Professional Frisbees back and forth in front of an array of clicking Instamatics.

Shortly after discovering the village we had made an arrangement to board with the Lopez family and share their daily *comida* (afternoon meal). We cooked breakfast in our room on a backpacker's stove, buying what food we needed in local *tiendas*. Entertainment consisted of long chats with townspeople, hikes into the jungle, evening strolls along the short rock and sand beach and daydreaming. Time moved as smoothly and quietly as the dull green river where we rinsed salt water from our bodies after a swim in the sea. Two weeks had somehow slipped by and boredom was creeping in.

Getting Lorena away from this beach, however, would probably be about as easy as prying an abalone off a rock with my fingernails. I'd have to offer something very attractive, something that combined sun, beaches and salt water with a wild card . . . That afternoon I confronted her in the patio of the Lopez home.

"It's time for Adventure," I announced. She happily sorted through a tangle of unidentifiable leaves, flowers, vines and roots grubbed out of the patio garden for some noxious health brew.

"The call of the Unknown!" I continued, catching a flicker of interest in her eyes. "Distant horizons!" Her face lifted from the shrubbery collection. "And maybe . . ." I hesitated, waiting until her eyes widened with genuine curiosity, ". . . the Seven Cities of Cibola or even the Lost Elephant Graveyard!"

"OK. Sounds good to me. When do we start?" Lorena asked.

Leaving required a concentrated burst of organization and preliminary footwork. That evening I visited my fishermen friends as they mended nets. Did anyone know of a place where we might find fantastic skin diving, few people, good weather, fresh water, cool shade and what else? . . . Oh, yes, tropical fruits dangling at hand? A sort of Big Rock Candy Mountain with coconuts.

Various places were suggested, discussed and rejected.

"What is it you want most?" an old man finally asked, squinting at me as his hands flew deftly over the torn webbing of the gill net.

I thought for a moment. "*Pescado.* I want fish and, *si es posible,* oysters and lobster." He nodded. I didn't have to explain a love of seafood to a fisherman.

"*Pues . . .*" he said, "you should visit *Paraíso.* The sea there is *caldo de mariscos,* seafood stew!" The other fishermen agreed. Yes, Paradise was just what this fish-crazy *gringo* needed.

A delicious shiver of anticipation went up my spine. Mexicans are explicit when it comes to place names, at times *too* explicit: San Juan Without Water, Valley of the Dead and Big Dust were all places I'd carefully avoided. But *Paradise*! It could only be reached by boat. Even mules balked at the long arduous trek required through virgin jungle and unexplored *barrancas*. The old man offered to arrange a boat ride.

Later that evening Geraldo, a young fisherman, stopped me on the street. After shaking my hand and vaguely discussing the weather for five minutes, he said, "They say you might be thinking of passing by Paraíso?" The impersonal "they," the vague "thinking," "might" and "passing by" were all polite escape hatches in case I wasn't truly serious about the journey.

I assured him that we lived only for the moment when, God Willing!, we could finally visit that fabled place. Money, of course, was no object . . . as long as it didn't cost very much.

Geraldo hemmed and hawed, thought, re-thought, considered the cost of gasoline for his twenty-five horsepower outboard motor and the earning power of his battered fiberglas *panga,* not to mention the incredible distance involved (fifteen miles one way), the weather (good now but *¿quién sabe?*), the need for a crew (one of his family of twenty might, perhaps, break away for a day?) and, last but certainly not least, the danger involved.

"*¿Peligro?*" I asked. "What kind of danger?"

He shook his head sadly. He hated to spread tales, but quite frankly the people in Paraíso were thugs, bandits, hoodlums, poachers and worse: true-to-life *pirates!*

"*¡Vaya!*" I laughed. "Go on! You have relatives there! The fishermen told me so! Isn't your mother from Paraíso?"

Geraldo gave me a twisted grin and an eloquent shrug. *Bueno,* if I insisted.

I got up at five a.m. and turned my attention to supplies. My excitement about visiting Paradise demanded that I work off some excess energy. Lorena would rise from bed like bread dough: over a period of hours.

There are two types of Explorers: those who go with boxes, bales and bearers on full-scale expeditions and those who 'go light,' with nothing but a sharp knife and an unwavering determination to survive. We, of course, would travel in the latter style, living by our wits and the bounty of the sea.

"Two oranges, *por favor,*" I said to the sleepy woman behind the scarred wooden counter of the town's largest *tienda.* "Fifty grams of noodles, fifty grams of oil, twenty-five grams of salt and . . ."

"What are you doing, buying *samples?*" Lorena was leaning over my shoulder, scowling at the brief list I'd penciled onto the back of a road map. "If you're into that 'live off the fat of the land' kick again, you can forget it right now!" she flashed the proprietress a knowing smile. Before I could object, Lorena produced a tickertape length list and began reciting: "Fifty oranges, two kilos of *limones* . . . no, *que sean tres kilos,* two liters of cooking oil, a kilo of salt . . . " She gave me a hard look, "You know we'll need salt for smoking fish! A box of candy bars, a dozen spools of thread, six needles . . ."

I retreated to the doorway. We could trade all that for Manhattan Island!

It took hours to ready the boat and load our gear and foodstuffs. Geraldo had shanghied two younger cousins as crew. They appeared at the last moment with diving and fishing gear, a large gill net, homemade anchors and several boxes and burlap bags stuffed with small merchandise and staples.

"A gift for the pirates?" I joked.

"My father is sending a few things to his *compadres* in Paraíso," Geraldo explained patiently, "And we will stop on the way to set the net." I nodded; such side trips were to be expected. After all, why waste the opportunity, especially since we were paying for the gas?

We left El Rincón in early afternoon, delayed at the last moment by the unexpected arrival of the Lopez clan. Lorena and I had given them a few small gifts the night before, out of appreciation for their hospitality and as a means of lightening our overloaded packs. They returned the favor in a mini-potlatch — several ripe papayas, a large cracked conch shell, a newspaper-wrapped bundle of venison jerky and the dried, hairy skin of some unfortunate jungle rodent. This last treasure, we were assured, would make Lorena a fine purse. I stowed the odorous pelt in the bow of the *panga*, promising to get a leathersmith on it as soon as possible.

They waved us off with cries of "*¡Vayan con Dios!*" as we pushed the heavy canoe into the sea, headed directly toward Paradise!

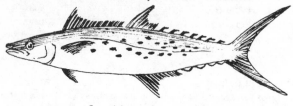

Spanish mackerel   *Sierra*

It was a long hot trip, though the queasy motion of the overloaded boat and the choking smell of a leaky gas can were more than compensated for by the view. Mile after mile of almost unexplored beaches and jungle-covered headlands had us frothing at the mouth in anticipation. Geraldo passed the time by trailing a homemade feather jig behind the *panga*, nonchalantly hauling in more *sierra* mackerel and silvery jacks than I was able to clean in an hour. The 'crew' caught up on their sleep.

The sun was lowering toward the jungle when I realized . . . "Lorena, there's no more jungle!"

In the few minutes it had taken to clean Geraldo's last fish, the landscape abruptly changed from brilliant shimmering green to a dull lifeless brown. Geraldo caught my look of dismay and explained: "The wind and currents are very strange here. There is little rain. But don't worry, the same conditions somehow make many big fish and" his hands formed a circle as big as a dinner plate, "oysters!" He turned the boat in a slow curve toward the shore. "Paraíso is on the other side of that hill!"

My excitement returned. It might not be true Tarzan jungle but no matter, we'd soon find virgin diving, a fine campsite and adventure . . .

"What's *that?*" Lorena exclaimed, her face wrinkling with disgust. An awful smell enveloped the *panga*, the noxious odor of rotting fish.

Geraldo laughed. "You'll get used to it, *amiga*," he said. "It's the sharks drying and the remains of the big *meros* and *pargos*." I cleared my mouth and spit over the side, distracted by a flash of silver in the clear water. The desolate shoreline and terrible smell were forgotten as Geraldo and I pointed out the fish to each other.

". . . and over there," he said, waving toward a wave-washed pinnacle of rock, "there are *langosta!*" The distance between his hands promised a lobster of truly record proportions. I was ready to leap into the water when Lorena groaned and said, "Paradise? *That?*"

I looked up. The bow of the *panga* was pointed directly toward a dismal collection of rough sheds and improvised sun shades, crouched between a crumbling grey rock cliff and a narrow beach. A hot dusty wind stirred the gagging smell that hung over the tiny bay, rattling sheets of torn plastic and rusted tin. Visions of quaint native dwellings of bamboo and palm thatch were replaced by soot-blackened cardboard, rotting burlap and flattened tin cans. In the midst of this squalid slum, dogs snarled over rotting turtle carcasses as children poked idly at sun-bleached sharks' jaws, discarded like grinning bear traps next to crude racks of drying flesh.

"Paradise!" Geraldo announced, running the boat slowly toward the beach. Before I could dispute this outrageous misnomer, the cousins were in the water, hauling the *panga* onto the sand. A horde of shouting children and curious adults poured out of the fish camp like refugees greeting the Red Cross. Before we could decide if we were being attacked or welcomed, our gear was snatched up and carried to the base of the cliff. Geraldo shook hands with several men, any of whom could have easily won a C-grade movie role as pirate, thug, robber or worse.

"We must return at once," Geraldo said, passing the last of the merchandise to a sinister character he addressed as "uncle".

"Wait a moment!" I said. "How will we leave here?" My thoughts were already on the quickest way of making this Paradise Lost. Lorena just stood on the beach, staring vacantly at an enormous mound of sea turtle skulls as little kids pestered her with questions.

"Leave?" Geraldo puzzled. "I have no idea. It is very difficult."

"But . . ."

"We'll see you!" he shouted, gunning the big outboard in reverse as the cousins, energized by a few whiffs of Paradise, pushed the boat off the beach. He waved at the pirates and turned the *panga* out to sea.

"At least Paradise isn't on the Tourist Circuit," Lorena quipped, poking at the meager cookfire we'd coaxed from twigs and dried burro cookies. Our camp sat at the mouth of a brush-choked arroyo, on the only spot of beach not littered with the fetid remains of slaughtered fish, sharks and sea turtles. High cliffs behind us created a natural reflector oven. The children assured us, "There is no shade anywhere, only where you make it."

Once the *panga* had departed, the adults returned silently to whatever occupied their leisure time, leaving us at the mercy of their semi-wild kids. A few well-placed bribes of fruit and hard candies soon organized them into trusty bearers. It was from the oldest child that we learned Paradise was dry.

"What do you mean?" I said, shielding my eyes from the still intense glare of the sun. "How can you live here without drinking water?"

The boy retreated a few steps. "*Pues, señor,*" he mumbled nervously, "our fathers bring it in boats and others bring it on the *bestias*.

"Beasts? Beasts?" I tried to control the screech in my voice. "What kind of *beasts* can bring water? Camels?"

He reached protectively for another boy's shoulder. "Burros," he said, "in big jars. The water is very expensive."

"What about *licores?*" I gave him my best cross-examiner's stare. "And food. Eh? Food and liquor? How about that?"

"*Tampoco!*" he said, a note of mourning in his voice. "Neither of those."

"Come on, *hijo!*" I coaxed. "There has to be liquor. At least *mescal*, eh?" He could confide in good 'ole Carl, tell him whose uncle's brother's cousin had a bit of white lightnin' under the bed.

"It is *prohibido, señor,*" he answered, ignoring my groans as he explained that warm beer was sometimes available but at very high prices. There was no store, no restaurant, no *cantina* and no spare food. "But there are fish," he said, brightening at the thought, "*mucho pescado!*" Fish were not only plentiful but free! Did we want some right away?

I waved him off. A flock of voracious gulls wheeled overhead, shrieking in glee as they fought over the corpse of a freshly butchered hammerhead shark. Lorena stared bleakly into the smouldering fire.

The marines landed shortly before dawn, encircling Paradise in a combined land/sea operation that left no avenue for escape. My first indication of trouble came when ten soldiers in full combat regalia woke me with angry shouts of, "Where are the oysters?" The question was repeated several times as flashlights probed our camp. Sentries were posted around us.

"Huh?" I answered, jerking up from the sleeping bag. A parachute flare drifted over the fish camp, cruelly illuminating the sad little shacks. Groups of armed men in dark uniforms roamed up and down the beach, scouting the arroyos.

"Where are the oysters?" a soldier barked, a submachinegun cradled in a no-nonsense manner in his arms.

"Why, I . . . I . . . I . . ."

"The oysters, *hombre*! Where are they?" His tone was menacing. The others darted their eyes nervously from side to side. Why was this fool stalling; could it be a trap?

"I have no idea, *señor*," I finally managed to stammer, "We're just *turistas*."

"Don't give me that!" he snarled. "What would you be doing *here*, in a place like this, if you were a tourist? *Pah!* Where are the oysters? *Andele!*"

Angry shouts and cries drifted from the direction of the fish camp. A large boat patrolled offshore, loaded with more marines. They were taking no chances.

"*Pues*, in the sea?" I answered, shrugging my shoulders to emphasize both my ignorance and innocence. What was this, a military seafood coup? "Why don't you ask the fishermen?"

He growled with irritation, but menace suddenly turned into shock and embarrassment as Lorena finally stuck her head from beneath the edge of the sleeping bag. Her eyes were half closed, heavy with sleep.

"Whattatheywant?" she mumbled, her mouth stretching into a tremendous yawn. The marines stared in disbelief.

"You are . . . you are . . . *tourists*!" the leader gaped at us as though he'd discovered a strange new race of beach dwellers only previously rumored to exist.

"Well . . . *pues* . . . sorry to bother you . . . uh . . . *hasta luego!*" He snapped a command and led his men at a trot toward the fish camp. Lorena gave them one last curious look before snuggling back under the covers.

"What did they want?" she asked drowsily, eyes slowly closing.

"Some oysters," I answered. "They were desperate for an oyster cocktail."

She mumbled incoherently as she faded off.

Sunrise revealed a grim scene, all too reminiscent of the Evening News: sullen soldiers guarding sullen civilians, as wailing children cowered in the background.

"A place like this could get on your nerves," I said, sipping a cup of tepid, bitter, instant coffee and scratching my latest sand flea bite. Lorena busied herself with the tarp, trying to arrange protection from the already blistering heat of the sun. Our gear was neatly sorted and re-packed. Some primal instinct warned us to prepare for evacuation.

Lorena was examining some interesting pelican bones she'd discovered under her sleeping bag, when the crunch of footsteps came from the arroyo.

"*¡Buenos días!*"

It was our head bearer from the previous afternoon, followed by a group of nervous companions. Lorena gave them a reassuring smile and asked if they'd like coffee.

"*No, gracias,*" the boy said shyly. "We have to go soon. We are all leaving here." I noted the excitement and relief in his voice. Even for a kid, Paradise had little to offer.

"*¿Qué pasó?*" I asked, waving toward the fish camp and the marines.

"They found our oysters," the boy began, hesitation giving way to the excitement of the story, "and because we do not have the *permiso*, the permit, they are taking them all! And they say there will be a big *multa*, a terrible fine!" He shook his head in dismay. "We had gathered almost fifty thousand oysters. *A fortune!* They were all alive and hidden in a giant hole underwater. But somehow . . ." His skinny brown shoulders moved in a classic 'So it goes' shrug.

"My father says you can come with us in the big *panga*. By tomorrow, everyone will be gone."

I flinched. Stranded in Paradise, without any water or way out?

"But where will you take us?" I asked. "Back to El Rincón?"

"No, *señor*," the boy answered. "I think to the south. But my father has not said. "*¿Quién sabe?*"

I admired the kid's nonchalance but would have preferred something more specific than just "south." How far south? Ten miles? A hundred?

"We'd better go with them, Carl," Lorena said. "It's got to be better than staying here on our own. What could be worse?" She waved toward the garbage around us.

"*Muy bien*," I sighed. "Tell your father *muchas gracias*. Have an orange."

The marines took little notice of our departure; they were too busy counting oysters. Relays of carefully guarded divers recovered the shellfish from their hiding place a few hundred yards offshore, then dumped them into commandeered *pangas*. When I asked a scowling fisherman what would become of the illegal catch, he shrugged and said, "The soldiers will sell them and keep the money. What else?" His eyes flickered toward a group of non-coms sharing a bottle of expensive brandy, smiling and joking as if they'd just won the lottery.

If I'd thought Geraldo's boat had been overloaded, it was nothing compared to that of Victor, the fisherman who had offered us an escape from Paradise. Dogs, chickens, a young hysterical pig, an outraged parrot and a resigned-looking squirrel were wedged between bales of empty burlap sacks, hundred-kilo bags of rock salt, coils of heavy line, blankets, furniture, gas cans, spare outboard motor parts, kitchenware and all the other odds and ends of a fish camp family's rugged life.

"*¡Vamonos!*" Victor ordered, lifting another excited child into the boat. We took our assigned places. With a few final curses for the marines, he pointed the boat toward the mouth of the bay. In the confusion I'd found it impossible to pin Victor down on his proposed destination. "*¿Quién sabe?*" was all he'd say, though his brusque reply was softened with a smile. Lorena finally divined that he was keeping it a secret, to avoid being followed by the marines. Other *pangas* were leaving, their destinations equally vague.

With Paradise an hour behind us, Victor relaxed and began to smile. A fishing line was dropped astern and the oldest boy ordered to tend it. Other children calmed the menagerie while their mother nursed the baby. Lorena dozed on a warm nest of burlap sacks and I contemplated the large blank area on our map. We were somewhere in the middle of that uninked expanse, heading *where*?

I looked up from the map to find Victor studying the sky, his brow wrinkled in concentration. He gave me a quick troubled glance, hesitated, then said, "La Soledad, *amigo*. I must take you to La Soledad."

Our destination was now revealed. But *Solitude*? After the desolation of Paradise what could be waiting for us in *Solitude*? The name made my skin crawl. And then the full meaning of what he'd said struck me.

"What do you mean, take *us*?" I said. "What about you?" I waved my hands somewhat desperately at the family and the *panga*.

Victor gave me a shrug and a weary smile. "I'm sorry, friend, but the boat is very heavy. We must pass the Cape this evening. If the weather changes the sea will be very *feo* there, very ugly. Soledad comes two hours before the Cape. *Entiendes?*"

Yes, I understood. All too well, in fact. It was his boat and his family; if safety required that we be marooned in La Soledad . . .

"Thank you," I said. "We appreciate the favor very much." I tried to cover apprehension with a smile. Victor's relief at my acceptance was obvious. He launched into a description of Solitude that wiped the grin from my face.

"It is a sad place, La Soledad." He shook his head with appropriate solemnity, "few people. Not many fish, either. *Muy retirado*, very isolated."

His wife's eyes widened; she glanced shyly at Lorena, her thick braids bobbing sympathetically at the thought of the hardships this *gringa* must now face . . .

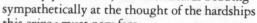

". . . surrounded by *puro monte*," Victor's description of La Soledad continued with morbid good humor. "*Monte alto!*" He looked up, as though gauging the heighth of 'pure high jungle'. "And the *barrancas!*" His hands chopped the air to emphasize the awesome depth of the canyons cutting Solitude off from the outside world.

"But how will we . . . ?"

"Don't worry!" Victor said, reading my mind, "All the fishermen will know where you are." He turned to stare at the shoreline, lost in thought. "You can get another ride out . . . someday . . ."

> *Dear Friends,*
> *Well, here we are, stuck in Solitude and trying our best not to suffer too much . . .*

I sniffed to the left, trying to find a more solid position in which to continue writing. The swaying of the coconut palms transmitted a gentle rocking motion to the hammock that made my penmanship even more erratic than usual.

> *. . . after six days of uncertainty and privation. God only knows what tomorrow may bring . . .*

I bit off a laugh. If the hunting were good, tomorrow would bring venison tenderloins roasting over open coals, basted with a sauce of fresh pineapple juice, oil and wild honey. Gregorio had promised a feast we'd not soon forget; our nearest neighbor was now combing the *barrancas* for a plump deer while his wife prepared stacks of golden *tortillas*. Their children searched the gardens and thickly forested hillsides for papayas, aromatic *guayabas*, pulpy sweet *guanabanas* and other tropical delights.

> *. . . The desperate lack of water is a continuing problem, but we hope to find some solution without sacrificing . . .*

I glanced over the edge of the hammock. A glistening earthenware jar sat at the base of a palm tree, filled with cool fresh spring water. Gregorio's children had carried it from the well that morning. If only we didn't have to walk that long quarter of a mile to the swimming hole! Deeper thirsts would also be quenched soon: I had commissioned an old man from the village to search out a few liters of the local moonshine. He assured me that it would be delivered in plenty of time for the next day's festivities. There was so much to do before the guests arrived! The weight of my responsibilities crushed me deeper into the soft webbing of the hammock.

> *. . . what puny comforts we've managed to wrest from the ominous jungles . . .*

I thought for a moment and then struck out the word 'ominous'. Hiking among the colorful butterflies and blossoming plants wasn't so much ominous as awesome. Gregorio took great delight in pointing out edible curiosities, such as the shining red berries of coffee trees we'd chewed for energy as we trekked far into the jungle, eventually climbing high above the coastal plain to the open oak forests where he and his brother planted small fields of corn and beans.

> *. . . Lorena has carefully rationed our food supplies, which I have attempted to supplement by foraging the beaches and nearby reefs . . .*

I paused, mentally inventorying my cache of fishhooks and line. It was costing us about five hooks a day, in trade to the kids, for enough *barrilete* and *cabrilla* to fill the cook pots and the fish smoking racks. When my bartering stock was exhausted, I'd don my diving gear to retrieve hooks and line the kids had lost on the rocky snags along the shore, then recycle them for yet more fish. I yawned; it was almost time to get busy. Some spear work on my part was required to fill out the seafood portion of the next day's menu. Now what would go best with venison? A light delicate fish like pompano? Decisions! Decisions!

My gaze wandered down the beach to a flock of pelicans resting on a white spattered rock. *Lobo*, a bowlegged yellow mutt Gregorio had retired from active hunting duty, shambled out of the bushes with a hopeful gleam in his eye. Lorena tossed him a day old *tortilla*. He gulped it down and wagged his tail for more. His favorite snack was coconut meat, but we'd used all we had for baking into banana breads and soft candies for the *fiesta*. The dog studied the faint trail to the village of Soledad, almost a mile away. Was it worth the walk in hope of finding a coconut? He yawned and flopped sideways onto the hot sand. Maybe later.

> *. . . As you can imagine, the extreme isolation has been something of a hardship for us, though we manage to amuse ourselves . . .*

The first question we were asked after being marooned was Gregorio's anxious, "Do you play music?" When I'd said "No," he covered his disappointment with "Well, at least you can *listen*!" His nightly concerts on a wheezing accordion, accompanied by his brother's untuned violin, were more than a match for Lorena's and my rendition of *Over the Garden Wall* and *Mother's Not Dead, She's Only A-Sleeping*.

> *. . . so that's about all the news, for whatever it's worth. Think of us this winter and don't forget: "It's a tough life if you don't weaken!"*

I heard the distant buzz of an outboard motor. A *panga* was leaving Soledad, heading south. The few fish not used locally or traded to *campesinos* in the mountains behind us, were taken to a distant market town beyond the Cape. These runs, infrequent and unscheduled, were the only real contact Soledad had with the rest of the world. I yawned again. We'd probably have to take that boat . . . *someday . . .*

Unknown Mexico

Rivers

Mexico's rivers fall into two basic types: 'young' fast-flowing streams with steep vertical drops forming many rapids and waterfalls, often funneled through deep narrow canyons; and 'old' slow-flowing rivers, with deep meandering channels. The first type is the most common and includes the majority of the rivers along the Pacific coast and the steep eastern slopes of the Sierra Madre Oriental facing the Gulf of Mexico. Most slow-flowing rivers are in southern Mexico, with the exception of the Río Bravo, more commonly known to *gringos* as the Rio Grande.

For pleasure boating 'old' rivers are generally considered best, though if you enjoy white water, 'young' rivers will provide plenty of thrills.

Because so little information is available on Mexican rivers, boaters tend to overlook the possible trips that can be made. I know people who have rafted and kayaked great distances on rivers no one knew anything about, including local natives. One river may be known by many names and the name will change along a river's length. "Where does this river go?" is a question that puzzles those who live along its banks as well as curious boaters.

One of the most exciting aspects of exploring Mexican rivers, especially those leading into the sea (about 95%), is the amazing variations in topography, wildlife and vegetation you'll encounter. A brisk mountain stream, surrounded by pines and hardy cactus, slowly works its way seaward through warm, subtropical canyons and deep, shaded gorges, gradually transforming itself into a lazy jungle waterway or vast mangrove-lined lagoon.

The term 'navigable' is used in the following description of Mexican rivers. Unfortunately, the definition of navigable is open to wide interpretation, depending on the draft of the vessel and the season of the year and rainfall. In general, however, the word navigable as used here, refers to deep draft vessels: large barges, ships and other commercial craft. Obviously, smaller boats will find much more navigable water, including thousands of miles of tributary rivers and canals not listed here.

As a general rule, subject to changes in the weather, the months from July to January produce the highest water volumes. In rivers such as the Micos, boating isn't considered safe until the water level has dropped in the spring. Local river-running regattas are becoming popular in some areas, with the usual craft nothing more than a raft of innertubes. Those I've heard of usually take place in September and October, depending again on the intensity of the rains.

Although the following lists of rivers, lagoons and estuaries represents a lot of research it is obviously incomplete and sketchy. I hope that readers will take the time to send me more detailed information to be published in future editions. Without such help a great deal of fine boating will be missed by all of us.

The following seven rivers are Mexico's largest, at least in terms of water volume (given in billions of cubic meters of annual flow). Together they drain over one quarter of the country's surface area.

Usumacinta	58.9 billion	Pánuco	18.9
Grijalva	46.3	Balsas	12.2
Papaloapan	41.1	Santiago	11.5
Coatzacoalcos	22.4		

Eastern Mexico, Texas Border to Quintana Roo

Nuevo León: *Río Bravo* (Rio Grande): 2,800 km long but because of many dams the river is not navigable for commercial purposes. For small boats, however, the potential is enormous. Major tributaries are *El Salado* (480 km long) and *El San Juan* or *Salinas* (390 km long; lower 5 km navigable).

Tamaulipas: *Río San Fernando:* 352 km long; 40 km navigable. *Soto la Marina:* 332 km long; 58 km navigable. *Pánuco:* 680 km long; 285 km navigable. Major tributaries are the *Tamesí* or *Guayalejo* (353 km long; at least 35 km navigable) and the *Tamuín*. *Río Carrizal* or *San Rafael:* 60 km long. *Río Sabinas:* "Exceptionally beautiful."

Veracruz: *Río Tuxpan:* 161 km long; 67 km navigable. *Cazones:* 156 km long; navigable by small craft. *Tecolutla:* 184 km long; 20 km navigable by small craft. *Chachalacas:* Navigable upstream to town of Úrsulo Galván. *Nautla:* 88 km long; upper reaches fast and shallow, but lower 20 km navigable by small craft. *Jamapa:* 112 km long; many tributary streams. *Blanco:* 184 km long; numerous canyons, rapids and waterfalls in upper stretches. *Papaloapan:* 540 km long; 242 km navigable. "The River of Butterflies" is said to be one of the world's most beautiful waterways. Navigable stretches decrease considerably during the winter dry season. *Río Culebra:* 10 km navigable by small craft; joins the Río Papaloapan at the town of Tlacotalpan. *Coatzacoalcos:* 332 km long; 222 km navigable.

Tabasco: There is a saying in Mexico that "the entire state of Tabasco is navigable." This isn't an exaggeration; Tabasco is one of the world's most extensive wetlands and is often called "the Holland of Mexico." *Río Tonalá* or *Pedregal:* 145 km long; "partially navigable to small craft." Crosses the rainiest area in Mexico. *Mezcalapa* or *Chiapa:* 700 km long; virtually unexplored but at least 100 km are said to be navigable by small craft (and perhaps much more). *Grijalva:* 120 km long and all navigable. *Usumacinta:* 825 km long; 300 km navigable. There are dangerous rapids in the upper stretches. One of Mexico's finest rivers, nicely described in *Wild Rivers of North America* (see *Recommended Reading*). *San Pedro:* Navigable.

Campeche: *Río Palizada:* 140 km navigable; a tributary of the Usumacinta. *Candelaria:* 300 km long and almost entirely navigable. This river was an important transportation route for *chicle*, the tree sap used to make chewing gum in the good old days. *Champotón:* 110 km long; partially navigable.

Quintana Roo: *Río Hondo:* 250 km long and navigable by small craft. The only surface river in the Yucatán Peninsula.

Western Mexico: Sonora to Chiapas

Most of the following rivers are subject to fast changes in water volume during the rainy season. Some are almost dry by the end of the dry season (May-June). They still offer boating possibilities, though their courses are seldom travelled and remain virtually unknown. Travel with great caution if you are kayaking or rafting.

Sonora: *Río Yaqui:* 680 to 740 km long, depending on rainfall. There is said to be gold dust in this river. *Mayo:* 350 km long.

Sinaloa: *Fuerte:* 350 km long. *Río Culiacán:* No information. *San Lorenzo* or *Los Remedios:* 250 km long. *Piaxtla:* 200 km long; lower stretches navigable. *Presidio:* 160 km long.

Nayarit: *Río Acaponeta:* 210 km long; lower stretches navigable during and after the rainy season, but there are many waterfalls upstream. *San Pedro* or *Mezquital:* 700 km long; very turbulent but supposedly navigable in lower stretches.

The state of Nayarit shares many rivers with Jalisco and Colima; the following are the most important: *Santiago* or *Bolaños:* 412 km long; navigable with caution by rafts and kayaks. Dangerous obstacles in upper reaches; see *Wild Rivers Of North America* for details. (See *Recommended Reading*.) *Huaynamota:* A major tributary of the Santiago; no information. *Río Ameca:* 230 km long; 100 km navigable.

Colima-Jalisco: *Río Armería:* 294 km; lower 35 km navigable by small craft.

Guerrero: *Río Balsas:* 840 km long. The Balsas has lots of whitewater and is the scene of an annual high speed powerboat race right through the rapids.

Oaxaca: *Río Verde* or *Atoyac* or *Nochistlán:* 275 to 340 km long, depending on who you talk to. *Tehuantepec:* 240 km long.

Other Rivers

Durango: *Río Nazas:* 300 km long; navigable for much of its length in rafts and small boats. An entirely inland river, the Nazas is subject to quick changes due to summer rains.

San Luis Potosí: *Río Micos* or *Tampaon:* The "Spider Monkey River" has many waterfalls but is said to be navigable by rafts and kayaks at the end of the dry season, May-June. *El Verde* and *El Santa María:* Join to form the Tamuín, which in turn flows into the Pánuco in the state of Tamaulipas. *Río Choy:* Said to be navigable by whitewater craft and of exceptional beauty; no information.

Major Lagoons, Estuaries

The boating potential in Mexico's coastal lagoons is difficult to even calculate, since most areas are visited only by the occasional fishing fanatic or birdwatcher. The usual catch-all description given in geography books and tourist literature for these unknown waters is "a veritable inland sea." How many inland seas can one country hold? Quite a few, judging from maps I've studied: the Gulf coast, for example, has a total shoreline length greater than 2500 kilometers (over 1500 miles). A good portion of this coast is bordered by lagoons, estuaries and flood plains, most of it ignored entirely by tourists rushing toward the Yucatán Peninsula. On the Pacific coast the situation is similar, though lagoons are farther apart and tend to be smaller, with such notable exceptions as La Laguna Superior in Oaxaca.

Lagoons not only offer protected waters for boating, but some of the richest fishing and seafood foraging imaginable. Many are designated *Parques Naturales* (Natural Parks) and teem with wildlife, particularly waterfowl. And if that isn't enough, the people who live and fish in these waters are among the most isolated and traditional groups in the country, their customs and lifestyles protected by a barrier of water that is rarely crossed by outsiders. Load the boat!

Note: Some lagoons and estuaries, such as the Laguna Madre of Nuevo León and the Mar Muerto of Oaxaca-Chiapas have been variously described as "desolate" and "paradises." The desolate opinion was from a traveller who loves vegetation; the paradise was from a fanatic fisherman and get-away-from-it-all type. I include such comments warily, mainly to give you a hint of what you might find, not as a nuts-and-bolts description. A hitchhiker put it quite well, if rather obscurely, when he waved toward a stretch of Death Valley that was particularly dead and said, "This place is scenic in its own beauty."

Mexicans often refer to inland lakes as *lagunas*. To avoid confusion the lagoons listed here are salt or brackish water and connect to the sea.

The length of a lagoon is only a vague indication of its overall area; many lagoons are made up of hundreds of kilometers of short twisting canals, lake-like open areas and dead ends. Carry a compass and ask directions from local people whenever possible.

Eastern Mexico, Texas Border to Quintana Roo

Nuevo León: *Laguna Madre:* One of those "veritable inland seas," though a shallow one, with an average depth of about three meters (ten feet). This lagoon is 150 km long and covers 2,000 km^2. The water gets very salty at times and has been tested at 21%: equal to the Great Salt Lake in the U.S. and saltier than the Dead Sea. The surrounding countryside is flat and rather desolate.

Tamaulipas: *Laguna de Chairel:* Connects to the Río Tamesí. *Laguna de Pueblo Viejo:* Connects to Río Pánuco. *Barra del Tordo:* No information.

Veracruz: *Laguna de Tamiahua:* 130 km long, with seven islands, the largest 32 km long. Navigable from Tampico to Tuxpan. *Laguna de Tampamachoco:* This is the southern stretch of the Laguna de Tamiahua, about 40 km long and connected to the Río Tuxpan by a canal. *Laguna Camaronera* and *Laguna de Alvarado:* Over 50 km long, connecting with many smaller lagoons and rivers, including the Río San Juan, which in turn flows into the Río Papaloapan. *Laguna Encantada* and *Laguna Sontecomapan:* near Catemaco.

Tabasco: *Laguna del Carmen* and *Laguna Machona:* 40 km long; "one of the most beautiful sights imaginable."

Campeche: *Laguna de Atasta:* No information. *Laguna de Términos:* 82 km long with an area greater than 4,000 km^2. This one really is an inland sea and connects to three large rivers: the Candelaria, Palizada and Chumpán. *Laguna Noh* or *Silvituk:* No information.

Quintana Roo: *Laguna Yalahau:* over 200 km^2. *Laguna de Bacalar:* very clear water, near Chetumal.

Western Mexico: Sinaloa to Chiapas

Sinaloa: *Laguna de Teacapan:* No information. *Bahía de Santa María:* 40 km long. One friend reports "too many islands to count" and "it's rather desolate but the fishing is sure good." *Bahía de Pabellón:* 50 km long. *Laguna Caimanera:* 32 km long.

Nayarit: *Agua Brava:* 97 km long. *Laguna Mexcaltitán:* 100 km^2. *Laguna La Tovara:* Near San Blas; "exceptional."

Colima: *Laguna Cuyutlán:* Runs south of Manzanillo for 50 km.

Guerrero: *Laguna de Tuxpan:* Near Iguala. *Laguna de Mitla:* 23 km long. *Laguna de Coyuca:* 40 km long, 3 islands, "very tropical." *Lagunas de Tres Palos:* 13 km; very close to Acapulco.

Oaxaca: *Laguna Chacagua:* A wildlife park of great beauty and crocodiles. *Estero de Manialtepec:* No information. *Laguna Superior* and *Laguna Inferior:* A combined area of more than 2,000 km^2, seldom visited. *Mar Muerto:* Over 60 km long.

Chiapas: *Laguna La Joya:* 25 km long. *Bahía de Paredón:* "A dead sea" over 50 km long. *Laguna Cuzo:* No information. *Laguna Las Palmas:* Connects to the Río Cintalapa.

Islands

Islands exert a romantic attraction for the footloose and adventuresome that is more powerful than the scent of spring clover to a bee. "Escape to the Islands" is a daydream that most of us have used at one time or another to get through a bad day, or month or year; visions of distant coco palms over the blue line of the horizon, the peace and solitude of a deserted coral sand beach . . .

Quite a number of Mexico's islands are uninhabited though reasonably accessible, at least by those who don't mind uncertain boating conditions and uncertain supplies of water and food once you get there. As an astute friend once observed after a long stay on a true desert island, "Most islands are uninhabited because people can't live on them." In other words, you can visit but don't plan to set up house.

Baja Peninsula: Pacific Coast (North to South)

Islas Coronados: Four small rocky islets; the largest 8 km long. *Islas Todos Santos:* Two rocky islets; 3 km long. No fresh water. *Isla San Martín:* Lies about 5 km off the coast; 1.6 km in diameter. Volcanic peak and crater; few plants but many birds and sea lions. *Isla San Jerónimo:* Lies 8 km offshore; about 1 km long. Very barren, with dangerous reefs, shipwrecks and excellent fishing. *Isleta Elide:* Lies about .5 km offshore; .5 km in diameter. *Islas San Benito:* Three barren islets; shipwrecks, sea lion rookery. *Isla Cedros:* Pine trees, fresh water, wild animals and a small settlement; 33 km long and up to 15 km wide. *Isla Natividad:* Barren and hilly, unpaved airstrip, fishermen's camp; about 6 km long. *Isla San Roque:* About 3 km offshore; 1.2 km long. Seasonal fishermen's camps. *Isla Magdalena:* A very narrow island; about 100 km long. No information. *Isla Santa Margarita:* Ranch and fresh water at south end, high and barren, shipwrecks; about 34 km long. *Isla Creciente:* Good fishing; 19 km long.

Baja Peninsula: Sea of Cortez (North to South)

Isla Montague and *Isla Gore:* At the mouth of the Colorado River; no information. *Isla Miramar* or *El Muerto:* About 4 km offshore; two deep coves. *Isla Salvatierra* or *Los Lobos:* About 6.5 km offshore. *Isla Encantada:* About 5 km offshore; fishing resort. *Isla San Luis:* Black volcanic sand beaches, lagoon; 2 km offshore. *Isla Ángel de La Guarda:* The second largest land mass in the Sea of Cortez: no beaches, fresh water or people but lots of rattlesnakes. A high volcanic island, 68 km long. *Isla Smith* or *Isla Coronado:* Very narrow and 65 km long. *Isla Estanque:* Sheer cliffs; about 1.5 km long. *Isla Partida* or *El Cordonazo:* Rocky beaches, wind and wave battered; 2 km long. *Isla Raza:* A migratory waterfowl sanctuary and Seri Indian burial ground; 1.2 km long. *Isla de Salsipuedes:* "Leave If You Can" Island is washed by very dangerous currents; about 2.5 km long. *Isla Roca Blanca:* No information. *Isla San Esteban:* Steep cliffs, gravel beaches; 6.5 km long. *Isla San Lorenzo:* Very barren, cliffs and small beaches; 16 km long. *Isla San Pedro Mártir:* Dwarf cactus, rich sea life; triangular, about 1.5 km on each side. *Isla Tortuga:* Hilly, barren, no fresh water; 3.2 km long. *Isla San Marcos:* An official Port of Entry; supplies. *Isla Santa Inés:* No information. *Isla San Ildefonso:* Flat and barren, no beaches but abundant sea and bird life; 2.4 km long. *Isla Coronados:* A small extinct volcano about 3 km long; sandy beaches, seasonal fishermen's camps. *Isla Carmen:* Fresh water, village, salt works, good fishing and diving; 28 km long and up to 11 km wide. *Isla Danzante:* Seasonal fishermen's camps; quite small. *Isla Monserrat:* Bird sanctuary, barren and uninhabited; 6.5 km long. *Isla Santa Catalan:* Giant barrel cactus and rattle-less rattlesnakes abound; 12 km long. *Isla Santa Cruz:* Spectacular cliffs, one beach; about 6 km long. *Isla de San Diego:* Unusual numbers of scorpions, mice and lizards; less than 2 km long. *Isla de las Ánimas:* Barren with narrow gravel beaches; about 2 km long. *Isla San José:* Comparatively fertile, coyotes and other wildlife; about 27 km long. *Isla de San Francisco:* Very small and rugged with sandy beaches. *Los Islotes:* Three rocky islets that abound with sea lions. *Isla Partida Sur:* A small extension of the following: *Isla Espíritu Santo:* Good fishing and diving, fresh water at military outpost; 12 km long and rugged. *Isla Cerralvo:* Barren, rocky and uninhabited; about 26 km long and 6.5 km wide.

Mainland Mexico: Sonora to Oaxaca

Sonora: *Isla San Jorge, Isla Patos:* No information. *Isla Tiburón:* Very large and formerly occupied by Seri Indians; about 1200 km^2, restricted access. *Isla Pelícano, Isla Turners, Isla San Pedro Nolasco, Isla Pajaros, Isla Lobos, Isla Huivuilay:* No information.

Sinaloa: *Isla de la Lechuguilla, Isla Santa María, Isla San Ignacio, Isla Macapule, Isla Saliaca, Isla de Altamura* (80 km^2): No information.

Nayarit: *Isla Isabela, Isla San Juanico:* No information. *Isla María Madre* and *Isla María Magdalena:* Penal colony, restricted access. *Isla María Cleofas, Isla Jaltemba:* No information.

Jalisco: *Bahía de Chamela:* Nine small islands, good diving.

Colima: *Islas Revillagigedo:* Far offshore; restricted access. *Isla San Benedicto, Isla Socorro* (244 km^2), *Roca Partida, Isla Clarión:* No information.

Guerrero: *Isla Grande* and *Isla Roqueta:* No information.

Oaxaca: *Isla Piedra Blanca:* No information.

Eastern Mexico: Texas Border to Quintana Roo
Note: many of these islands border large estuaries and lagoons.

Veracruz: *Isla de Lobos* and *Isla de Sacrificios:* The latter is an archeological site; good diving.

Tabasco: *Isla Ballitzia, Isla del Buey:* No information.

Campeche: *Isla del Carmen* (153 km^2), *Isla Aguada, Isla de Jaina:* No information.

Yucatán: *Isla Cayo Arenas:* No information. *Isla de los Alacranes:* Said to be the graveyard of many ships, ancient and modern.

Quintana Roo: *Isla Holbox* (100 km^2): No information. *Isla Contoy:* Wildlife sanctuary, excellent diving; 3 km long. *Isla Blanca:* No information. *Isla Mujeres, Isla Cancún* and *Isla Cozumel:* Beautiful but developed; easy access and all facilities. *Banco Chinchorro:* Superb diving.

3. Backpacking

"We're lost."

"You're probably right. Now what?" I sag to the ground, easing the strain of the shoulder straps, enjoying the fresh cool air that evaporates the sweat from my sticky flannel shirt.

"Let's check the map," Lorena says.

"Can't do that," I answer. "I gave it to the mayor of the last village. He said they'd put it up on the wall of the *municipio* building."

She gingerly eases her own dusty pack to the ground and begins rummaging through the bulging side pockets. Lorena's rule-of-the-trail: when in doubt, brew tea. Ah, well; we've got a patch of welcome shade on the side of a red dirt arroyo, a down-sloping trail and a full day of walking ahead of us.

"Shall we worry?" Lorena pokes through half a dozen small blue stuff sacks. When she locates the miso paste, she'll search the next set of sacks for thin strips of dried pressed seaweed. There is nothing quite like a delicious mouthful of fermented soybean and boiled seaweed to give a trail-weary body a blast of pure raw energy.

I squint up at the sun, now well above the tops of the scrub oaks. "Let's put off worrying until later. We're heading west, or sort of, anyway. Bound to reach the coast one of these days. Do you still hear music?"

She cocks her head, brushing her well-crushed straw hat to the ground as she rearranges long blond braids on the back of her neck. We've listened to the distorted sounds of a battery-powered record player for a full day and night now. Mexican polkas echo on the clear mountain air from some distant *pueblo*. These public entertainment systems are like foghorns, marking the positions of villages and *ranchos* with much more accuracy than any maps we've found.

"I can barely hear it now," she says. "Sounds almost like Saturday Night Fever."

"Maybe we can find out where we are when we get there," I say, "But it's not really that important. I'm more worried about water." I shake my well-dented Boy Scout canteen. Half empty. With the liter bottle in my backpack it's enough to get me through the afternoon.

Lorena energetically scrapes together a pile of dry twigs. The stove is deep inside my pack, useless since the day I forgot to screw the top down tight on the fuel bottle. I still smell like a barrel of kerosene and can taste *petróleo* in everything I eat.

"Any idea of how far we've come?" She crumbles the dark seaweed into the water and casually reaches a long arm for my Piggly Wiggly cup, tied to my pack with an extra shoelace.

"Drop it!" I warn. "Get out your own."

Lorena sighs and begins digging for her enameled tin cup, the one with the boring design of insipid blue flowers. She covets my dancing pig openly.

"We've come at least half a mile since breakfast." I lay back and enjoy the graceful sweeping flight of a curious *zopilote*. Do vultures eat seaweed?

"*Half* a mile?" She sighs as though she'd expected me to say twenty miles. I check my watch.

"We finished our oatmeal at exactly 10:15 this morning, remember? Then you just had to write in your journal. Couldn't wait another second. Then you sewed up that tear in your pants and rearranged your pack. It took you another ten minutes to give up trying to identify that weird-looking cactus."

"What time is it now?"

"Noon."

"I thought so. I'm feeling kind of droopy."

I don't bother to answer; the droops hit Lorena every day within an hour of breaking camp. Her reaction is just as predictable.

"Why don't we find some nice spot to lay over for a day. We can cook something really nourishing." This means a massive dose of garlic and cooking oil, preferably poured over a pot of steaming noodles or rice. If Lorena had set the pace for Cortez he'd never have gotten beyond the beaches of Veracruz.

I pick up the thin branch I've peeled and swat at a few curious flies circling my face. Unless we start making some miles I figure we'll need another month to get within close range of a road or major access trail to a city. We've been hiking for a week, delayed by visits to villages and friendly *rancheros*. We spent half a day exploring a crumbled stone wall that might have been a pre-Columbian ruin, but was actually a farmer's abandoned corn crib, and twice made camp early to enjoy good views of the sunset. Time to get the lead out!

"Tell you what," I say, "Let's just go to the bottom of the next *barranca*. We should hit water down there." Lorena perks up.

"Think so?"

"I'm almost sure of it." I've been saving this as an ace-in-the-hole. While wandering around our camp the night before I'd come upon a perfect viewpoint into the deep canyon below us. There was definitely the sparkle of water down there, perhaps enough to bathe in. The problem, of course, would be leaving it. Water means comfort and security and delicious cool shade trees in the midst of miles of dust and dry rock.

With tea time over we heft our backpacks again and head down the trail. Lorena soon drops back; no matter how many years we hike together we can never match our paces. After fifteen minutes I stop, resting the weight of my pack on a convenient outcropping of rock.

I hear voices and Lorena soon appears, followed by a short Indian woman and her young son. The woman's thick dark braids, woven around strands of bright green yarn, almost touch the ground as she bends beneath a load of heavy oak, cut and split into firewood lengths. Although Lorena towers over the woman and carries but a fraction of her weight, the *campesina* clucks disapprovingly and eyes me as though I am a slave driver.

"She says we're on the right trail. Do we want to buy potatoes from her?" Lorena smiles down on the woman. The slave driver will buy potatoes, don't worry. Her dark face eases into a tentative smile; hard cash is scarce in this part of the country.

Steamed spuds! The woman helps us stash our packs well out of sight behind a clump of thorn bushes. Her house is "very close" she assures us, just a short detour down the side of this impassable cliff. With a shy "¡*Vamonos!*" the overloaded mother and son sprint homeward.

An hour later we regain the trail, our sweat-soaked shirts and pants pockets bulging uncomfortably with at least three kilos of tiny potatoes, enough fresh *chiles* to last us a year and some bitter red berries that only the truly hungry would find appetizing.

"If I'd known she lived at the bottom of the world I might have settled for seaweed," I gasp, draining my canteen at one gulp. Lorena staggers into the shade, gnawing a dried apricot for energy.

"Don't collapse," I warn her. "It's at least two salt tablets down to the water." To emphasize that we've got to beat the afternoon sun I shake out salt tablets and hand her one. As she tips back her canteen I wipe the sweat from my forehead and kick myself once again for buying a wool *serape* a few villages back. Who would have thought it would gain a hundred pounds?

We rest a while longer and then continue on.

"Carl, look!" Lorena points straight down, a thousand feet. I see the tops of giant mesquite trees, sunlight shimmering off a shallow stretch of rapids. A good place to devour several pounds of potatoes.

Though still a good hour or more above the stream, Lorena begins snatching twigs and dead branches scattered along the trail. This is a trick another Indian woman taught her, insurance against not finding enough fuel to prepare the evening meal. The growing bundle under her arm is an unmistakable signal that we will soon camp for the night.

But two steep switchbacks later, still far above the water, we come upon a weather-grayed crucifix, the hand-hewn oak beams towering unexpectedly over a lichen-encrusted cairn of granite boulders. A major intersection. Left or right? We silently study the burned out candle stubs at the base of the cross. Other travellers, perhaps equally puzzled about their route, have rested here, leaving simple offerings to compensate the Gods for a safe journey. Would the Gods accept a *serape*?

"This goes toward the music," Lorena says, waving her hand wearily to the left, "but this other one definitely goes to the water." A real dilemma. If we detour down to the stream we'll have to backtrack, straight up, to regain the main trail to the village. Unless, of course, we decide to change our plans completely and follow the trail past the stream, to whatever lies beyond.

"If we go to the village now we'll have to spend the night there," Lorena says, her eyes drawn toward the peace and quiet of the mesquite grove.

"Well?" I face equidistant between the two branches of the trail, forcing her to make the decision. She continues to the right, down into the canyon.

The campfire burns low, with the rich red-orange glow of hardwood coals, the pungent scent of smoldering mesquite. We comb the knots from our hair after a long soak in a deep shaded pool. The potatoes are almost tender and garlic gravy teases me as it bubbles in the frying pan. Lorena blows gently on a cup of steaming vegetable broth, gives a tentative sip and says, "Where to tomorrow?"

I fall back on my air mattress, trying to ignore the tiny hiss of escaping air that will lead to midnight cursing and half-awake attempts to puff more comfort between my bones and the hard ground. A swath of stars glow overhead, trapped between the high dark walls of the canyon. There is a flutter of wings as a night-hunting owl rides the breeze, followed by the sweet acrid odor of distant cornfields being burnt off after harvest.

"Backtracking to the village isn't going to be easy," Lorena yawns. "Maybe we should just follow this trail. Do you remember anything from the map about where it goes?"

I shift onto my left side and feed another dry branch into the fire. Flames lick upward and claim a careless mosquito.

"This wasn't even on the map," I answer.

"How about the village?"

"Nope. I think we're genuinely lost this time. Might be better to just continue downhill. We have to hit a road eventually."

Lorena is quiet for a moment. With *campesinos* such as the lady-of-the-spuds living in almost every arable nook and cranny it is unlikely that we could lose ourselves completely, with no hope of another trail or a meal of beans now and then. On the other hand, as carefree and footloose as we might wish to be, there is something rather unsettling about walking right off the map. The general feel of the countryside is reassuring: tough but negotiable, but what greater obstacles might wait for us around the corner?

"Let's flip for it."

"For what?" I stall.

"Heads we stay here for a day or two and keep going on this trail. Tails we go up to the village." The temptation to throw the decision to the Gods is great; after all, they deal with the local people all the time and must know the country . . .

"Call it for the village!" Lorena warns, squeezing her eyes shut as her imaginary coin tumbles upward into the sky. Heads or tails? Heads or tails? My mind races, hesitates, stops . . . no! Heads?

"Tails!" I shout, leaning eagerly toward her. She lifts her eyes slowly from the back of her bare hand. There is nothing here but mutual trust.

"Heads!" She cries happily, "We can spend all day tomorrow taking baths."

I lay back on the mattress. Mutual trust. Odd, though, how these imaginary coins always fall in favor of water, rest stops and downhill trails.

"Flip you for the dishes," I say.

Lorena gives me a wry look and reaches for the pot scrubber.

Mexico is covered by an extensive interconnecting network of trails and water-ways, many in constant use for thousands of years. Of the estimated 100,000 small villages and *ranchos* in the country, each is the center of its own web of trails and rough roads: trails to neighboring *pueblos* and market towns; trails to water holes, cornfields and grazing land; trails to shrines, caves, hunting grounds and wood-lots. People from the *alta sierra* (mountain highlands) follow ancient trails to the lowlands for the annual coffee harvests; their route may cross high deserts, ranges of isolated mountains, pine and oak forests, tropical jungles and lowland savannahs. In areas that remain unknown to the outside world, there is a small but steady traffic, by foot, *bestia* (animalback), canoe and small plane. Traders, prospectors, missionaries, archaeologists and many others are now being followed by increasing numbers of tourists and curious independent explorers.

Very few of the travellers you'll meet on Mexico's trails consider themselves to be 'backpackers,' though they may be embarking on foot for a journey of hundreds of miles. The term *mochilero* is used almost exclusively for tourists carrying backpacks. When traveling with pack animals you're an *arriero.* If you've got nothing but a walking stick and a sack over your shoulder, you may think of yourself as a *vagabundo,* but it's best not to use the word with people you meet along the trail. In Mexico a *vago* (bum) and *vagabundo* are almost one and the same. Even lower on the social scale come Gypsies (*húngaros, gitanos*), almost universally distrusted and feared by Mexicans.

To further complicate the picture, our friend John pointed out that most of our backpacking trips should properly be called 'treks.' "Trekkers rely on the land and people they visit for supplies," he explained. "You take what you can get from the natives."

Ringtailed cat   *Cacomixtle*

I asked what would happen if the 'natives' didn't feel like handing over tortillas upon request. "You'll really be on your own, then," he answered, a note of excitement in his voice. "You'll actually be exploring. Explorers suffer. They travel in unknown country, *terra incognita,* without maps or other aids." He gave a wistful sigh at the thought of being without other aids. "They aren't lost," he quickly assured me, "because they don't know where they're going."

Now that your excitement and curiosity have been aroused the big question must be answered: where do I start and how? The answers are the real purpose of this chapter, to get you out of the daydream and onto the trail. Backpacking in Mexico requires a degree of independence and self-reliance seldom necessary for hiking in the U.S. It will be many years (I hope) before Mexican trails are so well known and travelled that guidebooks will offer step-by-step descriptions and hand holding. This book is just a starting point; the moment you put it down and step onto the trail you're on your own. Don't be surprised if the tingle of excitement this gives you is mixed with another tingle of slight worry and fear; once the trip is over you'll find it was a richer experience than any backpacking you've done before.

Planning Your Hike

The map of Mexico is pinned to the garage door and you've just reached for a sharp dart. Trip planning is about to begin with a bang. Before you let fly, consider this: what do you want out of your hike? Excitement? A glimpse into another way of life in an Indian village? A nature trek through remote canyons? Fishing and bird watching on an unspoiled river? Danger and hardships on a 'bring 'em back alive!' expedition through impenetrable jungles? Or a simple walk with the kids away from the noise and smell of the cities and truck-filled highways? The possibilities are so numerous that you'd better grab a handful of darts; Mexico offers all of the above and far more.

Although I've always advocated a rather loose, come-what-may approach to travelling, I prefer to tighten things up when planning a backpacking trip. Advance planning is especially helpful if you aren't very familiar with Mexico and want to avoid disappointments: "You mean the trail is now Highway 6?," over-equipping ("Ask that lady in the red bathing suit if she wants an ice axe.") and mindless wandering from one end of the country to another in search of a good starting point. One of the most important lessons to learn is that any trail in Mexico is probably going to be interesting; the hardest step is the first one, away from the familiar and into the relatively unknown.

Start by reading over *Unknown Mexico* at the end of various chapters. Does the Yucatán look too warm for hiking in August? Is your Spanish too weak to carry you comfortably through a month-long trek into the rugged *Espinazo Del Diablo* (Devil's Spine) mountain range? You might be better off hiking the eastern slopes of the Sierra de Puebla, high enough in elevation to beat the summer heat but not so far into the boondocks that you feel totally out of touch.

When planning a hike we ask ourselves: will it be a short trip or an open-ended odyssey? Can we afford to hire a guide, pack animals or a boat? Do we want to go completely on our own or with friends? Will the trip be easy and relaxed or really challenging?

The answers to these questions quickly add up to a series of clues about where to look on the map for a departure point. There are, for example, great hiking opportunities just south of the Mexican-American border. Much of northern Mexico is completely overlooked by travellers who automatically head for Oaxaca, Chiapas or the Yucatán Peninsula.

The *idea* of hiking Mexico is both romantic and exciting but some travellers find themselves all but overwhelmed by Mexico's foreignness. It takes a while to adjust to the sights, sounds, smells and rhythms of a new country, especially one as varied as Mexico. This is quite natural and there's nothing to be gained by forcing yourself into situations that don't yet feel comfortable. Take it slow: hike an hour or two to a village, drink a warm soda and spend an easy afternoon chatting with the people you'll meet. Your confidence will soon grow, especially after you've seen for yourself that *campesinos* (country people) are very friendly and accommodating. One thing easily leads to another; before you know it you'll be off on a truly memorable hike.

Typical Backpacking Trips

The following brief description of trips we and others have made can't begin to cover the possible hikes in Mexico, Guatemala and Belize.* The purpose of these suggestions is to help you find a starting point for your own adventures. Be flexible and confident; the people of the back country will generally do everything they can to help you out. Patience, respect and an open mind will lead you to far more valuable experiences than any map or guidebook.

End Of The Line

The ultimate decision of where to hit the trail can be very difficult, if only because there are so many trails in Mexico. I discovered one simple solution by accident, when the second class bus I was travelling on pulled into a tiny village at the mouth of an

*The depressing political climate in Guatemala and the rising incidence of violence make it advisable to travel with care, especially in the back country. Hiking in Belize usually means jungles; I recommend that you find a guide or consult local people for detailed advice.

intriguing looking canyon. The majority of the other passengers continued on foot, burdened with crates of fresh food, sacks of beans and other market goods. I'd hopped onto the bus on a whim, for a very cheap and interesting side trip. I had my backpack with me (it was my only luggage), but hadn't really thought of hiking.

"Let's go, *amigo*." The man sitting next to me said, motioning toward the trail.

"Why not?" I thought, and obediently headed after him.

The bus driver shouted, "Maybe we'll see each other tomorrow, *güero!*" (paleface).

It was that simple; I tagged along with the crowd from the bus for two days, not making very many miles but visiting quite a number of isolated *rancherías* (small rural villages). I later checked a map and saw that my short excursion could have easily been extended in many directions into thousands of square miles of unknown country.

To reach the end of the line, just do as I did and hop a bus to a small town. When you see an intriguing place, get off. If you have time (and if you don't you're probably pushing too fast), get a room for the night. People will be very curious; when you've answered their questions ask them about the surrounding countryside. In one village a storekeeper generously gave me a simple letter of introduction to his *compadre* (close friend, god-relative) far back in the hills. The man I rented a cot from offered his son's services as a guide; the lady who ran the only *fonda* (small restaurant) sold me a stack of tortillas and a handful of dried beef. By the time I'd spent an evening in the general store, sipping warm Superior with the local cops, I had a fair knowledge of what lay beyond the edge of town. And by the next morning, when I set off with my backpack, I had an eager escort of excited children to lead me beyond the first confusing tangle of trails surrounding the village.

Cargo Trucks & Hitching

Thousands of miles of unmapped dirt roads penetrate much of Mexico's back country (see Chapter 10). When you get to the end of the line you'll often discover that someone has managed to open a rough track even farther. Trucks of all sorts travel these unknown roads (called *brechas*), hauling vital supplies like beer, Coca Cola, food and farm equipment into the interior. They also serve as unscheduled buses and rarely travel without at least a few passengers. To get a ride just put out your hand or thumb. In some cases you'll be expected to pay, since the only alternative is to walk. *Gringos* are such a novelty, however, that you'll often be given the ride for nothing.

The advantages of this type of travel are numerous: you're with people who know where they're going, where to eat, sleep and buy food supplies; you'll arrive tired and perhaps a little shaky, but it's not nearly as demanding as hiking the same distance; you'll find opportunities for other rides and side trips, especially invitations from other passengers to visit their *ranchos* or some special local attraction; and, last but not least, it's a very inexpensive way to visit areas you might not otherwise be able to reach.

Cargo trucks also congregate around the marketplaces of large cities and small towns. Finding one that's going your way may take time and patience. If you don't have a specific destination in mind, just ask *el chófer* (the driver) for *un aventón* or *un ride*.

Let's assume that you want to go into the high forest country. Look for cargoes that are typical of the highlands and timber regions. Bananas are from the hot lowlands; keep an eye out for forest products (from logs to furniture), sheep, bales of wool and grain. Incoming passengers are a good indication of where the truck has come from. Indians in traditional costume are almost a certain sign that the driver has come from a very remote region.

Don't waste your time or the driver's patience by pressing for exact details about route and departure time; he probably plans both very casually. If he agrees to let you return with him and he's leaving at five a.m., *más o menos* (more or less), you'd better sleep in the truck or underneath it.

You'll probably be charged for this type of ride, since you've sought it out rather than thumbed it. Don't be surprised if the price is relatively high compared to the cost of a second class bus. This is normal and the other passengers will be paying the same — or even more, if they're heavily burdened. The driver is charging for gas, wear and tear, and the convenience offered by the ride. When you finish the trip and look back at the country you've crossed, you'll feel it's a bargain.

Now where are you? Probably a village or *rancho*, but perhaps at an isolated mine, lumber mill or temporary fishing camp. Ask the truck driver, "*¿Cuándo regresa usted?*" (When will you return?) or "*¿Cuándo va usted a . . .?*" (When are you going to . . .?). You may find that he won't be going *anywhere* for a week. although truck drivers are very helpful and will often find a return or continuing ride for you, it's best to be prepared to wait.

Lorena and I waited three days for a ride out of a remote coastal fishing camp we'd arrived at by boat. When a truck finally appeared, the driver urged us to hurry; we piled into the back of his stake truck as fast as we could. Then he had an idea: without a word to us, he turned to a woman and asked if she'd cook him a meal. "Of course," she answered. It would take only a moment.

We used the extra time to lash our backpacks securely to the truck's high sideboards. I wrestled some of the heavier cargo — bales of very odorous dried shark meat, empty gas drums and crates of live oysters, into a semblance of order. We'd been warned that the road wasn't just rough; it was downright murderous.

Suddenly, the truck gave a lurch as the emergency brake slipped. We took off downhill toward the bay, rolling out of control backwards. I was thrown to the floor, pinned under a huge tire and rim, my knee badly scraped and sprained. Lorena had time for one startled yell before we crashed directly into the side of a house. The truck driver ran out of the same house, a piece of tortilla dangling form his mouth, eyes wide with shock. The back of the truck had gone far enough into the kitchen so that Lorena could almost serve herself from the bean pot, bubbling away on a wood fire.

The lady of the house laid into the truck driver with an amazing variety of insults and threats. He did his best to choke down the tortilla while convulsing with laughter. Without so much as a backward glance at the wreckage he hopped into the driver's seat, started the engine and pulled away.

"You're lucky the house is flexible!" he hollered back to the indignant woman, who was already angrily repairing the huge hole with broken palm fronds.

We once hiked directly into the heart of one of Mexico's most forbidding mountain ranges. After seven grueling days we came upon a small village surrounded by mountains that soared up in a vertical barrier — a barrier that appeared impassable. There seemed no alternative but to backtrack to our starting point. The thought of recrossing all those steep, waterless canyons was too much to bear . . .

A couple of hours later I was poring over our totally inadequate map in the shade of a crumbling adobe wall when the village mayor, who had introduced himself earlier, approached with a large jar of homebrewed mescal. Between sips we analyzed our predicament: the country that lay ahead was obviously far rougher than I'd expected; we were too tired to continue and our best alternative was to detour to the nearest highway. But how? One look at the formidable granite wall that hung over the town was enough to give a mountain goat the shakes.

"Could we descend into the canyon," I asked, "and follow the river out?"

The mayor shaded his eyes against the afternoon sun, thinking hard. The roar from the gorge nearby had taunted us for days with glimpses of deep, clear pools and misty waterfalls. Many times we'd watched, dry-mouthed, as the water flowed temptingly below our feet. A thousand feet below, straight down.

"Nooo . . ." he sighed, "It is far too dangerous."

I was hardly surprised; such gorges were one of the reasons the area was so sparsely settled.

"What of an *avioneta*?" I asked. We couldn't really afford to charter a small plane but if one just happened along, who knows?

"¡*Híijole!*" he laughed. "The radio no longer works to call them and besides . . ." His hands spread eloquently, "Since the rains of last season we have not yet repaired the landing place. Maybe next month."

I sipped at the jar; backtrack or mountain climb? I'd rather walk fifty miles than risk falling fifty feet. I folded the map with a sigh of defeat.

"If you want to go to the highway," the mayor said, "why don't you go in the truck?" I followed the direction of his pointing finger. To my complete amazement I could see the cab of a green pickup truck parked behind a cluster of mud huts. Before I could ask for an explanation his finger lifted and began to slowly trace a winding path up the sheer cliffsides. What I assumed were fractures in the rock and the scars of landslides was actually a road. A sudden rush of relief was tempered by the thought of what driving up it would be like.

"The truck comes just once a week. Sometimes less. If you ask a friend, they will take you up in the morning." The mayor winked; maybe that river gorge wasn't so bad after all.

The next day, a full hour before dawn, we lifted our packs into the back of the truck. The driver cautioned us to place them carefully; he was taking out a load of fresh eggs and didn't want any crushed. Several people surrounded the truck, gently shaking hands and muttering goodbyes. Occasional nervous laughter reminded me somehow of scenes on television, as the men in jaunty silver suits closed their helmets and eased into the space capsule . . .

Lorena and I were shown to the front seat, the guests of honor. My stomach began tightening and a trickle of perspiration ran down my back. As the driver reached for the ignition key I couldn't help asking how we could possibly scale that mighty cliff. He gave a sharp laugh.

"¡*Con Dios, amigo!*" he said, slamming the truck into gear. "¡*Con Dios y cuatro al piso!*" His right hand moved quickly in the sign of the cross as his foot stomped the accelerator pedal to the floorboards.

"With God! With God and four-on-the-floor!"

Note: Many large, well-organized trucking lines do not officially allow women to ride in their trucks. This rule, like many others in Mexico, is flexible. Just don't be upset if a driver asks you to get out; there may be an inspection station ahead and his job could be at stake. The driver of a logging truck let us out on the outskirts of a large city, explaining that he couldn't be seen with a woman aboard. He'd already given us a two-day ride and then generously offered an invitation to stay with his family — if we'd only take the bus to get there.

Airplanes

Avionetas (small planes) are competing with foot and burro power for travel into remote areas of Mexico. Airstrips, some nothing more than a line of whitewashed stones across a stretch of brush-cleared hilltop, are found near many isolated villages. Service varies from fairly regular, like once a week, to whenever someone decides to hire a plane for a business trip or a visit to the doctor.

Chartering small planes is not expensive, especially when you look down and see what you're soaring over rather than hiking. Many places that require a tough one or two week hike to reach take only an hour by plane.

To find a plane and *piloto* visit the airport of a fair-sized city and ask, "*¿Hay servicio de avioneta a . . . .?*" (Is there small plane service to . . .?). The best bargains will be to regularly visited places, but you may also get a deal by waiting for a pilot to complete a load. He might be carrying a passenger to visit a relative and have space left over at a discount.

The very convenience of plane travel is also one of its biggest drawbacks. Dropping out of the sky, uninvited, right into the insulated lives of small villagers (especially Indians) can easily blow their minds. Hikers, on the other hand, approach slowly, creating both interest and a definite respect for the effort they expend in the journey. Even the most cautious Indians will offer a bit of sympathy or hospitality to a trail-weary foreigner. However, they might offer a very cool reception to rich sightseers flying in and out of their lives, asking rude questions about their customs and exposing miles of film. This is considered intrusive and insensitive, so don't be shocked if you are given the cold shoulder. It takes time and mutual respect to overcome such poor impressions — and though you may be innocent yourself, others have often been inconsiderate.

Unless you have a definite purpose in flying directly into a village, I advise you to go in by foot. You'll see and experience much more and meet people, literally, on their own level. If your time or energy are limited, make arrangements to fly out after hiking in. Some villages have government-supplied short wave radios for calling in planes; other radios are operated by missionaries, mining and oil prospectors, and well-to-do farmers and merchants. (Many radios are also broken down; so don't plan too definitely.)

If you're really well organized, arrange to be picked up by plane before you begin your hike into a remote area. This has the disadvantage of creating an inflexible deadline for your arrival.

A friend who enjoys exact planning has a trick to ease his fears that the pilot will find something more interesting to do than meet him at the scheduled time and place. He cuts a banknote in two (he says American money is best: looks flashier and U.S. banks don't balk at replacing damaged bills) and gives half to the pilot. The pilot gets the other half when he meets the rendezvous. (Symbolically, since the friend promises an undamaged note of the same denomination. Torn money is hard to get rid of in Mexico.)

Roads Are Trails

In discussing roads and trails with Mexicans you'll often notice a confusion between the terms used to describe each. *Camino* means both road and trail, depending on whether you're talking to a truck driver or a muleskinner. This confusion probably stems from the fact that many bad roads aren't as good as the average foot trail. Most traffic on them, in fact, will be on foot or animal back, with only the occasional truck or battered bus daring the trip.

Don't restrict your hiking to foot trails, especially if you're worried about getting lost. Dirt roads make fine paths and they have the advantage of offering at least an occasional chance for a lift should you find yourself too worn out to enjoy more walking.

Camp and Hike

Unless you have detailed information about a particular trail, you'll have to rely on what we call the Three Guides: Luck, Local Knowledge and Curiosity. Hikers accustomed to conditions in the U.S. and Canada, where every landmark is carefully described in detailed trail guides, may find this come-what-may approach to be downright unnerving. To break down your natural reluctance to strike off into the unknown, camp out for a while to familiarize yourself with the local countryside and people before hitting the trail.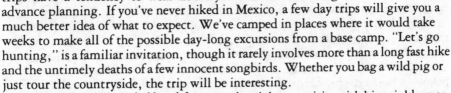

"I'm going to visit my aunt Felicia at her *rancho* over there." The young man points vaguely in the direction of a distant valley. Here's your golden opportunity; even if visiting aunts isn't your idea of exploring, it'll get you moving in the company of someone who knows the country. One or two days will be enough to pay your respects to Felicia and from there you can continue onward or return for another trip in a different direction.

Start with simple day trips, rather than full scale treks. Long trips have a tendency to wear down your nerves with long advance planning. If you've never hiked in Mexico, a few day trips will give you a much better idea of what to expect. We've camped in places where it would take weeks to make all of the possible day-long excursions from a base camp. "Let's go hunting," is a familiar invitation, though it rarely involves more than a long fast hike and the untimely deaths of a few innocent songbirds. Whether you bag a wild pig or just tour the countryside, the trip will be interesting.

One expedition included breakfast at my host's house, visits with his neighbors to borrow a rifle, visits to more neighbors to borrow a pack of scruffy hunting dogs (which promptly deserted out of boredom), visits to even more neighbors to discuss where the game was hiding and finally, by high noon, a brisk walk to a mountain top. We checked out the magnificent view, ate an orange and shot a tree. We were back in time for a swing in a hammock and a long dinner of stewed chicken.

Several other hunting trips that were amazingly similar to this one led me to realize that hunting was only an excuse to visit and tramp through the underbrush. Having a *gringo* along made it all the more interesting. One fellow took innocent delight in playing practical jokes on me, *campesino* style. "Let's cross here," he'd say, sending me crashing into a mudhole. "Go up there, we'll meet at that tree." An hour later I escaped from an impenetrable thicket to find him snoozing in the shade. "Try this wild fruit," turned out to be the world's most bitter excuse for a berry and so on, until I'd fallen for them all, like a child going though a hilarious manhood ceremony. Later, when he'd run out of tricks, I'd say, "Why don't we hike up this river?" or "Where does this trail go; let's find out." Like most *campesinos,* he wasn't so tied down that he couldn't drop his chores and lead me on a side trip.

I once camped with a friend in the cemetery of an almost deserted old mining town, tucked away at the head of a high, spooky canyon. Every day we followed a new trail, carrying food and water for a picnic lunch in the cool mouth of some long abandoned mine shaft. We covered almost one hundred and fifty miles in the time we were there, none of it done with heavy backpacks. At the end of a hard day we'd eat a meal in the town's sole surviving restaurant and then enjoy a restful night among the tombstones. Cheap rooms were easily available for those who preferred less ghostly surroundings. We soon came to be known by the local people and were given many suggestions for hikes, bits of interesting folklore and town history and the inevitable invitations to return one day as friends.

Travelling Merchants

You probably won't have to hike very long before you meet with one of the most common romantic sights of Mexico's back country: *recuas* (mule and burro trains) loaded heavily with canvas-wrapped bundles and stick crates, driven by half a dozen men, women and children. The animals plod relentlessly onward, encouraged by cries of "*¡Mula! ¡Mula! ¡Andele mula!*" Carefully thrown sticks and stones remind the animals not to lag. If time is pressing, the people driving the animal train will eat as they walk, perhaps dipping handfuls of cold beans from a communal enamel pot, washing them down with a swig of tepid water from a gourd canteen. Such scenes never fail to excite me. Never mind that they are carrying cases of crude bar soap, *piloncillo* (lumps of cane sugar), sardines, salt, candles, flashlight batteries and seed corn. To me those bundles are the Treasure of the Sierra Madre.

Such moments of romanticism can usually be purged by trying to keep up with the *recua*. "*¡Vamos despacio!*" They cry, "We go slowly!" They motion you to fall in with them, to have a tortilla and a turn at the bean pot. How can any normal human walk up a mountainside, carrying a backpack while chewing on a taco?

In spite of the tough pace they set, the advantages of travelling with traders are numerous: they know the trails intimately and have excellent local contacts (for further side trips or connections with other traders and guides); they carry food for trade and resale so you won't go hungry; they tend to be open and friendly and very free with information; and finally, traders are rarely ignorant. Their experiences with the outside world (i.e., the rest of Mexico) are much broader than the majority of people living in the back country, especially the more traditional Indians. Traders are therefore easier to deal with than their often shy and reticent country cousins.

"*¿A dónde van ustedes?*" (Where are you going?) is a good natural opening when you wish to tag along with traders. "*¿Cuánto tiempo van a estar en el camino?*" (How long will you be on the trail?) may bring an answer as vague as a shrug; after all, business is business. If they hear of a good bargain in homemade cheeses in the next valley they'll probably make a detour.

I once planned an ambitious trip with an *arriero* (trader, muleteer): we were in a small town in the high sierra and I proposed to hike to the ocean. He suggested instead that we take a bus to the coast, buy a string of burros, load them with dried shark and shrimp and miscellaneous merchandise and trek back into the mountains. We would sell and barter our goods along the way and once we'd returned to his town, resell the burros for a nice profit. I'd get a long guided trip through fantastic country and make money in the bargain.

"How long does it take to travel from the *costa* to here?" I asked him.

"Two weeks, *más o menos.*"

"So we'll return at the end of the month, *¿verdad?*"

"Oh, no!" he answered, "Two months, maybe even three . . ."

When I asked for an explanation he gave me a curious look. "Two weeks of *travel, amigo*. We must also move our *negocio*, our business. And visit my *compadres* and my *tios* and my older *hermana* who now has a *ranchito* in Las . . ."

Although I did my best to talk him into a quicker trip, he just couldn't lose those opportunities for business and pleasure. "Well, another time." he said, adding a significant, "When you are not in such a hurry."

One of the best ways to travel with a trader is to join them before they begin their trek, as they form up their *recua* and collect merchandise. To find them visit the market area of a medium-sized town. The closer the town is to some undeveloped area or mountain range, the more likely you are to find groups of *comerciantes* (business people, traders) preparing for a trip.

When you strike a bargain for the journey make it clear that you intend to walk emptyhanded, with your baggage on board an animal, not on your own back. The fee for this service is dependent, of course, on such factors as the length of the trip, the weight of your pack, etc. A friend who travelled with a mule train of dried beans paid a fee based on the weight and value of the beans represented by his luggage. The return trip was much cheaper because the trader carried cow hides, bulky but not so heavy. To make things simple ask for a flat rate and agree on it firmly before you leave.

Does the price include your *comida* (meal, food)? It probably does, since I can't imagine them eating and not offering you anything. In any case, carry a good stash of candy, nuts and munchies unless you can subsist on the Basics: beans and tortillas.

Pare your gear to a minimum and carry plenty of drinking water. The people who travel the back country are like camels; they often do a full day's walk without a sip.

Guides

My image of the perfect guide is a combination of Ricardo Montalban, Edward Abbey and the Galloping Gourmet. He must photograph well, especially when peering in profile over the mane of his trusty pinto, entertain and amuse with bits of arcane local knowledge and manage to make beans and tortillas as satisfying as grilled steaks and hashbrowns. In Mexico, a *guía* (guide) is more likely to be a shy farmer or ranch hand, willing to take a few days from his chores to lead you over the next mountain or two. His cooking may involve nothing more than flipping tortillas over a pile of hot coals. Conversation will probably be limited by your own command of Spanish but chances are he'll make a good companion.

Because hiking and camping out for pleasure are still relatively new in Mexico, the concept of a *guía* often baffles people, especially *campesinos*. "*Una persona que me acompañe*," (A person to accompany me) is a more familiar idea and skirts the often delicate question of 'employment'. A *campesino* who will happily throw down his plow to guide you to a distant canyon may refuse to do the same trip for money or be too proud to discuss payment.

Finding a guide can take time but it's usually worth it. First of all, you might as well forget about getting help from tourist agencies or travel agents. They'll advise you to take the $199, five-day-package-tour to Palenque; any questions about hiking in the boondocks will be met with blank stares or gasps of horror.

Make inquiries in and around the marketplace, in old-fashioned *tiendas* (stores) and at cheap hotels catering to travellers from the back country and small-time traders. Rehearse your lines well before asking questions. It tends to make people nervous if you can't seem to remember why you want to go somewhere or even *where* you want to go. If you don't have a *motivo* or *misión* (motive, mission) to justify the trip, make one up. "I want to photograph birds" sounds much better than "I have no purpose," since this latter reason is no reason at all.

I once tried to find a guide to take me by mule into a very beautiful desert canyon. Rather than explain my reasons for the trip (which boiled down to wanting to ride a mule) I hemmed and hawed. No one wanted to take me, though one man was obviously interested in making some money and kept plugging away, asking time and time again why I wanted to do the trip. Finally, in great exasperation, he said, "Surely you want to at least visit the hot springs?" It was the first I'd heard of it but I quickly agreed. "Why didn't you say so at first?" he laughed and the deal was quickly made. Later, when we'd spent some time together, he told me that the area was famous for its illegal mescal stills, not to mention hidden patches of marijuana. I'd acted more like a spy than a tourist with my inane non-answers to people's questions and had made them too nervous to want to guide me.

Once you've found a person who is willing to do a trip with you, be patient; they may have to finish plowing the lower forty before they can leave. Others will just grab a blanket and be off and running. It is considered bad manners to show impatience, but if delays become too inconvenient don't hesitate to drop hints.

Make a clear arrangement before you commit yourself to hiring a guide and reaffirm it shortly before leaving. Haggling for personal services like this is a delicate exercise in economic diplomacy. If you shout, "You robber! You aren't worth that much!" your prospective guide is going to make a very disgruntled companion. Mexicans are very fond of saying, *"Lo que me hace el favor."* (Whatever you do me the favor of.) This puts the ball squarely in your court. Fortunately, there are some commonly accepted guidelines for wages: a day's pay at the local rate (higher on the coast than in the mountains) for the guide; a day's pay for each mule or horse (burros are cheaper); you pay for food and lodging (and perhaps fodder), especially if you want to eat more than the bare minimum, and long trips cost more than short trips, on a daily basis. This is a sort of 'dislocation' bonus, since the guide will have to put aside normal business for extended journeys.

The simplest way to find out what the going rate is for labor is to ask a third party, *"¿Qué es el jornal (El sueldo minimo)?"* (What is the daily wage. The minimum wage?) This gives you a starting figure; I prefer to err on the side of generosity.

You may be asked to pay *un adelanto,* an advance. This is normal, especially on longer trips when the guide must leave money at home for food and household expenses.

A guide may have an entirely different style of travel than *gringos. Campesinos* and traders make few rest stops, travel from dawn to dusk and try to camp in or very near villages and *ranchos* whenever possible. Age-old fears of *fantasmas* (ghosts) and bandits die hard; if your guide refuses to camp out, be gracious and work on him slowly, rather than demanding that he conform. (See Chapter 4.)

Travelling with a guide is an experience in itself. Once you've adjusted to each other you'll appreciate the value of his services much more: a guide introduces you to people and quickly explains what you're up to (such explanations can wear you out if your Spanish is weak); a guide will explain local customs and legends, identify landmarks, plants and wildlife; he will scout out food, firewood and water and steer you away from places you shouldn't see, like marijuana fields, stills and unlicensed mines. It's quite doubtful that you'd stumble on these places on your own, since they're quite well hidden, but a guide will make sure there's no mistakes.

If you prefer to leave all the planning, preparation and coping to someone else, a number of organizations and individuals offer guided camping trips in Mexico, Guatemala and Belize. I've never taken one of these tour-type trips but if you're pressed for time rather than money, they're probably a good introduction to camping in a foreign country. (See *Guided Tours & Adventures: Appendices.*)

Pack Animals

Although *gringo* hikers and explorers can find a *bestia* (beast, pack animal) to be a welcome relief from humping a heavy backpack, it does take time and sometimes more than a little patience to find the proper animal and an agreeable owner. Because of the high value of pack animals, especially mules and horses, many people will be understandably reluctant to entrust them to the care of a stranger. In most cases it is far easier to hire an *arriero* (who may be a young boy) with the animals. Fodder and water can be very scarce and a guide/helper will relieve you of the responsibility of keeping the beasts in good running order. As a friend put it, "Herding a string of burros is about as easy as maintaining half a dozen Edsels."

One of the easiest ways to find a pack animal for rent is to visit a *tienda* (small store) or marketplace in the village or small town near the area you'd like to travel in. Once you've gone through the brief but important ritual of explaining in simple terms what you're up to ("Getting to know the country" is my favorite), simply ask for help from the store owner or a customer. *"Quiero rentar (contratar) una bestia"* (I want to rent a pack animal). An interesting custom of the back country will now work in your favor: it is considered highly unusual for a person 'of means', especially a woman or a foreigner, to carry a burden on the trail. Obviously your backpack must be borne by an animal and the rules of hospitality usually cause someone to volunteer help. If you're lucky, in fact, you'll get the services of a pack animal and helper *gratis*, especially if the trip is to be a short one.

The cost of renting an animal is open to some negotiation but as a general rule a large expensive *bestia*, such as a mule or sturdy horse, costs as much per day as a man's wages. Burros cost less and are all but impossible for *gringos* to ride: too short, too weak and just too bony for any but the most well padded human posterior to bear.

Horses are not as strong as mules, nor as sure footed, an important consideration if you don't have riding experience and are travelling in rough country. I will never forget the mule that carried me along the sheer edge of a crumbling precipice. By carefully leaning out of the saddle I was able to take an excellent bird's eye photo of the river hundreds of feet below us. In the course of the day my guide's horse fell or stumbled dangerously several times; only his skill and nerve prevented a fatal accident. My mule plodded on as relentlessly and steadily as a tractor.

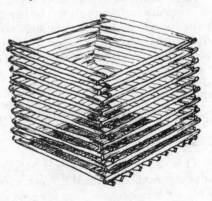

Because few *campesinos* can afford fancy 'tack', your saddle may be nothing but a hand-carved framework of sticks covered with a rough piece of cowhide or a tattered burlap sack. Gear is lashed to the animal's back with ropes, thongs, wire or even vines. Small items are stuffed into bags, homemade stick boxes (called *huacales*), empty lard cans or baskets. If you've got a backpack you'll probably find it inconvenient for loading onto an animal and may have to carry your gear in the owner's containers.

If you are renting an animal for riding, take a close look at the saddle before making a deal. Do the toes of your hiking boots fit into the stirrups? I doubt that they will; Mexican stirrups are very small. You must have good toe support or your legs will gradually feel as though they've been through a long session on the Rack. If you can't improvise something (loops of rope will do in a pinch) it could be easier to walk.

A tennis shoe might fit into the stirrup but a pointed cowboy boot is obviously what you need.

Renting pack animals and an *arreiro* might seem an unwanted complication to your trip but consider this: the muleskinner will also be your guide and companion, able to direct you to the more interesting campsites, arrange for food and shelter, explain details of life among the people you meet, ward off trouble if necessary (over-talkative drunks at fiesta time are your most likely problem) and generally ease your way into an area. And last, but certainly not least, you can ride an animal or walk the trail without your backpack weighing you down. This saves a great deal of hard work and leaves much more energy for seeing the sights, photographing, note taking and quick side trips.

One of the easiest ways to find a burro or mule for rent — or loan — is to shoulder your pack and strike off down the trail. Unless the area is especially remote you should soon meet people coming and going with *bestias*. Many will be loaded with gear but at least a few will be empty or able to carry more. Give a friendly greeting, strike up a conversation and casually ask, "*¿No se puede llevar (cargar) un poquito más?*" (Can't it carry a bit more?) Point to the empty pack animal and raise your eyebrows inquiringly. You're on your way to striking a bargain, whether it's for a short hop to the owner's *rancho* or a longer trip deep into the interior. When you get to the next village and unload, someone will inevitably wonder, "How will you continue?" and you're on your way to finding another pack animal.

Here are a few more ideas that should make travel with pack animals and their owners easier:

• Don't drive too hard a bargain; if the animal's owner is unhappy with the deal you may find yourself with an unhappy guide — or left alone in extreme cases.

• Never overload an animal. It will only lead to problems and is very inconsiderate. A *large* burro can carry about one hundred pounds, a mule two hundred pounds and more and a horse between one and two hundred pounds. These weights vary according to the animal's health, stamina and size, the nature of the load and the way it is packed and, of course, the difficulty of the trail. If the owner says your gear requires two animals rather than one, it rarely does much good to argue.

• Your proposed route may have to be modified to accommodate the pack animal. Burros, for example, can't follow really steep foot trails. Alternate animal trails are common in rough country so heed your guide's advice.

Beach Hiking

There are so many beaches in Mexico that it is difficult to give more than general advice about hiking them. In most cases, however, beaches are not used for travel. They are considered too soft for good walking, too exposed and hot, and beaches rarely lie along the shortest line between two points. Other than that, of course, they're absolutely great for camping, fishing and loafing.

The combination of beach and jungle is common in Mexico and nothing would seem to fit a backpacker's daydream more than ambling along beneath the shade of tropical vegetation with a cool sea breeze on your cheek. I once attempted to hike a coastline in an area where the foothills (up to 3,000 feet high) ran directly into the sea. Alternating ridges and deep forested *barrancas* ran at right angles to the shoreline. The beaches were too short to provide good walking and the main trail ran inland about half a mile. The terrain was passable — if you had a heart like a buffalo and the stamina of a rhinoceros.

I soon gave up and hitched a ride on a passing *canoa*. The fisherman who picked me up explained that the trails had been used before outboard motors were introduced and only when the trip to town was urgent. "That is why this place is so beautiful," he said. "No one can get here except by sea." When I asked if I could rent *bestias* I got a similar response. "The trip takes seven days by *mula,* following the shore. It is only a few hours by boat. Why bother?"

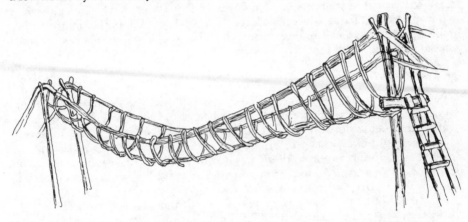

This doesn't mean that fine beach hiking isn't available. There are many long stretches of good firm sand beaches along the Gulf of Mexico, Isthmus of Tehuantepec and on some northern portions of the Pacific coast. Buses sometimes use these beaches as highways. By hiking at night, especially with a full moon, you can avoid the problem of sun and heat.

Short beach hikes can lead to rewards that are out of proportion to the actual effort involved. An hour's hike from a crowded beach can make the difference between camping with other people or finding relative privacy. There are a lot of beautiful unspoiled nooks and crannies along Mexico's coastlines that are accessible only by foot; with a little persistence you'll discover one for yourself.

Jungle Hiking

Nothing satisfies my image of Adventure more than the sweaty explorer hacking through tangled lianas and grasping vines, surrounded by the mysterious exotic cries of jungle birds and animals. You pop the top on a can of chilled Budweiser, adjust the color on the Tube and watch in fascination as some poor fool fights off bloodsucking leeches, pythons, quicksand and restless, spear-throwing natives. All this just to discover some Lost City paved with gold. It hardly seems worth the effort.

Although I tend to discount the fears most urban Mexicans express about camping out, I take them much more seriously when faced with a genuine *selva* (jungle). Mexico is not just deserts; some of its jungles rival anything found in the Orient and South America. Jungles, and the creatures that live in them, are quite simply beyond most people's experience. It's easy to get lost and easy to *stay* lost — not at all like the carefully planned and groomed National Parks that many people consider 'wilderness'. Mosquitos, snakes, choking heat and humidity, confusing trails, no landmarks and plenty of unidentified crawling objects all have to be expected and dealt with, either one at a time or all together.

Discouraging? Don't lose hope yet; the unanimous opinion of jungle-wise Mexicans I've spoken and hiked with is very simple and very sensible: go with a knowledgeable guide or don't go very far. In some areas the trails will be clear and easy to follow, but unless you're sure of it, don't take chances. Take the time to acquaint yourself with local people and they'll inevitably teach you a great deal about the area.

Camping and hiking in the jungle can be a rare and unforgettable experience. For this reason, as well as your personal comfort and safety, the price of hiring a guide is well worth it. You'll not only feel more comfortable about camping out for the night, supplies, directions and avoiding hazards, but once you've studied under an expert, you can consider jungle trips on your own.

Downhill Hiking

Backpackers tend to see mountains, peaks and hilltops as goals rather than starting points. That attitude is fine for short trips, when you've got nothing more to carry than a camera and a bottle of wine to enhance the view. For longer hikes, however, when the weight of my backpack brings back sweaty memories of Boot Camp, I prefer to start at the top and work my way down. You'll still have some challenging ups and downs in *barrancas* and inconvenient mountains, but your general progress will be with gravity, rather than against it.

Downhill hiking has other advantages: if high altitudes bother you (and I automatically get a headache at 10,000 feet), it shouldn't take long to reach a lower elevation. It's much more difficult to escape altitude discomfort if you're working upward. Trails in Mexico tend to take the path of least resistance. In the mountain highlands bordering the Pacific, for example, a typical trail will drop into the first canyon that leads to the lowlands. In most cases you'll have to select trails very carefully to avoid descending before you want to.

On one hike we took a second class bus into the heart of a large range of mountains, getting off in a small village near the crest of the sierra. Local people told us of two possible routes to the coast: a path that led almost parallel to the road and another that followed the ridge line to distant *ranchos* and eventually to sea level. We took the second, longer route.

Because the trip began at almost 10,000 feet our initial progress was very slow. Clouds and fog helped keep us cool. At night we were grateful for plentiful firewood to cook and warm ourselves with. The views were staggering and compensated me for shortness of breath and midnight gasping sessions that disturbed my sleep. In the first few days we dropped a couple of thousand feet and adjusted comfortably to the elevation.

In spite of the inevitable descents into canyons and climbs up the other side our general progress was steadily downward. By the fourth day the trail grew steeper and our descent was quite dramatic, both for the rate at which we dropped and the amazing changes in vegetation. In just one day we went from cold cloud forests of pine and oak down through semi-tropical regions of bananas, mangos and sugarcane fields. Next came a lower area of grassy brown foothills and clear, rocky streams, reminiscent of northern California. A few hours later — and lower — we were in towering forests and coffee plantations, filled with birds and the promise of tropical heat. Beyond and below the forest came low scrub jungle: dry, hot and dusty. The next day it was a short distance to the beach. We shook the pine needles from our clothes and spread sleeping bags beneath the coconut palms. There had been more to see in the space of two days' walking than we could absorb in a few weeks. By the time the hike had ended, in fact, we couldn't help lamenting the campsites and side trails we'd so casually bypassed on our way down.

Religious Pilgrimages

Every year hundreds of thousands — if not millions — of devout Mexicans embark on long and often arduous *peregrinaciones* (pilgrimages). A pilgrim may hike hundreds of miles cross country to honor a favored saint, to complete a *voto* (vow) or to demonstrate faith before requesting a favor at a shrine. The spectacle of tens of thousands of people converging on one particular spot, the vast majority on foot — old women, children, entire families, cripples, the blind and whoever else feels the urge — is something that has to be seen to be appreciated. The mind is compelled to images from Cecil B. DeMille movies, particularly at night, when the pilgrims gather around thousands of camp fires to catch a few hours of sleep before continuing their journey by starlight.

Although *gringos* are a rare sight among these multitudes, a small number (mainly faithful Catholics themselves) do accompany the *peregrinos* (pilgrims). It is a unique opportunity to meet people while at the same time participating in a sort of spiritual forced march. If you decide to join a pilgrimage make no mistake: suffering along the way is considered part of the greater scheme. Although baggage is usually carried by trucks and buses that meet the pilgrims at night, few people can trudge twenty to thirty miles, day after day, without experiencing discomfort. Larger pilgrimages include the services of the *Cruz Roja* (Red Cross) and private ambulances for those who must fall out and seek medical care. The main problems, according to friends who have gone on long (a week or more) pilgrimages, are blisters, muscle cramps and diarrhea. Carry alcohol to bathe your feet, plenty of adhesive tape, calcium and Lomotil tablets (see Chapter 8).

One of the great advantages of pilgrimages, especially the larger and better organized ones, is that services are provided along the way: food vendors sell everything from barbecued meat to *atole* (corn gruel), invigorating drinks of hot *canela* (cinnamon), some laced with alcohol, fresh fruit, beer and whatever else might tempt a footsore hiker.

The routine of a pilgrimage is quite simple: everyone rises at an unholy hour of the night and hikes well into the next day, arriving at some traditional camping and gathering place. They'll be met by their baggage trucks and hordes of food vendors, hawkers of religious momentoes and day-trippers from the surrounding area who want to join into the festive mood without sacrificing shoe leather. Everyone eats, has a beer or two (drunkenness isn't appreciated though it happens) and then immediately falls asleep. Mariachi bands and transistor radios blare all night, but the weary find them to be no obstacle to a much needed rest.

Gringos who accompany a pilgrimage should keep in mind at all times that they are involved in a protracted religious ceremony, not just a tough country outing. It is perhaps best to say that you are a Catholic, even if you aren't. On an overnight pilgrimage that Lorena and I made, a Mexican acquaintance said, "You may not be Catholics but you acted with respect, and that is what is important."

Pilgrims prefer to travel in groups, usually formed around a banner bearing the name of their neighborhood or village religious 'society.' A *cofradía* (union, association) may provide its members with food, transportation and other support along the march. Other groups will be led by a village or town elder; everyone sticks together and cheers each other on. Gringos find it quite easy to adopt a group and will probably be invited at an early stage to join in. Once you accept, however, you'll probably find it difficult to leave the group, since they'll be protective of you. This, too, is just part of the experience. Friends who have made long pilgrimages say that strong bonds are often formed in the course of the journey.

Here are a few tips for those who follow a pilgrimage:

• Carry at least two liters of water for stretches when you'll be beyond the services of food and drink vendors. Use purifying agents liberally in your water, especially at over-crowded camping areas.

• Carry a daypack with a good supply of candy, nuts and other high energy foods. Some pilgrims deliberately go short on food and water as a sign of faith or atonement.

• Leave your main luggage with your group's truck (if you bring it at all; consider storing it at a hotel), but keep medicines, water, hat, toilet paper, a flashlight and a warm shirt or sweater with you at all times. If you feel up to it, carry your sleeping bag, too, especially if you want to camp away from the main assembly points and won't be dependent on the baggage trucks.

• If you must drop out and can't connect immediately with your baggage, don't worry, just ask someone where the next assembly/rest place is and take a bus there.

• Don't be disappointed by your goal, many shrines aren't particularly exciting to casual visitors. The pilgrimage itself is the experience to be remembered.

The dates, routes and other details (history especially) of pilgrimages in Mexico are difficult to find. There are two major points, however, for cross country pilgrimages: Chalma, state of México and San Juan de los Lagos, Jalisco. Many other pilgrimages are made, some along ancient routes that were followed by Indians carrying annual tribute to their leaders. In general, however, a saint will have a main shrine (often in an out-of-the-way place) and pilgrims will visit the shrine on its 'Saint Day' or 'Feast Day' (*Día de Santo, Fiesta*). Pilgrims converge from many different points; you can try to find out where they'll be leaving from or join them along the way.

The annual pilgrimage to see the 'Little Virgin' at San Juan de los Lagos, Jalisco is probably the longest and grandest of them all. It is estimated that up to half a million pilgrims participate, many walking all the way from Mexico City. This is about a two-week hike, so groups must leave around mid-January to arrive on the Feast Day in San Juan on February 2. The pilgrimage follows high ground and frost can be expected at night, though it'll be quite clear and warm during the day.

Solo Hiking

I have no special reservations about men hiking alone in Mexico, other than such obvious precautions as not breaking your neck in a lonely spot. Solo hiking tends to push you into closer contact with local people. If you enjoy human company at all you'll find it very easy to involve youself. There's always room in a *campesino* house for another bedroll and another plate at the table.

Women, however, should never hike alone. The hassles and hazards of *machismo* will be constant, irritating and even dangerous for women on their own. I'm sorry to say that this applies to short hikes and day trips as well as longer journeys. A woman alone is considered 'fair game.' *Gringas* often get more attention than they enjoy, even when in the company of husbands or other men. (See *Machismo:* Chapter 4.)

Hiking With Friends, Groups

Unless you're quite familiar with Mexico or unusually independent, you'll probably feel more comfortable by hiking with a companion. Although Lorena and I have done some long group hikes, we generally prefer to go as a couple. It's much easier to make plans and to change them on the spur of the moment if two people rather than a group are involved. "Left or right?" can become a complicated summit conference when several opinions have to be considered.

Groups do have advantages, the most obvious are the comfort of company and the feeling of safety in numbers. The latter can be especially valuable for anyone who is new to Mexico and feels understandably nervous about plunging into the boondocks on their own.

The initial excitement and enthusiasm for a backpacking trip shouldn't be allowed to overwhelm common sense and good planning. First, and most important: agree to a loose plan of activity and a route. If you can't settle any differences that arise before you leave, don't be so foolish as to think they'll be resolved any easier on the trail.

Untested groups should start with a conservative plan, one that can be quickly adjusted to meet unexpected developments. If you find, for example, that one person just can't keep up at all, it might be time to split up. Don't delay such important decisions until you're fifty miles into the high sierra.

If one person in your group is more experienced at travel in Mexico or assumes the burden of speaking Spanish, he or she will probably become the unofficial leader or guide. This is efficient, since it tends to eliminate time-consuming group decisions over which trail to take, where and when to camp, and so on. Nothing creates resentment quicker, however, than a group leader who imposes decisions on others, rather than considering what the group as a whole would enjoy. I remember one hike in particular, where the leader had the legs of a mountain goat and the endurance of an Olympic runner. Our group included a couple of candidates for early coronary arrest. By the time we got the front runner to slow down, our mood was murderous and beyond hope of reconciliation.

Groups of hikers should also take into account conditions of life and travel in Mexico's back country. Of special concern are food and water. In remote areas, people often exist on the outer edge of poverty. Problems of transportation make supplies of food and other essentials uncertain at times (especially the rainy season). Because the custom of hospitality requires that guests and travellers be offered food and shelter (Indians sometimes make exceptions as they tend to distrust all outsiders), you may be a real burden on them, especially if your group is large. Refusing hospitality is not polite, but you can restrain yourself in other ways. Half a dozen famished hikers, accustomed as most gringos are to eating heartily, can make a serious dent in a village's reserves.

"Buy all they've got!" is a familiar cry when spying a stock of macaroni or sweet cookies in some remote *tienda*. *Don't* buy them out and don't complain if prices seem unusually high; it costs a lot to carry supplies overland or to bring them in by plane or boat. If there are no *tiendas* (a store may be a shelf in someone's house) or travelling *comerciantes* laying out their wares, requests for food may lead to a house-to-house search. An egg here, a few limes there.

On a group hike we made through dry mountains and drought-stricken villages, drinking water was a real problem. One evening we lucked upon a tiny seep of water, trickling drop by precious drop into a neat hole gouged into a hillside. We happily filled our canteens and made camp nearby, filling our reserve bottles during the night.

At noon the next day, we were overtaken by a man and his young son, leading a *recua* (train) of pack burros. The man very hesitantly asked us for a drink of water, explaining that the seep they normally rested at had been strangely dry.

"I don't understand," he said, "wild animals must have visited the water. We must hurry now; there is too little to give to the *bestias*." His burros licked their dry lips.

We looked back toward the seep, realizing just what type of greedy two-legged animals had raided the water and reached for our full canteens . . .

Be very careful of accidentally splitting up; maps are so poor and inaccurate that advance rendezvous can be impossible to determine. "Meet us *here*, at this river bend," may well be the last you see of your friends for a long time. If someone wants to do a side trip the group should wait until they return before continuing on.

Signals and clever trail signs, such as forked branches and scratchmarks in the dust, have a way of fading when burro trains scuffle over them or curious *campesinos* accidentally rearrange their direction. Wait at cross trails and junctions until everyone catches up. This is the conservative approach but it beats arguing over who made what mistake and where.

If some of the group drops back along the trail try not to let the women get separated from the company of a man. A shrill whistle makes a good signal if a woman finds herself being hassled. A whistle can also warn others if someone twists an ankle or decides they aren't going any farther for the day.

No matter how well organized your group may seem, don't let other people carry your drinking water or emergency food. Lorena and I like to carry our basic gear, including cooking utensils, even if we are eating communally. When the rest of the group gets too far ahead, we can stop and prepare a meal rather than having to make an exhausting sprint to catch up for lunch.

Backpacking Tips

• Be very careful while hiking in remote country. A minor injury or illness can turn into a serious problem if not given immediate and proper attention. Read Chapter 8 carefully, especially if you plan to go far into the boondocks where medicines and medical care are very scarce. Precautions to avoid diarrhea are minor inconveniences when compared to the physical and mental discomfort of the 'trots' a hundred miles from the nearest flush toilet.

• If you find that you're so uneasy, nervous or just plain scared by backpacking in Mexico that it takes the fun out of it, it's time to slow down or stop. Don't continue just because you've made plans or don't want to lose face with friends. Abandon your two hundred mile mountain trek and head for the nearest quiet beach. Suffering builds character but it's a hell of a way to spend a vacation.

• One of the problems of hiking unknown trails is that you never quite know where you'll find water or a good campsite. This leads to a case of "let's just go another hour," as you search for the mythical Perfect Spot. Take the first place that looks reasonable, even if it's a little earlier in the day than you'd normally stop to camp. If you don't, you may wind up like we did, sleeping in the middle of a steep trail on a sheer rock mountainside. A nervous Indian, caught out after dark, came racing down the trail and stepped right on a friend's chest. It not only scared both of them out of their wits but our friend was badly bruised: the Indian was carrying a hundred-kilo sack of corn on his back.

On other nights when the search for the Perfect Spot failed again, we carved miserable sleeping trenches out of a mountainside with our plastic trowels, built inadequate stick beds over mushy bogs or literally tied ourselves to trees on slippery pine needle slopes. Stop early; it's well worth it.

Asking Directions

"I wonder where we are in relation to what?" our friend Morgan mused, staring off into the purple late afternoon haze that clung to the peaks of the distant sierra. We'd been on the trail for almost a week and had at least that long to go before getting . . . where?

Easy relaxed hiking is fine, especially if you're interested in more than setting speed and distance records. On the other hand, it's often convenient and comforting to be a little more specific about your location than "somewhere south of nowhere". Fortunately, getting lost in Mexico rarely means losing complete contact with people. *Campesinos* live almost everywhere; someone inevitably comes around the bend, leading a pack mule or staggering under a load of firewood.

"*¡Buenos días, señor!* Is this *la vereda* a San Simón?"

The man straightens slowly under his burden. He looks carefully at the dusty trail, wore to a narrow ditch by countless years of passing feet and hooves. Yes, he nods, it is a trail.

"To San Simón?" you repeat, smiling encouragingly so that he knows you are a friend.

He stares into the distance, apparently lost in thought. Finally he speaks. "*¿Quién sabe, señor?*" The flicker of panic on your face causes him to add, "I am from La Magdalena."

A quick look at the map fails to produce evidence of La Magdalena. You're pondering this development when an *arriero* appears, roundly cursing a balky mule that staggers beneath a pair of corn-filled *costales* (gunny sacks). The woodcutter fades away with a final *¡Adiós!* as you approach the next prospect. The man removes his hat, draws a forearm across a sweaty brow and says, "Do you mean to say San Simón de Limón? El Limón? Yes, the trail goes there."

Reassured, you thank him profusely and move on. So they call it El Limón, huh?

Just for the hell of it you stop at the first *milpa* (cornfield) and ask an old woman husking corn if this is the trail to El Limón.

"Quizás," she mumbles, eyeing you nervously. "Perhaps?" Your newly found confidence evaporates with a sigh. Rather than bother with further questions, however, you take the chance and forge ahead. Half an hour later you overtake two men carrying huge baskets of squash on their backs, their foreheads bent low toward the ground, straining against cowhide *mecapales* (tumplines).

They turn curiously and offer greetings. You ask the question. They exchange a blast of rapid-fire Spanish, heavily laced with incomprehensible Indian words. You can't follow it at all, even though you thought your Spanish was pretty good.

"Bueno, amigo, look," one says pointing up the trail. "You want to go down the next arroyo to the big oak tree, but do not go left there, it leads to La Concepción. Keep to the right for two hours until you find a big *milpa* that belongs to Emilio's son, Geronimo, who is visiting my brother now in El Peñasco, but you don't want to go there either so pass the small tank of water and walk two leagues . . . Or is it three *leguas?"* His friend can't help him there, he's never been beyond Tres Cumbres, over towards La . . .

You stagger off in a daze, not sure now whether you're coming or going to El Limón.

This type of frustration can be avoided by following a few simple guidelines when asking for directions and distances.

• *Gringos* ask too many questions and expect to learn too much from the answers. For example, if you are looking for water and are told that there's a river nearby, don't confuse the basic issue (getting water) by asking how deep it is, its name, its origin, etc. Stick with what you *need to know*. After you get there and fill your canteens you can indulge in idle questions and speculations.

• A seemingly simple question (to you, a world-wise traveller) can boggle someone else's mind. "How many people live in the next *pueblo?"* I asked an intelligent-looking *campesino* one day. He looked at me in utter amazement. "We don't count people here," he answered, as though I'd asked how many hairs he had in his moustache.

• Phrase your questions in simple comparisons. Is the next village as large as this one, the one we're in? Smaller? *¿Más o menos igual?* (More or less the same?) How is the trail over that mountain? As *feo* as this one, as ugly? More difficult?

• Use short simple sentences and you'll probably get short simple responses. *Campesinos* are often close mouthed, especially when confronted with foreigners. Work into conversations slowly, allowing plenty of time for meditative silences. Don't skip the polite formalities that are so essential when dealing with polite people, especially in the back country (see *Speaking Spanish:* Chapter 4).

Many *gringos* who think they speak excellent colloquial Spanish are often confused by conversations with *campesinos* and Indians (who speak Spanish as a second language). Don't let your ego take over; repeat questions and answers until there's no doubt that you understand what's been said. We once hiked with a woman who was very proud of her Spanish. She made a point of being in front when it came time to ask someone for directions, barraging them with rapid-fire questions before they could even say hello. Pride wouldn't allow her to admit that a mumbled answer might be incorrectly translated or misunderstood. We had to make several tedious and tiring detours before she finally accepted that clear comprehension meant more than fast talking.

• If the person you are asking about directions cannot seem to understand you or gives confused answers, look for someone else. Some people are honestly ignorant, others are too proud to admit they don't know and a few are just plain dumb. You won't make things clearer by getting angry, indignant or loud.

• When approaching someone with a question, lead off with one you already know the answer to (or hope you know). If ten people have confirmed that it is two hours to the next water hole and the eleventh person says "ten hours", the rest of their information will also be suspect.

• The people most likely to know the trails and countryside are those who have reason to travel themselves: village officials, priests, traders, storekeepers, teachers and prosperous ranchers. Women and children know the immediate area and little else. "Uy! It's very far!" can mean that the next village is three hours away, a journey that a woman might make once a year if she's lucky.

When you find someone who seems to know the country well, write down their comments and directions, rather than trying to rely on memory. This is especially important when you are travelling in a group and everyone is doing their own sleuthing. After a day of questions and varied answers, you'll wish you had a computer to sort things out.

• There are often several trails between two points. One is for people, the other is for animals and a third for the rainy season. Trails for people tend to be more direct. They are not, however, always the quickest or easiest route for backpackers. Country people have amazing strength and stamina. Their trails will ignore obstacles and make very steep ascents and descents. I prefer animal trails; they are gentler and usually quite well marked by many hooves. "¡Siga la caca!" a friendly horseman once called back to me when I complained that the trail was faintly marked and difficult to follow. "Follow the shit!" was one of the best tips I've been given and saved me many lost miles. Whenever I was in doubt I dropped my pack to the ground and walked until I found a fresh 'biscuit' confirming that it was the main trail.

• Keeping your Spanish terms straight can be difficult. Camino means both road (and sometimes highway) and trail. Vereda means foot trail or path but is not commonly used; Indians and many campesinos prefer to say camino real (royal road) for well travelled trails. La carretera, the highway, may be a poor dirt road but still a major improvement over local trails.

• Maps of the Mexican back country are not only inadequate but often lead to more confusion than they're worth, especially if you depend on them very heavily. Campesinos are barely literate at best; when faced with a map they are completely baffled, though they absolutely love to look at them. I carry maps primarily as gifts and general outlines to refer to at the end of a day's travel. (See Appendices: Maps & Sources.)

A travelling music teacher (known in the area as El Maestro Sinfónico) who spends a good deal of time in a rugged stretch of mountains, demonstrated to us a simple and effective map-making technique that is easily understood by campesinos. It's just a straight line, connecting dots or circles that represent towns and landmarks. Major turns may be shown but otherwise the line is straight ahead, as the crow flies. In between the circles, write down the number of hours of estimated travel from one place to another. Anyone can follow this type of map, even a gringo.

• Villages, rivers and prominent landmarks may have more than one name. Map makers and local people rarely agree on which name is correct; when in doubt, use whatever name locals prefer when asking questions and directions.

• Many long place names are abbreviated or substituted by nicknames. San Simón de Limón, as already described, can become San Simón or even El Limón. In most cases the official name of a village includes its governing municipio (municipality, county). San Juan Tecolote and Santa María Tecolote are villages in the county of Tecolote. They will be commonly known as San Juan and Santa María, though if one is the cabecera (county seat) it may be called Tecolote.

Other names are shortened to leave only the last name. San Juan de Los Pinos and

San Juan de los Robles become Los Pinos and Los Robles. Simple, right? Don't worry; you soon get used to it.

• Time and distance have their own meanings in the back country. Watches are a great *campesino* status symbol but they are worn more for ornament than marking the hours. There are two important times of day: sunrise and sunset; the time between will be divided by the routine of work, eating and gossip with neighbors.

Asking for advice on travel times satisfies our *gringo* urge to keep time well regulated and in its place. Popular U.S. trail guides sometimes advise us how many *minutes* it is between landmarks. In Mexico, you're damned lucky to be within hours, or even days, of predicted schedules.

Travel times, as understood by people you'll meet along the trail, are given according to the load on one's back (or on your *bestia*), the mode of travel (foot, canoe, horseback), the terrain to be covered and the total distance. This latter can be most confusing: a predicted two days of travel, for example, might mean only ten hours of walking but ten hours that will exhaust you so quickly that they'll have to be taken in two shifts. The same ten hours over flat land might be called "one day".

The safest approach we've found is to automatically double the times given: if a man carrying a two hundred pound bale of onions says "six hours" to the village, we plan on twelve and rejoice if it's less. Mounted travellers rarely push their animals very hard and we've found that doubling their predicted times works out surprisingly close to foot times.

If you are told that it's "one day" to a place, that means a day that begins at dawn — or earlier — and ends when the sun is down. "One day" is a long way, however you look at it. A *legua* (league) is approximately three to five miles, the distance a person carrying a load can walk in one hour. By 'person' I mean a well muscled *campesino* or *campesina*, who steps out under a heavy burden as if it didn't exist.

Millas or miles are often used by Guatemalan Indians.

• When hiking near borders pay attention to where you are. I met a hiker who made the mistake of casually going cross country from Chiapas to Guatemala. The border is not heavily patrolled there and many Indians refuse to recognize that it even exists. The *gringo* found out, however, that to bureaucrats the border is a sacred line. When he walked into an Immigration office inside Guatemala to request a tourist visa and bragged about his journey, he was promptly deported. To make matters worse, he was told that his name was now on the 'blacklist', supposedly barring him from entering Guatemala in the future.

• Lost? Can't decide whether to go left, right or backwards? Tired, pissed-off and hungry? All of the above? It's time to brew a cup of tea, pull off your boots and take a relaxing nap. There's no point in rushing anywhere, since you don't know where to rush to.

If the trail you're on is heading in the 'wrong' direction, but is well marked and seems to definitely go somewhere, consider going ahead rather than backtracking to pick up another trail you missed earlier. Why not? There's plenty of new country to see in four directions; one trail is often just as good or better than another. Suddenly, in fact, you realize that you're not lost, you're just *exploring*. Feel better?

Trail Etiquette and Customs

Backpackers in Mexico find themselves moving through another world, a world that has much more in common with the eighteenth century than modern times. Mexicans are very tolerant of strangers and will go out of their way to help you, especially outside of the cities. It makes things much easier for everyone, however, if you take the time to study a few customs in advance. Most of these customs are quite simple and often logical but whether you agree with them or not, it is important to respect what others believe.

Note: A more general discussion of customs, etiquette, polite phrases and superstitions can be found in Chapter 4 and *The People's Guide To Mexico: Custom and Superstition* and *Viva Mexico!*

One of the most important aspects of hiking in Mexico is trail etiquette. Some is obvious and common to hiking anywhere in the world: it is impolite to shoulder someone off the trail, especially along a cliff; it is not proper to burn fenceposts for firewood; etc.

Always yield the trail to people walking faster than you or those with clumsy burdens and pack animals. Some trails you'll hike are quite tricky; one misstep and it's all over. We once met several men carrying sheets of corrugated tin roofing to a very isolated mountain village, their contribution to a communal work effort to build a school. They'd been walking for two days over really rough  terrain. I remarked that it seemed a difficult load to negotiate over the steep mountains. One answered, "On the last trip the wind struck us very hard and a friend was blown over a cliff, just like a kite."

Take the inside of the trail when meeting burro and mule trains. Stand quietly until the animals have passed and don't try to pet them or prod them on their way. These animals are naturally skittish and the look and smell of strangers can easily spook them.

You will sometimes meet women alone, though a woman usually travels with at least one child when out gathering firewood or tending livestock. She will probably be nervous or scared at the sight of you, especially if you have a beard. I give a ritual greeting to be polite but leave any conversations to Lorena. Old women are much more open with men: one old crone took a quick look at my backpack and called out, "What is that young man, your parachute?"

The key to establishing some sort of rapport is patience. Don't talk too much or too loudly, don't ask for anything unless you really need it and don't pester anyone with curious questions. The pushier you are, the more resistant and suspicious they'll become.

Our experience has been that some Indians you'll meet on the trail will seem very pleased to see you (especially those who trade with Mexicans and are more cosmopolitan) and others will react as if they've seen a *diablo* (devil).

I was once working my way up a very steep mountainside, my nose almost touching the toes of my hiking boots. I came around a bend and collided head-on with an Indian man, also bent double under a load of firewood. It was difficult to say who was the most surprised; by the time I'd recovered my composure the Indian was watching me closely, his lips twitching with a tentative smile. Two younger men behind him, however, were obviously alarmed by me. I didn't think much of it until I made to pass the older man. The trail was very narrow, skirting a dangerous precipice on one side and constricted by a rock wall on the other. It was a tight squeeze but could be done with caution. Since I don't like heights at all I moved to pass him on the inside. His smile vanished; with a quick step *he* moved to the inside, blocking me.

I stopped. The man's fear was obvious; one nudge and this bearded *güero* (paleface) would send him over the edge. Then a thought occurred to me: he can do the same and he's got two strong friends to help with the job. I instinctively flattened against the cliff.

"Where are you going?" I asked nervously.

"Down," he answered, watching me intently. He looked like such a nice man, hardly the sort to . . .

"Where are *you* going?" he asked.

"Up," I answered.

The man's face suddenly wrinkled in thought. With a quick unintelligible command to the men behind him he shrugged off his load of firewood and placed it on the path at his feet. With a tight smile he motioned that I do the same with my backpack. Once our loads were on the ground, we easily switched places on the trail. I carefully dragged my pack around their bundles of firewood as they sat several yards away, engrossed in sharing a cigarette. Once the switch had been made the old man smiled and called out, "*¡Vaya con cuidado, amigo!* Go with care, friend! And don't fall!"

Always warn people of your approach by whistling, singing or calling out "Good day!" well before approaching a house or camp, especially if it is isolated. Children can be easily frightened by *gringos* and it makes everyone nervous if they run shrieking into the forest. If men are working nearby they will probably spot you and come immediately to check you out. Walk up slowly, with a smile and a further greeting. If dogs appear, and they usually do, don't come too close to the house until they've been called off or tied up. Dogs are expected to guard the family and they take their work seriously. I like to carry a staff, since it makes a good club as well as a walking aid. Avoid using it, however, unless a dog makes a serious try for your leg.

People may respond from inside the house, "*¿Quién?*" (Who?) Answer, "*¡Soy yo!*" (Me!) or "*¡Un amigo!*" If no one answers your warning call, don't snoop around.

Never enter a house until invited to. The standard invitation is, *"Pasala, por favor,"* and the response, *"Muchas gracias, muy amable."* (Many thanks, you're very nice.) Take off your hat; it may not be expected but they'll take it as a sign of respect.

If you've stopped for a reason (to buy food, ask for directions, water or a place to camp) or been hailed over in passing, you'll be expected to pass a certain amount of time in conversation before getting down to business. The average *campesino* family also expects to offer you food or refreshment, if only a glass of water or fresh goat's milk. Even though something may be offered with apparent casualness, it should not be refused without good reason. "I don't like goat's milk," for example, isn't a good reason. How can you not enjoy something so *rico* (rich), so refreshing and so nourishing? Drink it and read Chapter 8 again.

I once accepted an offer of a 'small meal' shortly after entering a village. When I'd finished my cooked potatoes, tortillas, fried jerky, two glasses of milk, one of hot chocolate and a bowl of candied sweet potatoes, my hosts graciously passed me on to my neighbors, who had already set their table.

"But I just ate!" I protested. Everyone smiled in agreement.

My first host said, "It was such a poor meal we gave you. You must fill up with our *compadres*!"

When I finally staggered to a nearby shade tree, the day was too far gone for more hiking. I dug out a sack of hard candies and passed them around to a circle of curious men and children. They asked the usual questions about my *tierra* (country), discussed the problems of wet-backing to *el otro lado* (the other side — of the border) and invited me to play a fast game of *fútbol* (soccer). I begged off, explaining that I was tired from a day's hiking. One of the men promptly grabbed my backpack and insisted I rest inside his house. The corn stalk mattress wasn't exactly a water bed but it served quite adequately for a short nap. By the time I'd woken up, dinner was ready and my evening's activities carefully planned. Bedtime came at some outrageously late hour; this time I slept in a real bed, displacing four children onto the floor.

The family woke hours before dawn and after a hearty breakfast of heavily sugared coffee, hot *atole* (corn flour gruel) and a fried egg, I was allowed to continue on my way.

Such scenes of hospitality are not unusual in Mexico; in fact, they're almost routine. On a long hike through a remote sierra we found that people's hospitality threatened to delay our hiking to the point where we began to avoid villages and *ranchos*.

Since most *pueblos* straddle the trail, slipping through without being seen is impossible, but we did learn a few tricks to avoid attracting crowds. First, time your arrival for mid-morning rather than afternoon. Most people will be working and the afternoon meal is far enough away that any invitations can be gracefully declined. "Thank you very much, but we want to walk to . . . " Instead of reaching the next village, however, we usually find a place to camp along the way. "We're very tired; we will be there tomorrow," is a good explanation for why you've stopped for the night. You are also telling people, if only in a small way, that you will see them the next day and they shouldn't be concerned about you.

If you pass through a village in late afternoon, however, you'll hear, "It's too late! Stop and rest with us! What's your hurry? You don't want to be out after dark, do you?"

Villagers can be quite insistent. If they think you're weakening, they may give dark hints of bandits ahead or exceptionally rough trails. Take this with a liberal dose of salt. It is the custom in the back country to avoid camping out whenever possible. Villages and *ranchos* are seen as rest stations for weary travellers and people are often eager to put a gringo up for the night.

Many of the tall tales, myths and scary stories told of life and travel in Mexico's back country have their origins in long-past revolutions and regional armed conflicts. Rural people are very superstitious and believe whole-heartedly in *fantasmas* (ghosts). Hints of danger in the night can often be traced to a sincere belief that Pancho Villa and his men are still on the loose in spirit form. Don't laugh at such tales but at the same time, don't allow yourself to be frightened by local legends.

Privacy

Although backpackers will have many opportunities to get away from it all, complete privacy is often impossible. Your attempts to find peace and quiet may be misinterpreted by others. "Why are those *gringos* hiding from us? What can they be up to?" All this just because you camped a quarter of a mile from a village rather than spending the night inside someone's house or yard.

When camped near a trail you'll often notice that other travellers approach cautiously. Don't ignore them: stand up, give a smile and call out a greeting. If you don't, even though you're dead-tired and not in the mood for more idle chatter in Spanish, they'll think you're acting suspiciously. When you need privacy, move well away from the trail. If someone spots your fire and comes to check you out, wave at them or call a greeting. It is important to ease any fear *they might have* that you're up to no good.

Most *campesinos* believe strongly that sleeping outside can be unhealthy. We once asked permission to camp in front of a family's house. They wouldn't hear of it. We'd have to sleep inside because of *mal aire* (bad airs, wind). We could contract something awful, from a stiff neck to *pulmonía*. When I pointed out to the father that the air temperature was in the upper 60's he just shook his head, "It hits much harder," he said, making a chopping motion against his neck.

Space was cleared for us on the floor. Our hammocks, which would have swung comfortably from the porch, were bundled into pillows. I've always had difficulty sleeping in other people's houses, mainly because of unfamiliar night sounds and movements. Laying there on the hard dirt, with the snores of almost a dozen people around me and the wind sighing down a deep canyon, I had to play every trick in order to fall asleep. Lorena's snores finally provided a soothing rhythm and I drifted off slowly.

When my eyes opened, I knew at once that it was the middle of the night. What was that sound? Oh, no! There was something on the floor . . . coming toward me . . . scrabbling with *claws* to reach me. I choked back a cry of alarm. What could it be? Monster scorpion? Giant rat? My heart swelled; above the slithering scrabble came another sound, a ragged wheezing gasp. This was *IT*: King Rat creeping out of some fetid cave in search of *gringo* meat. It was almost on me now. The blood hammered in my ears. I drew in breath for a scream of . . .

"Whaazaat?" Lorena jerked up suddenly, her short cry reverberating loudly in the small room. There were several answering groans and mutters from the communal bed and the reassuring sound of a match being scraped to life. The awful scrabbling turned, drawn to a new prey.

I saw it then, a low dark shape hugging the floor like a monstrous hairy beetle.

"*Muñeca*," a child's voice called sweetly from the bed. The loathsome creeper increased its pace with a sudden flurry of legs thrashing for a grip.

"Come on, Doll," the child urged, "Come to the bed."

"What is it?" I cried. "*¿Qué es?*" In all the strange stories I'd been told by *campesinos* of night roaming creatures, none had mentioned *this*.

"It is our dog." Our host's voice was heavy with sleep but I couldn't miss the humor in his tone. "Poor Doll had an accident with a cart. She is *bien chueca*, well crippled, and likes to come out only at night. Do not worry, she only wishes to sleep with you."

Last-minute preparations for a backpacking trip to Mexico involve complex strategy sessions and command level decisions. To make organization as efficient as humanly possible, Lorena and I categorize each item of gear we are considering taking under three headings: Essential/Definite, Possible/Probable and Hopeful/Doubtful. A flashlight falls into the first category, an extra pair of socks into the second and a four-inch-thick hardbound copy of the I Ching into the third.

"Are you serious? Are you really taking the I Ching?"

Lorena looked up from her position on the living room floor, the heavy volume held reverently in front of her. I continued to pour over my lists, certain she would come to her senses. I glanced back. Damn! She was actually moving the book from Hopeful/Doubtful up to Possible/Probable. This was madness! I bit my tongue, reminding myself for the hundredth time that we each have our requirements, our own Basics.

I shuffled my lists, satisfied that nothing had been overlooked; all my equipment had withstood the acid tests of merciless evaluation. My lists were models of clarity, conciseness and detailed planning, neatly typed out and as fresh as a new leaf.

"When are you going to get *your* stuff together?"

I ignored her. One entry on the Essential/Definite column caught my attention. With a ruthless lash of my pen I reduced *Safety Pins: 3* to *Safety Pins: 2*.

"In about five minutes," I said, checking my watch. In a flash of inspiration I slipped off the watch and removed the thin plastic wrist band. The watch fit quite nicely in my front pants pocket. Always vigilant!

I got up from the desk and made my way across the room, stepping cautiously through Lorena's scattered piles of clothing, maps, cooking gear, yarn, books, herbal medicine bottles and bags, cloth hand-puppets, star gazing charts, colored chalks and pencils and other vital hiking paraphernalia. My own equipment sat against the living room wall, neatly arranged in open cardboard boxes, awaiting final confirmation before packing. My backpack hung empty from a nail above the boxes, a constant reminder to *keep it light and keep it small!*

I was reaching for the Hopeful/Doubtful box when the front door opened. It was Denny, my uncle, and his fifteen-year-old son, Rick. Both wore new backpacks and excited grins.

"Aren't you guys ready yet?" Rick asked, slipping his pack to the floor. He gave Lorena a puzzled look. "What's all this stuff?" He pointed to her piles of gear. "Are you going to the Swap Meet again?"

Lorena managed a weak grin.

"Let's take a look in your pack, Rick," I interrupted. It would take a little time, but she'd get it pared down to the true Basics.

Rick eagerly unzipped his pack. I couldn't help smiling; neither he nor Denny had been to Mexico before. The thought of backpacking in a foreign country was obviously especially exciting for them. I smiled again as Rick pointed out each item, nodding patiently as he emptied the side pockets, proudly displaying his toothbrush, penlight, pocketknife and water purifying tablets. But something was puzzling me . . . there was something not quite right about . . .

"Is that it?" I asked. "Is that *all* you've got?"

Rick stared intently at the tiny pile for several seconds. "Yeah," he answered uncertainly. "I did just like you said and brought the . . . the Basics. A few clothes, my sleeping bag, a dictionary and the little stuff."

He looked up. "You kept saying, 'Keep it light, keep it small,' didn't 'ya?"

"Sure, Rick, sure. I just hope you didn't forget something *essential*." I left him brooding over this and returned to my lists. Denny perched on a stool near the front door, shaking his head silently from side to side as I eliminated a spare Frisbee and a How-To-Tie 5,000 Knots book from my boxes. I could hear Lorena behind me, muttering as she labelled small plastic bags of powdered roots and medicinal teas. "Don't worry!" I shouted, reaching reluctantly into the Essential/Definite box for my trusty bedroom slippers. "It'll all come together like clockwork. Remember: a journey of a single step begins with a thousand preparations!"

Two days later we met again for a final pre-departure planning session. The living room was still strewn with Lorena's things, but she assured me it would be straightened out the following morning. Denny and Rick's faces look Hopeful/Doubtful.

"Rick," Lorena said. "I've been thinking a lot about this garlic press."

Rick looked at the curved metal object in her hand as if it were a smoking .38 Police Special.

"Oh, yeah?" he stalled.

"I was thinking that this is going to be a long trip and all of us are going to eat a lot of garlic that is put through this one press and . . ." Her voice was controlled and reasonable, a tone that never fails to arouse a feeling of dread when I find it directed at me, like a plump mouse being charmed out of its hole by a kindly cat.

"No way!" Rick blurted, backing toward the kitchen doorway. *"No way!"*

"You'll regret that when it comes time to make spaghetti!" Lorena snapped, tossing the garlic press into the Hopeful/Doubtful pile. Rick retreated into the kitchen, chanting "No way!" until safely out of sight.

To ease the tension in the room I began regaling Denny with vivid descriptions of remote beaches we'd hike to, of the fantastic skin diving that waited for us, the reefs, the fish, the . . .

"I'VE GOT IT!"

A sudden and blinding inspiration ended my monologue. I looked around the room, gripped with the passion of a Good Idea. Rick peeked suspiciously from the kitchen as I leaped to my feet and began pacing between Lorena's slowly diminishing junk piles. Denny's face was characteristically bland but hinted curiosity. It was all so simple . . . so ridiculously *simple!*

"Look, you guys," I said, trying to control my excitement. "There's just one thing, *one thing,* standing between us and some of the most fantastic diving you've ever seen!" I had them well hooked; Denny actually rubbed his hands together in anticipation. I stood silent, waiting to hear . . .

"What?" Rick asked, edging into the room. I turned with dramatic slowness, raising my right arm and pointing wordlessly into a corner.

"Hang that on the back of a dugout canoe and we can go anywhere!" My shout faded away. All eyes were on the corner of the room, mesmerized by the pure logic and brilliance of my idea. I walked slowly to the outboard motor, propped against the wall. I rested my hand lovingly on the smooth cowling. A pre-War three-and-a-half horsepower outboard; a model of precision engineering and American dependability.

"This baby weighs less than forty pounds," I said, "and can be field stripped into three highly portable parts in less than five minutes." I faced them head on, hoping my voice conveyed the admiration I felt for this motor, purchased at the local flea market for a mere fifteen dollars and some odd change.

Denny fidgeted on the stool, his eyes darting between the motor and Lorena's backpack.

"Are you actually *serious?*" he asked.

"Absolutely!" I said, giving the motor a reassuring pat. "Look, it's as simple as . . ." I quickly lowered the motor onto the floor. "Rick, pass me that crescent wrench." I bent over the cowling and swiftly dismantled the outboard. "Okay, Rick, this is your part. Denny and I will take the rest." I held out the upper unit, the engine block itself.

"You want me to put this thing *in my pack?*" Rick protested, looking wonderingly toward his father. Denny's head was bowed, his fingers massaging his temples.

"Of course," I said. "You've got lots of extra room. Think of this as just part of the Basics? Right? The Basics? Rick?"

He was backing away as if the motor was a coiled rattlesnake. His face was red and flushed. "I think you're . . . I think you're *nuts!*" He escaped into the kitchen once again, chanting his irritating litany of "No way, man! *No way!*"

I turned beseechingly to Lorena. Surely, if anyone could grasp my idea, it would be . . .

"No way!" Lorena snorted, glaring defiantly as she dredged the I Ching from under my desk and dropped it squarely back into her Essential/Definite pile.

Unknown Mexico:

Canyons and Rock Formations

Canyons are especially fascinating for their dramatic variations in topography, flora, fauna and climate. A canyon that cuts through a barren Mexican desert may be a veritable oasis at its deepest and most sheltered points, with pools of cool water, ancient shade trees and semi-tropical vegetation. The awesome Barranca del Cobre (Copper Canyon) reaches from the often snow covered mountains of western Chihuahua to the steamy Pacific lowlands. A few days of hard (and preferably downhill) hiking can be an amazing experience.

Although some of the canyons and rock formations listed here were discovered hundreds of years ago, few are heavily visited and the majority remain virtually unexplored. As a general suggestion for hiking and camping, canyons in particular are hard to beat. A special attraction: canyons are usually formed by rivers. Even in the dry season you'll have a good chance of finding water, if only in isolated *tinajas* (tanks, pools) eroded into the rock.

The canyons listed here are among Mexico's largest and most spectacular, but they represent a small fraction of the total number to be found by the curious traveller. See *Unknown Mexico: Rivers, Lakes & Dams* and *National Parks* for more ideas on where to discover your own unknown canyon.

Aguascalientes: *Sierra de Laurel:* A rugged and beautiful range of mountains. Rock formations located south of Calvillo.

Chiapas: *Cañón del Sumidero:* The canyon is one of Mexico's most spectacular sights, more than 30 km long and 1,000 meters deep. To the horror of nature lovers, Mexican and foreign, the Chicoasén Dam will soon flood much of the lower canyon floor. El Sumidero is considered ecologically unique. The canyon contains the Río Grijalva and some dangerous rapids.

Chihuahua: *Barranca del Cobre:* The Copper Canyon is several times larger than the Grand Canyon in the U.S. Approximate length: 600 km; depths up to 2,166 meters (over 7,000 feet!) and an average width of 6 to 8 km. The *Barranca* is actually made up of several smaller canyons, many virtually unexplored. Access to the area is very limited, though unmapped dirt roads can be found. Approached from the city of Chihuahua, both by highway, dirt road and railroad. The views from the train are said to be good but to fully appreciate the canyon's size it must be explored by foot, animalback or jeep. *Basihuare:* Colorful belts of rock, some miles long. Access is from Creel, 40 km of dirt road. *Valle de los Monjes:* Rock formations. The words *monja* (nun), *monje* (monk) and *fraile* (friar) are commonly used throughout Mexico to describe unusual rocks and formations. It helps to have an active imagination.

Durango: *Espinazo del Diablo:* The Devil's Spine is another 'clue term' for very rugged country, but this particular Espinazo probably deserves first prize. Located south and west of Durango City and crossed by the Durango-Mazatlán highway (Méx 40). Spectacular views for the passenger and hundreds of sharp curves for the driver. I've hiked this area and heartily recommend that you go with care, keep your canteens full and your bootlaces tight. During the rainy season most trails are completely impassable. *Mexiquillo:* Unusual rock formations at km 96 on highway 40 from Durango to Mazatlán.

Guanajuato: *Cañada Grande:* On the highway from León, 52 km toward San Felipe. *Malpaís:* The word *malpaís* is used for badlands and other interesting but

Mountain Ranges

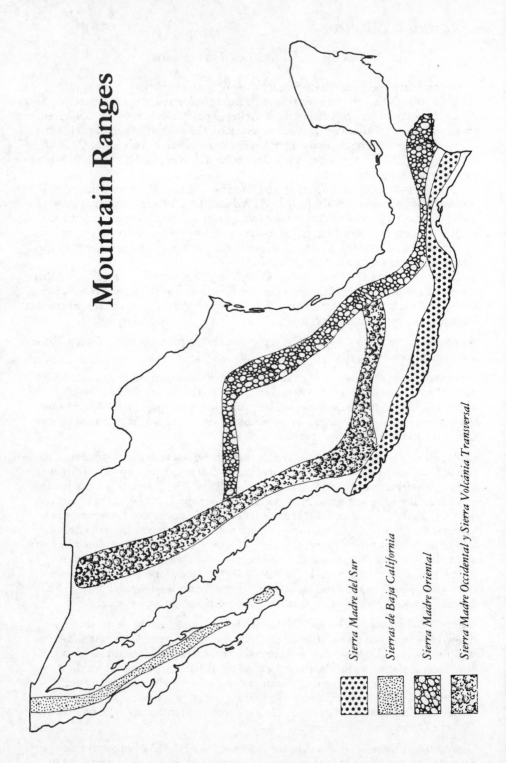

Sierra Madre del Sur

Sierras de Baja California

Sierra Madre Oriental

Sierra Madre Occidental y Sierra Volcánia Transversal

often rugged country. Located near Valle de Santiago; many craters, some filled with water.

Hidalgo: *Barranca de la Luna:* Also known as *Chicomoztoc;* near Metztitlán. *Valle del Mezquital:* Beyond Ixmiquilpan and Orizabita. *Santa María Regla:* These spectacular basalt formations were first described by Alexander von Humbolt. Located near Huasca. *Piedras Encimadas:* Between Presa El Tejocotal and Zacatlán-Apizaco. *Encimadas* loosely translates as "stacked" and is a clue to interesting rock formations. *Valle de las Monjas:* Located 4 km from El Chico National Park.

México: *Chapa de Mota: Mota* is slang for marijuana, which has nothing at all to do with this area of canyons, streams, rock formations and small lakes. Located between Tapaxco and the town of Chapa de Mota.

Michoacán: *Cañon de Tepuxtepec:* Located near San Juan del Río, Tepuxtepec and Epitacio Huerta. *Barranca Honda:* Near Nueva Italia on highway 37 from Uruapan to the Pacific coast.

Morelos: *San Antón:* Basalt formations near Cuernavaca.

Nayarit: *Jumatán:* Unusual and very tall basalt formations.

Nuevo León: *Cañón de la Huasteca:* Located near Monterrey; no other information.

Oaxaca: *Cascada de Sal* or *Hierve El Agua:* A 'frozen' waterfall of accumulated mineral deposits. Located northeast of Mitla, near San Lorenzo Albarradas.

Oaxaca-Puebla: *Cañón de Tomellín:* Geography books describe this canyon as "an enormous fracture in the earth's crust." It is considered one of the oldest inhabited areas on the North American continent. The canyon runs between Oaxaca City and Tehuacán, Puebla; access is by train and paved highway.

Puebla: *Las Derrumbadas:* An area of high mountains (to almost 11,000 feet), canyons, rock formations and rattlesnakes located near Perote and Zacatepec. Virtually unexplored.

San Luis Potosí: *Macizo de Cerro Grande:* An area of many peaks and streams located between Ciudad Valle and Tamazunchale. *El Lugar del Rayo:* Many rivers, canyons and mountain ranges; located near Tamasopo. *Valle de los Fantasmas:* Rock formations and fossils, 40 km east of San Luis Potosí, toward Río Verde.

Sonora: *El Pinacate:* A vast volcanic zone dotted with more than 600 craters.

Tamaulipas-Hidalgo: *La Gran Barranca:* A huge canyon running between Tampico and Pachuca, Hidalgo. Access is by highway 105.

Veracruz: *Tenexamaxa:* Basalt formations.

Zacatecas: *Los Organos: Organos* is a common name for rock formations that suggest organ pipes. A good area for camping and short hikes. Located near highway 45 and the Durango border; access is by dirt road.

Mountains and Volcanoes

Mountain tops attract adventurers like giant irresistible magnets. Unless you're a skilled *alpinista,* however, take great care when scaling anything steeper and tougher than an average mountain foot trail. The lure of the unknown can lead you to disaster.

Many of the peaks listed here are high enough to require special equipment, clothing and training to climb safely. Several of the tallest peaks have perennial ice and snow (polar climate zone) on top and are not for the unguided novice.

Qualified guides and mountain rescue service are available on most peaks near Mexico City; elsewhere you're definitely on your own, though people will certainly do what they can to help in case of an emergency. It is vitally important, however, to realize that you are basically *on your own* while mountain climbing in Mexico.

Many of the peaks listed are difficult to reach by road. The standard mountain climbing procedure is to visit a village or *rancho* near the mountain, hire guides and pack animals and approach on foot. Many mountains are planted in corn and grain to a surprisingly high elevation. A guide will be invaluable when you confront the confusing network of trails that farmers have created around their fields.

The elevations given are in meters and feet, *sobre el nivel del mar* (above sea level; abbreviated in Spanish as s.n.m.). When different sources disagree on a mountain's elevation — a very common occurence — I have given the benefit of the doubt to the mountain and used the higher figure.

	Meters	Feet		Meters	Feet
Pico de Orizaba, Pue.	5747	18850	Sabanilla, Méx.	3283	10768
Popocatépetl, Méx-Pue.	5452	17882	Paricutín, Mich.	3170	10398
Iztaccíhuatl, Méx-Pue.	5286	17338	Huehuento, Dur.	3150	10332
Nevado de Toluca, Méx.	4550	14924	Cerro Calentura, Qro.	3100	10168
Malinche, Tlax.	4461	14632	Cerro Laurel, Ags.	3090	10135
Nevado de Colima, Jal.	4330	14202	La Encantada, B.C.N.	3069	10066
Cofre de Perote, Ver.	4282	14044	Cerro de la Ardilla, Ags.	3003	9850
Tacaná, Chis.	4057	13306	Volcán de Tequila, Jal.	3000	9840
Mohinora, Chih.	3992	13093	Cerro Sombrero, D.F.	3000	9840
Cerro del Ajusco, D.F.	3950	12956	Cerro del Pinal, Ags.	2890	9479
Volcán de Fuego, Jal.	3960	12989	Volcán de Ameca, Jal.	2800	9184
Tancítaro, Mich.	3845	12612	Cerro Temeroso, Zac.	2800	9184
San Miguel, D.F.	3775	12382	Cerro de Cuervo, Zac.	2800	9184
Patambán, Mich.	3750	12300	Tlacotepec, Gro.	2800	9184
Sehuiloya, D.F.	3740	12267	Volcán Colli, Jal.	2800	9184
Cerro Teotepec, Gro.	3705	12152	Yubay, B.C.N.	2787	9141
Las Palmas, D.F.	3700	12136	La Campaña, Ags.	2768	9079
Tláloc, D.F.	3687	12093	Cerro del Muñeco, Jal.	2743	8997
Peña Nevada, N.L.	3664	12017	Chiquihuite, D.F.	2717	8912
Pelado, D.F.	3620	11874	Cerro Pajaritos, Nay.	2700	8856
Picacho, D.F.	3600	11808	Los Frailes, Sin.	2680	8790
San Andrés, Mich.	3589	11772	Cerro de Cubilete, Gto.	2560	8397
Monte Alto, D.F.	3577	11733	Cerro Grande, Col.	2530	8298
Cerro Borrado, Tamps.	3533	11588	Cerro Blanco, Zac.	2400	7872
Tepetlixpa, Gro.	3474	11395	San Juan, Nay.	2300	7544
El Rosario, Tlax.	3418	11211	Cerro Jumiltepec, Mor.	2300	7544
Yucuyacua, Oax.	3376	11073	Volcán de Ceboruco, Nay.	2164	7098
Los Llanitos, Gto.	3360	11021	Volcán de Sangangüey,	2150	7052
Cerro del Gallo, Qro.	3351	10997	Nay.		
Zirate, Mich.	3340	10955	Volcán de las Vírgenes,	2054	6737
Quinceo, Mich.	3324	10903	B.C.S.		
Las Derrumbadas, Pue.	3300	10824	Picacho, B.C.S.	2000	6560
			Cerro Calamajué, B.C.N.	1657	5435

4. Stranger In A Strange Land

The following advice for travellers is freely adapted from a letter written by Isaac Newton over three hundred years ago. Its value is timeless, especially for those who will be visiting areas of Mexico where the passage of time is not very noticeable.

When you come to any new company observe their humor and mood.

Adapt your own to suit them and this will make their conversation and manner more free and open.

Let your conversation be more in questions and doubtings rather than quick assertions or arguments. It is the design of travellers to learn, not to teach. Besides, it will persuade your new acquaintances that you think better of them and make them more ready to communicate what they know to you. Nothing brings disrespect and quarrels quicker than rudeness.

You will find little or no advantage in seeming wiser, or much more ignorant, than your company.

Seldom criticize anything or you might find yourself unexpectedly forced to make an embarrassing apology. It is safer to praise something more than it deserves, for praise rarely meets with disagreement.

You will find favor with others by approving and commending what they themselves like, but beware of doing it by comparison and at another's expense.

If you are insulted, it is better in a foreign country, to pass it by in silence, and with a jest. Even though you may feel dishonored, what value is there in revenge, especially after you have returned home? If you do meet with trouble, control your temper and language to avoid provoking people even more.

In a word, keep reason above passion; that and watchfulness will be your best defense.

Excuses for violence may pass among friends, but among strangers they are insignificant and only demonstrate the traveller's own weakness.

Time travel exists in Mexico. The thin veneer of the twentieth century is easily left behind by anyone willing to make a short detour off the tourist circuit. When hiking in Mexico we turn back the clock a hundred years for each day's travel; we take the same backward leap after an hour of paddling down a jungle river or a brief stint of determined, back road driving. Nothing more effectively insulates people and preserves their traditions and culture than physical obstacles.

In spite of an increasingly modern facade, much of Mexico remains well off the beaten track, rarely visited and virtually unexplored. The opportunities this offers to curious campers are almost beyond calculation.

While researching this book I visited the offices of a Mexican government agency involved in mapping the country by air. When I was shown an aerial survey I commented that a great deal of the country remained blank. Whole mountain ranges and expanses of jungle as large as entire states had yet to be filled in with anything more detailed than major cities, highways and obvious landmarks.

"What can you expect?" the project director said. "We've only had a relatively modern highway system since the '50's and '60's. Many areas are inaccessible, even by small plane. It can take a survey team weeks to map a single *municipio* (county)."

His job was further complicated, he said, by extremes in topography, climate and vegetation, not to mention the differences in language, culture and traditions of the people living in the back country. An estimated eight million native Indians live in Mexico, divided into more than eighty distinct groups, many with entirely different languages.

These differences might complicate a surveyor's job but they make travelling in Mexico, and camping in particular, both varied and highly interesting. One day you're camped with people who scratch a meager living from a high mountain desert, the next day you're chatting with tropical lowlanders, to whom the word *desierto* is as meaningless as a snowstorm.

In spite of many differences, however, there are certain attitudes and experiences common to most rural Mexicans. Whether your contacts with them will be limited to shopping for food in small *ranchos* or asking for directions deep inside *tierra desconocida* (unknown country), you'll want to observe basic polite manners and customs. By understanding and respecting these people's beliefs, your trip will be more relaxed and enjoyable and far more rewarding.

Speaking Spanish

Communicating with others is a fundamental need, whether by improvised sign language or by the spoken word. The degree to which you can express yourself and understand others often affects the success of your trip. This is especially true if you want to get away from it all and to meet people who rarely, if ever, have contact with *gringos*. Not only will you need to ask such obvious questions as, "Where can I find drinking water?", but you'll be expected to provide a few answers yourself: "Who are you? Why do you come here?" Tourists are taken for granted only on the 'tourist circuits': Mexico City, popular beach resorts, well-trammeled archaeological sites, etc. In the back country you are basically just a stranger. The burden of communication is therefore on *you*, not the local people.

Learning Spanish is a big step in communication, but simple words and phrases only a beginning. Your attitude will tell others a great deal about you, especially when meeting people who are naturally close mouthed. A life of goat herding or tilling lonely cornfields doesn't make for great conversationalists.

"*¿A dónde van?*" a fisherman calls, his castnet draped over one shoulder as he crouches in the bow of a low dugout canoe.

"*Río arriba,*" you answer, raising your paddle to point upstream. He stares into deep space, unblinking. Your canoe drifts in the gentle current; long seconds drag by as he digests this scrap of information. You cough nervously, anxious to be on your way. His eyes widen slightly; nervous are you? In a hurry? Why? What's upstream that's more interesting than this wide pool, filled with fish?

You pull your sweaty *sombrero* off your head and wipe your brow. The silence continues. At a loss for anything more to say you mutter, "*Adiós,*" and bend over the paddle with a sigh of relief. "Strange character!" you think, feeling his eyes boring into your back.

The man continues to stare, then shrugs and prepares to throw his *ta'raya* at a promising ripple. "Not very polite, that one!" he thinks. "I was just about to mention the fine mullet up there near my mother's *rancho*. I wonder what that fellow is really up to?"

Country people tend to be very sparing of words. Long silences are normal; after all, what's the point in blurting it all out at once?

We camped in a small coconut grove, five miles from the nearest village. Nonetheless, every day we had visitors, silent, staring and potentially unnerving. The routine was quickly established.

"Carl," Lorena called, "here come your buddies."

I dragged myself from the hammock. Through the palms I could see men approaching on horseback. They reined in a polite distance away and I called, "*Buenas tardes.*"

"*Buenas,*" the oldest of the group answered. He was the talkative one. They slid from their saddles, their mounts wandering off in search of grass.

We sat in a rough circle on the ground and began fiddling with twigs, silently . . .

"*¡Uiii!*" one said, wiping his damp throat with a large bandana.

I had to agree, it was awfully hot. Wish it would rain. Be good for the bean fields.

"*¿Eh?*" another asked, looking at the coconuts overhead.

I smiled. Sure, I'd love a fresh coconut. After all, it isn't often that . . .

"*Ten.*" He handed me a heavy green nut. I opened it carefully with his razor sharp machete, offered without a word.

"*¿Eh?*" the old man asked, joining the conversation for the first time since his initial lengthy greeting.

I nodded. Yes, coconut milk is quite delicious, reminds me of a drink they make in San Francisco called a . . .

"*¿Hrrmmp?*"

I raised my hand, palm toward my chest. No thanks, I don't smoke. It's really bad for your . . . oh, well, forget it . . . We settled into a long and very deep silence.

"What's up? Still there?" Lorena called.

"Yup!" I answered. The men raised their eyebrows. Talkative people these *gringos*. Ten minutes dragged by.

"*¡Bueno!*" The old man got to his feet. The others followed, whistling up their horses and winging into the saddle. All tipped their hats carefully toward the *señora* in the hammock.

"*Hasta,*" one muttered.

"*Hasta,*" I replied, biting off the word *mañana* lest they think me a babbler.

Lorena gave me a curious look as I walked back to my hammock. "Have a nice visit?" she asked.

"Wonderful. They were more talkative than ever. I'd say the ice is definitely broken. Yup!"

The old cliche, "A picture is worth a thousand words" applies well when fumbling with an unfamiliar language. Smiles, shrugs, frowns, handshakes and general arm waving are almost telepathic when used with genuine feeling. This works both ways. A very slight frown or a quickly suppressed smile are meant as signals: no, you should not stare at my child and give her the Evil Eye; yes, do help me lift this sack onto the burro. These are very simple but very important communications. The greater the superficial differences between people, the more important small avenues of communication become. Anyone can overlook a few blunders when they know the other person is doing their best.

The simplest acts can have exaggerated importance. The casual offer of a cigarette, for example, should not be brushed aside; it's also an offer of friendship. As a confirmed non-smoker I have to refuse, but I always do it with profuse thank-you's and a friendly smile. Even a small piece of candy can work wonders with a group of silent *campesinos*. I carry a supply at all times and pass them out as liberally as a politician offering campaign promises. Small overtures such as these will usually open the flood gates of conversation and hospitality.

Polite Phrases and Manners

Polite expressions are an important part of any language and culture. In Mexico, they are absolutely *vital*, especially in the back country. The farther you travel from the cities, the more important polite language becomes and the more attentive you should be to using it. Traditional *campesinos* and Indians often have little to say other than polite phrases until the ice is broken. Your initial contact with people gives them a chance to measure your mood, character and attitudes. "How 'ya doin' grandpa?" is no way, for example, to address an elderly *campesino,* though he'll probably give you the benefit of the doubt for being an ignorant foreigner. Minor social blunders can be overlooked, but if they persist they become as irritating as a burr in a saddle blanket.

One of the biggest mistakes *gringos* make in Spanish is choking up out of a fear of looking stupid. Swallow your pride and open your mouth. Polite phrases are easy to learn, but you've got to leap the hurdle of embarrassment and start talking. The best rule is: when in doubt, say something polite, even if it's just *"Lo siento. No entiendo."* (I'm sorry. I don't understand.)

Some people try to mask nervousness with laughter. Avoid the habit; mindless laughter not only gives the impression that you've got a screw loose, but it can also be very offensive. I once travelled with a guy who laughed at everything he didn't quite understand, under the mistaken impression that it made him look agreeable. His giggles fell on unsympathetic ears when he laughed at a *campesino's* rambling story of how his son had died of a spell cast by a *bruja* (witch). I explained to the horrified father that my companion thought it was just a ghost story but he never really trusted my companion again.

Although handshakes may be given silently they are as important in Mexico as any polite phrase or greeting. A *light* handshake is given upon meeting people and when parting company, even after the briefest of encounters.

A man-to-man knuckle buster handshake is considered both aggressive and insulting.

Indians often kiss the backs of each other's hands, but this is rarely done with strangers.

Hand salutes, head nodding, slight bowing and tipping hats are seen between *campesinos* and appreciated from foreigners as well, especially if circumstances don't allow a handshake.

Don't laugh if children shake your hand and greet you with the formality of an adult; they learn manners very early and by the age of ten or twelve are considered mini-grownups.

The following words and phrases should carry you through almost any situation. In many cases they'll be worth far more than money in terms of the favors and friendship you'll receive by using them liberally. Practice them frequently and you'll soon appreciate their power.

Buenos días: Good day. Used only before noon.
Buenas tardes: Good afternoon. Between noon and sundown.
Buenas noches: Good evening, good night. When greeting and parting.
Buenas: A contraction of the above, handy when you are unsure of the hour. *Muy* is often added for emphasis: *¡Muy buenas tardes!* Very good afternoon!
Adiós: Means both "goodbye" and "hello" when greeting someone in passing. Repeating *adiós* in quick succession means you're in a hurry and can't stop to chat. Never pass anyone on the trail without saying *adiós* or *buenas.*
Disculpame: Excuse me.
Perdón: Pardon, pardon me.
Perdóname: Pardon me.

Use any of these to stop someone after you've greeted them. Excusing yourself before asking a question is considered polite. "*¡Buenos diás, señor! Perdóname, por favor, pero dónde está el volcán?*" "Good day, sir! Pardon me, please, but where is the volcano?"
Gracias: Thank you. *Muchas gracias* (Many thanks) is even better and *Muchisimas gracias, se lo agradezco mucho* (Many, many thanks, I appreciate it very much), even better yet.
¡Está bien!: It's fine, good, okay! Use this one liberally: when you want to agree to anything, dismiss something as trivial (spilled coffee in your sleeping bag) or to show approval. *No importa* (It's not important) can be offensive in some situations since it may imply disdain.

A positive expression is safer than a negative: *Está bien*, for example, when the farmer's baby twists your nose rather than *No importa*. What isn't important, your big nose or our precious one-of-a-kind *bebé?* This works in many ways: "*Estoy bien*" or "*Estoy contento*" (I'm well, content) is a more polite way to say "I've eaten plenty" than "*No tengo hambre*" (I'm not hungry). The implication may be taken as, "I can't eat any more of this stuff!"
De nada: It's nothing; you're welcome.
Al contrario: On the contrary. Used as an emphatic expression of thanks, especially in a mutual exchange of favors.

Most conversations and casual encounters begin with some sort of question. The following examples will be heard often, especially if you travel into areas where campers are a real novelty. Keep in mind that every person's curiosity deserves an answer, even when you've tired of having to explain yourself.

¿De dónde viene?: Where do you come from?
Soy (somos) de . . . : I (we) are from . . . *Campesinos* will say, *Soy de México y mi tierra es*

Jalisco. Mi tierra, my land or home place, means far more to them than a vague word like Mexico.

¿De dónde radica usted?: Where do you come from? From where are you rooted? Like many archaic expressions, this one is popularly used in the boondocks.

¿A dónde va?: Where are you going?

Voy (vamos) a . . . : I(we) are going to . . . I like to begin my answer with *"Quisieramos ir a . . ."* "We should like to go to . . ." is vague, more formal and less assertive. Mexicans avoid flat definite announcements. The *gringo* custom of being 'loud and clear' is considered aggressive and rude.

"We should like to visit the river," implies that you may not, since you don't know the future or control it, much less the condition of the road, who owns the property in between or what obstacles God may place before you.

Si Dios quiere: If God wishes. You'll soon learn this one; anytime people must risk committing themselves they'll add "If God wishes" just in case He doesn't. "We will meet you with the horses in the morning, if God wishes." "I'll bring a fish, if God wishes." "The day will be warm, if . . ."

Si Dios nos da licencia: If God gives us permission. Used similarly to, "If God wishes."

¿Cómo le va?: How is it going? This can be a vague question (How is life?) or specific (How is the trail treating you?).

¿Cómo le ha ido?: How has it been going for you?

¿Cómo está usted?: How are you?

¿Qué tal?: How are things?

Any of these inquiries can open a discussion of the weather, your route, the distance to the next water hole and so on. The situation you find yourself in determines, of course, your response.

Muy bien, gracias: Very well, thanks.

Así-así: So-so. You broke your arm earlier, but like a true Mexican you won't mention it unless you absolutely have to.

Pues, no muy bien: Well, not so good. To a Mexican, this would be heard as a shout for help. The reaction will be sharply raised eyebrows and:

¿Qué pasó?: What happened?

¿Qué pasa?: What is happening?

¿Qué es?: What is it?

¡Digame, hombre!: Tell me, man!

You launch into your tale of woe, which the other person frequently interrupts with exclamations like:

¡Vaya!: Go on!

¿De veras?: Really?

¡Ay, qué caray!: Oh, wow!

¡Valgame Dios!: God bless me!

¡Hijole!: Yipes!

¡N'ombre!: Name of God! Also a slang contraction of "No, man!"

Obviously the situation calls for outside help; your new friend immediately takes you to someone and makes introductions:

Quiero presentarle a . . . : I want to introduce you to . . .

Mucho gusto: It's a pleasure. Time to shake hands; gently now.

Mucho gusto en conocerle, señor(a): It's a pleasure to know you, sir (madam). Slightly formal but don't think it's stuffy; many people add *"A sus ordenes"* (At your orders, command) or *"A su servicio"* (At your service). *Campesinos* may go even farther and address you as *Patrón* (Boss) or *Jefe* (Chief). Don't let it go to your head.

¿Cuál (Cómo, Qué) es su gracia?: What is your name? Another archaic form that country

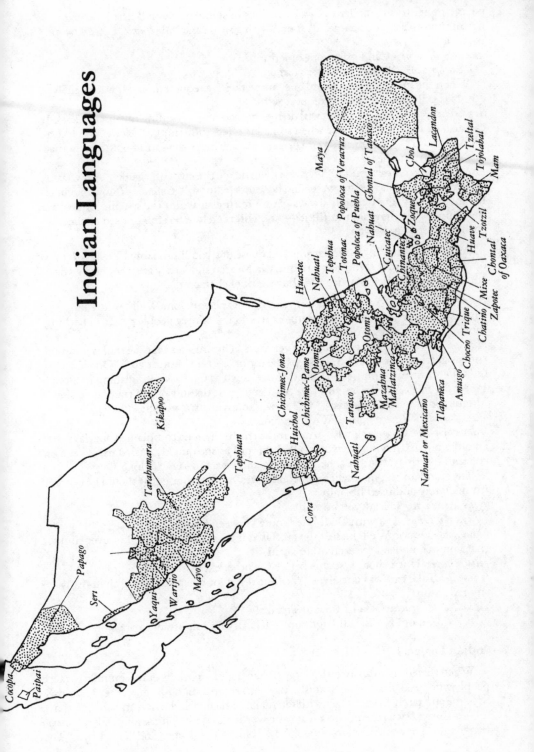

Indian Languages

Maya

Lacandon

Popoloca of Veracruz

Chol

Tzeltal

Tojolabal

Chontal of Tabasco

Mam

Nahuatl

Zoque

Tzotzil

Popoloca of Puebla

Nahuatl

Chontal of Oaxaca

Cuicatec

Huave

Huaxtec

Nahuatl

Tepebua

Chinantec

Mixe

Totonac

Popoloca of Puebla

Zapotec

Chatino

Otomí

Trique

Chocho

Amusgo

Chichimec-Jona

Otomí

Mazahua

Matlatzinca

Huichol

Chichimec-Pame

Tlapaneca

Kikapoo

Tarasco

Nahuatl or Mexicano

Tepehuan

Nahuatl

Tarahumara

Cora

Papago

Mayo

Seri

Warijio

Yaqui

Cocopa

Paipai

people prefer to the modern *¿Cómo se llama?* In some cases you'll first be asked permission to ask your name. Respond with a smile and *"Me llamo . . . (My name is . . .)."*

¿Le ofrezco algo?: Can I offer you something?

¿Qué le ofrezco?: What can I offer you?

When the question is a general one, answer with a request for food, water, shelter, etc. It is polite to preface the request with:

Si me hace el favor de . . .: If you will do me the favor of . . . (selling me some beans). It can also be used as a response when someone offers something. "Would you like a glass of water?" *"Sí, gracias. Si me hace el favor."* This is the sort of polite extra that *campesinos* love to hear.

Lo que me hace el favor, gracias: Whatever you do me the favor of, thanks. You've asked a man if you may have some water and he wants to know *"¿Cuánto?"* (How much?). By answering vaguely you'll always get more. It also avoids the specific request and the danger that they can't fulfill it — and will therefore be embarrassed or short themselves to satisfy you.

After these greetings, salutations and questions you'll probably be ready to move on, but don't rush it. No one is in a hurry in Mexico and if they are, they often won't admit it. Impatience is a vice and shows lack of character.

Bueno, ¿Con permiso?: Good (Well), with (your) permission. Well, excuse me, now. This is the short, casual leave-taking expression. Country people prefer something more elaborate. My favorite is:

Hay que ir a llegar: You have to go to get there. This implies that the trail is long and time is getting short. It also sidesteps the use of "I" as in "I must go." "One must go" or "One must eat" implies an outside force, such as God's Will, pushing us along.

Vamos llegando: We go arriving; we are arriving. It doesn't pay to translate these idioms too closely. It means, "Well now, 'bout time we were headin' out."

Vamos yendo: We are going. We go by going.

Vamos despacio: We go slowly. "Ain't it the truth?" Lorena complained one day, after an old woman carrying firewood called this out as she quickly passed us. People on the trail use this as both a cheery greeting and a way to say "So 'long."

The standard response when someone leaves you is a phrase that should be learned immediately and used liberally:

¡Qué le vaya bien!: May you go well!

¡Vaya con Dios!: Go with God! Used more between friends.

Nos vemos (vimos): We'll be seeing you. Used if there's any chance, however slight, that you may indeed see each other again.

Hasta luego: Until then. Use this before the other expressions, for emphasis.

Cuidense: Take care of yourselves. We hear this a lot when backpacking in really rugged country.

¡Igualmente, gracias!: Same to you! Thanks!

¡Andele!: Go on! Go ahead! Right on! This is a very important expression.

Indian Dialects

When travelling in areas with a large Indian population, it is quite common to meet people who speak little or no Spanish. Women are often mono-lingual; they stay closer to home and rarely have contact with foreigners (which includes non-Indian Mexicans).

We always try to memorize a few basic words and polite phrases in the local *idioma* (language). They can be as simple as "Yes," "No," "Thank you" and "Good-bye." The point is not to be fluent, but to demonstrate respect for their language, which in turn shows respect for them as people. Your small effort will often be taken as a major event.

On my first trip to the Yucatan I learned one phrase in Maya: "Let's eat!" I not only got to use it at least twice a day at mealtimes, but the Mayan family I was living with often called upon me to spout my phrase at odd hours of the day and night. It always brought smiles, whoops of laughter and encouragement to try new words.

Indians (and *campesinos*) commonly refer to Spanish as *castellano* (Castilian) and their own Indian language as *la idioma*.

For a brief vocabulary in Spanish, English and several common Indian *idiomas*, see *Appendices: Vocabulary*.

Meeting The People

Who's Who

The word *gringo(a)* is very commonly used by campesinos and Indians to define all foreigners. It is considered a legitimate name, not an insult. The only people who feel nervous about the word *gringo* are those Mexicans who have worked in the States and heard it used insultingly there. Foreigners are often called *gabacho(a)* and *güero(a)*. The former originally meant French or 'Frenchified Spaniard'; the latter is 'blond, pale, paleface.' *Güero* is also used without insult to describe a light-skinned Mexican.

The word *campesino(a)* (country man, woman) is used with pride, but city folk often refer to *los del rancho* (those of the ranch) as we would say 'hicks' or 'hillbillies.' "*Es del rancho*" (He's from the ranch) is a taunt used when someone's table manners, clothes or haircut are slightly *rústico* (rustic). Among country people, however, the term *ranchero* (rancher) is used proudly. When someone says, "My place is very small, it is only a *rancho*," they are being deliberately modest to avoid the sin of bragging.

A *patrón* (boss, owner, host) is a person of substance and standing, at least in relation to poorer neighbors. A *peón* is a landless person or unskilled laborer; the very bottom of the ladder.

The word *indio(a)* is often offensive to genuine Indians. Many proudly say, "*¡Somos mexicanos!*" (We are Mexicans!) or "*¡Somos cristianos!*" Christian is synonomous with 'civilized'. Indians have been despised since the Conquest and are still considered to be savages by many *mestizos* (mixed blood Mexicans). "There are no *cristianos* in that *rancho!*" means the village is predominantly Indian. This is insulting, since it implies that Indians have no culture or morals.

Educated Mexicans often use *gente indigena* (indigenous people) as a synonym for Indian. Visitors to Indian communities would be wise to tread carefully. Asking "Are you Indians?" may make you quite unpopular.

Who Are You?

Gringos often fail to appreciate how strange they appear to Mexicans, especially in areas where any visitor is an event. You expect people to be curious, but have you considered that you might also frighten them?

Imagine this: you are living in rural Ohio, on a little known back road. Your nearest neighbors, the Smiths, live more than a quarter of a mile away. Mr. Smith is fond of his bourbon and Mrs. Smith is half deaf. They go to bed right after the Evening News.

Late one afternoon, a couple of hours before sundown, you notice a group of unfamiliar people hiking across your lower forty, leading a string of horses or are those . . . *burros?* They stop near the creek, not more than two hundred yards below your house. Before you can even begin to figure out what's going on, they unload crude wooden boxes and bulging saddlebags. The men produce machetes and hack the lower branches off your favorite shade tree as the women briskly erect a large stained tarpaulin of hand-sewn flour sacks.

Though it is early winter, the children scamper about barefoot, gathering twigs and *dried cow pies?* for a cook fire. The men wear wide-brimmed straw hats, sandals of loosely woven leather thongs with tire tread soles, white knee-length muslin breeches, scarlet sashes and strangely patterned *ponchos.* The women have babies bundled across their backs in brilliant shawls, ankle-length dresses in loud patterns and colorful beads and bangles around both wrists and ankles. Like the children, the women are barefooted.

The unintelligible sound of their voices drifts up to the house, along with the smell of scorched corn and meat. An eerie wailing flute answers the mournful call of a guitar. Who are they? What in hell are they doing? Shall we load the shotgun? Call the sheriff?

I'll never forget the unfortunate impression my brother and I made on a Mexican woman and three small children living on a remote ocean beach. We had beached our kayaks about half a mile from their small house. Our food supply was low and our drinking water almost gone. We hoped that a house might also mean a well. Rob and I headed off on foot, leaving Lorena with the boats.

As we slogged through the scorching sand I took quick stock of our appearance. After a month of hard paddling and rough camping, our hair and beards were matted

with salt and bleached an irregular blond where hats failed to protect us from the sun. Our bodies were streaked with a thick crust of salt, our skin blistered, scabbed and peeling from over-exposure to the elements and many hours of seafood foraging around coral and sharp rocks. I wore a rotting bathing suit while Rob sported remnants of a pair of denim cut-offs. He had also lost a front tooth on a dried apricot. Combined with the wicked fillet knife and seashells that dangled on a string around his neck and a gallery of tatoos on his arms. Rob looked the perfect cutthroat pirate.

As we approached the house I attempted to whistle a cheery tune through dry cracked lips. My warning rendition of *When The Moon Comes Over The Mountain* was answered by a frightened squeal and the desperate slamming of the crude wooden door. We heard odds and ends of furniture being piled up in a hasty barricade.

"Shall I go get Lorena?" Rob asked, quickly assessing the situation.

"I think so," I answered. "And while you're there why don't you hide under the kayak."

It took Lorena almost fifteen minutes to coax the woman from the house. The children weren't so easily fooled; as the door opened they bailed out of a rear window and were last seen heading east, like jackrabbits on opening day of hunting season.

Our visit ended on a friendly and productive note — fresh eggs, tortillas and plenty of sweet water — but I'm sure that the family didn't breathe easily until we'd paddled well out of sight.

It's difficult not to draw attention when you enter a remote village but you don't have to draw a crowd. I've seen *gringos* who came on like a three ring circus: dogs and children erupting from a car or motor home in a wild excited melee; adults frantically snapping photos of anything that moved, and so on, until no one could possibly ignore them. Take it slow; park near a *tienda* (small store), quietly sip a soda or warm beer and give people a chance to see that you're basically normal. I've backpacked into villages that had seen so few outsiders that it took hours of patient squatting in the shade before people would approach us without looks of suspicion. In some cases, in fact, it was necessary to lure them in by setting up the backpacking stove to prepare a cup of instant coffee. Take it slow; you'll get much farther in the long run.

Why Are You Here?

What do you want? Where are you going? Why are you here? are questions every adventurous camper will hear when travelling far off the beaten track in Mexico. As a stranger it is *your* responsibility to give clear, respectful answers. Your tourist card (see Chapter 11) does not automatically entitle you to diplomatic immunity from questioning by local people, though at times you'll wish it did.

Answering questions can be tiring, though many are often rather quaint. "Are there trees in your country? What color eggs do your chickens lay? What noise do the cows make?" These are asked seriously, though your attempts to answer may bring grins and restrained laughter. *Campesinos* are very curious about crops and livestock; they may express genuine amazement to learn that bananas do not grow well in Minnesota. When Lorena casually told a *campesina* that tortillas were not as common as bread in our *tierra,* the woman's hand flew to her mouth and she gasped, "How barbaric!"

Indians and *campesinos* have a long and very sad history of being exploited by Outside Interests: the federal government; oil, mining and timber companies; big landowners (*latifundistas*) and U.S. controlled agri-business. Unless you're obviously a family group you may be suspected of being an agent of a large company or Mexican federal agency (Indians often think *gringos* are just people from Mexico City). In some remote areas, dope smugglers and missionaries were the only people to have visited before we backpacked in. Never laugh off an inquiry; just calmly explain what you are doing and that you are a simple tourist and nothing more.

The best general response to questions about the *motivo* (motive, purpose) of your visit is to say *"Paseando, no más."* This means, "Passing through, no more" and also "Looking around, having a good time," etc. Why anyone in their right mind would hike through a barren desert or paddle slowly up a jungle river should be answered in a positive way. "The life of the people is very interesting here" or "My land is very different. I want to know your land" (*Quiero conocer su tierra de usted*). If you've got photographs or picture postcards of home this is the time to break them out and make your point even more clearly.

"I want to take photographs to show my family how Mexicans live" is always a good one, since most campers carry a camera. A general response such as this avoids the hazard of saying "I have no *motivo*." As they will see it, no apparent 'motive' means you're hiding the real one.

We once drove our VW van on a wild goose chase in search of a fantastic skin diving area. We followed fishermen's rumors and a tattered road map to the end of one of the worst roads I've ever seen in Mexico. It ended high in the mountains, in a small village more than thirty miles from the coast. A quick look at the map solved our dilemma.

We would just have to leave the van there, hire burros and hike overland to the sea. It seemed a perfect opportunity for a side trip.

"Where can I rent a burro?" I asked a man behind the counter of a *tienda*.

"For what?" he answered.

"To go skin diving," I said. His eyebrows shot up. He looked inquiringly at several other customers, silent men who slouched against the thick adobe walls, sipping warm Cokes liberally laced with cane alcohol. They shrugged: *¿Quién sabe?*

I realized my error and began to explain that we wanted to skin dive on the coast, not here in the mountains. More shrugs; like country folk everywhere they didn't bother to tell me my own business.

I left the *tienda* and began asking men on the street if they knew of an available burro.

"People seem awfully uptight," I said to Lorena, after another prospect had scurried away from my question as though I had an infectious disease. We continued the search for a burro from house to house.

"Excuse me. Who owns these burros?"

"Excuse me. But is that a burro behind your house?"

"Excuse me. Who owns burros? Are there burros with owners?"

"Excuse me. Is this perhaps a burro?"

The woman looked at the large hairy ear I held firmly in my hand, attached to a large hairy beast tied to her front porch. "*¿Quizás?*" she answered, closing the door firmly in my face.

Perhaps? What was going on here? Some sort of anti-*gringo*/burro conspiracy? It was absolutely baffling. Suddenly a small boy touched me furtively on the elbow and hissed, "Follow me, please, to *el señor de los burros.*" Now we were getting somewhere!

It was a short walk to the burro man's house; we were quickly shown inside and given low wooden stools. A little girl shyly offered a plate of saltines. The burro man, a middle-aged farmer with a stubble of beard, looked us over appraisingly. I still didn't get it; what was all the fuss and mystery about? We wanted to *rent* a burro, not adopt the damned thing.

Conversation opened slowly; after the required remarks about the condition of the road and weather the man gave me a sly wink and said, "So, it is true then, that you want to take a burro swimming?"

"No, of course not," I explained, launching into a detailed description of snorkels, spear guns and the problem of getting our gear to the beach. He listened impassively, then suddenly waved me to be silent.

"It is not your mission that interests me," he said, "but the price. Burros are costly. How many do you require?"

I thought for a moment. One burro would do but several would do even better. I'd always fantasized having my own burro train, rather than one lonely beast. Hell, yes, six or twelve burros would do the job in fine style!

The man mentioned a price for six burros that was so astronomical I couldn't help crying out, "But that is more than our van cost!"

He nodded, then gave me a mischievous grin. "Expensive? Of course, *señor*, but then to skin dive in the *sierra* is a . . ."

"*¡Papá!*" The boy dashed into the room and buzzed into his father's ear. The man's eyes widened. He looked at us guiltily and began pounding a fist against his chest. His body was wracked with a dry hacking cough.

"*Gripa,*" he said, "I have the flu." He wheezed painfully. "Give me . . . *back* . . . one-half of the . . . money . . . and leave here *immediately* . . . cough . . . choke . . . and the animals . . . are all yours!"

"There's something really fishy going on here," I said to Lorena. "This whole town is a little crazy. I think it's time to move out." I told the burro man we'd give his offer some thought. Lorena stepped out of the door. I followed her. Right into the waiting arms of the Army.

" . . . and so you see, that is why we said we were going skin diving. The trail starts way up *here*," I waved to the surrounding peaks, "but ends way down *there!*" I pointed vaguely westward, to the sea.

The Army officer in command of the anti-marijuana and opium poppy patrol sighed for the hundredth time, scowling at the road map I'd been waving in his face. Five long hours with this mad tourist and he still claimed to be a skin diver! What would these *contrabandistas* try next? But the sweating soldiers had found nothing inside the van, not even a seed! Where were the guns, the Radio Shack walkie-talkies, the plastic trash bags, the bundles of cash? All the tricks and tools of the dope smuggler's trade?

"*¡Basta! ¡Ya!*" the officer commanded, "Enough!" He took a deep steadying breath and waved the tired troops back to their jeeps and pickup trucks. We smiled gratefully.

"Don't smile!" he warned. "And next time, *amigo,* you'd better be able to show me a fish!"

Presenting Yourself To The Authorities

In many isolated communities it is considered proper to present yourself to *la autoridad,* the authority, upon arrival. This is especially common in the mountain highlands and in traditional Indian areas. Along the coasts of Mexico people are much more relaxed and you'll rarely have to deal with this situation.

The authority may be the *alcalde* or *presidente* (mayor), *gobernador* (mayor, governor), *jefe* (chief), *juez* (judge), *comisario* (commissioner, usually of an *ejido* — rural collective), *alguacil* (bailiff) or *jefe de cuartel* (chief of headquarters).

"*¿Quién es la autoridad aquí, por favor?*" (Who is the authority here, please?), is a good way to take the bull by the horns and introduce yourself. You'll be taken to the man (I've never heard of a woman *autoridad*) or to his office. The office is usually called *la presidencia, la municipal* or *el cuartel.* It may be nothing more than a bare adobe room with a few hand-hewn wooden benches, but treat it with respect. This is the setting for an introduction to the town so don't act flippant. On the other hand, don't be nervous, either; once formalities are over the authorities will revert to their normal roles as farmers and small businessmen.

The *autoridad,* his assistants and other leading citizens (such as the schoolteacher) may gather in an impromptu town meeting. Everyone will be curious about you and eager to hear why you're visiting. Don't be surprised if the meeting is delayed while someone is summoned from a distant cornfield. In one village the mayor was also the captain of the town's soccer team. He examined our papers as we shared a bottle of tequila on the side of the playing field.

Don't be put off by questioning; it is both their right and obligation to their office to establish who you are, why you're there and perhaps, if you're well received, what they can do to be of assistance to you. When visitors are few and far between, they deserve attention.

"*¿Qué es su misión?*" (What is your mission?); "*¿Qué es su comisión?*" (What is your commission, assignment, purpose?); "*¿Con qué motivo llegan aquí?*" (With what motive do you come here?); "*¿Qué hacen aquí?*" (What are you doing here?). These are commonly asked of travellers and should be answered honestly and seriously.

We onced hiked with a group of friends into a remote area populated almost entirely by Indians. It didn't take long to learn the ritual of presenting ourselves to the authorities, but one woman in our group was increasingly irritated by what she saw as time wasted answering the same questions over and over. The crunch came late

one afternoon, as we confronted an Indian mayor who had obviously never dealt with *gringos* before. He seemed to have the idea that we worked for the Mexican government and were visiting the area for sinister reasons. Perhaps we would recommend that the forests be cut down for lumber? Whatever he had in mind, it was clear that he distrusted us.

"What right do you have to stop us?" our friend suddenly demanded. "Who do you think you are? Let us go immediately. This is stupid!" We tried to calm her down but the damage had been done; with a snarl the mayor ordered us to sit on the porch of the town hall while he and his advisors huddled in a summit conference inside. After two very long hours a man emerged from the room with an antique brass trumpet. He raised the instrument to his lips and ceremoniously blew a series of raucous blasts into the distant canyons. An hour later an old man puffed into view. He was the former mayor, summoned to advise his younger successor.

At this point we became slightly anxious. One of the mayor's aides squatted down beside me and whispered confidentially that only one other *gringo* had visited the village in recent memory.

"He was a missionary," the man hissed, "or so he claimed! It took us a week to confirm his mission."

"What did the *gringo* do during the week?" I asked.

"He prayed," the man laughed, adding, "*In jail!*" and pointed a finger toward a nearby squat adobe structure with a heavily barred door and windows. I took a long look at the jail; at least it had a nice view.

Suddenly the mayor emerged onto the porch, carefully winding a large alarm clock, another fine antique. He glanced up toward the sun and arbitrarily set the hands at five o'clock. I was motioned inside, having earlier assumed the role of spokesperson for our group. The town council was in full session.

The bailiff, holding his silver-tipped hardwood staff of office, directed me to a wooden stool. The room was dark and gloomy; I sat several feet from a long wooden table where the council had assembled. Our passports and tourist cards were spread out in front of the mayor and the ex-mayor. From time to time their unintelligible discussion would be interrupted by the passing of a bottle of *mescal*, a very necessary part of the local legal ritual (see *The People's Guide To Mexico: Booze and Cantinas*). I was given occasional nods and inquisitive stares. The candles flickered as the evening wore away.

I was doing my best to appear interested in the proceedings when the mayor suddenly straightened up and took my tourist card carefully in hand, holding it to the light so that his predecessor could read the fine print. As the older man read from the tourist card, stopping frequently to translate or comment in his native tongue, a scribe dutifully recorded everything in a cheap ruled notebook.

When the front of the card had been studied, it was flipped over to the back. As the man's voice droned on I realized that he was reading *everything,* including the printer's miniscule trademark and address on one edge. That finished, my passport was opened to the first page. As the young mayor picked it up several color photographs I kept between the pages fluttered to the floor. There was an embarrassed silence as these were carefully retrieved and spread out near the candle. The mayor bent over them, studying each intently, as though they might provide a conclusive answer to our *misión.*

"What are these?" he finally asked, a note of genuine interest in his voice.

"Those are cows," I answered. "They belong to my brother. He is a farmer." It wasn't the exact truth, since the cows were a 'herd' of just two animals, but I thought it might establish a common connection between our ways of life. There were a few more barnyard scenes and a couple of spectacular shots of snow-capped mountains in the Cascades. These were passed around and eagerly discussed, except for one photograph that held the mayor's undivided attention. He stared at it in the poor light, obviously baffled.

"What animal is this?" he finally asked, tapping the photo with his forefinger. "Is it a he-goat?" I crossed the room to get a better look.

"That is my brother. He is standing next to a cow. He has a beard and long hair." The confusion was obvious; Rob was shown bent over the calf's neck, facing away from the camera.

The room fell deathly silent. The men looked at each other nervously and failed to meet my eye. A voice muttered something in a strained, sarcastic tone. The mayor flinched. He turned to me with an embarrassed frown and I suddenly realized what had happened: he had called my brother a *cabrón,* although indirectly, and the powerful insult was hanging in the air between us. They watched me intently; would I take offense?

I gave a slight smile and a wave of low laughter swept the room. The *mescal* bottle made its round and for the first time, I was included.

The mayor's face gradually hardened into a familiar frown as he fiddled with my passport for a few face saving moments. He stood up — rather unsteadily after the pressures of the evening's ritual drinking — and announced his decision: we would spend the night sleeping on the roof of the jail (*would,* not could) and would be allowed to depart the village at dawn. No earlier and no later. He gave me a rather chilly smile, then turned to the *alguacil* and barked in Spanish, "Arrest that man!"

My heart hit the floor. It wasn't until the bailiff rushed past that I realized one of the drunker council members had moved behind me and lay stretched out on the floor. He was hauled roughly to his feet and dragged out, protesting loudly that he was not drunk, not by a long shot.

When the door to the jail had been carefully chained shut, the bailiff smiled at me and said, "That is how the town makes a little money. It is legal to drink but not legal to be drunk. On a good night we arrest almost everyone. Sleep well." He cocked an ear toward the jail, where the drunk had begun a loud protest that would last into the small hours of the night. "That bird will sing you to sleep!"

Life In The Back Country

Customs and Superstitions

Good travel literature inevitably includes descriptions of quaint customs to amuse and entertain the armchair traveller. We learn to our astonishment that Dodo Islanders worship the Toad Goddess and eat popcorn only during the last quarter of the full moon, lest they anger sleeping volcanoes and bring dreadful eruptions that will destroy their crops of sacred pipi nuts. Tourists, we are told, may eat popcorn discreetly in the better hotels and clubs. Other than that, don't worry; the natives are a happy-go-lucky bunch.

Typical customs and superstitions of rural Mexico may be less romantic than those of the Dodo Islanders, but to the people themselves, their beliefs are as real as the sun and sky. Don't worry too much about violating a local custom, however. Mexicans are very tolerant when dealing with *gringos,* especially if you demonstrate sympathy and an open mind. The safest approach to learning new customs is an attitude of caution, careful observation and self-restraint. Shyness, real or pretended, is also a good cover for ignorance. It puts you in the position of having to be taught and told what to do: "Here, take this seat, please," or "Would you care to pass the night in our house?" Barging in with questions and requests is definitely not the custom, nor good manners.

Travellers should try to develop a sixth sense for detecting when people are subtly telling you how to behave — or not to behave. Mexicans generally avoid correcting others openly. This is especially true in small closed rural communities, where open criticism is carefully avoided. "That man over there is very drunk," you comment to a Mexican acquaintance. His noncommital "Um?" or no response at all means, "Drop the subject, would you? That's my brother-in-law's best friend."

The word "Why?" should be used with great restraint, if at all. "Why do you believe that burning cornfields creates rain clouds?" "Why are deer sacred here?" "Why can a person die of a 'bad wind'?" There are no answers to these questions; their beliefs have evolved as slowly and complexly as the surrounding country. It's like asking someone why their eyes are brown instead of blue. If you do ask "why?", the usual response is a laconic, "It's the custom." Leave it at that.

Gringos tend to be embarrassingly open and aggressive in their questioning of *campesinos* and Indians. "How many sleep in this bed?" "How much corn do you grow?" Don't come on like Oscar Lewis researching a book on the private lives of rural Mexicans: respect their right to privacy. Even if your motives are genuinely innocent, others may resent the prying.

Questions about drugs are especially hazardous. Carlos Castenada and other popular writers have unleashed a horde of self-styled apprentice sorcerers and pseudo-ethnologists on the innocent people of Mexico. There seems to be a hollow-eyed *gringo* behind every hallucinogenic plant, asking a bemused Indian for the recipe to his favorite mind-blowing concoction. Even in communities where hallucinogens such as magic mushrooms are used, a good portion of the population may heartily disapprove of the practice.

Witchcraft, sorcery and hallucinogens seem to form a supernatural partnership, at least in popular literature, but to superstitious Mexicans *brujería* (witchcraft) is often highly feared. "I am told that María is a *bruja*" can be like saying to a *gringo*, "I hear your son is a child molester." Tread very carefully 'round the subject. If your interest is more than casual you'll need time, patience and mutual trust to overcome people's natural reluctance to discuss such sensitive and personal subjects.

Some Mexican customs, especially *machismo*, (discussed later in this chapter) conflict directly with our own. Take the expression *A cada quien su vida* (To each their own life) to heart. Meddling in others' lives seldom pays off in anything but resentment and distrust. You won't make yourself popular, for example, by insisting that a husband drop his attitude of *machismo* while you're around. *Machismo* is the most irritating, and at the same time, one of the most entrenched customs in all of Mexico. Grin and bear it; save criticism for discussions with more 'enlightened' people.

Churches and shrines in very remote villages and traditional Indian communities are generally considered the property of the community, rather than public places. Ask permission to enter and to take photographs. The *sacristán* (sexton) will probably appreciate a donation, especially if you ask him to unlock the church so you may enter. In spite of relaxed customs in urban Mexico, women should cover their heads inside a rural church and men must remove their hats.

Backpackers often come upon trailside shrines, some decorated with colorful offerings and religious mementoes. Treat them with respect; they're not placed there to provide souvenirs for curious tourists. Picking up a gourd filled with incense, a crudely worked crucifix or a pottery image is not only a form of desecration, but can lead to very serious trouble if you're caught — or even suspected of such thievery.

Never intrude on a religious ceremony, especially if it is being held by Indians. I know of several cases where curiosity overcame common sense and courtesy, and prying *gringos* were shown the gate with a shower of sticks and stones.

You will often be asked what religion you practise. If you don't have a preference, pretend to be a Catholic; they're in the majority. An Indian once refused to let us enter his village until we'd answered his question "Are you *cristianos* or *ateos?*" When we said, "Christians!" he smiled broadly and said, "Very good, we don't like atheists here."

Mexican Indians do not see themselves as tourist attractions. As in many Indian communities in the American Southwest, the Indians of Mexico have realized that their culture must often be protected by closing themselves off, both to casual tourists and well-meaning scientists and social worker-types. This statement by Santiago Gutiérrez Toribio, President of the Supreme Mixe Council of The Oaxaca State National Native Peoples Congress sums up the Indian position quite well:

> *We formally demand that your government order all repressive acts against our communities be stopped . . . In short, we want an end to the discrimination we are being subjected to . . .*
>
> *The substitution of our culture by degenerated cultural forms imported from abroad, the television and radio broadcasts that encourage alcoholism, envy and strange ways of living without considering our heritage other than as museum pieces should be changed.*

It is interesting to note that "your government" refers to the Mexican federal government. Native groups definitely consider themselves isolated from Mexico, both culturally and politically.

Always ask permission to take photographs. In Indian communities it is best to keep your camera out of sight until you're certain it won't provoke trouble. Most *campesinos* love to have their picture taken, but some Indians will toss you into the local *jaula* (cage, jail) at the first sight of an Instamatic. Ask, "*¿Se puede retratar* *aquí?"* (May one take photographs here?) and if the answer is less than an emphatic "Yes!" I'd be cautious.

Campers are often approached by people offering to sell *monitos* (little monkeys, figures), *antigüedades* (antiquities, artifacts), *figuras* (figures, artifacts) and other interesting lumps of worked clay or stone. Some of these turn up during the plowing and seeding of fields, others are excavated with an idea toward selling them to traders who deal in illicit artifacts. It is incredibly tempting to buy an artifact, especially when the price is ridiculously low and the object is beautifully made and obviously authentic. They may even take you to the hole and show you other artifacts in place.

Avoid the temptation, please. It is not only quite illegal but artifacts are the property of the Mexican people and should rightfully remain inside Mexico. Small artifacts of "no significant value" can be collected but the interpretation of "value" is up to the government, not you. At the least it would be embarrassing to be caught with artifacts, at the worst a downright disaster.

I once made the mistake of admiring a small pottery figure that an old man showed me when we camped near his *rancho*. His price went from cheap to ridiculous in about five minutes; I finally gave in and bought it just to do him a favor. I had no intention of carrying it out. The figure wasn't just ugly and poorly done; it weighed a good ten pounds. The last thing I needed in my backpack was ballast. I paid the man, however, and as soon as he'd left, stuck the figure behind a bush, where it could wait another few hundred years for an archaeologist.

The next morning, to my horror, the old man returned, bearing a huge basket stuffed to the brim with broken pottery bowls, fragments of figures, bits of obsidian knife blades and all the floor sweepings of the average Aztec tomb. He'd been up half the night, madly excavating a local ruin and canvassing all the nearby *ranchos* to gather together this treasure trove of ancient junk. When I clearly refused to buy any of it, the old man was crushed. As he left our camp, he muttered disgustedly, "I shouldn't have sold you the best piece first!" A collector later explained to me that buyers of such artifacts always count on getting the worst items at the beginning of a bartering session, with the very best held out as long as possible to raise its price to the limit.

People in the back country will be very interested in your clothing and gear. Dress modestly and you'll attract less attention (see *Clothing:* Chapter 9 for more).

Nudity in public is absolutely unacceptable and the farther into the back country you go, the more unacceptable it becomes. Men and women never bathe together, even with underwear to protect their modesty. You may notice men or women bathing nude or semi-nude but it is impolite to 'see' them or make comments.

If you spend much time in rural communities you'll notice that sanitary facilities aren't just crude, there often aren't any at all. Everyone 'does their business' in the bushes or behind the nearest wall or fence. This is obviously unhealthy but *gringos* are more offended by a lack of privacy. Just as you squat down behind the meager protection of a dried thistle, half a dozen curious youngsters pop their heads around the corral. A wise Mexican man told a *gringa* the secret to achieving privacy in such a situation: "Close your eyes until you've finished." The kids are just budding anthropologists, investigating intimate habits of the elusive *gringo*.

Beards and hair attract a great deal of attention. Lorena's long blonde hair is often touched or tugged by both children and adults (especially Indian women) for luck and just to feel the texture. I am constantly razzed about my beard. "How is Cuba, Fidel?" or "Hey there, *barboso!*" (bearded, but distressingly similar to *baboso*, drooler).

Unfortunately, beards are also associated with the Devil by many Indians and they are instinctively distrustful of bearded strangers. I trim my beard down to the nubs when making trips into remote areas. Bearded men should be careful about staring at children or pretending to chase or frighten them. The kids may love it but their parents might take it as a sign of the Evil Eye (*mal ojo*). I have frequently heard parents warn their children when I approach, "Here comes the Devil!" or "Be good or this *gringo* will eat you!" It's funny until you see how seriously the little brats take it.

Ghosts and Witches

I once asked a group of farmers about what I could expect on a long hike into a remote mountain range. We discussed the usual problems of food, water and trail conditions, plus interesting people and landmarks to visit. When I had the information I needed, I asked casually, "Is it dangerous there?" Experience has shown me that if something is going on that a *gringo* should avoid, someone comes up with a timely warning. Warnings, however, are often indirect.

"Yes!" one of the men answered, with surprising abruptness. "It is very dangerous there! Never sleep outside at night."

"*¿Hay gente mala?*" (Are there bad people?) I asked, assuming that he meant trouble in two-legged form.

He quickly shook his head. "No, they are just poor people like us. The problem is . . ." He launched into a hair-raising description of mythical wild beasts and headless horsemen that would have sent Boris Karloff scurrying to the safety of the Acapulco Hilton. When he'd finished I promised to take all precautions. The trip went without a supernatural hitch, perhaps because I'd been forewarned and carried plenty of garlic to ward off the spirits.

Gringos should not laugh off such tall tales. *Campesinos* and Indians firmly believe in what we call the 'occult' and they take their beliefs very seriously indeed. Witches, for example, exist throughout Mexico. The cross-eyed woman in the next village may be considered responsible for a child's sudden loss of appetite and raging fever. Many *brujas* (witches) have been killed by frightened neighbors who are convinced that the supernatural has been used against them.

Envidio (envy) is also considered a very powerful force, one that can bring ruin and ill health to the person (or animal) it is directed at. If you covet your neighbor's pig and the animal just won't gain weight, it is your fault for being envious.

Sightings of ghosts are very common among *campesinos*. If you are warned about a *fantasma*, accept the warning gracefully rather than expressing disbelief. You may even have to move your camp. Lorena and I once camped next to a haunted sawmill. Every morning we were asked by local people, "Have you seen *her* yet?" The ghost of a woman who had died ages before was considered as real as the next person, but a lot more dangerous.

If you are asked for an opinion or advice on repelling a 'spell' or dealing in any way with magic, take it very carefully and seriously. "*No entiendo eso,*" (I don't understand that) or just "*No sé*" (I don't know) are much safer than dabbling with things that can have serious and very real consequences. (See *The People's Guide To Mexico: Custom and Superstition* for more.)

Food and Drink

The unwritten code of rural hospitality in Mexico says that travellers must be offered something to eat or drink, if only a glass of water or a few hot tortillas sprinkled with coarse salt. In Indian communities this custom is usually reserved for Indian visitors; *gringos* will probably have to ask for food and be expected to pay for it.

Men and guests are served first. The cook (the wife or elder daughter) won't eat until the others have finished. Don't make a scene by insisting on a more democratic arrangement; you'll only embarrass everyone.

"Está muy sabrosa" (It is very tasty) is enough of a compliment to make most women blush. Giving compliments is considered rather unusual, but I've never noticed anyone objecting. If you're a man complimenting a woman, keep it very simple to avoid appearing too forward. Women, of course, can be much freer in their conversations with each other. If your host or hostess makes disparaging comments about food, their house or their hospitality, respond positively: *"Está muy rica"* (It is very rich, tasty) or *"Estamos muy contentos, gracias."* (We are very content, comfortable, thank you).

If you are not given a spoon (forks don't exist in the boondocks), use your fingers and tortillas as utensils. If you are clumsy (and few gringos aren't when dealing with tortillas as spoons) and make a mess, don't worry about it, they'll pretend not to notice and thoroughly enjoy the spectacle.

Never ask for more food. If it isn't freely offered or more likely, actually forced on you, it means they don't have enough to go around again. You'll usually be given the most and the best, even if someone else in the house has to do without. It is difficult to protest without giving offense or embarrassing the household. Since your visit is going to become a colorful piece of local history, be as gracious as you can and it will repay them adequately.

When leaving the table say, *"Con permiso"* (With permission, excuse me). The response will be *"Andele," "Es propio"* or *"Pasale"* (Go ahead. It's yours. Pass ahead.).

You may be offered water to wash up with, either before or after the meal. It is polite to use it.

If you are served something that you just cannot deal with, such as a hunk of fried armadillo, don't say *"No me gusta"* (I don't like it). Any excuse, no matter how feeble, is better than the truth in this situation. One of the prices of visiting foreign places is that you must often close your eyes and chew. Do it; if nothing else it will make a nice story for the folks back home.

Paying For Food and Services

When it comes time to pay someone for a meal of beans and tortillas, to pay off your guide or to buy an interesting wooden flute from a local artisan, don't make a big fuss over the deal. Transactions involving money, either small or large amounts, are done quietly and often slowly, without great displays of emotion. *Gringos* often mistake this indifference for ingratitude. Pride is the real reason, plus the macho law that prohibits revealing our true feelings, good or bad.

Many people will refuse to accept money for food or lodging, especially if they have invited you into their house. Men are particularly reluctant to take payment since it offends their pride. The best solution is to make the exchange as simple and impersonal as possible: *"Algo para la casa"* (Something for the house), is the classic phrase when slipping the *señora* a few bills. I like to have Lorena give the money to the woman of the house, since it makes it even easier for the man to ignore while at the same time giving a more personal contact between the women. If Lorena isn't with me, I leave the money on the table as I am leaving. Don't give money, however, if it is emphatically refused or you'll insult the household.

When in doubt, I quietly ask, *"Se puede ofrecerles algo?"* (May one offer you something?). A positive response may be as subtle as a half-smile or a shrug. Refusals are usually obvious: *"¡No, señor! ¡Le invitamos!"* (We are inviting you). Some people respond, *"Lo que sea justo"* or *"Lo que me hace el favor"* (Whatever is fair. Whatever you do me the favor of.) This isn't the time to be a tight wad.

When paying for a meal I calculate roughly what it would have cost in a simple restaurant, then give at least that and preferably even more. Remember: supplies are hard to come by in the back country and raw foodstuffs cost more than in town. Err on the side of generosity, without playing the role of the Big Spender. You'll make it up in good will and free meals another day.

If you find yourself being obviously over-charged, I suggest that you grin and bear it. Bartering may be expected, especially when buying a souvenir or discussing a prospective trip with a guide, but if you've already eaten or used a room without agreeing beforehand on the price, give what is asked. Arguing will embarrass everyone. Even if you are in the right, you are exposing someone's greed and making a scene. No one will thank you for that, believe me.

It can be very difficult to find small change in the back country. Carry enough cash to last for the trip but don't carry large bills. Fortunately pesos come in notes of ten, twenty and fifty. Coins are very handy but they're also heavy. On one backpacking trip we were forced to 'rob' the church collection plate. Actually a friendly priest agreed to exchange our large bills for sacks of small change he'd collected from his parishioners. The total value of the coins wasn't much but the weight was considerable. After that experience I now take the trouble to visit a bank before leaving the city.

Gifts

Gifts are an excellent way of repaying favors while camping. It really doesn't have to be much to be greatly appreciated. Food is always welcomed and makes a natural payment when someone gives you a meal. When backpacking we carry spices, candy, honey, instant coffee and dried milk to give away. Offer it after your visit or your hostess will probably serve your gift to you as part of your meal.

Travellers may ask a local woman to prepare a meal for them, giving her all or part of the ingredients from their own supplies. When offering a gift, just say *"Un regalito"* (A little gift) to make things clear. *"¡Dios se lo pague!"* (God will pay you!) is a commonly heard response when someone thanks you for a gift or favor.

I prefer to give things as we are parting company, rather than at first meeting. This doesn't put the other person on the spot quite so much if they don't have something to give in turn. While backpacking we have often been given giant twenty-pound squashes, six-foot lengths of sugar cane, whole stalks of bananas, enormous papayas and in one memorable case, a hand-hewn chair of heavy mesquite wood that I'd admired (admiring things in Mexico is hazardous in this way). We accepted all of these, with the notable exception of the chair, but passed them on to others as soon as we were a polite distance away. This can lead, of course, to a vicious circle: you give a *campesino* a monster squash and he desperately combs his fields and orchards for an even grander gift. The secret is to unload the item and then make a hasty exit.

We once gave a very ragged *campesino* we met along the trail a gift of two sleazy plastic bowls, worth no more than twenty-five cents each. It was during one of our periodic weight purges, when I regretted packing anything that wasn't constantly in use. Nothing demonstrates the value of camping gear like carrying it up and down mountains for several days. To our surprise, the man tracked us to our campsite the next morning and presented us with several large slabs of dark dried beef. He swatted a few pesky flies from the meat and launched into a speech that went something like this: "Well, I just happened to look around the house after I presented my wife with those beautiful new dishes and what do you know, there was some meat! We don't need it, of course, and I suppose you don't either, but there it is!" He'd hiked eight miles before dawn to deliver this treat.

He was back again, the following morning, with fresh tortillas. As we made to leave he grabbed two packs (he was about five feet tall and skinny) and raced off down the trail. When we protested, he just laughed. "This trail is ugly and I have much practice." He led us a merry chase for ten grueling miles. Late that afternoon he gently lowered the backpacks to the ground and said, "Well, I must return home. Have a good trip." He absolutely refused to accept money for his prodigious labors. I finally forced him to accept a pair of pants, after threatening to leave them hanging on a bush if he wouldn't take them off my hands.

Gifts are often much more useful and certainly involve more feeling than the cold clink of metal pesos. Give practical things rather than novelties: knives, small tools (hacksaw blades, pliers, chisels), penlights, fishing gear, cigarette lighters, needles and thread, cloth buttons and sturdy toys.

Cultural Shock

One of the hazards of being a "stranger in a strange land" is that things sometimes get a little too strange and you feel like you're losing control. This is commonly known as 'cultural shock'. Most travellers suffer from it at one time or another and campers are no exception. If you've backpacked into Indian country for a hundred miles and wake up one morning wondering, "What the hell am I doing here, anyway?" or feel vaguely uneasy and apprehensive every time you point your motorhome a little farther South, you're suffering a mild case of cultural shock. Severe attacks can be quite disturbing: you can't sleep, lose your appetite, feel constantly harried and nervous and have a strong inclination to grab the first northbound bus. Here are some suggestions that should alleviate or even eliminate the symptoms of cultural shock. Don't be embarrassed to use them; it is a natural reaction to a sudden and complete change in diet, language and surroundings.

Go ahead and daydream about home but don't overdo it. Why did you come to Mexico in the first place? Try to recapture that feeling of excitement you had when you first decided to go south. If you keep a journal, go over it now. Write out how you feel and why you're upset. Write a detailed letter to a friend and get it all off your chest.

Don't get mad at Mexico or Mexicans; it's not their fault that you feel weird. Think of all the adventures that await you. Maybe you'll do them next year. Don't dwell on any unpleasant experiences you might have had recently. If you find yourself in uncomfortable surroundings, keep in mind that travellers have the freedom to move. At the very least it's got to be better than going to work, *¿No?*

Find a comfortable spot (how can you beat a hammock at the beach?) and *relax*. Maybe you're pushing too fast and too hard. Lots of campers are content to follow the tourist camping circuits. Leave the jungle bushwhacking to others if you don't really enjoy it.

The constant pressure of speaking, listening and dealing with the Spanish language can be exhausting. Find a friendly *gringo* and bend their ear. Some travellers feel guilty if they don't spend half of their trip learning Spanish. This is a narrow attitude; you're probably in Mexico to have a good time and learn how others live, not to take a degree in linguistics.

Don't listen to other campers' horror stories; most are 90% hot air and 10% rumor. Stick your nose in a thick novel and by the time you pull it out again, you'll be ready to hit the trail for another adventure.

Scared? Bandits?

We are often asked if we don't get scared while camping in Mexico. The answer is complicated: scared of what? Bandits? They exist primarily in legends and lurid scare stories and on the marquees of neighborhood movie theaters. The popular *gringo* image of a mustachioed *bandido,* thundering over a cactus-studded hill brandishing a rifle in one hand and a smoking *pistola* in the other went out with silent movies and the decline of the narrow gauge steam locomotive. The word *bandido* in Mexico means "thief, criminal, perverse person." Forget the picturesque wide-brimmed hat and crossed bandoliers of ammunition, they're as rare as Indians firing arrows into a circle of motorhomes.

What about *ladrones* and *rateros* (thieves)? Or *mala gente,* 'bad people' as Mexicans refer to general bad-ass types? We have run into a few, as anyone who travels for long periods of time must. Every town, whether in Michigan or Michoacán, has its bad-tempered type, its loudmouth and bully. There are universal rules for handling these characters: stay calm, stay cool and don't stay around any longer than you have to.

Our experience, and that of many friends, has shown that camping in Mexico is at least as safe as camping in the U.S. In fact, we've been hassled a lot more while camping at home by drunken hunters, joy-riding drugstore cowboys and teenage vandals. Mexico can be a violent country but fortunately tourists are rarely involved.

In the many years it has taken to research and write this book, I've asked a number of people "Do you think camping is safe in Mexico for *gringos?*" The answers I got, from archaeologists with years of field experience in remote areas of the country, from cops, *federales,* soldiers, ranchers, guides, tourist officials and other campers were almost unanimously "Yes!" One point was repeatedly made: the people of rural Mexico, *campesinos* and Indians, are basically very honest, hardworking, proud and willing to give visitors more than a fair chance to prove themselves worthy of trust and friendship. And among this nation of Scout-like folks there are the inevitable drunks, petty thieves and malcontents who can so easily give an entire area a bad name. Dealing with this latter group tends to overshadow the good qualities of people you'll meet while camping in Mexico. Paul Theroux wrote, ". . . travel writing is a funny thing . . . the worst trips make the best reading." What better way to get someone's attention, either in a book or sitting around the living room swapping tales, than with some awful horror story? It doesn't matter if you have to exaggerate the drunk into an armed *bandido,* the point is to hold your audience's attention at any cost, even if the cost is truth and accuracy.

It is common to hear urban Mexicans refer to *campesinos* as lawless, rowdy, uncultured, low-class people. This is far from the truth and just an obvious example of the classic distrust between country people and city dwellers. Mexicans are very class conscious and the average middle class Mexican considers camping out to be an insane way to spend a vacation (this attitude is slowly changing, fortunately). They'll warn you of *tigres,* snakes and *mal vientos* (evil winds) and if that doesn't deter you, they'll start on the bandit legends. None of these stories, of course, are based on their own experience; it's all "A friend of my father's said" or "Once upon a time . . ."

Campesinos themselves are also at fault for giving outsiders the impression that the back country can be dangerous. "You mean to tell me you hiked through San Juan without trouble?" a man exclaims, shaking his head in disbelief. (In San Juan they had warned you that here, in San José, everyone was very untrustworthy.) "Well," the man continues, "whatever you do, don't go through San Pablo! Very bad people there!" San Pablo lies across the trail ahead and you must pass through it. When you get there, as usual without trouble, everyone asks, "*¡Caray!* How did you get through San Juan and San José?"

It can make a camper nervous to hear all these sincere warnings. What they don't tell you, however, is that they've been feuding with the neighboring village for fifty years over a minor boundary change or who should get the most water from the irrigation ditch.

One of the greatest mistakes *gringo* campers make when plunging far into Mexico's back country is a failure to realize, in advance, that you are about to be *on your own*. A long and arduous hike into the sierra in Chihuahua might sound fantastically romantic and exciting in the comfort of your living room in Berkeley, but what about when you actually get there and find yourself short on food? Can you handle it? Are you going to be frightened or so irritated and uncomfortable that the experience is ruined? Let's add a few more common camper's problems: a blistered big toe, an inadequate map and an encounter with a surly man who just lost his best cow. Will you turn this into just another day on the trail or a classic horror story?

Gringos are overly sensitive to unfriendly treatment by Mexicans. "Why is that woman rude?" "That man was very uncooperative!" The same people who laugh off an insult from a bus driver at home or a passing obscenity from a cantankerous neighbor will be horrified by anything less than a toothy grin in Mexico.

Rip-offs

Take reasonable precautions while you are camped and chances are you'll never have a problem with thievery. Be especially careful, however, while in the larger cities. Ironically, we've heard of more campers being robbed on their way to Mexico than south of the border. Professional rip-off artists in the U.S. know that a loaded motorhome or van makes a fat target.

Backpackers should keep their gear neatly stowed at all times. We like to keep our things out of sight as much as possible, without being obviously paranoid. "Don't touch that!" isn't the way to deal with a curious visitor. Rural people are very open about handling your things, though they'll often make polite hints before looking at something. Sleeping bags, stoves, lanterns and kitchen gear interest them a great deal. Oblige their curiosity but don't leave things lying around carelessly lest you tempt someone beyond reason to take it with them.

Most rip-offs take place on the beach (or in cities) and are often the direct result of a camper's own laziness and lack of even normal vigilance. It is very common to see excited campers fling their valuables to the sand and run into the surf— only to return ten minutes later to find they've been robbed. Let's face it, the temptation is incredible when a thief or poor person is presented with a golden opportunity to snag a camera or a wallet. If you must leave things, ask someone (in a store, restaurant or another camper) to keep an eye on your stuff.

We always carry our money and important papers inside a 'hidden pocket'. This is the safest method I know to keep such valuables close at hand and out of sight. It takes just a short time to make your own Hidden Pocket and will save you untold hassles and worry. (See *Clothing:* Chapter 9.)

If you are sure that something has been filched, quietly mention it to the local authority. Don't make a loud stink; it will embarrass people horribly and almost insure that your visit will be ruined. Petty thievery is not common but when it happens it's sometimes best to take more precautions rather than demanding 'justice'.

Drunks

There are times when I'd almost prefer to face down a full dress Mexican bandit than another bleary-eyed *borracho*. Drunks, in my opinion, are far more of a hassle to campers than mosquitoes, scorpions or itching sunburns. Dealing with them requires the greatest self-control and patience. A classic confrontation goes like this:

You are hiking in a remote area and are stopped in a village by a drunken man, waving his arms and attempting to tell you something in unintelligible Spanish. Passersby give you both a wide berth or smile knowingly from the sidelines. Your embarrassment and confusion soon become dismay and irritation as the harangue continues. Who is this jerk, anyway? Why not just push him aside and go on your way? Don't; drunks are not treated like bums in the back country and you may be making a serious mistake by being rude, no matter how much *you* feel it's justified. The man may be the mayor or a respected citizen out on a toot. The tolerance of local people toward such drunks is phenomenal; they tend to see it as just a crazy interlude in the often tedious routine of daily life.

Ritual drinking is very common in Indian communities. This custom is depressing to outsiders but you must put up with it. Basically, ritual drinking means that town officials and leading citizens get totally smashed whenever there is an official function, *fiesta* or other excuse for heavy boozing.

To minimize hassles with drunks, never accept an invitation to join them, even if you have to tell a whopper like, "I have no liver." Once you're hooked you won't get away without giving even greater offense. I've gotten myself into some uncomfortable situations because I was afraid to refuse an offer of a drink and ended up in the midst of a *borrachera* (binge).

Women should carefully avoid drinking scenes. It is very unusual for *campesinas* to drink in public (with the occasional exception of *fiestas*) and the sight of a *gringa* hoisting a glass of tequila will be considered scandalous.

If a drunk appears at your camp, hide the booze as fast as you can. Once you break out a bottle your company won't leave until it's finished off. I'd lie and say, "I'm sorry, I have no liquor to offer" rather than deal with a drunk and perhaps my own hangover the next morning.

For more on booze, drunks and Mexican drinking customs see *The People's Guide To Mexico.*

"*¡Toma! ¡Toma!*"

My hand reached for the offered gourd cup; I drank another searing gulp. My head throbbed painfully. How long had this been going on? I groped in a pocket for my watch. Five p.m.!

The cowboy next to me stretched lazily, lying on his back in the warm afternoon sun. His clothes gave off the rich odor of hot leather and wet horse hair. Five o'clock! We'd been sprawled in the middle of the peanut field since dawn, drinking from a dirty plastic jug of local moonshine *mescal,* liberally adulterated with chilis and unknown herbs.

I waved the buzzing green flies from my face and looked at my three companions. They lay around the campfire in the careless postures of the *bien tomado* (well drunk), eyes heavy from lack of sleep. Pistols were stuffed casually inside the waistbands of their pants, two had rifles and all sported wide bladed knives in tooled leather sheaths. Well-honed machetes in saddle scabbards completed their armaments. With sweat-darkened leather chaps, horsehair lariats, hand-stitched saddlebags and rough, well-patched clothing, they were obviously the real thing, cowboys from head to hoof. I wondered once again just what I'd managed to get myself into.

I'd met the cowboys the previous afternoon, my fifth day on the trail. The hike had become a grueling ordeal of deep rocky *barrancas* and arid treeless ridges, about to be complicated by torrential rain. Massive cloud banks piled against the highest peaks, their dark boiling contours highlighted by flashes of lightning. I was 'pouring on the coal,' hoping to find a sheltering tree or overhanging rock, when I'd heard a scramble of hooves on the loose ground behind me. "*¡Apurate! ¡Te vas a bañarte!*" a voice called. Hurry up! You're going to take a bath!

Three horsemen reined in, looking me over with the curious but polite disbelief I'd come to expect in the back country. The curved brown body of a young deer was lashed behind the lead rider's saddle. Fresh blood dripped from wide black nostrils, spattering the rocks at my feet.

"*¡Súbate, hombre! ¡Vamos a la casa!*" (Get up, man! We're going to the house!)

I didn't question the invitation, I handed my backpack to one man and crawled up behind another, precariously straddling the horse's well-defined backbone. I grabbed at the saddle as the horse leaped forward.

It took an hour to reach the house, one of several tucked into the head of a narrow valley, bordered by a sheer mountain on one side and a raging river on the other.

"*Mira,*" the first cowboy said, pointing below us. A group of *campesinos* stood on the near bank of the river, waving their arms and shouting. Across from them, separated by fifty feet of foaming brown water, were two small boys.

"They must have been watching the goats when the river came up," the second cowboy said, quickly assessing the situation. He waved toward the village, to the approaching storm. "It's the *ciclón.* A very late hurricane. This is just the *orilla,* the edge." He looked back at his companions for a moment, then reached for his lariat. "They are trapped over there. There is no place for them to shelter for the night." He began to shake a loop into the lariat.

"*Bajate, por favor.*" I slid to the ground. "See you in a moment!" the first cowboy called, leading his friends quickly down the trail. I picked up my pack and hurried after them.

There were cries of greeting and anxious explanations punctuated by near hysterical wailing from a woman who was probably the boys' mother as the three horsemen reached the group of villagers. I had just made the valley floor when the cowboys abruptly kicked their horses into a fast sprint away from the river.

Suddenly they turned, racing back toward the water with wild yells, a dozen hooves spraying gravel. They hit the river at a full gallop, three abreast, lariats spinning overhead as they urged their mounts into the powerful current.

"¡Madre de Dios!" a voice cried. One of the riders had lost control. He was swept downstream in a wild tangle of flailing arms and legs, the horse's head straining upward, eyeballs crazy with fright. Men rushed waist deep into the cold flood to help the fallen rider. At the same moment the remaining two cowboys' lariats snaked across from midstream, landing in the water at the boys' feet. They dove for the ropes, quickly tightening the loops around their chests. With triumphant yells the cowboys reeled the children in like obedient trout, urging their horses back into the shallows.

A man and woman rushed from the crowd, freed the dripping kids and ran toward the village, both clutching a soggy boy to their chests.

There was no time for congratulations; the storm struck with a roar of wind and water that threatened to raise the adobe roof tiles. I passed my backpack to one of the horsemen and ran behind them to the village.

"Estás en tu casa," the leader of the cowboys said, ducking through a low doorway into a gloomy dirt-floored room. The only light came from a small votive candle and a smoky cook fire on a raised platform of adobe bricks. I was casually introduced to Ramón, father of the rescued boys. His wife gave me a quick glance and turned back to the fire.

"Get out the trago, little brother," the cowboy laughed. "It's going to be a long night!"

"¡Tómate otro! ¡Andele!"

My turn again. The mescal burned into my stomach. Mixing fresh chiles with raw moonshine was definitely a case of adding insult to injury. I belched painfully and passed the gourd to the man on my right. Enrique? Eduardo? Eugenio? It didn't really matter, I'd forgotten their names, just as they'd forgotten mine. To them I was the peregrino, the wanderer in strange lands. They were the Good, the Bad and the Ugly. At least in my imagination; I certainly wasn't drunk enough to call them that to their faces. Trouble was, the Good was also quite ugly and each swallow of mescal made his temper noticeably more bad. His brother had thought it wise to warn me, in fact, that the Good was "muy bravo." 'Very brave' is a Mexican term that can also mean tough, mean, and aggressive. From the cautious look I'd been given by Ramón I gathered that I could take it any or all ways.

I reached into the ashes for a scorched peanut. Earlier they'd scraped together a pile of twigs for a quick fire. The Ugly had dug into the soft, wet earth and pulled out handfuls of fat raw peanuts. Roasting was as simple as tossing them into the flames. I liked that, it had real cowboy style. I wouldn't have been surprised to see Clint Eastwood mosey up.

"How long have you been hairy?"

I raised up on one elbow, leaving daydreams behind.

"What?" I answered, looking across at the Ugly. He had a scar across his face worthy of a million-dollar malpractice suit.

"I said, how long have you been hairy?" There was menace in his voice. The Good and the Bad perked up.

I stroked my beard thoughtfully. "I've had a beard for about ten years," I said. "Why don't you have one?"

"Why?" he persisted, ignoring my attempted diversion, "Why do you have long hair?" I gave this even more thought. I had long hair because I had been too lazy to get my semi-annual haircut. I didn't like my hair long; it just kept growing and growing until one day I'd notice and have it shorn off.

"I forgot to get a haircut," I said. There was a long and meaningful silence. I reached for the *mescal*. I took a long drink. "Many deer around here?" Silence. I took another drink. The Bad got to his feet and walked unsteadily toward his horse. The Good and the Ugly looked at each other. I started to ask another question when I heard a strange swoosh! swoosh! behind me.

"Hey!" I yelled, fighting to free myself as the lasso dropped around my shoulders. A hard jerk pinned my arms to my sides, spilling the *mescal* across my legs. More loops were deftly thrown, firmly and irresistably hog-tying me. *Clint, baby, where are you when I need you?*

The Good and the Ugly whooped joyously, then jumped to their feet and ran to their horses. The Good brought a long narrow machete; the Ugly thrust a small hand mirror in front of my face. "You should see your hair at least once more, *peregrino!*" He laughed, giving my beard a painful tug. I struggled hopelessly against the coarse horsehair rope, my mind racing. The sight of the Good stropping his machete against a flat rock brought a flutter to my guts. Obviously they meant to shave me, right down to my 'chinny chin chin'.

"*¡Un momentito!*" I said, steadying my voice against a nervous tremor. The Bad was standing behind me, absentmindedly running his fingers through my hair. I'd be lucky to get out of this without shaved legs.

"This is a very important moment," I continued, launching into a *mescal*-inspired monologue on the history of my hair, bringing in four years of enforced shaving in the Navy, the long struggle to grow a beard, the cost of brushes and shampoo . . . "And so this moment must be recorded. Somehow we must do that!" One of them held the *mescal* cup to my lips and I drank gratefully.

"How?" the Ugly asked.

"A camera!" I answered. "We need photos. Photos of all of you and me. Photos you can show to your friends." I was blatantly playing on the *campesinos'* love for photographs, especially of themselves.

They looked at each other, smiles growing as they thought of the great picture this would make: the helpless *peregrino* shaved like a cue ball.

"*¡Está bien!*" one said. "Go get your camera." I was quickly freed.

My plan of hiding out in the village was squashed when the Bad mounted his horse. "Don't say anything to anyone," he said, motioning me to walk ahead of him. Escape was impossible. If I made a fuss it would only turn their practical joke into genuine anger and resentment. I walked slowly toward the nearby houses.

Ramón gave me a questioning look as I pulled the camera from my backpack. I answered with a shrug and what I hoped was a martyr's all-forgiving smile. What would Lorena think when I emerged from the mountains, looking like a well-gnawed Yul Brynner?

"Here's your customer!" the Bad laughed, interrupting the Good's intense fine tuning of the razor-edged blade. I thought of three feet of cold steel against my naked face and shuddered. This would make Boot Camp dry shaves look like . . .

Swoosh! Swoosh!

My last hope of a reprieve vanished as the Bad once more roped me with an expert throw. I gritted my teeth against his laughter, determined not to lose my temper. Good clean fun between drinking buddies; that's the way it had to stay. I might look odd for a few months but my hair would grow out again. Eventually.

"Here's the camera," I said, nodding toward my hand. The Good took it curiously, laying aside the wicked blade. It was a Pentax 35mm, single lens reflex. Easy enough to use with a bit of practice. He looked as though it might bite off a finger.

"How do you take a picture?" the Good asked, tentatively thumbing the film advance lever.

"No! Not that, *por favor!*" I said. "That will ruin the film!"

He took my lie seriously. The camera was cupped gingerly in the palms of his hands, like a red-hot potato.

"It is *very complicated*," I said. "You must not turn that but do push *that*," I nodded vaguely. "And then you must turn the other thing and another, move that one and push this . . ."

They looked confused. "Here, let me show you," I said struggling gently toward the camera. The Bad immediately loosened the rope. I couldn't quite raise the camera to my eye. The rope fell from my shoulders. I stepped aside helpfully as the Bad automatically recoiled his lariat.

"I should take the pictures," I said, "or I'm afraid they won't come out." They all nodded agreement, then immediately looked distressed. How could I take my own picture while tied up and being shaved. Impossible, right?

"*Pues,*" I said slowly, knowing this was my only hope, a desperate gamble. "If only *we* were to shave someone else . . ." The words were barely out of my mouth before the Bad's right arm spun the rope again. The Ugly gave a startled curse, dashed nimbly to his horse and hopped into the saddle, just as the lasso snapped around him in a deadly flat loop. The startled horse bolted out from under him, dropping the helpless cowboy onto his back. The air rushed from his lungs in a painful *whoof!* The Ugly was halfway to his knees, clawing at the rope, when his friends fell upon him, trapping him inside a thick wool *sarape*. A few more deft twists of the lariat and he was ready.

"Perfect!" I cried, madly snapping pictures. Like a true photo-journalist, I would only observe, not actually get involved. I got him from the front, snarling at his friends as they pounded their knees with glee; from the back as he hissed curses and threats; from the top as they first scraped the machete over his thickly-forested skull, from below as they pared a week's chin whiskers down to the roots — and then some. I quickly finished the roll but kept snapping like a news photographer at a train wreck. Ten minutes later the Ugly sat as still and hard as stone, eyes staring rigidly ahead. Sad little tufts of hair sprouted from behind his ears and poked from natural dents and hollows in his otherwise naked skull.

The Good suddenly had an inspiration. He dragged a large faded bandana from his back pocket and dipped it into the ever-present cup of *mescal*. "So you will smell like a *catrín* (dude)!" he said, swabbing his victim's painful scrapes and nicks with burning raw alcohol.

The Ugly rose a foot from the ground, howling like a scalded wolf.

"*Está bien,*" the Bad laughed, helping his peeled friend to his feet. "We will just lift him onto his horse and go hunting. Tonight, when he is not so angry, we may let him go free." The Ugly was unceremoniously thrown into the saddle. With final hearty thanks for taking the pictures, the cowboys led their snarling companion into the sunset.

Machismo

Although sophisticated Mexicans publicly deplore *machismo* (manliness, maleness), it still has a strong influence, especially in Mexico's back country. Campers should be aware of how *machismo* works and how best to handle it. Whether you find *machismo* amusing or downright disagreeable, it's best to accept that it won't soon go away. By dealing with *machismo* as objectively as possible, you'll save yourself a great deal of frustration.

The macho code says that any woman on her own is a woman on the loose. This makes camping alone very impractical for women. You'll be constantly visited by local Romeos and leering drunks, and the farther you are from other campers the greater the pressures will be. Violence isn't common but aggressive 'courting' can quickly ruin your vacation.

Camping near other *gringos* or even with them will reduce the attention you get from Mexican men but certainly won't eliminate it. Unless you're an obviously attached woman (and even that doesn't stop all machos), you're fair game.

Don't despair; there are a number of ways to camouflage yourself that will reduce hassles by men. Mexican women have been dealing with *machismo* for centuries and you'll do well to observe them in action.

Be conservative in your dress and hair-style. Bare skin is like waving a red cape in front of a bull. The fairer your complexion and hair, the more attention it will attract. Don't wear shorts while hiking or tops that expose your upper body or back. *Campesinas* go well covered, with a shawl on top of regular clothes.

Roadrunner   *Curasson*

Lorena keeps her hair in braids, pulled to the back of her head or pinned up on top. She wears a scarf to cover her blond hair, especially when first entering a strange town. Loose swinging hair is rarely seen on Mexican women in the country and is commonly associated with younger women on the lookout for a boyfriend.

Wear long pants, preferably loose fitting. Tight pants or blouses, especially those that emphasize the breasts, are going to attract men immediately. White clothing is saved for 'dress up' by Mexican women. Darker solid colors are less noticeable and also more practical for camping and concealing dirt.

When you find yourself alone, either while travelling, strolling through a village or just lazing around camp, do not respond to Mexican men in any way unless you want even more attention soon afterwards. Mexican women avoid eye contact with strange men, rarely answer questions or respond to comments (some get downright lewd) and generally act as though men don't exist. This can be a very difficult attitude for a friendly *gringa* to adopt, but most women soon find it easier than dealing with *machos* day after day.

Watch a Mexican woman walk down the street: The eyes look ahead and a purposeful stride says quite clearly, "I'm going somewhere so don't bother!" A leisurely strolling attitude is about as attractive to machos as a shiny fishing lure tossed in front of a school of hungry mackerel.

Whenever possible, deal with other women rather than men. When we're hiking, for example, Lorena usually does the house-to-house food search, with me in close attendance. Women respond to her much more naturally than to me, a strange bearded man. "A woman's place is in the house" is a rather harsh fact of life, especially in the back country. When visiting with a *campesino* family, for example, Lorena seeks out the women and sits next to them. This not only reduces attention from men but gives the women an opportunity to talk with a foreigner, too.

Machismo is usually just irritating, like a background swarm of mosquitos on a sunny day. At times, however, it can be dangerous, especially if you refuse to recognize an impending crisis. Men should avoid arguments, challenges, insults, taunts, dares and any display of 'courage', even as apparently harmless as arm wrestling. Proving yourself is an important part of a *macho's* self-image. In the same way, never indulge in self-deprecating comments. "I'm not very strong" might be the truth, but a *macho* will see it as a blatant display of personal weakness — and a golden opportunity to demonstrate his own prowess. I avoid discussions of sex, religion, politics and other sensitive topics unless the person I'm talking with is both sober and reasonable. Drunks often find the courage to ask for titillating stories of *gringas'* sex life. I do my best to look offended and embarrassed and maintain a careful silence on the subject. If you're with a woman and make lewd comments about other women, it will be assumed that you don't respect her. Mexican men will then feel less restraint and may move in on her.

Gringas often respond to *machismo* as if it were a personal challenge to their right to freedom of thought and action. This can lead to serious problems. Ironically, men who travel with women can find themselves the unwitting victim of a macho's offended pride.

A group of campers, three men and three women, decided to take a day-long raft trip down a tempting river. Along the way they stopped at a small village for lunch. They found a *tienda* that sold beer and were soon involved with a group of local men who were taking a day off and getting loaded. Everyone was very friendly and in the course of the afternoon, one of the *gringas* found herself in a corner with the neighborhood *macho*.

The *macho's* amusing flirtatious comments weren't quite so funny and quaint after a while, but the *gringa* couldn't seem to get away from him. Finally, when he openly propositioned her, she got up to leave, obviously angry. He grabbed her roughly by the arm and pulled her back down. The husband, finally noticing the situation, jumped across the room. Being slightly drunk himself, he grabbed the fellow and shouted an insult in Spanish. Before the other bystanders could move, the *macho* whipped out a .22 pistol and shot the *gringo* in the leg. If he hadn't been a tourist, a local was said to have joked, the bullet would have probably been in the head.

Everyone in the village was shocked by the violence but they all seemed to find it justified: after all, hadn't the woman led the poor fool on? And how could the local man ignore the *gringo's* 'attack'? The *macho* went to jail for a short spell and the *gringo* spent the last weeks of his vacation in the local hospital.

I once hiked with a young man and woman who had never been to Mexico before, much less dealt with *machismo*. The woman, who I'll call 'Jill,' was not attached to either of us and made the fact quite clear to people we met. I finally asked her to pretend to be with the other guy, if only to avoid the obviously scandalous behavior of a woman travelling with two single men. She went along with this for a while, but soon insisted again on being 'one of the boys'.

Then we made the mistake of joining a group of cowboys for an evening with a jug of *mescal*. Jill drank her share and jokingly fended off the more aggressive of our new friends. The next day as we continued our hike, she lagged behind. Two of the cowboys came up behind, realized she was alone and decided to take advantage of it. Jill let out a bloodcurdling scream, dropped her backpack and ran quickly down the trail. By sheer luck she came into sight of a house before the men could catch her. The cowboys turned and hurried off. After that incident she became my 'sister' and I treated other men with the classic attitude of the over-protective elder brother fending off unwanted suitors.

One of the best safeguards for women is a loud whistle. Lorena carries a whistle with her at all times, and in her hand when walking alone at night.

Don't be discouraged by these stories; *machismo* is more often like the weather . . . you'll learn how to dress for it and deal with it and it soon recedes into the background.

We were awakened in our tent late one night by a strange sound coming over the low moaning of the wind. Angry cries drifted in the air, punctuated by a metallic banging, as if a bucket were being beaten with a broom handle. Occasional dim flashes of light through the trees indicated that someone was approaching our camp. Who could it be? And at this hour of the night, when all respectable and superstitious *campesinos* were safely barricaded inside their houses?

I crawled out of bed and quickly kicked dirt over the coals of our campfire. There seemed little hope that we would be overlooked. A partial moon reflected off the tent, erected almost in the middle of the trail. My instinctive reaction was to hide, but where? The ridge was too steep and confining to make a strategic getaway. Could this be a genuine bandit attack?

"Sounds more like a snipe hunt to me, " Lorena said, pulling on her clothes and wrapping herself in a shawl to ward off the chill.

I wanted to agree but my imagination had taken control: it was a drug-crazed band of Indians bent on exorcising the intruders (us) from sacred ground. We would be dragged off by our hair to . . . no, it was too awful to contemplate. I would have to amaze them with my Bic lighter, convince them we brought only goodwill and gifts of garlic powder, soy sauce and flashlight batteries . . .

We listened intently but the cries and shouts were meaningless.

"Here they come," Lorena nudged me with her elbow, pointing to a break in the dense pine trees a hundred yards away. I saw an odd twinkle of light, followed by a shout of "¡Vapor! ¡Vapor!", a string of curses and a tinny crash. What did he say? Steam? Steam? Before I could puzzle this out a huge knock-kneed burro staggered into view, its ragged dusty coat gleaming an eerie silver in the moonlight. Its head tossed crazily from side to side as the rider, a hunched up old man who looked as eroded and scarred as the mountains themselves, thrashed the beast about the neck and ears with a long crooked stick.

"¡Vapor! ¡Más luz!" the old man cried, delivering a mighty blow between the animal's flopping ears. The burro shook its head and to our amazement a dim light beamed out of its forehead. Another angry shout of "Steam! More light!" and a jab in the neck with the stick intensified the glow.

In our travels in Mexico we have often heard wild tales of mythical creatures: the whistling deer of Quintana Roo that lures hunters to an unknown fate, dwarves that steal naughty children and snakes that fly and grab you by the nose. But this! Nothing had prepared us for a burro that glowed in the dark!

We stood transfixed as the unearthly pair bore down on us. Running, I knew, would do no good. No one escapes the Glowing Burro.

"¡Buenas noches!" a quavery voice called, the greeting punctuated by a final THWACK! of the stick as the burro steered toward us. "Sorry I am so late," the old man added, gingerly easing ancient bones from the crude wood and leather saddle. He hobbled over with his hand extended, eyes glittering brightly in the moonlight. I automatically shook his frail hand.

"Allow me to present my identification, *señor*," he said in a tone of formality tinged with humor. He thrust a small tattered piece of paper into my hand and raised his arm in a sloppy salute. "Just a moment," he added, "and I will bring you the light. Come *Vapor!* Come you grimy son of a . . ." He turned and grabbed "Steam" by the nearest ear, twisting and tugging until the beast relented and took a few steps forward. With no further ado, the old man raised his club and clobbered the burro on the forehead. Each blow brought a tremendous shake and clatter as the animal tried to avoid the stick. Within seconds the light reappeared on its forehead, gradually increasing in intensity, like a weak flashlight beam.

"It's a carbide miner's lantern!" I said to Lorena. The light was lashed onto the burro's head with wire and string. When Steam shook his head to avoid the stick, the motion agitated the carbide and water mixture inside the well dented lantern, producing carbide gas and light.

"My identification?" the old man reminded me, leaning heavily on the burro's neck to direct the light downward.

"It's some sort of ID," I said to Lorena, bending closer to read the faded print. "Zapata? Good lord! This is his ID from Zapata's Army!" The old man grinned triumphantly as I returned the card, replacing it with great care in a handmade leather pouch on his belt. There was only one more mystery to be solved: what did he want with us, late news from Pancho Villa's Army Of The North?

He anticipated my question; reaching for a Revolutionary era blown glass jug that dangled by a thong from the saddle, he smiled and said, "*Amigos,* my neighbors told me that *gringos* passed through today." He paused for a long gurgling swallow before passing the bottle to me, "and I came just as fast as I could. Uiii! You walked farther than I expected! Such energy!" He took a deep breath of air and continued, "I am going to tell you stories of my adventures, all of my many adventures." He watched with an appraising eye as I took a tentative sip. It was homemade *aguardiente,* smooth but very potent. "I have *many* stories," he said, reaching behind the saddle to untie his bedroll, "and I know that you will enjoy them. What else is there," he added, "to do on such a long night as this?"

Unknown Mexico:

Caves

Mexico has an extraordinary number of magnificent caves, with at least a dozen *known* caves more than one thousand feet deep. (Carlsbad Caverns in New Mexico are officially just over one thousand feet deep.) There are literally thousands of unknown and unexplored caves and even those known by local people are seldom investigated for a significant distance. We've often come upon caves while hiking and camping. One of the simplest ways to spot a cave in a dry area is to look for green spots on the sides of cliffs and otherwise bare mountains. Cool moist underground air acts as a water source for hardy plants and trees that grow around the cave entrance.

Caves have great religious and mystical significance and many show evidence of ancient ceremonies. Some, in fact, are still in use. Anyone seen lingering around a cave after dark is almost invariably suspected of dabbling in witchcraft. Caves are also renowned for holding buried treasures and you may be suspected of hunting for gold rather than merely exploring if you spend much time in a cave. Explain what you are up to ("*Paseando, no más.*" Looking around, nothing more.) and never disturb offerings or artifacts you might find in a cave. It is both illegal and stupid, especially if you get caught. *Campesinos* and Indians can be very jealous and protective of a place they consider sacred.

Few Mexican caves are *acondicionado* (fixed up, prepared for tours) and you might be tempted by curiosity to go farther into a *cueva* than you should. Think twice, then a third and fourth time for good measure. Rescue services are very scarce and it could take many days before help arrives, if it does at all.

Should you venture inside, carry at least two good flashlights, spare bulbs and batteries, water, warm clothing and a stout rope. At the first indication of doubt or danger — *stop.* You can always come back later with better equipment and experienced companions and do the exploration safely.

The most commonly used words for caves are *cueva, gruta* (grotto, often extensive), *hollo* or *olla* or *joya* (roughly "hole"), *caverna, pozo* (well) and *sótano* (cave, hole, cellar). The word *mina* (mine) is often applied to caves that have been mined, if only on a very small scale.

Aguascalientes: *Caverna de Tepozán; Cueva de la Barranca; Cueva del Pastor; Gruta de los Murciélagos.*

Campeche: *Gruta de Ixtacumbil-Xunaan,* west of Campeche. *Cueva de Bolonshén:* Located between Campeche and Hopelchén. Like many caves on the Yucatán Peninsula this one contains *cenotes,* deep pools of subterranean water. Be careful: *cenotes* often have sheer walls and are very treacherous.

Chiapas: *Grutas de San Cristóbal* or *de Rancho Nuevo:* South of San Cristóbal de las Casas. "Very beautiful." *Cueva El Chorreadero:* Near Tuxtla Gutiérrez. There is a waterfall of the same name, formed by a subterranean river within the cave. This cave has been explored for about 5 km and is at least 345 meters deep (1,130 feet). *Grutas de Bolantón:* In the *municipio* of Citalá. *Grutas de Cintalapa: Municipio* of Jiquipilas. *Grutas de Jusnajab: Municipio* of Comitán. *Grutas de la Trinitaria:* Near Zapaluta, 18 km southeast of Comitán, *Grutas de El Mormón:* Near Comitán. *Grutas de San Rafael del Arco:* Caves and a natural arch just beyond Lagos de Montebello.

Chihuahua: *Grutas de Chumachi:* In the *municipio* of Bocoyna; extensive cave but difficult access. *Grutas de Coyame:* Near Coyame. *Grutas de Santo Tomás* or *Los Socavones:* Near Ciudad Guerrero. *Grutas del Diablo: Municipio* of López. *Grutas de la Gloria: Municipio* of Jiménez. *Grutas de Santo Domingo:* Very large caves but difficult access. Near Guadalupe and Calvo.

Coahuila: *Cueva de la Candelaria; Cueva de la Paila; Cueva de los Indios. Cueva de los Supremos Poderes:* "The Cave of The Supreme Powers" gives you an idea of just how seriously local people take their caves in Mexico. *Cueva del Agua; Cueva del Macho; Cueva Hundida; Cueva del Coyote; Grutas de las Cuevecillas:* Not fully explored but very large. Near Villa de Arteaga in Cañón de Carbonera. *Grutas de la Sierra; Grutas de la Ventana; Grutas El Caballero.*

Durango: *Grutas de Mapimí:* Not fully explored but "of notable beauty." In the Sierra del Rosario; guides in Vicente Suárez.

Guerrero: *Grutas de Cacahuamilpa:* Mexico's version of the Carlsbad Caverns with lights and tours. Near Alpuyeca. An extensive zone of caves runs from Cruz Grande to Taxco and beyond. *Grutas de Juxtlahuaca:* One of the most extensive caves in Mexico. Guided tours of several hours are available. Near Colotlipa. *Grutas de Pacheco:* Near the Grutas de Cacahuamilpa. *Grutas de Chontalcuatlán:* Close to

Cacahuamilpa, near the end of Barranca de Chontalcuatlán. *Grutas de Acuitlapan:* Near Las Granadas. *Cueva de Oxtotitlán:* Near Chilpa; rock paintings. *Cuevas de Agustín:* Near the Río Amacuzac. *Gruta del Agua:* Near Paxtepec. *El Hoyo:* Near Ayotoxtla. *Cueva de Cualac:* Near Cototolapan. *Grutas de San Miguel Guerrero: Municipio* of Taxco.

Hidalgo: *El Laberinto:* Subterranean river near El Chico National Park. Dangerous without a guide. *Tolantongo:* Caves and hotsprings near Ixmiquilpan.

Jalisco: *Templo de Dios:* Near Ahuijullo.

México: *Gruta de La Estrella:* Subterranean river. Near Tonatico. *Cueva de San Agustín:* More than 612 meters deep.

Nuevo León: *Grutas de García:* A vast cave area with tours. Near Monterrey. *Grutas de Bustamante:* Considered equal or even better than Las Grutas de García but undeveloped and access is difficult. Near Villaldama.

Oaxaca: *Sótano Río Iglesia:* The state of Oaxaca is rich in unexplored caves. This cave is 535 meters deep (1,750 feet). *Cueva de Santa Cruz:* Approximate depth 314 meters.

Puebla: *Grutas de Xonotla* and *Zoquiapan:* Near Cuetzalán.

Querétaro: *Sótano del Barro:* The world's deepest sheer drop inside a cave: more than 1,350 feet, straight down. The total estimated depth is 455 meters (1,500 feet). Don't slip. Located in the Sierra Gorda, *municipio* of Arroyo Seco. Access is difficult. There are many other major caves nearby, including: *Sotanito de Ahuacatlán* (288 meters); *Hoya de La Luz* (190 meters); *Sótano del Puerto de Lobos* (178 meters); *Hoya de las Guaguas* (150 meters). This area of the state is little explored.

San Luis Potosí: *Sótano de las Golondrinas:* This cave has a sheer drop of 376 meters and a total depth of 514 meters (1,686 feet!). It is said that the entire Empire State Building could easily fit inside this awesome shaft. There are many caves in this area. Located near Aquismón. *La Gruta de la Catedral:* This and other nearby caves are not fully explored. Estimated depth: 200 meters. Located in the Sierra de la Equiteraria. *Sótano de la Trinidad:* Information is conflicting on this cave but one source estimates its depth at a staggering 559 meters (1,833 feet), making it one of the world's deepest. Caves in this area of the state are often claimed by neighboring states and there is a great confusion over exact locations and local versus published cave names. *Sótano del Arroyo:* Said to be more than seven kilometers long. *Hoya de las Guaguas:* Depth 422 meters. *Cueva de Tlamaya:* Depth 454 meters. *Sotanito de Ahuacatlán:* Depth 320 meters. *Hoya de Zimapapán:* Depth 320 meters. *Cuevas de Amagol:* Depth 283 meters.

Sinaloa: *Cueva México:* Near Cosalá; access is by foot trail.

Tamaulipas: *Joya de Salas:* This cave illustrates the difficulty of confirming depths. It is reported as 376 meters deep by one source, 272 meters deep by another, and hang on: "more than 1,000 meters" (over 3,000 feet!) by yet another. Located near Gómez Farias; access is difficult. *Sótano de los Pinos:* Located three kilometers east of Joya de Salas. *Sótano de Harrison:* Near El Cielo. *Cuevas del Encino:* Near El Encino.

Veracruz: *Grutas de Naranjal* and *La Santa Escuela:* "Very extensive." Located near Rincón del Mexicano. *Cueva del Águila* or *La Carbonera:* Near Ixhuatlancillo del Borrego.

Yucatán: *Gruta de Calkehtok* or *Calcetok:* Between Maxcanú and Opichén. *Caverna de Loltún:* Near Oxhutzkab. *Cueva de Balankanché:* Near Chichén-Itzá.

Natural Arches

The term *puente de Dios* literally means "Bridge of God" and is a 'Mexicanism' for a natural arch, usually formed by a river or ocean wave action. Arches, like caves, are considered very special places.

Chihuahua: *Basaseachic:* A small graceful arch channels the water flowing over the famous Cascada de Basaseachic. Mexican visitors love to pose for pictures while casually sitting or standing on the arch. One misstep and it's *adiós,* over a thousand feet straight down to the rocks.

Chiapas: *El Arcotete:* An arch almost 100 feet high and 150 feet long; near San Cristóbal de las Casas.

Guanajuato: *Puente de Dios de Bernalejo:* A large and impressive arch reached by a difficult trail from *ranchería* Mesa de Jesús, north of San Luis de la Paz.

Hidalgo: *Puente de Dios Amajac.* Near Amajac on the Río Amajac.

Nuevo León: *Puente de Dios Huasteco:* Near Cañón Huasteco and Monterrey. *Puente de Dios:* Near Galeana.

Puebla: *Puente de Dios:* A river forms a tunnel several hundred feet long very near Molcaxac.

Querétaro: *Puente de Dios:* Near Jalpan.

San Luis Potosí: *Puente de Dios Tamasopo:* The Tamasopo region is famous for its waterfalls, caves, canyons and scenery. *Puente de Dios Santiaguillo:* True arch lovers take note: by rough dirt road go 8 km from Santiaguillo, then 1 km on foot to the shore of the Río Tamuín and fifteen minutes by canoe. Got that?

5. Camping Skills

Have you ever found yourself next to a Model Camper? The type who leaps from the car after a marathon journey, brandishing a foxhole shovel and a machete and who, within an hour of frenzied activity, is relaxing in a perfectly constructed thatch hut, surrounded by ingenious tables, shelves, fireplace and a taut clothesline. In the bushes there's a freshly dug hole for garbage that has a dog-proof lid made of driftwood and fronds; nearby is the outhouse, complete with a 'toilet' of lashed sticks, carefully peeled and of matched sizes. A roll of paper is conveniently at hand, suspended like a Modern Art mobile on an arrangement of twine and twigs.

You quietly survey your camp and feel the rising pressure of envious resentment in your chest. It looks like a capricious tornado has swept through some desolate refugee center. Clothes and bathing suits dangle from scraggly bushes, half of the cookware lies unwashed on the ground, the tent is sagging dangerously and paper plates and rotting orange peels drift underfoot. The Model Camper ignores this pitiful scene and drives another nail into a nifty dishrack. Blood rushes to your face, turning sunburned cheeks an ominous scarlet. You are embarrassed.

"Let's get organized!"

Your friends lie about the camp in various stages of suspended animation, reading dog-eared copies of *Time* Magazine and wondering who will be hungry enough to fix lunch. "Go to hell!" they answer in unison, adding an unnecessary, "Do it yourself!"

Grabbing a foxhole shovel and machete, you plunge into a multitude of wonderful projects, sweating, swearing and slashing under a blazing tropical sun. Several hours later you collapse in a dirty heap in the center of the rejuvenated camp. It is complete.

"Hey!" a friend drawls, wiping his back with your towel after a long relaxing swim, "What do you call that?" He is pointing at the native-style hut, the *tour de force* of all your efforts. He looks as if he may laugh.

"That is our *palapa!* It says so right here," You thrust a sweat and dirt stained copy of this book under his peeling nose.

"Wow, excuse me! I thought maybe it was a duck blind or a tank trap," he laughs, ignoring the blazing light in your red rimmed eyes. "You really get *involved* in camping, don't you?"

A few seconds later, a long animal cry of pain cuts through the warm, early evening air. It is your friend, collapsed in the bottom of the freshly dug garbage pit. He is bleeding slightly from a cut on the knee and makes an interesting whining sound through his nose.

"And that is the garbage pit," you explain quietly. "I suppose you didn't notice the neat lid I made for it out of sticks and fronds that looked almost as natural as the rest of the ground?"

As others gather to haul the poor wretch out of the deep hole you quickly slip behind the hut, ducking a sharp pole that sticks out at eye level. "Maybe it does sag a little," you mutter, propping up the roof with a convenient scrap of board. There is a sudden splintering crash of wood and human bodies. Running around the *palapa*, you almost stumble over two more friends, laughing and giggling as they extricate themselves from a tangle of blankets, boards, sticks and rope.

"What have you done to the table?"

Your friends look very sheepish as they explain that they thought it was a bed and had decided to try it out. "It was a Japanese style dining table," you moan. "It even had bamboo legs that I found on the beach. Look!" and there indeed are several bits and pieces of wood that look like bamboo.

You wander away disconsolately, staring at the ground, when . . ."Arrrggkkk!" You stagger back, clutching your throat, gasping and glaring at the newly strung, cable tight clothesline. In a mad rage your hands grab the machete. Whack! Whack! You turn slowly from side to side, eyes glazed, the long shiny blade flashing signals of mayhem to your friends, the table, the hut and especially the Model Camper. Your companions gape in horror, backing away. Just that morning you'd been happily sucking on a fresh coconut, staring at the ocean and counting waves.

"Hey, there, take it easy," they say softly. "Come have a nice cold beer. Let's talk this over. We can work it out!" They coo gently, motioning to the only aluminum reclining chair. Others are furiously washing dishes, folding clothes and trying to restore order to the demolished table. Everyone is very kind.

Camp Projects

Tools and Materials
Better Huts and Gardens
   plastic strips
   cup hooks
   shelves
   food containers
   bug proofing
   dogs
Mats
Garbage and Litter
Outhouse
Coleman Stoves: Care and
   Maintenance

Adobe
Mud Stove
Adobe Oven
Tin Can Oven
Tin Can Lantern
Table
Bed and Bench
Finding Water
Digging a Well
Conserving Fresh
   Water
Washing Clothes
A Mobile Laundromat

Palm Frond Hut
Palmetto Hut
Tipi *Palapa*
Pitching Tarps and
   Tents
Drip Cooler
Ice Chest
Sleeping Bag Ice
   Chest
Sharpening a machete
Smudge Pots
Hanging a Hammock
Baby-in-a-Box

I've met a number of people who have a love/hate relationship with camping. The thrill of a sunset from a remote mountain top or wave-lapped beach palls before the thought of a night on the ground and the hum of bloodthirsty mosquitoes. These people think of camping as 'roughing it'. When the going gets too tough they retreat to a hotel or return home, saying only half-jokingly, "We have to recover from our vacation". After a few months back at work their memories take on a rosy glow and they find themselves planning another camping trip.

There is a popular myth that good campers were either born that way or had an authentic Mountain Man in the family, training them from the time they were children to face the rigors of outdoor life. Others place their faith in modern technology, as represented by the amazing variety of complex and expensive camping equipment that floods the market. The secret to comfortable and enjoyable camping is not an encyclopedic knowledge of woodcraft and arcane survival skills, nor is it ultra-lightweight tents and portable kitchen sinks. Learning to camp well is as simple as learning to recognize what you need and what you *don't* need. I like a comfortable, insect-free night's sleep; campers who can sleep on sharp rocks are as amazing to me as fakirs snoozing on a bed of sixteen penny nails. My first camp project is therefore a bed of some sort: a place to hang my hammock, a cozy nest of leaves or pine needles, a fresh patch on my air mattress, an improvised cot or a dry area of fluffy sand. Next comes the mosquito netting, chosen according to the type of camping we're doing. We have a mosquito net that fits over the bed in our van, a larger one to hang under a hut roof or between trees and smaller, individual nets for backpacking and boating trips.

The next requirement is food and that means firewood or a good place to set up the stove, a sand-free surface for dishes, utensils and a sharp knife. None of these require special skills or equipment; in fact, almost all of our camping gear can be found in the average house (especially the kitchen and attic) and the local Salvation Army store.

Some of the projects described here, such as the palm frond hut, are quite ambitious. Others are very basic, as simple as digging holes for garbage and an outhouse. These simpler projects will soon become automatic (the first sign of a good camper). Garbage, after all, is inevitable. "Toss it in the bushes," gets it out of your sight, but what about the next camper? A forked stick jammed into the ground next to your cooking fire will keep sand and dust out of cups, spoons and cookpots. Water stored in a cool porous pottery jug or canvas canteen tastes better than water from an overheated plastic bottle. These are simple things that add up to a sense of well-being and satisfaction: in other words, good camping.

Tools and Materials

Having been raised in a tool and machine-oriented culture, we *gringos* often mistakenly think such modern wonders are indispensable. How can you stick two pieces of wood together without a drill, screws and screwdriver? Easy: patiently bore the holes with the tip of a knife or machete (crude, yes, but it does work), drive in a carved wooden plug or lash through the holes with tough strips of bark, vines, twine or wire.

Many of the houses you will see while camping in Mexico are built entirely of native materials, using no other tools than human hands and a machete. Even the holes for upright supports and basic foundations are gouged out of the ground with the blade. If a hand saw is available to cut rough boards from logs, the builder's projects will know no bounds.

It takes more than just a strong arm, however, to be successful with a simple tool like a machete. Experience is hard to beat. For this reason I suggest that you carry a few basic hand tools and simple materials rather than risk frustration and time-consuming mistakes. The following will help a great deal and are not expensive:

Hand saw	Tin snips	Nails
Hammer	Hand drill, bits	Baling wire
Machete (short blade)	File	Twine, rope
Small shovel	Sharpening stone	

If you enjoy camp projects as a pastime, I'd also bring a wood chisel, wood rasp, wood glue, coping saw and wood plane. Now you can whip together anything from a couch to a bamboo hang glider.

When camping from a vehicle I carry a few odd boards, sticks and scraps of light plywood. They can be used for a multitude of projects when other materials aren't available.

One problem with camp projects is materials. In a country where an empty rum bottle isn't considered trash but a useful container, things like boards, old pieces of tin roofing, sticks, bent nails, frayed ropes and other 'junk' have some value and are very difficult to scrounge. Never use materials that have been previously gathered; they belong to someone.

Cutting poles is risky. Even in the most heavily forested areas of Mexico, it is technically illegal to cut a tree without permission from the federal forestry agency. When you can't find the necessary poles by beachcombing, it's best to get local people to cut them for you. (They know how to get away with it and will usually do it for a very modest sum.) It never hurts to take the precaution of asking before you use something. If you're diplomatic enough, you'll probably be given both permission and help.

We once asked the manager of a coconut plantation for permission to camp on his land, going so far as to offer him money for rent. He countered our offer with one even better: if we would agree not to pick green coconuts or cut living palm fronds, he and his workers would build us a house. We said that we only intended to stay for two weeks, but he answered, "It would benefit the *rancho* (meaning the local workers and their families) to have you here as neighbors. And besides, when you leave you could send others to live in the house."

Note: Although Mexican beaches are all legally owned by the federal government, many tourists mistakenly believe that this allows unlimited public use and access. This isn't true: many beaches are leased, controlled by *ejidos* (cooperatives) or managed by a *concesionario* (concessionaire). You may be asked to pay a nominal rent, especially if you're building a lavish camp or hut. If the price isn't reasonable and can't be lowered, it's best to move on rather than hassle over it. Even if you win the battle, you may well spoil things for the next camper who comes along.

Better Huts and Gardens

Living the good life in a thatched hut is the frosting on most camping fantasies; the following suggestions should help you cope with minor hutkeeping chores. Most of the ideas here can also be used or adapted for tenting, camper vehicles, backpacking or even regular houses.

• A fairly effective fly barrier can be made from a sheet of *plástico* (also called *ule,* rubber, and *nilón,* nylon). Clear and colored sheets of plastic are sold in dry goods stores and around the marketplace. Buy one larger than your doorway and cut it into strips that are connected at the top so that it becomes a kind of hula skirt. Make the strips about half an inch wide. Tack this over the doorway (or window holes) and the fluttering strips will keep flies out. If the flies are persistent, put one or more additional 'skirts' over the first.

• Pound nails into stout sticks (not living trees) and hang them around the hut or campsite for pot holders, clothing racks, cups, tools, shoes, wet bathing suits and shopping bags. Hooks can also be bent out of stiff wire (*alambrón*) to hang things from. We carry large cuphooks to screw into convenient rafters and upright posts. Ten minutes work can make hutkeeping much simpler.

• Use small boards, squares of light plywood or pegboard and foot wide pieces of masonite for improvised shelves, tables, cutting boards, counter tops and night stands. Drill holes in the board and tie on loops of elastic cord to make holders for kitchen utensils, sunglasses and other easily misplaced gear.

• Drill two holes in each end of a board and suspend it from a wall, rafter or tree limb to make a shelf. If you don't have a drill, just tie a sturdy loop of twine or wire around the ends of the board and hang it up. Don't use this type of shelf for dangerous things like burning candles or pots of boiling iguana stew; they have an unfortunate tendency to wobble and sway when bumped into.

• Store food in closed containers or in baskets or boxes covered with cloth or mosquito netting. Whenever possible suspend the container by a rope or piece of wire. Soak the rope in kerosene to stop crawling insects. Rat guards can be made by cutting out the ends of a large tin can. Slice from the edge of the tin can end to the center. Slide this over the rope or wire, so that it comes between the unwanted visitor and the basket.

• Lash the ends of three strong sticks together (about three feet long or more) so that they stand as a tripod. Hang a basket, bag or box from the top of the tripod. This makes a great food and utensil 'caddy' for the fireside. Paint the sticks liberally with kerosene (away from the fire) to deter insects.

• We carry a lightweight lawn rake in our van and when other campers see what a ten minute sweeping will do they inevitably want to borrow it. Thorns, broken glass, bottle caps, burrs, cigarette butts and other carelessly strewn but common camp litter is quickly gathered up with the rake. The camp not only looks nicer but is safer for bare feet. A daily raking keeps down flies and other bugs that come to dine on tiny bits of food and garbage.

• A frequent dampening of a hut floor with a sprinkler can (use seawater) keeps bugs and dust down and eventually compacts loose sand.

• Kerosene is widely used in Mexico to repel scorpions. Add one cup of *petróleo* (kerosene) to a bucket of fresh or salt water and sprinkle it liberally in and around — and on — your hut. The smell soon goes away. Paint table and bed legs, rafters and wooden supports with pure kerosene every week or two. Kerosene can also be used in a hand pumped *rociador* (sprayer, flit gun). A *rociador* works nicely on thatched walls and ceilings, but don't get kerosene mist in your eyes or food.

• Place bed and table legs in tin cans half filled with a strong mixture of kerosene and water. This stops crawlers cold.

• Mix sugar and water together and place it in cans or half filled bottles where bugs congregate. They'll crawl in and drown.

• Does the hut have a crudely lettered *CNEP* number daubed on the door or upright post? If so, it's been sprayed by the National Commission to Eradicate *Paludismo* (malaria). This is an admirable and highly effective program; spray teams try to hit every dwelling, no matter how humble, twice a year. Unfortunately they spray with DDT. Don't argue with them; it's useless. Just ask for enough time to move your gear outside and quickly vacate. It takes about twelve to twenty-four hours for the smell to go away. If you leave your things inside (the sprayers insist, of course, that DDT is utterly harmless), they'll be sprayed and temporarily stained with the water and chemical mixture.

• Harden your heart and never allow stray dogs into camp. They always have fleas and once your camp is infested, you'll have a hell of a time getting rid of them (dogs and fleas). The most friendly Mexican stray dog will turn into a ravaging monster the moment you leave camp, devouring everything from the hand soap to your Nescafé. If you weaken and encourage the mutt to come in, the next camper may greet the dog with a boulder or a bullet. Mexicans make short work of camp robbers.

Mats

One of the nicest camp improvements involves nothing more than spreading a few *petates* (woven reed or palm mats) on the ground. We usually put one near the side doors of the van for a doormat and a couple of others to designate the kitchen area.

Petates are sold in markets, in small stores and on the street. There are many types, some extremely well made and decorative, but the most common mat is about the size of a twin bed mattress (which it can be used for) and fairly thick.

If your mat is folded and creased, pour water on it. When the mat is reasonably damp, but not soaked, tramp on it for a few minutes and it should spread out with no creases. We have used the same mats for several months, refolding and reflattening them many times. When you're camped on the beach, mats will stop most of the upward movement of sand, keep it out of food and cameras and allow you to lie down without filling your hair and ears.

Mats make it much easier to keep the kitchen area clean. Spilled food can be swept or washed away rather than soaking into the ground and attracting bugs. Turn the mats occasionally to avoid mildewing, but keep your eyes open for scorpions that may have taken up residence underneath.

Because they are flammable, don't place your mats near a fire.

We once left our most elaborate and ingeniously arranged camp for a few hours and returned to discover a problem of using *petates:* cows. An entire herd had been lurking nearby, just waiting for us to let down our guard before moving in to eat our mats. The effect of twenty cows jostling for a mouthful was catastrophic. Everything, from our fireplace to our beautifully built kitchen table, was crushed and ground under-foot during the banquet.

When your mats are worn out, leave them where someone can find them. As tattered and useless as they appear to you, some poorer person will be able to use them.

Garbage and Litter

Tourists often complain about litter in Mexico, but many of them unknowingly aggravate the problem by improperly disposing of their trash. After a summer storm, for example, an apparently clean beach will suddenly cough up unwanted treasure troves of tin cans, plastic bags, broken glass and buried beer bottles. Whatever the wind and waves don't turn up, dogs and bands of hungry pigs will. Animals aren't discouraged by a few inches of dirt or sand. Dig it deep, then go down another half a foot or more just to be sure. When you fill in a garbage hole, top it off with layers of rocks and clumps of cactus spines or thorn bushes. If possible, dig your garbage hole in the dirt rather than sand.

Most village garbage dumps are just a corner of a field, covered with cans, bottles and drifting plastic bags. This may not be very neat but it's better than having the stuff underfoot. I always make my contribution to the mess after first burning everything flammable. Bottles and cans should be left at the dumping area intact; poor people will forage and recycle them. Rinse them out well if they've held food or anything poisonous.

Mexicans are becoming increasingly conscious of litter but there's no better temporary solution to the problem than picking it up instead of complaining. I've seen a number of camping areas that were all but ruined by litter — and quickly restored by a spontaneous communal effort among both Mexican and foreign campers. On one especially dirty beach, a Mexican businessman who had no intention of spending his vacation picking up garbage solved the problem by hiring a local family to do the job. The idea soon caught on and other campers chipped in, getting the beach clean and providing a welcome income for people who appreciated it.

Outhouse

Choosing a place for an outhouse should be done without delay, especially when you're camped near others or with a group of friends. Get a general agreement on where to dig the hole (consult the neighbors, too) and *dig it deep*. If the sides threaten to cave in, a friend suggests this: cut the top and bottom from three five-gallon metal cans (sold in the marketplace) and stack them on top of each other inside the hole. The top of the highest can be at ground level or even higher. Fit it with a toilet seat or a tightly sealing lid. Sprinkle ashes from your campfire into the hole after each use. Lime is also very effective in reducing odor and flies: it is called *cal* and is sold in hardware stores, some *tiendas* and construction supply outlets. *Cal* is very inexpensive; when combined with the tin can outhouse, you've got cheap health insurance and an excellent way to keep a camping area clean.

When cans aren't available use cardboard boxes, heavy paper, sticks, old mats, cloth or whatever to line the hole. Pound long stakes along the sides of the hole to hold the retaining material in place. Crude but very effective.

We use our outhouse hole to burn trash in; it saves another shoveling session and kills flies.

Coleman Stoves: Care and Maintenance

"Hey buddy, can 'ya spare a cup of white gas?" is a familiar sound to anyone who camps in Mexico for very long. Although Coleman stoves and lanterns are very popular with *gringo* campers in Mexico, *gasolina blanca* is very scarce. The solution to the fuel problem isn't necessarily to carry enough white gas from home to last the entire trip but to use unleaded automobile gasoline (Extra, the silver pump).

"What? Use car gas in my stove? It says on the Coleman can that . . ." Forget it; the main difference between Coleman fuel (white gas) and unleaded gasoline is additives that clog and crud up the stove's generator. (Coleman lanterns don't work as well as stoves on unleaded gas but they will give light.) If you use unleaded gasoline you'll have to clean the generator *regularly* to remove these deposits before they plug things up beyond the point of no return (which takes about 4 to 8 weeks, using the stove every day). We clean our generator every week or two . . . or three or four if it seems to be burning well. Just don't let it get too dirty or you won't be able to get it properly clean again and will have to replace the generator.

Unleaded automobile gasoline burns with a stronger odor than white gas and the flame is often yellowish. Keep the stove's tank well pumped up with air and try to

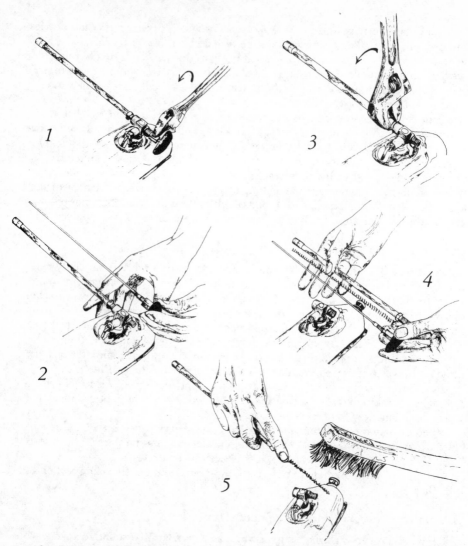

avoid long periods of simmering. If you do use the stove for simmering foods, turn the flame up very high before shutting the stove off. This helps clean out accumulated carbon from the inside of the generator. The more you simmer, the more frequently you'll have to clean the generator. Here's how:

Step 1: Loosen and remove the packing nut located just behind the control knob. Your control knob probably isn't as large as the one shown in the illustration; we broke ours and carved a replacement out of driftwood. Remember: to loosen the nut turn it to the left, counterclockwise.

Step 2: Remove the long skinny 'needle' from inside the generator tube. Be careful; there's a very delicate tip section that is easily damaged. If your generator is hopelessly crudded up, removing the needle may be difficult or even impossible. If it just won't come out you'll have to replace the entire generator assembly. Soaking the generator assembly in solvent might eventually dissolve or loosen the deposits but don't count on it.

Step 3: Loosen the generator tube by turning it to the left, counterclockwise. Use a wrench rather than pliers. Pliers tend to chew up the metal.

Step 4: You've removed the tube, so now shake out the long coiled spring that sits inside. If it's crudded up and won't come out you can drag it out with a hooked wire, needle-nosed pliers or some other improvised device. Once again, if it refuses to come, the generator tube may be beyond cleaning. This is why it is important to do this cleaning procedure frequently, to avoid heavy deposits that literally ruin the generator.

Step 5: The object of this last, crucial step is to remove the crud from the needle and the spring and also from inside the generator tube itself. There are several ways to do this but the important thing is to avoid bending any of the parts (though the spring is relatively tough and flexible) or altering them so that they won't work properly.

I prefer to use a stiff wire brush or very fine sandpaper. Big chunks of crud can be carefully scraped away with a sharp knife but don't cut the metal, especially on the delicate needle. Try laying the needle on a piece of flat smooth wood. This prevents bending.

The method shown in the illustration is also good. After you've removed the generator tube and spring, slip the needle back inside the spring and slip both these back inside the tube. Let a couple of inches of the spring and needle extend out beyond the end of the tube and brush them lightly with the wire brush. Don't bend them! When one section is clean, slip out another inch or so of spring and needle and brush them. This method works best if the parts aren't heavily encrusted and can be cleaned with *light* strokes.

Be patient; if you screw something up here you'll have to throw the old generator away and replace it with a new one — or dig out your firewood saw.

Step 6: This step isn't illustrated here since it's just the other steps in reverse. To reassemble the generator first slide the spring inside the tube. Screw the tube (spring inside) back onto the tank assembly. Get it tight but not ridiculously tight. The tube should screw in most of the way with finger pressure. If it won't go you've probably got the threads crossed. Take it off and try again. Cross threading will really foul things up and may ruin the tank assembly, too.

OK, now slide the needle and control knob *very carefully* back inside the tank and on into the generator tube. The delicate tip of the needle must go inside the spring. Do this gently. If the tip section bends or catches on something, stop — pull the needle out — straighten the tip and try again. These reassembly procedures should go quite smoothly, but if you do it too fast or too stoned, you'll probably regret it.

Tighten the packing nut behind the control knob and you're done.

WARNING: Test your stove after this procedure and if it doesn't work properly, I strongly advise you to replace the generator with a brand-new one. Cleaning the generator can extend its life but when in doubt, don't risk using one that is obviously faulty. These stoves use gasoline and gasoline is just plain dangerous. Faulty generators may gush fuel into the burner or give a very uneven flow of fuel, with dangerous spurts at unexpected settings of the control knob. If your generator acts like this, get rid of it.

Campfires and Firewood

A fireplace — either a circle of rocks or just a shallow hole in the ground — will serve both as a stove and as a means of paper trash disposal. It should be large enough for cooking and for sitting around at night, but not so large that it consumes huge quantities of wood. It is a rule of fireplaces that they are always filled. If you build one with the capacity of a blast furnace, you'll spend your days collecting fuel and your evenings watching it go up in smoke.

Build the fireplace away from the center of the camp; someone will invariably step on a hot coal or a spark will land on a dry mat and lead to excitement. Don't locate it too close to the car or tent, not only to avoid the possibility of a dangerous accident, but to keep the smoke from spoiling someone's peace when they are trying to read and you're heaping green coconut husks on the coals (keeps mosquitoes away).

We all love a good blazing bonfire, but such fires are very wasteful. Do your fertility dancing around a blazing candle and save the wood for cooking. To make small fires appear even larger and give better light, build a reflector of stones behind the fire pit. When it's cold outside we sometimes reflect more light and heat by erecting a wall with a foil-backed blanket or tarp. This is risky, however, since popping coals can burn holes or even ignite the material.

Build a cooking fire no larger than a dinner plate. Feed small pieces of wood into the fire as needed. Give the wood time to burn down to hot coals; most cook fires are built much larger and hotter than needed. Hold your hand palm down over the fire, six inches above the coals. If you can count to three without being burned or starting to scream — but not to four or five — the heat is just right for normal cooking and barbecuing.

Very dense hardwoods are often found in the desert and on the beach. Small pieces will burn for hours, though with little flame. These are perfect for cooking and smoking meat and fish (see Chapter 7). Start your fire with soft wood, stoke it with hard stuff and when cooking is finished, use more soft wood as you need it for heat and light.

A good bed of coals is best for cooking, but doesn't satisfy people who want a fire for rubbing hands over and telling lies about their day's adventures. When cooking in the dark, we sometimes build two fires. The cook fire is kept very small and when it cools down too much I steal a few coals from the other, larger fire.

Douse your fire well, even if there is no obvious fire hazard. You or another traveller will appreciate the few charred sticks that remain. Covering the fire with several inches of sand will usually produce charcoal.

Mexico has a forest fire problem and very little firefighting equipment. Be extremely careful: never build a fire on top of roots or thick ground cover (leaves, pine needles, rotten wood). We once spent half a night digging out a smouldering patch of pine needles and roots that had been ignited by our miniscule cook fire. It also took most of our precious supply of drinking water to finally subdue it.

When in doubt about the fire hazard, don't build a fire. Your noble self-restraint could save others from disaster. *Campesinos* don't have insurance for their trees, houses, crops and livestock. It would be a terrible thing to have on your conscience.

Scorpions love dead wood. Handle it carefully and when a piece is burning, watch for escaping scorpions. Campers are sometimes bitten when they block a fleeing *alacrán*.

Leña (firewood) is sold throughout the country. The price varies considerably with the time of year and availability. A burro load is called a *carga*.

Carbón (charcoal) is unpressed and still in the shape of twigs and branches. It makes an excellent fuel. *Carbón* is sold in and around the market, in small stores or by individuals who make it themselves and pack it into town. When used for barbecuing, *carbón* should not be ignited with gasoline, oil or *petróleo* (kerosene) as they will taint the food with obnoxious fumes and soot.

Charcoal briquets are sold in bags in some large supermarkets. *Carbón* is cheaper and better, though it tends to spark a lot.

Although millions of Mexicans use *leña* and *carbón* for cooking and heating, the source is limited. Don't waste it.

After renting a small beach front *palapa* from a woman, Lorena casually asked, "What do we use for firewood?" The beach had been picked clean of driftwood and we didn't want to cut wood indiscriminately. The landlady shrugged and answered, "Go ask your machete!"

A friend who had a similar problem finding firewood joked, "Fuel doesn't always grow on trees" as he prepared a pungent blaze of dried cow pies.

Corn cobs, corn stalks, dried citrus peels, dead cactus, pine cones, twigs, dried dung (of grass-eating animals), straw and dead grass can all be used for miserly cooking fires. They are especially handy for use in a tin can stove.

Grills

A good fire grill can make the difference between relaxed cooking and fuming tempers. Barbecue grills sold in the U.S. are rarely designed to withstand the weight of anything heavier than a hamburger or wiener. Stewpots and heavy skillets sag toward the coals, waiting until you've turned your back to spill into the fire.

If you can't find a heavy duty grill (oven grills are about the best bet) consider having one made in Mexico. A *parilla* (grill) can be built to order, usually while you wait. Just look for a backyard shop, advertising *soldadura* (welding) and describe or draw what you want. A rough model of light wire or sticks is even better.

Grills of heavy gauge *varilla* (steel reinforcing rod) may sag slightly when used over very hot coals, but they won't burn through in less than several years of hard use. To straighten out a grill, just lay it on a paved or cement surface and run your car over it a few times. Don't use a hammer; it might fracture the welds.

WARNING: never use a refrigerator grill for cooking; some contain dangerous substances that will be released into the air (and your food) when heated.

Tin Can Stove

Gringos call this modern appliance a hobo stove. Mexicans use them when fuel is scarce or an open fire is inconvenient. They can be used, with *great caution*, inside a hut.

The first type of tin can stove is very simple, very cheap to fuel and very messy. Fill a can (soup size to gallon) half full of dirt, sand, sawdust or other material (shredded paper would probably work). To improve the draft and decrease the amount of greasy soot produced, first punch a bunch of holes in the upper half of the can.

Now pour in half a cup of alcohol or kerosene; *not gasoline* — you'll blow yourself right out of camp! Light the stove and start cooking. It helps if you hold the pan about six inches over the can. Never add more fuel until the fire has gone completely out and the can's contents are well cooled or fuel vapor may explode violently.

The second type of tin can stove uses solid fuel and isn't nearly as messy. A one gallon can works very well, but both smaller and larger cans can be used. Mexicans prefer a rectangular five gallon tin can. (Fancier versions of this stove are sold in the market.)

First remove the top. Punch a row of holes around the can, two-thirds of the way up (pencil to thumb-sized, depending on the size of can). If you can't remove the top, ventilate it as best you can to allow the heat and hot air to pass through (like a stove top).

Cut a 4" x 6" hole near the bottom on a side and carefully peel back the tin flap. Crimp, round or file the edges of this opening or you'll cut yourself for sure. Stuff in some firewood, light it and reach for the cooking pots.

Adobe

Adobe is a very versatile building material and great fun to work with. The proper attire for adobe work is a bathing suit.

Take a pile of dirt and form it into a mound with a depression in the center, like a doughnut or volcano. Pour water into the hole and work dirt from the inner edge of the hole into the water. While this mixture is still soupy, add handfuls of dried grass, pieces of shredded dry horse or burro 'cookies', shredded palm fronds or any straw-like material.

Mix in more dirt until the adobe is fairly stiff. Then, if there is still dirt left in the mound, add more water, very sparingly, and mix it all together. The object is to use up all of the dirt without making the adobe too moist.

Test the adobe by forming it into balls and holding them in the palm of your hand for a minute or so. The adobe will lose its shape and ooze between your fingers if too moist. Adobe of the proper consistency is fairly firm — and *almost* crumbly.

It is often best to wait a few days before starting ambitious projects such as huts, mud stoves and ovens. You may find that your camp is also the favorite haunt of a herd of cattle who just happened to be somewhere else when you arrived or the wind may shift and bring back the bugs.

Mud Stove

When you've decided to stop in one place for a fairly long time, you might enjoy building and using a mud stove. It's excellent for cooking as the temperature is easy to control and it conserves firewood. The type described here is much simpler than some I've seen in Mexican homes (which were works of art), but it's quite functional.

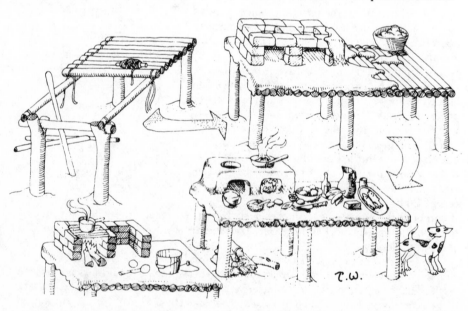

Begin by building a table (see *A Table* later in this chapter) of very sturdy materials. The legs should be a minimum of four inches in diameter and the top sticks a minimum of two inches. A big stove will require a table several feet long, although much of this will be counter space. Long tables should have at least six supporting legs, if not more. A small stove without a counter and just one 'burner' can be as short as two feet. Whatever the size, make it sturdy or you'll have it collapsing on your feet; fire, mud, bricks, sticks, pans and all.

After finishing the supporting table, you're ready to start with the adobe and bricks (rocks can be used but it's more difficult). Cover the top of the table with two or three inches of adobe. While still soft, cover the adobe with a layer of bricks or flat stones (optional). The entire table surface does not have to be plastered or bricked, just the area where the fire will be used. Using adobe, mortar the bricks or stones into the shape of burners.

Fired or unfired adobe bricks can be used. They are inexpensive at a brickyard. Some are huge, some are small, so you will have to figure out how many you need by measuring the table and the bricks. Get plenty; extras can be used for other projects.

The burners can be simple affairs with three sides and a front opening for air and fuel, or they can be carefully built with a round opening at the top that will just fit a pan or piece of pottery cookware. Leave enough table space in front of the fuel opening to catch coals and sparks that would otherwise fall on your feet.

When the stove is finished, you can improve its rough appearance by plastering it with thin mud. Designs can be etched in this surface coating and shells and rocks stuck to it before it dries.

Adobe Oven

The first model of this oven was built near a remote beach in western Mexico, to the great delight and amusement of the local people. They thought it was a grave marker. It eventually collapsed because guests insisted on using it as a seat.

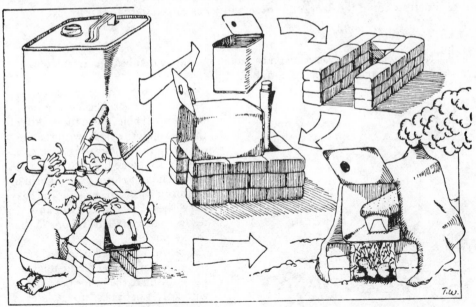

Cut the top of a rectangular five gallon can on three sides and fold the flap back. This is the oven door. File or hammer down any sharp edges. Clean the can thoroughly, especially if it's been used for oil or gasoline.

Now build a U-shaped base for the can, allowing six to eight inches of space for a firebox underneath. (If you have two cans, one can be placed on top of the other and the lower one used as a firebox.) Bricks or rocks can be used for the base, but it's much more difficult to build a firm level support with rocks. Two metal bars or rods (*varilla*) placed across the base structure, one at each end of the can, will make this procedure easier and the oven much sturdier.

Place the can on its side so that the lid opens upward. The open end of the can will be over the open end of the U-shaped base. The rear of the can should be about two or three inches from the back, closed end of the U. This narrow space will be used as a chimney for the firebox.

The chimney is made by wrapping a stick, two or three inches in diameter and two or three feet long, in paper and placing it upright, behind the can in the space provided. The stick should go to the bottom of the firebox and be centered in the opening.

The next step is to insulate the oven. This can be done with bricks or adobe. When adobe is used, it must be placed over a base of rocks or bricks piled around the oven (except, of course, for the front) and up the sides of the can. It takes a lot of adobe to cover the entire thing. Taper the mound of adobe towards the top of the can. When it appears that there's not going to be any major shifting of the adobe, cover the top of the can with a layer about two or three inches thick. Allow an hour or so for the adobe to firm up and then slowly pull out the stick behind the can. It should leave a nice neat chimney hole.

Build a small fire in the firebox and keep it going several hours. This speeds the hardening of the adobe. Without a fire the oven should be hard within a day or two, depending on the air temperature and humidity.

When using the oven, don't build a roaring fire. A small fire will heat surprisingly well without great fluctuations in cooking temperature. Should the fire become too warm, just place something over the chimney hole until it cools down.

Small stones in the floor of the oven will act as a makeshift grate.

Tin Can Oven

This is an excellent variation on the adobe oven, one that has the advantage of weighing very little and being portable.

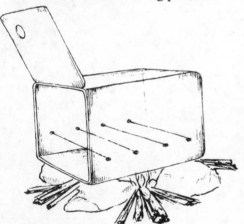

Cut the top of a five gallon can as described in the adobe oven. Punch a row of small holes down the middle of the two opposite sides (with the lid cut along three sides and opening upwards). Run wire between these two rows of holes to form a sort of grill or platform; this is the rack for the baking dishes. You can also wire in a ready-made grill (look for one in the marketplace).

Use the oven directly over a camp stove, bed of coals or on the mud stove. Insulate the inside bottom with a layer of bricks, stones, tiles or even sand. This will act as a heat sink and give a more even temperature. Insulation on the top and sides would be nice, but isn't absolutely necessary.

Tin Can Lantern

I call this ingenious device a *Campesino* Flashlight. It is used by country people throughout Mexico and Guatemala. For nighttime hiking, an activity I definitely don't recommend but sometimes find myself doing for one reason or another, this type of light is indispensable. It may not be as intense as a battery light, but it can be made anywhere and its softer, more diffused beam reduces night blindness. Several lanterns will illuminate an entire campsite or hut. Their rich warm glow is the perfect background to a relaxed evening of fireside stories or mindless wave listening.

The most practical lantern size is a one gallon tin can, though both smaller and larger cans also work. Tin cans are sold in the marketplace, if you can't find any along the highway or in a garbage dump. The large *chile* cans (sometimes called a *banco,* stool, for ribald reasons) are ideal. I personally prefer large Nido cans (powdered milk); they are shinier inside.

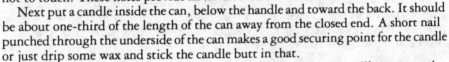

Here's how: remove one end of the can and lay the can on its side. Punch a small hole on the side of the can near each end with a nail or awl. Use a piece of wire to rig a simple handle between the two holes. String won't do; the lantern gets hot and it will burn through.

Now punch several holes around the area of the handle (which is now the top area of the lantern when in use). Don't put too many holes directly under the handle or it may get too hot to touch. These holes provide an air draft for the candle.

Next put a candle inside the can, below the handle and toward the back. It should be about one-third of the length of the can away from the closed end. A short nail punched through the underside of the can makes a good securing point for the candle or just drip some wax and stick the candle butt in that.

Light the candle and see how it burns. If it's too tall the lantern will soot up or the candle may melt itself. Both problems can be cured by using a shorter candle. Enlarging the draft holes may also help, but you run the risk of creating too much air flow and the candle will burn up quickly. Short stubby votive candles (without a glass holder) are excellent, especially in a smaller can.

With a little practice, you'll soon learn how your lantern handles in the wind and the best way to carry it.

If your candle must be pared down, save the extra bits of wax. Melt them down and pour the wax into improvised molds with a wick of string, cotton threads or strips of your most ragged pair of undershorts (if cotton). Molds can be made from foil, paper, cardboard toilet paper rolls, clam and lapa shells, the covers of this book, etc.

Fancier candle lanterns of tin and glass are sold in most Mexican markets. They are cheap, convenient to use and make nice souvenirs.

WARNING: don't leave a candle lantern unattended; it is a fire hazard of the first order! Never use a candle lantern inside a tent!

A Table

This is a very simple table that has the disadvantage of not being very smooth on top so you'll probably curse me when the cooking oil turns over, or worse yet, your beer bottle. Its main advantage is the cost — nothing, and the neat way crumbs, bits of garbage and spilled liquids drop right through the top.

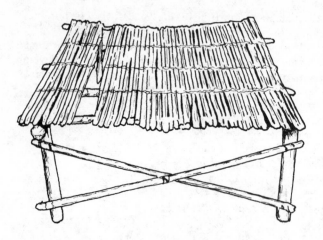

Place four sticks in the ground with forked ends up. (Before you do this, it is wise to investigate the supply of available sticks for the top of the table. You may find that most are very short and the table will have to be narrow.) Use heavy sticks for the legs to insure that it will be stable.

Now lash four more sticks between the forked tops of the legs. If the table is a big one, lash extra sticks at both the top and bottom of the legs and diagonally between them.

To make the top of the table use sticks of as nearly equal diameter as possible or the cleaned center ribs of palm fronds. Lay these sticks or ribs (alternate small and wide ends when using ribs) between the 'rafters' of the table and lash them down.

By frequently coating the legs with kerosene you can prevent ants from climbing onto the table.

Bed and Bench

Build a basic table frame stout enough to support your weight. Instead of sticks, however, use rope or heavy twine for the top. The idea is to stretch and tie the line tight enough to support your body, but not so tight that it won't give a little. Don't worry; unless you're extremely strong, you probably won't be able to overtighten the top.

Run the rope or twine back and forth around the upper sticks, close enough together to give a firm, even surface. When plenty of line is available you'll be able to make a surface that can be used without an additional covering. A *petate,* blanket, tarp, palm fronds, corn husks, banana leaves, burlap sacks or flattened cardboard boxes will fill out a loosely woven top and give extra comfort.

If you're short of rope, tie half a dozen lengths across the width of the frame and another three or four lengths down the length of the frame. This loose webbed pattern isn't as comfortable as the other, but with an additional covering will work quite nicely.

Paint the frame with kerosene to repel scorpions and bedbugs.

Finding Water

Look for signs in town that say *Agua Purificada* or for trucks and hand carts bearing large five gallon glass *garrafones* of purified water. If you want your own *garrafón,* a refundable deposit is required; otherwise, just have them empty the bottles into your containers. If you find the pure water plant they'll probably fill your jugs from a hose. No other water, no matter where it comes from or whomever swears that it is pure, can be trusted absolutely.

Always ask, "*¿Se puede tomar el agua?*" when using water from a tap or hose. If the water cannot be drunk, most people will say so quite emphatically. When in doubt, don't.

Pure ice is sold in supermarkets, liquor stores, *some* factories that make *paletas* (frozen flavored ices) and big ice plants, called *fabricas de hielo. Cubitos* (cubes) are becoming popular but most ice is sold in big blocks. One eighth of a block, an *octavo,* will fill most ice chests. Some ice plants sell it by weight, others by size, others by-guess-and-by-gosh. Friendly beer truck drivers will sell, barter, give away or match coins for ice.

Locating fresh drinking water can be a real problem for hikers and saltwater boaters. The dry season (November to May in most of Mexico) is often truly dry. Small streams evaporate, shallow wells become even shallower and funky, lakes recede, and so on. The mournful song of the Sons of the Pioneers, "All day I faced the barren wastes, without a taste of water," always runs through my head when my canteen gets light.

To avoid serious shortages carry plenty of spare water containers (see Chapter 9) and ask everyone you meet, *"¿Dónde hay agua?"* (Where is there water?) Drinking water is often called *agua dulce,* sweet water. I never pass up the chance to top off my canteens. The stream that someone swears is "just over the mountain," may be a ten-hour hike away, or you may want to camp on top of the mountain rather than go down to the water immediately.

Finding water in the trackless wastes is a desert rat skill I've never acquired. I have to rely on more obvious signs of a waterhole than bowlegged mouse tracks heading northwest on the east side of a sand dune.

Spots of green, no matter how small, in an otherwise dry landscape are indications of moisture, though you may have to dig. At the very least you'll find leaves and green stuff to gnaw on.

When in doubt go down: to the bottom of arroyos, canyons, large cracks, holes, etc. Mine shafts are extremely dangerous (in Mexico many are very old and have no internal supports), but often have trickles of water inside. Don't go in more than a few yards without a rope and a good light.

If a spring is nearby, there'll almost always be a path to it, either a human footpath, livestock or wild animal trail. Watch closely: I've seen small springs in rock cliffs that could easily be missed. Even in remote areas local people enlarge springs and dig water catchments on the sides of mountains. Look for rock walls, mounds of earth and cement work. On one very dry hike we were directed to a *tanque,* a big cement trough stuck to the side of a mountain and filled with green (but delicious) water.

Birds are a good sign of water, especially in the morning and evening when they drink and bathe.

If you find water that is just too awful looking to drink, dig a hole a few feet away and wait for it to fill. The sand and earth between the two holes will filter the larger crud out. (For a compact water purifying unit, see Chapter 9.)

Fresh water that flows into the sea mixes with salt water where the two meet. If the tide is coming in, salt water can spoil the fresh water for several hours. Wait until the tide reverses and the fresh has a good seaward flow. Take your water from the surface; salt water is heavier and sinks toward the bottom. If you can't wait for the tide to change, go further upriver, away from the salt water.

Dig for water near lagoons, estuaries and beaches. The soil between your hole and the salt or brackish water will often filter it enough so it is drinkable.

Don't drink salt water; it will increase your thirst and give you an unforgettable gut ache and case of the trots.

Always purify water from shallow wells, rivers, lagoons, etc. (See Chapter 8.)

Digging a Well

You will rarely live in a place for very long where there is absolutely no fresh water

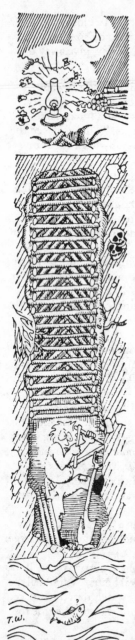

for drinking. It is common, however, not to have enough fresh water for bathing, washing dishes and clothes or other luxury uses.

If the thought of digging a well already has you weak-kneed and sweating, read on before hiding the shovel; my sympathies are with you.

A well that can supply enough water for washing doesn't have to be very deep, at least not if the conditions are right. You will often see shallow pits in dry river beds that have been scraped out by local people searching for water. To do this yourself, just find the lowest point of ground near your camp (preferably in a river bed or near the beach) and start digging.

Water should appear within three or four feet of the surface if there is a fair amount around. The well may take a few days to fill up with enough water to be useful.

After you've found water, improvise some sort of protection from cave-ins. A triangular box is the easiest method. It can be made from driftwood planks or sticks wedged into place. Animals may foul the water by standing in it (or worse). Make a fence around the well or cover it with a thorn bush.

Conserving Fresh Water

When fresh water is scarce, it should be reserved for drinking and cooking. Just as you would not guzzle down a bottle of vintage wine, you shouldn't use fresh water to soak your feet. When you've developed the proper attitude towards fresh water and the habit of not wasting it, you'll be amazed at how far you can stretch a gallon. (See Chapter 7 for using salt water in cooking.)

Washing dishes: When near the beach, scrub dishes thoroughly with sand and rinse them once or twice with salt water. To prevent the build-up of grease, particularly on frying pans, soak all dishes and utensils in boiling hot soapy seawater every couple of days. Grease inevitably leads to diarrhea and upset stomachs.

Before washing greasy things, rub them vigorously with dry table salt. An iron skillet or a water glass will look and feel cleaner than you would have believed possible. After the salt rub, rinse well and wash with soapy water. (The salt technique is particularly valuable when you don't even have seawater to wash dishes in.)

When camped at the beach for a long period, we buy a plastic dishpan and three plastic buckets. After being washed in soapy seawater the dishes are rinsed in each of the buckets (also filled with seawater). The first rinse bucket will quickly get soapy, but the last one should stay clear enough for a good final rinse. A table with a top made of palm fronds is great for drying dishes.

When there is no source of wash water, dishes can be cleaned fairly well in dry sand. Remove all crud from the dishes with a rag or scraper (coconut husks work very well).

Rub with sand until the dishes are as clean as you can get them. Now, if you can afford it, heat a cup of your drinking water. Add a *small* amount of soap — not too much; most people use more soap than is necessary. Wash the dishes well with a rag dipped in the hot soapy water. To rinse, repeat the process with another cup of clear hot water and a clean rag.

Dishes can also be washed and rinsed over a pan to collect water that runs off. This extra bit of water should not be too dirty if you have previously cleaned the dishes with sand and a rag. It can be used again for washing.

After rinsing, wipe the dishes dry, if possible, to remove any soap you might have missed.

Washing Clothes

Many people ask how we get our laundry done while camping. If we stay in one place long enough to get to know the local people, we sometimes find a woman to do our washing. Otherwise we wash them ourselves. After long hours hunched over a rock we have pared our so-called wardrobes to the very minimum. Our method of washing is not the same as that of Mexican women. Instead of rubbing the clothes against themselves, we scrub them with a heavy bristle *cepillo* (brush), available in most stores.

Lay an article of wet clothing on a rock, board, mat or patch of clean dry grass. A rock works fine, but it may cause minor damage to parts of the clothing that are scrubbed against bumps and sharp edges. The mat is best since it's flatter and larger than most rocks and can be moved about. Sprinkle a little powdered soap or liquid detergent on the clothing, flip a handful of water over the soap and start scrubbing. It doesn't take much soap, but it does require a lot of arm work. This method is tedious but practical. It will encourage you to have fewer clothes and will also keep your fingernails clean.

A Mobile Laundromat

This modern camper's appliance can be made from any large closed container with an opening big enough to stuff clothing through. A plastic trash can with a tight fitting lid is the most practical thing to use, but milk cans, metal ammunition boxes or any fairly watertight and water resistant container will do. My brother uses his ice chest: "Let's drink up this beer, Carl, so I can do the laundry."

The only other thing needed is a vehicle, preferably a car or van; carrying a load of wet clothes on the back of a motorcycle is difficult.

The idea is to create washing machine action by the natural bouncing of the car as you drive. If you have a roof rack, the 'washing machine' can be lashed above without worrying about suds and water should it leak. You can use the trunk of a car, but keep the machine away from anything that might be damaged if your clothes are suddenly burped up on a bad bump.

Throw a few items of clothing into the machine (avoid overloading), cover with water and add soap. Secure the container well and forget about it until you stop for the evening. The clothes should be washed reasonably well. You might like to time the rinsing with a stop at a gas station or village communal faucet.

A very crafty way of washing clothes without using your own car is to ask someone camped nearby to take your washing machine with them when they make a side trip. They might think it strange but it beats washing by hand.

This technique also works with tightly sealed plastic bags, though the risks of a puncture are great. To heat the water just fill the bags, add the clothing and soap, and leave in the sun for an hour or two. Works with dishes, too.

If more agitation is needed to get the clothes clean or you don't have access to a car, try this: a five gallon plastic bucket with a tight fitting lid (the type commonly used for food storage) can be converted into a churn-type washing machine. Just drill or cut a hole in the center of the lid large enough to allow the handle of a plumber's helper (plunger) to slide through. Put the lid back on the bucket, with the big rubber end of the plunger inside bucket. Don't forget the dirty laundry, water and soap. Go easy on the soap; you can add more later if you need it.

Fix your gaze on the horizon and begin churning. Up and down. Up and down. Pre-soaking the clothes for half an hour makes the churning process more effective. When your arms are tired, your clothes are clean. Open the lid, dump the soapy water, wring out the garments and add clean rinse water. Repeat the churning and replace the rinse water until clothes are free of soap. If you used too much soap this may take quite a few rinse cycles. Wringing as much water as possible from the clothes betwen cycles will cut down on the amount of rinse water you need.

Washing in Salt Water

"How do you get your clothes so clean in salt water?" many grimy campers have asked us. The answer really isn't too startling: we just pretend it's fresh water and wash our clothes as always. Other than that we wring them out as well as possible to remove what salt water we can. Salt that dries in the clothing will attract moisture, especially on damp mornings. This makes your clothes feel uncomfortable and slightly grubby. The only solution is to do a final rinse in fresh water. Even a very small rinse will remove most of the salt.

When camped near the ocean, we prefer to wear lightweight wash and wear clothes. They are easier to wash, rinse and wring out and are cooler than heavy fabrics such as denim.

If your clothes are wearing out at an alarming rate from primitive washing methods and over-exposure to the sun, dry them in the shade or inside out. The sun's rays are very hard on cloth of all types and most clothes wear out unevenly — from the outside in. Store them inside out, too, to avoid getting them dirty before you've even had a chance to wear them.

Do-It-Yourself Sinks

Your source of water may not be convenient for on-the-spot laundering. Washing out your BVD's in a Pemex station or next to the village communal tap is rather embarassing. Rural water sources such as lakes, springs and streams can be contaminated by detergents and dirty rinse water. To avoid problems of privacy and pollution, use a cheap plastic washtub or make your own. Dig a hole in the ground or scoop a depression in the sand and line it with a sheet of plastic. Fill this 'sink' with water, soap and dirty clothes (or dishes). To be very clever, cover everything with another piece of plastic and let the sun's rays heat the wash water for an hour or so. Another sink can be made nearby for rinsing.

Bathing

Unless you can afford to rent a hotel room just to take a bath, you'll find that keeping clean while travelling is difficult. *Baños Públicos* (public baths) are located near the marketplace, in some gas stations, trailer parks and dirty factory districts. For a very reasonable charge you can have a long shower or both a steam bath (*baño de vapor*) and shower (*baño de regadera*). Soap and towels are extra; bring your own if you wish. Their soap may be very harsh and their towels very tiny.

When travelling, rivers and lakes never seem to show up at the right moment, especially if you enjoy a good wash before going to bed and not just whenever you're lucky enough to find water. If you're travelling in a car, the answer to this problem is to carry your own shower.

A cheap five gallon plastic water jug with a sprinkler head can provide two to four baths per filling, if the water is used sparingly. To make the shower, just remove the cap from the container and plug it with a large cork fitted with a sprinkler head (the type used for watering flowers). This isn't going to be the kind of shower you loll around in, but it will get you clean.

Fill the jug whenever you stop at a gas station. The water will be surprisingly warm within a few hours when lashed to the roof of your car, stored in the trunk or placed in the sun.

To take a shower, have someone stand on something (the car roof) and slowly pour the water over you. Use the 'Navy Shower' technique: just enough water to get wet, just enough soap to get clean and then just enough water to rinse.

Camping outfitters offer a simple and very effective portable shower: it's basically a heavy-duty black plastic water bag with an attached hose. Hang the bag in the sun until the water is hot, then spray yourself with the hand operated nozzle. This type of shower is great for miserly rationing when water is scarce.

The greatest complaint that people make who must wash themselves in salt water is that they feel sticky and greasy afterwards. Hair and beards have the texture of cotton candy and are almost impossible to comb. The solution is to wash yourself with liquid detergent or coconut oil soap (often called 'salt water soap' and sold to yachting types for outrageous prices). Inexpensive bars of coconut oil soap, *jabón de coco*, are sold in grocery stores and drugstores. A rinse with a handkerchief and a cup of fresh water will get the salt off and leave you feeling clean.

When no salt water is available for personal bathing, pretend that you're a greasy skillet (but skip the salt rub) and wash yourself with a cup of water and rinse with another. Believe it or not, it can be done.

Brush your teeth with salt water.

Palm Frond Hut

A *palapa* (hut, also *choza* or *jacal*) is basically a shelter made of sticks and palm fronds (called *palapas*). They are very common on all the coasts of Mexico. Although many *palapas* are torn down when not in use to prevent the theft or natural loss of the poles, you may find one ready built.

Building a hut that will be waterproof and long lasting is not simple. A *palapa* of your own construction will be adequate as a sun and wind shelter, but if you're hoping to live in it for several months, it's quite easy and inexpensive to have a really good one built for you. An experienced hut builder can finish a small one in four or five days. In most cases the only tool he'll use will be his *machete* — even for digging the holes — and all of the materials will be gathered in the surrounding coconut groves or jungle.

If you are building the *palapa* yourself, you should determine its size; spectators and their endless suggestions are to be ignored completely. When they become persistent, go swimming until the heat changes their attitudes.

Begin by finding four sturdy poles about eight feet long and forked on one end. These stout poles are called *horcones*. (Shorter poles can be used but eight feet will give about six foot head room inside.) Dig four holes, two or more feet deep and place the poles in an upright position. If sand threatens to fill the holes, use water to moisten and firm it up as you dig.

The easiest shape to use for a *palapa* is a square. It is even easier if the distance between the poles is the length of your palm fronds. It takes a lot of fronds to cover both roof and walls so keep the size within reason. (*Petates* can also be used if fronds are scarce.)

When the corner posts are in place, find at least four more poles for the roof rafters. These do not have to be forked, but they must be sturdy enough to support the weight of the frond roof, usually considerable. Place the four rafters between the upright corner posts and lash them together. Additional rafters spanning the roof area will help support fronds that are small or broken.

Next locate some coconut palm fronds. WARNING: If you are building a hut from fallen fronds or from materials scrounged from another hut, watch for snakes and scorpions! They like to sit in piles of fronds, leaves and coconut husks and will often be in the walls and roof of old huts. Move heaps of fallen fronds with a stick and don't thrust your hands or feet into these piles. Never carry an old frond (or piece of dry driftwood) on top of your head. A scorpion may pop out and nail you on the nose. When cutting fresh fronds, check first to be sure no snake is resting its weary bones on top.

Dry, rather than green fronds, are best for building as they are lighter and much easier to split. Half fronds are also neater and more efficient than whole ones. Don't try to split them from the large end. Slip the blade of a machete into the thin end and use it to keep the split even and to avoid breaking the frond off short.

Begin roofing by laying the half-fronds at a ninety-degree angle to the roof rafters, overlapping them as closely as you can afford to. The center rib of the frond should be up. In this way each frond acts as a weight for the leaves of the frond beneath it, preventing your *palapa* from looking like a wild head of hair. Alternate large and small ends of the fronds to keep the weight evenly distributed. It is not necessary to lash the fronds down as you do the roofing. However, it's best to determine the direction of the prevailing wind, if there is one, and to begin roofing at the side away from the wind. When it blows hard, the resistance will be less and the weight of the fronds should keep them from blowing away.

During the rainy season sheets of thin plastic (*plástico*), laid under the roof and inside the walls (preferably before placing the fronds) will give reasonably good protection from water.

To make walls, just lash frond halves between the corner posts, starting at the ground. Your *palapa* will look very neat and trim if you overlap the fronds with the loose leafy side facing inward. This works fine for three of the walls but if you'd like a fourth to be covered too, you'll have to allow for a doorway.

A doorway and window can be made by adding two more poles to the framework. This can be done after finishing the roof and three walls.

Plant another upright pole (it doesn't have to be forked but should at least be lashed to the roof rafter) about two and a half feet from any corner post. This is the doorway. You can completely cover the remaining wall space with fronds or leave a long window in the wall by lashing another pole, horizontally, between the door post and the other corner post. (If this crossbar is about waist-high, it can also be used as the main support for a table or counter, inside and outside the *palapa*.) Lash fronds beneath the crossbar from the ground up.

Palmetto Hut

The sturdiest and most attractive huts are not made from coconut palms but from the leaves of the palmetto plant. Houses of this type are very common in Yucatán and Quintana Roo. A properly built house of palmettos will be rainproof and cool inside and should last ten years if there are no hurricanes.

Unfortunately, building one is no easy matter. It takes an experienced person four or five days of really hard labor to finish a very small hut. You can use the technique yourself; it may not be waterproof, but it will be as good as a coconut palm *palapa*.

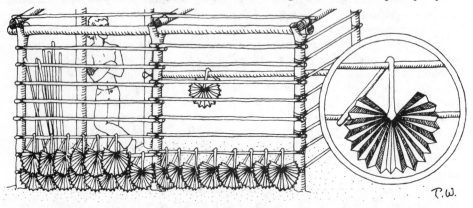

First build a framework of poles like the Palm Frond Hut. However, the rafters must run in the *opposite direction*. When there's a breeze you'll find that the palmettos will blow all over if they are not arranged correctly.

When you have a frame with rafters, lash on more sticks, eight to twelve inches apart, called 'stringers'. These go on at a ninety degree angle to the rafters. They can be very thin, but it's best to use sticks as long and as straight as possible. They should be well lashed to the rafters with string or twine, but to be completely authentic use strips of palmetto leaf. This is very ethnic.

Build a fire and toast the palmetto leaves that you're going to use for lashings. This doesn't take long; about fifteen seconds or so on a side will make splitting them easier. When a palmetto has been toasted, pull it into strips along each rib. If one of these strips is not long enough for a lashing, tie two of them together. This type of lashing can be used for any part of the construction, including larger poles and rafters but remember: a piece of leaf is not a piece of rope; you can't jerk and pull on it too hard or it will break. Use a firm but gentle presure when tightening the strip of leaf around the poles. Tie it off gently with a square knot. The whole thing is going to be pretty flexible when it's finished so you don't have to get everything tight.

Now take your machete and plunge off into the jungle in search of palmettos for thatching. This can be nasty work since hot, humid, bug infested places best support the growth of these plants. When you have located palmettos, cut only large mature leaves; the small ones won't do. Cut the stem at the point where it joins the trunk of the palm. If you do this in one stroke, the leaf will drop to the ground at your feet. And if you cut it properly, the end of the stem will be like a spear point and may stick in your foot, arm or head. Be careful.

Cut until you are ready to collapse; it takes a lot.

After you've staggered back to camp with five or six huge bundles of palmettos, you'll probably have enough to start thatching. It is amazing how humble a hut can become when it's time for the cutting and thatching. People who wanted a house the size of an airplane hangar are suddenly glad to settle for packing crate proportions.

To thatch, bend the stem about four inches from the base of the leaf and slip it between the stringers in such a way that it is hooked over one and prevented from falling out again by another. (See *illustration*.) If the stems are very long and the bodies of the leaves very broad, you could space the stringers farther apart. Start at the lower edge (if the roof is slanted) or at the edge farthest from the prevailing wind.

As the thatching progresses (midst screams and curses), it will be obvious whether or not you're using enough thatching. It takes thousands of palmetto leaves arranged in four tight layers to be really waterproof.

A very real hazard of living in a *palapa* is fire. If your hut is dry, and most of them are like tinder, it will burn to the ground in a matter of *seconds*. Although it's true that many people cook over open fires in palm houses, it takes long experience to develop the necessary sense of caution that prevents disasters.

Candles are particularly hazardous and should never be placed near a wall or where they might fall into the thatching. Never build large campfires upwind of a *palapa* or burn piles of old fronds nearby. When heated to a certain point, dry fronds and palmetto leaves will burst into flame with a sudden, explosive force.

During windstorms, place several heavy poles on the roof to prevent the thatching from flying away. Wet down the sand in and around the *palapa* to keep flying particles out of your food and eyes.

Short coconut fronds or palmetto leaves can be stuck upright in the sand to form windscreens and fences. This is particularly nice around garbage pits and crapping places.

Tipi *Palapa*

Commercial fishermen often build these quick shelters on exposed beaches. The basic hut takes ten minutes to throw together. With the addition of a few supporting poles and more fronds, it would be quite adequate for one or two people to use for an extended time.

Find half a dozen palm fronds and drag them to the building site. Short fronds work fine and long ones can be whacked in half and both pieces used. Long fronds, in fact, are too long: they'll catch the wind and the hut will fall down. Don't expect full headroom. This is a hands-and-knees shelter.

Draw a circle about six feet in diameter in the sand with your big toe. Place the base of three fronds (the wide part where it grows from the palm tree) an equal distance apart around circle. Now stand them up on the thick ends and hold the tops together. Lash them with a hunk of twine or *bejuco* (liana, vine). If your fronds are full and wide you may be finished already. Is there enough shade and privacy inside? If not, add more fronds to the circle until you've got it as tight as you want. The door and windows are just cut out after the tipi is finished.

Because the fronds are 'upside-down', leaves pointing upwards, rain will come in very easily. To beat this, tie on additional layers of fronds to the basic frame, but with the natural direction of the frond leaves pointing *down*.

If fronds are scarce, tie a tarp around the basic frame. Banana leaves, brush and grass can also be used.

Weaving the fronds together makes the tipi both stronger and more attractive.

Pitching tarps and tents

Lorena and I were camped along a sluggish desert river, in a deep narrow canyon a few miles below a large dam. The afternoon was hot and still, the flies rather thick and the beer cold. I remember the cold beer because when the ice chest blew over it dumped the beer, ice and ice water over the *petate* I was dozing on. I woke at the same moment our tarp burst its grommets like an overstrained spinnaker. Within seconds the sleepy canyon was transformed to a wind tunnel, with gusts rocking the van wildly from side to side. Our maps were sucked out through the open driver's window and joined a dust devil pelting us with thorns, gravel, uprooted bushes and fallen leaves.

An incident like this is irritating to a car camper but can be extremely dangerous to a boater or hiker. Lost gear (such as maps) is *gone*.

On another occasion, while kayaking the Sea of Cortez, we were struck by a similar wind in the middle of the night. Fortunately the kayaks were beached and fully loaded or they might literally have blown away. Rocks the size of marbles peppered us steadily and sand immediately filled every available crack and crevice, cup, piece of clothing and sleeping bags.

The following suggestions soon become second nature when erecting a tent or tarp. Lorena and I often take turns setting up our shelter since it's a rare day indeed that we can agree on just exactly how it should be done. Once it's in place we take turns trying it out before moving the gear in. This saves sharp discussions later on, when the cook finds that the blazing afternoon sun makes the kitchen area unbearable.

• Erect your tarp or tent with the unusual and the unexpected in mind. A few extra stakes, a few extra lines or a few minutes selecting a more sheltered site can mean the difference between disaster and just temporary discomfort while riding out a blow.

• Tarps (and some tents) are very effective airfoils: i.e. *wings*. Ours proves this everytime it escapes and goes flapping away. To reduce the airfoil effect or lift caused by air rushing over the tarp, set it up with a broken or irregular surface pattern rather than a flat plane.

• If your tarp is billowing too much and has grommets or tie points in the center, fill a stuff sack, large sock, shopping bag or other container with rocks or sand and 'anchor' the tarp. Should the strain be too great, reduce the weight of the anchor. We've often used several adjustable anchors to restrain a wild tarp. It may look odd to see bulging socks hopping up and down, dangling and bobbing in the breeze, but it is very effective.

• 'Grommetless ties' are indispensable for the complete tarpologist. Here's how they work: lay an egg on a handkerchief. Pick up the ends of the handkerchief (egg inside) and give them a twist. Tie a string around the twist, trapping the egg. The handkerchief represents a corner of the tarp. The string represents the tarp line or grommetless tie. The egg is . . . probably broken by now, but it's the tie anchor — a small rock, ball, wad of dirt, seashell or, my favorite — a peanut. When I take down the tarp, I eat the peanuts.

• Inexpensive line tensioners and adjustors are available in outdoor shops. They are very handy and save a lot of knot tying and line cutting.

• We carry our tarp lines jammed into a stuff sack. When it comes time to pull them out they are a tangled mess. To avoid this, roll them up individually and secure with rubber bands. Confused about which is the three foot line you need to tie off the last corner? Tie a knot for each three feet of length in one end of each line. A twelve footer, for example, would have four knots (each representing three feet), and a six footer, two knots. The knot system makes identification in the dark much easier, too.

• To avoid unnecessary toe stubbing and midnight cursing, bury anchoring stakes and rocks. This increases their effectiveness, too. When using our large tarp (eleven by fourteen) in windy areas, we've often had to resort to a 'deadman'. This is basically a log or large branch, buried as deeply as possible at a right angle to the attached line. It may move a bit under extreme strain, but there's nothing much more secure than this method.

• When fierce winds drive sand under the edge of your tarp, lash it directly to a 'deadman' or to rocks or pegs set in a trench. Now fill the trench, burying the edge of the tarp at least four to six inches. Drifting sand should complete the job.

• Keep a few extra stakes or rocks on hand at night in case one portion of the tarp begins to get out of control or needs further adjustment.

• When anchoring a line to a rock use a big rock, not a small one. There's nothing quite as painful or irritating as being lashed across the shins by a baseball sized stone attached to a wildly flapping tarp.

• When placing a stake in a rock crevice, don't pound it in so far you'll never retrieve it, but also not so loose that it will be shaken out by wild flapping. Pointed stakes flying around on the ends of long lines are dangerous, oversized darts.

• When in doubt about the grip of a stake, place another stake nearby and join the two with a piece of line. Now run another line from the tarp to the line connecting the two stakes.

• Shock absorbers between a tarp and a pegging point prevent tearing and allow the tarp to move with the wind. They are sold in outdoor shops or you can rig your own from steel springs, surgical tubing, pieces of inner tube, bungee cords or whatever.

• When rigging a tarp to poles or sticks that must be set into dirt or sand, use the most flexible rather than the stoutest. I'd rather have a broken pole than a torn tarp if something has to give.

• Take advantage of natural terrain to give additional protection from the sun and wind. Does the afternoon sun scorch one side of an arroyo while the other, just a few yards away, is in cool shade? If so, put your shelter in the shade.

Keep in mind that the sun sets in the west and is hottest in mid to late afternoon. A compass will help you orient yourself.

• The sun's rays are very hard on tent and tarp material. Build a simple *ramada* (palm frond roof) over the tarp or tent. *Ramadas* can also be made of brush; they're not very neat looking but any shade helps. The offensively bright colors of many new tents can be muted with a few palm fronds or corn husks.

If you're using an expensive tent, one that you'd like to have around for years, consider making a 'sun fly' — a protective cover out of flour sacking or *manta* (muslin). A simple square sun shade is inexpensive and will greatly increase the protection from the sun.

• *Lonas* (tarps) are also available throughout Mexico, though the materials used tend to be heavy by backpackers' standards. Tarps are widely used by truckers and having one made to order can solve your shelter problems. Tarp makers can also modify your present tarp or tent: add grommets, tie points, reinforce stitching, etc. (See Chapter 9 for more on tents and tarps.)

Drip Cooler

Don't laugh at this until you've tried it; it really works. Put a thick layer of cloth in the bottom of a basket (one with a handle is best). If you don't have cloth, use your extra clothes, shredded fronds, grass, newspapers or whatever. Soak it well with fresh or salt water. Place whatever you want cooled onto this wet layer and cover it with more wet material. Now hang the basket in the shade, preferably where it will be exposed to wind. Drape another wet cloth over the basket, the thicker the better. Keep the cloth damp and within a few hours the food or beverages will be chilled. They won't be so cold that they make your teeth hurt, but they'll definitely be cooler than the outside air. This type of rustic refrigeration can prevent seafood from spoiling for a full day beyond its normal 'shelf life'.

An even simpler variation is to put whatever you want cooled into a woven plastic, cloth or burlap bag, dip it into water and hang it from something. When it begins to dry out give it another dunk.

Model Campers may prefer to rig a drip bottle over the cooler to provide a slow but steady source of water for evaporation. A plastic sack with a tiny hole also works. To build a luxury model Drip Cooler, replace the basket with a well ventilated box.

Those who doubt the principle of Drip Cooler should try this: dip a T-shirt in warm water and put it on. Now run as fast as you can. The wind you feel against your chest will get colder and colder, even though it may be a hot day. That's the wonder of evaporative cooling.

Ice Chests

What can be done to avoid the dreaded Meltdown of a precious block of ice or bag of ice cubes? Here are several ways to delay the inevitable:
• Some fancy ice chests with hinged lids can be used either lying down or standing up. If possible don't use it in a standing position. Opening the door immediately spills heavier, cold air and greatly speeds up melting. Lay the chest down so the top opens upward.
• Don't drain off melted ice water until it threatens to submerge the butter; it is keeping things cold too.
• Precool things before putting them in the ice chest. A bottle of beer or a watermelon, for example, will be much cooler in the morning or after a few hours in the Drip Cooler. Think of food and drinks as lumps of heat.
• Keep your ice chest shaded at all times. We wrap ours in a sleeping bag or cover it with a foil-backed blanket. If your chest doesn't have a tightly securing lid, keep something heavy on top. Make sure the lid seals well and if it doesn't, use a plastic sack for a gasket.
• Put ice cubes in a plastic bag and keep it tightly sealed. This slows melting and protects the cubes from dirty water or unwashed food. By wiping off bottles and purifying food before storing them in the ice chest, you'll reduce messes and health hazards.
• Bury your ice chest, even if it's only a few inches into the sand or dirt. The deeper you go, the longer the ice will last. A chest kept buried to the lid, in the shade and with additional insulation over the top (blankets, sleeping bag, *petates*, palm fronds, etc.), will keep ice up to three times longer.

Sleeping Bag Ice Chest

What do you do when a friendly beer truck driver hands you a dripping forty pound mini iceberg and your backpack doesn't include an ice chest? An improvised ice chest can actually keep ice longer than a cheap styrofoam one. The only problem is that someone has to donate their sleeping bag (although a jacket works, too) and run the risk of having it get a little damp.

Put a block of ice or bag of cubes into at least one and preferable two heavy-duty plastic bags. If bags aren't available, a large sheet of plastic can be used. Just be sure it's large enough to wrap around everything without dribbling out the sides.

Spread out your sleeping bag and place the ice bag in the center. Wrap the sleeping bag snugly around the ice bag. If you're using a jacket zip it up, turn it upside-down, slide the ice bag inside and tie the jacket arms together.

A foil-backed blanket can also be wrapped around the ice bag before it is placed in the sleeping bag or jacket. Put the foil side facing in toward the ice.

We've used this type of cooler with great success while staying in hotels, on the beach and camping from a small car. The 'cooler' can also be partially buried for additional insulation. Lay a sheet of plastic in the hole before spreading the sleeping bag to protect it from dirt. The person who donates the sleeping bag is always given the first and last cold beers.

Sharpening a Machete

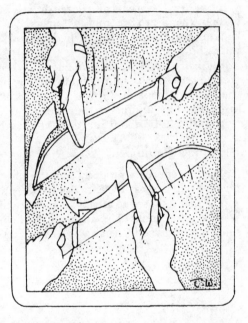

The usual temptation is to buy the biggest, heaviest, nastiest looking blade there is in the market. This is a real mistake; those without long experience of handling a machete often injure themselves seriously with these wicked knives. Unusually long machetes and those with unusual shapes are designed for specific uses — cutting sugar cane, husking coconuts, clearing brush, etc. The camper who buys one of these special-use machetes increases the chances of an unfortunate accident. For general camp use — cutting poles, firewood, opening coconuts — the most practical type of machete is short with a broad blade and not razor sharp. Machetes, especially long ones, have the nasty habit of richocheting when you least expect it. A very sharp blade is not essential for the use it will be put to while camping.

New machetes are as dull as butter knives. By far the easiest way to sharpen them is to have it done by a metal shop or wandering knife sharpener. He can put a good edge on it in just a few minutes.

To do it yourself, a file will be needed and a six-pack of beer or a fat joint. It is a long laborious process.

Brace the machete against something solid with the edge of the blade toward you. Hold the file at a low angle to the blade and run it in long even strokes from the handle to the tip. Do this three or four times and then turn the machete over. Now repeat the same number of strokes, running the file from the *tip toward the handle.* You should always be filing toward the blade, a slightly risky motion but necessary for a good clean edge. Keep the strokes even in pressure and number on each side to avoid a lopsided or wavy edge.

Once you've got the edge to the point where it might just cut something, you are ready for the sharpening stone. I use a regular carborundum machete stone, the type sold in every market and hardware store. (See *illustration.*)

Pour a shot of cooking oil, beer or water on the stone and drip the excess onto the blade. Smear it around on both. Hold the machete as you did while filing and repeat the same motions with the stone. Always keep the stone at a very low angle to the blade. When the beer runs out, it's time to quit.

Work the machete over with the stone every time you use it and it will never degenerate to the point where it must be refiled. When the blade gets black from oxidation, slice a lime in half and rub it vigorously over the metal. Before the juice dries, wipe it off with a rag.

Smudge Pots

Smoke definitely repels mosquitoes and nothing makes smoke like coconut husks, green or dried. Gather half a dozen dried husks (be careful of scorpions hiding inside), and put them into fireproof containers. Tin cans work very well or use a discarded cooking pot, fry pan or improvised foil bowl. Our favorite is a hanging pottery flower pot or bowl.

Put half a husk in each container and then add a few hot coals. If you don't have coals give the husk a squirt of kerosene and light it. When it's burning well, snuff out the flames. Smoke should pour out: thick, smelly, choking clouds that will drive visitors and mosquitoes to the edge of your camp.

If the husks burn too fast, dampen them with seawater.

Hanging a Hammock

The procedure for properly hanging a hammock is simple, but even a simple mistake will destroy the entire purpose — to have a comfortable bed.

The method used to attach the ropes to the ends of the hammock is important. S-shaped iron hooks are available in the market, but if you don't have them use a short piece of wood (see *drawing*). When ropes are tied directly to the ends of the

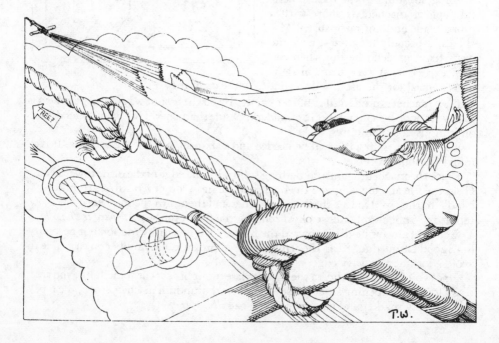

hammock the knots soon become too tight to untie and may chafe through the end of the hammock after long use.

The hammock should be tied so that it hangs symmetrically; that is, both ends should be the same distance from the ground and tied with equal lengths of rope. The middle of the hammock should be lower than the ends but not so low that your chin touches your knees when you lie in it. The worst mistake is to hang a hammock too low. It takes only a few scrapes against the ground to weaken or break the strings, even on a new hammock.

Once the hammock is hanging properly, you shouldn't pile in and lie any old way you want. There is a proper position for the body. Lie at a thirty to forty-five degree angle to the long axis of the hammock. This prevents the hammock from sagging and stretching and gives your body the type of support needed for comfortable sleeping. Don't let your friends violate this rule, either, or you'll soon find that your hammock has stretched and isn't as comfortable as it should be.

Sleeping in a hammock, particularly outdoors, is wonderful. Lie with a blanket underneath you, especially if there's a breeze. Mosquitoes enjoy a rear attack but a blanket will stop them.

Getting into the hammock and keeping covered up with a blanket at the same time can be a real trick. First of all, put a blanket cape-like over your back, allowing enough length so that your feet will be covered when you get in. Clutching another blanket to your chest like a parachute, back slowly into the hammock until it's safe to fall backwards. If you haven't opened the hammock far enough you will do a neat back flip — to the great delight of anyone nearby. Once inside, form the blankets into a cocoon. If another person is getting in, the procedure is the same except that the second person just drops in next to the first without being wrapped in a blanket.

Before doubling or coupling in a hammock, check it to insure that the ropes and whatever it's tied to will take the strain. If you're in a crude *palapa* (at least one built from my instructions), this is especially important. The posts, if not properly placed, will be pulled together by your weight and could knock you silly.

Baby-In-A-Box

In areas where scorpions are hazardous to small children and babies, Mexicans suspend their youngest from mesh-bottomed wooden boxes. This basic cradle can be hung from a tree or rafter. The bottom is covered with a rag or blanket and at night the top is draped with a square of mosquito netting.

Larger children aren't so easy to get off the ground but it can be done. Carry a playpen and either set it on blocks of wood soaked in kerosene (to stop crawling insects) or hang it from the rafters of a *palapa*. An overhead tarp protects the child from scorpions that may drop out of the fronds.

Hanging seats that allow the baby to sit upright will also let them see what's going on, eat, play, gurgle, etc.

Mosquito Nets

When the Devil invented the mosquito, God came up with mosquito netting, properly named by Mexicans *manta del cielo* (heavenly blanket, also *mosquitero, tela mosquitera*). For those who rate chemical insect repellents only slightly above the insects themselves, mosquito netting is truly a godsend. It is inexpensive (especially in Mexico), easy to rig in a variety of ways and provides almost total protection from bugs when kept in good condition and properly hung.

We prefer the loose, gauze-like *manta del cielo* over synthetic mosquito netting for

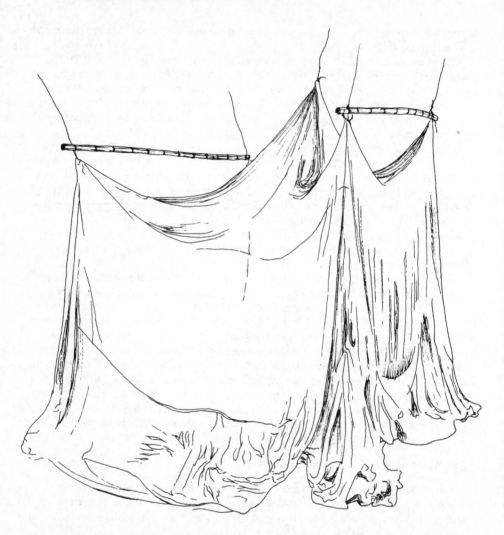

several reasons: it's cheaper, very lightweight, easy to do emergency repairs with thread (or even rubber bands, tape, paper clips or string), compresses into a very small soft bundle and is so flexible that it drapes over irregular surfaces without providing entry to furious mosquitoes. Mexican netting is sold by the meter and can be quickly sewn into a small or large net (go to a *sastre* or *sastrería,* tailor, seamstress or tailor shop).

Our largest netting, called a *pabellón* (pavilion) is a huge rectangle of almost fifty square meters of material. It cost about fifteen dollars to make and has saved us many times that in repellents, not to mention the comfort provided. With our *pabellón* we can sleep without blankets in hot weather or read and play cards (sitting up) when the bugs attack.

Backpackers can carry smaller nets. It doesn't have to be large to protect your face and upper body, but when in doubt, make it bigger; you can always trim it down later.

Sew on squares of light cloth or strips of cloth to use as tie points. Grommetless ties (see *Tarps and Tents* in this chapter) will also support a mosquito net, but the loose weave tends to wear and break after long use, especially if it's windy.

Extra material allows the net to be draped in loose folds rather than stretched tight. Your foot, elbow or head will burst the netting if there's not enough slack. We tie large rubber bands between the netting and the supporting lines or sticks to act as shock absorbers. Light thread works too; it breaks under strain and saves the net from tearing.

Store the netting in a stuff sack. If it's attached to a framework, just stuff as much net in the bag as you can during the day and let the bag hang until you need it at night.

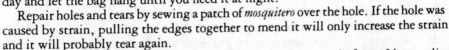

Repair holes and tears by sewing a patch of *mosquitero* over the hole. If the hole was caused by strain, pulling the edges together to mend it will only increase the strain and it will probably tear again.

Lower the net before you need it, not after the bugs are out in force. I love to lie naked in bed, listening to the hungry buggers beating their stingers against the material.

Nets can be suspended from roof rafters, tent poles, a bamboo or stick frame, lines tied between trees, branches or a tripod of sticks set over your sleeping space. A stick will stretch the netting to give more room: tie it either inside or outside of the net. Two sticks lashed to form an X or 'cross' will give even more room inside. Or form a big circle of wire and drape your net over it like an embroidery hoop. Mosquito nets, like tarps, are very versatile.

Ready-made mosquito nets for hammocks are sold in the Yucatán (they're called *pabellón*, too), but you can easily make your own. Sew a large box, long and high enough to cover the length of the hammock and deep enough to reach the ground, and suspend it over the hammock. Hem a hole in each end of the netting for the ends of the hammock. It helps keep mosquitoes out if you put a drawstring in these holes, with strings long enough to pull tight after you've climbed in the hammock. Tie a short stick across each end of the netting to cover the hammock when occupied. Now rig a tarp overhead for sun and rain protection and you've got a real explorer's jungle hammock. I once met a fellow who lived in a hammock for six months. It literally held all of his gear; at night he just crawled in and rearranged things to give enough sleeping room.

WARNING: a mosquito net is highly flammable. Don't use candles inside one or drape it too near open flames or spitting fires. When they burn, they burn like roman candles.

Stuck Again?

Don't pass over this section just because you've traded your Hudson Hornet for a pair of hiking boots and a backpack; one of these days you'll be asked to help a driver who doesn't know how to get a vehicle out of a sandtrap or mudhole.

The following suggestions can be used one at a time or all together. I prefer the full scale approach; in the long run it saves time and energy and avoids worsening the situation by frustrating failures which tend to soften the ground.

Start by straightening the vehicle's wheels. Keep them straight throughout the entire rescue operation.

Clear any obstructions from in front and in back of all four tires and from under the frame. If one or more tires are in a hole, jack the vehicle up. I always carry a jack pad, a thick square of tough plywood for jacking on soft sand and mud. Rocks make lousy jack pads; they're slippery and therefore very dangerous. When the tire is out of the hole slip a bunch of rocks beneath it. Enlarge the hole if necessary before filling it with stones, especially in very loose soil. Branches, grass, fronds, brush, boards, floormats and pieces of your nice carpet will also give better traction. In a pinch, use blankets.

Be careful while working under a raised vehicle. Jacks usually fail when someone is under them.

When the vehicle is back down on all fours, release air in the tires to about ten pounds pressure (almost flat). This is too little pressure to drive on, so I hope you didn't forget the tire pump.

Now unload passengers and cargo. This is optional, since in some cases the weight increases traction (especially uphill). I'd give a first try at getting unstuck with the extra weight and then jettison the baggage if it doesn't work.

If you've got a tow chain or heavy rope and another vehicle, connect them (bumper to bumper or frame to frame; not to the tie rods: they bend like pretzels). If the nearest solid ground is ahead of you, the first move will be forward, in second gear (or Drive for automatics). This strains the poor engine, but helps prevent over-revving and tire spinning. Tire spinning will get you nowhere. Ease your foot off the clutch and gently press down on the gas. Don't look back; your friends should keep pushing and screaming until you've definitely reached solid ground.

Didn't make it? Try rocking the vehicle back-and-forth by alternately shifting into first and reverse. The idea is to get a rhythm going, assisted by the weight of the vehicle, that will swing you free (forward or backward; at this point either way out is better than staying stuck). A friend at each end can help a great deal.

No luck? Look for large and strong levers, something the size of a fencepost. Have your friends use them under the frame and/or bumper (VW bumpers tend to fall off at this point) as you move the vehicle forward or backward. Don't rock it; you'll hurt the people with the pry bars.

Still can't get out? Turn to the *Appendices* and study some Spanish. You're going to have to wait for more help.

6. Fishing, Diving & Foraging

There is something deeply satisfying about eating food that you foraged yourself. The flavor is better, the aroma more tantalizing and the nutritional value at least seems superior to any other food you've eaten.

We've found that it is possible, at least along the coasts of Mexico, to live almost completely independent of stores by catching seafood and eating only locally grown fruits and vegetables. The amount of money saved is considerable.

Scrounging your own food requires only time and a great deal of imagination. *Keep your equipment simple;* the initial cost and upkeep will be less and it will be easier and more satisfying to use than lavish, complicated gear. (See the discussion of equipment later this chapter.)

Going out on your own for fish or coconuts can be quite productive, but a little help will go a long way. There may be types of food in the area that you'd never find on your own. One of the tastiest fruits I've eaten was pointed out to me by a little kid who extracted it from the center of a strange cactus-like plant. At the time, we were living on fish, beans and coconuts and the new fruit was a very welcome addition to our diet.

Local knowledge has its drawbacks, however. The advice you get is often based on superstitions, misconceptions and just plain ignorance. A man once asked me if I'd like to collect oysters. Naturally, I accepted. As we were prying them loose from the rocks, I noticed there were two distinct types: one large and easily removed, the other small and very difficult to pry loose. When I asked about this, he told me very seriously that the small oysters were 'bad' and not to collect them.

A few days later, I returned to the same place and gathered a few of the smaller 'bad' oysters. We ate them and they tasted good. I questioned several people and got the same responses, from "not very good" to "poisonous". Finally a young Mexican diver told me that because the small oysters were harder to pry loose and also tedious to clean, no one ever ate them.

A small village on the Carribbean suffers from ignorance of this sort in a more extreme form. Although the town is just a short walk from the sea, many of the women have never seen it. Everyone there loves to eat fish but they rarely do, even though the water is teeming with them and they are easy to catch. I asked various people why they didn't fish more often, particularly because they had been complaining about a lack of meat. One man summed up the problem when he said the people in the village 'knew' the land and the forest but they did not know the sea and distrusted it.

What can you do if someone tells you that something is poisonous or inedible and you don't believe them? Eat it in small amounts or invite someone to dinner and don't tell them it's an experiment. A safer method is to ask as many different people as you can whether or not something is good to eat. If everyone says "don't," then don't.

Sometimes tasting even small amounts can backfire; a friend invited us to share a dish of string beans cooked with what she described as 'wild squash'. One bite had us running for the bushes. It was *calabaza hedionda* (stinking squash, *Apodanthera undulata*), a wild gourd that is used by Mexicans to repel bedbugs. Mash it up and smear it on the bedframe; the smell will even repel unwelcome two-legged visitors.

Conservation and Self Control

It can't be news to anyone by now that the world's resources are limited. Almost everyone can remember a time, often not long past, when something that is now scarce was very abundant. Oil is the most obvious example, but forests, river systems and even entire oceans are now threatened with pollution, extinction or slow death. Dramatic stuff, so dramatic and difficult to imagine, in fact, that when you slide into the water with your speargun and kill some harmless reef fish or knock off a souvenir chunk of coral, you can't imagine that such a minor event has any real impact. It does make a difference, however, especially when hundreds of people a year do the same thing in the same place.

When foraging for food, please keep in mind that the pleasure you receive may not be available to others (or yourself) in the future unless you use great self restraint. On one of our favorite beaches in Mexico, a small coral reef has formed in a sheltered corner of a bay. The reef is in shallow water and easily accessible to waders and novice divers. Hardly a day goes by when some eager tourist doesn't say, "I'm going to try out my new spear," or "Let's go get a hunk of coral". The result: there are now few reef fish over two inches in length and the beautiful coral formations look as gnawed and chipped as an Aztec ruin. If it could be fenced off, it would still take hundreds of years to revive; as it now goes, the reef will never recover.

Although Mexican law prohibits or restricts the taking of coral, oysters, lobster, cabrilla (a very tasty reef fish), turtles, abalone and other sealife (see Chapter 11), enforcement is almost impossible. I've witnessed wholesale turtle slaughters within a few miles of a major tourist town (killed for the tourist market, especially Mexican seafood lovers). I've seen Mexican commercial fishermen dump hundreds of pounds of dead and dying fish into the sea because they'd caught more than their boat could hold. And so on . . . We've all seen the waste and more than a few of us have participated in it at one time or another.

Now is the time to stop: take only what you need, not what you *want*. Don't wait for someone else to set a good example. Take the initiative and be the good example yourself. When friends come back with a hundred pounds of fish in the boat and say, "What shall we do with these?" let them know just how wasteful they're being rather than running for the camera.

This book includes advice on gathering seafood that is protected by Mexican law. I know, however, that when faced with an oyster-covered rock few people will be able to resist the temptation to take "just enough for dinner". The decision is really up to you. But if you do weaken, please don't break down entirely and go hog wild. If everyone uses reasonable restraint the problem of shortages might even go away. Let's hope so.

Fishing

Gear

Fishing is probably the most practical method of supplementing your food supply. The basic equipment is cheap, easy to obtain and not difficult to use. All you need is a length of monofilament line, a sinker, a hook and something to wind the line onto — a thick stick, discarded bleach bottle or tin can. Wire leader is advisable but not always necessary. When you hook a monster fish, a glove will protect your hand from line cuts, a very real hazard.

Although the simplicity and cost of a handline are quite attractive, those of us who write down 'Fishing' under Religious Preference on application forms are compelled to own more lavish gear. I have four fishing outfits myself, though I rarely carry all of them on the same trip. The first is the handline, which I use when going very light. It fits into a pack or knapsack. If it doesn't get used for fishing I generally rob short lengths of the monofilament for camp projects. I also carry my handline in my gear bag (just a gunny sack) when skin diving from a boat. I picked up this habit from Mexican divers who invariably troll to and from the diving ground.

The second outfit is an ultralight backpacking rod and reel. This gear is so light that it probably should not be used in the ocean, but I do anyway, which is why the rod is missing the delicate tip

Snook   *Robalo*

section and the reel's drag mechanism doesn't always work. I was cautiously fishing in the surf when a small roosterfish (five pounds or so) slammed my lure halfway across the bay. I now reserve this rod and reel for fresh water, though judging from the size of bass commonly taken in Mexican lakes, I'll probably overstrain it there, too, one of these days.

My all time favorite outfit is a Mitchell Garcia 300 reel my parents bought for me about twenty years ago and a fairly stiff and fairly worn out seven-foot spinning rod. I crowd twelve-pound test line on the spool for salt water and pray the fish will turn before the line runs out. The rod just manages to fling bait and jigs into the surf and is the bare minimum for most trolling. A larger spinning reel and longer rod would be ideal for surf fishing and trolling for fish over ten pounds.

My fourth set up is a Hemingway Macho Special — a large conventional reel with star drag and a short stout trolling rod. It cost me a total of thirty dollars in a flea market. I occasionally use it instead of a handline when someone offers to take me fishing. It doesn't work that much better but sharpens my image as a fisherman. This rod and reel is just one of a series of similar secondhand marvels, which I usually trade off or give away at the end of a trip.

Unless you plan to go for big sport fish, the Mitchell 300 spinning reel or equivalent is the most versatile. These reels are often featured in sales and package rod and reel offers. You don't need an expensive rod to go with the reel, but don't skimp on the line; ask someone knowledgeable (the clerk in a fishing tackle shop) for the name of a good quality line. Get enough to fill your reel at least twice and more if you expect to fish for longer than a few days. Salt water fish have sharp teeth and even a good line begins to lose its elasticity with hard use.

Bait

Finding the bait is frequently the most difficult and enjoyable part of fishing. It's a good excuse to spend time poking around in tide pools when other people are doing the dishes. "Have to get some bait," you say authoritatively as your friends glare at you with suspicion.

There are two kinds of bait: natural and artificial. Of the natural baits, the easiest to find and collect are those that don't move very fast. These include chitons, limpets, clams, mussels, various worms, oysters, etc. Most of these are also good to eat themselves, so if you find enough it may not be necessary to go fishing at all.

Other baits such as fish and conch require diving or some other involved procedure to capture them. These more elusive baits are ususaly the best type.

Lures, jigs, artificial baits

"Big and shiny or small and shiny" might seem a vague guideline to use when shopping for tackle, but Mexican fish are very cooperative when offered artificial baits. I've caught big lunkers on tiny trout spoons and tiny fish on giant casting plugs. Unless you want to stock a large tackle box, however, I recommend a few basic types of jigs and lures: heavy trolling and casting spoons (such as Krocodile, Hopkins, Kastmaster, Salas); large plugs (four inches or more in length — Rapala is a favorite of Mexican fishermen but almost anything works); medium to very small trout and bass spoons and plugs for surf and lagoons, not to mention lakes and river fishing; 'hootchies' or plastic hula skirt jigs with weighted trolling heads, heavy hooks and wire leaders, and feathered trolling casting jigs: all-white, white-and-blue or white-and-red. The all-white feather jig is the classic all purpose lure for Mexican salt water fishing; it catches everything from rock fish to blue water gamefish. This is one of the few lures made in Mexico and available for a reasonable price. Look in hardware stores in coastal towns.

Lures can be improvised from pieces of metal and foil. This type of bait must be kept in action either by fast retrieving, trolling or up-and-down jigging.

Artificial baits and lures often appeal to really voracious fish and you may get more than you bargained for. Our friend Steve once caught a four and a half foot barracuda using a handline. To the utter disgust of some better equipped *gringos* camped near us, he had used the lid from a sardine tin for a lure. Their efforts had been fruitless but they still refused Steve's gracious offer to make them a lure from one of their empty beer cans.

A strip of white cloth about two inches long and a half inch wide is a good artificial bait for any type of fish. A crude but effective jig can be made by lashing pieces of dried grass, chicken feathers or colored string to a hook. A Mexican fisherman demonstrated the effectiveness of a very simple jig by catching several sierra mackerel in just a few minutes. He tied half a dozen rubber bands to the shank of a large hook, then cut open the trailing ends of the bands to make a basic 'hootchie' or hula jig.

These jigs can be trolled and cast by hand or with a fishing rod. They are also effective for rock fish when jigged straight up and down a foot or so over the bottom.

If you are backpacking carry at least half a dozen 'worm' hooks (a few size 8, a few size 12) and some light split-shot sinkers. If you don't have a rod and reel, buy a small plastic spool of six pound monofilament line before you leave home. This keeps the line neat and though it isn't much, it will drag fish out of creeks and lakes. If you want more line, carry it wrapped around an aluminum beer can or small plastic bottle. (See how to cast it under *Fishing Techniques* in this chapter.)

Maintain your equipment carefully. Check the line for nicks and if you find any, chop them out and throw that section away. Sharpen the hook occasionally and check to see that it's well tied on and that the line is not wearing thin where it touches the hook.

Fishing Techniques

The method used for casting a handline is almost universal. Hold the 'reel' (stick or can with line wrapped on it) in one hand pointed toward the spot where you're going to cast. Don't allow your fingers to creep over the line or it will stop short. In your other hand, hold the line so that about three or four feet dangles free. Start swinging the line slowly around and around, moving your arm upward until the bait is revolving over your head. You now look like a helicopter. Don't try to swing the line too fast or your cast will be wild. When everything feels comfortable and controlled, release the line as you throw your arm forward toward the target point. If you hit the beach, you released it at the wrong time.

Never wrap the line around any part of your body you don't want to lose! Keep a sharp knife handy, too, just in case you or a friend becomes entangled. Battling a fish on a handline is heavy drama; I was almost pulled right out of a boat by a fifteen pound *toro*. Fish have awesome power, though most cannot exert it for extended periods of time.

Handlining from rocks and around reefs is tricky; you'll undoubtedly get snagged and occasionally lose gear. To avoid continual snagging, use a fast retrieve. Haul the line in rapidly, hand over hand, as if coiling a rope or in short fast bursts to simulate the movement of a wounded fish.

One of my favorite pastimes combines beachcombing (or jogging if you're really enthusiastic) with fishing. The gear can be a handline rigged for casting or any casting rod and reel. Here's how it goes:

Get up just before the sun and grab your gear. Better put on a bathing suit or shorts and a light shirt since you'll undoubtedly get wet. I carry sandals around my neck or, if the beach is sandy, just go barefoot.

Stroll to the water's edge, keeping your eyes peeled for obvious signs of fish: birds diving or wheeling above a certain spot, splashing caused by feeding fish or tiny bait fish, unusual ripples or swirls in the water that indicate something below. If none of these pulse-quickening sights greets you, start walking. I make an occasional cast, just to limber up, but never stop searching, both ahead and behind, for signs of fish. Fish usually travel parallel to the shoreline and tend to concentrate when they reach a point of land, either a definite jutting peninsula or subtle bulge in the beach.

See something? Start flogging the water and don't let up until you've caught something or no longer see evidence of fish. If they leave you empty handed, just look for the next target; it shouldn't take long.

Repeat this procedure in the afternoon and evening. You'll soon develop a healthy physique and a sharp eye, not to mention a reputation for fanaticism. But once you tie into an early morning, eye-opening fish you will, in fact, be a fanatic.

It is a popular misconception that the longest cast catches the largest fish. This is not at all true; some of the largest fish are found right behind the bait fish they have chased into shore. I once fished along a stretch of beach for several days without success. All of the indications, from diving pelicans to shimmering schools of baitfish, indicated that there were a large number of fish near the beach. Then one afternoon a young boy came along just as I was pulling in my line and we started to talk. The line was forgotten and the bait lay in the water a few yards from my feet. Suddenly a tremendous strike interrupted our conversation and several minutes later I landed a large bonefish.

A few more short casts and I had more fish than we had seen in days. All were hooked in knee deep water. After making this discovery, I rarely failed to bring fish to camp, to the consternation of my neighbors who insisted on using large surf casting rods to fling the bait well beyond the fish.

When fishing 'blind' from the beach, don't stay in one place if you don't get a bite within five or ten minutes. You'll have a much greater chance of success by moving than if you sit for hours waiting for something to pass by.

Your overall chances of meeting feeding fish are best at sunrise and sunset but fishing at midday can also be rewarding.

I've found that one of the problems of fishing in Mexico is the constant temptation to try for something too large for my gear to handle for more than a few heart thumping seconds. When angling for food, it is best to go after the smaller fish and leave the world's records and your gear intact.

A boat or raft increases your chance for success. There seems to be some sort of fish for every imaginable bait, trolling speed and location. Acquaintances of ours hooked large tarpon and sailfish from a slow moving rowboat using handlines and scraps of fish for bait. They didn't land the fish but they revised their opinion of the myth that only expensive gear will attract sport fish.

A good general guide for trolling is to move fast and fish fairly close to the shore, offshore reefs or rocks. Troll a jig fast enough to keep it at the top of the water or to skip from wave top to wave top. Don't overtighten your reel's drag; a friend watched a relatively small fish snap a twenty pound test line when the fish met the jig in a head-on collison.

When all else fails, another method remains: trade fish-hooks or line for fish. In many isolated areas, hooks and line are scarce and people will offer to trade or buy your equipment. I've found that supplying the gear for a portion of the catch is often more efficient than using it myself.

Sport fishing is just becoming popular among Mexicans. Because of this and because commercial fishermen tend to be conservative about trying new gear, techniques and fishing grounds, many areas are almost untouched. I once ran into a wild-eyed *gringo* carrying a stringer of big freshwater perch. He had casually tossed a small lure into a nearby stream, not really expecting anything because no one else ever fished there. To his amazement he found himself hauling in fish after fish, urged on by the delighted yells of children swimming nearby. "Unbelievable! Un-be-lievable!" he kept muttering as he headed back to his tent.

Diving

Diving involves more equipment, effort and personal risk than sitting in the sand watching the birds as your bait drifts unnoticed in the surf. The equipment, however, doesn't have to be complicated or expensive to be effective. Once you have the basic gear to get into the water and spear a fish, you have all that is needed.

Gear

Mexican-made diving masks, fins and snorkels are available in coastal resort cities and large sporting goods and department stores in Mexico City and Guadalajara. It is not of the best quality, nor inexpensive, but it will do the job. I try to buy my diving gear at home, preferably in a discount store that carries name brands: White Stag, Voit, Dacor, etc. Unless you're very serious about diving, get a simple mask and snorkel and a pair of standard 'shoe fins'. Fancier and much more costly gear just isn't necessary.

If you have a small face, extra large nose or beard and moustache select your mask carefully. After years of trial and error I now prefer the simplest model masks over those with wide angle vision, purge valves and so-called 'custom' features. A simple mask is easiest to seal against a small face and they eventually mold themselves around moustaches, giving a good tight fit. If your mask persists in leaking, smear a gob of plain non-medicated Vaseline around the edge and this should stop the leaks and drips.

Your pole spear or speargun will be the center of your equipment. If you already have a speargun and it works, don't buy something newer and more powerful. The best speargun is one that has been used for years without being a problem. When you know the limitations of your equipment, you can buy spare parts for *anticipated* failures.

Unless you have spare parts, spearing big fish is foolish. Any fish larger than your frying pan will have the strength to raise hell with your gear. If the fish struggles and manages to bend the shaft or sever the line against coral, your spearfishing is over if you don't have spares.

A small well-made speargun with a *permanently attached* spear head and one or two rubber bands is ideal for both novice and experienced divers who want fish to eat, not trophies. Small guns are easy to cock, an important consideration if you're not a good shot or you're spearing many small fish. The force needed to spear the average fish is not great; one rubber band is sufficient but two will give you greater range.

Although pole spears require more skill than a speargun they have several advantages: cheaper to buy, almost no maintenance, easily stowed (especially break-down models), and handy to use as a sort of underwater 'walking stick' to fend off rocks, coral and curious moray eels.

Surgical tubing of the type used for spearguns and pole spears is expensive in Mexico and often extremely difficult to track down. Ask in fishing supply stores, large hardware stores and *farmacias* for *liga, liga para pistolas* or *ule para torniquete*.

The spearhead is as important as the speargun or pole spear itself. Many spears are sold with a trident-type head, in my opinion not worth using. It will not penetrate far enough to prevent most fish from tearing free; eventually it will bend and break. Fancy detachable heads are even less practical for normal spearing. They are designed for big fish that will not be killed or stunned by the impact of the spear and will struggle, possibly bending a shaft. It is significant that Mexican commercial spearfishermen, who can't afford to buy something ineffective or short-lived, prefer spearheads made of plain steel. It's greatest advantage (although it does rust) is that it can be filed to a sharp point and occasional collisions with rocks won't flatten it so badly that it can't be resharpened.

Most pole spears are now sold with paralyzer heads rather than trident or barbed heads. The paralyzer is very simple and extremely durable: three steel prongs several inches in length are set at slight angles from each other in the base of the spearhead. (See *illustration*.) When the prongs strike a fish, they are forced apart, holding the fish in place. The impact also stuns the fish.

I've used the same paralyzer head for years and though it's been bent, hammered out, flattened and generally abused, it still works fine. Its only disadvantage is that the paralyzer does not hold well on fish larger than a few pounds, and even smaller fish can thrash off if not hit hard and securely. When hunting large fish I carry another head with barbs, and trade the paralyzer for the 'Warhead' rather than risk wounding and losing a fish.

An extra spearhead is a good idea, but if you don't have one, glue the spearhead to the shaft. Be sure: use epoxy or hardening-type gasket cement. Don't just tighten it on with pliers. Even a small fish can twirl around a few times and then sink into deep water with your spearhead (your only spearhead, of course).

Gloves are almost indispensible for diving around rocks and coral reefs. I usually wear one glove, on my left hand, and use that hand to steady myself when peering under rocks and into caves. Stinging sea growths, razor sharp coral, sea urchins and other hazards make indiscriminant groping quite painful. My free right hand is used for the spear. When sightseeing underwater, I wear a glove on each hand.

Diving knives, like spearguns, often reflect the owner's fantasies rather than reality and common sense. The most common use for a diving knife is opening coconuts and prying the tops off beer bottles. Other than that, you'll use it occasionally to clean a fish or extract a spearhead.

Instead of bringing a beautiful stainless steel diving knife and plastic case, wait until you get to Mexico and buy a cheap steel knife in the market. It will rust and not look too cool, but it will be easy to sharpen, easy to handle and even easier to replace when you lose it.

You'll need an inner tube and some type of bag for your catch if you don't have a paddleboard or boat. Buy your inner tube in the U.S.; a used Mexican tube is truly used. A flour sack will cost a few pesos in the market. The bag should be attached to the inner tube, but not so securely that it can't be removed quickly and easily. If sharks are attracted to your catch, you may want to ditch the bag rather than tow it along as a giant lure.

Diving Techniques

There are three basic approaches to spearfishing and three basic types of divers: hungry, curious and macho. The curious diver is often the novice, paddling happily in the shallows, ogling the colorful reef fishes and occasionally sending one to its Maker. When curiosity is combined with more self-confidence or hunger the novice leaves the protection of the shallows and ventures into deeper waters and even more curious adventures.

The macho diver can be seen lurking in unlikely and often uncomfortable waters, a genuine predator, armed with a speargun of hideous power. Long after the curious and hungry divers have sought shelter in a palm thatched beer joint, the macho diver is pursuing some hapless shark or enormous gamefish. When successful he will draw gasps of amazement and admiration as he drags his catch from the sea. With fingers as wrinkled as California raisins he traces the course of his undersea battle, giving his respectful listeners a good profile of any cuts or injuries sustained in the struggle. As his fabulous tale comes to an end, he withdraws a bayonet-sized diving knife from its sheath and casually hacks an enormous slab from a corner of his catch. This is tossed to a curious or hungry diver (especially those wearing two piece bathing suits) with a few expert words of advice on how it should be prepared. The curious and hungry return to their beers, riddled with self-doubt.

As a hungry diver fully committed to filling my belly rather than entering the Record Books, I've found a number of tricks and shortcuts to help keep fish on our table.

The best time to dive is usually mid-morning to early afternoon, when shadows are short and the light brightest. Individual places, however, depending upon their location, will be lighted more favorably in the morning or afternoon. Make a mental note of the best times to visit these spots.

The easiest fish to spear lurk around rocks, reefs and other natural cover. Reef fish usually have very definite territories and feeding habits. By studying their behavior, you'll greatly reduce the time and effort it takes to spear them.

Don't churn around like a motorized surf board. Drifting and very slow swimming not only allow you to see more but do not frighten the fish.

Patience is essential. Don't chase one fish for half a mile; as soon as it's out of range forget it and wait for a better target. Up-and-down diving will wear you out rapidly. Spot your fish from the surface and move as close as possible while still on the top, then dive after it.

Most fish will move a short distance and then attempt to hide, either by sitting under a rock or by holding perfectly still. This is the moment to strike, not while they're racing madly from side to side. If the shot misses, rise quietly to the surface and study the surrounding area. The fish may not move at all or may move just a few feet.

Although spearing is usually more entertaining around rocks and reefs, with more to peer and poke at than in open water, it is not always more productive. Schools of *lisa* (mullet), *boca dulce* (sweetmouth, perch-like bottom feeders), *cocineros* (tuna-type), *gatos* (catfish or similar), *jurel* and *toros* (jacks, bulls, crevalle), *palmeras* (pompano) and many others can be found in open water, from knee deep to too deep to worry about. The most efficient method for spearing fast swimmers like these is to paddle very quietly and slowly on the outside (deeper edge of the surf or to drift, turning quietly from side to side like a radar scanner. A pole spear with a paralyzer head is ideal if these morsels are under a pound; any larger than that are pure hell to hang onto with a pole spear.

When you spot a fish or a school, give them the opportunity to swim to you. If they don't, or if they circle warily, dive as quietly as possible below the surface and swim toward them, spear ready. The moment to strike is when the fish turns its side toward you. Pompano, for example, are impossible to chase down, but have the fatal habit of pausing for a quick curious look at their pursuer. If you're prepared for this, their next stop will be an open bed of coals and a basting of butter and garlic.

Lisa and *boca dulce* rove the bottom in schools and are best approached from above, diving to meet the school in the middle. This confuses them and gives you a better chance for a shot. *Lisa* have a habit of returning to the same feeding spots, even after fleeing in panic. Patience, again, and visual bearings with the shore or underwater landmarks, can greatly increase your catch.

One of the most exciting aspects of shoreline diving is that sooner or later you'll meet one of the big blue water cruisers. The first time this happened to me I almost swallowed my snorkel. One moment I was listlessly paddling in several feet of water, pursuing some agile minnow, the next I was face to face with an enormous *dorado* (dolphin, mahi-mahi). This is the moment macho divers dream of, as they blast small fish to pieces with their super-powered spearguns. The *dorado* came within four feet of me, hovered for a few vulnerable seconds and then disappeared into the deep with a flick of its tail.

When your efforts in open water fail to meet your needs, consider the lowly sting ray (*raya*). These bottom fish are not just a hazard to waders and curious divers), they are also quite edible. In some areas, especially in the springtime, they are thick as flies. Choose one less than two feet long. A large ray will tow you off or wrench your speargun from your grasp.

Dive down slowly, approaching from the rear. Don't worry about scaring them; rays are very calm about being speared. A paralyzer spear head is best or a barbless spear (a sharpened stick works fine). Aim at the head and let fly. Hold the ray against the bottom and push the spear firmly into the head. If it gets off it may go wild and swim right into you.

Never, ever attempt to put them into a bag or onto a stringer. Being struck by a ray's sharp bone-like 'stinger' while swimming would be a terrible stroke of luck.

The minute the ray is out of water (and before taking it off the spear) cut its tail off and discard stinger. Don't leave the stinger lying about where someone might step on it. Bury it or put it in the fish bag until you can dispose of it later.

While spearing rays you may luck upon a much finer bottom fish — the halibut. The procedure for spearing them is the same as for rays. Halibut up to ten pounds are not uncommon and cause for a tasty banquet.

I was drinking beer in a small beach restaurant, scanning the area for likely

spearing spots, when a nearby *gringo* asked if I was going diving. Since I had my fins, mask, fish bag and spear in my lap, I knew he was a keen observer. I nodded. "Know any good spots?" I asked.

"Gotta go *way out!*" he said, pointing towards Japan.

"How about the mouth of that creek?" I suggested, nodding to the sluggish tropical stream that dribbled into the surf nearby.

He laughed.

There is a simple equation for dedicated foragers that goes: fresh water plus salt water equals fish. In this case the fresh water looked a little murky, but the telltale cloud of silt where it poured into the sea meant that *something,* even though it might be small, had to be in there feeding. I put on my gear and eased into the water. Visibility wasn't very good; I couldn't see my hand in front of my face.

I drifted quietly for a few moments, adjusting my mask and feeling out the situation. There were occasional patches of clear water, like breaks in a cloudy sky. And within a few minutes I had spotted fish, ranging in size from one inch (even I don't usually go for those) to almost two feet. Without exception they were open water fish — that is, not the type that hold still for more than a second. I waited until one passed just a little too close . . . fry one! Its struggles on the end of my spear brought others, curious and vulnerable. The pole spear flicked out again . . . a miss . . . and again . . . fry two!

After half an hour in the water and very little swimming, I had four tasty fish weighing about half a pound each. I returned to the restaurant for another beer.

"Where'd you get those?" my acquaintance asked incredulously.

"Way out," I said. "Way, *way* out."

Lagoons, Lakes and Rivers

Although I prefer to fish these waters with a line rather than a spear, many Mexican divers do quite well in murky lagoons, lakes and rivers. Some aren't murky at all but for some reason the best fishing always seems to involve very limited visibility. Luis, a Mexican diver friend, will float for hours in a chilly lagoon, working his way through tangled mangrove roots covered with sharp little oysters and stinging growths in search of snappers, snook and Creatures. On the few times I've accompanied him, the chill up my back came more from the setting than the temperature. His technique is to patrol the edge of the mangroves and reeds like an alligator. Move silently, with your finger poised on the trigger and don't ask questions if you catch a glimpse of a fish — blast 'em. If you hit a hundred pound tarpon, your friends will tell the story of your last ride through the swamps for years.

Poking

I learned this classic hungry-diver technique from some helpful Mexican children. Later I found that even professional Mexican divers practice poking. The usual gear consists of a diving mask (no fins) and a three to five foot length of *varilla* (steel rod). One end is filed or beaten to a point and the other has a loop of rubber tubing or innertubing lashed to it. This crude pole spear is used on everything from lobsters and crabs to minnows and monsters.

The technique is simple: in a shallow rocky area or coral reef the poker looks into every hole, searching for fish and lobster. Most pokers prefer to stand on the bottom or to scramble from one rock to another, dipping their heads into likely pools and holes. It takes a sharp eye for camoflaged fish and a quick hand, but poking can be very productive. It is also a lot of fun, especially if you go with kids.

When I go poking I wear gloves, tennis shoes and sometimes a shirt and pants in order to protect myself from sharp rocks, coral, stinging mysteries and sea urchins. Be extremely careful of large waves; I once dislocated my knee and cracked a few ribs when my enthusiasm overcame caution. The force of even a small wave can throw you dangerously off balance and into something painful.

I learned another hazard of poking in Baja. I stuck my head under water into a fair sized hole and was face to face with a fifteen pound snapper. It took me about one second to break my firm resolution never to spear a large fish with my breakable aluminum pole spear. And it took the snapper less time than that to snap the spear in two. I wounded a fish that I had no hope of catching and ruined my only spear.

Spearguns can be used for poking, but be careful. I once blasted a large parrot fish with a very large gun. I had the fish trapped in a hole and couldn't miss. And I didn't: the spear went through the fish and into the rock, ruining the head and bending the shaft.

Safety & Sea Monsters

Contrary to the 'buddy system' I prefer not to swim with another person if that person has a pole spear or speargun. I'd far rather take my chances alone than get it in the neck from a freak shot. I've narrowly avoided being speared on two memorable occasions: when a friend's brand new speargun suddenly went off on its own (with the safety definitely 'on') and when a novice diver lost his grip on a cocked pole spear and nearly skewered me through the stomach.

The following safety rules should never be broken. A spear wound is extremely dangerous, especially if it happens in the water.

• *Spearguns should never be cocked when the weapon is out of the water.* Cock it after you've left the boat and when returning to the boat, uncock it underwater, before you get within range of the boat. A slip of the hand or safety mechanism could spear a friend, the motor or the boat.

• Swim with the spear pointed down or straight ahead, not trailed behind. If it goes off, you may bag an innocent person behind you.

• Never swim in surf with a cocked speargun.

• Do not hunt with your pole spear cocked; wait until you've spotted a fish and are within reasonable striking distance. Swimming with the spear cocked will tire your hand and arm and it will 'go off' when you least expect it.

• Protect both the spearhead and the people around you from accidental injury by keeping the spearhead covered when not in use. I carry chunks of inner tube, rags, soft wood or coconut husks to bind to the speartip. This is especially important when travelling by boat. A mishap in the surf or a sudden wave lurch can lead to a painful accident.

• Last, but not least, practice with your gun or pole spear before taking it on the hunt. Don't use those beautiful and highly vulnerable reef and rock fishes for target practice. Find a calm spot of water, not too deep and well away from casual bathers. Fill a plastic bleach bottle with air and anchor it to a stone by a short piece of fishing line. It will float above the bottom — but below the surface, like an underwater buoy. When it won't hold air any longer, just throw it ahead of you several feet, let it sink a ways, then let fly.

One of the greatest hazards of skin diving is that excitement often overwhelms common sense and the diver is suddenly half a mile from shore, laden with fish and completely exhausted. Add a strong current or a cramp and the result could be tragic.

Give your body time to condition itself to swimming, heat and the strenuous daily routine that most campers follow. When you feel tired, stop diving; don't allow the thought of going without fish keep you from heading back to camp.

Short initiation swims will familiarize you with local currents. Later, when you begin to spend hours every day in the water, use currents to your advantage by planning to drift toward shore at the end of the trip rather than away from it.

Floating on the surface of the water for one or two hours is more than enough to roast your back and legs to a salty crisp. Have a shirt along to wear in the water, and another for protection from sunburn on the return walk, swim or boat ride to camp. That last half hour of exposure may do you in. Sunburns retard tanning and a bad burn will last for weeks. (See *Remedies:* Chapter 8.)

Perhaps the most dangerous hazard for the inexperienced diver or swimmer is the *surf*. It's very easy to say to yourself, "All I have to do is get beyond that first wave and I'm okay" This may be true when you go *out*, but not when you come in. Surf conditions are rarely constant and may change drastically several times a day. If the tide turns and the

surf suddenly springs up to twice its former size, your return to the beach will be quite thrilling.

Have an alternate return route in mind just in case it builds up dangerously high before you can get back to shore. A wave that's as high as your head when you're in ankle deep water will look like a mountain while you're swimming and will hit you just about as hard.

When it appears that you'll have a hard time crossing the surf line, remove your mask to avoid losing it. Tie it securely to the inner tube or stuff it inside your fish bag. Your spear should also be lashed to the inner tube and never left cocked.

When your gear has been secured, swim into the beach, always keeping a close watch behind you for monster waves. If one does appear, release the inner tube and dive to the bottom. You can body surf to the beach but unless you're adept at it, surfing may mean a rough ride along the bottom.

Beaches with an undertow or currents caused by erratic wave action should be avoided like the plague. When there's any doubt in your mind about going in the water, *don't*.

While diving around a reef, allow for the surge and flow of the water to avoid being rasped against the sharp coral. I learned this the hard way on my first dive in the Caribbean. The top of the reef was surprisingly flat and only a few feet underwater. I was drifting slowly, admiring the coral, when a large wave on the ocean side of the reef began to build up, drawing water toward it. I started to move toward the wave, sucked along by the shallow fast-moving water. It was exciting, drifting even faster than I could swim and watching the different colors flash by beneath me.

Suddenly I realized what was about to happen and fought desperately against the current. It was hopeless; by then the water was just a few inches deep and I was dragged at high speed over the coral like a carrot across a vegetable grater. Several painful rolls and I was left scraped and bleeding from head to toe.

Some corals also sting and will give you an itch-

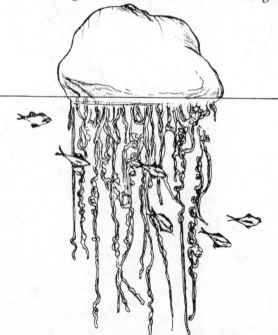

Portugese man-of-war   *Malagua*

ing rash that is quite painful. Look but don't touch.

Stinging jellyfish (*malagua:* bad water) such as the Portugese Man-Of-War, occasionally drift into the beaches. The man-of-war is a small purple jellyfish with a distinctive bubble-like growth on top that acts as a sail. A fleet of these devils can drive the hardiest swimmers onto dry ground.

Most jellyfish do not sting (the stingers are on the long tentacles that hang below the creature), or do not sting badly. The man-of-war, however, is a painful exception. If you are stung while swimming, don't panic! Thrashing the water won't do any good, in fact it can make matters much worse by wrapping more tentacles around you. Even broken off tentacles retain their stinging capabilities (which is why some swimmers and even beachcombers never see a jellyfish but still get stung).

When you get stung, stop moving. If you have a diving mask on, look carefully for thread-like tentacles around you. Brush any you see away with your spear or fins, not your bare hands. Swim very slowly out of the area, keeping a sharp eye out for more tentacles.

If you find yourself surrounded, dive down at least ten or fifteen feet (or more, if you can) and put as much water between you and the jellyfish as you can before surfacing. (See Chapter 8 for treating stings.)

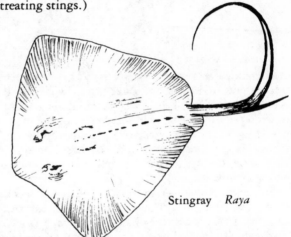

Sting rays can make casual wading a very nervous pastime. They lie flat on the sand and are very difficult to spot. When you step on the ray's back, the tail arches over and the barb is jabbed into the top or side of your foot. To avoid this, wade slowly and shuffle your feet rather than prancing like a gazelle. If your foot bumps into the ray's side, it'll probably scuttle off and give you nothing but a scare.

Stingray   *Raya*

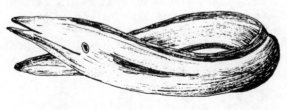

Moray   *Morena*

Avoid spearing moray eels, sharks of any size and fish with very sharp teeth. I almost lost my left thumb to a two foot *sierra.* Moray eels live in crevices and caves of every size, even in holes of large sponges. Don't antagonize a moray; they bite.

When speared, they have the annoying habit of working their way snake-like up the shaft towards you. A speared moray is dangerous and very difficult to kill.

A shark two or three feet long might seem like a vulnerable target, but it is not. A Mexican spearfisherman working near our camp was bitten four times by a three foot shark he'd speared. He survived the attack but the wounds were extremely painful.

When you've speared enough fish for a meal, don't linger around; sharks may be attracted by the blood and struggles of the fish you've killed. Should a shark appear, you'll probably want to get out of the water. Keep your eye on it at all times and swim steadily, but not wildly, away. Thrashing around makes them think you're wounded. If you are near a boat, don't jump in and then let your feet dangle over the side while you remove your swim fins. A shark once tried to eat our anchor just as it was lifted out of the water. This happened a few seconds after we'd leaped into the boat ourselves.

Striking the surface of the water with the palm of your hand is reputedly a good method of frightening sharks. I've tried it and they didn't seem to notice. A solid punch on the end of the snout is supposed to frighten them — if you haven't fainted by the time they're that close. Don't think that a shark won't follow you into very shallow water; if they want to, they will.

Sharks are a dramatic hazard but fortunately, the chances that a reader of this book will be eaten by one are slim. *Erizos* (sea urchins), on the other hand, are a very real danger for both divers and beach foragers. Their distinctive pin cushion appearance indicates exactly what they'll do if you so much as brush against them. One of the types found in Mexico has spines so thin and brittle that touching it without being punctured is almost impossible. Sea urchin spines easily pass through clothing, swim fins and shoes. When collecting food on urchin infested rocks, remove those that present the most immediate danger. You can do this with your knife. Be careful that the urchin doesn't become a floating 'mine' and nail you on the next wave.

Seasnakes can be seen in the Pacific Ocean, especially when warm currents bring them close to shore. Although all sea snakes are poisonous none are known to be aggressive. The worst they'll do is cause you to swallow your snorkel if you unexpectedly swim near a sea snake. Avoid them but don't panic if one happens to swim toward you. It's undoubtedly just confused rather than attacking. Sea snakes have very small mouths and even if they wanted to bite you, they'd find it very difficult. All the same, give them a wide berth.

The greatest hazard of sea snakes is to curious beachcombers, especially children. Sea snakes often wash ashore and it wouldn't do to step on a live one or to allow a child to play with it.

Some Common Edible Fish of Mexico

Pargo is a general term used for many types of snappers, though specific types may have regional names. *Huachinango* usually means red snapper — highly esteemed by Mexican seafood enthusiasts, it brings a good price. *Huachinango* is usually fished by handline and lives in very deep water. I don't know of any type of snapper that isn't good to eat. They come in a wide variety of shapes, sizes and colors and any big enough to catch is big enough to eat. (See *Recipes:* Chapter 7 for ways of preparing the fish you catch.)

Sierra (Spanish mackerel) is a fast swimming gamefish, usually caught while trolling or in gill nets. It is excellent grilled over coals, raw in *ceviche*, baked or smoked. Leftovers can be boned and flaked, then used as a sandwich filling with mayonnaise, fresh lime juice and black pepper. It makes an excellent smoked or kippered fish.

Mero is a general purpose name for groupers, rock fish and seabass. These are favorites with sport and commercial divers, though they are also caught with fresh bait, feather jigs and bright lures. They range from good to excellent eating; my favorite is most commonly called *cabrilla*. *Mero chino* or *tigres* (Chinese grouper or tigers) are very common along the rocky areas of the Pacific coast. They average about one to two pounds, though *chinos* up to five and six pounds are common too. They live in crevices and are relatively easy to spear. I no longer try to remove their tough scales or skin, and just cook them whole. The flesh can be quite tough. Try them in fish stew.

Sharks (*tiburón*) are an important commercial seafood in Mexico. When prepared it is usually called *cazón*. Big and little sharks are eaten; baby hammerhead is a favorite and makes great *ceviche*. Shark fishing camps are interesting places to visit, if you don't mind the mind-numbing smell of drying shark and rotting scraps. Spearfishing and fishing in front of a shark camp is usually excellent, since many fish move in for the free leftovers.

Toro and *jurel* (jacks) are dark-fleshed and not popular with Mexicans, though in my opinion they are quite tasty, especially when slow cooked over an open fire. Fortunately for the dedicated forager, dark-fleshed fish are often caught in netting operations. In most cases the fishermen will be happy to sell these fish for a low price or even give them away. Some are also taken trolling and I often put in a special request to save the *toros*. This backfired one time when a fisherman proudly returned with fourteen *toros*, all in the ten to fifteen pound range. It took me an entire day to locate enough hungry *gringos* willing to take my word that the fish were good eating.

Mexicans will eat dark-fleshed fish when they are prepared as *tatemado*. In one of my favorite diving areas on the Pacific coast, when the net fishermen return at dawn from their rounds, the local children meet them with buckets and washtubs. Dark fish, oddballs and anything too small or damaged to sell at the market are all dumped into these containers. The fish are then carried to nearby restaurants, each of which operates a crude kippering pit. The fish are rinsed and the sides slashed several times with a razor sharp machete. The shallow cuts are rubbed with coarse salt and the fish spread over a wide bed of coals on a rack, often of green sticks. Banana leaves may be used to cover the fish and to trap the smoke.

Within three hours the smaller fish have been turned many times and are ready to eat, though they'll be left on the grill with the others. The flavor of the fish is excellent — smoky, salty and fairly dry. Leaving the guts in cuts down on their storage life but adds a stronger flavor that goes well with fresh lime juice, hot sauce and chopped onion. These fish are sold as snacks for beer drinkers or as a very delicious meal when combined with tortillas.

Fish Poisoning

Ciguatera (fish poisoning) can be a problem in the Atlantic and Caribbean areas. It is said to be most common in snappers, barracuda, moray eels, parrot fish and jacks. Symptoms are a tingling in the lips, mouth and throat, followed by extreme weakness, nausea and diarrhea. In the West Indies (where it is much more common than in Mexico), this is called "the light footsies," since it supposedly feels pleasantly weird in mild cases.

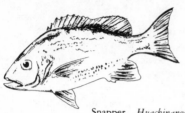

Snapper   *Huachinango, Pargo*

Drum   *Corvina, Roncador*

Convictfish, Sheepshead

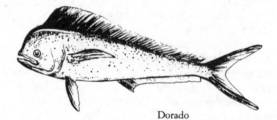

Scorpionfish   *Sapo*

Dorado

Sea trout   *Corvina, Trucha*

Striped grunt   *Ronco, Mojarra*

Bonito   *Barrilete*

Amberjack   *Coronado, Atun*

Rock grouper   *Mero, Cabrilla*

Long spine sea urchin   *Erizo*

Yellowfin tuna   *Atun*

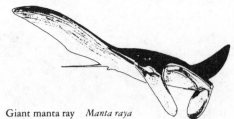

Giant manta ray   *Manta raya*

Damselfish

Soapfish   *Pez jabon*

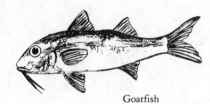

Goatfish

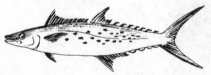

Wahoo

Spanish mackerel   *Sierra*

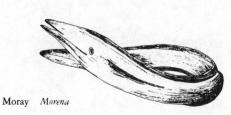

Parrotfish   *Loro*

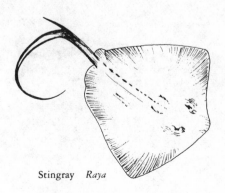

Stingray   *Raya*

Moray   *Morena*

Lookdown   *Joroba*

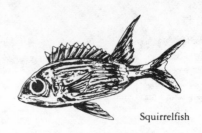

Squirrelfish

Needlefish   *Agujón*

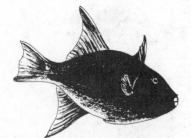

Jack, Crevalle   *Jurel, Toro*

Mojarra   *Mojarra*

Filefish

Triggerfish   *Bota*

Snook   *Robalo*

Sea catfish   *Bagre*

Bonefish   *Macobi*

Pipefish   *Trompeta*

Mullet   *Lisa*

Sailfish   *Pez vela*

Barracuda   *Picuda*

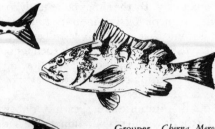

Grouper   *Cherna, Mero*

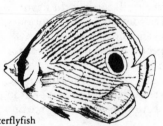

Blue marlin   *Marlin, Espadón*

Angelfish

Butterflyfish

Tarpon   *Sabalo*

Porcupinefish, Spiny Pufferfish

Pompano   *Palometa, Pompano*

When diving in the Caribbean I always ask local people what fish are safe to eat. "*¿Se puede comer este pescado?*" (Can one eat this fish?) is all it takes. As with any dubious food or water: when in doubt, don't.

Keep It Fresh

Spoilage is always a great worry. You crawl dripping from the surf, proudly clutching a ten pound snapper. Your friends race to your side; "Is it still good?" one asks anxiously. By the time you're ready to cook the fish a few hours later, people are sniffing it suspiciously and muttering about food poisoning.

It is ironic that many people will expend great amounts of money, time and energy to catch fish or other seafood and then ignore a few quick procedures that will insure that they enjoy eating it too. The following suggestions should be followed as soon as possible. Nothing can restore the flavor of a fish that has lain in the hot sun several hours before dinner.

Your first impulse after spearing or hooking a fish should be to clean it. This may also be the downfall of your dinner unless it's done properly. Bacteria will attack and multiply in any cut or puncture in the fish's flesh. Keep cut surfaces to a minimum. Do not cut off the head, fins or tail until just before cooking. Begin cleaning by slitting the belly open far enough to remove the guts. Leave the head intact but remove the gills. Scrape the kidney (sometimes called the blackline or bloodline) carefully away from the body cavity. Avoid tearing the flesh as you scrape. A teaspoon is ideal for this. Do not remove the scales; they will protect the flesh from heat and bacteria.

Now wash the fish *thoroughly* in fresh or salt water removing any bits of guts, gills or blood.

The next procedures are not absolutely necessary but they will enhance the flavor. Put the fish on ice, well wrapped in paper or cloth. It is a common misconception that warm water fish won't keep very long on ice. This is not at all true; when properly cleaned, they will last much longer than most people would want or need to keep them. Remember: all fish smell fishy; spoiled fish smell awful.

When ice is not available, wrap the cleaned fish in a piece of wet cloth and place the package in the shade, preferably where there's good air circulation. The evaporation of the water on the cloth (or paper) will drop the temperature of the fish enough to be noticeable when you feel it with your hand.

Should you want to keep the fish for several hours on a hot day, sprinkle it with salt, inside and out, paying particular attention to cut surfaces or punctures. Now wrap it in a damp cloth and place in the shade. Before cooking the fish, give it a quick rinse and there should be no noticeable amount of salt left.

Never fillet a fish until just before cooking. Filleting causes unavoidable loss of fluids from the flesh and this will detract from the flavor.

Shellfish

There are many excellent seafoods in addition to fish. Most do not require diving gear to collect, although it helps.

Conch

Caracol are easy to capture but it usually requires a diving mask. Conch are found sitting quietly on the bottom in water six to fifteen feet deep. They prefer calm water and a sandy or slightly rocky bottom with seaweed to feed on.

Conch resemble a melon-sized rock and once you've learned to recognize them, they are easily spotted from the surface.

When you see a *caracol*, dive down and flip it over; if the 'foot' of the animal suddenly retracts, it's alive. Many empty shells are inhabited by crabs and small moray eels. If the shell does not shine brightly when turned over, the animal is dead. *Caracoles* will live about twenty-four hours when kept under a wet sack and out of the sun.

Because *caracoles* are easily collected, there's always the temptation to take as many as you can. That's why *caracoles* are now scarce.

Oysters

Ostiones are a magical word and we go to ridiculous lengths to get them. However, my introduction to oyster diving almost cured my taste for them.

A diver named José came by our camp and invited me to go along in his tiny boat to a good oyster spot. We rowed to a place where huge ocean swells were crashing against a high cliff. I thought he was just showing me the view and had no idea that this was the area in which to dive. José very carefully measured out a length of anchor line in order to drift close to the cliff. I looked at the foaming white water in horror; it went against all Water Safety lectures I'd ever heard.

After elaborate instructions to me about where to swim and where not to, he took several sacks and a huge iron bar, quickly made the sign of the cross and jumped into the water. I swam cautiously behind him, almost certain that we'd both be tossed against the rocks. Just before reaching the point where the largest waves broke, José dove out of sight with the sacks and iron bar.

After what seemed an impossible length of time, he reappeared and waved at me to come closer. I swam apprehensively to his side. José motioned that I was to follow him down on the next dive. He floated on the surface, inhaling deeply, then suddenly sprinted down through tingling clouds of tiny air bubbles, I saw him reach the bottom and enter a large hole that descended several more feet into the rocks. The iron bar lay nearby.

Taking the bar in one hand and bracing himself against the powerful surge with the other, José began to chip at the surface of the rocks. I watched, eyes bulging from lack of air, as he pried the oysters free and slipped them into a sack. He collected several, then dropped the bar and headed to the surface. This was repeated until he'd filled all of the sacks and had made at least fifty long dives.

"Don't you want to try?" José gasped after a particularly long dive.

"*Bueno,*" I answered lamely. I dove quickly to the edge of the hole but the oysters were at least another eight or ten feet deeper. With a lunge, I pushed down to the bar and began hacking desperately at the thickly clustered shells. The heavy bar was so difficult to manipulate that I was forced to use both hands. The surge threw me off balance and into the side of the hole, scraping my back along jagged oyster shells. "The hell with this!" I thought, dropping the bar and shooting to the surface.

José only commented, "It is not easy."

On the Pacific coast, oysters are found in most rocky areas. They are often exposed by low tides and you won't have to imitate José's diving feats to get enough for a meal. Where local people have depleted the supply, you'll have to go farther away or deeper.

Oysters are not easy to spot if you aren't familiar with their well camouflaged shells and rock-like appearance. The best way to identify shellfish like oysters, rock scallops, limpets and chitons is to hit them with a piece of metal such as a hammer or knife. Shellfish absorb much of the force of the blow and will feel different than rock.

If the alleged oyster is underwater, put your face very close and look for the division in the two halves of the shell. A thin white or pinkish line will indicate that the oyster is partially open and passing air through its body. A light tap will cause the shell to close, confirming that the oyster is alive.

An oyster bar (*barra*) is a length of pointed iron rod or a piece of flat iron about the size and shape of a small human hand attached to the end of a short stout pole. A *barra* is without a doubt the best tool to use for collecting shellfish attached to rocks. Other tools such as claw hammers, large diving knives, abalone irons and crowbars are also effective but not as easy to handle. *Barras* are sold in hardware stores and junk stalls in the market. If you can't find one ready-made, a blacksmith will make one for you. The heavier they are the better.

Use short sharp blows to the rim of the shell in order to slip the edge or point of the *barra* under the shellfish. When this is done correctly, the shell can be pried off quite easily. A small knife should be at hand to clean the meat out of broken shells still attached to the rock.

Because the shells are quite sharp, it is advisable to wear gloves. Be extremely careful of surf; a large wave can smash you against the rocks with rib-crushing force.

Lapa

While diving for oysters, you may notice a large shellfish also attached to the rocks that looks like a flattened cone. These are *lapas,* a type of giant limpet that is similar in appearance and taste to abalone. The shell, however, doesn't have the distinctive row of holes that the abalone has. *Lapas* are most often found on rocks that are well washed by waves and currents. They can be removed with a *barra* or by beating on them from the side with a rock or hammer.

Lobster

Langosta are among the favored prizes of any diving trip. In some areas nonswimmers can collect them at low tides. The most common way to nab a lobster is with a *gancho* — a large fishhook lashed to the end of a stick. The *gancho* is used to gig the lobster and pull it from its hole. (*Ganchos* can also be made from lengths of very heavy wire.)

Lobsters hide under rocks, in caves and in holes. Approach slowly and look for the long antennae that the lobster will usually extend from his hiding place. If you don't see antennae from the surface, dive down and peer into holes and crevices.

When you've spotted a *langosta,* ideally at least a foot long (it will look huge underwater), either hook or spear it. Grabbing it with your hands isn't too wise. These are spiny lobsters and don't have claws, but their shell will rip your hands to shreds. The antennae are also covered with tiny sharp spines and are too brittle to use to pull the lobster out of his hole.

When spearing lobster, try to hit the head rather than the soft meaty tail.

Clams

Almejas are not as common as in the U.S. Although we've been directed to clam beds on several occasions, we were never able to gather enough to make it worth while. If you're interested in clams, ask for help from local people and if possible, get them to go with you.

Crabs

Tiny crabs can be seen scurrying by the hundreds over rocks near the beach. They are not easy to capture but it can be done. Use a long pole with a nail in one end as a spear. Be quick. Several small crabs will make a good soup. They can also be cooked whole.

Crabs that live in lagoons can be captured with bait. Use a big hunk of fish that will not fall apart on a hook or when tied to the line. Throw the bait out — but not very far. The object is to drag the crab out of the water or into range of a spear or dip net.

Fashion a dip net from heavy wire or sticks lashed to the end of a pole in the shape of a triangle. Cover the opening with a net-like pattern of wire or twine. When a crab is within range, scoop the net under it quickly. I put the bait directly in the net and submerge it if the crabs are close enough to shore.

You can improvise crude traps from large tin cans, sticks lashed together to form a box with a narrow entrance or even large bags (plastic shopping bags or feed sacks) held open with sticks. Fish, meat or scraps of chicken make good bait.

Crayfish

Crayfish are found in many streams, lakes and brackish lagoons. They are variously known as *langostinas, cucarachas* (cockroaches) and *camarones del río* (river shrimps). They are commonly caught by hand (grope very carefully under rocks, ledges and roots; they can pinch!), with traps (coconut meat is said to be a good bait) or with bait (see *Crabs* in this chapter). Spearing is also possible but it takes sharp eyesight and excellent aim to hit them. I find it easier to buy *langostinas* from local people; children are especially good at capturing them. They are prepared for eating in the same way as lobster and shrimp.

Chitons

Chitons make excellent bait and good food. A large chiton may provide as much as two or three bites. They must be well pounded to tenderize the tough flesh. Chitons are found attached to rocks where waves can wash over them frequently. They vary in color according to the rock they are attached to, so look closely.

Limpets and Others

Limpets or Chinamen's Hats are quite good to eat, but they are about as tender as bubble gum off the end of an iron bedpost. Collect a batch of limpets, then clean and prepare them according to the suggestions for *lapa* (see *Cleaning and Preparation of Shellfish* in this chapter). You will probably decide, as we did, that limpets are fine when there's nothing else, but too much trouble for large meals.

Sea urchin eggs are considered a delicacy by some people. Crack the shell and remove the tiny yellow roe (egg) sacs located along the upper inside surface of the 'test' or shell. Eat them raw on crackers, with a squeeze of lime juice or shot of hot sauce.

There are many types of marine *snails* that can be collected on the rocks; they are quite tasty, though rather rubbery. One snail produces a dye. Pick a likely snail and press your thumbnail gently against the operculum (the horny piece that protects the body). A 'dye' snail will immediately begin leaking white stuff on your hand. It smells like sour milk and turns whatever it touches purple. (This dye used to be highly valued by native weavers.) Collect the dye if you wish and return the snail to the water.

Cleaning and Preparation of Shellfish

Oysters, conch, clams, crabs, lobster, *lapa,* snails and other shellfish should be kept alive until just before eating. It is not true that some seafoods *must* be cooked alive. However, they will taste better if they are. A lobster that has been kept on ice for several hours will not be as tasty as one dropped live into boiling water. Oysters, clams and *lapa* that have been beaten around badly while collecting should be placed on ice or eaten within a few hours. Exposing the flesh to the air for several hours is not advisable in hot weather. (See *Recipes:* Chapter 7 for ways to cook shellfish.)

Opening and Cleaning Conch

There are various methods of extracting the meat from a conch shell, all of them brutal. The first method is the easiest and most efficient once you've had practice.

You must first pound a small hole over the point where the animal is attached to the inside top of the shell. The best tool for this job is the claw of a hammer or the pointed, heavy end of another conch shell.

Begin by laying the conch in the sand or on a board with the big opening down. The muscle is attached on the first row or spiral of the shell up from the top edge of the opening. Make the hole on this row (knobs on the shell mark each row) about two inches back from the edge of the opening. The hole should be about an inch or so wide, just large enough to slip in a screwdriver or long bladed knife. (See *illustration.*)

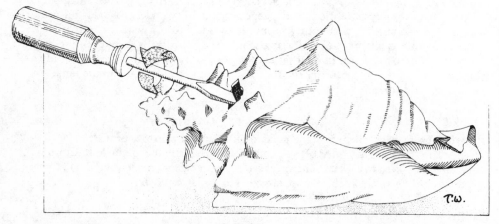

Slip the screwdriver or knife into the hole and push it in as far as it will go. On a large conch this will be about three to six inches. When the tool is all the way in, lever it back and forth and up and down. You might feel it cutting through the stiff muscle, but often you won't know if you have or not.

Check to see if you've cut it properly by grabbing the animal by the foot (not a joke; the foot is the part in the big opening) and pulling. You may have to tug quite hard and steadily before all of the attachment has been ripped free and the meat loosened. If the meat won't come out, put the tool back in the hole and twist it around until you cut something. The hole may be in the wrong place or the tool not far enough into the shell.

Another method is to smash the entire shell. This is no easy matter; the walls of the shell are very thick and hard. The fragments look much like broken china and are just as sharp.

Lay the conch on something sturdy. A rock or thick board is best. The opening of the shell should be pointed almost straight up. Strike the shell next to the opening, on the shiny colored area that's so pretty. If you're using a hammer or the back of a hatchet, it will take a good series of sharp blows. A rock or another conch shell can be used but they're difficult to handle. Break the shell along its entire length. Usually you'll have to work through one or more layers before the meat can be easily removed. Be very careful of flying fragments and of cutting yourself on the shell.

Boiling the conch in the shell until it dies and can then be slipped out preserves the shell but requires a large pot. The conch can also be thrown directly into a fire and killed. This takes five or ten minutes.

Hanging is the most ghastly and also the most tedious way to extract the meat, but it does not destroy the beautiful shell. Tie a sharp fishhook to a piece of strong line about three feet long. Stick the hook into the body or foot of the conch. Once hooked, hang it from something and let the weight of the shell do its awful work. It will take hours. Prepare the conch for eating right away or refrigerate the meat. After hanging for so long it will soon spoil.

Cleaning conch meat is slimy work so continually rub your hands with sand and don't hesitate to pour some over the meat too. A sharp knife is a great help. Remove everything that just hangs from the main chunk of meat. Some of this stuff can be pulled off but most of it will have to be cut. Trim off the various knobs and bumps (siphon tubes for food and water) and make a slit along the edge of the body. Work your thumbnail under the tough outer skin and pull it off.

When the skin has been removed, clean out the small amount of guts at the wide flat end and cut off the operculum (the beak-like thing on the foot, opposite to the guts). The operculum can be removed sooner but it is handy to hang onto when the meat is sliding around. When you're finished, all that's left is white meat.

The meat is now ready to prepare but no matter how you eat the conch, cooked or raw, it must be pounded to tenderize it. Split the entire piece of meat into two thinner portions and pound them with a board, mallet, hammer or the edge of a dinner plate. The meat may lose its shape and begin to go to pieces, but it's best to pound it well rather than eat something like a rubber band.

Dispose of the shells by burying or dumping them well away from camp. Conch shells not only smell rotten but are very dangerous for bare feet.

Opening Oysters

An experienced 'shucker' can make opening oysters appear quite simple. A heavy short-bladed knife is inserted in the tiny crack between the two halves of the shell and with a quick motion the oyster is open, lying beautifully on the half shell, ready to devour.

On the other hand, inexperienced oyster shuckers (which includes almost everyone) attack brutally with a hammer. First knock off the edge of the shell in order to insert a knife blade, then twist it savagely from side to side to cut the strong muscles that hold the two halves of the shell tightly together. It's messy, but it works.

When the oyster has been opened, trim off whatever pieces of the muscle your knife did not cut from the shell; this meat is excellent. Gloves will protect your hand from tiny cuts on the sharp shells.

There is another method of opening the shells that is slower but not so messy. Build a fire and throw the oysters onto the coals. As soon as they begin to bubble, pull them out; they're ready to open and eat.

To avoid burning myself, I prefer to lay the oyster on a wire grill and set it in the fire. If you don't have a grill, oysters can be lined up on a board as close as possible to the coals or arranged around the edge of the fire. This takes longer but once you start opening them, there will be plenty of time.

You can open the shell with your hands if the oyster has been killed and cooked by the heat, but it will require a knife if you prefer them almost raw. The blade should go between the shell halves quite easily after the oyster has weakened.

Cleaning Lapa and Limpets

This is a tedious job that requires hunger for motivation. Two or more people should join together when cleaning *lapa* to keep one person from foul humor and mutiny. Take a sharp knife and run it around the outside of the strange creature residing under the *lapa* shell. Push the knife firmly into the shell at a slight angle to avoid leaving any of the flesh behind. One quick cut around the meat and it should drop out. It will look like a thick gray oval with guts on one side. The idea is to remove and discard anything that is not white. Trim and scrape away the guts and head (notice the resemblance to a snail?), then slice off the tough outside edge of the meat. This done, you're left with a piece of meat that seems to be coated on one side with a soft art gum eraser. This is the bottom of the animal's 'foot' and must be scraped off with a sharp knife, piece of *lapa* shell or glass.

Tenderizing, cooking and other methods of preparing *lapa* are exactly the same as for conch.

Small limpets can be eaten whole (without the shell) or they can be cleaned and prepared similarly to conch and *lapa*. Cleaning a limpet is about as tedious as skinning a worm so you will probably prefer them cooked whole in soups or stews.

Preparing Lobster

This is perhaps the easiest of all seafoods to clean and prepare. Lobster should be cooked whole if possible. Many people ignore the meat in the head and concentrate their efforts on the tail. An average sized lobster has enough meat in the legs and head to make the effort of breaking them apart worthwhile.

There is nothing that needs to be done to a live lobster before cooking it. Should the lobster be dead and dinner more than a couple of hours away, it's best to clean it immediately. Tear the tail from the body and thoroughly rinse out the body cavity, removing any bits of guts that may be inside. Break off one of the antennae and insert the small end in the lobster's asshole. Run the antenna back and forth through the length of the tail, reaming out the passage entirely. Rinse the tail and the head and wrap both in a clean wet cloth.

On The Land

One of the simplest ways to get a quick preview of what can be foraged on the land is to visit a village or small town on market day. *Campesino* families will offer every conceivable kind of food, from regular crops of beans and fresh squashes to home cooked armadillos and live iguanas.

I once took interest in a woman's strange wares, tasting several oddities she'd brought in from the countryside and enjoying her easy going manner. The armadillo was good, but I think I preferred the roasted rattlesnake.

"Try this, *güero!*" She picked up what appeared to be a football-sized lump of baked mud and cracked it in half with a deft karate chop. Inside the mud casing was a pinkish-purple goo. I dipped my fingers into it and dredged up a wad. I tasted it.

"Delicious!" I lied. "Where did you get it?" I thought I'd let it digest slightly before asking what it was.

She gave me a sly look. "I found it in the mountains. Under a rock." When I became even paler than a normal *güero*, the woman laughed and said, "It is some type of squash, I *think*."

When the fish aren't biting and there is no source of meat, you must either become a vegetarian or take up your spear and set out into the jungle. There you will find the last bastion of living and breathing protein — the iguana.

Iguanas

Iguanas are lizards and some get very large; a specimen two or three feet long is not uncommon. They are hideous creatures, the type of thing that scuttles through childhood nightmares. They are very plentiful in many areas of Mexico, particularly along the coasts. The meat of the iguana is considered a delicacy by many and disdained by others. Those willing to overlook the appearance of these lizards will find them truly delicious.

Iguanas come in many colors: brown, green, yellow, blue, red, striped and almost black. They can be found sunning themselves on rocks and in trees. They prefer to sit around fresh water or lagoons and if you discover a good sun-bathing area, they may be there by the hundreds.

Capturing and killing iguanas is a grisly business. They are difficult to murder. Throwing rocks, sticks, spears or shooting at them with arrows are common methods of attack. I prefer to use my special weapon — an alert and agile child. Mexican kids are notorious for the havoc they wreak on the surrounding wildlife, from grasshoppers to songbirds. They are extremely accurate with slingshots and can pick an iguana out of the top of a tree with little effort.

To attract children to the hunt just go off with a long stick and make feeble clubbing motions at an iguana. As if by magic, all children not shining shoes or selling chewing gum within a ten mile radius will converge on you. Tell them what you want and be specific; don't just say, "Bring me some iguanas," or you'll have to open a reptile garden. Say, for example, "*¡Quiero cuatro iguanas, pero grandes!*" (I want four iguanas, but big ones!). Hold firm or they'll bring every iguana they can lay their hands on, from those the size of your little finger to veritable dragons.

Tell your hunters that you want iguanas *muertas* (dead) if you don't relish the thought of doing them in. For a small additional fee, the kids will also skin and clean them for you. This is a tedious job.

Prepare and cook iguana as if it were chicken.

Hunting

Gun regulations are so rigorous in Mexico that only the most serious hunters will want to bother with the hassles involved (see Chapter 11). Casual hunting is not only complicated by bureaucratic paperwork but also by a general lack of game. Unless you mount a serious trip to some remote area or concentrate on small stuff like birds and rabbit, you'll probably be disappointed. *Campesinos* never pass up the opportunity to blast edible creatures, including parrots, robins, squirrels and other small game.

I've often gone hunting with Mexican friends, primarily for the experience and sightseeing rather than for the meat and hides (which never materialized anyway). Sometimes I was offered a gun, other times not. On one occasion I was elected to carry the dynamite. When the forests failed to produce dinner, my friends used the

Papaya Tree   *Papaya*

dynamite to stun and kill fish in a small stream. Total bag for the day: one sparrow and half a bucket of pulverized minnow.

Fruits and Vegetables

Scrounging fruits and vegetables is much more difficult than collecting seafood or iguanas. Most fruits and vegetables are planted intentionally and the owners don't appreciate your taking them. Since small farmers cannot afford wire or posts to fence off their crops, stealing from farms, plantations and unfenced fields is very easy. Very few tourists can imagine what the impact of losing one squash or one bunch of bananas can be to a poor farmer. If you have to steal, don't do it from the people who can't afford to lose a single bean.

Before you rush off with your face charcoaled for a midnight raid against some large *hacienda,* you should know that many large farms will give away or sell ripe produce very cheaply. This is because most produce is picked just before it ripens to avoid spoilage on the way to market. By politely asking for ripe or slightly overripe produce, you can often get an open ticket to pick whatever you need.

Nopales

One of the most common foraged foods is the *nopal* cactus and its fruit, called *tunas.* The young leaves of the *nopal* are carefully cut from the main plant. After the spines are removed with a sharp knife, the round flat *penca* is cut into narrow strips, which are called *nopalitos.* These are rinsed several times (to remove a rather slimy texture), then cooked. They are prepared like young stringbeans and are excellent in tacos, with potatoes and onions or just mixed with *chile,* garlic and lime juice as a salad. The big *pencas* can also be used as containers for roasting meat and vegetables (see *Recipes:* Chapter 7).

The *tunas* grow from the outer edges of the mature *pencas.* They vary in color from deep purple through yellow to pale green, depending on soil conditions, ripeness and the type of cactus (*tuna* is a general term for round cactus fruits). Don't grab one! They are protected by tiny but vicious spines that must be carefully cut away before eating. I once stuffed one into my mouth before trimming the spines and spent days with swollen tongue and lips, not to mention painfully sensitive fingertips.

Here's the safest method: before cutting the *tuna* from the *penca,* spear it with something sharp like a long thorn, twig or the tip of a maguey leaf. When it's firmly skewered, slice it off at the base. Now without removing the 'handle' hold the tuna on a board, stick or rock. Make a slice down the side, about half an inch deep, from top to bottom of the fruit. From this starting point run the knife blade around the fruit, cutting away the thick pulpy skin. If there are plenty of *tunas* available, don't worry about wasting some by sloppy cutting. When the fruit is peeled you'll have a juicy, seed-filled center. Eat it, seeds and all, or spit them out after sucking and slurping the pulp. *Tunas* are delicious when cooked into jam.

Coconuts

I look upon the coconut palm with awe and reverence. They not only provide water, food, shelter and fuel, but can also give you relief from diarrhea and constipation, should the latter ever occur. (The *coco* water alleviates diarrhea; the oily meat, constipation.)

Although many coconut palms have sprouted from drifting nuts cast up by waves and tides, the vast majority have been planted intentionally. Many people mistakenly believe that a fallen coconut is of no use to the owner and they collect these instead of 'stealing' nuts off the tree. Actually any nut that is not rotten will be harvested for the meat (dried it is called *copra*). Most Mexican copra is used to make coconut oil.

Ask if you can buy coconuts. If the owner can afford to let you take them *gratis,* he probably will, but if he's hard up, he'll charge some small price for each nut.

Keep coconuts that are going to be used for drinking in the shade. The husk has excellent insulative properties and will retain the coolness of the night long after the sun is blazing away.

Should you open a coconut and find that there is no meat or very little, don't despair; it still contains something to eat. Immature nuts will be lined with a jelly-like substance (the unhardened meat) that can be scooped out and eaten like pudding. It is delicious; I greatly prefer it to the harder mature meat.

Picking *cocos* is not a simple feat. Climbing the palm is very difficult and should not be attempted unless you're agile and strong. (Children are often sent up the palms because they can stand on the fronds at the top without too much risk of breaking them loose and falling.) Should you safely reach the top, have a rope tossed up and passed over a sturdy frond, close to the trunk. A machete can be tied to one end of the rope and hauled up. Select a good stem of coconuts and tie one end of the rope to it. Someone on the ground should be holding the other end and be prepared to stop the nuts from falling when the stem has been severed. Cut the stem and carefully lower it to the ground. Individual nuts can be twisted off like apples and tossed down.

Coconuts are very brittle and a short drop to the ground can split a large one in half. To avoid breaking the nuts and losing the water, you must either catch them or heap fronds beneath the tree to act as a break-fall. The latter is preferable to missing a catch and having a heavy nut smash your foot. Make a huge pile of fronds and recover each nut as it is thrown down.

If there is no one around foolhardy enough to climb the palm, you have three alternate methods remaining, all of them rather difficult and tedious.

The most difficult is to throw rocks or sticks at the tree in an attempt to knock a coconut down. This is hard work but it does yield an occasional nut.

Use a long pole to knock the nuts down. Insert the end of the pole between several coconuts at the point where they join the main stem. Push, prod and twist the pole to break the nuts loose. This may take time but when it is successful, you'll often have two or three *cocos* in the air at the same time. Be prepared to drop the pole (undoubtedly on someone's head) and to start catching.

When the coconuts absolutely refuse to break loose, a machete can be securely lashed to the end of the pole to sever the stems. Use a sawing motion rather than hacking wildly. If you puncture the husks — very easy to do — you will get a shower for your efforts instead of a refreshing drink.

WARNING: Never cut down a coconut palm without the owner's explicit permission. I know of misguided people who have chopped down palms just to get a few coconuts. This is very stupid and a good way to end up in jail. You will pay not only for the value of the tree, but also for whatever it *might* have produced in it's long life span. This can be a surprising number of coconuts, especially if official opinion is against you, which it almost certainly will be.

When collecting coconuts, be careful of falling or crawling snakes and scorpions that may be living in the top of the tree and in the dead fronds beneath. Ticks are often the greatest annoyance; they love to take up residence in fallen dry limbs.

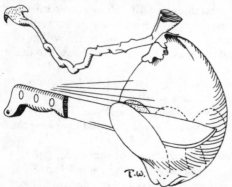

Whacking open a coconut with a few deft strokes of a machete looks easy and is, *if you know how*. The first thing you need is a sharp machete or very heavy knife. The coconut may be opened at either end but the end with the stem is easier to hold. Grasp the nut securely and don't allow your fingers to stray toward the end you're opening. Lay the *coco* in soft sand or better yet, on a piece of wood or a palm branch to avoid dulling the machete when you miss or cut completely through.

Opening a nut so that it can be drunk from without pouring half of the water down your pants is the object of this lesson. The desired opening in the hard inner nut will be about the size of a quarter. This requires a sure hand. Start whacking off slices of the outer husk, working your way slowly toward the inner nut. If you do it properly, the last crucial stroke of the machete will cut just inside the nut. This takes practice but it's worth it, especially when a group of Mexicans are passing the machete around and appraising everyone's technique. It gets to be embarrassing when you have to have a five-year-old kid open your *coco* for you.

When you've finished drinking the water, lay the coconut on another husk or palm frond and cleave it in half from end to end to get at the meat. If you are using a long machete, be careful of a deadly ricochet.

Unknown Mexico

Lakes and Dams

With a few notable exceptions, the largest and most interesting lakes in Mexico have been formed by dams. Although some are well-known among *gringo* fishermen for the tremendous size and quantity of bass they hold, most remain relatively unexplored by boaters and campers. Lakes make excellent base camps for short hiking trips into the surrounding country and those formed by dams are often on interesting canyons and river systems.

Boat launching ramps are built into or very near *la cortina* (curtain, face) of many dams. Others have commercial launching facilities or spots where careful launching can be done from a beach or other access point.

Mexicans commonly use the word *laguna* to describe both freshwater lakes and saltwater lagoons. Lakes formed by dams may also be called *laguna, lago* or *presa*. Ponds are usually called *estanque* or *ojo de agua* (eye of water, spring).

When known, the capacity of a lake is given in millions or billions of cubic meters of water. Lake levels vary greatly, with the highest volumes found in late summer through early winter.

Aguascalientes: *Presa Calles;* 340 million m^3 (cubic meters).

Baja California Norte: *Presa Abelardo Rodríguez;* 137 million m^3.

Coahuila: *Presa La Amistad;* 7 billion m^3, 147 km long. *Presa Don Martín;* 1.4 billion m^3.

Chiapas: *Presa Malpaso* or *Netzahualcóyotl;* 13 billion m^3. This lake is 95 km long and averages 5 km wide. Its shoreline is 400 km long and the water is up to 80 meters deep. *Presa Chicoasén;* One of the world's largest dams, as yet uncompleted, on the spectacular Cañón del Sumidero.. *Presa La Angostura;* 18.6 billion m^3. *Lagos de Montebello;* More than one hundred small and very colorful lakes. National park; excellent camping, hiking and small boating. *Lago Miramar;* Considered one of Mexico's finest lakes. Access is very difficult, though a highway is planned.

Chihuahua: *Presa La Boquilla* or *Lago Toronto;* 3 billion m^3. *Presa El Granero* or *Luis León;* 850 million m^3. *Presa Las Vírgenes;* 425 million m^3. *Presa El Tintero;* 130 million m^3, *Presa Las Lajas;* 90 million m^3. *Presa Guadalupe* or *Abraham González;* 70 million m^3. *Presa del Chuviscar;* designated a Natural Park. *Lago Arareco;* difficult access and "exceptional scenery."

Durango: *Presa Lázaro Cárdenas* or *El Palmito;* 4.4 billion m^3. *Presa Las Tórtolas* or *Francisco Zarco;* 438 million m^3. *Presa Guadalupe Victoria* or *Tunal;* 81 million m^3. *Presa El Bosque* or *Francisco Villa;* 101 million m^3. *Laguna de Santiaguillo; Presa La Tinaja;* No information. *Presa Garabitos;* "Good boating." *Presa de Durango;* Popular boating area. *Presa Peña de Águila;* Eucalyptus forest, boating.

Guanajuato: *Presa Solís;* 850 million m^3. *Presa Ignacio Allende* or *La Begoña;* 251 million m^3.

Guerrero: *Presa Vicente Guerrero* or *Palos Altos;* 250 million m^3.

Hidalgo: *Presa Endó;* 201 million m^3. *Presa Requena;* 70 million m^3. *Lago de Tejocotal;* No information. *Lago de Metztitlán;* good boating but launching is difficult.

Jalisco: *Presa Cajón de Peña;* 707 million m^3. *Presa Basilio Vadillo* or *Las Piedras;* 182 million m^3. *Presa Santa Rosa;* 420 million m^3. *Presa Tacotán;* 149 million m^3. *Lago de Chapala;* Mexico's largest natural lake; 82 km long with an area of 2,300 km^2. Islands, fishing, boating and an impending ecological crisis due to industrial pollution from Guadalajara.

México: *Presa Valle del Bravo;* 458 million m^3. Forests, camping and boating. *Presa Villa Victoria;* 254 million m^3. *Presa Huapango;* 130 million m^3, 20 km long. *Presa Tepetitlán;* 70 million m^3. *Presa Brockman; Presa Colorines; Presa Santo Tomás;* No information.

Michoacán: *Presa El Infiernillo;* 12.5 billion m³. Creation of this lake flooded over one hundred known archaeological sites. Ninety kilometers long; connects to the Río Balsas. *Presa La Villita;* 700 million m³. Located immediately below El Infiernillo; good boating. *Presa Melchor Ocampo* or *El Rosario;* 200 million m³. *Presa Tepuxtepec;* 585 million m³. *Presa El Bosque;* 249 million m³. *Presa Cointzio;* 85 million m³. *Lago de Cuitzeo;* A large shallow lake with many areas choked by weeds. Good motorless boating, however. Islands; total length of 48 km. *Lago de Pátzcuaro;* One of Mexico's most publicized lakes. Large and very beautiful, with islands. *Lago de Zirahuén;* "Small but beautiful." *Lago de Janitzio; Laguna Magdalena; Presa Mata de Pino; Lago de Camécuaro;* No information.

Morelos: *Lago de Tequesquitengo; Laguna de El Rodeo; Laguna de Coatetelco;* No information.

Nayarit: *Laguna de Santa María del Oro;* 2 km long, forested shores. *Laguna de Santa Teresa;* Small. *Laguna de San Pedro Lagunillas;* Small. *Laguna de Tepetiltec; Presa del Bañadero;* No information.

Nuevo León: *Presa Rodrigo Gomez* or *La Boca;* Boating. *Laguna de Sánchez;* Forests. *Presa Sombreretillo;* In the Sierra de la Iguana.

Oaxaca: *Presa Miguel Alemán* or *El Temascal;* 8 billion m³. *México Desconocido* magazine calls this "The Lake of A Thousand Islands." Eighty kilometers long. *Presa El Marqués* or *Benito Juárez;* 942 million m³. *Presa Yosocuta;* 47 million m³. Fishing, boating and camping.

Puebla: *Presa Valsequillo* or *Manuel Camacho;* 424 million m³. *Presa de Apulco;* A small lake, just 6 km long by 1 km wide, described as one of Mexico's finest with "extraordinary vegetation."

Querétaro: *Presa Hidalgo;* 75 million m³.

San Luis Potosí: *El Lugar del Rayo;* There are four lakes in this area: Toro, Grande, Patos and Tampasquín. *Laguna de Media Luna;* No information.

Sinaloa: *Presa Miguel Hidalgo* or *El Mahone;* 3.4 billion m³. *Presa Adolfo Mateos* or *El Humaya;* 4.1 billion m³. *Presa Guamúchil* or *Buelna;* 343 million m³. *Presa Sanalona;* 845 million ³. *Presa El Sabino* or *Josefa Ortiz;* 600 million m³.

Sonora: *Presa El Novillo* or *Plutarco Calles;* 7.3 billion m³. Described as "an island sea in the desert." *Presa Oviáchic* or *Alvaro Obregón;* 3.2 billion m³. *Presa Mocúzari* or *Adolfo Cortines;* 1.1 billion ³. *Presa La Angostura;* 921 million m³. *Presa Abelardo Rodríguez;* 250 million m³.

Tamaulipas: *Presa Falcón* or *Internacional Falcón;* 5 billion m³. *Lago* or *Presa de Guerrero* or *Las Adjuntas;* 5.3 billion m³; 60 kilometers long and 20 km wide. *Presa Marte Gómez* or *El Azúcar;* 1.2 billion m³. *Presa Las Ánimas;* 665 million m³. *Presa Anda La Piedra;* 160 million m³. *Presa El Empalme;* 90 million m³. *Presa Real Viejo* or *República Española;* 75 million m³.

Veracruz: *Lago de Catemaco;* 657 million m³. Very beautiful and popular, though rarely crowded. Good boating and camping. *Presa Chicayán;* 570 million m³.

Zacatcas: *Presa Trujillo* or *Leobardo Reynoso;* 75 million m³.

7. Camp Cooking

Imagine a group of seasoned campers sprawled around a blazing fire, all lost in their own thoughts after yet another hearty meal of undercooked beans and pasty rice. Bob, drafted as Cook-of-the-Day by popular vote, has just finished an impassioned monologue on the nutritional and moral values of a pure bean and tortilla diet. In the distance, a donkey's sarcastic gulping bray seems to sum up the group's reaction to their cook's philosophies.

"This fire'd be perfect for some weinies," Fred mutters only half-jokingly, stirring the mesquite embers with a greedy look in his eyes. He has just returned from a three-week van trip in the mountains west of Oaxaca, where he never quite got his kitchen gear unpacked. His belt now goes around his narrow hips twice.

"Junk food!" a woman from the Bay Area sneers, prying a grain of rice from between her rear molars with a convenient thorn. She has travelled a full year on less money than most *gringos* spend on their pet canary. The last time she was elected to cook a meal the scavenging dogs didn't even bother to pass by the camp afterwards.

The mere mention of the words 'junk food' throws the group into a frenzy of righteous self-denial. Ever since they caught Steve in bed with a Twinkie Wonder they've watched each other with the suspicious curiosity of castaways counting ship's biscuits.

"I hiked from Punta del Sol all the way to Tres Piedras with nothing but a sack of bananas!"

"I know a guy who can make bread out of avocadoes!"

"Has anybody else ever eaten *huitlacoche,* that gooey black corn fungus stuff? I love it!"

"I once ate with a Tarahumara family for three months. It was really an experience!"

"You're kidding!" Lois says, shifting her considerable bulk for a better look at the emaciated fellow across from her. "How much weight did you lose?"

"Well . . ." he smiles, embarrassed, "I didn't lose much . . . in fact I think I *gained* a few pounds. They ate a lot of sugar." There is a hushed silence at this outrageous confession. He tries desperately to recover his position by describing in clinical detail the case of dysentery he's just cured with a ten-day regimen of boiled garlic and milk. No one is impressed.

There is a strained silence, broken only by the familiar sound of pumpkin seeds being cracked between front teeth. All exclaim over the exquisite flavor of the seeds and agree on their obvious nutritive value. Wendy, tomorrow's cook, proposes that eating nothing but seeds for twenty-four hours would be a good thing and perhaps even a Complete Protein.

There is a dull silence as the group digests this proposal; the alternative, after all, is another meal of — you guessed it — beans and rice.

Suddenly a loud voice booms out of the night. "Hey! You folks wouldn't want some of this leftover food would 'ya?"

It's Herb and Phyllis, the retired couple in the luxurious motorhome. They are on their way back north in the morning and want to jettison some extra groceries in order to increase their gas mileage. The group has avoided Herb and Phyllis since the day they bragged that they'd been in Mexico for two months and had yet to eat Mexican food. Their freezer and cupboards look like a mini-Safeway.

"Got some Hearty Hunks," Herb says, "and some Crispy Crunchies and some Sugar Soggies and a half case of Chunky Chowder and some Salty Snappies and . . ."

The group responds like the Faithful to a celestial trumpet; with a communal cry of gut hunger they thunder through the thorn bushes, shouting and laughing with glee.

Campers are often surprised to find that shopping for food, cooking, eating and KP chores take up a major portion of their free time. Lorena's detailed journals of our hiking, boating and van expeditions tend to read like gastronomic tours, giving casual readers the impression that we don't do much but cook and eat while camping. This might sound like an exaggeration when you're sitting in the kitchen at home, surrounded by cupboards of food and a bulging refrigerator, but wait until True Hunger strikes at the end of a long adventurous day in Mexico. I've seen food-crazed campers run amok like rogue elephants, trampling trees and children that came between them and the larder. Lovers rise furtively from cozy sleeping bags to rummage for a hidden chocolate bar or a cache of limp cucumbers, old friends squabble over miserly portions of gooey oatmeal as if it were gold dust and insatiable teenagers plead for more as if posing for a CARE poster.

Although food is generally abundant in Mexico and of excellent quality and freshness, the deeper you travel into the boondocks the less variety you'll find. We've all read that the basic staples of Mexican cuisine are corn, beans, squash and *chiles,* but it always comes as something of a shock to find out that this limited selection really is *it* for most of the people.

"Lorena, come look! I've found an onion!" This sort of scene is typical when travelling far off the beaten track. The trick is not to be discouraged, even when it means filling out your diet with imaginary banquets of Greek olives, golden barbecued chickens and mugs of chilled beer.

The longer your camping trip is, the more important food and regular meals become. Establish a cooking routine as quickly as possible. Most people don't realize how rigid their present cooking and eating schedules are until they've hit the road and broken the familiar cycles of shopping, cooking and setting the dinner table. The sudden transformation from a well organized and brightly lighted modern kitchen to a sandy, windswept campsite can wreak havoc on the most determined and experienced cook. For those who normally waver between a dinner of canned noodle soup or no dinner at all, this transformation can lead to severe weight loss and a sharp drop in morale.

When we stop at the end of the day our first consideration is food. It takes just a minute to start a fire or set up the stove. While one of us scouts the sleeping possibilities or gathers fuel, the other gets out the cooking utensils. Before we've even had a chance to appreciate the view, the teapot is jumping. A hot cup of tea, coffee, broth, chocolate or instant soup is just what we need to sip on while setting up camp. Once we've relaxed, planning and preparing dinner is a lot easier to face.

When fatigue threatens to overcome hunger, don't give in. Your body needs to replenish itself, and not with a bag of potato chips and a long drink of José Cuervo.

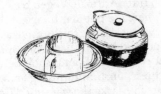

When exhausted, our standard ploy to force ourselves to cook is simple: Lorena peels garlic while I heat a small amount of butter or cooking oil in a skillet. There's got to be something to fry, if only the garlic. The next step is something to put the garlic on — noodles? rice? or add more vegetables and water for soup?

Advance planning can save you a great deal of extra work while cooking in camp or on the road. Let's assume that you've stopped for the night and are camped on the edge of a cornfield, just a little too tired to feel enthusiastic about making dinner. This is the time to fall back on a simple meal, like steamed potatoes and other vegetables. Cover them with a gravy and grated cheese, add a simple salad on the side and you're all set.

Here's where advance planning comes in: cook enough for both dinner and breakfast. In the morning slice and fry the leftover potatoes and vegetables with onion, then scramble in one or two eggs per person. (Cooked vegetables keep overnight without refrigeration except in the hottest weather.) Part of the advance planning of these meals is also having the right food on hand: vegetables and eggs.

When camped in one spot for a few days or more we always keep a pot of beans at the back of the fire. When I'm struck by hunger but don't want to bother cooking, I just heat the beans or eat them cold. Plain steamed rice can also be used for quick meals: fried in butter, plain or with eggs; with vegetables, seafood or meat, etc.

Pack your cooking gear and food so that everything is easily accessible and just as easy to put away when you're finished. We carry our basic utensils and food in boxes or baskets that are stuffed in a corner of the van. It's not very neat but when we want to whip up a quick meal the kitchen isn't lost under the books or hidden behind the diving gear. When backpacking we stow the food and kitchen last, making it the easiest to get at when we stop for a snack or a night's camp. (See *Travelling Kitchens* later in this chapter.)

Cooking two or three times a day while camping is real work. Something as simple as rinsing off the vegetables can turn into a major chore: going for water, finding a place to put things down without dirtying them, locating the purifying tablets, filling a large pan or leakproof bag and so on. How can the cook keep this under control while stoking the fire, adjusting the lantern, locating the tableware and topping off the salt shaker?

Unless you're a combination of Julia Child and Sourdough Sam, you'll need help — help from those deadbeats who are reading paperbacks and watching the sunset while you sweat over a hot cookfire. I always wait for someone to ask, "Hey, when is dinner going to be ready?" That's my first volunteer. The next one is, "Sure am getting hungry!" They get sent into the bushes for firewood. "Wow, that smells good!" doesn't fool me; that person makes the salad.

Sharing cooking chores isn't done just out of a spirit of cooperation. In most camps, if everyone doesn't help, things don't get done or don't get done well. This is especially important if one person is doing most of the cooking, voluntarily or otherwise. Rather than force someone to prepare meals that look like bad accidents and taste even worse, assign them a support task. Leave the actual cooking to a cook.

The simplest meal takes about twice as long to prepare while camping as in a home kitchen. Anticipate this, especially for the evening meal when a slight delay can mean finishing up in total darkness. It's not only easier to cook in daylight, but most people like to see their food as they eat it rather than play Twenty Questions with each bite: Animal, Vegetable or Mineral?

There is a popular image of the gourmet cook that has been propagated by television shows: smiling, vivacious, witty, energetic and delightfully outraged at minor kitchen mishaps, like spilling boiling oil onto the floor. I've found that the reality of a good camp cook lies somewhere between Idi Amin and the Godfather: ruthless, uncompromising and generally ill-tempered. (When I worked on fishing boats in Alaska the warning, "Cook's savage!" would send fear into the hearts of every crewman, from the lowliest greenhorn to the captain.) Treat camp cooks, especially those working under arduous conditions, with the respect due to a brilliant but potentially homicidal artist.

Give the cook preference on work surfaces: if there's just one table, move the poker game to the ground and let the cook work in comfort and cleanliness. Your reward for such noble behavior will come on your dinner plate. The same goes for lights: nothing makes cooking more tedious and difficult than darkness. If the meal is prepared over a campfire, the cook determines its temperature, not idle spectators who want a bonfire instead of a gentle bed of coals for sauteing.

True or False?: If one spud bakes in 40 minutes at 350° then two spuds will bake in 10 minutes at 1400°.

If you answered "True," I'm afraid you've won two hours of KP. When in doubt use less heat and more time. Don't rush the food or the fire, it only leads to burnt meals and hot tempers. Camp stoves tend to cook hotter than home gas and electric ranges, and campfires are truly scorching: most are several times as big and hot as you'll need to cook even the most elaborate meals.

Have all the dishes and utensils washed before the cooking starts and keep them readily at hand. True 'one-pot' meals are very rare and if you're like Lorena, you'll need at least two spoons to stir the soup. Nothing aggravates the cook more than having to interrupt the creative process with a frenzied session of dish scrubbing.

"A little sand never hurt anybody," is a line that every camper hears at least once a trip, usually after someone has broken a filling on a small rock hidden in the refried beans. It takes extra care on the cook's part to keep sand and miscellaneous debris out of the food, but it is precisely this bit of extra work that distinguishes a good cook from a galley slave. The kitchen area should be treated as reverently as a Buddhist shrine, kept religiously clean and neat, and not allowed to become a hangout for hungry camp followers.

An important rule of good camp cooking is *"What you see is what you've got."* Don't fret over what you want or feel you need; use what's on hand and apply your talents to turning those ingredients into a good meal. Cookbook-trained cooks may find improvisation difficult at first, but hunger usually carries them through to success.

Keep your food in sight, not hidden away where it will be forgotten until it starts to reek. We carry fresh foods in baskets, one or two with lids or cloth covers to keep flies off the bananas and tomatoes. A typical meal or snack begins with "What's left in the baskets?"

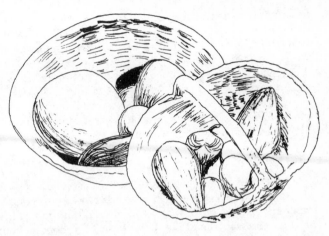

By using what's on hand and locally available, you'll not only simplify your life, but save money and needless shopping trips. When you'd prefer to spend the day relaxing rather than on a supply run to town, you'll find a variety of new uses for those sprouting potatoes and limp carrots.

One of our favorite camping spots in Mexico is on a beautiful but relatively isolated beach, miles from the nearest village or store. Food is available, but the variety runs heavily to the Mexican Basics.

In spite of the beach's beauty and an abundance of fresh fish, many campers leave before they really want to because they aren't able to buy what they *assume* they need in the way of food. (See *Food & Water:* Chapter 1.)

This is an opportunity to learn how the local people cope and to imitate, to a certain degree, how they eat. Do you find tortillas boring? Smear them with your secret stash of peanut butter or shred them into soup. How many ways are there to prepare the humble spud or noodles? A lot, believe me; use the *Recipes* and plenty of imagination.

Backpackers and boaters should be especially attentive to minor changes which create new tastes and dishes. When supplies are limited to what you can carry, forage or luck upon in a remote *tienda,* the smallest variation can be important.

We made a long boat trip on the spur of the moment, with almost no time at all to shop or gather food carefully. I bought a gunny sack near the marketplace and grabbed whatever looked good and not too perishable: onions, garlic, potatoes, limes, cabbage, cooking oil, salt, bananas and honey. A typical meal (breakfast, lunch or dinner) would be fresh fish cooked on a stick (see *Recipes*), chopped cabbage with lime juice dressing and a potato or onion baked in the fire. By the end of the trip our taste buds were as sensitive as a cat's whiskers. A simple variation such as a tablespoon of minced onion in the cabbage salad was noticed and really appreciated. One meal was just broiled fish followed by roast bananas and melted honey. Ambrosia!

On an extended backpacking trip we learned another simple fact of camp cooking: strong flavors are often more satisfying than subtle flavors. We found ourselves munching raw onions and even whole cloves of garlic. I remember eating a cucumber, skin and all, and wondering why I'd always peeled them.

Simplicity is the next lesson: when in doubt, leave it out. Too many cooks add a pinch of this and a piece of that, just because it's on hand, not because the dish really needs another flavor or ingredient. Such simple dishes as baked potatoes garnished with minced green onions are often more memorable than multi-flavored stews or giant fried concoctions that taste okay, but all taste the same.

Which brings me to 'gorp' and 'glop,' four-letter words that have no place in a good camp cook's vocabulary. Campers who equate eating with the grosser body functions substitute these 'dishes' for the most elementary yet genuinely tasty meals. Open a package of dried beef: dump it into boiling water. Open some dehydrated vegetable mix: dump it in, too. Here's some instant rice: dump it in. How about this stuff: Yeah, dump it in. Wait a minute, that was instant tea. Ah well, what's the difference? Stir it a few times; I think it's burning. How does it taste? Like sh . . . gorp!

In more civilized cultures a cook would be consigned to the rack for even considering such a gastronomic atrocity. If you must eat gorp, please do it late at night in the privacy of your own tent.

Cravings and Snacks: A Stitch in Time

Sudden changes in your daily routine, especially the increase in physical exercise that most campers experience when they head outdoors, may cause intense food cravings. After a long day of skin diving, hiking and gathering firewood, I can count on a merciless attack of the Killer Munchies about an hour after dinner. When the munchies strike, nothing is safe: stale tortillas with mustard, cold oatmeal with jelly, lots of smoked fish, crackers, candy bars, the honey jar . . . lick it to the bottom . . . pass the catsup and *chiles* . . .

When routine foods can't quite satisfy your needs, don't fill the void with expensive and nutrition-low junk foods. Take the Scout approach and *Be Prepared:* cheese, nuts, fresh and dried fruits, juices, smoked fish or meat jerky. Eat these foods first, then allow yourself to dip into the sack for things like candy bars and potato chips.

Many campers confuse a craving for carbohydrates with protein and sugar cravings. While on a very long ocean kayaking trip we found that huge servings of noodles, rice or potatoes, with a simple sauce of garlic and oil with herbs, were extremely satisfying. It also went well with a heavy diet of fish and other seafoods. We often ate noodles for breakfast, lunch and dinner. Monotony was never a problem; our appetites and a variety of spices took care of that.

One of my favorite camping snacks is just cold boiled potatoes, garnished with salt and pepper and eaten with a green onion or canned jalapeño chili. *Atole* (see *Recipes*) also provides a good combination of sweets and carbohydrates and can be served hot or cold.

Uncontrolled snacking can make serious inroads on your food supply and budget, especially if anyone in your family or group has an appetite as ferocious as mine. If there are stores nearby, or you've stocked up in advance, this won't be a problem. But what if you're at the end of a fifty-mile dirt road or three-day's paddle from a *tienda?* You're out of luck; start daydreaming about food and jot down a list of what you wish you had along. Use this list when you stock up for your next adventure into the boondocks. Cravings aren't easily recalled when you're full and wandering the aisles of a market or store.

On a long kayak trip I was obsessed by chocolate bars. The *idea* of chocolate bars that is. I hadn't eaten candy since I was a kid and hadn't even thought of taking any with me. I'll never forget my intense feeling of relief when I spotted a dirty glass jar filled with stale hard candies in a remote *tienda*. I cackled with glee as the old woman behind the counter wrapped those precious nuggets in a twist of newspaper.

Food and candy stashes are useful for more than just casual cravings, especially if you're backpacking or boating. We sometimes find ourselves in situations where cooking is just too much to face, either because of the physical circumstances (five miles from shore in a boat or torrential rain trapping you inside a tent), exhaustion, no fuel, etc. That last four-kilometer stretch of rugged trail or hour of frantic paddling to reach a perfect campsite can leave you incapable of anything more than unwrapping some delicious treat and rolling into a sleeping bag for the night. Moments such as these will be much less of a hardship if you have a really tasty and nutritious snack on hand.

Constant snacking isn't a vice, especially while exerting yourself physically. Forget that childhood brainwashing about not eating between meals; steady snacking gives steady energy, rather than the tiring 'highs-and-lows' that come from gorging at widely separated mealtimes. Gorging also uses up your food supplies faster than moderate but continuous munching.

Many people mistakenly buy cheap food, especially cheap snacks, in order to save money. An apparently expensive bar of chocolate, for example, goes a lot farther than one that is basically just sugar and flavorings. Tuna fish is a favorite Mexican snack and although it isn't cheap, a can of good quality tuna will make several sandwiches or tacos, a tuna salad or a large tuna and noodle casserole. Or just open the can and eat it with your fingers. By indulging yourself more on snacks, *when you really need them,* you'll save money in the long run and be healthier.

The best place to buy snack foods in Mexico is a large supermarket (salami, sausages, cheeses, economy-sized bags and cans of nuts, canned meats and seafoods, candy bars by the box, instant soups, etc.) and in stores and stalls that sell sweets, nuts and dried fruits in bulk. Shop around; the prices can vary quite a lot between two stores. Packaged dried fruit, for example, is expensive in small bags, but if you find a store that sells it *suelto* (loose, in bulk), the cost will be much lower.

Try homemade Mexican sweets before you stock up on prepackaged candies and confections. *Ates* are fruit jellies, molded into rolls and large bricks. They are very tasty and inexpensive. Nuts and seeds are mixed with brown sugar or honey and prepared similar to peanut brittle. Look for them in the market or in candy shops. You'll usually get a sample taste if you ask with a smile, *"¿Puedo probarlo, por favor?"* (Can I try it, please?).

For a lot more on food in Mexico, including candies, nuts and typical confections, see *The People's Guide to Mexico: Restaurants and Typical Foods* and *Markets and Stores.*

Reluctant Vegetarians

Dedicated carnivores often find meat difficult to come by while camping. Small villages rarely have refrigeration and most rely on a weekly or monthly slaughtering of a pig or other large animal for fresh meat. In between times they eat dried meat, the odd chicken or two, or do without. Meat will be sold early in the morning, usually before ten a.m. Get there ahead of the rush or you'll have to be satisfied with snouts and elbows. Poultry is sold live, though in most cases you can ask the seller to do the dirty deed, including plucking, for a reasonable fee. Mexicans love chicken heads and feet, so give them away if you don't use them yourself.

If you crave the flesh of innocent animals and birds but can't find a meat market near your camp, your only alternatives to becoming a reluctant vegetarian are foraging (see Chapter 6) or eating canned meats and fish. We always try to carry a supply of smoked fish (Lorena is a confirmed vegetarian but eats fish these days) and I often prepare a batch of jerky when meat is available. Cheese will keep for a long time when properly packaged (see *Food Storage* in this chapter) and by using it liberally you shouldn't go hungry.

Food and Guests

When travelling in the back country you'll often find that you've got a much more interesting stock of food than the local people. If someone comes along while you're cooking it can be a tough decision as to whether or not to share your meal. When in doubt — offer. In most cases they'll turn you down or accept a token portion. But if they accept eagerly you know it's from hunger. The rule of Mexico's back country is hospitality; don't forget that it works both ways.

Sharing your food with local people often has unexpected rewards, and not just in good feeling. I especially remember the two men who rode for several hours to give us a huge block of the most delicious cheese I've ever tasted. We'd given their wives a can of condensed milk the day before. Or the lady who came shyly out of the jungle, offering a pile of thick tortillas in return for a head of garlic. The divers who dropped by with a sack of oysters and lobster; the *campesina* with an apronful of fresh garbanzo beans; the giggling children lugging a wooden box of papayas and bananas and many, many others.

Shopping

Shopping for food in Mexico is quite different than a routine visit to the local A & P for a cartload of groceries. The following information is necessarily brief; for much more on food shopping, booze, bartering, weights and measures, packaging and brand names see *The People's Guide to Mexico: Markets and Stores, Restaurants and Typical Foods, Travelling Cheap* and *Cooking in Mexico*.

Food is sold in *tiendas* (small stores), *supermercados* and the traditional marketplace, where open food stalls cater primarily to morning shoppers. Although some foods are packaged, especially in supermarkets, the vast majority are sold loose. Fortunately for campers, most packaged foods are offered in a range of sizes, including very small. Cooking oil, for example, comes in tiny cans and bottles, just about enough for one meal. Always carry a good supply of sturdy food containers; even if foods are packaged they often break open. Loose foods will be wrapped in a cone of newpaper or dropped into a weak plastic bag, a banana leaf or a corner of your shirt. If you don't have a bag and one isn't offered, you'll have to buy one on the spot.

Foods are sold by weight and volume, *kilogramas* and *litros* (2.2 pounds and 1.1 quarts). The most commonly used fractions of these amounts are:

medio kilo:	1.1 pounds
cuarto de kilo:	.55 pounds
medio litro:	.55 quarts (close to a pint)
cuarto de litro:	.27 quarts (close to a cup)

Many foods are sold by the gram: *"Dáme cien gramos de arroz, por favor"* (Give me one hundred grams of rice, please). It takes practice to learn how many grams of beans are equivalent to the familiar packages you used to buy at home. When in doubt, buy less, especially of fresh foods that may spoil.

Loose foods are also sold by the *mano* (handful), *montón* (mound, pile) and *pieza* (piece). Eggs, for example, may be sold *por pieza* (by the piece, individually) or *por kilo* (by kilos, also *por peso,* by weight).

Bartering over the price of food is not too common in larger marketplaces. In most cases the vendor will prefer to give you a bit more food rather than take a bit less money.

Two other types of food stores will interest campers: Conasupo (the name of a government agency) and mobile *tiendas* that travel from village to village, some operated by Conasupo, others private. Conasupo stores usually sell below the normal price, especially for staples. Tourists are welcome to shop in the Conasupo, but if the stock is very limited don't clean out all the goodies (such as canned juices). Local people can't compete with your buying power and if you take everything, they'll go without until the store is restocked.

Mobile *tiendas* come in all shapes and sizes, from semi-trailers to broken down pickups and old cars, loaded to the gills with canned goods, staples and fresh produce. Some have regular routes, others just happen along and set up wherever there's a crowd. If you camp in one spot for a long time they may make a special visit.

When shopping in remote areas keep in mind that prices are usually higher than in the cities due to scarcity and the cost of transportation. If something seems outrageously expensive, don't complain; it won't do you any good and may cause hard feelings. Slightly higher prices are usually offset by the savings in time, energy and gasoline to do your own supply runs.

Food Storage

There's nothing quite like dipping into the food larder at the end of a long, hungry day to find that the tomatoes and bananas have gotten together with the peanuts and garlic to make a strange and disgusting sauce. Food spoilage is a constant problem while camping, especially if the weather is warm and refrigeration just a dream. Before you give up and buy a case of canned food, read over this section and plan both your food lists and storage to take advantage of foods that resist spoilage or can be encouraged to last longer with simple precautions.

First, and simplest, is to buy some produce that is ripe and ready to eat, and some that is still green or hard. By buying both ripe and unripe produce you should be able to cover your needs for at least a full week in one shopping trip.

Fresh food is rarely treated with preservatives in Mexico and many *gringos* don't recognize a banana or mango that has been allowed to ripen naturally, rather than being ripened under controlled artificial means. A natural ripe banana is usually spotted brown or black and is not only still good inside but incredibly sweet and flavorful. Taste them before you toss them into the garbage bucket.

Spoilage caused by natural bacteria on the surface of produce can be delayed for a considerable time by simply washing the food in a cleansing bath of *yodo* or bleach (see Chapter 8) to kill anything in the water or on the produce. For good measure we increase the dose used for purifying drinking water by 50 to 100%, depending on how dirty the produce looks. (This is the same procedure, by the way, that you should use for all produce, regardless of whether you want to store it away or use it immediately.) Soak the food for at least half an hour, then remove and drain until completely dry. Don't rinse it off; what little purification agent remains will also help retard spoilage and will have little if any effect on the flavor of the food.

Now wrap the individual pieces of produce in paper, taking care not to bruise or break the skin. Newspaper works fine but don't use plastic, aluminum foil or other impermeable wrappings. The food has to 'breathe'. Plastic bags are fine for food storage inside a refrigerator (dry air), but while camping they actually speed up spoilage by trapping moisture, heat and bacteria. Arrange the wrapped food in a basket or box and store in a dark place or at least in the shade. If you are unable to purify the food first, try the wrapping method anyway. Check all the produce daily, using up any that is ripe or shows signs of spoilage. Under ideal conditions a green tomato will keep for weeks. Cucumbers, chayotes, onions, limes, cabbage and other fairly durable fruits and vegetables will also last a surprisingly long time.

Store food for immediate use in baskets or boxes that have good air circulation. In humid weather you may have to dry your food in the sun every morning to avoid rapid spoilage from condensation and dew. Line the container with paper or cloth,

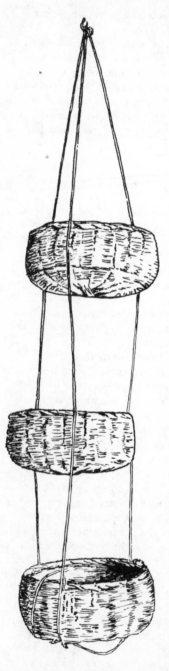

not plastic. If you are heading into a remote area and want to stock up on food in advance, select your fresh produce with special care. Cabbages and cucumbers are classic long-lasting foods. Buy the best you can find and reject any that have started to spoil or are very ripe. Limes with thin hard skins and oranges with thin skins (very difficult to peel) last far longer than thick, easily peeled varieties. Thin-skinned oranges are usually called *naranjas para jugo* (oranges for juice).

To soften limes that have formed a very hard skin, drop them into boiling water for one minute. You can also roast them quickly right in the coals of a fire. You won't believe how juicy they'll be.

We use a great deal of cheese while camping and rarely have any way to refrigerate it. Buy a large block of *queso de chihuahua* (a very popular cheddar-like cheese) and wrap it well in several layers of paper or clean cotton cloth (cheesecloth was invented for this purpose). When you want a piece of cheese, carefully shave off any mold — which won't hurt you but tastes funky. Remember, the moldy outside layer is protection for the cheese, so only trim it off the piece to be used. If the weather is warm the cheese will exude water and natural oils. This is part of the aging process and actually improves the flavor. A block of mild cheese will gradually turn sharp, though we usually eat it up before this happens. Carefully wrapped cheese that is kept well aired and away from prowling dogs and rodents will last for weeks, even in warm weather.

Mexican supermarkets are excellent sources of dried and lightweight prepared foods. New products appear constantly — the latest is Mexican-made Japanese Ramen noodles and soups — and campers can find interesting and tasty bargains by touring the shelves. Look for instant refried beans, instant soups and potatoes, dried meat, fish and shrimp, quick desserts and cake mixes, etc.

Alpura 2000 is a 'super pasteurized' whole milk sold in Mexico. It can be found on supermarket shelves, in squat paper cartons that do not require refrigeration. Alpura is said to last up to six months (unopened). This makes it an excellent camping food, though once the carton is opened the milk should be used as if it were regular milk.

Salt has an annoying tendency to get damp, harden and block the holes in the shaker. Cover with a plastic bag at night to keep the moisture out.

Camp Kitchens

After thousands of camping meals we have divided our kitchen gear into three basic categories: the Backpacker Kitchen, the Suitcase Kitchen and the Colonizer's Kitchen. The type of trip we plan to make determines which of these three kitchens we'll use. We also make liberal adjustments: while boating in Baja we didn't need a stove, fuel bottles or primer and spare parts. When firewood wasn't available we just ate our food cold.

The Backpacker's Kitchen is our most basic, lightweight set-up and it also forms the heart of the Suitcase Kitchen. The Suitcase Kitchen, as the name implies, fits into a small suitcase or sturdy box. We use it on short van trips or long car camping expeditions where space and weight are important. The Colonizer's Kitchen is for extended vehicle trips, when we're not sure when we'll get back and don't care if we ever do, and for trips to favorite beaches where eating is a major entertainment.

Backpacker's Kitchen

This kitchen is for two people but we've fed as many as six for short periods of time. With the addition of another cup, an extra spoon and a bowl, it served three of us quite well on a seven-week kayaking voyage. We sometimes had to use hats for salad bowls but otherwise we had few problems.

The equipment listed is of backpacking weight, that is, as light as reasonably possible. When you're travelling in a vehicle or boat, you can substitute standard kitchen items for many things without overloading.

Stove
Grate
2 Fuel Bottles (1 liter)
Stove Primer (if needed)
2 Pots (nesting)
2 Pot Grabbers (I lose 1)
Frying pan (Teflon, 7-9 in.)
Spatula (plastic or wooden)
4 Bandannas/Dish Towels
Frisbee

Knife (We carry Lorena's sm.
    filet knife and a veg. knife)
Pocket Steel
Can and Bottle Opener
2 Cups (metal)
2 Bowls (plastic with lids)
2 Plates (metal)
2 Spoons, Chopsticks
Jars & Bottles (plastic,
    assorted)

Tea Pot (metal, 4-cup)
Zip Loc Bags (assorted)
Aluminum Foil
    (sev. yards)
Pot Scrubber (plastic)
Lighter, Matches
Storage Bag (for kitchen)
Purifying Pills or Liquid
Napkins
Soap
Comal (tortilla griddle)

Stove, Fuel bottles: See Chapter 9.

Grate: We improvised our backpacker's grill: buy an oven grate or light barbecue grill at a junk shop and hacksaw out a piece about 6" by 12". Carry it in a drawstring bag to avoid dirtying other gear. (See Chapter 5 for more on Mexican grills.)

Pots: We use aluminum 'nesting billies' with wire handles and tight-fitting lids. We call the larger pot (about a two-quart) Bill and the smaller, Billy. Billy fits inside Bill. Bill is perfect for boiling potatoes, stews, clams and noodles. Billy is just right for cooking coffee, rice and sauces.

Bill and Billy travel inside the Billy Bag, a light, waterproof sack with a zipper along one side. The bag can be attached to the outside of a backpack, a burro saddle or canoe thwart. The Billy Bag also holds the pot scrubber, pot grabbers, lighter and matches, aluminum foil (folded up), spoons, spatula, cups (inside Billy), plates or bowls and other odds and ends.

Pot Grabbers: The most useful piece of special camping gear ever invented. Using a metal pot grabber turns a tin can into a cooking pot. Watch your pot grabbers around sand; they can sink and disappear in an instant. Pliers also make good pot grabbers.

Spoons, Chopsticks: Forks are a luxury since real campers don't mind slurping or tearing food apart with their fingers. Chopsticks make good stirrers, tongs, pokers and utensils for unexpected guests who might eat more than their share if they had a fork. The best spoons are long enough to scrape the bottom of a pot but not so large they won't fit into your mouth.

Bandannas or Dish Towels: For wrapping *tortillas,* making bundles of dry beans or loose foods, hot pads, small tablecloths (especially on beaches), drying dishes and even blowing your nose when smoke gets in your eyes.

Frisbee: This isn't a joke; we use our Frisbee for a plate, lid, soup and mixing bowl, cutting board, sand shovel, fire fan, serving dish, emergency kayak paddle, hat (drill two holes, lash to head with shoelace) and even a toy, if that sort of thing amuses you. Its final function comes at the end of the trip: a Frisbee makes a good gift.

Cups: Mexican enameled tin cups are ideal for camping, superior, in my opinion, to the overrated Sierra cup. The enamel tends to insulate the metal, but take care when cooking in the cup to avoid popping the enamel from the metal.

Bowls: Plastic bowls are cheaper than metal and often come with tight-fitting lids. Look in discount stores. Our bowls are labelled as refrigerator containers; we use them to carry leftovers, too.

Plates: We carry two very sleazy tin plates that make good lids and temporary food holders (for complicated meal preparations). I consider them optional, since most meals on the trail can be eaten from bowls and cups.

Zip Loc Bags: I hate 'em. I don't know how many of these bags I've torn open when groping in the dark for a midnight snack. All the same, we carry a wide assortment, from tiny ones for spices to great big ones for maps, the camera and emergency food. Carry spares.

Plastic bags are sold everywhere in Mexico but wire twist clamps aren't. I prefer to seal bags with strong rubber bands.

Plastic Jars & Bottles: Assorted sizes with tight-fitting screw lids are excellent for dry foods, liquids and leftovers. Wide-mouthed jars are easier to clean than narrow-mouthed. Get good quality containers that will survive rough handling (see *Canteens & Water Jugs:* Chapter 9).

Aluminum Foil: Foil can be folded to make bowls, cups, plates and even cooking pots. Get heavy duty foil; it can be washed after use and survives refolding, at least for a while.

Napkins: Cheaper than paper towels and good for toilet paper.

Tin Comal: This is a simple piece of round tin, sold in the marketplace. They are used to bake and reheat tortillas and for simple frying.

Suitcase Kitchen

Imagine the looks of amazement and envy on the faces of other campers when you wheel your Mini Motor into the camp area, leap briskly to the trunk, whip out what appears to be an ordinary suitcase, pop it open on the hood of the car and lo-and-behold, reveal a complete kitchen! Their mouths will drop open, especially when you add the master touch of conjuring up a five-course meal that sends them drooling to their own camps for another can of hash.

This list is in addition to the Backpacker's Kitchen. If you stock the Suitcase with food before you leave home, you'll save a great deal of money by cooking your own meals on your way down to Mexico. This kitchen should fit into the smallest cars, on the back of a motorcycle or in a corner of a van.

Forks	Drinking Water (1 liter)	Herbs and Spices
Paper Plates	Rice (200 grams)	Coffee, Tea
Salt Shaker	Noodles (200 grams)	Dried Fruit (500 grams)
Cutting Board (thin plywood)	Cooking Oil (half liter)	Cereal (200 grams)
Egg Container	Honey (half liter)	
Grater	Dried Milk (Nido brand, small can)	
Vegetable Peeler	Cheese (1 kilo)	
Mixing Whisk	Vegetables (onions, tomatoes, etc.)	
Small Strainer	Eggs (dozen)	

By keeping a basic stock of food on hand, especially non-perishable things like rice and cereal in good tight containers, clearly labelled and easily reached, you'll find cooking on the road and while camping to be much easier.

Here's how to put it all together. Assemble everything on your living room floor. Put the foodstuffs into their containers, or if you haven't got the containers yet, use bags and small boxes. The idea is to calculate how much space it will all take, without putting it together into a tight, interlocking Chinese Puzzle. If things aren't easy to get at and put away again, confusion will quickly become chaos.

Okay, now pack it all into a cardboard box. Use a shallow box, one that roughly resembles the dimensions of a suitcase or a small foot locker. Does it fit without piling too many things on top of each other? If so, head for the Goodwill or discount store and find a suitcase that will hold everything. Ours is a small cheap tin and cardboard suitcase we bought in Mexico. After many years of use, it is rusty but still serviceable.

The best kitchen will be in one suitcase or box, but two or even three containers are fine, just as long as each has its own internal order and logic (condiments and spices in one, food in another, utensils and stove in another, etc.).

Dividers inside the suitcase or box will improve the organization. Use stiff cardboard, thin plywood, masonite, pegboard, thin aluminum or plastic. Discount stores are great places to find 'organizer' containers used for kitchens, workshops and offices. Attach a piece of pegboard inside the lid with clips, lengths of elastic and strong magnets to hold knives, spatulas and other utensils.

I love to use our Suitcase Kitchen in hotels. By cooking our own meals we can justify paying a little more for a room. Just go easy on the garlic or you'll have curious guests and hotel employees lined up outside your door.

The Colonizer's Kitchen

If you take eating as seriously as we do, the Colonizer's Kitchen should satisfy your needs, both for long camping trips and short bouts of complex gluttony. This kitchen is based on the Suitcase Kitchen and will fit into a medium-sized footlocker with careful packing and luck. Items under *Buy in Mexico* are cheaper there and make attractive, utilitarian souvenirs. They also take up the most space; if adding them flattens the springs on your Ford, you'd better do without.

Pressure Cooker
Blender
Electric Skillet
Dutch Oven or Covered Skillet
Butcher Knife

Buy in Mexico:
Bean and Potato Masher
Orange Juicer
Lime Squeezer
Casserole Dish

Large and Medium Kettles
Food Mill
Plastic Funnel
Measuring Cup, Spoons
Vacuum Bottle
Apron
Folding Oven or 5 Gallon Can
Baking Pan
Towels and Rags
Bucket or Dish Pan
Large Fire Grate (see Chapter 5)

Buy in Mexico:
Bean Pot
Salad Bowl
Wooden Utensils
Enamel Spoons (all sizes)
Fire Fan
Shopping Bags
Baskets
Mortar & Pestle
Tortilla Press

Pressure Cooker: Saves lots of fuel and time and is a great convenience for camp meals. A pressure cooker can even make tough Mexican beef almost tender. Use it to sterilize water (see Chapter 8).

Blender, Electric Skillet: Luxury items, indeed, but if you stay in trailer parks you'll enjoy having both. Blenders are perfect for *licuados* (fresh fruit and milk blended with sugar or honey), quick soups, homemade mayonnaise (see *Recipes* in this chapter), grinding coffee beans and much more. An electric skillet saves fuel (trailer parks often include electricity in the bill) and is good for fast, one-dish meals. Take a good, long extension cord, too.

Electric appliances are very expensive in Mexico. They make excellent gifts and trade goods, even when they are used or beat up.

Dutch Oven or Covered Skillet: Iron cookware is perfect for campfires but if you can't afford the weight, buy a good-quality, coated skillet with a tight-fitting lid. Use it carefully; a campfire can scorch the synthetic inner coating and make the pan a hopeless mess. Coated cookware fries food with very little oil or butter and is very easy to clean (don't scrub with sand). When water is scarce, a coated pan can be wiped clean with a rag or napkin.

Food Mill: A food mill is really a hand-powered blender. Very useful for soups. Available in Mexico.

Vacuum Bottle: I like lots of coffee while on the road and by making my own at rest stops I can save a considerable amount of money during a long trip. A wide-mouthed bottle for soups is also nice: make soup in the morning for quick lunches and snacks later in the day.

Apron: Staying clean while camping is next to impossible. Aprons are for getting dirty and make laundry day easier, with fewer tomato stains on your shirt and pants.

Folding Oven or Five Gallon Can: Folding ovens that fit on top of a camp stove (the most common is made by Coleman) are excellent for baking small casseroles, banana bread and drying beef for jerky. A five gallon can also works (see Chapter 5), but is bulkier.

Bare Bones Kitchen

If you have a spur-of-the-moment urge to hike or boat in Mexico but don't have cooking gear, the only item not easily available there is the backpacker's stove. This bare bones kitchen can be assembled in almost any fair-sized *tienda* in Mexico, in less time than it takes to describe it. We used this kitchen on a ten-day beach hike and found it quite adequate. Its total cost is less than ten dollars; with the addition of a pot grabber and a few tin cans, it would almost be lavish. Use your imagination and ingenuity when pots and utensils run short.

Cook pot (one liter, enameled, with lid)	Aluminum Foil
2 Cups (large, enameled)	Matches
Knife (6-8 inch blade)	Flour Sack
2 Spoons (enameled)	Tin *Comal*

The cups serve as bowls. Our meals ran heavily to soups, fish cooked on a stick, salads, vegetables baked in foil and whatever fresh fruits we could luck upon, mainly bananas.

The flour sack holds the kitchen and whatever food you pick up in the market.

If you can't figure out what to do with your Bare Bones Kitchen at the end of your trip, just give it away; someone will really appreciate it.

Food From Home

You can find just about anything in Mexico, *if* you know where to look and have the patience to do so. I prefer to take the easy way out and bring some foods from home. The following items are difficult to find in Mexico or of noticeably lower quality or higher price.

Brown Rice	Whole Wheat Flour
Dried Brewer's Yeast	Dried Fruits and Vegetables
Unusual Herbal Teas (see	Mung Beans, Alfalfa Seeds
Staying Healthy)	Olive Oil
Peanut Butter	Sourdough Starter
Dried Yogurt Starter	Soy Sauce
Ginger Root	Imported Teas
Wheat Germ	Vitamins

If your diet includes special foods (salt free, for example) consult *The People's Guide to Mexico* for a detailed discussion of foods found in Mexico or take along a supply that will last your entire trip.

Health foods are available in larger Mexican cities, but they are expensive and the selection is often quite limited.

"Carl, you aren't going to believe this," Lorena said one afternoon, "but I've come up with the mythical Perfect Camp Meal!" I looked up from my improvised couch of sleeping bags and reed mats.

"Oh, yeah?" I didn't bother to disguise the doubt in my voice. "What is it?"

"It's super fast," she said, dodging the question, "warm, filling, inexpensive, flavorful, uses just one pan and . . ." she hesitated for a moment, ". . . highly nutritious."

I propped myself on my elbows; this sounded too good to be true. "What?" I repeated.

"We'll have it for dinner," she hedged, rummaging in the Suitcase Kitchen for the skillet, "since it's my turn to cook." I slumped back and closed my eyes, exhausted from a tough day of casual hiking and surf fishing. ". . . flavorful and filling" just exactly what I needed. I dozed off, dreaming of hamburgers and french fries . . .

"Come and get it!"

I jerked awake, my nostrils twitching at the rich smell of hot garlic. Lorena approached with a covered pan, laying it carefully on a convenient rock next to me. Dinner, at last! She whipped off the lid with a flourish, revealing the Perfect Camp Dinner.

"Popcorn?"

Recipe List

Eggs
　Scrambled & Omelettes
　With Beans
　With Chorizo
　With Rice
　With Tortilla Bits
Potatoes
　Mashed
　Baked Without an Oven
　Crisp Fried
　Fried With Onions
　Potato and Fish Hash
　Mexican Potato Patties
Beans
　Boiled, *de la Olla*
　Refried
　Magic Bean Ball
Rice
　Steamed White Rice
　Steamed Brown Rice
　Pressure Cooker Brown Rice
　Rice Ideas
　Mexican Quick Fried
　Rice and Smoked Fish
Noodles & Pasta
　Super Quick Mexican Spaghetti
　Fast Clam or Shrimp Spaghetti
　Noodle Ideas
Bananas
　Steamed, Baked, Fried
Soups & Stews
　Quick Vegetable Soup
　Lentils & Split Peas
　Lima Bean Soup
　Thick Stew With Gravy
Cooked Vegetables
　Stuffed Cactus
　Steamed Cactus
　Vegetable Ideas
Salads & Dressings
　Cabbage Salad
　One Vegetable Salad
　Fast Potato Salad
　Fast Macaroni Salad
　One Bean Salad
　Bean sprouts
　Fish Salad
　Fruit Salad

Salads & Dressings (cont.)
　Salad Dressing
　Handmade Mayonnaise
Drying Fruits & Vegetables
Breads & Tortillas
　Fried Biscuits
　Pancakes & Pan Bread
　Coconut Banana Bread
　Flour Tortillas
　Sweet Tortillas or *Buñuelos*
Sandwiches, Tacos, Etc.
　Egg Sandwiches
　Luncheon Meat Sandwiches
　Sandwich Ideas
　Instant Tacos
　Tortilla Pizza
　Quesadillas
　Gorditas
　Tortilla Ideas
Sauces
　Rich Tomato Sauce
　Teriyaki Sauce & Marinade
　Gravy
　White Sauce
　Cheese Sauce
　Red Chili Sauce
　Green Chili Sauce
Yogurt
Fish
　Fish Ideas
　Fish On A Stick
　Grilled Fish
　Fried Fish
　Tempura
　Baked Fish
　Ceviche
Smoked Fish
　Fish *Tatemado*
Jerky & Smoked Meat
Other Seafoods
　Conch
　Lapa
　Limpets
　Lobster & Crayfish
　Oysters
　Shrimp
Desserts
　Key Lime Pie

Note: Seawater cannot be used full strength for cooking; it's just too salty. Dilute it with an equal measure of fresh water, however, and seawater will be fine for cooking noodles, spuds and vegetables. If the water is not to be discarded after cooking and will boil off— soups for example — use one part seawater to two parts of sweet water. Taste the water as it boils away and adjust the salt content very cautiously with more salt or fresh water. Remember: once you add salt or salt water to a dish there's no practical method for removing it, you can only try to dilute it with more fresh water.

Eggs

Brown eggs (*huevos rojos, del rancho*) cost more than white eggs but they also have more flavor. When hiking or boating we carry some eggs hardboiled for immediate snacking and crack others into a wide-mouthed plastic jar. Open the eggs one at a time into a cup, just in case one is rotten. Eggs will keep for weeks in their shells but boiled or broken-open eggs should be eaten within a day or two.

Most people overcook eggs. Seven to ten minutes in boiling hot water should hardboil them adequately; fry eggs gently, not hot enough to crisp or burn the thin edges.

Scrambled Eggs and Omelettes: The camper's lifesavers, with an infinite number of variations. My favorite: for each person saute one small sliced *calabacita* (zucchini) and a very small onion in butter, margarine or oil. When *just* tender, add two eggs per person, gently beaten together with a shot of warm water or milk. If eggs are scarce use more zucchini. I also saute quite a lot of garlic and perhaps a tiny fresh chile. Cook slowly, stirring as little as possible and serve with a stack of fresh hot tortillas. Makes an excellent sandwich filling, too, hot or cold.

For a quick non-authentic omelette or semi-souffle repeat the above procedure but don't stir the eggs as they cook, just pour them into the pan, cover as tightly as possible and let them fluff up as they cook. For variations add any or all of the following: grated or chopped cheese, fresh sliced tomatoes, mushrooms, chopped meat or fish, capers, *nopalitos,* parsley, cooked asparagus, olives, fresh greens, bean sprouts or chopped meat or seafood (like shrimp!).

Eggs With Beans: Heat a cup of cooked beans per person in a lightly oiled skillet, then stir in one or two eggs per person. Serve with tortillas or bread.

Eggs With Chorizo: A Mexican truckdriver's special. Fry one link of *chorizo* sausage per person, breaking it into bits as you cook. Add two eggs and/or cooked beans; serve with tortillas.

Eggs With Rice: Saute one cup of cooked rice per person and scramble in two eggs per person. Serve with tortillas and a mild hot sauce (see *Sauces* in this chapter). Saute vegetables before adding rice for variety.

Eggs and Tortilla Bits: Saute bits of fresh or stale tortillas for a few minutes in a small amount of fat. Stir in eggs and crumbled or grated cheese. Serve with yogurt or sour cream on top and more tortillas. Add chili and vegetables for variety.

Note: for more egg ideas see the other recipes, especially *Sandwiches.*

Potatoes

At high elevations in Mexico *papas* are an important staple, replacing rice and even corn to a certain degree. Wash your spuds thoroughly and cook them with the skins on; they'll be tastier and far more nutritious.

Mashed Potatoes: About a handful of potato per person will do for a single meal. Cut large potatoes into egg-sized pieces and steam gently in lightly salted water until tender, not mushy. Don't submerge the potatoes; use just enough water to keep them steaming rather than drowned and diluted in flavor. When they are done, drain the water off (use it to make powdered milk or soup) and mash with a fork or spoon. Add a shot of milk and/or a fresh egg. You can also whip them with salad dressing, strong bouillon, butter or cooking oil. For variation add chopped fresh onion, minced *chile* or herbs.

Mexicans use mashed potato as a taco and sandwich filling, hot or cold, baked or fried, sometimes with a sauce on top.

Potatoes Baked Without An Oven: Lightly oil a scrubbed potato and wrap it tightly in aluminum foil or banana leaves. Place it directly on the coals of your camp fire. Turn the spud every ten minutes until it can be easily pierced to the center with a fork or twig.

This method works quite well for onions, carrots, cabbage and other vegetables. To get fancy coat the potato or vegetable with garlic, salt, herbs and cooking oil before you wrap it up.

Crisp Fried Potatoes: Cut well scrubbed potatoes into 1/4 inch thick slices. As they dry off on a cloth or piece of paper, heat 1/4 to 1/2 inch (or more) of oil in a skillet. Get it hot but not smoking hot. Fry the slices until lightly brown but not quite fully cooked. Remove and drain for at least five minutes, then refry the slices again, until fully browned and crisp. The thinnest slices will become chips. Serve with slices of lime and hot sauce.

Fried Potatoes and Onions: Excellent with fish, for dinner or breakfast. Add thick slices or chunks of onion to the potatoes when frying them for the second time (see above). Remove with the browned spuds and drain. Sprinkle potatoes and onions with grated cheese (especially Parmesan) and hot sauce or mild chili powder.

Potato and Fish Hash: Norwegian fishermen call this plugfisk: with a cup of strong coffee and a brilliant sunrise, it's a great way to start the day. Steam whole potatoes, drain, cool and cut into bite-sized chunks (I do this the night before). Saute a good portion of onion in oil, add the chopped potatoes and an equal amount (or less) of cooked, boned fish. Smoked fish is excellent. Heat and serve with black pepper and catsup. A fried egg on top is nice, too.

Mexican Potato Patties: These keep well and are tasty hot or cold and as taco and sandwich fillers. Prepare mashed potatoes, blending in cheese (1/2 cup for two or three servings) and a pinch of salt. Shape the mashed potato into round, thick patties, called *tortas*. Now separate the yolk from an egg white, beat the white until it's stiff and fluffy, beat the yolk (separately) and stir it into the stiffened egg white. Got that? Dip the *tortas* into the egg mixture and fry them in 1/4 inch of hot oil until browned. These patties are traditionally served floating in a rich tomato sauce (see *Salads* in this chapter), but we usually eat them with our fingers, right out of the pan.

Beans

Buy the best quality beans available; they'll cook faster, taste better and have fewer rocks and other tooth-breakers. Pay close attention when cooking beans or they'll be bland, burnt or under-done. Well-prepared beans are very satisfying, can be eaten hot or cold and are quite nutritious.

Boiled Beans or de la Olla: Carefully clean the debris and stones from one cup of dry beans (serves three or four). Rinse the beans three times in fresh water. Bring a large pot of *unsalted* water to a brisk boil, dump in the beans and let them boil vigorously until they begin to swell up. Reduce the flame, cover the pot and simmer until tender. Keep plenty of water on the beans. When they need more, add boiling hot water, not cool, or they'll be grainy and never really soften properly.

When I reduce the flame I also add a pinch of cumin, oregano, garlic, mild chili and perhaps chopped onion. Never add salt until the beans are quite tender or they'll stay hard. If you keep the beans in a cool place and reboil them for a few minutes at least once a day, they should keep for a long time, even in very warm weather.

Refried Beans: *Refritos* are excellent for camping; they keep well and can be eaten on tortillas, bread, by themselves or even dissolved in water for soup.

Heat a few tablespoons of butter, oil or lard in a skillet. Drain three to four cups of boiled beans, saving the liquid. Fry the beans over a hot fire, mashing and stirring them constantly with a fork or bean masher. Add squirts of the bean juice as you stir, until the beans are thick and pasty but not dry. Serve garnished with minced onion, tomato and lettuce.

Magic Bean Ball: A friend introduced us to this ancient miracle dish while we were climbing a volcano in Guatemala. It is perfect for backpackers and kayakers. Refry a large pot of boiled beans, adding lots of garlic powder or finely minced fresh garlic and salt to taste. Use as little oil as you can while refrying and be careful not to burn the beans. When the beans are the consistency of proper *refritos,* keep frying and stirring, until they're as thick as damp adobe and beginning to crumble. Remove from the pan and when they've cooled, mold the beans (they won't look at all like beans by now) into a ball, cube or thick cake. Wrap the ball in a clean cotton cloth, brown paper or newspaper (the ink might come off). Don't use plastic bags; they trap moisture and cause quick spoilage.

A properly fried Bean Ball will keep for several days, or even longer in cool weather. Eat it cold or: sliced and fried with onions; mashed with fresh tomatoes; fried inside tortillas; dissolved into soup or hot water as a quick energy drink.

Rice

Buy the best quality rice and check it for rocks. Experts say that rice will lose food value if washed but Mexican rice is often dusty. It also tends to be gummy and a quick rinse or two improves its texture.

Steamed White Rice: Patience is the secret for properly cooked rice (and beans). Clean one cup of dry rice (serves three or four) and dump it into a pot with a tight fitting lid. Add just enough fresh water to cover the rice to a depth of one thumbnail. That's right: one thumbnail of water. Don't ask me why but this works, regardless of the pan used or amount of rice. Cover and bring to a boil, then reduce the heat as low as possible and steam for about 20 minutes. If you often burn your rice, try this: remove the rice after 15 to 20 minutes (don't open the lid), wrap the pot in a thick towel and let it cook in its own heat for another 15 to 20 minutes.

Steamed Brown Rice: Add one cup of rice to two cups of boiling water, cover the pan tightly and simmer for 40 minutes or remove after 35 minutes, wrap the pot in a thick towel and let stand for another 15 to 20 minutes.

Brown Rice In A Pressure Cooker: Cook equal measures of brown rice and water for twenty minutes. If the rice looks old or especially hard, give it five more minutes. Too much water makes mushy rice. Every grade of rice cooks differently so be prepared to experiment. When in doubt, use less actual cooking time, wrap the pressure cooker in a towel and allow it to stand unopened for fifteen minutes. This prevents scorching and gives the rice time to absorb all of the water.

Rice Ideas: Saute chopped vegetables until almost tender, then stir in a portion of cooked rice. Fried rice has a better texture if the rice has cooled for several hours after being steamed. Eggs can be scrambled into the rice but I prefer to cook the eggs separately, then add them to the fried rice as it is served. This looks nicer and the rice isn't as gummy.

Cold fried rice makes an excellent trail food; try adding lots of toasted sesame seeds or salted peanuts. Experiment with rice and it'll never bore you.

Mexican Quick Fried Rice: A perfect one pot camping dish, with many variations. For two very hungry people or if you want leftovers: fry 1/2 cup of uncooked dry rice in 2 tablespoons of cooking oil or lard until the grains are golden brown. Add chopped onion, garlic, thinly sliced carrots and a chopped tomato or two, stir it all together for a minute, then add *enough water* or bouillon to cover the mixture, seal with a lid and simmer until the rice is done. Add more liquid if necessary but if the rice looks too moist, remove the lid and stir for the last five minutes of cooking. Use this recipe when you can't think of anything else. If you don't have vegetables, add strong broth instead of water and the rice will be quite tasty.

Rice and Smoked Fish: This is our 'hands down' favorite: for four servings, steam one cup of dry rice (preferably a few hours in advance to allow time to cool). Saute garlic and a large chopped onion in two tablespoons of butter or oil. Add 1/2 teaspoon of thyme and half a cup or more of flaked, boneless, smoked (or canned or plain cooked) fish or other seafood. Heat this mixture, then add the rice and fry until hot. Stir in at least 1/2 cup of grated cheese, wrap the pan in a thick towel and set aside for 15 minutes (or more if you can resist). Don't add salt until the rice is served; the smoked fish may have plenty.

Noodles & Pasta

Mexican *fideos* (very thin noodles, elbows, stars, etc.) should be prepared Mexican-style or they'll probably be gummy. As a general guideline, cook 100 grams of whatever shape *fideos* you have for two people.

Super Quick Mexican Spaghetti: Brown 100 grams of *fideos* in 3 tablespoons of hot oil. Add just enough plain water or bouillon (chicken flavor is a Mexican favorite) to cover the noodles, seal with a lid and steam over a low flame until tender. For a richer sauce add chopped onions, tomatoes, garlic, peppers, oregano, salt and what-have-you a few minutes before adding the water or bouillon. A small can of tomato paste and a piece of *chorizo* sausage will really fancy this dish up.

Fast Clam or Shrimp Spaghetti: If you're using *fideos* this is just a fast variation on the dish described above. When the *fideos* are tender, lift the lid and add canned or raw clams (whole if you like, with shells and natural juices), a pat of butter or squirt of olive oil, fresh black pepper, parsley or oregano. Close the lid again, simmer for a few minutes and then dive in.

Cooked Noodles: Noodles will be gummy if they are cooked in too little water. For two people add 100 grams of any noodle to at least 2 liters of boiling, lightly salted water. Cook at a rolling boil until tender, usually ten to twenty minutes, depending on the type of noodle. Less water can be used in a pinch, but keep a close eye on the pot or the noodles will stick and scorch into an unholy mess. If possible add one cup or more of cold water or ice to the cooked noodles before you drain them. This helps to remove gummy starch.

For spaghetti or noodles just prepare a sauce of butter, garlic, parsley, clams (or shrimp, steamed and peeled) and salt and pour over the cooked pasta.

Noodle Ideas: Mix cooked noodles with cream sauce or fried vegetables, cheese, evaporated milk, cooked meat or seafood and serve as a casserole. Drop raw or cooked noodles into thin soups for a heartier meal.

Bananas

Bananas, especially the *platano macho,* or cooking banana, are an important staple in many parts of Mexico. They can be eaten as a main course for dinner or breakfast or prepared as a dessert.

Steam or bake whole bananas, in their skins, until they can be pierced to the center with a fork. Serve them chopped or mashed, with butter, gravy, sauces or grated cheese. They are excellent, too, with honey or jam or drenched in sweetened condensed milk. Regular bananas are so sweet when cooked that you'll hardly need anything else on them.

Banana chips can be made exactly as fried potatoes (see *Potatoes*), then rolled in sugar or eaten with garlic salt.

Banana tacos are good, especially with beans and hot sauce.

See *Coconut Banana Bread* in this chapter.

Soups & Stew

Soups often taste the same, since it's tempting to put one of everything and a pinch of this-and-that into the pot. A single-flavored soup can be much more interesting and takes just a few minutes to prepare.

Quick Vegetable Soup: Slice whatever vegetable(s) you have on hand into small pieces and saute until almost tender in 2 tablespoons of butter or a single tablespoon of oil (or less, if you have a coated fry pan). When the vegetable is tender, add broth or lightly salted water and simmer until done. For an Oriental flavor, add two dried shrimps. There are enough variations on this type of soup to keep you busy for months. One of my favorites is to add boned fish or whole peeled shrimp. And a tomato, *chile,* garlic, oregano, cumin . . .

Lentils & Split Peas: Hearty one pot meals; either can be served as a thick stew or watered down as a soup. Cook lentils or split peas (see *Beans* in this chapter) until soft and then add chopped vegetables, especially carrots, potatoes, celery, onion and garlic. Thyme is an excellent spice for split peas. Simmer until tender.

Lima Bean Soup: A special dish in Mexico for Lent. Cook half a kilo of *habas* (lima beans) until tender (see *Beans* in this chapter). Add a small chopped onion, a tomato, garlic, a pinch of cumin, one fresh or canned *chile* (small), salt and a sprig of *cilantro* (Chinese parsley). Serve with crumbled cheese and tortillas.

Thick Stew With Gravy: This is a full one dish meal and certainly the richest vegetarian stew I've eaten. It can be prepared with meat, too, if you wish. To avoid filling a washtub with stew, try this for two people (with leftovers): cut into bite-sized pieces: two medium or large spuds, one large carrot, one medium onion, one zucchini, one small chayote, a few green beans . . . garlic, celery and whatever else is around. Strong flavored vegetables such as cabbage, broccoli and turnips are best left out, though I use them in a pinch.

Now mix half a cup of flour (white, whole wheat, corn or a combination) with salt, pepper, oregano, rosemary, thyme, bay leaf, etc. The total amount of spices shouldn't go beyond a tablespoon or so. Shake it all together in a tight sack or large pan, drop in the vegetable chunks and give them a thorough coating of flour.

Heat 4 to 6 tablespoons of butter, oil or lard in a skillet, the bigger the better or you'll be frying in two batches. Brown the vegetables well and add any extra flour mixture. Add enough water or broth to cover everything, seal tightly and simmer until done.

If you use tough meat, flour and brown it separately and cook until tender in a small amount of water, then add it to the vegetables when they've finished cooking (or just before).

Cooked Vegetables

When you're tired and don't want to cook it's easy to think, "If I can't fix a big meal I'd rather not eat at all." Don't give in; a simple cooked vegetable dish can be the answer to going hungry.

Cut whatever vegetables you have into bite-sized pieces and steam them over a gentle fire. Sprinkle in a little salt and one or two spices. When the vegetables are tender, serve with a dressing (see *Salads* in this chapter) or a sauce (see *Sauces* in this chapter). In the morning scramble the leftovers with eggs or fry them with rice.

Stuffed Cactus: Mexican *campesinos* use the thick fleshy leaves of the nopal cactus as a container for baking meat and vegetables. (See *Nopales:* Chapter 6.) Cut a large *penca* (nopal leaf) from a cactus and carefully trim away the spines. Now open the stem end of the *penca* with a knife, forcing your fingers inside the leaf and opening it up like a narrow sack. Stuff this cavity with chopped vegetables (tomatoes add needed moisture) and a plump skinned *mayaguera* (maguey rat) if you have one. Close the end of the *penca* with spines and cook on top of the coals, 30 to 45 minutes.

Steamed Cactus: Young tender nopal leaves are known as *nopalitos*. They are very high in vitamins and minerals and important to many *campesinos'* diets.

Trim the spines from young, thin *pencas* and slice them into narrow strips. Rinse well to remove the slimy texture and steam or bake until tender with garlic, onions and a bay leaf. Cooked *nopalitos* can be garnished with salad dressing, lime juice and *chile* sauces. Use them in bean tacos or any recipe calling for vegetables.

Salads & Dressings

Cabbage Salad: Cabbages are much more common than lettuce in Mexico's back country. They are cheap and keep a long time, two good reasons to learn to love them, even if it takes time.

Most people prefer to slice cabbage very thinly for salads. My favorite cabbage salad is the simplest: sliced or grated with a dressing of vinegar or lime juice, oil and herbs. Add chunks of tomato, raisins, nuts and seeds, crumbled cheese or almost any raw, finely chopped vegetable. Fruit is also good with cabbage, especially pineapple and oranges.

One Vegetable Salad: Another Mexican tradition that suits camping quite well: chop or slice whatever vegetable you have into bite-sized pieces and serve with fresh lime juice, salt and mild chili powder. Don't hesitate to try raw zucchini, cauliflower, jicama, onions or even fruit. Vegetables can also be dipped into salad dressings or mayonnaise (see *Salad Dressings*).

Fast Potato Salad: One of my favorite camp meals, hot or cold. Cook potatoes (see *Potatoes* in this chapter) whole and when they've cooled enough to handle, chop into bite-sized pieces. Mix in minced onion, garlic, herbs, chili, mayonnaise (and/or mustard or catsup) and boiled eggs. Serve with avocado, tomato slices and lettuce. For variety, garnish the potato salad with vinegar and oil salad dressing. I like to carry cold steamed spuds while backpacking and munch on them with mustard, salt and fresh onions.

Fast Macaroni Salad: Prepare 100 grams of elbow noodles or any small shaped pasta (see *Noodles & Pasta* in this chapter) and allow them to cool if you have time. Stir in raw (celery, onion, bell pepper) or cooked vegetables, a salad dressing (mayonnaise is traditional) or oil and lemon juice with herbs (celery, dill or caraway seeds). Makes a full meal if you wish. Try adding smoked fish or whole peeled shrimp.

One Bean Salad: Drain cooked beans and mix them with chopped raw onion, tomato, garlic, lime juice and cooking oil (or a previously prepared salad dressing). Serve immediately or allow to marinate for a few hours. Makes a great cold taco filling or just a substantial snack by itself.

Bean Sprouts: Lentils are easy to find in Mexico and make good sprouts. If you use alfalfa be sure to ask, "*¿Se puede comer esta semilla?*" (Can one eat this seed?). Most Mexican alfalfa seed is chemically treated and absolutely shouldn't be eaten.

Soak 1/4 cup of lentils in fresh water for 12 hours (optional), drain and place them in a plastic bottle or jar. The seeds need air so cover the mouth of the container with a clean handkerchief or fine-meshed screen. A rubber band or string works well to hold the cover on the bottle. Wrap in a towel to keep the sprouts dark and leave near the water jug so you don't forget them. Rinse them with fresh water two or three times a day, leaving the container upside down to drain well. Sprouting takes three to five days, so you might want to start a new batch every two days in order to have a constant supply. Backpackers and boaters will find sprouts very useful in areas where green vegetables are scarce.

Use sprouts in salads or just garnish them with lime juice and salt and eat them like a refreshing hay.

Fish Salad: Use smoked, canned or cold cooked fish. Tuna is the standard, but we also use parrot fish, shark, and when really lucky, lobster tails. For a full meal for two people: mix one or two cups of boned and flaked cooked fish with a small minced onion, enough mayonnaise to moisten everything and salt, pepper and garlic to taste. If possible add chopped lettuce, bean sprouts, minced celery, mushrooms, olives . . . serve with saltines, bread, tortillas or crisp fried potatoes.

Fruit Salad: Cut fresh fruit into bite-sized pieces (the bigger they are, the longer they'll stay firm and juicy) and garnish with fresh lime juice and a bit of salt (optional). For variety mix equal parts of La Lechera sweetened condensed milk and mayonnaise, or just use La Lechera. We sometimes add a shot of orange or pineapple juice, a dash of nutmeg and cinnamon. Seeds and nuts, especially grated coconut, go well in fruit salads.

Salad Dressing: I make a jarful of dressing and then add squirts of oil and lime juice and various herbs as the level drops. It makes for a constant supply and a constantly changing flavor. Mix 1/4 cup of lime juice or vinegar with 3/4 cup of cooking oil; add salt and pepper, mashed garlic, one teaspoon of oregano or other spices and one well-mashed chicken bouillon cube (optional but nice). If you have it, substitute olive oil for part of the cooking oil; it doesn't take much. For a small serving of dressing use tablespoon amounts of oil and vinegar and small pinches of herbs.

Handmade Mayonnaise: Lorena likes this so well I call her Madame Mayonnaise. In a large bowl put one egg yolk, a pinch of salt, the juice of an average-sized lime and garlic powder (optional, also dry mustard or herbs). Beat vigorously with a fork or wire whisk. Add cooking oil (part olive oil is good) drop by drop or 1/2 teaspoon at a time, beating constantly. Be patient; it takes a while. This yields about half a cup of mayonnaise. Use it up as soon as you can, especially if the weather is warm. Fresh egg mayonnaise should be eaten within 12 hours or less if it's hot out.

Did your mixture curdle rather than turn to mayonnaise? If so, you probably added too much oil, too fast. Save the mixture. Crack another egg yolk into a clean bowl and begin whipping, adding the curdled mixture, drop by drop as you beat it up.

To make mayonnaise with a blender, use both yolk and egg white and blend slowly as you add the oil.

Drying Fruits and Vegetables

Dried foods are very convenient for camping: lightweight, relatively imperishable, compact and easy to handle and prepare. Dried foods are also expensive, even in Mexico, where the raw fresh materials are plentiful and cheap. Do-it-yourself dried foods are obviously the answer, especially if you find yourself in a sunny spot with a load of bananas and some free time on your hands.

Although many books have been written on the subject of drying and preserving fresh foods, *campesinos* have reduced the entire topic to its basic elements: sun and food. The final product may not be as beautiful or long-lasting as food that comes out of a commercially built dryer, but it will adequately serve your purposes and taste fine. Here's how they do it.

Thoroughly wash and disinfect the food to be dried (see Chapter 8) and slice it into thin strips or rounds. Hang these pieces on a thorn bush or cactus (keeps dogs away as a bonus), on a tightly strung piece of twine or wire (rust may stain the food but it shouldn't hurt you). Food pieces can also be placed on paper (tends to stick), mosquito netting, the hood of your car (wash the car first), a length of board or tree limb, a canoe paddle or what-have-you.

If flies land on the food you may want to protect it with mosquito netting. If it doesn't dry out in one day, take the food in at night or the dew will restore its moisture and delay the process.

Dried food is ready for storage when it feels pliable but not brittle. Keep it in cloth or paper, not plastic bags that trap moisture.

If you happen to be in Mexico during Lent, look for home-dried foods in the marketplace, especially *orejones*, thin dried slices of zucchini that can be eaten raw or cooked.

Breads & Tortillas

Fried Biscuits: If you make a double batch and don't have friends drop by your camp at the first whiff, you just might have enough biscuits left over for breakfast. Mix 2 cups of flour (white, whole wheat, corn or a blend) with one teaspoon of salt and one tablespoon of baking powder. Add 6 tablespoons of vegetable shortening (Inca brand, *manteca vegetal*), butter, margarine or lard and mix it well with your hands. Now add one cup of boiling water and stir until the shortening has dissolved.

Form the dough into inch thick balls, then flatten them between the pages of this book (well floured) or your hands. You want round patties about 1/4 inch thick. Fry in 1/2 inch of hot oil until browned and cooked through. The oil can be filtered (napkin in a funnel) and reused. If you're short on oil, fry the biscuits over a lower heat in a well-greased pan or on a *comal* (tortilla griddle of clay or tin).

Serve with gravy, honey, jam or use as a bread with meals.

Pancakes & Pan Bread: Mix 2 cups of flour (we prefer a blend of 2/3 cup each of white, whole wheat and *masa harina* tortilla flour) with one teaspoon of salt and 2 to 3 teaspoons of baking powder. Add a teaspoon of powdered cinnamon if you like and one tablespoon of sugar or honey. If you use honey dissolve it in the milk or water (next step).

In a second bowl mix: 3 eggs, 2 cups of sweet or sour milk (or water) with 1/2 cup of yogurt (optional) and 1/2 cup of oil or melted butter or margarine. Add this to the flour mixture and allow to stand for 15 minutes. Fry the pancakes on a hot, lightly greased griddle or frying pan. Avoid flipping them more than once or they'll go flat and gummy.

For extra fluffy pancakes try this: separate the egg whites from their yolks and add the yolks to the milk mixture. When the fifteen minutes are up, beat the egg whites stiff and fluffy with a fork or whisk. Fold them gently into the final mixture and fry.

This same recipe makes a very nice pan bread; just grease a pan lightly (use a cook pot if you have to), add an inch or so of batter and cook slowly in the coals of a campfire.

Coconut Banana Bread: One taste of this brings back many memories of the beach. Mix: 2 cups of flour (we prefer whole wheat) with one teaspoon of salt and one tablespoon of baking powder. Add 1/3 cup of dry powdered milk and a cup of chopped or finely grated coconut. Other nuts are good, too. Now mash three or four overripe bananas and add them to the mixture along with 3 tablespoons of cooking oil and 1/2 cup of honey or molasses (or sugar).

Bake for about 45 minutes at 350 degrees in a well-greased pan. Mexicans often use sardine tins (the long oval ones). The bread is done when a toothpick comes out clean from the center.

Flour Tortillas: This is the answer to the camper's eternal craving for bread. If you use some whole wheat flour in the recipe they'll be even more nutritious. Don't be discouraged if your first batches aren't perfect; like all very basic foods, it takes practice to make them taste authentic.

This recipe makes enough tortillas to feed four people, if they aren't accustomed to eating as many tortillas as most Mexicans are. Mix half a kilo of flour, about 4 to 5 cups, (white, whole wheat or combination) with a teaspoon of salt and a heaping teaspoon of baking powder. Mix in 2 heaping tablespoons of lard (for authentic flavor), margarine or shortening. Butter makes the dough stick to the *comal*. Mix everything with your hands, adding enough warm water to form a dough that won't quite stick to the bowl or your fingers. If the dough is too wet, add more flour. Form the dough into a ball, put it in the bowl, cover with a cloth and set aside for 15 minutes to an hour.

When the dough has risen (it may not be obvious to the eye) break off small lumps and roll them into balls about an inch to an inch and a half in diameter. Keep your hands covered with dry flour. Dust a clean board or sheet of heavy plastic with flour; do the same to a rolling pin or clean glass bottle. Pat the dough ball out with your palms, then give it a good even ironing with the rolling pin, until it's 1/8 to 1/4 inch thick. Pick up this raw tortilla and flap it back and forth between your hands to knock off excess flour. A properly rolled-out tortilla won't tear or break.

Heat a *comal* (pottery or tin griddle) or frying pan over a medium hot fire. Don't grease it. Lay the raw tortilla on the *comal* or pan. Bubbles will form on the upper side but don't flip it until the cooked surface has begun to brown.

These tortillas will last without refrigeration (don't store them in plastic bags, however) for a long time, eventually hardening into a sort of ship's biscuit that is rock-like but edible.

Sweet Tortillas or Buñuelos: The 'Mexican doughnut': make a batch of tortillas but add 3 eggs to the batter and fry the raw tortillas in lots of hot oil until crisp, then sprinkle them with sugar.

Sandwiches, Tacos, Etc.

Whenever someone asks how we manage to live and travel on a budget that is less than many people pay in yearly taxes I answer, "Egg sandwiches." We once met a fellow who travelled all over Latin America eating nothing but avocado sandwiches and avocado tacos, occasionally splurging for an avocado salad.

A steady diet of one food, egg sandwiches or T-bone steaks, eventually becomes boring and unsatisfying. Learn to use fast sandwiches and tacos as a back-up for those moments when you don't want to cook but are too hungry not to (and feel tempted to splurge in a restaurant). Sandwiches have fallen into disgrace in the U.S. because of nutritionless white bread and fast food joints that crank out burgers and submarines faster than Detroit can make hubcaps. Put some imagination and creativity into your sandwiches and tacos; the reward is right on the plate in front of you.

Egg Sandwiches: My best egg sandwiches are just one egg omelettes, laid reverently between two pieces of warm bread or toast. The Mexican *bolillo,* a small oval roll, is perfect for sandwiches, as many *gringos* who have travelled in Mexico on five *tortas* a day can attest.

Luncheon Meat Sandwiches: The standard Mexican cold meats are *jamón cocido* (cooked ham loaf) and *queso de puerco* (pork 'cheese', head cheese). *Salami* is becoming popular too. Buy 150 grams of sliced meat and 4 *bolillos* and you've got a good instant lunch for two, for a rock bottom price.

Sandwich Ideas: Try melted cheese and avocado (or tomato) with garlic or melted cheese with boned bits of smoked fish. A 'salad burger': compress a green salad between two halves of a *bolillo* and douse with vinegar and oil dressing. Make fried potato sandwiches (a variation of potato tacos, a Mexican favorite), etc. etc.

Instant Tacos: When *bolillos* aren't available, I prefer tortillas to Bimbo bread, the standard Mexican bland bread. If fresh corn tortillas aren't available, look for packaged white flour tortillas. They aren't bad, especially if you warm them up a bit. One package of tortillas and 150 grams of luncheon meat will keep me going for quite a while. Tortillas can be wrapped around anything ready-to-eat: avocado, salad, cooked beans, peanut butter and jelly, canned seafood, cheese and so on. This is how *campesinos* eat when they come to town; find a nice doorstep or park bench and have a picnic.

Tortilla Pizza: This looks much more like a pizza when you're in some remote camping place in Mexico. Make a rich tomato sauce (see *Sauces* in this chapter). If you have salami, cold meat or *chorizo* sausage, the pizza will have more flavor. For two people: grease or butter a skillet (or aluminum foil) and lay a tortilla on the bottom. I much prefer white flour tortillas for this but you can use corn, too. Put a dollop of sauce on the upper side of the tortilla and smear it around, then sprinkle on a few tablespoons of grated or crumbled cheese (and meat). Cover this with a second tortilla, more sauce and cheese, adding layer after layer, until it's an inch or two thick. Place the pan on a very gentle fire and heat until the cheese melts and oozes between the layers of tortillas. If the bottom tortilla burns, the fire is much too hot. Add a squirt of water or wine if the sauce begins to dry out.

Quesadillas: Vegetarians travelling in Mexico soon learn to love *quesadillas,* the Mexican equivalent of grilled cheese sandwiches. Mix finely chopped raw onion and tomato with salt, a sprig of minced *epazote* (optional) and grated cheese. Fold or roll a tortilla around a few spoonsful of this mixture. Fry gently in butter or oil until crisp or the cheese melts. Serve with chopped lettuce or cabbage and hot sauce. There are many variations on this recipe; I'll leave them to your appetite and imagination.

Gorditas: An excellent camping food. *Gorditas* are basically extra thick tortillas, some small, others a foot across. The best are *gorditas de trigo* (whole wheat). *Gorditas* last a long time, like a ship's biscuit.

Gorditas are usually sold by little girls and women around the marketplace and bus stations. Wrap them in paper or cloth. *Gorditas* are softer and tastier if warmed before serving. Smear them with refried beans, honey, peanut butter or hot sauce. Some can be split open like pocket bread and stuffed. Fill and fry.

Tortilla Ideas: Leftover tortillas puzzle *gringos*; what can you do with a dozen rock hard corn discs? Here are a few ideas:
• Keep *tortillas* wrapped in cloth or paper, not plastic. If they can't breathe they'll go sour.
• Sun-dried *tortillas* can be used for snacks. Garnish with refried beans, hot sauce, cheese, vegetables or even peanut butter.
• Bake *tortillas* in a warm (not hot) oven until brittle to make chips.
• Fried chips: sprinkle the *tortilla* with salted water and dry. Cut or break into pieces and fry until golden in hot oil. Fried *tortilla* 'chips' require lots of oil and are less nutritious than baked or sun dried.
• Saute hard *tortillas* in butter. When soft, sprinkle grated cheese on top, roll tightly, and eat like a breadstick.
• Add hard *tortilla* pieces to soups just before serving or bake in casseroles.

Sauces

A clever cook uses sauces the way a bricklayer uses plaster to conceal mistakes and irregularities. Sauces convert leftovers into 'new' dishes, disguise plain rice or noodles, give fresh interest to old vegetables and otherwise make camp cooking a lot easier. Most sauces will keep for a couple of days in warm weather without refrigeration but the safest bet is to recook them every morning and evening. A spoiled sauce won't kill you but it can taste rather odd.

Rich Tomato Sauce: This is basically spaghetti sauce, but we also use it liberally on rice, potatoes, fried tacos, fish and even melted cheese sandwiches. Saute chopped onion, garlic, green pepper, minced carrot, celery, zucchini, chayote and/or other vegetables in a few tablespoons of butter or oil. A shot of olive oil is very nice. When the hardest vegetables are almost tender, add a few chopped tomatoes and pinches of herbs, especially oregano, basil, thyme, rosemary, pepper . . . Cook at low heat for half an hour or more; the longer the better. Add tomato sauce or puree for a richer sauce. Beer, wine or bouillon instead of water adds more flavor when it needs thinning down. I also throw in one fresh green *chile,* a small one, seeds and all.

Teriyaki Sauce & Marinade: Excellent on venison, pork or fish, especially *dorado* (mahi-mahi). Mix equal amounts of soy sauce and sugar (1/4 cup of each for an average meal) with powdered or grated ginger and garlic to taste; we like lots of both, say 3 tablespoons. Marinate the raw food for at least half an hour. Cook over open coals, gently, basting constantly with leftover sauce. Try variations: mustard, worcestershire sauce, lime juice, chili powder, herbs . . .

Gravy: Brown 2 to 3 tablespoons of flour (any type) in 3 to 4 tablespoons of hot oil, lard or butter, stirring constantly. When the flour is well browned, add milk, water or bouillon, a few tablespoons at a time. Keep stirring and adding liquid until the mixture has thinned down to the proper consistency. It will get even thicker as it cools, so if you add too much liquid just simmer it for a while to evaporate the extra away.

Cook the gravy for fifteen minutes, then sprinkle in herbs and salt and pepper to taste.

White Sauce: Make gravy with white flour and milk, preferably using butter or margarine rather than lard or oil. Add paprika or one herb.

Cheese Sauce: Sprinkle a cup of finely grated or crumbled cheese (ranch cheese won't melt) into a white sauce and simmer slowly, stirring constantly until the cheese blends with the sauce.

Red Chili Sauce: If you don't like *chile,* leave it out; the sauce will still be tasty. Chop and mix 2 red ripe tomatoes, one medium onion, garlic, *chiles* (to taste, canned or fresh), salt and a dash of lime juice. Remove the seeds and veins from the *chile* to cool it down a little. Serve the sauce as is or cook it for a while.

Green Chili Sauce: Cut and mash together 6 to 10 small green tomatoes (the type covered with a dry leafy membrane or use 3 regular green tomatoes), one medium onion, 2 to 3 cloves of garlic, one *chile* or less, salt and pepper. Simmer until fully cooked and serve hot or cold.

Yogurt

Yogurt makes a good sauce for baked spuds, tacos and steamed vegetables. Or put it on fried bananas for breakfast, with honey and grated cheese. Yogurt is becoming very popular in Mexico and is called *yogurt, bulgaro* and *leche bulgara.* It can be used as a starter if you don't have a dry culture, though read the label carefully and if it says *pasteurizada,* it may or may not be a live culture.

Mix one cup of boiling water with one cup of cold water, one cup of dry powdered milk and one yogurt culture or 1/4 to 1/2 cup of fresh yogurt. Pour the mixture into glass jars (plastic is okay, too), cover and set in the sun or other warm spot. We put ours in a plastic tortilla bucket (sold in dry goods shops) or a small ice chest. Wrap it in a sleeping bag or jacket if you don't have anything else.

Don't handle the yogurt until it sets up, usually about six to ten hours. Make fresh yogurt frequently or it will begin to go sour.

Fish

Very few fish are not edible and those that are considered marginal (skipjack, jacks, rays) can be prepared in ways that will pleasantly surprise you. One of the most important secrets to preparing good fish and seafood is to cook it slowly but not too long. Fish can safely be eaten raw but once the flesh is hot and the protein congealed (exactly like cooking an egg), the fish is done. More cooking will only dry it out. The following suggestions are just a beginning. When faced with an unfamiliar fish, compare its flesh with others you recognize and cook accordingly.

WARNING: don't eat puffer-fish; their guts can be very poisonous. Properly cleaned puffers are delicious, but it's best not to take chances. In rare cases some fish from the Caribbean can be poisonous. (See Chapter 6.)

Snapper, Rock Fish: Excellent all ways but outstanding filleted, breaded and fried, or in tempura

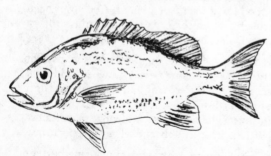

Snapper   *Huachinango, Pargo*

batter. Scale small fish (under two pounds) and fry them whole. Use the heads for soup stock.

Sierra or Spanish Mackerel: Perfect for *ceviche* (see *Ceviche* in this chapter). The flesh is very tender but the fish can be grilled whole or filleted and fried. Delicious smoked.

Parrotfish: Fillet, skin and batter fry.

Triggerfish: Fillet and tear off the very tough skin. Cut the meat into chunks for chowder. Slow fry or grill.

Jacks and Skipjack: Fillet or split the whole fish and grill slowly over coals, basting frequently with oil, garlic, herbs and black pepper. Small jacks can be fried whole or roasted on a stick. Douse with lime juice.

Mojarra: A general term for anything perch-like. Scale and fry whole or grill quickly, taking care not to overcook them.

Mullet: Practically a trash fish in the U.S. and highly regarded in Mexico, with good cause. Split and slow grill over coals or scale and fry whole. Excellent smoked.

Tigre, Mero Chino: A common rock fish, easily speared or handlined. The flesh is tough but makes good chowder. Grill very slowly or it turns to rubber.

Sting Rays: Fillet the meat from the 'wings' and use in chowder or batter fry.

Halibut: Almost too tender to grill but excellent all ways, especially batter fried. The head is great in soup.

Pompano: Fried, whole or filleted, or slow grilled, whole, on a stick. Baste frequently.

Moray Eel: Skin and fillet, grill over a low fire or smoke. Chunks of meat are good in chowder.

Barracuda: Fry or cut into steaks, baste and grill over coals.

Shark: All ways, especially *ceviche.*

Needlefish: Fry gently or bake in foil. Very bony.

Roosterfish: Grilled or fried. A good smoking fish.

Robalo, Snook: Ambrosia all ways, including raw with lime juice. Almost too tender to grill but if you do it carefully it's well worth the trouble.

Dorado, Mahi-Mahi: Batter fried or marinated and grilled. Don't let it dry out. The heads are fantastic if split and grilled.

Wahoo: A religious experience, both in catching and eating. All ways but especially smoked.

Fish-On-A-Stick: This is how Mexican fishermen do it, no muss and no fuss. Skewer a whole fish, guts, scales and all, from head to tail with a sharp stick or heavy wire. Slice the flesh on both sides several times, not too deep and sprinkle the cuts with coarse salt. Prop the skewered fish over the coals of a fire or jam the end of the stick deep into the sand, angling the fish over the coals. If you don't have salt, dunk the fish in the sea several times during the cooking. Eat with tortillas, limes and *chile.*

Grilled Fish: Cook small fish whole or scale them and remove the guts and gills. Larger fish can be split in two but filleting removes too many bones and the flesh may fall to pieces as it cooks.

Brush the fish with cooking oil and lay it, skin side down, onto the grill. Hold your hand over the coals at grill level, palm downward, and count to three. Couldn't stand the heat? Raise the grill until you can comfortably make the 1-2-3 count and adjust it accordingly as the fish cooks. Grilled fish should never have scorched skin or flesh. Turn the fish as little as possible to avoid drying out and baste frequently with oil.

Fried Fish: Gut, gill and scale small fish (under a pound) and fillet and skin larger fish, cutting the meat into six inch long pieces. Roll the fish in flour (any kind, with or without spices), then dip the pieces into a mixture of beaten egg and milk (or beer) and roll through the flour again. It's messy. Fry the fish in hot oil until browned and just tender. I add sesame seeds to the flour for variety.

If you don't have egg or want less of a mess, just roll the fish in flour and fry.

Tempura: Frankly, a box of premixed tempura batter is a lot easier than making your own, but when I'm full of energy it's well worth the trouble. Use this batter on all seafoods and slices of vegetables and fruit, especially bananas. Sift a cup of white flour together with a cup of cornstarch (optional), then mix in one teaspoon of salt, a heaping tablespoon of baking powder (also optional but good) and one or two egg yolks (optional). Stir in enough water, beer, mineral water or even 7-up to make a thin batter. Avoid stirring it too much.

Dunk small chunks of fish into the batter and fry them in deep, hot oil. If the batter is too thin, add more flour and cornstarch. If it doesn't puff up, add more baking powder.

Serve with mustard, soy sauce and sesame seeds, and catsup with a dash of chile.

Baked Fish: Remove guts, gills and scales from small whole fish or fillet larger fish. Use a pan with a tight-fitting lid or a piece of foil. Rub the fish with oil, sprinkle a few pinches of herbs, salt, garlic and pepper, drop in a slice or two of onion, a bay leaf, a sliced banana, pineapple . . . you name it; it'll taste good. Add a shot of water, beer or wine, seal tightly and place directly on the coals. Bake it gently and if the package can't be easily turned, heap coals over the top. It shouldn't take more than half an hour.

Ceviche: Fillet a mackerel, wahoo, small shark or use finely chopped oysters, shrimp, conch or octopus. Scrape the raw flesh from the fillets with a spoon and put it into a bowl. Stir in lime juice until the flesh is saturated and some sits on top; it takes quite a bit. Now mince onion, tomato and *chile* and mix with salt and garlic to taste. Some Mexican recipes call for equal measures of fish, onion and tomato but it doesn't really matter. Mix the fish and lime juice with the chopped vegetables. Add a shot of bottled hot sauce if you wish; oregano and parsley are nice, too. Allow everything to marinate for at least ten minutes (several hours is best), then drain the mixture and squeeze out the lime juice. Serve on saltines or crisp tortillas with lots of cold beer and tequila.

Smoked Fish

There are many ways to smoke a fish and after years of experimentation we've come to rely on what I call the Stone Age Method. Forget fancy smokehouses, portable smokers, hickory chips and other modern complications; the following technique produces the finest smoked fish I've ever had.

Preparing the Fish: The first 'secret' for high quality smoked fish is to clean the fresh fish as soon as possible, preferably right in the boat. Cut out the gills and guts and keep the fish damp and out of the sun. As soon as you get to camp, remove the head (I often leave it on; heads are very tasty) and split the fish lengthwise, along the backbone, into two separate pieces, or 'butterfly' it. Don't fillet it; those bones add flavor and hold the fish together. Cut large fish into pieces that are easy to handle and not too heavy for the smoking grill.

Clean the split fish well, removing every bit of guts and blood, and rinse thoroughly in clean salt water. Lay the pieces out on a clean board, paper or cloth. Sprinkle a liberal amount of salt over both sides, taking care to hit all the nooks and crannies. Don't smother the fish but use more salt than you'd want on a regular fried fish. Some of the salt will dissolve and run off into the fire later. The idea is to preserve the flesh with salt and smoke (both kill bacteria) without making it too strong to eat. You'll soon learn just how much to use. (You can actually smoke fish without any salt but it won't keep as long and just doesn't have the flavor of salted fish.)

If the fish will be smoked within a few hours, place it in a cool shady place and allow the salt to soak in. Fish that will be smoked the next day should be salted very heavily or kept in brine (add enough salt to the water to float a raw potato or egg). The warmer the weather, the more salt you should use when storing raw fish.

The Smoker: After many elaborate construction projects we've become firm believers in using a very simple smoker. It must be tended carefully to avoid burning up the fish, but when you taste the final product you won't begrudge the time. A simple smoker actually works better in warm weather (especially humid beach conditions) than a smoker that is completely enclosed and traps moisture.

The basic idea is to suspend the pieces of fish about twelve to eighteen inches over the top of the coals. Support a metal grill with forked sticks, rocks or bricks or, if you don't have a grill, improvise one with green sticks. When the sticks begin to burn through, replace them and feed the burnt sticks into the smoke fire. Be careful; drops of fish fat can suddenly catch fire and send the whole works up in a mini-inferno.

To get fancier, build some sort of sides around the grill's supporting legs or framework. We use mats, fronds, cardboard, aluminum foil, pieces of tin and even newspaper. This traps the smoke and helps control the fire, especially on windy days. The fire should not be hot enough to scorch anything: the fish, the supporting sticks or the sides. This looks like a hobo set-up, but it's all the more satisfying because it will turn out really fine smoked fish and meat.

The Fire: Build your fire from dry wood but keep it small. When it starts to cool down later you can add more small bits of dry wood to rejuvenate it. Driftwood is fine, but don't use any that is painted or has tar stuck to it. (Tar is becoming a real problem on some Mexican beaches, the result of oil spills and passing ships pumping their bilges.) Don't use coconut husks: they put off a thick greasy smoke like old rubber tires. Pull out any wood that produces dark or obnoxious-smelling smoke.

Once the fire has burned down to a nice *small* bed of coals, add several pieces of green wood. Give it ten minutes or more to heat up and produce smoke. As the wood dries, it will begin to smolder and perhaps burst into flame. If this happens, beat out the flames with a stick and spread the coals around. Add more bits of green wood (if needed) and let it begin smoking again. This is where time and patience come in; nothing can substitute for a very careful watch over the fire to maintain constant smoke and the proper temperature. If you don't have green wood, use dry stuff and watch the fire even more closely.

Place the fish on the grill with the skin side down. Test the fish by carefully touching the side facing the coals. If it's hot but not sizzling (fish that are fatty will gently ooze fat at the proper temperature), you've got it just right. The darkening of the flesh should be caused by smoke, not from cooking.

Leave the fish skin side down until the flesh has firmed up, then turn it gently. Very tender fish may fall apart at this point. The only solution is to use a fine-meshed grill. Bony fish hang together better.

How long does it take to smoke a fish? It depends on several factors: the heat of the fire, the thickness of the fish, the degree of dryness and smokiness you prefer, and the length of time you'd like to keep the fish afterwards. Here are a few examples: a thick slab of *sierra* takes about four to six hours, start to finish. This is enough smoke to preserve the fish for at least several days, if not weeks. *Sierra,* however, is a tender and relatively thin fish. Fatter fish, such as *dorado,* snapper and wahoo, and thick slices of shark, can be smoked for eight to twelve hours. Fast smoking is okay, but it dries out the fish and makes it tougher than a patient, slow smoke.

Storage: Smoked fish should be kept in a shady, cool, well-ventilated place. We wrap ours in brown paper, newspaper or cloth (never use plastic) and keep it in a loosely woven Mexican shopping bag. The bag is easily suspended from the rafters of a hut or tree branch, out of reach of dogs and other pests. Check the fish every day or two; if mold appears on the surface don't toss it out. Put the fish back onto a smoke fire for an hour or dry it carefully in the sun. The mold won't hurt you and another round of smoking disguises its flavor. Smoked fish does spoil, especially if you don't use enough salt or smoke (a hazard of thick fish). Give it a close whiff. Spoiled fish smells really awful.

Try variations: baste the fish as it smokes with a mixture of soy sauce, water, ginger powder and garlic. Don't use too much; as the fish dries out the flavors will be concentrated.

Use smoked fish in soups, casseroles, salads, tacos or other dishes that call for meat or fish. Tough smoked fish can be tenderized by soaking it in warm water.

Fish Tatemado: Mexican fishermen rave about the smoked fish we give them, but very few we've met know how to do it themselves. They complain that it's not just too much work but there's no reliable market for the product. One exception is a process called *tatemado,* very similar to kippering.

Prepare a smoke fire, exactly as for regular fish smoking, but build the grill higher and the fire hotter. This is a relatively quick process and you'd better plan on tending the fire closely or you'll end up with fish cinders.

The best fish for *tatemado* are *lisa* (mullet) and other smallfry, less than two pounds or so. Remove the gills (optional) and cut shallow slices in the sides of the whole fish, about an inch apart. Rub salt into the slices and place the fish on the rack. Don't gut the fish unless you're really squeamish; they give a special flavor that is essential to good *tatemado.* Turn the fish about every half hour or so. If the fire is the proper temperature, the fish will be thoroughly cooked and quite smoky within two or three hours. The more green wood you heap on, the more they'll have a rich smoky flavor.

Fish prepared *tatemado* are salty and go very well with cold beer. Tear off chunks and place on a hot tortilla. Squeeze fresh lime juice over the fish, add chopped onion and chili. It's hard to beat!

Other Seafoods

Grilled Conch: Cooking time is critical for conch; overcooking makes them tough and chewy. Dip well flattened and pounded conch into a mixture of oil, pepper, garlic and paprika. Place them on a hot grill over coals. Cook no more than 30 to 45 seconds, *total time.* This means you'll have to work fast. Try overcooking one piece and you'll see the reason for such a short cooking time.

Fried Conch: Conch are good fried but the cooking time necessary to brown a flour coating toughens most of the flesh. Fry dried unfloured pieces of conch in oil or butter with garlic and onion. Eat them as they come out of the pan. This helps keep cooking time to a minimum, especially if you're feeding a group.

Deep Fried Conch: Cook exactly like fish. Conch in tempura batter are really a delicacy. If they tend to become tough while deep frying, add more baking powder and/or water to the tempura batter. This should make it lighter and faster cooking.

Clams: Steam living clams in a couple of cups of salt water until the shells open. Don't drown the clams, steam them! Dip in melted butter mixed with garlic and parsley and eat.

Use them in rice, spaghetti, macaroni or scrambled eggs. Clams are good with almost everything.

Crabs: Boil in salt water until the shell turns red (no more than 5 to 7 minutes). Small crabs can be used whole in soup or rice.

Lapa: Prepare as conch.

Limpets: Prepare as conch or clams.

Lobster and Crayfish: Boil, living or dead, in salt water until the shell turns red (don't overcook), or extract the uncooked meat from the shell and cook in tempura batter. Lobster can be grilled. Split the entire lobster lengthwise (leave it in the shell), coat well with melted butter, margarine or oil and grill the same as fish.

Oysters: Cook as clams or eat raw, garnished with lime juice. Heaven!

Shrimp: Bring a large pot of salted water to a boil. If you're using sea water dilute it half and half with fresh or it might be too salty. Drop the raw shrimp, heads and all, into the water. They should be done before the water comes back to a boil. When in doubt, remove the pot from the heat and start testing: remove a shrimp, peel and eat it. If it isn't done, remove and eat another. The shrimp will still be cooking in the scalding water. When you decide they're done, drain them quickly and rinse with cold water. If you don't rinse the shrimp, heat retained by their bodies will continue to overcook them. *It is a sin* to overcook shrimp!

Jerky and Smoked Meat

Campesinos can't depend on refrigeration to preserve extra meat. What isn't eaten immediately or sold or bartered is cured, usually by salting and sun drying. The meat is often rubbed with a mixture of spices, mainly *chile,* and eaten roasted, fried or in stews. It is almost always very tough and the strong flavor, especially the *chile,* may cause *gringos* to chew quite slowly.

Smoked and dried meat is an excellent camp and trail food. I usually try to prepare a supply before making a long back country trip. At other times I may buy a piece of venison or receive meat as a gift. Some goes right into the cook pot and the rest is jerked or smoked.

Lean meat makes the best jerky. Fat eventually breaks down and gives a slightly rancid flavor. Fattier meats should not be passed over, however, especially if you don't intend to keep it around very long. *Lomo* (loin) is excellent and more tender than most other cuts. A full *lomo* from an average Mexican deer will weigh 3 to 6 pounds and make a fine batch of jerky.

Boil a large kettle of water (seawater is okay) with enough salt to float a raw potato or egg (about 1/2 cup per gallon).

Cut the meat into long thin slices, thin enough to be translucent. Thick spots can be beaten out later. If you buy your meat from a butcher ask for *bistec de res aplanada* (flattened beefsteak). Don't try to make the slices as neat as commercial jerky or you'll just waste time and energy. Large strips are easier to handle but small pieces can be used too.

Dump the thin slices of raw meat into the boiling brine, stirring constantly. You can add garlic and spices to the water or wait until later, and sprinkle them directly onto the meat strips. Don't turn your back; this is a fast operation. When the meat is grey on the outside (within a minute or so) remove and spread it out to dry. Discard the salt water.

An oven works great for the drying process but I prefer an open fire (follow the instructions for Smoked Fish). If you use an oven put it on a very low heat. Spread the meat on the oven rack or in shallow pans. Don't use waxed paper; it melts. Prop the door open to increase air circulation. The jerky will be done in four to eight hours, depending on the temperature and thickness of the meat. It's done when it bends but feels tough and is on the edge of brittleness. It will get more brittle as it cools, so don't overdo it.

• Try different flavors of jerky. I brush some lightly with soy sauce before drying. Garlic powder works great but if you use garlic salt be careful or the jerky may be too salty. A mixture of oregano, garlic powder and dried mild red chili powder is good, though go very easy; the shrinking of the meat will concentrate the flavors.

• If the jerky is too salty soak it in fresh water for a few minutes and redry it. Jerky that is too salty can also be added to soups and stews *before* other spices are added. Give it time to release the salt before adding more.

• When a fire isn't practical the meat can be sun dried. Put more salt on the meat to prevent spoiling since sun drying may take 2 or 3 days. Drape it over strings, wires or thorn bushes. The salt should keep flies away but if it doesn't, you'll have to cover the meat as best you can without blocking too much sun. When the sun goes down, take in the meat. Put it back out as soon as possible in the morning. Finish the drying off with a short session over a smoky fire to enhance the flavor.

Desserts

Key Lime Pie: This doesn't require cooking, only mixing. Mash a package of cookies or sweet graham crackers into crumbs and mix it together with a stick of butter or margarine. Pat this into a pan to form a crust. Mix the juice of two limes with a regular sized can of La Lechera (sweetened condensed milk, about 6 ounces).

This is going to jell into a fairly thick pudding. If it doesn't, add more lime juice. Pour the lime pudding into the crust and serve. For variety add raisins, nuts, fruit and more La Lechera on top. If you don't have crackers just eat the pudding by itself.

Popcorn: The perfect camping snack, though Lorena even eats it for breakfast, with a glass of powdered milk. To each their own . . .

A large frying pan with a good lid works best for this but we've used an empty tin can on occasion, with a foil lid. Heat a few tablespoons of cooking oil and drop in four kernels of *palomitas* (popcorn). When they go off, drop in enough kernels to cover the bottom of the pan. Start shaking the pan gently; if you stop and turn your back, you can bet they'll scorch. When the corn pops keep shaking until the main volley has passed, then remove from the fire. It's better to leave some corn unpopped rather than risk scorching it all. Dust with garlic powder and salt. Tasty options: use garlic butter or garlic and oil, chili powder, parmesan cheese or sugar.

Fruit Pudding: Campers often have to face quantities of overripe fruit. The solution is simple: peel, mash and cook it with water and sugar (or honey) into a thick pudding or jam. Serve with bread or tortillas, on pancakes or just eat it as it is. Add dissolved cornstarch as a thickener or mix with *atole* (see *Drinks*).

Drinks

Agua Fresca: A healthy, inexpensive substitute for soft drinks. 'Fresh water' can be made from almost any fruit, though I suggest you first try pineapple, melon, strawberries or limes and then begin experimenting. Start with about a pound of fresh trimmed fruit. Blend or mash it well and mix with 2 or 3 liters of fresh water, sweetener to taste and ice if you have it.

Hibiscus Flower Punch: Dried *jamaica* flowers are sold in stores and in the marketplace. Pour a liter of boiling water over a small handful of flowers, steep until cool, then add the juice of a few limes, oranges, pineapple or what-have-you, including canned juices. Dilute to taste with more water or juice and add sweetener. This is a very refreshing punch and mixes well with booze.

Drink Ideas: When water is scarce or has been treated with purifying agents that taste awful, it seems to go farther and definitely tastes better if it's flavored. While backpacking we just stuff a few dry *jamaica* flowers in our canteens (don't forget to clean them out later). It gives the water a pleasant tartness and satisfies your thirst. A few squeezes of lime juice, with or without sweetener is also nice. I also put a spoonful of Nescafé in my canteen (not with the lime juice or *jamaica,* though), or if we have it, Tang or some other commercial flavoring (sold in Mexico under familiar brand names). Herb teas are good but most of them tend to get bitter after a few hours.

Atoles: This might be called the Mexican national beverage. Like most 'national' dishes and drinks it often takes getting used to. *Atole* is basically just mush or gruel, thinned with milk or water and laced heavily with sugar (and often cinnamon). It is very cheap, nutritious, easy to prepare, almost imperishable in dry form and . . . well, that's reason to learn to like it. We use basic Mexican recipes for atole and then spice them up quite a bit. The most basic poor person's *atole* often tastes like wet cement.

Corn Atole or Atole Blanco: There's nothing quite like a giant glass of hot cornstarch to start the day! This stuff tastes better than it sounds: bring one liter of milk or water to a boil. Put a cinnamon stick in, too, or add powdered cinnamon later. Stir 5 tablespoons of cornstarch (Maizena brand) into half a cup of the hot milk or water. When it's fully dissolved blend it into the remainder of the milk liquid and sweeten to taste. In general, the sweeter it is the better. Cook for 15 minutes over a low flame, stirring constantly. It may get too thick to drink. If so, dilute it with more milk or water.

Prepared *atole* mixes in all flavors are sold in small packets. They make good trail snacks and emergency meals. I like to add raisins, dried fruit, instant chocolate mix and even Nescafé. A big serving of *atole* is a full breakfast.

Oatmeal Atole: *Atole de avena* is my favorite; it has a strong resemblance to runny tapioca pudding and a very pleasant flavor. Boil a liter of milk with a cinnamon stick, add 1-1/2 cups of oatmeal and sweetener and cook for 15 minutes, stirring constantly.

Atole de Pinole: The Aztecs invented this one; it's just *atole* made from toasted ground corn. The traditional sweetener for *pinole* is *piloncillo,* crude brown sugar.

Rice Atole: *Atole de arroz* is also good served thick and cool, as a simple rice pudding. I always associate the taste with misty cold mornings in some high forested canyon. Boil a cinnamon stick in a liter of water, add a few pinches of salt and 1/2 cup of rice, white or brown (you may have to add more water to get brown rice fully cooked). Boil until the rice is puffy and very tender. Remove from the fire and add a can of La Lechera or dry milk. Sweeten and if you have them, add raisins and chopped or mashed bananas.

8. Staying Healthy

Staying healthy while travelling and especially while camping in a foreign country requires constant attention and self-discipline. Don't put that carrot in your mouth until you've washed it, no matter how hungry you are, and yes, stop for the night before you're exhausted rather than forging ahead to the next mountain top. Campers who take a "What the hell! We're on vacation!" attitude, often find themselves stuck in bed with hangovers, indigestion, sunburn and assorted aches and pains rather than enjoying themselves hiking or beachcombing. The temptation to overdo things can be overwhelming, especially if your trip is short and you want to cram as much into it as possible. How can you stop fishing when the big yellowfin tuna move in? So what if your nose is purple and blistering from the sun? This is *it,* the whole point of your trip, right out there beyond your rod tip!

Health precautions actually take little time and pay great dividends in terms of how enjoyable your trip is. The secret to staying healthy is quite simple: pay attention to what you're doing to yourself and imagine the consequences if you get sick. I once casually accepted the offer of a "quick trip around the bay" with some friends who wanted to catch a *sierra* for lunch. I was fresh from the States, with a typical *gringo* pallor. I jumped at the chance for a boat ride in the sun. Two hours later, when I crawled back onto the beach, I had a sunburn that forced me to hide in the shade for the next three frustrating weeks. If I had simply grabbed my pants and a shirt rather than going out in shorts, I would have saved weeks of discomfort, not to mention untold lost hours of fishing and diving.

Medical assistance is readily available in Mexico and anyone who stays close to the Tourist Circuit (trailer parks, campgrounds, motels, popular beaches, etc.) should have no problem finding professional care and medicines should they be needed. The farther you go into the *campo* (country) however, the scarcer such help becomes.

If you enjoy camping in remote areas, I strongly recommend that you take personal health care and precautions seriously. This doesn't mean carrying a bale of medical supplies whenever you head into the Unknown. In most cases a few medicines will cover normal health problems. The real danger lies in stupid accidents that quickly turn into life-endangering situations.

A friend learned this lesson the proverbial hard way: he happily canoed by himself into one of Mexico's most extensive lagoon and estuary systems, penetrating more than fifty miles into a region of jungle shaded canals inhabited by the scattered families of fishermen, hunters and subsistence farmers. He camped along these uncharted waterways, often sharing food and visiting with local people he met. It was truly the trip of a lifetime; his sense of excitement and accomplishment grew day by day as he paddled well beyond the limits of his maps and into areas that had seen very few outsiders.

"It was a perfect trip," he said. "At least until I got into that damned machete-sharpening contest." An Indian man felling trees for a new *milpa* (cornfield) invited my friend to stop for a lunch of tortillas and roasted venison. In the course of the afternoon, the man jokingly stroked his thumb over the blade of the *gringo's* machete and said, "The trees must be very soft in your country to be cut with this." He picked up his own blade and casually lopped off a four-inch hardwood sapling with one easy stroke.

Not to be outdone, my friend set to work on his machete with a sharpening stone while the Indian whetted his own blade with nothing but a flat smooth rock from the river bed. The contest was quite simple: both men stood in front of a huge banana plant, its fleshy stalk as thick as a man's thigh. The Indian took the first swing, neatly slicing the top off the plant with one slash. He motioned to a place lower on the stalk; they would take turns cutting thicker sections, working their way toward the base of the plant. The first to fail to cut the stalk in one blow would be the loser.

"I swung so hard I almost fell over," my friend said, "and the blade went through that banana plant like it was hot butter." The machete then hit the ground, ricocheted and buried itself deep in my friend's leg, just below his left knee.

"Just before I passed out the guy looked at me kind of funny and said, 'You win, gringo.'"

It took the Indian two days to paddle the canoe and casualty to the nearest road, where a ride could be found to a hospital. "It was a scary trip, believe me. The worst part was whenever I opened my eyes I'd find the guy staring at me, looking really worried. He kept asking over and over: 'Do you feel like dying?' What a way to end a good trip!"

This is a rather dramatic example of what can go wrong by being careless, but it pays to plan for the worst when there's no one around to take the blame but yourself. When preparing for a camping trip, especially one into a remote area, I always indulge in a brief bout of 'creative paranoia' to help plan our Health Kit: what if the bugs are vicious? Pack another bottle of repellent. What if my skin is too pale? Another tube of sunscreen. What if the water is especially suspicious? More purifying tablets. These, in fact, are the three most common camping health hazards. An amazing number of people shrug off the possible discomfort of biting insects, sunburn and *turista* (diarrhea) with a bland, "Ah, don't worry about it!" that quickly turns into a cry for help when they find themselves swatting mosquitoes or crouching behind a thorn bush half the night.

Physical Conditioning

The very words 'physical conditioning' conjure up unpleasant memories of sweaty tennis shoes, red-faced gym instructors and scabby elbows. *My* idea of conditioning is a few fast laps around the living room, energetically waving my arms while describing to Lorena the wonderful time we're going to have on our latest camping expedition. I once filled a new backpack with old newspapers and did a brisk two-mile walk in the suburbs, trying to strengthen my legs but instead arousing the curiosity of a diligent cop. I got a ride home in a squad car and a strong hint to head for the mountains without delay.

Although a slothful approach takes its toll, especially if you go hiking in a rugged area of Mexico or immediately set off on a long kayak trip, it probably won't kill you. The secret to avoiding a coronary or even a bad muscle cramp is to *take it easy*. Don't sprint to the top of the Temple of the Sun until you've had time to adjust to a new climate, new foods and a different style of daily living. Camping takes a lot of energy and if you expect to maintain a fast pace from the crack of dawn to the closing of the last *cantina,* you'll soon be a real wreck.

Lorena claims that being slightly out of shape is actually an advantage: while hiking your body cries out for rest stops. These are ideal opportunities to appreciate small things: a wild fuschia in bloom beside the trail, the good taste of a fresh brewed cup of coffee, the shy questions of a passing *campesino* family . . . These small and seemingly insignificant images will combine with hundreds more to form the mood and memories of your trip.

Lorena and I once made a hike up a volcano with a genuine mountain climber, a fellow who thought nothing of inching painfully up a granite precipice by his fingernails. He took one look at our standard casual gear (Lorena wore sandals and I took a few back issues of *Esquire* I'd scrounged in a hotel lobby), gave a snort of disgust and immediately set a pace that would have felled a Sherpa. As we gasped and groaned behind him, he regaled us with hair-raising tales of 'real' hikes, hikes that made this volcano jaunt look like a stroll in the park. Lorena finally rebelled, dropping back and letting our friend disappear into the mist. We continued at a much slower pace, guided by his echoes from above, muttering about our snail-like progress.

By the end of the day, however, the tune had changed: our friend had developed a nasty chest cold and was thoroughly exhausted by the climb. He was too tired to eat much but it didn't matter, he bragged, why one time on Mount Misery he'd gone without food for more than . . .

The next morning he was really sick, too sick to enjoy himself at all. We left him huddled inside his sleeping bag while we savored the view and explored the heavily forested canyons leading to the summit. By the third day he could hardly talk and on the fourth, when we finally descended, he looked like the sole survivor of a major mountaineering disaster. The last we heard of him was a weary groan of *"Sandals? Magazines?"* as he stumbled to the bus.

Don't let your memories of Mexico be nothing but a blur of campgrounds, bus stations, poorly lighted restaurants and ear-splitting hangovers. If the old cliche "I have to go back to work in order to rest up from my vacation" applies to your current style of camping and travelling, you're pushing far too hard. Slow down and you'll actually see and enjoy more in the long run.

Here are a few additional suggestions that should prepare you for camping in Mexico and help keep you healthy:

• Don't rush to Mexico, especially if you're driving long distances or riding buses. Arrive rested rather than road weary; you'll need extra energy to help cope with the 'foreign-ness' of a new country.

Wombat *Agouti*

• Don't go on a vacation binge, either with booze or food, just because you're suddenly away from home. Overeating and overdrinking are bad for your health and don't do much to improve your general mood, either.

• The sun is one of Mexico's greatest tourist attractions, but beware of sunburn. If you have the opportunity to sunbathe or to use a sunlamp before your trip, by all means take advantage of it. Nobody likes to wear clothes on the beach, but if you're sensitive to the sun you have no choice.

• Don't 'tough it out' when you begin to feel tired or ill. Take a good long rest, even if it means missing another beach or another mountain top. Look for alternatives to more strenuous activities. Instead of running yourself into the ground take a day to sit on the porch of a back country *tienda* and gossip with the locals or accept an invitation into a house and watch the daily activites, learn to make tortillas, etc.

Staying Healthy

Campers in Mexico often find themselves in places where supplies of food and sources of water are less than reliable or sanitary. Think of this as a challenge, not as a threat. Shall we break out the shovels and dig for water here or give up and move to Pancho's Trayler Parque? Shall I drink this glass of fresh goat's milk I've just been offered or give up this hike and head for a hotel? What should I do? *Help!*

The following suggestions should be followed religiously, though if you're as religious as me you'll often backslide. Do your best; none of these precautions takes much time or energy, especially after they've become a part of your normal daily routine.

• *Purify all drinking water.* I sometimes get lazy and drink some fairly awful looking water. I sometimes get awfully sick, too. It doesn't really take much to purify your water and to protect your health. Guzzling dubious water isn't a sign of bravery in the face of the amoeba; it's just plain foolish.

Here's how: boiling purifies water, but contrary to what most people believe it takes time, *at least* thirty minutes of boiling at sea level and at least forty-five minutes at 7,000 feet. This is a lot of boiling and a lot of fuel. (A pressure cooker would probably reduce these times by one half.)

Water purification tablets (called *hidroclonazone* in Mexico) are very convenient but they taste awful. Let pill treated water stand for at least thirty minutes before drinking.

Liquid bleach can be used instead of tablets: 8 to 10 drops per quart of water, then allow to stand for thirty minutes or more. If you purify a bucket of water at a time and leave it uncovered for several hours much of the bleach flavor will go away.

Iodine is the most common water purifying agent in Mexico. It is sold in *farmacias* and is called *yodo*. The usual dose is five to seven drops per quart of water. New products are now appearing, both in *farmacias* and supermarkets. The best we've tried is Elibac. It has almost no flavor and takes only five drops per liter of water. Ask for *gotas para purificar agua* (drops for purifying water) or *pastillas para purificar agua* (pills for . . .). Remember, if you can't find anything else, use plain *blanqueador* (bleach).

Lime juice will purify water, but I'd add enough to make it taste like limeade just to be sure. Water treated with lime juice makes terrible coffee.

Small water purifying units for campers remove microorganisms and also some noxious chemicals. They aren't cheap but considering the relatively high cost of purification tablets, their awful taste and inconvenience, a purifying unit looks much more attractive. Palco makes a plastic, EPA approved unit for less than $30 that can purify 1,000 gallons of water.

The Survival Straw is a compact water purifying unit that can even make urine drinkable (that's thirst!). Its capacity (300 gallons) makes it a very useful item for travellers and campers. The straw is available by mail from Survival Straw, 2148 Jimmy Durante Blvd., Suite FC, Del Mar, Calif. 92014.

• *Purify all fruits and vegetables.* Forget that old cliche about purifying only food that can't be peeled; *do it all*, even the oranges and bananas. Any food can get dirty and contamination can easily find its way from peeling-to-hand-to-mouth. Keep a bucket or large sturdy plastic bag on hand. When you've finished a marketing trip, put your fresh fruits and vegetables into the container, cover them with water and add enough pills, bleach (cheapest) or *yodo* to purify both the water and the food. Add a bit extra for good luck. Leave the food in this bath for *at least* half an hour. This simple operation will do more to protect your health than a suitcase stuffed with modern medicines.

If water is scarce use seawater or put the food into a plastic bag with just enough water to coat everything well. Add enough purifier to make a strong solution.

When the food has been well soaked, remove from the bath and drain until dry. Don't rinse it; the rinse water itself may be impure. Any slight aftertaste from the purifying agent will usually be lost in cooking or disguised by salad dressings, lime juice or whatever.

Although cooking purifies food, very few dishes are actually heated enough to wipe out tough microbes. The purifying bath is the only sure method I know of. Once you get into the habit you'll find it takes very little time. Produce should be washed off anyway before using it.

• *Avoid as best you can any unpasteurized or uncooked dairy products.* Notice that I said "as best you can". Raw milk and cheeses, especially the very common *queso del rancho* (white cakes of homemade cheese) are considered special treats in the back country of Mexico. We often find ourselves eating raw dairy products and hoping for the best. Raw milk and cheese aren't always hazardous, of course, but you're safer without them.

Raw dairy products should be cooked well before eating. To sterilize raw milk, bring it slowly to a boil, stirring frequently to avoid scorching. Mexicans generally boil it twice, which is doubly safe.

Queso de Chihuahua and *queso de Oaxaca* style cheeses are almost always pasteurized. Dried pasteurized milk (Nido/Nestle) is safe and very common.

• *Go very easy on fried and greasy street foods, baked goods, chiles, green fruits and local moonshine and homemade beverages.* Hell, you say, what does that leave, tortillas and Coca Cola? These foods don't have to be passed over entirely, just take it very easy until your body has adjusted to Mexico. People who forage at random and without self control often suffer indigestion and frequent bouts of *turista.* After you've become more familiar with Mexican foods and new flavors you can begin sampling with less risk of a sudden revolt from your stomach.

• *Use liberal amounts of soap and water on your dishes and yourself.* Some people seem to think that camping means living like Neanderthals, without benefit of soap and simple hygiene. In areas where water is scarce, even the most fastidious campers may be lax when it comes time to wash their dishes or hands. Either attitude can lead to health problems. It is important to take special care in washing up. At least once a week we put all of our dishes and utensils through a purifying ritual: fill a bucket with hot soapy water, another with a mixture of water and one-quarter cup of plain bleach and a third bucket with clean rinse water (purified). Run the dishes through this cycle until they're spotless. If water is really scarce keep a bucket of bleach and water to use for casual rinsing of cups, forks and not-so-dirty plates and bowls. This purifying rinse takes the place of a full-scale soap wash (but not permanently). For your hands, keep a bucket or tin can of soapy water in a convenient spot and *insist* that everyone use it at least a couple of times a day, especially after trips to the outhouse. You'll feel better by not being grubby and substantially reduce the risk of health problems, especially hepatitis.

• *Clean minor wounds, insect bites and infections often.* It is far easier to prevent infections than to cure them. (See *Remedies: Infections* in this chapter.

• *Camper's Tonic:* Conditions in the back country, especially on hikes and boat trips into really remote areas, often put you into a position where getting ill would be extremely inconvenient. The following 'tonic' is very effective against intestinal problems and was given to us by a Mexican herb doctor. We use it and swear by it. Every day (preferably in the morning) take two (or more) cloves of garlic and the juice of at least three limes. I chop the garlic and wash it down like aspirins with water. Lorena chews hers. Now chew several pumpkin seeds. Yes, it does sound weird, but all these have known medicinal properties — in other words, they really work. I also take an occasional cup of *epazote* tea for good measure. (Don't use *epazote* if you're pregnant.) If you eat something suspicious, such as raw milk, take a double dose as soon as possible and increase your morning tonic for a few days.

Health Care and Medicines

Doctors and dentists are usually easy to locate in Mexico and excellent hospitals can be found in larger cities. Most people, however, rely heavily on the local *farmacia* (pharmacy, drugstore) for both medical advice and medicines. Drugs of all sorts are dispensed without a prescription and injections are often given on the spot.

In the country, however, medical care is unreliable. Small towns and villages may boast of a *clinica,* but the staff will be small and often unqualified to do more than dispense aspirins and antibiotics (greatly overused in Mexico). The *Cruz Roja* (Red Cross) has emergency facilities in many small towns; look for road signs that show a red cross and telephone number. Some can be reached by CB radio.

Curanderas (healers), *brujas* (witches) and *espiritualistas* (spiritualists) are very commonly consulted by poorer people in Mexico. They may even honor a healer with the title *doctor de campo* (country doctor). Don't laugh; many are highly skilled in the use of medicinal plants, folk remedies, healing massage and the setting of broken bones. The farther you go into the back country, the more you'll find local people depending on traditional methods of healing. I've been fed some strange brews and potions, but not too surprisingly, these remedies often worked just as well or even better than standard medications.

What should you do if you need a doctor? First, and most important, ask yourself, as calmly as possible, *do I really need to see a doctor?* Am I overreacting or just plain scared? Don't be embarrassed; when you feel lousy everything tends to look a lot worse than it really is. Calm down, have a cup of soothing tea (see *Nervousness & Tension* in this chapter) and give yourself time to relax before heading to town. In many cases a good night's sleep or holding someone's hand will do the trick. Combine a gut ache with a sunburn and a case of diarrhea and many people automatically head for the hospital. If it's close by, that's fine, but if you're out on the trail somewhere you'll probably find that you can get over this temporary crisis by taking it easy and treating yourself.

Still feel rotten? Read over the *Remedies* section carefully. If you don't find anything encouraging, start moving toward a road, village or some other contact with civilization. However, don't hesitate to seek a doctor if you really feel you can't handle the situation.

I once got sick on a long hike and spent a week in a very hospitable village, being cared for by a family who made room for me in their small house. It was a strange time; I didn't feel like talking very much and just lay in bed, listening and watching the people around me. I soon got better, due in large part to loving care and lots of herb tea. In the end I was glad it had happened in a village rather than in an impersonal city or lonely hotel room.

Helping Others

Anyone who travels far off the beaten track in Mexico will eventually be asked for medical advice and medicines by local people. This can be very unnerving. The dilemma is complicated by the fact that *campesinos* have an almost mystical faith in the ability of *gringos* to repair things and to doctor people. Medical missionaries may be the only foreigners they've ever seen; their need for help will compensate (at least in their opinion) for your lack of a medical degree.

Before you stuff a stethoscope and scalpels in your backpack, however, consider this: first aid and simple health care can do a great deal for people who have no knowledge themselves and no alternatives, but playing doctor isn't a game. The consequences of making a mistake or trying too hard, however well-intentioned, can be very grave. Use common sense and if you can't assist someone on the spot, lend a helping hand to get them to a real doctor or offer money to finance their treatment. A few dollars can save a poor person's life.

Superstition is a very powerful force in Mexico and people literally die because they've somehow become convinced that the End is at hand. Strange complaints should be taken seriously. If Juan has fallen ill because of *envidio* (envy) from his neighbor, he'll feel just as sick as if he actually had a 'real' illness. Lending moral support can often do wonders; once again, your status as a *gringo* will give your opinion special weight.

I was hiking with a couple of friends in a remote area when we were suddenly hailed by a very excited man running down a mountainside. When he reached us he hurriedly explained that his son had fallen off a cliff and was badly injured. Could we please come and cure him? Our hearts hit the ground. What could we possibly do? None of us knew how to set bones or treat internal injuries. But the man persisted, begging us to at least take a look at his boy.

It took us an hour to reach the house, perched on a ridge in an area of steep mountains and sheer box canyons. The boy had slipped while tending goats and fallen onto the jagged trunk of a lightning shattered tree. One look at his left foot and leg was enough to send us out of the house; splinters had been driven well into the leg and he'd obviously lost a lot of blood. The mother and smaller children huddled in a corner, wailing as though the boy's fate were sealed. Jode, watching the scene with a face as pale as bleached flour, suddenly took charge, ordering the mother in halting Spanish to heat pots of water. While John and I stood by, feeling very helpless, Jode bent over the injured boy and began the long laborious job of removing splinters, cleaning the wounds and bandaging them as best she could. When she finished the boy was out cold but looking somewhat better.

"Will he die now?" the father asked.

"*¡No! ¡Absolutamente no!*" Jode said, with far more confidence than I felt myself. To reassure the family — and especially the boy — we spent two days with them, doling out our limited supply of aspirins and sulfa as the boy steadily improved. When the worst danger had passed and the boy could be carried to town if necessary, we continued on with our hike. As soon as we'd reached the trail I asked Jode, "How did you know what to do? I didn't know you had medical training."

"I don't," she sighed, "but I thought about all these corny Late Night Movies I've seen about pioneers. After I told his mother to heat water, the rest just sort of came naturally."

In spite of the extra weight, we carry a copy of *Where There Is No Doctor: A Village Care Handbook* by David Werner. This book is based on Werner's work in remote Mexican villages and clearly explains prevention, cure and diagnosis of many injuries and illnesses, medicines (including dosages, brand names and side effects), how to give injections, herbs and simple hygiene. I cannot recommend it enough, even for people who never go camping.

The book was originally published in Spanish and is available in that language. Copies of *Donde No Hay Doctor* make fine gifts, especially when you travel in areas where medical care is hard to find. (See *Recommended Reading: Appendices* for ordering information.)

Camper's Health Kit

The following suggestions for a health and first aid kit are very complete. It has evolved to this stage after years of travelling and camping in Mexico. The odds are in your favor that you won't need or use much of this stuff on every trip but like any backup or survival equipment, a health kit is basically for moments that can't be predicted. The longer and more adventurous your trip, the more complete your health preparations should be.

After once again learning 'the hard way,' we now carry a small kit of antiseptic and bandages in our van at all times, in addition to a larger all-purpose kit that is kept in camp. It went like this: I left Lorena at the beach and drove into the mountains. Twenty miles from nowhere I gashed my wrist open on a piece of torn metal. Naturally I'd left our first aid kit — in camp. In the ensuing bloody saga I got patched up by *campesinos*, returned to camp with a painful infection and spent more than a month recuperating in a hammock. My new motto is: Don't be paranoid; be prepared.

Look over the list and read through the *Remedies*. Many of the herbs are available in Mexico but you might find it easier to buy them at home in your local health food shop. If you prefer standard medications to herbs, almost anything imaginable is available in Mexico, usually much cheaper than in the U.S.

Ace Elastic Bandage	Garlic	Scissors
Adhesive Tape	Gauze	Skin Conditioners
Alcohol	Hydrogen Peroxide	Snake Bit Kit
Aloe Vera Gel	Insect Repellent	Soap, Antiseptic
Ammonia Solution (10%)	Iodine	Sting Ointment
Antivenins (scorpion, snake)	Limes	Sunscreen, PABA
Aspirin	Lip Balm	Butterfly Bandages
Baking Soda	Lomotil or Paregoric	Teas, Herbal
Band Aids	Moleskin	Thermometer
Burn Ointment	Needle	Tweezers (fine point)
Calcium Tablets	Pain Pills (Mecoten)	Water Purification
Clove Oil	Penicillin (Pentrexyl)	Vitamins A, B, C, E
Cornstarch	Salt Tablets	

Lime juice and garlic have proven antibacterial qualities and have been used by Mexicans for centuries as disinfectants. Squeeze lime juice liberally over fresh and cooked foods; it's one 'medicine' that tastes really good. Lorena and I rarely suffer stomach troubles while travelling and camping, even in areas where sanitation is very poor. We attribute this to a little luck and a lot of lime juice and garlic.

Mexican brand names for specific medicines and many more detailed recommendations for both herbal and standard remedies are included in the *Remedies*. Read them over carefully and expand your Health Kit to meet your own health needs. Do it now, not when it's too late.

Some items on this list require a doctor's prescription in the U.S., but everything mentioned is 'over the counter' in Mexico. When you return home don't forget to declare any Mexican medicines at U.S. Customs. If you don't, they might well seize the medicines and fine you. Most Customs agents will allow small amounts of prescription drugs even without a prescription, *if they are properly declared*.

Cormorants
Cormoránes

The simplest way I know of to assemble a really good camping Health Kit, one that meets the requirements of a short trip or full fledged expedition is by mail order from Indiana Camp Supply. (See *Equipment Sources: Appendices*.) (Also see *Vocabulary: Appendices* for Spanish translations and more health related terms.

Remedies

Altitude Sickness: Symptoms are headache, nausea, loss of appetite, mental confusion (I absolutely could not spell 'mountain' at 12,000 feet), poor memory, weakness, yawning, chills, shortness of breath (especially while sleeping) and fatigue. Avoid overexertion, alcohol and drugs. Rest, relax and eat even if you're not hungry; take lots of liquids. If you don't adjust to the altitude within 48 hours go to a lower elevation.

Amoebic Dysentery: See *Diarrhea, Dysentery & Food Poisoning* in this chapter.

Bites & Stings: Light muted colored clothing attracts fewer *mosquitoes*. Commercial 'bug dope' containing diethyltoluamide is strongest. The most common Mexican *repelente*, Seis-Doce (6-12), isn't very powerful. Lorena makes her own: mix 1/4 cup of fresh crushed garlic in 1/4 *cup of light cooking oil, coconut oil or massage oil, let stand for ten days and strain. Add a few drops of pennyroyal oil to repel* **no-see 'ums**, a few crushed eucalyptus leaves for fleas, and parsley to help kill the garlic odor. This is also a good balm for bites and stings.

Repellents of any type are much longer lasting if applied to clothing. Have a shirt, pair of pants and socks that you use only when needed for protection against bugs. Don't wash them until they're really ripe; most repellents will be effective for weeks. We keep our bug clothing in a plastic bag when not in use.

Smoke repells mosquitoes, especially smoke from greasy coconut husks. See *Camping Skills* for more on smudge fires and mosquito nets.

Don't scratch insect bites; the itching and swelling will only get worse. No-see 'ums bites go away in about ten minutes, *if you don't scratch them*. If the itch becomes unbearable, apply finger pressure for a few seconds and it should be relieved. Once you scratch, it'll last for days.

Fleas: Often a problem in small villages and crowded ranch houses. Eucalyptus leaves (or oil) repel fleas; put a bag of leaves in your sleeping bag and another in your backpack or shirt pocket.

Bees: Remove bee stingers by scraping, not pulling. Apply baking soda paste or aloe vera gel, garlic, lime juice, wet teabags or tobacco, saliva, ashes or crushed match heads mixed with saliva, Windex or mild ammonia solution, crushed parsley, or equal parts of camphor and chloral hydrate.

Wash all bites and stings frequently with soap and water and/or fresh lime juice to prevent infections.

Cortico-steroid ointments ease itching and swelling. They are sold in sporting goods shops and drugstores. In Mexico ask for *pomada para piquetes* (salve for bites) or by brand name, Synalar or Fusalar.

Ticks and Chiggers: To remove a tick that has burrowed into your skin, coat the body of the tick with oil, kerosene, fingernail polish or some substance that will suffocate them. Touching a hot match or cigarette to the tick will shrivel the body, but may make it difficult to remove. Wash with soap and water — both the bite and your hands. Ticks carry diseases.

For ticks and chiggers apply a salve of one part sulfur (*azufre*) to ten parts of vaseline, lard or shortening. A mixture of 25% camphor and 5% phenol in mineral oil is good for chiggers.

Horseflies (*tabanos*): Wear more clothes. Treat as a bite.

Vampire Bats: Place cloves of garlic between the toes and sleep in an enclosed space.

Jellyfish: Apply a mild ammonia solution, urine, Windex or other sting balms. Meat tenderizer or papaya juice also helps. Mix ashes with saliva and rub on the stings.

Scorpions: The effects of a scorpion sting have been greatly exaggerated. The sting is rarely fatal, especially to a healthy adult, though it will probably be quite painful. Lorena and I have both been stung and suffered very little discomfort (after an initial strong pain) — about like a bad bee sting.

Unless you have a serious heart or respiratory problem or weigh less than about thirty pounds (children under three years), *don't worry!* The pain may persist for some time but you aren't going to croak! Think about this: more than 250,000 people a year report being bitten by scorpions in Mexico. Of these, only about 30 adults die; the majority of victims are kids under four years of age from *campesino* families (and probably undernourished).

What should you do if a scorpion nails you? First, and most important, *lie down and relax!* Don't panic; it will only make you feel worse. The symptoms can be quite unpleasant: an immediate burning pain and swelling, followed in most cases by stinging sensations, numbness or prickling in the throat and perhaps a 'thick' tongue. You may have some trouble breathing, too, especially if the scorpion was large and full of venom. There's still no need to panic.

Immediately apply crushed garlic and several drops of lime juice to the sting. Drink the juice of ten limes, and/or take several thousand units of Vitamin C and swallow at least half a dozen large cloves of garlic. This classic Mexican folk remedy was also recommended to us by a Mexican physician who treats scorpion stings almost every day. It seemed to help us a great deal, though the lime juice made my throat and stomach burn.

The sting can be soaked in ice water or covered with a piece of ice wrapped in a cloth or T-shirt. If the pain seems unbearable, take aspirin but *NO opiates or morphine derivatives* (no codeine, Darvon, Demerol or paregoric).

Avoid eating (especially dairy products), smoking and booze for 24 hours. Fruit juices are fine. Some doctors advise doses of antihistamines; if you have some on hand take a reasonable dose, not a handful.

Antialacrán (anti-scorpion) serum is available in drugstores, especially in areas where the most dangerous species (*Centruroides sculpturatus*) is found, mainly the states of Jalisco, Nayarit, Colima, Michoacán and Durango. Keep this in mind however: more adults die from a reaction to antivenin shots than from scorpion stings themselves.

The serum must be tested on the victim before being administered, in case of possible allergic reaction (when adrenalin should be given quickly).

If you have kids and are worried about scorpions, buy *antialacrán* and adrenalin before you need it, not after. Have the pharmacist or a doctor give each child the reaction test; it's just a simple 'skin pop' that takes only a few minutes to complete. Read the instructions carefully on the antivenin and adrenalin — you'll probably have to translate them with a dictionary.

Use the antivenin on children only if you can't get to a doctor and the child is in mortal danger. Bites on the head and upper body are the most hazardous. Don't let a kid's yells be mistaken for a bad reaction; it's natural for them to feel pain. Antivenin is most effective when administered within two hours of being stung.

In areas where scorpion stings are common, nearly every village will have the antivenin and someone (often a nurse) who knows how to do the reaction test.

Scorpions hang out in brush, under rocks, in old coconuts, under mattresses and inside blankets, in rotten wood and driftwood and under anything damp and dark. Shake your blankets out before going to bed and in the morning check your shoes, socks and pants before you put them on.

Snakebites: Mexico has an amazing variety of snakes, some of them amazingly poisonous. Fortunately very few tourists will ever see a poisonous snake, much less have the misfortune to be bitten by one.

It is vital to keep in mind that most bites from poisonous snakes are not fatal, though they'll undoubtedly hurt like hell. Remain calm and *keep still*. Have someone carry you to a doctor but don't go into a panic, it will only increase the speed that the venom travels through the body — if there is any venom. Non-poisonous snakes also bite, so your problem may be nothing more than a simple puncture wound (see *Infections & Wounds* in this chapter).

According to Mexico's *Instituto Nacional de Higiene,* only about 135 people a year die from snake bites and that figure is expected to drop as more villages receive antivenin. There are two types of antivenin: *suero anticrotálico* and *suero antiviperino.* The first is for rattlesnakes only, the second for rattlesnakes, fer de lances, pit vipers and others. Neither is good for coral snake venom, but true coral snakes are quite rare and their small fangs are easily stopped by shoes or clothing. If the snake has a black ring between two yellow or white rings, completely circling the body, it is a true coral; all other color combinations are false corals.

Antivenins should be used quickly (within 2 to 3 hours or not at all) and precautions taken in case of allergic reaction to the antivenin (adrenalin and anti-histamine injections). Be prepared; have the antivenin, adrenalin and antihistamine all together and don't wait to read or translate the instructions until you need them. *Where There Is No Doctor* explains all this quite clearly, including how to administer the drugs (see *Recommended Reading: Appendices*).

Tarantulas: Tarantulas look awful and though their bites are not poisonous they infect easily. Treat as a wound: wash thoroughly and bandage.

Birth Control: Pills (*pastillas anticonceptivas*) and injections for one or three months (*inyección anticontraceptivas*) are easily available in *farmacias* (birth control pills were first developed in Mexico). Condoms (*condones*), however, are not of the best quality; one brand is ominously called *Buena Suerte* (Good Luck). Diaphrams are available only in Mexico City; elsewhere they have to be ordered by a doctor. If you use one, consider taking an extra.

Bleeding (external) can almost always be stopped by applying pressure directly over the wound (lean on it, even if it takes an hour!) and by elevating the wounded part as high as possible.

Tourniquets should not be used unless all other measures fail, as they are very dangerous themselves. Loosely tie a strong piece of wide cloth above the wound, insert a stick inside the cloth and twist only until the bleeding stops. Try to locate and tie off any severed blood vessels as soon as the tourniquet has slowed the bleeding. The tourniquet can then be released. (It must be released every 30 minutes and circulation allowed to continue for at least one minute, if possible.) (See *Infections & Wounds* in this chapter.)

Sherpherd's Purse, (Capsilla or *thlaspi* in homeopathic stores) is good for any internal or minor surface bleeding. It is used for excessive menstrual bleeding or bleeding caused by miscarrying or after a delivery. Make Shepherd's Purse tea (*bolsa de pastor*) by steeping 1/2 ounce (14 gms) per cup of water. Drink a cup of this tea every half hour until bleeding has stopped. If you think you're miscarrying head for a hospital.

Blisters: Swab you feet frequently with alcohol to toughen the skin. As soon as you feel a sore developing, stop and pad it with tape or moleskin before a blister forms. Bulging or broken blisters should be thoroughly washed with soap and water or alcohol. Bandage with gauze and tape. Clean and bandage.

Broken Bones: Don't try to set a fracture; it's too dangerous. Immobilize the broken limb with padded splints or by binding the arm to the body or both legs together. Not too tight or you'll cut off circulation. Clean open wounds well and bandage. Treat the patient for shock and move them with great care.

Burns: Clean gently with soap and warm water. Compresses of cool water or ice relieve pain, as does aloe vera gel or the juice of any succulent cactus, wet black tea bags or grated or mashed raw potatoes and onions. Vitamin E oil or cream can be used, but no salted grease, especially butter. Lorena keeps a Vitamin E capsule handy and immediately squirts a few drops of the oil on burns. Bandage with sterile, fine-meshed gauze. For serious burns drink lots of liquids; see *Diarrhea* for a special cocktail. (See *Sunburn* in this chapter.)

Colds, Coughs & Sore Throat: *Prevention:* Lots of Vitamin C and garlic. Lorena's favorite remedy is 2,000 units of Vitamin C and four 00 capsules of goldenseal powder or osha or echinacea powder and two 00 caps of cayenne powder, followed by half dosages of each, three times daily, one hour before meals. The same mixture can be taken as an awful tea. Try teas of sage, cinnamon, bay leaves, mint, camomile, lime juice and honey: all together or separate. Coughs are soothed by honey and lime juice (with or without hot water or tequila), bougainvillaea blossom tea and orange leaf tea. Gargling with warm salt water soothes coughs and sore throats. Chew garlic.

Goldenseal is also known as *hydrastus* in homeopathic stores.

Cramps: For both prevention and treatment of all kinds of cramps take calcium tablets (increases the body's tolerance to pain and should be taken for any injury) or eat more tortillas, milk, greens, unhulled sesame seeds and sprouts. Camomile tea, rest and massage do wonders. Don't overeat or overexercise. Take hot baths and relax. Taking calcium for the 10 days preceding a menstrual period not only prevents cramps, but usually eliminates depression, headaches and other menstrual problems.

Cuts: See *Infections*.

Diarrhea, Dysentery and Food Poisoning: 'Traveller's diarrhea' as the medical community now calls this ailment, is almost impossible to avoid. If you stay in Mexico long enough, you may experience another case when you return home. Consider it a natural side effect of travel, like a hangover after a night on the town.

Because doctors now recognize that traveller's diarrhea is almost inevitable, even 'natural,' they have begun to change their approach to treatment. The change has been toward remedies that sound suspiciously like those used by natural healers.

First, do not take anything that will stop bowel movement. The body needs to flush out, not plug up. This eliminates the use of Lomotil, Entero-Vioformo, Kaopectate and other classic diarrhea medicines. Using them will only prolong the problem and may even aggravate it, by forcing the body to delay healing.

A normal case of diarrhea is often more severe than a person expects: cramps, nausea, vomiting, chills and fever as high as 103°F. It lasts from one to three days and may end suddenly, leaving you weak but happy. Don't resort to antibiotics or 'liquid cork' until you've given yourself enough time for normal recovery.

Avoid coffee, black tea, alcohol, chilies, black pepper, raw fruit, anything greasy, spicy or extremely hot or cold. Rest and relax; it will probably go away.

For all internal ailments drink plenty of liquids. Beware of dehydration, especially in children. The following drink is recommended by the U.S. Center for Disease Control. It can be used for prevention as well as relief from diarrhea.

Diarrhea Cocktail: Put eight ounces of fruit juice in a glass and add half a teaspoon of honey (or sugar) and a pinch of salt. In another glass mix eight ounces of water (mineral or carbonated is okay) and one quarter teaspoon of baking soda. Drink them down, alternating sips from one glass to the other. An adult should take several doses a day and a child at least four.

The classic Mexican diarrhea remedy is dog tea, *té de perro*. It really works. Add a handful of the herb to one liter of boiling water. Let it stand (not boiling) for up to 30 minutes. Drink a glass whenever you're thirsty. It's good with lime juice. *Té de manzanilla* (camomile) is also popular and if you can get them, *tuna de cardón* (cardon cactus fruits). Eat four a day until you're recovered. Coconut milk is good, though eating the oily meat will only aggravate the problem.

What if you're in a situation that makes immediate relief necessary? When I'm travelling by public transportation I carry a few ounces of *paregórico* or Lomotil tablets. Both contain opium and will stop uncontrollable diarrhea. Opium makes you very sleepy, a desirable state to be in when you've got diarrhea. Paregoric has no other ingredients, but Lomotil is adulterated with belladonna. This produces a slight nausea, the drug company's sneaky way of preventing Lomotil addiction. The only advantage of Lomotil over paregoric is the size of the tablets; tiny and easily carried in your pocket.

If symptoms persist beyond four days see a doctor. When antibiotics are used follow them up with yogurt. This helps to restore beneficial forms of bacteria to your system.

Disentería is used in Mexico to decribe both dysentery and diarrhea. This leads many *gringos* to erroneously believe that they're suffering from a case of amoebic dysentery when in fact, it's either traveller's diarrhea or food poisoning.

Don't assume, just because the symptoms are severe, that you've got a case of dysentery. Dysentery should be diagnosed by a doctor, not by some sympathetic tourist. When I had amoebas my main symptoms were headache, depression and sore muscles — not diarrhea.

Papaya contains digestive enzymes that soothe the stomach. Many Mexicans eat 3 papaya seeds a day to prevent dysentery and 9 a day for 9 days to cure it. One teaspoon of chia seeds in a large glass of water, juice or soft drink will soothe your stomach and plug you up. We also use goldenseal (one or two 00 capsules, 3 times daily).

An awful Mexican remedy is to boil 1/2 liter of milk with a handful of *epazote de zorrillo*, three cloves of garlic and three *pepitas* (squash seeds). Boil it down to one cup of liquid and drink first thing in the morning. A real eye opener. Repeat daily for a few weeks.

Cuasia (quassia) bark is used both in Mexico and the American Southwest for intestinal problems. It is very bitter and best taken in gelatin capsules. Take one large capsule a day as a preventative and three caps, three times a day for several weeks as a cure. Teas made from *cuasia* are also good — effective, that is; the taste is terrible. Boil a small handful in two quarts of water for one hour, allow to stand for several hours, then drink a cup an hour before every meal.

Food poisoning: The symptoms are similar to diarrhea, but usually come on much faster and are more severe. Food poisoning also tends to end quickly; a common variety lasts about twelve hours.

Use the same treatment for food poisoning as for diarrhea. You'll probably have no choice but to rest.

Drowning: The procedures for resuscitation should be learned from a manual on first aid. What many books fail to mention, however, is that in order to be effective, the resuscitation must not be delayed by such procedures as loosening the victim's clothing or making them a nice place to lie down. Get your hands on the person as quickly as you can and go to work, even if you have to do it in neck deep water. Other things can be done later or when help arrives; the critical factor is to get air into the victim's lungs *as quickly as possible.*

Ears: If your ear is plugged with water after swimming and can't be shaken out, try this: lie on your side and carefully fill your ear with warm water. Lie there for a minute, then roll over and drain for five more minutes. Repeat several times. Hydrogen peroxide (diluted 1/2 with water) or alcohol can also be used but they dry out the delicate skin inside your ear; follow with a drop of warm oil or suntan lotion. A persistent earache is cause to go to a doctor. Middle ear infections can be very dangerous.

Eyestrain: Drink lots of carrot juice, take Vitamin A and wear sunglasses. Soak a cloth in *té de manzanilla* and press it gently against the eyes.

Fever: If the temperature goes above 102°F (see *Appendices* for conversion to Centigrade), take aspirin and uncover. Fevers about 104°F should be cooled by bathing with wet cloths and placing damp cloths on the chest and forehead. Alcohol or aloe vera gel rubs also help.

Fever caused by sunstroke can go very high. Check it with a rectal themometer and if the temperature is over 106°F immerse the patient in an ice water bath or wrap in a soaking wet blanket. Massage the skin vigorously until the temperature falls. Check the rectal temperature every ten minutes and remove the patient from the ice water before it drops below 102°F.

If you're alone and have a bad fever try to find someone to keep an eye on you. I've always found Mexicans very sympathetic; hotel employees will usually be glad to bring you tea and drinks.

Some common Mexican fever remedies are teas of lime juice, hibiscus, borage, alfalfa and parsley. Toast an aloe leaf, slice it open, coat with cooking oil and sprinkle with a few petals of *rosa de castillo* (optional). Place this against the soles of the feet, wrap and leave overnight.

Grippe, Flu: See *Colds, Coughs & Sore Throats* in this chapter.

Hangover: *Treatment: Té de perro,* raw eggs and hot sauce, and lots of Vitamin B.

Heat Prostration and Sunstroke: Although both heat prostration and sunstroke (also called heatstroke) are caused by excessive exertion in heat and prolonged exposure to the sun and heat, the symptoms and treatments are distinctly different for each.

Heat prostration is relatively common. To avoid it, take it easy in the heat; wear light, loose clothing and a broad-brimmed hat. Drink lots of fluids, eat high energy foods and salt (tablets or table salt).

Angelfish   *Angelote*

Common symptoms: unusually pale skin, cool and clammy; heavy sweating; headache; pulse under 100, vertigo, dizziness, blurred vision, cramps and irritability. In other words, you feel really rotten. At the first sign of heat prostration (a headache usually), I take two salt tablets, guzzle half a quart or more of water and get out of the sun. That usually does the trick. If not, lie in a reclining position in the shade with your feet higher than your head. Loosen your clothing and rest; you'll soon recover.

Sunstroke is uncommon but quite serious. It is often brought on by very hot weather, when even the nights are unpleasantly warm. Take the same precautions as for heat prostration. The symptoms may appear suddenly and, at first, be similar to heat prostration. There may also be a reduction or even cessation of sweating several hours before the attack. The victim is flushed and the skin is hot and dry. Cramps, twitching and a listless and anxious attitude, pupils contracted at first but dilated (open) later. The pulse can go to 160 or more, with the body temperature 105 to 106°F (see *Fever* in this chapter right now!). The victim should lie down with the feet *lower* than the head. It is time to get a doctor! Don't wait; just do what you can to lower the fever on your way to the hospital.

Hepatitis: 'Hep' as it is called, is highly contagious and spread by food and drink, saliva and sexual contact. Keep your dishes washed, your hands clean and your mouth shut. The symptoms are jaundice (the whites of the eyes and eventually the skin look yellowish), loss of appetite, fatigue (sleeping 14 hours?), aches and pains, nausea and brownish urine. If you have hepatitis or have come into contact with a victim, take extra care to avoid passing it on to someone else. Avoid communal meals, wash all dishes with hot soapy water every day and keep your camp clean. Never share food or dishes with a hepatitis case; the risk of passing it on ends when all signs of jaundice have disappeared.

The treatment is quite simple but slow: good diet (lots of fresh fruit and vegetables, juices), B vitamins (brewer's yeast is good) and plenty of rest. Avoid alcohol and tobacco entirely. The only cure is food and rest. If you don't rest and eat well, you may have a relapse. Very few victims require hospitalization. Because drugs are sold so freely in Mexico, many hepatitis sufferers mistakenly take lots of antibiotics.

Gamma globulina injections are recommended by some doctors if you have been exposed to hepatitis. They are available in *farmacias* everywhere.

Hypothermia or Exposure: Hypothermia is basically caused by chilling. Anyone who camps in Mexico, especially at higher elevations, should take suitable precautions. First, and most important, *stay dry.* Wet clothing exposed to a breeze creates a dangerous chilling effect, the same effect that is described in Chapter 5 for cooling your beer. We always carry foil-backed emergency 'blankets' (the size of a bandanna when tightly folded) for quick rescue warm-ups. One of hypothermia's greatest hazards is that the victim seldom recognizes the symptoms until it's too late. The three steps toward death are: *uncontrollable shivering* followed by a *sudden stop in shivering* (the body can't fight the cold any longer) and finally, *unconsciousness and coma. Adiós!*

At the first sign of hypothermia (shivering, memory lapses, irrational behavior, clumsiness, poor coordination) get out of the weather and under cover. Change your clothes, cuddle with a friend, drink sweet warm liquids (never alcohol), eat chia seeds, bee pollen, a protein bar or candy — have a good time, but get warm and dry. If the victim refuses help, someone else has to crack the whip; this refusal is a symptom of hypothermia. This happened to a companion on a hike in Mexico; he sprawled out in a gully and absolutely refused to move. It took some very vivid threats, plus forcing several cups of hot tea on him, before he recovered his senses.

If the victim reaches the shivering stage or beyond, you must act as quickly as possible. Take off your clothes and climb into a sleeping bag with the victim. Give them warm sweet fluids as long as they are fully conscious but don't force anything if they're unconscious; the liquid might go right down a lung.

Once the victim has recovered it's time to take a good long rest. Don't forge ahead or you'll just bring on another attack.

Infections & Wounds: Wash the wound with soap and water, or alcohol. If it is too painful to scrub, flush well with soapy water and hydrogen peroxide or soak the wound or infection in a bucket of warm soapy water. You have to clean out all those tiny particles of dirt and grime. Hot compresses used for 20 minutes, four times a day, will improve circulation around the wound. Lime juice is good on minor cuts or wounds, but stings like crazy.

Infections and wounds can be bandaged with crushed garlic compresses. Coat the surrounding skin with light oil (not industrial oil) before putting the garlic on. If the garlic burns, remove it, clean the skin and apply even more oil. The wound should be thoroughly cleaned three (or more) times a day and a fresh poultice applied. Goldenseal powder can be sprinkled on wounds and infections. Covering the wound with honey is said to prevent infection. Cover with gauze, and/or a cloth.

Puncture wounds should be cleaned as thoroughly as possible as they can infect rapidly if not properly cleaned. If infection sets in (pus and swelling) it may be necessary to enlarge the wound (time to bite the bullet) and clean it again.

Persistent Infections: Itching, open sores are common in tropical areas. These are usually 'staph', the most common type of impetigo. The common remedy of antibiotic salves is rarely as effective in the long run as frequent and diligent cleaning with soap and water and/or lime juice. Keep the sores dry; don't go swimming.

Blood Poisoning: Blood poisoning can develop quickly (within 48 hours of an injury) and should be treated quickly. If you see a red line near a wound or infection, take 250 milligrams of penicillin four times a day for five days. Stop immediately if you have any allergic reaction. Take all the tablets; the infection can reappear suddenly if you don't. Treat yourself for blood poisoning if you have to, but find a doctor as soon as possible if the red line grows.

Minor Urinary Infections: Have to pee but can't? Drink vast quantities of *jamaica* (hibiscus) tea. Pour one liter of boiling water over a handful of dry flowers and steep, or soak the flowers in cold water for several hours. If the symptoms seem worse, try *boldo* or eucalyptus leaf tea. Any herbal tea or just plain water will also help. Avoid coffee, booze and black tea.

Vaginal Infections: If symptoms are mild (burning, itching) a douche one to three times daily should be sufficient. Add one to two tablespoons of vinegar or lime juice to a liter of pure water. Don't use antibiotics until the douche treatment has been given a good try. Antibiotics actually cause some yeast infections (burning, itching, perhaps a thick whitish discharge) and shouldn't be used to treat them.

For yeast infections, use a yogurt douche or the mixture mentioned above. Another remedy is to carefully peel a clove of garlic (don't cut or nick the garlic) and tie it in a gauze strip with a tail for easy removal. Insert the garlic high in the vagina for 24 hours. Repeat in a few days if necessary.

It is best to avoid intercourse until the infection is cleared up. If you take antibiotics and have intercourse, your partner should follow the same treatment.

Insomnia: See *Nervousness & Tension* in this chapter.

Intestinal Parasites: Worms and amoebas are unpleasant but easily avoided by eating lots of fresh garlic. Swallow a few chopped cloves at least once a day as if they were aspirin. Drink lime juice and *epazote* tea (pregnant women should avoid using *epazote*). Purify your food and water religiously. See *Diarrhea* in this chapter for cures.

Nausea: Camomile tea is a classic Mexican remedy. Also try *té de perro* (dog tea), *té de canela* (cinnamon), soda crackers and Alka Seltzer.

Nervousness & Tension: Eat a delicious and slightly narcotic *zapote borracho* (drunken *zapote*, also *zapote negro*) or a *zapote blanco*. Make tea from camomile, *zapote* leaves, valerian, mint, rue, orange leaves, linden, or lemon leaf. Mixed teas are sold by sidewalk herbalists. Ask for *té para nervios* or *té para insomnio;* they really do the trick. Calcium and B vitamins also help. Eat more tortillas, bean sprouts, sesame seeds, milk, greens and egg shells (dissolved in lime juice).

Poisoning: Induce vomiting by sticking your finger down the victim's throat or give warm water mixed with a little soap, mustard or salt. Follow this with milk, beaten eggs, honey and flour mixed with water or a tablespoon of powdered charcoal.

Don't induce vomiting if gasoline, kerosene, acids or corrosive substances were swallowed. Vomiting will force irritating fumes or liquid into the lungs and increase the chance of pneumonia. If pneumonia does develop (usually within a day or two), it will be indicated by a high fever. Go to a doctor right away.

Pain: Try aspirin first. For stronger relief Mecoten and Prodolina tablets (one every 4 hours) are sold without prescriptions and are effective for toothache and minor injuries, muscle pain, etc. Also available in injectable form. Pain indicates that something needs to be taken care of and if it persists, consider seeing a doctor.

Rashes: Dust yourself with plain cornstarch (*Maizena*) and occasionally swab the rash with aloe vera gel. Wear loose clothing.

Sea Urchin Spines: The spines are next to impossible to dig out. Mexican divers put lots of lime juice on them; it dissolves the spine and cleanses the wound. Treat as a puncture wound (see *Infections & Wounds* in this chapter).

Seasickness: I have been seasick many times and I hate it. Motion sickness pills (*pastillas para mareo*) cause drowsiness. I prefer this: slowly drink one or two warm beers while staring at the horizon and breathing deeply. Don't look down at the water and don't go below decks or hide your head in your arms; it'll just get worse. Pray a little and try to think positively. Bathe your face in cool water and if you puke, eat crackers and drink lots of water to avoid dehydration.

Shock: Sit down, with your head between your knees. Severe shock causes a faint rapid pulse, fast breathing, dry tongue and sweating. Lie down and elevate your feet twelve inches. Cover up well but don't get overheated. Small amounts of liquids can be taken in mild cases but none at all if the shock is severe. (See *Hypothermia* and *Heat Prostration* in this chapter.) (For *Cultural Shock* see Chapter 4.)

Stingrays: *Rayas* are common in shallow water. Contrary to popular belief, the stinger (actually a barbed shaft) is not poisonous, though it does produce a nasty, easily infected wound. To avoid being hit, shuffle your feet along the bottom rather than taking regular steps. When you bump into a ray, it will swim harmlessly away. If you step on its back, however, the tail arches over and the stinger is planted in your foot or ankle.

Treat as a puncture wound (see *Infections & Wounds* in this chapter). A common folk cure is to gather a bunch of leaves from a low-running, green, thick-leaved vine found at the edge of the beach (known in some areas as *yerba de raya*). Boil them for 20 minutes and wash the wound in the liquid.

Another remedy, one that sounds suspiciously like drowning the pain, is to have a friend rub your entire body with rags soaked in hot water, then wrap up in warm blankets and chug-a-lug a liter of tequila.

Sprains: Keep the sprain (or break) as still as possible. Wrap it well to give firm support. For the first 24 hours after the injury soak the sprain in cold water to reduce swelling and pain. Afterwards, soak it in hot water several times a day.

Sunburn: Sunscreen and 'sunblock' ointments prevent sunburning, but some suntan oils (including natural coconut oil) actually promote burning. Ask your druggist to recommend a sun-screen and buy more than you'll need; you'll certainly meet some fried tourist who could use a few dabs. To test your skin for burning, press one or two fingers firmly over the exposed area and hold down for several seconds. Now quickly release the pressure. A pale spot will mark the finger impression. If the spot is still there after you've said aloud, "I've got a sunburn," you're right, you do. Use this test all over your body; some places burn faster than others.

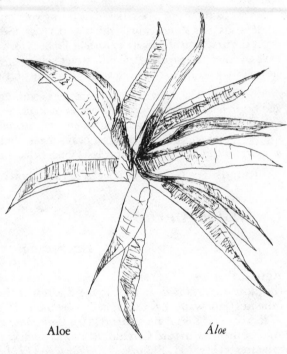

Aloe   *Áloe*

PABA (para amino benzoic acid) is a Vitamin B ointment that prevents burning, relieves sunburn pain, promotes tanning and conditions the skin. Red petrolatum is a very effective anti-burn ointment.

Treat burns with liberal amounts of aloe vera gel (Lorena's favorite), compresses of grated or crushed raw potatoes or onions, fresh or canned milk, vinegar or wet tea leaves. Peeling can lead to infection; leave blisters alone!

Use soothing lotions liberally but avoid any that contain more than a trace of alcohol. Pure coconut oil (*aceite de coco*) is inexpensive in Mexico. Use as a skin conditioner *after* you've come out of the sun. Bag balm (an herbal salve used for livestock) is very good for rough and chafed skin.

Sunstroke: See *Heat Prostration* in this chapter.

Toothache: A few drops of clove oil (*aceite de clavo*) on a piece of cotton or tissue (or just the oil alone) can be placed on the aching tooth. Whole cloves also work; put a couple as close as possible to the ache and hold there until the area is numb. Use clove oil carefully it can burn the gums. An aspirin can also be used, though it is most effective if the ache is caused by a cavity. A swallow of *paregórico* will kill the pain and cause drowsiness.

Mexicans use a prune or a raisin, split open and held against the aching area. You can also suck on a bag of black tea.

Raging toothaches are often caused by infections at the base of the tooth. I've suffered this agony on several camping trips; the only effective relief came from antibiotics. Take penicillin tablets or tetracycline (usual dosage is 250 mg four times a day) and continue treatment for two days after the pain has eased and any swelling disappeared. This is only a temporary measure. Consult a doctor or dentist as soon as you can.

Severe pain can often be relieved by filling your mouth with warm or cold water. It all depends on the individual which works best. (See *Pain* in this chapter.)

At the first sign of a severe toothache I'd head for a dentist, especially if you don't have antibiotics on hand. Pain pills won't help if it gets really bad. If you can't sleep, sit up or lay with your head elevated to relieve pressure.

Vomiting: The main danger of persistent vomiting is dehydration. Wait two hours and begin taking sips of water or diarrhea cocktail (see *Diarrhea* in this chapter). Wait a couple of hours more and try again. When water is kept down progress to juice and light soups. Wait awhile before eating a heavy meal. Vomiting with abdominal pain but *no diarrhea* can be dangerous if it lasts longer than one day. Seek medical help.

Wounds: See *Infections & Wounds* in this chapter.

Unknown Mexico

Hot Springs

Aguascalientes: There are more than sixty known areas of hot springs in the state; the most important are in and around the capital city, appropriately named Aguascalientes (Hot waters). *Ojo Caliente* or *San Rafael:* 44°; Aguascalientes. *Los Arquitos* or *El Refugio:* 42°C+; Aguascalientes. *Ojo Calientillo:* zone of springs; 50 km from Aguascalientes, toward Calvillo. *El Salitre:* undeveloped zone; 28 km from Aguascalientes on Hwy 45. *El Salitral, El Tilamo* and *El Manatial de San Lorenzo:* municipio of Jesús María. *La Alameda:* Rincón de Romos. *Balneario Ejidal Valladolid:* 25 km north of Aguascalientes on Hwy 45.

Baja California Norte: The Baja Peninsula has a large number of springs, many of them difficult to reach without tough vehicles, guides or hiking. *Cañón del Agua Caliente:* 42°C+; SW of San Felipe, 75 km rough road. *Cañón de Guadalupe:* 42°C+; between Tijuana and Mexicali; 65 km dirt road and 5 km on foot. *Ejido Jacume:* 50 km from Tecate on dirt road, rustic. *San Carlos:* 40°C; 24 km SE of Ensenada, 14 km rough road. *Punta Banda:* 12 km SW of Ensenada. *Ejido Uruapan:* 20 km south of Ensenada, 3 km of dirt road. *Cerro Prieto:* 22 km SW of Mexicali.

Baja California Sur: *Las Vírgenes* and *Huerta Vieja:* municipio of Comundú. *San Pedro:* 28 km south of La Paz. *San Bartolo:* from La Paz, 99 km toward Buenavista. *Agua Caliente:* 123 km from La Paz toward Buenavista.

Chiapas: *Municipio de Tonalá:* zone of medicinal springs. *La Trinitaria:* 30 km SE of Comitán. *El Burrero:* 37 km east of Tuxtla Gutiérrez in Ixtapa. *El Carmen:* 36 km SE of Tuxtla Gutiérrez, near Acala. *Amatan:* SE of Comitán. *Las Rosas:* near Tapachula on Hwy 200. *La Flor:* 40°C; in Camactitlán between Huixtla and Motozintla. *Manantial de Tolimán:* 42°C+; on Hwy 200. *Manantial de Escuintla:* 42°C+; on Hwy 200 just before Huixtla. *Sesacapa* and *San Luis:* municipio de Mapastepec. *Ixtapangojoya:* 42°C+; near La Esperanza and Tapachula.

Chihuahua: *San Diego de Alcalá:* 57 km from Chihuahua, near Bachimba. *San Buenaventura:* south of Galeana. *Carrizal:* 4 km NW of Villa Ahumada. *San Borja:* 12 km south of Cusihuiriachich.

Coahuila: *La Cascada:* in Múzquiz. *Los Sabinitos:* 10 km SE of Nueva Rosita on the highway to Múzquiz. *Ojo de Agua:* 62 km SW of Piedras Negras, in Nava. *La Azufrosa:* 42°C; SE of Torreon, between Villa Unión and Allende. *Los Carricitos:* 42°C; 2 km from La Azufrosa. *Estación Hermanas:* on Hwy 57 between Saltillo and Monclova. *Bilbao:* near Torreón. *Ojo Caliente:* "medium hot"; 8 km from Saltillo on Hwy 40. *Agua Verde:* 15 km from Ocampo on highway to Cuatrociénegas. *Escobedo* and *El Antojo:* 46 km NW of Monclova on Hwy 57.

Colima: *Agua Caliente:* 9 km east of Colima. *Cayetano:* 4 km from Colima. *El Hervidero:* south of Colima, in Tepames.

Durango: There are more than twenty-five zones of hot springs in the state, many difficult to reach. *Navacoyan:* 42°C+; 10 km east of Durango. *Valparaíso:* 42°C+; 90 km SW of Fresnillo. *Hervideros:* 85°C; 12 km NW of Santiago Papasquiaro. *Atotonilco de Santiago Papasquiaro:* 45°C; 20 km from Santiago. *El Saltito:* "medium hot"; on Hwy 40, 28 km from Durango. *La Boquilla:* on Hwy 40, 56 km from Durango, near Francisco Madero. *Noria No. 3:* 22 km NW of Gómez Palacio, between Agostadero and Renoval. *Peñón Blanco* and *La Concha:* near villages of the same names. Difficult-access springs. *Zape, Pelayo* and *El Peñón:* municipio of Guanaceví. *El Pueblo, Los Brasiles, El Mexicano* and *El Castillo:* municipio of Topia.

Guanajuato: *San Bartolo:* on old road between Celaya and Queretaro. *Aguas Buenas:* 46°C; 16 km from Silao, toward Cerro de Cubilete. *San Luis de la Paz:* near Victoria. *Agua Caliente:* 5 km from Acámbaro. *Salados* and *Los Tanques:* near San Francisco del Rincón, between Silao and León. *Los Organos:* south of Manuel Doblado. *Tupátaro* and *San Gregorio:* 6 km from Cuerámaro. *Puroaga* or *Puruahua:* 10 km from Jerécuaro. *Churipitzeo:* near Pénjamo. *San Miguel de Allende:* several near the town. *Salvatierra:* several in area. *Puroagüita* or *Puruahuita:* 4 km east of Jerécuaro; *Cuerámbaro:* several east of town. *Marroquín:* 7 km SE of Apaseo El Alto.

Guerrero: *Agua Caliente:* 80°C; on Hwy 200, 51 km north of Zihuatanejo, in La Unión. *Agua Caliente:* 42°C+; in Coyuca de Calxán. *Las Piñas:* SE of Tlapehuala, 3 km from Ajuchitán. *Dos Arroyos:* 40 km west of Acapulco. *Atenango del Río:* many springs in the area. *El Chorro:* 42°C+; municipio of Cuajinicuilapan. *Atotonilco:* 55°C; 19 km south of Copala on Hwy 200, near San Luis Acatlán.

Hidalgo: *Tolantongo:* many springs, caves, pools. *Pozo de Vapor:* in the western part of the state, near the border with Querétaro; geyser and hot baths. *Pathé:* a large geothermic zone (don't confuse this with the Pathé in the state of México). *Río Moctezuma-Pozo de Vapor:* many springs in this region. *Huichapan, Agua Nacida:* Amajac; others nearby. *La Cantera:* Tula. *Tephé* and others: near Ixmiquilpan. *Tzindeje:* Tesquillo. *Barranca de San Pablo:* Tulancingo. *El Salitre:* Metztitlán.

Jalisco: This state has many hotsprings; this list is just a few. *Río Caliente:* 64°C; 2 km from La Primavera and 20 km from Guadalajara off Hwy 15. Many springs in the area; hot river. *Tizapán el Alto:* 36°C; south shore of Lake Chapala. *Cañón de las*

Flores: 30°C; near Río Caliente. *Villa Corona:* 40°C; several in the area. 50 km from Guadalajara on Hwy 80. *La Toma:* near Tequila. *Chorros de Tala:* near Tala, 40 km from Guadalajara. *Oblatos:* 42°C; 10 km from Guadalajara. *Cortijo de Paráman:* municipio of Tlaquepaque. *Soyatlán del Oro:* near Soyatlán. *Los Camachos:* 15 km from Guadalajara.

Michoacán: The state is rich in hot springs and includes some of Mexico's most notable spas, which are included regardless of their extensive development; some allow camping on or near their grounds. *Los Azufres:* a zone of geothermal activity and multitudes of hot springs, running from the volcano of Sangangüey to the Río Santiago in Nayarit and across México to Villa Rica in Veracruz. Azufres is north of Ciudad Hidalgo. Nearby are *El Cráter de los Azufres, San Alejo, El Baño del Chino, Laguna Verde* and *Baño de la Muerte* (The Bath of Death!). An extensive zone is found northwest and west of Aguascalientes, near Acambaro: *Araro, Zinapécuaro, Cuamio, Indaparapeo.* Another zone is near *Ixtlán de los Hervores: El Salitre* and *Pajacuarán. Spa San José Purúa:* 32°C; near Zitácuaro. Very famous. *Spa Agua Blanca:* near San José Purúa. *Santa Rosa:* 30°C; near Tuxpan. *Chucándiro:* on the southern shore of Lake Cuitzeo; 40°C. Several springs. *Cointzio:* 30°C; 14 km from Morelia. *La Huacana:* 60°C; 171 km south of Uruapan on Hwy 120. *Los Chicos:* 26°C; Parácuaro. *Jiquilpan:* 103°C; mud baths, on Hwy 59, east of Zamora. *Los Negritos:* near Villamar.

México (state): *Ixtapan de la Sal, Tonatico, Atotonilco:* Almoloya de Juárez. *San José Villeje:* Jocotitlán. *Los Baños:* Ixtlahuaca. *El Salto de Ferrería* and *Ixlostoc:* Valle de Bravo. *El Molino:* Donato Guerra. *San Pedro Totoltepec:* Toluca. *Santa Cruz Atizapan:* Zaragoza. *El Bañito:* Apaxco. *Pathé:* Acambay. *Temascaltepec.* There are many more, a good number of them located within state and federal parks.

Morelos: *Atotonilco:* 32 km from Cuautla. *Agua Hedionda:* "Stinking Waters" is a common name in Mexico for natural mineral springs that give off sulfurous odors. Municipio of Yautepec. *Oaxtepec:* one of the country's most famous spas. *Las Estacas:* 30 km from Cuautla. *Palo Bolero:* on old highway to Taxco.

Nayarit: *Agua Caliente y Caramota:* municipio of Huajícori. *San Dieguito:* 38°C; 6 km from Acaponeta. Aguacaliente de Rosa Morada: at km 997 of Hwy 15. *Bella Vista:* "medium hot." 9 km north of Tepic. *Santa María del Oro:* village of same name. *Agua Caliente de Mazatán:* 40°C; 26 km from Mazatán. *La Canoa:* close to Zapotán, municipio of Compostela. *Amatlán de Cañas, Olga:* 30°C; 12 km south of Zapotán. *Comisaría del Terrero:* 6 km west of Ixtlán del Río. *San Blasito:* 42°C+; 44 km from Ahuacatlán, in Amatlán de Cañas. *Teotitlán:* 18 km NE of Ahuatlán.

Nuevo León: *Topo Chico:* 40°C; 8 km north of Monterrey. *Agua Hedionda:* 35°C; 20 km from Monterrey in municipio of Villa Garcia. *Manantiales de Mina:* 42°C+; 50 km NW of Monterrey, near Apodaca. *Las Huertas:* south of Montemorelos. *Manantiales de Linares:* a zone of hot springs, including *Loma Atravesada, Dolores, San Fernandito* (all in the hacienda El Fresno) and *San Ignacio* in the hacienda Guadalupe, 20 km east of Linares. *Rancho Potrero Prieto:* near Galeana.

Oaxaca: *Atonatzin:* in *Tamazulapan,* km 391 of the Puebla-Oaxaca highway. *Totonilco:* 42°C; just before Puerto Escondido, municipio of Nopala. *San José:* municipio of Tuxtepec. *Yucutindoo:* near Sola de Vega on Hwy 131. *Chazumba:* 42°C; 58 km from Oaxaca on Hwy 131 toward Tehuacán. *Tehuantepec:* within the area of the city.

Querétaro: *Amascala:* 25 km northwest of Querétaro. *Batán:* 11 km south of Villa del Pueblito. *Pathé:* 42°C+; 27 km north of Cadereyta on Hwy 122. *Ahorcado:* 8 km north of Pedro Escobedo. *Tejocote:* 8 km from Ajuchitlán, Hwy Querétaro-Colón. *Rancho Agua Caliente:* 20 km NW of San Juan del Río. *Galindo:* 10 km north of San Juan del Río. *Tequesquiapan:* numerous hot springs. *San Pedro de la Cañada:* near Querétaro. *Colón:* near the town of the same name.

San Luis Potosí: *Lourdes:* 49 km south of San Luis Potosí. *El Gogorrón:* 42°C+; near Villa de Reyes, developed extensively but other springs in area. *Ojo Caliente:* 38°C; in Santa María del Río. *El Bañito:* 34°C; 10 km from Ciudad Valles. *Ojo Caliente:* in Ciudad Valles. *Anteojos:* 68 km from Ciudad Valles on Hwy 70, municipio of Santa Catarina. *Rancho Gamotes:* near Cárdenas. *Rancho San Diego:* near Río Verde and El Refugio. *Los Laureles:* 10 km west of Matehuala. *Manantial de la Estancia:* 28 km from Matehuala, near El Cedral. *Taninul:* 40°C; 16 km from Ciudad Valles.

Sinaloa: The state has few developed hot springs and the following are grouped according to their municipios for easier map reference. *Choix:* Agua Caliente El Grande, Aguacaliente de Baca, Agua Caliente de Lamphar. *El Fuerte:* Lay Joya, Aguacaliente de Gastélum, Aguacaliente de Zevada, San José de Gracia, Bacubirito. *Badiraguato:* Atotonilco, Huerta de los Ríos or Alicama. *Culiacán:* Carrizalejo, Imala Aguacaliente or Rancho Macurimi. *Cosalá:* Potrerillo or Guadalupe de Reyes, Comedero, San José de las Bocas. *San Ignacio:* Santa Apolonia, San Ignacio, Agua Caliente de Yurear. *Mazatlán:* Santa Fe, Aguacaliente de Gárate. *Concordia:* Aguacaliente de Concordia (35 km SE of Concordia) and Aguacaliente Iguana. *Rosario:* Cacalotán, Potrerillos, Matatán, Chametla.

Tamaulipas: *Los Azufres:* near Cuidad Mier. *Pozo Azufroso:* 27 km south of Ciudad Mante. *Camargo:* municipio of Camargo.

Tlaxcala: *Santa Justina:* east of Tlaxcala on old highway to Texmelucan. *San Juan Buena Vista:* near San Martín Texmelucan (Puebla). *Manantial de Santa Cruz:* NE of Tlaxcala. *Atotonilco Occidental:* north of Apizaco. *Apizaquito:* west of Apizaco. *Totolzingo:* near El Carmen, eastern edge of state.

Zacatecas: *Apozol, Papiscuaro, Ojo de Agua de la Higuera, Ojo Caliente, Santa Fe:* 10 km from Jerez. *Atotonilco, Santa Cruz.*

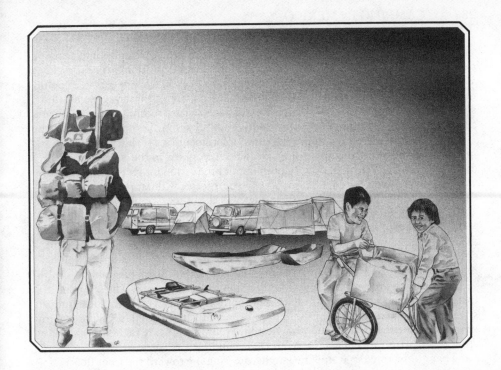

9. Preparations & Camping Gear

Several years ago my standard words of advice to anyone planning a camping trip to Mexico were: "Keep your gear, and therefore your life, as simple as possible." This still holds true but equipment manufacturers are doing their best to make simple camping a thing of the past. I have to admit to feeling like a slow learner when confronted by the complexity and sophistication of new camping gear.

Recently, I went to a fancy wilderness outfitters's shop in search of a stove . . .

"May I help you, sir?" The salesman approaches with the casual movements of a hunting shark. One false move and I'll leave the store wearing snow shoes and carrying a Himalayan Bivouac Pack stuffed with freeze-dried lobster tails.

"Uh, what kind of camp stove have you got?"

"Well, just exactly what are your *requirements*?" He flashes me a knowing smile. Last weekend he clung to the summit of Mount Endurance with his fingernails and boiled Russian Tea on a cloud top. He is very knowledgeable.

"Well, er, beans . . . making some coffee, frying fish. You know."

Barely suppressing a groan he leads me across the thickly carpeted shop to a walnut and plate glass display case. "Gas, pellets, solid, liquid, disposable, rechargeable or multi-use? Kersosene, butane, gasoline, naptha, alcohol or special blend?"

"Brass," I answer, licking my lips as my eyes roam nervously over the bewildering assortment of stoves that crowd the shelves.

"Brass? Did you say *brass*?" He repeats the word several times, peering at me as though through a dangerous winter white-out.

"Yeah, brass," I answer, plunging ahead. "I like shiny brass things. What have you got?"

The groan is no longer suppressed; I am off the Final Assault Team, obviously not summit material, just another low level load humper and gear hauler. He impatiently opens the display case and points at a stove. His description flows as quickly as a drawn-out yawn: "This is Model ZR Nine-oh-five-seven with twenty-four point two ounces dry weight, fuel capacity point nine liters, giving you an average boiling time at five thousand meters of three hundred and twenty seconds and total burn time of . . ." his eyebrows raise significantly, ". . . just over two point six hours!"

Before I can register the proper degree of amazement he continues to reel off information. "Stability factor is a bit low when compared to the XR Seven or the older DZ Ten . . . but then they've been out of production for seven years . . . anyway, it's rated well for ease of operation, compactness, durability and subzero — Celsius, of course — operation. What do you make of it?"

"It's pretty. Got a nice polish."

He stares at the stove for several seconds. His lower jaw is working back and forth as though clearing his ears at high altitude. His shoulders flex in the manner of a climber shifting the weight of an enormous backpack. "Yes," he sighs, a well manicured thumb idly polishing the sleek surface of the stove's fuel tank.

I impulsively make the momentous decision to buy the stove. The salesman's interest perks up as he equips me with spare parts and vital accessories: filter, funnel, spare O rings, wire orifice cleaners, a nifty vaporizer for improved fuel economy (my new burn time is hard to beat), windscreen, eyedropper, spare fuel flask and emergency priming pellets ("Once on Deadman Pass . . ." he tells me).

"That ought to wrap it up!" he laughs, steering me toward the front door. Another customer is inquiring about the loft factor of a cross-block baffle bivvy bag and it is nearly closing time.

"Just one more thing!" I say, ignoring the ice-axe grip on my left elbow. He stops, eyeing me suspiciously. What will it be this time, a canvas wall tent for twelve? "Yes?"

"Do you have a small can of Brasso?"

Begin preparing for your camping trip to Mexico as soon as possible; last-minute rushes inflict heavy damage on your budget and peace-of-mind. Lorena and I prepare, if only in such small small ways as making lists, for trips that are still dreams or half-formed ideas, rather than firm plans.

Does wintertime in the Uruapan Valley look more enjoyable than fighting ice and snow in Duluth? If so, begin preparations with casual reading about Mexico, inquiries to friends who might have camped in the area, a visit to a surplus store to see if they have a pith helmet in your size and so on.

The type of camping trip you plan to take will have a certain influence on your selection of equipment. Equipment, however, should not be allowed to plan your trip. Just because you bought three deep sea fishing rods at the local flea market, two with reels that almost work, doesn't justify scrapping plans to hike in Chihuahua for offshore fishing near Guaymas.

I'd bet a leaky air mattress against a broken folding chair that Murphy's Law ("Whenever possible something will go wrong") was invented while Mr. & Mrs. Murphy were camping. We've invented a new law for campers: Simplicity equals sanity. Amazing numbers of people spend every waking moment (which is often half the night) trying to keep their camping operation in motion. When not replacing a special mantle in a delicate lantern or adjusting the carburetor on the mini-motor bike, they are glueing, drilling, sewing, riveting and shrieking curses because everything is relentlessly falling to pieces.

A fellow camper once bragged, "I've got seven different kinds of glue in my tool box." I'd have been much more impressed if his camp life didn't require glue to hold it together at all, just the odd piece of twine or baling wire.

One of the easiest ways to keep camp life simple is to avoid equipment that claims to be "special for . . ." Special for camping often means "useless for anything else." Truly versatile gear may not be very attractive, compact or ingenious in design, but it's generally inexpensive, durable and easy to use. A bucket for example: a nifty plastic bucket that folds up when not in use works quite well for *carrying* water — but not for washing dishes (unless supported well) and not at all for heating over a campfire. A galvanized bucket will dip and heat water but an aluminum bucket or large cook pot does both of these and is also safe to cook food in (galvanized metal should not be used for cooking).

Versatility means more than multiple uses: a $.39 drinking cup is easily given away when it becomes unneeded, but an expensive backpacker's cup is a lot harder to part with, like it or not.

When in doubt, leave it behind. When weighing the delicate balance between useful equipment and excess baggage, I use this nugget of wisdom to tip the scale away from overloading and overspending. Chances are you'll never miss the extra tent, and spare stove and the emergency quart of boot oil. When the need for something arises, you'll either learn to improvise or do without, skills which are quickly fading in the modern world. The quality of your experiences while camping in Mexico depends on your attitudes and awareness, not the quantity or complexity of your gear. Keep it simple.

Buy new camping equipment only as a last resort. Look over the lists of suggested gear, then scour your house and garage. Don't spare friends or neighbors; some of them must have useful items they can be talked out of. Most camping equipment spends the majority of its life in the attic gathering dust.

Check out flea markets, swap meets, thrift shops, junk stores, garage sales and auctions for genuine deals-of-a-lifetime. Used kitchen utensils, for example, are very cheap in thrift shops. Think of substitutes: make your own nesting kettles by sawing the handles off aluminum sauce pans. Cheap metal coffee pots (with some part missing of course) are a dime a dozen in junk stores; they make great cook pots.

Watch the classified ads in local newspapers and check neighborhood bulletin boards for used equipment. Just because a tent is faded or looks slightly out-of-style, doesn't mean it won't serve you well, especially if the price is right. (Tents are very easy to sell to Mexicans before you return home.)

What if you can't beg, borrow or buy something cheap? Consider making it yourself. Tent kits, for example, offer substantial savings. Other gear can be made at home or even while camping (see *Recommended Reading: Appendices*).

Specialty stores have a reputation for high mark-ups on outdoor gear. Labelling a plastic bottle as a 'Backpacker's Flask' somehow justifies doubling the price. To avoid paying too much, leave the outdoor shops for the last resort.

Dime stores, supermarkets, discount stores and hardware stores can supply much of your gear at just about the lowest retail price. I needed a very lightweight grill for backpacking and kayaking. Specialty outdoor models were expensive and designed to support small kettles, not for grilling fish. In a discount store I bought an entire home barbecue kit, including a flimsy aluminum charcoal pan, a large but lightweight grill and several meat skewers. I reduced the grill to the size I needed with a few swipes of a hacksaw. The rest of the set went into the nearest Goodwill donation box. I got a very cheap grill and did a good deed at the same time.

In a dime store we bought plastic bottles sold as glue dispensers and used them for cooking oil, liquid soap, suntan lotion and other liquids. They've held up as well as expensive bottles we bought in backpacking shops.

Similar bargains on an amazing variety of plastic food containers, plates, bowls, cups and very lightweight pots and pans can be found in discount stores and large supermarkets. A good selection of plastic, tin and enamelware kitchen gear is also available in Mexico at supermarkets and dry goods stores.

Buying camping equipment by mail is tricky: I compared numerous mail order catalogs while researching this chapter and found a significant difference in prices from one company to another. At the same time, one catalog may offer a real deal on a popular item (known in supermarket jargon as 'loss leaders' to attract customers) but overprice other gear. Quality control may be sloppy; check their return policy and allow enough time to send defective gear back for replacement or refund. A number of mail order supply houses are listed in the *Appendices* of this book.

Once you've exhausted the alternatives and must shop in a specialty store to complete your equipment, here are some final hints:

• Ask a poor but knowledgeable friend to accompany you, someone who will wince at every price tag.

• Be rested and cheerful; weariness leads to "Ah what the hell?" spending.

• Take a list of what you *need*, not what you want.

• Examine the most pared-down models available. Once you determine that it fulfills your requirements, stop there; more elaborate and expensive versions aren't necessary.

• Look for slightly damaged goods or 'seconds'. We bought expensive backpacks for less than half price because the fabric color was irregular. Competition also creates good deals: ask for last year's models at substantially reduced prices.

• Watch for sales, especially end-of-season (late summer and fall), inventory (after Xmas and New Year) and pre-season (early spring).

• Don't sacrifice quality, however, just to save a few bucks. Careful shopping also means buying gear that not only works at home, but will also survive the rigors of a long camping trip.

What if you forget something and want to buy it in Mexico? Mexican-made camping gear is expensive and often of low quality; you're better off improvising or doing without. (There are a number of sporting goods shops concentrated on Venustiano Carranza Street in Mexico City, not far from the Zocalo.) Most equipment, however, can either be approximated or improvised from something easily available in Mexico. For example, a friend who wanted a backpack had one woven from reed basket material. He took the 'pack' to a shoemaker and had leather straps added. For a fraction of the cost of a real backpack he got a usable pack and a very interesting souvenir. Quick and cheap tarps can be sewn together from flour sacks; add a few pots and pans from the marketplace and you've got the Compleat Hobo Outfit.

Equipment Discussion

The equipment on the following pages is very extensive; there's enough here to fill at least one 3/4 ton pickup truck, if not two. The purpose, however, is not to overload you but to give an idea of what *might* be needed while camping, backpacking and boating in Mexico. In many cases you may find that conditions in Mexico will make a piece of gear completely unnecessary (backpacks are a good example). Rather than carrying extra equipment, throw in a notebook and pencil; when you want something note it down for the next trip.

Backpacks, Daypacks & Alternatives
Binoculars
Boats & Gear: See Chapter 2
Books
Bucket
Camera & Film
Candles
Canteens & Water jugs
Checkers, Chess & Playing Cards
Clothing
Fishing & Diving Gear: See
    Chapter 6
Flashlight & Headlamps
Gifts & Trade Goods
Hammocks

Health Kit: See Chapter 2
Insect Repellent
Journal & Notebooks
Kitchen Gear: See Chapter 7
Knives
Maps & Charts: See *Appendices*
Mattresses
Odds & Ends
Personal Stuff
Sleeping Bags
Spares
Stoves & Lanterns
Stuff Sacks
Tents & Tarps
Tools

Backpacks, Daypacks & Alternatives:

Gringo hikers take backpacks for granted. After all, the very name is synonymous with the sport. Consider, however, the amount of time you actually hope to spend on the trail in Mexico and some of the alternatives.

If you want to make short hikes, hire pack animals or travel in small boats or airplanes, a daypack and a suitcase or duffle bag should be quite adequate. Backpacks (especially with a rigid frame) are difficult to lash to small burros. You'll probably have to transfer your gear to burlap sacks or *huacales* (homemade crates of sticks and leather lashings). Frame packs don't fit well into the luggage racks of buses or trains, the trunks of small cars or the corners of dugout canoes. A suitcase or duffle bag, on the other hand, is easily handled in crowds, simple to pack and rummage through, cheap (especially secondhand) and reasonably sturdy. They also have an aura of respectability; backpacks are still associated with down-and-out travellers in most countries.

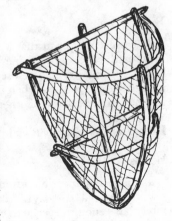

You might even consider what I call the Aztec Special: an *ayate* or woven carrying net slung over your back and supported by a *mecate* (skin strap) across the forehead. Your neck muscles will astound Charles Atlas after a few weeks of use. Other people you'll meet on the trail carry their loads in blankets, homemade boxes, huge baskets or even five gallon tin cans with wooden and rope handles.

Still prefer a backpack over a basket? For long

hard use under incredibly varied conditions we've found the 'frame sack' or 'touring pack' to be the best choice, with a rigid or flexible inner frame and a fully opening main bag. When laid on a bed or the ground the pack opens much like a suitcase, with the entire contents revealed and easily accessible. Outside pockets are large enough for canteens, food bags and small articles of clothing. The pack can also be carried by a strap handle, simulating a suitcase (hence the name 'touring' pack). Ours were made by Jansport and they have survived years of almost constant use, from Guatemala to Alaska.

Climber's packs, with simple flexible stiffeners or no internal frame are also a good choice for hard travelling, but they tend to be expensive and are not as versatile as a touring style pack. For most hikers, an extra large daypack would do just as well and is much cheaper.

Pack frames will surely be pushed to their limit (and beyond) if you travel by public transportation in Mexico. Can your pack survive being tossed from the top of a second class bus? If not, leave it at home. Mexican baggage handlers are notorious for putting the squeeze on when space is limited. (Load your gear onto the bus yourself; they rarely object to being helped.)

A friend backpacked throughout Latin America for many months, going to great lengths to protect his pack from damage. One day, after hoisting the pack from the roof of a bus and carefully placing it on the ground, he saw the Perfect Photo. As he turned his back and raised the camera to his eye the bus started up and drove directly over his pack, compressing it into an attaché case. It took him two days and two miles of twine to resurrect it.

The Law of Empty Spaces should be carefully considered when selecting a backpack: "All spaces will be filled, then overfilled." Pare your gear down to the minimum, then find a pack that barely holds it all. We've met a number of people who carried more useless junk on their backs than I'd care to have in a van. Needless to say, they did little actual backpacking and spent most of their time massaging sore back muscles.

Try to carry all of your gear, including your sleeping bag, inside the pack. This protects things from dirt, accidental loss or snatch-and-grab theft. Unfortunately I love loops, straps, tie points and strings; my pack is covered with strands of garlic, wet clothing, cups, canteens, spare pots and all the other handy extras that won't cram inside.

If your pack is honestly too small, just lash on a daypack. This is very handy for extra food and water and makes a good tote bag for market trips and side excursions.

Binoculars

We use a cheap pair that won't break our hearts when we lose them or drop them overboard, the seemingly inevitable fate of such fancy toys. Other than obvious uses as peeping and prying, we use our binoculars most while boating. They can save a great deal of detouring when looking for campsites along the shoreline. Binoculars also help to keep track of other boats, approaching whales, etc.

Blankets: See *Sleeping Bags* in this chapter.

Books

If you're like me, you'll find little time left over while camping to devote to reading. After a hard day of fishing, exploring, wood chopping and camp cleaning, I rarely have enough energy to crack open a cookbook, let alone a heavy novel or self-improvement tome. Many campers, however, find a sudden new interest in field guides, nature books and do-it-yourself language study. (See *Recommended Reading: Appendices* for more ideas.

Large picture books make great conversation pieces for Mexican visitors to your camp. They are very cheap in thrift stores at home and are much appreciated as gifts. *Campesinos* are particularly interested in pictures of farms, livestock, mountains and other natural wonders.

Boots: See *Clothing: Shoes* in this chapter.

Bucket

Very useful for washing dishes, produce and laundry, cleaning the car, carrying and heating water, building sand castles and adobe ovens, food foraging, water fights, sea anchors and soaking your head and feet after a long day on the road.

An aluminum or stainless steel bucket can be used to cook food, but galvanized metal can leach dangerous substances and should not be used as a cooking utensil. We carry a collapsible plastic bucket when hiking or boating. When not in use for hauling water we hang the bucket from a tree and fill it with spare food or small items of equipment that try to lose themselves in the sand and underbrush.

Rectangular five gallon cans converted to buckets are sold throughout Mexico, as are plastic and galvanized buckets of all shapes and sizes. Buckets made from empty tin and aluminum cans can sometimes be found.

Bug Dope: See *Insect Repellent* in this chapter.

Camera & Film

A 35 mm, single lens reflex camera with extra lenses, filters, tripod and carrying bag is ideal for anyone fully committed to taking pictures while camping. Once you get started, in fact, you'll find so much to photograph that you'll develop viewfinder squint. On the other hand, an inexpensive Instamatic will take a fine photo record of your trip. This type of camera is very cheap to buy, very lightweight and easy to give away if you suffer, as I do, from extreme laziness when handed a camera.

I've always regretted not having more pictures of some of our trips to Mexico. My regret isn't that we didn't have a camera, because we always did (sometimes two). The problem is that we seldom managed to use it. I remember one view of a high mountain canyon that had us gasping, both from awe and the effort of getting to it.

"Wouldn't that make a fantastic picture?" I puffed.

"Sure would!" Lorena agreed, sagging against a tree.

"Oughta get out the camera," I said, wiping my brow with a damp bandanna.

"Good idea!" Lorena said, sinking back and closing her eyes.

"People at home wouldn't believe it!" I said.

"Sure wouldn't!" Lorena sighed, fading into a trance.

Ten minutes later we moved on to the next awesome viewpoint, the camera still stowed in the bottom of one of our packs.

A camera can actually make your trip much more enjoyable: carry an inexpensive Polaroid and take photos of people you meet for instant and unforgettable gifts. Nothing breaks the ice quicker than a picture of the baby or even the entire family. If you're low on money, most *campesinos* will happily trade meals for a photo; in fact they'll often insist on an exchange of some sort.

Make the most of it when taking someone's photo. A family will want to change their clothes or at least straighten their hair. In the back country this may be a rare opportunity to record two or three generations at one sitting. Don't insist on smiles; the preferred family pose is with rigid backs and a direct stare into the distant horizon. I always fuss around, moving a child here or there, delaying the big moment.

Film of all sorts is available in Mexico, but costs more than in the U.S. You can find camera batteries, flash bulbs and other odds and ends in larger cities. Look for the yellow Kodak signs.

Keep your camera out of the direct sunlight and away from sand. Heat can melt plastic camera parts and will damage the film. We carry our camera in the pressure cooker, carefully swathed in a towel, or inside a plastic waterproof bag. If you seal the bag, make sure there's no moisture inside that might condense in the camera.

Carrying a camera, especially a heavy 35mm, is basically a drag. To ease the burden we use a Kuban Hitch, a somewhat complicated array of straps and snaps that holds the camera firmly against your chest. When I shout "Look at that!" and bend over a thousand-foot precipice, the Hitch saves the camera from falling off my neck. Hikers who suffer from camera bruises on their chests will love the Hitch.

A cheaper version of the Kuban Hitch can be easily improvised: attach snap clips to both ends of a wide camera strap, guitar strap or cloth belt (an elastic type is best). Hang the camera around your neck. Now put the extra strap with clips around your lower back and clip it to the same points on the camera that attach the neck strap. Lean forward; the camera should be held firmly against your stomach or chest. If it sags forward, shorten the waist strap.

Protect your camera's lens by using a clear filter or ultra-violet (UV) filter at all times. A polarizing filter will greatly reduce glare on the water and improve shots of clouds and sunsets.

Candles

Velas are very cheap in mexico. The best quality are sold in funeral parlors but good candles are available everywhere. When car camping we buy votive candles in drinking glasses or coffee cups. When they've burned up, the drinking glass or cup makes a good gift.

Candle lanterns of tin and glass are sold in the market and dry goods stores. Fancier versions are available in tourist shops; they make useful camp lights and nice souvenirs.

Backpackers should bring a candle lantern from home; candle flames are very hazardous. At the least, an open candle will drip wax on your best shirt or melt a hole in your sleeping bag.

Canteens & Water Jugs

A strong, leak-proof water container will be one of your most valuable pieces of equipment. Boaters and hikers will want to be very sure that their water supply is safe, especially when travelling in areas where replenishment is uncertain or difficult. Many trips we've made were limited by our ability to carry water. Water containers can be improvised (such as plastic bags filled with water and carefully carried inside cardboard boxes, stuff sacks or towels), but I'd be very leery of trusting my safety to them.

Buy the best quality water containers to carry your basic supply (survival minimum is two quarts per day per person). Several one liter jugs are easier to stow in a pack than one large container. Extend your supply with cheaper containers and always keep your jugs topped off. A simple pratfall in the desert can become a disaster if one or more containers rupture.

I always keep an eye out for used metal canteens when visiting flea markets and junk stores. Most need nothing but a good rinse and a new bit of gasket material inside the cap to be perfectly useable.

Collapsible water jugs, which we call 'elephant bladders', are one of the most useful items of modern camping gear I've encountered. They are durable, light-weight and stow easily in dugout canoes, backpacks, vehicles and saddle bags. When empty they can be inflated for emergency floats or used as buoys. We carry at least one each while backpacking (one gallon or larger) and when water holes get fewer and farther between we fill a bladder or two. By carrying extra containers and working like don-keys, Lorena and I were able to spend four days and nights camped on a barren volcano. When travelling by van, an extra ten or fifteen gallons of fresh water can save long and tedious backroad trips to a well or gas station.

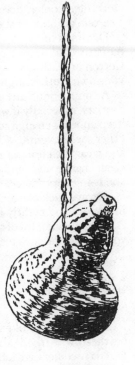

Plastic water jugs of all sizes are very cheap in Mexico, though the quality tends to be poor on the inexpensive ones. We often buy a few for extra water, then use them for gifts when we head for home. On a boat trip we found that water was easily available where we'd expected it to be scarce. We used our extra water first, then bartered the empty jugs for coconuts, bananas and tortillas.

When shopping for water containers I always subject them to a few tests: look for thin spots in the plastic, cuts, pinholes, etc. Remove the cap and blow into the jug. Feel any air leaking? If the store manager gripes about your mouth on the merchandise, fill the jug with air, close the cap tightly and discreetly give it a tremendous squeeze. Jugs that hiss or explode should be set aside.

Jícaras (gourds) are used as canteens by *campesinos*. They make beautiful souvenirs but be careful, the gourd is usually very thin and easily cracked.

Checkers, Chess & Playing Cards

If you enjoy cultivating the friendship of people who visit your camp, a deck of cards or game of checkers is a great way to establish communication. The Mexican checker game is considerably more difficult than ours, though the board is identical.

We carry a checker 'board' tie-died on cloth and a backgammon pattern on another. Beans, stones or colored shells make good markers. If you don't use your games, give them away or trade them for favors and food.

Clothing

I always start a camping trip with too many clothes, then purge the unneeded articles of clothing as I travel. Since my wardrobe is basically Early Salvation Army, discarding a shirt doesn't break either my heart or our budget. Clothing is always a much appreciated gift in Mexico and I enjoy giving someone the shirt off my back in return for a favor.

Campesinos are very fussy about clothing: not its style or cleanliness, but how much you've got on and what it shows underneath. Respectable clothing in the back country of Mexico can generally be taken to mean 'fully covering', whether it's a long-sleeved shirt and full-length pants or a neck-high blouse and long pants or dress. Revealing T-shirts, tight clothing or anything remotely 'exciting' (halter tops, for example) aren't proper attire, especially in the mountains. *Campesinos* wrap up in *sarapes* and overcoats when I'm sweating in a short-sleeved shirt; for women it's often ankle length dresses, heavy shawls and layers of blouses. When in doubt, put on more clothes.

Versatile clothing is best; a long-sleeved shirt protects your arms from sun and insect bites and keeps you warm at night. Pockets carry bug dope, sunglasses, pens and small change. Printed material or patterned T-shirts show dirt less. Loose fitting clothing is cooler, does not bind or chafe when hiking or mule riding, and eliminates a certain amount of staring if you're a woman.

Denim is not a good material for travelling and camping. Denim holds dirt and moisture and never feels entirely dry when camped on the beach or in the jungle. Cotton or wash-and-wear fabrics are much more practical. When you have to wash your own clothes, light fabrics will be greatly appreciated.

A comment on dirt and grime: rural Mexicans are not shocked at the sight of dirty tourists, especially if water is scarce. I wear one set of clothes until it's really dirty and keep another change completely clean. This second set covers town trips, visits and other social events. When we camp or rest near water I quickly wash my clothes out and wear the clean set until the others dry. At the end of the hike I've still got one clean change and can hop a bus or walk into a town without feeling self-conscious about my appearance.

Always pack clothing inside out to prevent accidental dirtying. Do it Navy style: inside out and tightly rolled, with all wrinkles smoothed.

The following list of clothing is about the minimum. Avoid dripping hot sauce down your shirt front, look for opportunities to do quick washings and it should be sufficient.

2 pants	3 pairs of socks	hat
2 shirts	underwear	bandanna
jacket, sweatshirt or	swimming suit, shorts	rain poncho
sweater	shoes, boots or sandals	Hidden Pocket

Women might like to add a wrap-around skirt for border crossings and nights on-the-town. It will also serve as a shawl for chilly nights around the camp fire. Lorena used hers as a tablecloth to impress visitors and once as an emergency sail for a dugout canoe with a broken paddle. A wide shawl also doubles as a skirt and can be folded up at night as a pillow.

Lorena advises women travellers who are worried about weight and space in their packs or luggage to forget dresses entirely; pants are acceptable on women almost everywhere these days. In the few places where a woman might feel more comfortable in a skirt (social gatherings and formal shindigs), you can improvise from yard goods, a shawl or whatever.

Boaters and beach campers will probably live in a bathing suit until sundown and spend only a few hours until bedtime wearing long clothes. While kayaking we carry just one pair of pants and pare the remainder of our wardrobe to the bone. It is unlikely that anyone you meet will be offended by your lack of clothing, especially if your swimming suit is more than a token covering.

Keep in mind that hard travelling and normal wear and tear can wear out the sturdiest clothing. Mexican clothing is expensive and not of the best quality; large *gringos* may have trouble finding a good fit. Leave your carefully faded and well patched denims at home — the newer clothes you take camping will probably look just as salty in a few short months of use. I once made the mistake of wearing almost worn out clothes on a long second class bus/hiking journey through northern Mexico. My socks dissolved, my pants fell to pieces and my shirts looked like they'd been attacked by army ants. I not only felt self-conscious wearing rags, but fought a constant battle with needle and thread to stay dressed at all.

Pants: While hiking I carry a wide assortment of lumps and bulges in my pants pockets: salt tablets, bug dope, extra film, notebook and pencil, pocket knife, money, bandanna, candy, interesting rocks and shells and so on. So many odds and ends, in fact, that I have extra pockets added by a tailor in Mexico. Lots of extra pockets are especially useful if the waistband of your backpack restricts access to some of your pockets.

Shirts: I have just one simple requirement for a good all-around camping shirt: it must be long-sleeved for sun and bug protection, with at least two front pockets that button down, not snaps (they break and can't be repaired easily); out of soft material, like flannel or well-washed cotton; preferably blue or brown . . . with little cowboys or animals in the pattern and no long tails. That's all. Lorena sews her own long-sleeved pullover shirts with pockets at the bottom.

Jacket, Sweatshirt or Sweater: An ultra-lightweight windbreaker and a hooded sweatshirt are just about the ideal combination for travellers who don't really know where they'll be or when they'll be there. On cold nights wear both over all of your shirts; when it's hotter peel off as many layers as it takes to reach the comfort level. You may suffer a few chilly nights but if you insist on total comfort at all times, you'll have to add to your wardrobe.

When travelling at higher altitudes, especially in wintertime, we carry light-weight jackets (rated as 'sweaters') insulated with polyester fibers. These jackets compress into a very small stuff sack and do double duty as pillows and ice chests (see Chapter 5).

Socks: Get good ones; socks wear out very quickly when travelling. I bought three pairs in a surplus store and wore out one pair a day while hiking. The hike, of course, was longer than three days so I finished with bare feet inside stiff new hiking boots.

The best all-around socks for varied travelling should give maximum foot protection with minimum heat and moisture retention. Ask for suggestions at an outdoor equipment shop. We use plain cotton work socks from Penny's or Sears.

Underwear: Cotton is best; it absorbs moisture and is easy to wash out by hand. I carry one colored or patterned undershirt to wear as a shirt when it's hot or for extra warmth at night. An undershirt makes a good all-purpose rag and dish towel. Friends get upset when you dry dishes with your extra shorts.

Swimming Suit, Shorts: Mexican women are just discovering the two-piece bathing suit and the string bikini. Judge from that how much impact your own bathing suit will have on others and what degree of attention you'll attract.

Mexican men often wear undershorts instead of bathing suits, but women should never bathe publicly in their 'unmentionables'. Public nudity is illegal and local dress standards are often very uptight indeed.

Hiking shorts draw a great deal of attention away from the beach. Unless our trip includes the beach I leave my shorts at home and wear long pants at all times. Bare legs on men or women in the mountains (unless you're an Indian and wear traditional dress) is nothing less than scandalous. At the least you'll be the butt of tiresome wisecracks and lewd comments.

Shoes, Boots, Sandals: Shoes or boots? Sandals or shoes? Decisions, decisions! Unless you plan to do lots of hiking, a strong pair of shoes should be adequate. Many people hike in running shoes or good quality tennis shoes. They are very lightweight, quick drying, durable, comfortable and have firm traction. They are also cheap in Mexico and widely available (Mexico exports footwear worldwide: look for known brands like Canada, Dunlop, Puma, etc. Men's sizes above 10 are extremely scarce, however).

I personally prefer light hiking boots or work boots for the additional ankle support and rock protection they give. I also carry very lightweight sandals for camp lounging, strolls and long stints of driving or bus riding.

Boots, however, have some disadvantages: they are very warm, heavier than most shoes, slow to dry out, relatively expensive and last, but definitely not least, almost impossible to fit into the stirrups of a Mexican saddle.

Whichever you choose, put durability first. I foolishly left my trusty hiking boots behind on a long kayak trip. In a fit of economizing I bought a pair of super cheap discount-store tennis shoes and a pair of equally shoddy shower sandals. The soles of the tennis shoes split lengthwise within a week. The shower sandals disintegrated upon contact with the ground. I spent five long weeks wearing Robinson Crusoe

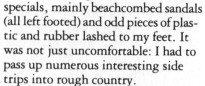

specials, mainly beachcombed sandals (all left footed) and odd pieces of plastic and rubber lashed to my feet. It was not just uncomfortable: I had to pass up numerous interesting side trips into rough country.

The vast majority of Mexicans outside cities and larger towns wear *huaraches*, sandals made from leather and used tire rubber. There are numerous styles, from a simple rubber sole and a single thong between the toes to beautifully made open weave 'shoes' of thin leather strips. Sandals can be copied or made-to-order by any good sandal maker for a very reasonable price.

Because Mexican sandals are cheap, durable and nice to look at, some *gringos* mistakenly decide to go native and use them for hiking. Do your feet a big favor first: take a close look at a typical *campesino's* foot. Looks kind of like a shoe itself, doesn't it? Those unbelievably thick calluses are as tough as a steel belted radial tire and are the results of a lifetime of bare feet and *huaraches*.

Soak your *huaraches* in water and wear them until they dry. Repeat this process until they have conformed to the shape and stresses of your foot. Don't be surprised

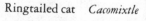

Ringtailed cat   *Cacomixtle*   if it takes several days for them to give in and become comfortable. Well broken-in sandals can be oiled occasionally, but give them another dunking if they begin to bind or chafe.

Any footgear should be well broken in and tested before trusting it to carry you through a long hike. If there's any doubt about durability, carry glue for repairs. I once had to sew up a flapping boot sole with baling wire. It's amazing what repairs can be done when faced with barefoot hiking in the desert.

On the advice of an experienced hot weather hiker, I have never oiled or sealed my hiking boots. He claimed that to do this would trap heat and moisture given off by the feet. Dry, unoiled leather would allow the feet to 'breathe' and both boots and feet would be less likely to rot. After three years of almost continuous use my boots are still alive and don't seem to have suffered from a lack of oils and lotions. So much for boot care.

Salt water is another matter. Nothing rots shoes and boots faster than a few weeks at the beach. If your footgear is soaked in seawater, give it a freshwater bath, even if it's days later. Salt left in the leather or fabric will continue to attract moisture and cause rotting and weakening.

Leather, especially if it has been oiled or soaked with perspiration, is considered a gourmet treat by rodents and their relatives. If your boots can't be hung in a tree or hidden in a tent or vehicle, put them in the bottom of your sleeping bag at night. I hiked with a friend who woke one morning to find that a nocturnal visitor had a bad case of the munchies and had reduced his expensive hiking boots to loafers.

Hats: I once left my hat behind when heading into a blistering desert canyon on the back of a very sweaty mule. I reasoned that the sides of the canyon would always provide shade, and besides, I don't like to wear a hat.

It took an hour before I realized that the canyon was actually an enormous reflector oven and solar cooker. By the second hour my guide was smirking at my beet red face. The third hour his smirk turned to an irritating giggle every time I gasped and wiped sweat from my sizzling forehead. When I finally dismounted, dropped my pants and transferred my Fruit of the Looms to my head, he was all but paralyzed with laughter.

Buy a hat; in Mexico they are so cheap you'll be able to afford two. Get a lightweight straw model, not heavy canvas or leather. Straw hats stretch, dry out quickly and don't make your neck muscles sore from over weight. If the hat is too small, just soak it in water, jam it on your head and let it dry in place. I 'block' my hat frequently, especially after sitting on it during long bus rides.

In extreme heat or glare, we dampen large bandannas and fit them under the hat, draped over the back of the head and neck, Foreign Legion style. I like that a lot; it cools my brain and makes me feel clever and adventurous.

An umbrella is a good substitute for a hat and *campesinas* often use them against the heat. Unfortunately, a man carrying an umbrella would be thought rather ridiculous. I use mine while boating or travelling in uninhabited areas.

Buy or improvise a chin strap, called *barbiquetes*. When riding in the back of a truck or on a burro, it will save sudden loss from wind gusts. A chin strap is essential while boating, especially if both your hands are occupied with paddles, fishing gear or the munchie bag.

We were hiking the mountains of Zacatecas, carefully picking our way down the side of a vast canyon. Far below on the bank of a shallow but very tempting stream, we saw the red tile rooftops of a small village. Three hours later, as the sun slid behind a mountain, we waded through ankle-deep water and squished right into a dusty plaza.

A number of people greeted us courteously but with frank curiosity. "So there aren't many *turistas* here?" I joked to an older man who took in our grimy backpacks and sweat-stained clothing with a good-natured "What next?" shrug.

"¡*Uiii!*" he laughed, making a flicking motion with his hand, "You're the first in many years. That's why we came in early from the fields to see you. My boy Juanito said 'Papa, here come some *gringos*' and here you are!"

I looked back across the valley but was barely able to make out the distant trace of the trail we'd come in on. "How did your son know we were *gringos?*" I asked, expecting him to produce a pair of Revolutionary era binoculars or an antique telescope.

"Why, your head, of course," the old man answered. "No one but a *gringo* would come down here without a hat." I looked around; everyone, from toddlers to grandparents, was wearing a straw *sombrero*. Their tentative smiles grew into wide grins as I dug into the top of my pack for a well crushed *sombrero,* punched it open and pulled it onto my head.

Bandanna: A truly versatile piece of equipment. Large Mexican bandannas make great sweat bands, hot pads, mini table cloths, wash rags, dust masks, tortilla and food wrappers, nose blowers, bikini tops, lens cleaners and when camped near suitable cliffs — parachutes to amaze local children. Buy several; you'll find a use for them all.

Poncho: A good quality lightweight rain poncho can do more than just protect you from rain: it makes a sun shade, sail, ground cloth, table cloth, temporary suit of clothing while doing laundry, rain catchment for drinking water, extra layer of insulation for freezing nights and more. If you don't have one, buy a two meter length of *plástico* near the marketplace. After a rain shower, *plástico* sellers appear like mushrooms, offering cheap plastic of all colors and sizes.

Hidden Pocket: "Hey, has anyone seen my . . .?" (traveller's checks, tourist card, passport, driver's license or other important paper) is a question all too frequently heard while travelling. The slight note of anxiety in the person's voice quickly turns to panic when everyone nearby casually answers, "Nope!" There's nothing that can quite match the gut-numbing feeling that comes from being unexpectedly penniless, without a shred of identification and thousands of miles from home.

The steps that some people take to avoid this unpleasant situation are seldom more secure than an ordinary wallet or purse: pouches that hang around the neck (these bang against your chest and chafe until the string breaks), money belts (won't hold anything else), secret compartments in luggage (not much good if the suitcase is misplaced) and so forth.

Our solution to this problem was inspired by Papillon, a French convict-turned-writer. He wrote that prisoners on Devil's Island hid jewels and large bank notes in small stainless steel cylinders. These cylinders, called 'chargers', were hidden inside a person's-. . . well, it's enough to say that it was very difficult to detect and to separate a man from.

The Hidden pocket (see *illustration*), is much easier to use than a charger, far safer than a pouch or wallet and more convenient than moneybelts or hidden compartments. It will easily hold a passport, traveller's checks and even small lumpy objects, if necessary. In a very short time the Pocket and its contents will mold against your hip and be almost indistinguishable from the natural curve of your body and clothing.

The greatest advantage, other than security, is that once you begin using the Pocket, you soon lose that nagging background fear of being separated from your valuables. At night it's a simple matter to put the Pocket in bed with you. Never leave it with your clothing when sleeping, showering or sunbathing; that's the first place a thief will look.

A belt, cord or stout string inserted through the top 'loop' of the Pocket allows it to be worn hanging from the waist, though placed *inside* your pants, shorts or skirt. Variations are also possible: with elastic straps at top and bottom, the Pocket can be worn on your leg like a knife sheath; pins or sewn-on ties will attach it to the inside of a skirt or dress.

The important thing is that the pocket be useable on all of your clothing. This not only saves the hassle of making permanent hidden pockets in every pair of pants or skirt, but increases your awareness of where your valuables are at every minute. You should be as aware of your money and documents as you are of cigarettes and eyeglasses.

If you're carrying more money, papers or valuables than one Pocket will conveniently hold, wear two Pockets.

In the many years we've used the Pocket, we've never lost a single thing from them

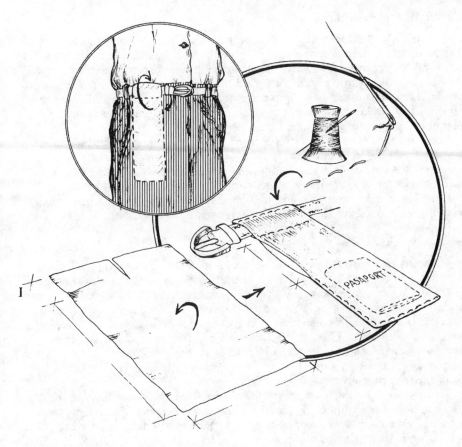

(knock on wood). Once you've become accustomed to it, you'll probably find that a wallet isn't necessary at all. I always carry whatever cash I need for immediate use in a buttoned shirt pocket and spare change in my pants pocket.

Sewing Instructions: The Pocket should be made of a durable but lightweight material. Plain dark colors will be the least noticeable on your belt. It is important to have something safe, sturdy and inconspicuous rather than fancily made.

The material can be cut in a long strip, 6" by 32" or in a rectangle 12" by 16".

If you start with the 32" strip, first fold it double, to 6" x 16". Leave 2" at at the top for the belt loop. Now sew down one side, across the bottom and back up for about 6". The remaining gap is for inserting your passport and money. Leave an opening large enough to easily insert and remove valuables but not so large that they might work their way out.

If you want to have the stitching hidden on the inside, turn the pocket inside out; now sew another seam 2 inches below the top to form the belt loop.

If your fabric is squarish (12" x 16"), fold it in half to 6" x 16". Now sew across the top and bottom and 6 inches up one side. Turn it inside out and sew the belt loop seam 2" below the top. Slice the fabric at the closed end of the belt loop. *Remember: The Pocket goes inside your clothing, not outside.*

Flashlight & Headlamp

We carry small pocket flashlights almost constantly, their bulge in a back pocket is as familiar as a notebook or wallet. We use the Mallory compact model (two AA batteries); its flat shape fits comfortably in a pocket and when two hands are needed, the light jams easily into your mouth. Flashlights are most useful when constantly at hand rather than stowed inside backpacks or stuck out of sight behind a car seat. Mine is in my pocket on night bus and train rides, either to track down drifting small gear or to locate a dropped ticket stub.

Hazards to pedestrians are rarely marked in Mexican towns and a small flashlight can save startling drops into dark trenches and deep gutters. Power failures — or no power at all — are common in small towns and cheap hotels. Groping for the bathroom in the dead of night makes a flashlight more than worthwhile.

Flashlights make great gifts and are a good substitute for money when paying for services, favors, food or lodging. We carry a few spares and trade them off as we travel.

Gifts & Trade Goods

Mexicans are often reluctant to accept payment from travellers they help out, whether it's a hand changing a flat tire or the use of a camping space in a coconut grove. Rather than forcing money on people who help us (which risks bruising their pride), we carry a small supply of inexpensive gifts and trade goods. It doesn't have to be fancy: Lorena gave a woman a few spools of thread in exchange for tortillas; by the woman's reaction you'd have thought it was a new sewing machine. In general, people don't expect anything and will be more than happy with something small and simple. Don't come on with piles of stuff, like Santa Claus or Foreign Aid. A fair exchange feels much better on both sides.

When space and money are severely limited consider giving something you make yourself: dolls from cornhusks, simple baskets (a friend makes them from pine needles), a sketch of a person or house, etc. In Mexico it is definitely the thought behind a gift that counts, not the value.

Frisbee or Soccer Ball: Teach the kids (and adults) how to throw a Frisbee but don't worry about the ball; soccer is part of life in Mexico, especially in areas that have no other entertainment. To avoid jealousy you might prefer to give the ball to a school teacher, village official or local priest.

Toys: Hand puppets, small balls, unbreakable dolls; you name it, some kid will absolutely love it. In many back country homes the only toy will be a block of wood or a 'ball' made of rags. The more durable the toy is, the better.

Clothing: Give good, simple, sturdy clothing, not discarded rags. Warm clothes are much appreciated in the mountains and baby clothes are a great hit everywhere. I once came through Mexican customs with a backpack stuffed with little girl's dresses. The customs inspector took a quick peek, turned two shades paler and hurriedly waved me through. When stuck for a gift, I buy a few yards of brightly patterned cloth.

Seeds: Since most of the people you'll meet in the back country are farmers, you can't miss by offering packets of seeds. The best are flowers and common vegetables (onions, corn, carrots, beans, peppers, spinach, lettuce). Anything weird (eggplant, for example) will be too far beyond their farming and cooking experience to be of use, even if it grows well. Try to buy seed packets that have planting instructions in both Spanish and English (more commonly available in the U.S. than you might think).

Pens, pencils, needles, thread, beads, mirrors: This sounds suspiciously like the shopping list that bought Manhattan Island from the Indians, but it's still a useful bag of tricks for back-country travellers. Crayons, notepads or anything resembling school supplies are very scarce and expensive in the boondocks.

Maps: In our many trips into unvisited areas of Mexico, our maps have served us better as conversation pieces and gifts than for orienting or following a trail. Maps of the world lead to hours of discussion and will give you an insight into how others perceive the outside world.

Tools: Any type of hand tool or kitchen utensil will be very welcome in households that rarely have more than a knife and spoon. Pliers are very good (baling wire is very widely used in Mexico) as are chisels, hack saws and blades, hand drills, hammers, files and adjustable wrenches. Knives are appreciated by everyone, from kids to adults.

Other ideas: Hand lotion, shampoo, perfume or any cosmetic; postcards from home, balloons, simple mechanical puzzles; any noisemaker or musical instrument; small radios; seashells (in the mountains); religious medals and costume jewelry; fishhooks and monofilament line (12 pound test or larger); artificial flowers (for the family altar) and any type of fairly sturdy Xmas decoration.

Hammocks

A hammock is more than just a piece of gear, it is a vital part of our romantic vision of camping under the sun, suspended in time and space between two picturesque coco palms. Most hammocks sold for camping, backpacking and mountaineering offer the absolute minimum, however, in comfort. Large hammocks are for lounging and sleeping; ultra lightweight and compact versions are for nights when there's no other alternative. When the terrain is just too rough or steep to sleep on the ground, the exhausted camper clings precariously to the webbing of a narrow hammock, praying for sunrise.

I sometimes carry a 'backpacker's' hammock, but use it mostly for daytime lounging and storing food and gear out of the reach of dogs and creatures.

Hot weather camping and sleeping are much more comfortable in a real hammock, especially one that is enclosed by mosquito netting. (See Chapter 5.) Large Mexican hammocks are world famous for comfort, quality and beauty but unless you intend to use one for regular sleeping (which means suitable trees to hang it from), backpackers will do fine with lighter Mexican models.

For more detailed advice on buying a Mexican hammock see *The People's Guide to Mexico: Buying Things.* Yucatan Hammocks can be ordered from John Muir Publications. See Order Blank at end of book.

Insect Repellent

Bring enough for the entire trip; any leftover repellent can usually be sold or bartered to other campers. People who don't have quite enough bug dope often act like secret drinkers — sneaking into the underbrush for a quick application of Cutter's or jungle juice. Offering your repellent to others is a sign of great friendship.

Make your own insect repellent: see *Bites & Stings:* Chapter 8.

Journals & Notebooks

A notebook can serve a much more useful purpose on a camping trip than simply recording each day's spectacular events.

My own reads like a cross between a cookbook and a ledger of lost thoughts: "See Eugenio day after tomorrow" is scribbled beneath "Remove spines rinse seven times steam tender." Under these entries the words "VERY IMPORTANT!" are printed in block letters. Important to what? — see Eugenio, whom I have no recollection of at all? — or rinse something with spines?

There is a special section devoted to numerology: do these figures represent a telephone number, address, winning lottery ticket or the serial number of a long ago cashed traveller's check? And what of this confusing tangle of lines and dots that leads to the note: "Best hotsprings in Mexico. Don't miss!"

Journal keeping requires discipline. I keep my nose to the grindstone by constantly reassuring myself that the information I'm gathering is of great importance and usefulness. I compile lists of cheap restaurants and hotels, bus and train departure times, fares, interesting handicrafts spotted in small markets, etc.

The organization of my journal is a little fuzzy but within a minute or two I can usually give you the name of a good Chinese restaurant in Guatemala City and directions from there to the bus depot.

Journals become personalized guidebooks to save time, money and hassles on future trips and for exchanges of information with others. Organizing a trip into a remote area, for example, is much simpler if someone who has done the trip passes along helpful information. I record as many details as possible: what kind of supplies are available and where; location of wells and waterholes; names of villages, *ranchos* and important landmarks; names of guides or good contacts; availability of firewood, shelter and booze; good diving and fishing spots; maps, with travel times and conditions and anything else that seems remotely useful, like the availability of shade along an especially exposed trail.

Your entries do not have to be lengthy to be useful. I record brief notes in a pocket notebook and transfer these to a journal at a later time. I prefer this method as it makes editing and a later review much easier, especially when passing information on to a friend. The following example is one full day during a two week hike in southwestern Mexico:

— 9 a.m.: left camp, half hour to top of ridge.
— Pine forest. Moderate descent along ridge. One hour through madroña and oaks.
— Steep descent with rocky trail. Switchbacks. Village to the left (west) several miles away. Should be San. F.
— 10:30: split in trail. Rested. Man leading pack burro said "go left".
— 11:30: Arrived San G. About twenty houses and school. Man gave us sugar-cane and sweet limes. Bought *mescal,* dry beans, tortillas, hard candy, chilis, macaroni, sour oranges and green coffee beens. Talked to young woman schoolteacher.
— 12:30: Left village, easy trail along small, clear stream. Many good campsites. Sugar cane and fruit trees. Shady but hot.
— 3:30: Crossed stream several times on rocks. Stopped to swim in large pool. Decided to camp. Old couple came along, gave us berry-sized tomatoes. Offered two tiny huts on mountainside above to sleep in.
— Ate noodles with tomato sauce. Incredible view of valley below from huts.

A friend in Guatemala gave us a copy of a similar 'journal-map' which made it possible to follow a very poorly marked trail for four days. Without his notes a hired guide would have been necessary.

When you're back home again a journal can be used to trigger memories of warm nights on a moonlit beach or a crazy bus ride through the mountains. It keeps the experience immediate and real and prods you along to the next journey.

One of the nicest journals I've seen was done by a fellow who combined a diary with photos, stubs of bus tickets, beer bottle labels, luggage claim tickets, pieces of maps and appropriate passages from guidebooks to create a vivid and highly visual account of his adventures. It even had a very brief introduction, lifted from Mark Twain:

"If you wish to inflict a heartless and malignant punishment upon a young person, pledge him to keep a journal for a year."

Lorena's journal is a small, loose leaf notebook, kept in the style of a 5-year diary. Each day is on a separate page, so that August 20, 1980 can be added onto August 20, 1979, which was added onto August 20, 1978, etc. When she reaches the end of a page, she starts another, August 20^{II}, August 20^{III}.

She likes to keep her journal this way because it allows her to recall what she was doing 'today', one year ago, two years ago, seven years ago. She refuses to get up in the morning until she's written in her journal and read 'today in History'.

"Hey Carl," a voice comes out of the mosquito net, "Five years ago today we were starting to pack for the hike in the Cañón del Cobre."

"Two years ago we were wondering if we'd get the camping book done by the end of the month. That afternoon you went to the bullfight with *compadre* Nacho. Last year we got stuck in that horrible traffic jam outside of La Lechera, remember? But then we found that great campsite beside the oil pipeline."

Knives

Although a simple pocket-knife will serve almost all of your needs while camping, knife cultists will want to carry an expensive 'hunting' knife. There are several reasons to leave these knives at home: few campers will get their hands on any wildlife larger than a lizard caught napping in the sun or an unfortunate snake squashed on the highway. Hunting knives, especially in the hands of children, are usually used to damage the local vegetation or for accidental self-inflicted wounds.

Sheath knives, some quite large, are commonly carried by *campesinos*. These

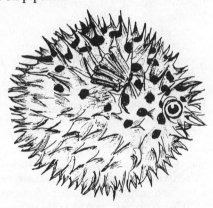

Porcupinefish, Spiny Pufferfish

knives are considered tools but their potential as weapons is obvious. If you are carrying a large knife someone will inevitably wonder *why?* This is especially true of the authorities. It is not uncommon for the police and Army to confiscate knives from tourists; arguments about whether or not this is legal are entirely meaningless. When your precious, stainless steel, bone-handled, drop-forged knife slips into a cop's back pocket, it is gone for good.

When we're travelling in an area where something more than a pocketknife is needed — the beach is the best example — I carry a small and inexpensive sheath knife in my pack or with the kitchen gear. It serves quite well for cleaning fish, opening oysters and small construction projects.

Mexican men love knives; if you carry a fancy one everyone will want to buy, borrow, trade or wheedle it from you. A young man visited me almost daily for a month in an attempt to talk me out of an expensive diving knife. I eventually gave in, vowing that I would never carry a flashy knife again.

Inexpensive sheath and pocket knives are available throughout Mexico. Many have interesting bone handles, hand-forged blades and attractive leather sheaths (*cubierta*). They are of low grade steel but take a good edge. They also rust easily (quickly removed with lime juice).

Because I am a fiend for keeping my knife sharp, I carry a very small sharpening stone or pocket steel. If you use your knife carefully and don't cut wire or chop onions on a rock, a good honing before your trip should be sufficient. If it gets dull ask a *campesino* to show you how to sharpen the blade on a rock. See *Sharpening a Machete:* Chapter 5.)

Lantern: See *Stoves and Lanterns* in this chapter.

Mattresses

A good night's sleep is as important to your health and happiness as food and water. You won't enjoy a strenuous day exploring Mayan ruins or skin diving on a coral reef if you spent the previous night cursing the rocks that jabbed your back and hips, or the cold that stiffened your aching joints. I've tried the standard alternatives to sleeping on the bare ground: mounds of leaves (scarce in the desert, believe me), piles of boughs (who said wooden branches are soft?) and 'fluffy' sand that compacts like dry cement. Give me four inches of foam rubber or a good tight air mattress and I'll snore away twelve hours on a jagged lava bed.

Backpacker's sleeping pads, sometimes inaccurately called 'mattresses', just barely take the edge off hard rock and earth, but do serve to protect you from cold and damp ground. For trips south, however, they have one big drawback: bulk. I've been jammed in the doorways of too many buses and trains to carry one of these supposedly compact pads. Even after cutting ours down to a width that barely protected our butts from grounding at night, our rolled up pads were still wide enough to scrape oranges off pushcarts and knock tottering old beggars to their knees.

I now carry a small (head to lower hip length) air mattress and a very complete patch kit. Although I spend a great deal of time Tracking the Elusive Leak, the air mattress is genuinely compact. Blowing it up at nights keeps my lungs in shape for skin diving. Lorena still uses a foam pad and tries not to look jealous when I take my air mattress into the surf for a few wild rides.

When camping out of a vehicle we carry a luxurious four inch thick foam mattress. If it has to fit into a car trunk, we roll the mattress tightly inside a strong blanket and tie it with rope or elastic shock cords. This mattress makes a great lounging couch; when covered at night by a mosquito netting it reaches the height of camping comfort and luxury.

Whatever your choice of mattress may be, keep it well covered while in use and while travelling. I store my air mattress in a strong stuff sack and before inflating it I carefully prepare the ground where it will lie. One small cactus spine can mean a long, long night of leaking air and sore hips and shoulders.

Foam rubber is available in larger Mexican cities. Look for stores that sell yard goods or furniture and ask, "*¿Hay espuma de ule?*" (Is there foam rubber?)

Odds & Ends

For odd jobs while camping at the ends of the earth. A full box or two of odds & ends completes what we call our 'Colonizer's Kit'. When a two-week camping trip turns into a two-year odyssey, these essential pieces of gear will keep you going. They also make good gifts and trade goods.

Anti-Rust Oil	Electrical Wire, Tape	Ass't Nuts, Bolts, Screws
Baling Wire	Gloves	Rope
Barge Cement	Glue	Solder & Flux
Cord, Twine, String	Liquid Wrench	Tape

Anti-Rust Oil is very important for lubricating metal that has been exposed to salt water and salt spray.

Personal Stuff

Brush & Comb	Lotions,Creams & Sun	Soap & Shampoo
Dictionary	Protection	Sunglasses
Fingernail Clippers	Needle & Thread	Tooth Brush & Toothpaste
Mirror	Safety Pins	Towels

Lotions: Sun protection is vital in Mexico. Take plenty of sunscreen, PABA cream, skin conditioners, Bag Balm and Aloe Vera gel. (See *Sunburns:* Chapter 8 and *Gear:* Chapter 2.)

Soap, Shampoo: For all around camp use nothing can beat cheap bars of *jabón de coco* (coconut soap), available in *farmacias,* CONASUPOS and other stores. They come plain or in flavors: my favorite, if only for novelty value, is tomato soap. The coconut oil base gives a good lather even in salt water.

When travelling by vehicle we carry a large bottle of Ivory Liquid, our favorite household soap. It lathers in salt water; few other liquid detergents will. Don't use very much, though, or it will take an ocean to rinse the dishes clean.

Laundry detergent is sold in plastic bags in Mexico. Carry a plastic container for powdered soaps; the bags always break and soap will flavor everything within ten yards.

Sunglasses: Cheap sunglasses are widely available in Mexico, as are prescription sunglasses. Some optometrists offer free examinations and eyeglasses-while-you-wait. They are a much better bargain than the frames; so take your own frames if you already have a pair.

Sleeping Bags, Blankets

Many years of 'trail'-and-error have led us to the following arrangement for sleeping bags and/or blankets: I use the lightest 'summer weight' bag I can find, insulated with polyester (Fiberfill II). Lorena uses a warmer version. The two bags zip together. When opened flat, each is almost wide enough to keep us fully covered on both sides. On warm nights we sleep on top of Lorena's bag and under mine. This is reversed if Lorena gets cold: my thinner bag on the bottom, Lorena's warmer bag on top. It rarely gets cold enough in Mexico to require additional covering.

Many travellers spare themselves the expense of a sleeping bag by carrying a blanket. This requires a combination of careful advance planning and an ability to accept at least short periods of discomfort. Mexicans I've camped with in the back country seldom use more than a well-worn *sarape* or a thin blanket. Going to bed is as simple as wrapping yourself up (they always cover their head; a good way to cut heat loss) and lying down on the cold, hard ground. It's easy to get up in time for sunrise.

A tent holds a great deal of heat; in fact, if your blanket is too warm you'll probably use it inside a tent for a pad, rather than as a covering.

A single blanket is usually heavier and bulkier than a lightweight backpacker's sleeping bag, but consider this: the blanket is inexpensive, easy to replace or part with and less conspicuous than a fancy bag. Whenever I sleep around people who are huddled inside blankets, I experience a few seconds of guilt before falling asleep.

If you go without a bag or even without a blanket and find yourself freezing, try to find something, *anything* to get under. I've slept beneath the idling engine of a semi-truck, under heaps of corn stalks, leaves, sheets of newspaper and cardboard, trees (vegetation protects you from cool, open air), sheets of plastic, dogs (it takes at least three) and once, in a freezing desert, under a pile of sand.

Still want a sleeping bag? If you plan to camp from a vehicle, a cheap bag from a discount store is probably more than enough. Carry a spare blanket and you'll be warm on the chilliest nights. When you head for home you might like to give the sleeping bag to someone who really needs it.

Get a rectangular bag, preferably one that can be opened at the foot without opening the entire bag. On warm nights your feet can stick out; a quick way to cool your body without providing a feast for mosquitoes. Rectangular bags that open fully can be used for blankets or sun shades. They are much less confining than tapered bags, an important consideration if you plan to use the bag inside a hammock.

Zippers should be extra large for nighttime groping and preferably not of metal, which corrodes quickly at the beach and leads to cursing and tearing. Carry large diaper pins if the zipper obviously isn't of the best quality; you'll need them.

Down bags are not good for Mexico unless your trip will be short and cool (high mountains). Down attracts and holds moisture; on dewy nights a down bag feels like a damp towel against your skin.

Polyester bags compress easily into small bundles, allowing them to be carried inside a backpack or suitcase. This protects the bag from dirtying and accidental loss.

We gently wash our polyester bags by hand, in warm and slightly soapy water. I don't know if this meets the manufacturer's suggested washing procedures, but it gets the bag clean, which is about all I hope for anyway. If it loses some insulative value through rough handling and washing it's probably for the best, since I prefer to sleep cool.

Spares

Camera Batteries	Generators	Lamp Glass
Eye Glasses	(stove, lamp)	Mantles

Stoves & Lanterns

Before you lose yourself in the complex questions of which type of stove and lantern to take to Mexico consider this: you may not need either one at all. Firewood

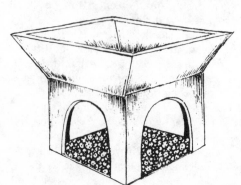

and *carbón* (charcoal) are used throughout the country and candles and flashlight batteries are as common as Coca Cola. You may have to cook dinner over a small pile of twigs or lumps of burro chips, but something is almost always available.

Stoves and lanterns really come into their own on a long trip, when foraging for fuel is no longer mildly entertaining but just plain tiring. An impromptu batch of tacos or an energizing mug of coffee is much easier to whip up on a stove, especially if you're staying in a trailer park or hotel, where loose fuel is scarce and open fires may create raised eyebrows. I know campers who went so far as to cook dinner over a newspaper fire on a side street in Mexico City, but if you're too self-conscious, you'll prefer a stove.

Many campers are surprised to find that their stoves are most useful when camping near civilization, rather than away from it. We use ours for cooking meals in hotel rooms more than we do on the trail, where an open fire is almost easier and certainly more enjoyable than a stove. Cooking your own food saves you lots of money; there's no better place to start economizing than while on the highway or staying in town. (See Chapter 7.)

Campfires and flashlights aren't the only alternatives to a regular stove and lantern; we often rely on a wood or charcoal fueled tin-can stove and a tin-can lantern. (See Chapter 5.) The stove cooks coffee as fast as most fancy stoves and does a much better job of barbecuing (when using the appropriate fuel). I must also admit to taking a perverse delight in cooking over a large, sooty tin can when others are adjusting the flame on an expensive three-burner stove that cost more than our entire kitchen set-up.

Fuel is the number one problem for stoves and lanterns, especially on a long, open-ended trip. Will you find disposable propane cartridges in Puebla? How about Panama and Peru? How many can you carry to delay the awful moment when the flame must go out? And what will you do when it does? The answers give dedicated campcooks and nighttime lantern lovers the cold sweats.

The most common fuels in Mexico (and the rest of the Third World, for that matter) are kerosene and natural gas. They are cheap and reasonably easy to find. The stoves and lanterns they fuel are also reasonably priced and reasonably simple to use and maintain. Parts for complicated stoves and lanterns (including Coleman) are not easily available — if they're available at all, once you leave the U.S.

Unfortunately, the most common stoves and lanterns in the U.S. are fueled by white gasoline (naptha). *Gasolina blanca* is scarce in Mexico. You may find it in drugstores (literally sold by the cup), hardware stores, the odd gas station or two and in tailor shops (for removing spots). But don't count on white gas to be there when you need it, especially in rural areas.

Fortunately there's still hope for Coleman users: *Extra gasoline,* in the silver pump, is unleaded and can be used in Coleman equipment. It does not work as well, however, as genuine white gas. Unleaded automotive gasoline eventually clogs the generator; while using it you may notice an unpleasant odor, yellow flame and sooting of pots and pans. These are caused by additives in the gasoline; the solution is to carry spare generators (at least two) and to clean the generator yourself (see Chapter 5). WARNING: never use leaded gasoline in a Coleman stove. It will contaminate your food — poison it — with lead. The lead also ruins catalytic heaters.

Propane is simply called *gas;* look for signs and large storage tanks on the side of the highway, especially on the outskirts of fair-sized towns and cities. Campers who spend long periods of time in one area may want to rent large propane tanks from the local gas dealer. This is a good deal, since it frees you from having to make numerous trips for a refill or doing without at times.

Propane stoves, lanterns and tanks of various sizes are sold throughout Mexico. Their drawbacks, however, should be carefully considered before investing in this equipment: first, and most important, the tanks do not always meet safety requirements in the U.S. Most propane dealers at home won't touch a Mexican tank with a ten foot pole. The quality and construction of the stoves and lanterns we've used is good . . . but not great. Give it a close check before you buy and whenever possible, light it up and make sure it works. Fittings are often poorly machined, clamps don't quite clamp and hoses swell and may even burst under full pressure. The motto is "Buyer beware!" so shop carefully.

Kerosene is dirt cheap in Mexico and lamps and stoves fueled by *petróleo* are very common in rural homes. Because kerosene is almost universal, travellers who have an eye on longer journeys should consider it carefully as a stove fuel. Kerosene lamps tend, unfortunately, to be fragile, heavy, dirty and not very efficient. They do give off light, however, even if it won't compete with mercury vapor.

Petróleo can usually be purchased in small stores or from government pumps near the market. In areas where the sale of *petróleo* is tightly controlled by the government (for some reason), you must buy it at authorized *Expendios* or under the counter. By asking discreetly, "*¿No hay petróleo?*" (Isn't there any kerosene?) you should eventually locate a source.

Expendios also sell wicks for kerosene lamps (*mechas*) and sometimes they have mantles for gas lamps. Mantles are called *camisas* (shirts), *capuchón* or *mechas*. They are inexpensive so when you find them, buy several extras to give to people who couldn't locate their own.

We've used a one-burner kerosene stove for many years and consider it to be almost perfect for varied travelling in Mexico. When carrying a stove is a debatable convenience — such as a short trip in a small car — our small stove fits almost unnoticed into a corner. We use it extensively for cooking in hotel rooms and when renting houses or *palapas*. With a very careful eye to maintaining ventilation, the stove quickly heats a cold van or tent; in rainstorms it saves the day with cups of coffee and hot meals.

Kerosene stoves have one drawback; they require an outside source of heat to prime them. I use alcohol; it is very cheap in Mexico and easy to find (liquor stores, hardware shops and pharmacies). One shot for the stove and another for the cook.

WARNING: Alcohol sold in plastic bottles in supermarkets and drugstores is not for human consumption. When in doubt, ask "*¿Se puede tomar este alcohol?*" (Can one drink this alcohol?) If the answer isn't a clear "*¡Si!*," don't drink it! Adulterated alcohol and industrial alcohol are very dangerous and many careless drinkers are poisoned.

I also carry a tube of priming jelly or pellets for a reserve, sold in camping supply stores in the U.S. When nothing else is available, just build a tiny twig fire around the stove's burner. When backpacking I use local moonshine; most is high enough 'octane' to do the job quite well.

Backpacking stoves need clean fuel for reliable operation, so carry a good filter, such as chamois skin, and use it religiously. I failed to do this on a long hike and spent two weeks carrying a hopelessly clogged stove. Spare parts are also important: O rings, cleaning tools and delicate fuel metering jets are not available in Mexico. Carry enough for the entire trip and a few more for good measure.

A high quality fuel bottle is very important. I once bought three, one-liter aluminum bottles that were inexpensive copies of the well known Sigg bottle. All three of these bottles failed on one trip. The tops stripped out and leaked and the sides dented as easily as aluminum beer cans. One developed a leak while my pack was inside the cargo compartment of a bus, seeping a full liter of kerosene into my pack and surrounding suitcases. I barely avoided being sued for damages. 'Fortunately' the driver's helper had spilled half a quart of motor oil on my pack and he got the blame for the entire disaster.

Never carry fuel in plastic containers. You won't believe how hot and swollen they'll be after a few hours under a broiling sun or stashed deep inside a second class bus.

A small funnel makes filling and filtering much easier. *Embudos* are sold in hardware and grocery stores and in hardware stalls in the market place.

If possible carry your stove (and lantern) in a sturdy box. My backpacker's stove fits inside a large cookie tin and the accessories go into a small plastic box with a tightly sealing lid. When camping from a vehicle we store our stove in an old plastic ice chest or metal ammo box. The box protects other gear from grease and stove dirt and protects the stove from denting and accidental damage.

WARNING: We have observed and participated in a number of camping disasters caused by careless use and handling of stoves and lanterns. They make slightly amusing stories but are no fun to deal with in reality. Be careful, all the time. Store your fuel away from heat and flame (including well away from heaters and engine compartments). Never light a stove or lantern that smells of leaking fuel. Never light up, in fact, without giving it a very close sniff. Lorena put a match to our two-burner Coleman one night — and torched off a blaze that took a fire extinguisher to cool down. Gas had leaked into the bottom of the stove after the flame had died out (the stove had been set to simmer beans).

Here's one that's hard to believe but true: After two weeks on the road, a group of campers finally reached the beach. They were busily setting up for the night in a *palapa* when their gasoline lantern went out, plunging them into darkness. One fellow lit a match, while his friend opened the tank on the lantern, assuming that it had run out of fuel. But the lantern was actually clogged up. As he removed the tank cap, pressurized gasoline sprayed out, hit the helpful match and exploded in a huge fireball. The guy holding the match ran for the ocean, shirt ablaze. The fellow holding the lantern laughed until he realized he too was on fire. Then he dropped the lantern and took off after his friend. A woman in the group laughed so hard she sat on the ground — right on a large scorpion that had been flushed out of the thatched roof by the flames. She also ran screaming into the night, leaving the rest of the group to fight the fire inside the *palapa*. Total injuries were amazingly mild: two hairless men, one very sore woman and a scorched hut.

Campers, including backpackers, should consider an electric light. A simple 110 volt light cord with a bulb socket and switch weighs only a few ounces and makes a very handy light for dark nights in trailer parks and cheap hotels. Use a soft glow bulb for reading and lounging and a brighter bulb for cooking and camp chores.

Small, coil-type water heaters used for making instant coffee and tea are very handy, but many people who have used them while travelling in Mexico complain that voltage fluctuations burn out the coil very quickly.

Stuff Sacks

In order to reduce confusion while

Pelicans   *Pelicanos*

packing our van or backpacks, we carry a confusing assortment of stuff sacks, in a confusing variety of colors.

"Where's the film?" Lorena asks impatiently. It's taken her a week to finally line up a shot of pelicans crossing the sunset.

"Right here." I toss her a small blue bag.

"This is your dirty underwear." She flings the bag back with a weary sigh. I rummage through my pack again.

"Here you go." I hand her a medium yellow sack.

"Ahhh!" Her hand withdraws quickly. Before she can turn a shout of pain into a curse, I hastily retrieve the sack and hand her another. No wonder I couldn't find those fishhooks; I'd swear I put them in the green bag.

"Carl," her voice is heavy with patience, a very bad sign, "would you please . . ." She chokes as she hands me back the last bag. I take a quick peek: odds & ends. Wait just a minute! "Hey, guess what?" I say. "You'll never believe what I found in this red bag!"

There's no answer. I look up and see her near the water, sitting in a meditation position. What the hell! At least we'll have garlic in our beans tonight.

The best stuff sacks are of waterproof nylon. This protects the contents from water, grease and dirt.

Stuff sacks hold everything from sleeping bags to cooking gear and small tools. On one hike we used a stuff sack as a bucket: by lashing sticks across the opening of the sack we were able to lower it into a deep well. It wouldn't hold much water but it was far better than nothing and eventually dipped enough to fill our empty canteens.

While kayaking long distances on the ocean we carried large bags of very odorous dried smoked fish and squid lashed to the deck. These stuff sacks endured weeks of rough treatment, including continual soakings in salt water. Our only problem was later convincing customs officials at the U.S. border that the smelly and stained bags were actually bags and not some ghastly form of sealife that we'd caught and dried.

Tents & Tarps

Travellers who have no definite plan or destination will probably find a tent more useful than a tarp. A tent provides a measure of privacy and security for your gear that makes spur of the moment camping much easier. Climb inside, zip up the door and close your ears to the sound of a soccer game ten yards away or the blare of a jukebox in a nearby restaurant. I've seen well-prepared campers erect tents outside of train and bus depots when faced with a long wait. It creates a momentary stir of interest but inside the tent, privacy is almost complete.

Quick protection from the elements, including insects, is the tent's main advantage over a tarp. A good, fast-erecting tent can turn the evening 'bug bite' into a pleasant period of relaxation and meditation on the day's events, rather than a minor ordeal of irritating repellents and heavy clothing.

Some fantastic campsites are also fantastic breeding grounds for mosquitoes: tropical lagoons are a classic example. As you sit on the bank, dangling your feet into the warm soothing water, admiring the flights of waterfowl that glide lazily through the palms at sunset, you hear the distant hummmm of . . . *ohmygod where's the bug dope?* Most insects relent their attacks as the evening cools: if you can tough it out inside a tent you'll find many more places to camp — and your privacy will be guarded by those clouds of bugs.

Tents give some security against over-curious children, dogs and chickens. Don't underestimate the damage a flock of chickens can do to your gear. Their uncontrolled bowel movements are trouble enough, but sharp beaks can make short work of stuff sacks, plastic jugs and other tasty bits of camping equipment.

In spite of how interested *campesinos* will be in your minor daily routine: eating, reading, brushing your teeth or polishing rusty fishing lures, they will respect your 'house', i.e. tent. Open and honest curiosity often upsets campers who aren't used to the Mexican communal style of living. By keeping loose gear out of sight, you'll greatly reduce your curiosity value for the local people. *Gringas* will especially appreciate the privacy of a tent, since they invariably attract attention.

A tent with a floor protects gear from dirtying and reduces nighttime fantasies of roving scorpions, snakes and other crawling mysteries.

Good ventilation is essential in a tent that will be used in a warm climate. If your tent doesn't have enough well-screened window and door areas, consider having it altered. A tent that feels cool and airy in the northern U.S. might become a stifling oven in coastal Michoacán. If it's not comfortable to live and sleep in, you'll regret carrying it.

Perhaps the best backpacking tent we've seen for Mexico is a dome style with large panels of no-see'um-proof netting. These panels do not open but provide sufficient window space to give an expansive view and lots of ventilation. With the addition of a rain fly or tarp overhead, this tent is perfect for summer and winter camping in warm countries.

Car campers should consider large and relatively inexpensive mosquito-proof tents with walls of netting and a simple flat roof. Most are large enough to stand up in and can shelter several people at bug-time. With the addition of a tarp wall or two, privacy can be provided when needed.

The size of a tent is very important, especially on a long trip. Your tent becomes a mini-home; the more you depend on it for shelter and comfort, the more you'll want it to be a pleasant space in which to live. This means that size and shape become very important, often more important, in fact, than the time and trouble it takes to erect the tent, or the weight and bulk. Campers who must slide into a tent with a shoehorn will do it reluctantly on the 30th night or the 100th afternoon siesta. Err on the side of more space; you'll rarely regret having extra elbow room. At the very least, your tent should be large enough to accommodate both you and your gear. Protection from the elements and casual thieves more than justifies paying extra for a tent that holds your pack, too.

Although some manufacturers make tents in eye-pleasing colors, the majority offer garish materials that belong on a carnival lot, not in the wilderness. There's nothing quite like the salmon-rose tones of a sunset reflected off a day-glo green tent to give a camper double vision. Garish tents and tarps have another disadvantage, one that is especially irritating in foreign countries: their shocking colors cry out "Hey! Look at us! Here we are, over here!" In a land where people build their houses of trees, fronds, grass, native stone and earth, the sight of a synthetic space-age tent is just too unusual to ignore.

If you'll be camping where it's definitely bright and hot — the desert or beaches — blue tents and tarps are the most pleasing to be in or under. They look and even feel cooler than hot reds, oranges or yellows.

A cheap plastic tube tent, or instant tent, is not very useful on a long trip. They are fragile, not very comfortable and ugly. One tube tent we tried, made of an 'improved' material, produced a deafening crackle and popping sound at the touch of a breeze. Another tube tent we used was so slick that our sleeping bags — with us inside them — slid out the lower end. We donated this tent to a rather puzzled Indian, who immediately solved the problem by cutting a hole in the center and wearing the tent as a poncho.

Because new lightweight tents are so expensive, you may want to save money by making your own. A friend went one step beyond this: she bought do-it-yourself plans and tent materials, took everything to Mexico and had the tent sewn by a professional seamstress. Another friend had a simple tent made in Mexico of flour sacks and mosquito netting: cheap, fairly lightweight, picturesque and totally useless in the rain, though a rainfly of plastic would be inexpensive and simple to rig.

Tarps: In spite of the many useful features of a tent, we prefer to use tarps whenever privacy and bug attacks are not major problems. This is mainly while boating or backpacking in remote areas. A few yards of *mosquitero* (mosquito netting) suspended beneath a tarp makes a great sleeping place. (See Chapter 5 for rigging *Tarps* and *Mosquiteros*.)

Tarps give good protection from the rain and wind, at least when properly rigged. I once adjusted a tarp line during a rainstorm and got ten unwelcome gallons of cold water down my neck.

We carry two tarps: a 9' x 12' and an 11' by 14'. Both are of lightweight tent-type material, with sturdy grommets along all sides. We've used them for years under a variety of conditions; other than a few holes and tears and a severe fading of the blue color, they're as good as new. Their combined weight and cost probably equal that of a three-person tent (a cheap one), but the shade area of these two tarps is unequaled by any camping tent. Depending upon the terrain and camping conditions (bugs, dogs and other people) we use the big tarp for shelter and the smaller for a ground cover or privacy wall. While camped in Baja during a hot spell, we rigged both tarps to provide shade and were able to survive the sizzling heat of the afternoon sun.

Spider monkey   *Mono de araña*

Tarps are much more versatile than tents, an important consideration for boaters and also for backpackers. We've used ours for sails, rain catchers for drinking water, as emergency blankets in cold snaps, for tablecloths, communal rain protection on the trail and so on. A tarp is ideal when rigged to the side of a vehicle for sunshade.

On many of our mountain backpacking trips in Mexico and Guatemala, we've found it difficult to locate enough level ground to pitch one or more tents on. Tarps can be rigged in countless ways to provide shelter; at the very least you can lie on one half and pull the other half over you.

While camped on a remote beach our tarp provided us with an unusual shelter. When I complained to a fisherman that marauding dogs were stealing our food and pissing on our bed, he suggested that we move into a large dugout that lay on the beach nearby. I rigged the tarp in an A-frame fashion over the canoe. We set up our kitchen in one end of the canoe (it was about 16 feet long and very wide) and our bedroom-living room in the other end. At night the dogs milled around, peeing in frustration on the canoe's high wooden sides.

Carry a good assortment of pegs, grommetless ties and various lengths of cord for rigging your tarp. One or more telescoping or folding poles are very handy, if space and weight allow them. While kayaking, for example, we found it difficult at times to rely on luck and beachcombing for suitable tarp poles. The two long aluminum poles we used more than made up for their weight; later they were very useful when rigging the tarp as an awning from the side of the van.

Lonas (tarps) are available in Mexico at reasonable prices but the materials used tend to be heavy for backpacking.

Tools

Axe	Hatchet	Scissors
Chisel	Iron Rods	Sharpening Stone
Crowbar	Machete	Shovel
File	Pliers	Wrenches
Hammer & Nails	Propane Torch	Vice Grips
Hand Drill & Bits	Saws	

Axe: A small hand axe or heavy hatchet is useful for splitting Mexican hardwoods, pounding tent stakes and flaying giant snappers for barbecuing. As with any hand tool, an axe is a fine gift to offer a *campesino*.

Hammer, Saws, Folding Shovel, Machete, etc.: These tools will not only be invaluable for camp construction projects but useful as well for repairing your car, digging it out of sand and mires, setting up a tent, hanging hammocks, cutting firewood and making adobe.

Regular handsaws are best for building things but a folding woodcutting saw (Swede saw) is handy for firewood. Hacksaws are indispensible for jury-rigged repairs on cars, spearguns and metal smoking pipes.

A sharp, three-sided file is another valuable tool for repairs and for sharpening spearheads, knives and machetes.

Iron Rods: Two pieces of iron rod about three feet long are very useful if you're building an oven with a five gallon can. (See Chapter 5.)

Electrical Wire, Solder, Propane Torch, Tape, Glue, etc.: With these miscellaneous items you can, and will very likely have to perform miracles of improvisation and repair. They will be invaluable for lashing your car back together if it tends to loosen up on poor roads.

A propane torch (non-refillable cylinder type) will last a long time if used sparingly.

10. Travelling South

". . . Natural pools of crystal-clear hot water surrounded by handmade walls of native stone, shaded by ancient mesquite trees, not to mention . . ."

"So don't mention it, okay?" I snapped, shifting down to first gear and grabbing the steering wheel with both hands as the van caromed from one dust-filled chuckhole to another. I heard the satisfying *thunk!* of Lorena's head against the doorframe. That would teach her to watch the road instead of tormenting me with guidebook visions of a desert oasis. Our never-ending quest for the Mythical Campsite had led us into this never-ending desert canyon, pounding over a sun-baked track of rock and choking dust.

"Just follow the road until it ends," a helpful *gringo* camper had casually advised, neglecting to mention just *where* the end was. My legs trembled with exhaustion from frantic pumping at the clutch and brake pedals; my shoulders were stiff and aching. The gas gauge had dropped ominously below half, plunging as quickly as the sun toward the edge of the mountains ahead.

"There's a dust devil," Lorena said, rubbing her head gingerly. A thick column of dust swirled high into the air. It appeared to be coming directly toward us.

"On second thought," she stared intently through the dirt-caked windshield, "I think it might be another car." I dropped our speed to a crawl, watching for a wide spot. I ran my tongue over dry cracked lips. My thirst was overpowering; while the car passed us I'd enjoy a stretch and a much needed drink of water.

The road turned slightly, disappearing between sheer walls of stone.

"LOOK OUT!" Lorena screamed, throwing her arms over her face. I swerved instinctively, running the van off the road and into the thorn bushes. A dusty blue pickup truck barrelled hell-for-leather toward us, all but scraping off our mirror as it charged past with a deafening, unmuffled roar. Voices screamed incoherently in Spanish, an arm waved in the air and a beer bottle exploded against a rock behind us. I watched in the rear-view mirror as the old truck lurched crazily from side to side. One dirt-caked brake light suddenly glowed.

"Oh hell! Looks like they're stopping!" I quickly let out the clutch and steered the van back onto the road, keeping an eye on the mirror. The doors of the truck sprang open. Two men leaped out. I stepped down hard on the gas pedal. The last thing I wanted was a confrontation with a couple of drunks. Their hoarse yells were audible over the loud growl of our engine.

"Don't look back!" I said. "Just help me watch for potholes and think about those natural pools of crystal-clear hot water we'll soon . . ." I reached up to adjust the rear-view mirror. "Oh, no, I don't like the looks of *this*!" The pickup truck had turned and was now pursuing us, headlights flashing in an unmistakable signal to stop. Arms waved from the windows, one of them clutching a foaming beer bottle. The gestures were insistent and considering the situation, menacing.

"Hang on!" I said, deciding to outrun them. Whatever they wanted from us, whether it was just a roadside party or the loan of a pair of pliers, I was definitely not in the mood.

"You watch the truck," I said, "and let me know if they try anything weird." I didn't let myself dwell on what 'weird' might include, but I had an awful feeling that this chase was somehow more than a drunken lark.

"Carl, they're right on our tail!"

The van was taking a terrific pounding; from the rear I heard the crash of pottery and the rattle of loose bottles. A thick, choking dust filled the air, coating my sunglasses, tongue and beard.

"The dust is so thick I don't see how they can even breathe," Lorena commented.

The walls of the canyon now began to spread apart. Small trees appeared alongside us. The road was very loose and sandy. I held the gas pedal to the floor and shifted into third gear. The van porpoised high into the air; the mess in back was now complete. I smelled smashed bananas, cooking oil and tequila, violently stirred together with books, bedding and rattling kitchen gear. Over the roar of the strained engine came an insistent honking from our pursuers. How they'd survived the last few miles I had no idea, but one thing was quite clear: the longer they chased us, the madder they'd be.

"LOOK!" Lorena yelled, pointing to our left, her eyes wide.

It was hard to believe, but the overaged pickup was now alongside, taking advantage of the sandy canyon floor to run off the road and cut us off. I pressed my foot down harder. A swarthy brown face emerged from the truck's passenger window. "*¡Parense!*" (Stop!) he shouted, a fist waving in the air.

My scalp tingled. There was grim determination on the driver's face, his thick black moustache was drawn in a hard line over tight uncompromising lips. His passenger was even more disturbing: the blinding dust couldn't hide the crazy glint in his red-rimmed eyes. His shouts were raw and violent, the words lost over the howls of the competing engines. He beat the door with his fist and pushed his hand upward with an open palm, the classic Mexican "*What gives?*" signal.

We barrelled through a thick stand of trees. Suddenly the pickup was gone.

"Can you see anything?" I asked, looking frantically in the rear-view mirror as I pushed the van to maximum speed.

"No sign of them. I think they gave up." We gave simultaneous sighs of relief. I eased my foot off the accelerator. The van slowed to a bone-crunching pace. There was a flicker of movement to our left, a flash of blue, a rising plume of dust . . .

"They took a short cut!" I tromped down on the gas pedal. "It must have branched back there in the trees." Seconds later the pickup burst out of the bushes ahead of us. I slammed on the brakes, blinded by an opaque wall of choking dust.

"Go left!" Lorena cried, pointing to a fork in the sandy track. I swerved, missing the truck's rear bumper by inches. The driver shouted, his tires spinning in the loose sand as they slewed after us.

Up ahead the canyon walls squeezed closer together. We had to beat them to this obvious ambush point. Once they were ahead of us we'd never have time to turn around, even if we lucked upon a spot wide and firm enough for the maneuver.

The smell of leaking tequila gave me an idea. "Lorena," I said, "reach that bottle of booze for me, would you? Just lay it there on the seat next to me." My plan was simple but chilling: if we were trapped I would grab the heavy bottle and run to the pickup before they could get out. The driver's window was sure to be open; I'd brain him with the bottle, grab the ignition key and run like hell. What happened then was anybody's guess, but at least the odds would be more favorable.

"Carl!" Lorena yelled, bracing against the dashboard. We skidded to within inches of a formidable barrier of weathered concrete and rusty steel pipes. A huge brass padlock secured the ends of a thick chain. The blue pickup shuddered to a stop behind the van. We were trapped.

"Wait here until I yell 'run'!" I said, grabbing the tequila and leaping from the van. My heart jackhammered in my throat as I dashed back to the truck, clutching the bottle by the neck.

The driver sat motionless, both hands gripping the steering wheel, a stunned look on his face. He eyes turned, widening as he saw me running toward him . . . lifting the bottle . . .

I raised it over my head. "¡No, gracias!" he shouted, slumping back in exhaustion. "I don't drink." His passenger sagged against the door, eyes closed. I hesitated.

"¡Híjole, amigo!" the driver blurted, shaking his head from side to side with a dazed grin. "You gringos drive like . . . like . . . locos!" He smiled apologetically, as though worried I might take offense.

"You have come to bathe?" he added, waving toward the gate. For the first time I saw the crude hand-lettered sign: "Eye of Water."

"Er, yes." I answered, lowering the bottle to my side. "We are looking for the hot springs."

"Well, then," the driver said, "you've found it. I am the owner. I thought you would want the keys to get in. That is why we followed you." He rolled his eyes heavenward. The mere mention of following us was obviously more than his nerves could stand.

"I have had no visitors here during the week, no clientes, so my helper and I were going to town to visit our families."

"Why are you in such a hurry?" his passenger now asked, leaning toward me with an intent and openly curious look.

"Well . . ." I stammered. "I thought . . . well . . . I thought that . . ." my voice trailed off.

The driver ran a wrinkled hand over his face. "I wanted to ask a favor of you. Would you watch the place while we are gone? Will you be here for a day or two? Is this too much trouble for you?"

"You mean," I croaked, "take care of the hot springs?"

"No, no!" he said. "It is only water after all." He gave a dry laugh. "What I mean is, would you keep the keys to the gate? And to the little *tienda* we have here. If someone comes, you can let them in. That is all. And sell them whatever they want. The prices are clearly marked." He must have misread the look of astonishment on my face. "Of course," he added quickly, "you can drink some beer *gratis* and use the springs. I'll be back in a few days. It is quite simple." He dangled a large ring of keys in the air. "*¿Por favor?*"

I stretched out in the bubbling pool, letting the scalding cascade from the rough-hewn stone spout fall directly onto the knotted muscles in my upper back. The last rosy tinges faded from the clouds as whippoorwills welcomed the cool of the night. A flicker of candlelight approached through the trees. I groaned luxuriously as Lorena appeared with another cold beer. Our campfire glowed nearby, outlining the van against a jade green backdrop of nightblooming jasmine.

"What was that you said?" Lorena asked, sliding into the water beside me with a sigh of pleasure.

". . . pools of crystal-clear water . . ." I said, ". . . surrounded by handmade walls of native stone, not to mention . . ."

Far in the distance, I thought I heard the low growl of an overworked pickup truck wending its way slowly and painfully to town.

Getting to Mexico: Car, Bus, Plane or . . .?

Your mode of travel often has a strong influence on where you'll camp in Mexico and what you'll do after you get there. We once made firm plans to go backpacking in Oaxaca. We would fly directly to Mexico City from Seattle, take the overnight train to Oaxaca City and then a second class bus into the mountains. At the last minute we decided to drive our van instead. The van would make camping more convenient, we figured, and would allow us to make several 'quick' side trips on the way to Mexico. Once we got to Oaxaca we could leave the van in a trailer park or parking lot and do our long-awaited hike. A few days before we left I impulsively loaded my small sailboat on top of the van. Why not? Maybe I'd do a little fishing . . .

Well, we never did get to Oaxaca and our backpacking was limited to a few overnight hikes. The problem was the sailboat: I just couldn't pass up a lake, river, creek, pond or salt water lagoon without pulling off the road and making a fast exploration. One thing led to another and before we knew it, the trip had turned into a camping/boating expedition.

Although your equipment shouldn't be allowed to plan your trip for you, in reality it often does. If you've got a nice van, equipped for camping and with four new tires, how can you leave it at home and hop on a Greyhound? This is a tough decision, especially for people who have always enjoyed the luxury and independence of driving their own vehicle.

Driving South: Pros & Cons

Whenever we begin to plan a camping trip to Mexico we carefully weigh three important factors: the purpose or goal of the trip, the cost of driving and the time involved. Any one of these can tip the balance between driving or going by public transportation. A firm desire to go backpacking on a tight budget, for example, almost automatically rules out taking our van. If our time is limited to less than a month, the thought of driving gives me an instant backache. We rarely make more than 500 miles a day, even when in a hurry, and prefer to do about 300. It takes only a few minutes with a map to calculate how many days of our camping trip will be spent barrelling down the highway. If you live closer to the border or have a large family, time and driving expense have to be weighed against the cost of public transportation, food and some lodging. It can get quite complicated but an hour with a pocket calculator will usually tell the tale.

Although gasoline prices have skyrocketed elsewhere, they are still a bargain in Mexico: about $.45 a gallon for *Nova* (regular) and $.65 a gallon for *Extra* (unleaded). Diesel is an astounding $.17 a gallon. These prices may go up in the near future, but it's unlikely that the increase will be too stiff. If you drive conservatively and camp out, cook your own meals and go easy on souvenirs, a long trip to Mexico can be very inexpensive.

Public Transportation in Mexico

Mexico's public transportation system astounds many foreign visitors, especially those from the U.S. and Canada, where buses and trains are usually considered a last resort rather than public conveniences. Mexico's train system may be old and a little shaky at times, but you certainly can't beat the price (less than two cents per mile!). Buses cost just slightly more and literally go almost wherever there's a road, no matter how rough it may be. In addition, there is excellent air service between larger Mexican cities and popular tourist towns, not to mention small aircraft, cabs, boats and *bestias* (burros, mules and horses). Once you've learned how to travel by public transportation and to minimize the expenses of food and lodging, being footloose and car-free can be a real pleasure.

Many examples of camping by public transportation can be found in the first chapters of this book. Hitching is easy, too, if you're travelling on a shoestring. (See *The People's Guide to Mexico: Public Transportation* and *Hitching*.)

Many people who travel by public transportation in Mexico fall into a habit of travelling too fast and going too far. Hundreds of interesting places flash by the windows of your bus, places that offer just as much as wherever you're headed. Learn to slow down and don't hesitate to get off when you spot a possible camping area or interesting side road. Check your road map before you buy your ticket. Do you really want to go all the way to Chiapas in one sitting? Consider going only until nightfall and taking a room in a small town. You'll probably be in a relatively unvisited place rather than stuck on the Tourist Circuit. Look around, check out the local countryside on foot and then decide whether or not you want to board another bus. These don't have to be long detours; just give yourself the chance to stop on a whim rather than holding to a rigid itinerary.

One of the greatest advantages of travelling by public transportation in Mexico is the people you'll meet along the way. If you're at all interested in speaking Spanish and getting to know people other than by chance encounters in gas stations and campgrounds, travel by bus and train can't be beat. It is definitely total immersion; let yourself relax and you'll have an unforgettable trip.

Bicycle Camping

We've met quite a number of bicycle campers in Mexico, all of whom seemed to be having a very good time. The following suggestions are based on their experiences.

Mexico is a large country and even the most dedicated cyclists can be discouraged by seemingly endless deserts and mountain ranges that never stop going upward. Rather than toughing it out to the last mile, put out your thumb and hitch a ride across the rougher stretches. Truck drivers are very helpful and will pick you up, bicycle and all. Second class buses can also be used (first class bus drivers aren't likely to allow a bicycle aboard), though you may have to pay extra for the bicycle. Load the bicycle yourself to avoid rough handling and if possible, padlock it to the bus's roof rack.

Carry your camping gear in tough, watertight bags or containers that can be easily removed from the bicycle. Theft isn't a great problem in the countryside, but in town you're better off taking precautions. Chain and lock the bike whenever you are separated from it. Don't hesitate to take it with you inside a hotel or restaurant, especially if your gear is attached.

Because most Mexicans (especially *campesinos* and the average working person) can't afford a car, bicycles are very common. Yours will attract attention and be an excellent way to break the ice when meeting people. Whenever you need repairs, just find someone else riding a bike and ask them for help. Bicycle repair shops are found in most small towns but if your bike is an unusual make or model, parts will probably be scarce. Carry a basic set of spare parts, plus a good tire pump and a patch kit.

One of the greatest advantages of bicycle camping is that you can easily explore the countryside and commute from a campsite to nearby towns for supplies and sightseeing. Cyclers stress, however, that riding in town takes extra care. Drive very defensively. Never let your guard down and never assume that other drivers are watching out for you. Even if they see you clearly, they'll often take advantage of their size and weight to force you into yielding the right-of-way.

If you tire of bicycling or don't wan't to bother shipping your bike home at the end of the trip, it should be quite easy to sell. Draw a large dollar sign — $ — on a piece of paper and tape it to the bike. Unless it's hopelessly wrecked or an odd model, you should be able to sell it quickly. In general, bicycles cost more in Mexico than in the U.S., so price a few before you strike a bargain. (If your bike is noted on your tourist card, you must take it with you when you leave Mexico or face paying a stiff duty.) The buyer will probably ask for a bill of sale, since Mexican bicycles are licensed almost as carefully as cars.

Private Airplanes

Many people fly to Mexico in their own planes and camp out, usually at remote airstrips that have few, if any, facilities. Fliers we've talked with strongly recommend that you do not leave your plane unguarded for very long or you may find yourself walking. There have been a number of cases where small planes were stolen by crafty smugglers.

We were once visited by a fellow who flew his plane to Baja from Los Angeles, arriving at the beach without any camping gear at all. He quickly set up an ingenious bartering system: plane rides in exchange for food and lodging. I'll never forget the look of utter amazement on a neighboring camper's face when we returned from a 200-mile round-trip flight for a cold six-pack.

For details of flying to Mexico, including red tape, check recent issues of popular magazines on private aircraft; the rules and regulations change as often as the wind.

Driving South

Mexico has an estimated 100,000 miles of dirt roads and unimproved side roads. If you're like us, you won't be able to resist getting off the main routes. All it takes is a vague hint of an untouched beach, a special hot springs or another waterfall to send us bouncing and crashing into the boondocks. The road may lead to nothing more romantic than a high mountain sawmill or a funky beachside restaurant, but who cares? There's always another road to explore and the next one will probably be *it*.

Backroads

Some dirt roads are shown on maps, but the majority lead into large, tempting, blank spaces and are known only by local drivers. Asking for directions can be very frustrating; even if you are given the name of the place or village where the road leads, chances are it won't be on your map either. We prefer to rely on a vague sense of direction and no firm plans to get anywhere specific. The inevitable unmarked crossroads is less of a problem if you just take the most tempting branch.

Important Note: Because of limited space, the discussion of driving in Mexico is confined to conditions away from the main highways. For a much more complete description of driving in Mexico read *The People's Guide to Mexico*. It you're driving I strongly suggest that you carry a copy. In particular see *Driving Hazards, Road Conditions, City Driving, At Night, Traffic Signs, Toll Roads, Cops, Parking, Asking Directions, Green Angels* (tourist assistance on the highway), *Breakdowns, Gas Stations, Garages, Mechanics, Body Work, Especially for VW's, Parts and Servicing,* and *Vocabulary*.

There are four types of back roads in Mexico: of these *la carretera*, the highway, is the best. By highway, however, I don't mean a paved highway with a neat white line down the middle. In the back country a *carretera* is the best of the bad roads, capable of rattling the loose fillings out of your teeth.

Next comes *terracería*, the typical dirt road, sporadically maintained. This road presents a challenge to the driver, but unless it heads straight up a mountainside, you can probably negotiate it (carefully!). When in doubt, wait for a Mexican taxi to come banging along, loaded to the gills with people out for a picnic or returning from market day. If they can do it, so can you.

Camino de mano de obra is a long name for hand built roads. A village or area that would like to connect itself to the outside world with more than a foot trail will mount a cooperative effort to construct a road, sometimes with government aid. Some *mano de obras* are better than the nearest *carretera* and some are a lot worse; it all depends on the terrain and the enthusiasm of whoever built it. Maintenance usually occurs only when the road deteriorates and is once again impassable.

Brecha (literally a breakthrough or opening) is the bottom of the line, the type of road that makes jeep drivers grin. A *brecha* follows the line of least resistance: down arroyos, through streams, up the sides of crumbling mountains. Many *brechas* are passable only a few months of the year, usually at the end of the dry season. When the men of the area aren't busy with crops and have extra time, they'll do a little rock clearing and hole filling.

One *brecha* we conquered was the bed of a small stream, littered with boulders and still trickling from the past rainy season. We humped over rocks and crawled through deep holes at an average of two miles per hour, but we made it.

Driving a *brecha* is almost always beyond the capability of a standard car or American van. A VW van is good, especially with oversized tires on the rear for higher clearance, but a truck or four-wheel-drive vehicle with a very low first gear and high ground clearance is best. Mexican-made Dodge pickups are a common sight on *brechas*, crawling along in 'granny-low', overloaded with *campesinos*, livestock and barrels of gas.

When in doubt about what lies ahead, check the road out on foot before committing yourself to what may be a very tight situation. Mexican back roads are often full of little surprises: unbridged streams and rivers, amazingly steep grades, switchbacks so tight they take two tries to get around, sand traps and even dunes, cactus spines and so on. All of the things that add up to Adventure rather than Sunday driving.

Anyone who drives back roads will be asked by *campesinos* for a lift. In areas where bus service is erratic or nonexistent, few vehicles travel empty. Giving a ride is both a Good Deed and an easy way to meet people. *"¿A dónde va?"* (Where are you going?), followed by a friendly *"¡Vamonos pues!"* (Let's go, then!) can, and usually does, lead to something interesting. (Also *"Sube."* Get in.) If you're open to sudden changes in plans and spontaneous side trips, your new passengers will almost certainly oblige you.

Passengers often expect to pay for their ride, especially if there's no bus service. If they insist on paying, I ask for a very small sum, one or two pesos, or a token amount of goods. Being repaid with a few sticks of firewood or a cabbage isn't unusual. (For more on back road hitching see Chapter 3.)

What To Drive

When the "take it or leave it?" question has been answered in favor of driving south, several more questions may arise. Risk this wheezing old VW bug or trade it in on a new Rabbit? Motorcycle or motorhome? Or how about a van? Or why not a schoolbus? Or tow a small trailer? Before you head for the nearest used car lot or reach for the classifieds, consider the following.

On my first trip to Mexico four of us crowded into a brand new Volvo sedan. Volvo prides itself on building a tough car but overloading and high speed driving on poor roads soon took care of the suspension and exhaust system, not to mention alignment, tires, motor mounts and miscellaneous parts torn or rattled away. Erratic maintenance and dirty gas kept the car permanently out-of-tune, reducing gas mileage to a bad joke. Instead of a car we needed a Sherman tank.

Whatever you drive to Mexico, try to strike a reasonable balance between convenience, economy, comfort and practicality. Careful planning, however, should not be allowed to mushroom into needless and expensive over-preparation. Remember: money equals time and new experiences. The price of a fancy chrome trailer hitch will hire a boat in Mexico for a long jungle river cruise you'll never forget. A one-week trip with lavish gear costs more than a month of camping with improvised equipment. Use self control; hide your trip money until you're on the road.

Small Cars

The temptation to trade in your faithful VW Bug on a mind-boggling Highway Yacht can be irresistible, especially for vehicle-crazy Americans. Unless you're related to an OPEC oil minister or don't fear the finance company, resist the impulse. A small car may not be perfect for camping but with patience, planning and a careful eye on the car's suspension system, you'll get along quite well.

The storage space available in a small car is far greater than even the most cavernous backpack — yet backpackers get along without such luxuries as folding chairs and ice chests. Follow their example. In fact, if you are a backpacker

Butterflyfish   *Baboso*

already, just stuff your gear into the trunk and leave. Whatever extra goodies you want later can probably be found in Mexico or improvised.

Consider the back seat: do you really need it? Pull it out and let hitchhikers squeeze in between the inflatable boat and the dog. Store your gear in cardboard boxes and when they fall to pieces, replace them in Mexico with inexpensive but attractive baskets and woven bags.

Friends resolved the dilemma of car vs. van or motorhome by converting their aging Ford sedan into a 'West Texas Winnebago'. They removed the rear seat and trunk partition, then installed a horizontal piece of plywood that extended through the trunk area. On top of this 'floor' they put a foam rubber mattress. Basic camping gear was arranged in wooden and cardboard boxes. (The spare tire was under the plywood.) Curtains were rigged behind the front seat and over the rear windows. They found this 'RV' more than adequate for an extended camping trip in Mexico and Central America.

A small roof rack will reduce clutter and crowding inside the car, but it will also reduce gas mileage and adversely affect the handling in strong winds. Streamlined fiberglas storage boxes are best; they also offer protection from the sun, rain and sticky fingers. Pack heavier items inside the car and lighter stuff on top. This lowers the center of gravity and improves stability.

European van and car campers often sleep *on top* of their vehicles. Small platforms and roof racks are ideally suited for getting off the ground. It saves space and keeps dogs from squirting your territory. Backpacking tents or tarps can be erected, though it's best to take extra precautions against strong winds.

The most ingenious type of sleeping arrangement we've seen was rigged by a fellow who slept on top of his VW Bug, in a canoe. When the weather looked bad, he rigged a canvas cover over the canoe. The looks on the faces of passing *campesinos* as he crawled out of bed in the morning absolutely made my day.

Station Wagons

We found camping out of our station wagon to be almost as convenient as a small van, undoubtedly because we lived outside and around the car, rather than in it. All of our gear was kept in boxes of an easily manageable size and weight. Loading and unloading took no more than fifteen minutes.

We quickly established a camping routine that went like this: once the daily argument about where and when to stop was settled, we'd briskly move everything from the rear of the station wagon to the front seat. Boxes were neatly stacked from the floorboards to the ceiling. According to how diligently we arranged any leftover odds and ends, our sleeping space varied from eighteen inches wide to more than three feet.

In the mild confusion of moving things around, we cleverly remembered to set aside the Suitcase Kitchen (see Chapter 7) and at least some of the food. All this went onto the lowered tailgate, which now served as a kitchen counter. We'd unfold our aluminum lawn chairs and sit around the stove, feeling very domestic and organized. Then, after eating and arguing about who had to wash the dishes (and putting it off until morning), we'd draw the curtains and crawl into bed. Once we'd settled down, the mouse we'd picked up somewhere in Oregon would begin to diligently fill our shoes with filberts and other goodies stolen from the food boxes.

Sometimes, as in any tightly run little ship, there'd be unexpected complications. The hassles usually came at night.

"Hey, Lorena, let's roll over."

"Mrrrr?"

"Roll over, would 'ya? My arm's asleep."

"Rnnnn?"

"Not that way! The other side. It's my *arm*."

"Ehh?"

"YOU'RE BREAKING MY WRIST!"

"Wha . . .? Huh? Whazzamatter?"

"My *wrist!* Wow, you almost broke it! Just go back to sleep, o.k.?"

Something wet presses against the back of my neck. Oh no! I've gone and made her cry by yelling.

"Hey, Lorena?"

"Mrrrr?"

"I'm sorry."

"Rnnnn?"

"Are you crying?"

"Whazzamatter? Crying? Who? *Me?*"

I grope around in the darkness. The wetness on my neck is now oozing down my back and shoulder blade.

"Hey, Lorena, remember your lost papaya?"

Pickup Trucks

Camping out of an open pickup truck is possible (Mexicans often do), but on a long trip it's complicated by the problem of carrying your gear exposed to the elements and potential thieves. Simple arrangements of poles and tarps provide protection from the elements and some privacy and security. Slatted wooden sideboards are even better, especially if they extend around the back and can be locked. It is well worth it to buy a large storage box (or build one of plywood) with a hefty lock.

When camping from a pickup we carried our things under a waterproof tarp. When parked in a city we took turns guarding the truck. In the country, however, we just tried our best not to worry about losing anything (and never did). Our real valuables, however, including the camera and diving gear, were always locked in the cab of the truck at rest stops and at night. For additional security we sometimes slept in the back. This is one case where a dog would earn its keep.

Motorhomes, Buses, Large Trucks

I am constantly amazed both by the numbers of tourists driving motorhomes in Mexico and the depth to which they penetrate into the boondocks. Although many prefer to travel in well-organized caravans, others strike off into the Unknown, braving poor conditions for the rewards of solitude and unscheduled adventures. Motorhomers generally agree that their portable accommodations and the low cost of gasoline in Mexico more than compensate for the hassles of driving a large vehicle.

"It doesn't cost me much more to drive this in Mexico," one tourist said, pointing to his enormous motorhome, "than it does to drive my compact in New York."

Driving conditions in Mexico can make handling large vehicles nerve straining. The shoulders of main highways may be abrupt, if there are any shoulders at all, or marked by rocks and dangerous cement curbing. The owner of a large pickup/ camper complained that he couldn't daydream while driving in Mexico because there was just too much risk of ending up in a ditch. Most people manage quite safely and this is largely a question of staying alert while behind the wheel.

Preparing Your Camper

Factory-equipped campers are basically miniature *gringo* houses, with all the modern conveniences reduced in size and weight. A small sink may *look* nice, but what do you do when it comes time to wash a large frying pan? Dig in the cupboard for a big bucket. When used on rough Mexican back roads, factory-built campers don't always make the grade. Cabinets may literally be stapled together. Soft chipboard is frequently used instead of plywood; it is heavy and doesn't withstand vibration well. Screws pull out, especially in humid, damp climates. Door and cabinet knobs and hinges may fall off after a few weeks of hard bouncing on dirt roads. This type of camper is designed for looks, not actually roughing it. Reinforce weak spots before you leave and carry plenty of screws, fasteners, clamps and strong glue.

A do-it-yourself camper can be more practical, comfortable and efficient, and also substantially cheaper than a factory model. Whether you use your camper for short trips near home or extended journeys, you'll find that simplicity and versatility pay off in more ways than one.

The first and most important design consideration is that experienced travellers live around their vehicle, rather than in it. Who wants to crouch over a hot stove, banging into the ceiling, when there's a cool breeze outside and a magnificent view? Your camper is best used as a storage room and bedroom, with normal daily activities centering around them. We often carry a tent for lounging and sleeping and use the van as a warehouse.

Living around your camper means that removable cupboards, storage containers, ice chests, water jugs and tables are much more practical than permanently built-in ones. You might find a *palapa* (palm thatched house) a welcome change from your camper. With movable furniture and gear, the bare hut can quickly be transformed into a temporary home, much more spacious than your vehicle.

Storage Containers

Building storage cabinets that are both portable and lightweight takes a certain amount of skill, not to mention tools. If you are as short on both as we are, consider alternatives. The best is the wooden fruit crate: very lightweight, surprisingly sturdy and extremely inexpensive, if not free. By adding a few wood screws here and there, lashings of string or twine and the odd nail, a fruit crate will give years of service. A paint job or lining of colored cardboard also improves the appearance if you enjoy interior decorating.

Plastic milk bottle boxes are also very good, though not as easy to find or as inexpensive as fruit crates.

A lightweight lid and seat top can be made for these boxes from a piece of plywood. Just drill a few holes along one edge and wire it loosely to the box.

Our favorite containers are cheap footlockers, made from very strong cardboard with tin corners and a sleazy hasp. They do double duty as benches and tabletops. One holds our kitchen and staple foods, the other is for clothing and odds and ends. It takes about ten seconds to drag them outside the van.

Miscellaneous gear and junk can turn the best organized camper into a nightmare of shifting debris. This is a phenomenon we call The Drift. You can reduce confusion in The Drift (but not eliminate it entirely), with an assortment of small baskets, boxes and drawstring bags. When I stumble on loose oranges, I grab a container and announce, "This is the orange box!" From that moment on we both use it for fruit. Our camera and film are also in a small basket. When the Photo of a Lifetime appears, we don't have to dig for them under the bed.

One of the best systems for storing small odds and ends is to sew pockets onto curtains, towels or rectangles of cloth. I like towels the best, since in an emergency the pockets can be dumped out and the towel used for drying things. A piece of wooden dowel or a coathanger can be hemmed in at the top and the cloth hung as a curtain. The arrangement is completely portable. Better yet, make the hanger removable so the cloth can be easily washed. They can also be rolled up (sew the pockets so that long things lie sideways or at an angle), tied and stuffed into a convenient corner.

Friends of ours carry an amazing amount of odds and ends this way: one towel fitted with pockets for kitchenware and utensils; another for toilet articles (each has one); another for film, stationary, pencils, maps and flashlights; one for eyeglasses and pocketbooks and even, believe it or not, a special towel for packets of teas and coffee. Each towel is a different color for quick recognition.

Once you've got your basic cupboards and containers, don't overpack them. By overpacking I not only mean overstuffing, but also excessively neat arrangements that won't survive the first bump or hasty rummaging. If it takes fifteen minutes to get your kitchen gear into a box, you can bet it will take four times that long to repack at the end of the first hard day of travelling. Camping gear has an irrepressible tendency to fluff up, pour out and sprout unpackable corners once you're on the road.

Furniture

A certain amount of furniture can make cooking, eating and general loafing much easier. The instant I relax on top of one of our footlockers, Lorena finds it absolutely urgent to get at something inside. The problem is easily avoided by carrying a couple of aluminum stools or lawn chairs. Very attractive and inexpensive handmade wooden stools and chairs are also available in Mexico. *Equipales* are our favorite: nesting stools and round tables of wood and stretched pigskin or woven reeds. They are very light, durable and make fine souvenirs and furniture when you return home.

Some counter or table surface should be easily accessible for cooking. A door shelf allows you to move the stove and cooking outside. However, using the stove outside

may become a hassle instead of a convenience if you have to climb in and out to cut vegetables or to set down a hot pan.

Small folding tables attached to the back and side doors of your camper are much more useful than a single large table that can only be used inside. All folding tables should be *very sturdily supported* when in use to avoid dangerous and irritating accidents.

Folding aluminum tables are very handy and very lightweight. I personally prefer a cheap lightweight pine table with the legs cut down to fit better inside the van. They are sold throughout Mexico; look in the marketplace. A quick coat of varnish or oil will prevent the soft wood from staining.

One of the simplest and most versatile tables imaginable is just a piece of plywood placed on top of a box or wide basket. Paint or woodburn a checker board on one side and you've got an instant rec-room.

Built-In Furnishings

Once you've used your camper under varied conditions, you may decide that certain things would be more convenient if built-to-measure. A nifty kitchen cabinet perhaps, with a fold-down table for the stove and a cutting board that slides out of sight. When the building urge strikes, consider having it done by a Mexican carpenter. The materials may not be cheap (wood is generally expensive in Mexico), but the labor will be a bargain. Look for a shop that is turning out good furniture; many Mexican craftsmen do fine hand joinery work and decorative carving. Just make sure they use plenty of *tornillos* (screws) and *resistol* (wood glue) to withstand hard road use.

Built-in cabinets and furnishings should be securely attached to the vehicle while travelling. A rubber burning emergency stop or unexpected speed bump at fifty mph can turn the best organized camper into a mess.

Water Storage

Built-in water tanks aren't worth the expense or trouble. When a hose for filling them is not available (often the case in Mexico), you'll have to do the bucket brigade trip, so you might as well start with portable jugs. Two five-gallon cans should be a sufficient supply of fresh water for two or three people for a considerable length of time.

Ice Chests

A sturdy ice chest that can be easily removed for use outside is much more convenient than a permanently built-in one. An ice chest with a lift up top is also better than an upright model when large slippery chunks of ice are used— usually the case in Mexico. (For more on keeping things cool see Chapter 5.)

Mattresses

I love mattresses that really work, not those thin pads backpackers toss and groan on, but spongy foam wonders, the thicker the better. Here's how to beat the incredible bulk while camping from a passenger car without sacrificing comfort: the width of your mattress should be slightly less than the width of the car's trunk or back seat. Lay a blanket on the ground (a thin, tightly woven blanket works best) and place the mattress on top. Now carefully roll the mattress inside the blanket, compressing it just as much as you can. This is easier with two or three people. Once you get started you should find that the mattress is greatly reduced in volume. (This procedure is for foam mattresses, not innerspring.) When you've got it tightly rolled, tie it well with short lengths of rope or bungee cords. To unroll the mattress just remove the bindings and jump back. It will pop open by itself. This simple discovery made camping out of a small car much more enjoyable for us. A removable, washable cover will keep the mattress from getting too funky.

Awnings

Living outside is more comfortable with some sort of protection from the sun and rain. We use a light tarp and extendable aluminum tent poles. The tarp is attached to the rain gutter of the van (drill small holes and make wire hooks or loops for tie points) and extends out from the side. Adjustable poles are convenient for irregular ground but anything will do. Two eight-foot lengths of light bamboo are ideal. Secure the tarp with lengths of twine and pegs. I tie strips of white rag to the twine so that when I trip over it, I know what's happened. Other tarps can be rigged as side walls for more privacy. (For more on rigging tarps see Chapter 5.)

If your tarp, poles, lines and pegs are kept neatly stowed, you'll be able to find them and erect a shelter within five minutes of parking. This can make even a brief highway lunch break much more relaxing and comfortable. The advantage of protection from the rain is obvious, especially if your vehicle isn't very roomy.

Skylights & Windows

Skylights and extra large windows, even heavily tinted, act as heat collectors during the day. The Mexican sun may be more than you expected when you installed that skylight in Minnesota. Our van, for example, has two skylights, each capable of heating us to the baking point on a hot day. To avoid this, we block them from the inside with newspaper, aluminum foil, a foil-backed blanket or whatever else can be taped or jammed into place.

Carry a good supply of silicone seal for emergency repairs. Skylights and plastic windows are notorious for leaking. When softened by the heat of the sun and then subjected to vibration they may develop annoying cracks and splits. A brief tropical shower can hammer through the tiniest of cracks. Lorena actually put her head through one of our skylights. It took a full tube of silicone seal and several feet of heavy duty duct tape to make it almost watertight again.

When bugs or rain force you inside, you'll want as much fresh air as you can get. If your vehicle is short on windows, install a few more, with strong, tight bug screens.

Windows that open will provide extra air, light and a better view. Crank-open overhead ventilators are also good.

Bug Proofing

Some type of bug screening is essential. Rig drapes or curtains or mosquito netting over side and back doors. The netting should be long enough to prevent mosquitoes from crawling underneath and loose enough so that you won't punch a hole in them with a foot or elbow.

We prefer a rectangular canopy of mosquito netting rigged over the bed. This allows all doors and windows to be opened without having to screen them. The canopy arrangement, however, forces you to stay in bed when the mosquitoes are out. This isn't always an inconvenience if you're into reading, sleeping, etc. (See Chapter 5 for more on mosquito nets.)

In many places where we've camped, bugs weren't a problem *most of the time,* but when they did attack it was merciless and all-out. This may happen during the day as well as at night. A screened refuge can mean the difference between evacuating a nice campsite or holing up for a short time.

Curtains

Unless you're an exhibitionist, put curtains on all windows or you'll be playing to standing-room-only audiences when camped in most areas of Mexico. This is especially true if you spend the night in a town, schoolyard, soccer field or other public place.

When sleeping by a highway, the lights of passing trucks can keep you awake with their near-lighthouse intensity. Dark curtains are especially good for blocking out unwanted headlights (and daylight too, if you enjoy an occasional *siesta*).

Curtains also protect your possessions from greedy appraisal by would-be thieves when you are not inside.

Interior Lights

The interior lights in a car or camper rarely shine when or where they're needed. Because light is important for cooking and reading, take the trouble to install lights that are really useful. When you wake up in the middle of a long night with the burning desire to re-read *War and Peace,* you'll be glad you did.

Lights are available in auto junkyards, discount stores, auto supply stores and, if you can afford the high mark-ups, trailer and RV supply outlets. I prefer portable, rather than permanently attached lights; they are more versatile and easier to install. Buy the type that plugs into the car's cigarette lighter. Spotlight models use a lot more juice than bulb types, but also give considerably more light.

Our van is a non-smoker model so I clipped the plug off the portable light's cord, stripped the insulation from the two ends and crimped (soldered is better) alligator clips to the bare wire ends. The light doesn't have a switch, so turning it on is a matter of attaching the alligator clips to two connections on the van's fuse panel. Clip one to any fuse holder and then touch the other alligator to other fuse holders until the light comes on. (You can also bare part of a hot wire for one clip and put the other on any good ground. There is a risk, however, of an accidental short circuit should something later touch the bared spot, but you can't have everything.)

Our light has a magnet built into the case. It almost sticks to the van's body. Magnets can also be glued to cabinets or strategic points that aren't metal.

A friend who burned down his 'fireproof' van, complete with all his worldly goods, suggests that candles be used with extreme caution. The votive type, sold in reusable glasses, can be held in plastic or metal devices sold as drink caddies.

Rugs & Carpets

Carpeted floors in vans and motorhomes can drive you to distraction when camped near sand or mud. After I reached the point of asking guests to go through a series of foot cleansings as complicated as those given to diseased cattle, Lorena suggested we remove our carpet. I immediately relaxed again though I quickly tired of bare metal floor. The solution was simple: we bought cheap *petates* (woven reed mats) of various sizes and one bright handwoven Mexican blanket to spread over them. The mats make a good rug pad for the blanket. They can also be used on the ground as doormats. The effect is much more attractive than carpeting and insulates against road noise. As a bonus when we get cold we pull up the rug and sleep under it.

Plumbing

A portable toilet can be very handy, especially if you suffer the inevitable attack of diarrhea in a traffic jam. Unfortunately there are few places in Mexico where dumping a holding tank will be appreciated. RV owners we've talked to suggest that you find a remote spot, dig a deep hole and flush. Don't do this near water, please.

Self-contained campers must also deal with dishwater and perhaps, lucky dogs, shower runoff. Make every effort to dispose of these wastes away from the campsite; there's nothing worse than discovering you've pitched your tent on an unpleasant wet spot. Think of others before pulling the plug. I know of one case where an uncooperative motorhomer was 'invited' by *gringo* vigilantes to leave his campsite after he refused to do anything about various obnoxious drains. When nearby campers tired of the smell and health hazard they spontaneously organized an 'Unwelcome Wagon'.

Mechanical Preparations

Car repairs are cheap in Mexico, but don't put off any obvious servicing or repairs. I force myself to take care of these tedious chores by constantly reminding myself that once I'm on the road, stopping to fix a leaky muffler or cranky carburetor is even more difficult than at home. "Hang on! We're almost there!" has led me to spend far too many hours — and even days — in search of a roadside *mecánico*. An ounce of prevention and all that . . .

Cars are very expensive in Mexico and even the most beatup *carcachas* (old wrecks) are still chugging away. Used parts are relatively scarce, relatively expensive and *well used*. And besides, the time to buy spares is before you need them, not afterwards. (I tell myself this every time I hitch to the nearest parts store.) The following spares should cover average driving anywhere, without breaking your budget:

Spares, Etc.

Tire.
Fan belt: check the size carefully.
Motor oil: enough for one change or more.
Filters; oil, fuel & air: enough for the trip if they're an odd size or brand.

Brake Fluid, Transmission Fluid.

Fuses, Bulbs.

Fire Extinguisher: cheap insurance — get two!

Flare or reflector: Repairs often take place in the middle of the road in Mexico, especially if there's no shoulder.

Repair manual: Jot down the settings for spark plugs, points and valves. If you've got a VW, buy *How To Keep Your Volkswagen Alive* or *How To Keep Your VW Rabbit Alive.* The former is also available in Spanish. (See *Recommended Reading: Appendices* for ordering information.)

Tools

Even if you avoid doing your own car repairs like the plague, it's wise to carry a basic selection of tools. A friend claims that the tools listed below will repair almost anything in the world, let alone an average car:

Large, medium and small *standard screwdrivers*

Medium *Phillips-head screwdriver*

Vice grip pliers, 10 inch

Regular pliers with wire-cutting jaw

Open end wrenches, metric or standard

Ten inch *Crescent wrench*

Jack and lug wrench

Tire pressure gauge (get a good one; cheap gauges are worthless)

Electrical tape and wire

Baling wire

Flashlight

Rags

Gull   *Gaviota*

No matter if you're a very conservative Sunday driver or a hell-for-leather type, don't neglect to do the following before you leave:

A Complete Tune-up and Lubrication

You'll save money on gas, cut down on wear and tear and pollute less.

Check and Test:

Tires and Wheels: Check the spare too. We've had consistently miserable luck with recapped tires on Mexican roads, especially on long trips. Heat and chuckholes will murder recaps; try to use real tires if you can afford them.

I suggest that you loosen and then carefully retighten the lug nuts on all four wheels before you leave home, especially if you haven't done this within the past few months. The lug nuts on our van were frozen tight, a discovery I made in the middle of the Sonora Desert when a tire suddenly went flat. I ruined our lug wrench and almost broke my back in a futile attempt to remove the tire. Lubricate the lug nuts with a bit of heavy grease or motor oil if you'll be near salt water for very long. On most vehicles a good cleaning of the nut threads with a wire brush will suffice but some, like our VW van, require careful light greasing. Check them again for proper tightness after an hour or less of driving.

Brakes: You'll need and want them, believe me. Check the brake fluid level before you leave and every few days while on the road. Check the condition of the brakes. If they need work, do it before you leave.

Battery: Check it frequently. Higher air temperatures in Mexico plus the heat of your engine can dry a battery up in record time. Carry distilled water, improvise a filter or 'remove' crud from ditch water by chanting, *"Pure! Pure! Pure!"*

Cooling system: You might want to change the thermostat. Clean air-cooled engines thoroughly and when the roads are dusty, clean 'em again.

Steering, Front-end suspension: If your tires are wearing unevenly or if the car shimmies or handles oddly, get the front end checked. Improper alignment and balancing can eat up new tires before your very eyes, especially on a long trip.

Horn: Mexican drivers use horns like *gringos* use CB radios. If you want to be heard . . .

Headlights: Clean the lenses and consider a set of driving lights for occasions when you violate the Golden Rule and decide to chance driving at night. It's best to attach driving lights permanently to thwart thieves.

Windshield wipers: Poor visibility is said to be a major cause of auto accidents. Having tried driving without wipers on various occasions, I firmly believe it.

Driving mirrors: Defensive driving is the absolute rule in Mexico. You are responsible for your own safety; don't expect other drivers to watch out for you, they're looking out for themselves. *Never* move out of your lane without checking both rear and sideview mirrors. If you use truck-type mirrors try to carry a spare. Driving on narrow city streets in Mexico raises hell with wide mirrors.

Roadside Repairs

Those who yearn for back country adventures should be even better prepared for roadside repairs. Our 'Damn the torpedoes!' approach is somewhat balanced by a well-filled toolbox, spare parts kit and plenty of reading material for those occasional long waits for assistance.

If you must leave your car unattended for any reason, make every effort to find someone to watch it for you. Offer a generous payment; after all, it's cheap insurance against theft or vandalism. Tell them *"Cuidalo día y noche, por favor"* (Watch it day and night, please), and agree in advance on what you'll pay.

I recommend that you carry:

Set of spark plugs, points and condenser.

Fine emery paper: For electrical contact cleaning.

Feeler gauges: For setting the points and valves.

Pure alcohol or commercial cleaner: For cleaning and drying the distributor on really dusty or wet roads.

Tire pump: If you don't need it, someone else will. A small air compressor that fits into a spark plug hole is great for those heartbreaking multiple flats and pumping up inflatable boats.

Tire and inner tubes: Slow leaks caused by slightly bent wheel rims are beyond most amateurs' abilities to repair; by installing tubes in your tires you'll avoid this problem. Tubeless recaps are the worst choice for rough roads; when they come apart, it's usually unexpected and irreparable. Carry patching materials — enough for all four tires in case you happen to blunder into a thorn patch. Mexico is the land of the slow leak.

Iron pipe or crowbar: The pipe will extend the leverage of your lug wrench handle and the crowbar is for emergency body work and prying giant limpets off rocks.

Gas and oil: A one-gallon can of spare gas is the minimum. I carry enough oil for normal changes plus extra oil for more frequent changes in extremely dusty conditions. Carry extra gas filters, too. (See *Maintenance Tips* later in this chapter.)

Siphon hose, chamois, funnel: For transferring gas.

Water: For drinking, filling the radiator and topping off the battery. If you drive in the desert, especially on bad roads, carry enough water to survive at least three or four days: two quarts per day per person is the *minimum.* Don't use anti-freeze or any other radiator additive if you want to use radiator water for emergency drinking. Don't laugh: almost every year someone dies of thirst in Mexico's deserts.

Got Stuck Kit: When you get stuck, your pathetic call of "Hey? Could 'ya gimme a hand for a minute?" will ruin a hot afternoon for some obliging soul. Before you go for reinforcements, give a valiant effort with: *a shovel,* preferably normal sized, but a folding 'foxhole' shovel will do; *gloves,* if you carry two pair your friend can help, too; *chain or heavy rope* for being towed or towing others (use snow chains even in sand and mud); and *salt tablets* for overexertion in the heat (see Chapter 8). Stay calm: wheel spinning, mindless shouting and frenzied fender beating should be used only as a last resort. (See *Stuck Again?:* Chapter 5.)

Gas, Oil, Parts & Mechanics

Gas stations are found along all of Mexico's major highways and arteries. Look for the big green *PEMEX* sign (*PEtróleos MEXicanos,* a government monopoly).

There are just two types of gas: *Nova* (blue pump, leaded, about 82 octane, $.45 a gallon) and *Extra* (silver pump, unleaded, about 90 octane, $.65 a gallon). Diesel is very common and ridiculously cheap: $.17 a gallon.

Although Mexico has vast quantities of petroleum and gas (which makes the country a motoring paradise for gasoline-hungry *gringos*), some stations do run out of *Extra.* Off the main roads *Extra* is rarely available, and you'll have to be satisfied with *Nova.*

It may come out of a battered steel drum, a milk can or a plastic jug, but at least it's gasoline.

When there's no gas station in sight, start looking for crudely lettered signs that say *gasolina.* A couple of dented gas drums outside of a house or *tienda* (small store) probably mean they sell it on the side. Ask anyone "*¿Dónde hay gasolina?*" (Where is there gas?). "*¿No hay gasolina?*" (Isn't there gas?) is also good, especially when accompanied with a smile and a sincere "*¿Por favor?*" (Please?).

Most backyard gasoline costs at least twice as much as it does at the pumps and often even more. It beats running out.

Truck drivers are very helpful and may offer a drain from their own tank. Always offer to pay: "*Muchísimas gracias. ¿Cuánto le debo?*" (Many thanks. How much do I owe you?)

Carry your own siphon hose, neatly rolled up and protected from dirt by a thick plastic bag. Because gas from casual sources may be dirty or contaminated with water, I always try to filter it through a piece of chamois. A good-sized funnel makes filtering much easier. If I suspect water in my gas (likely along the coast or during the rainy season), I also dump a pint or so of pure alcohol (not tequila; it's half water) into the gas tank to help burn off the moisture.

Before buying gas from a barrel, give it a close sniff to make sure it really is gasoline. Mistakes are rare but all it takes is a few gallons of diesel in a gas-fueled engine to cause dramatic problems. We once got a tank of kerosene. Surprisingly enough the car actually ran, though not very well.

Once you've located enough gas to continue your journey, ask if there's more ahead: "*¿Hay gasolina allá?*" (Is there gas there?) Wave your hand vaguely in the direction you're headed and they'll understand. "*¿Está muy lejos?*" (Is it very far?). Remember that the word 'far' can mean just about anything in Mexico, from around the next bend to well over the horizon.

Unless your engine is a real oil burner, you should be able to bring enough from home to last your trip. Oil is sold in Pemex stations and auto parts stores, but it's hard to find in the back country. Auto parts stores are the best places to look for additives; only the largest Pemex stations carry them.

Should you need a *mecánico* (mechanic) look for signs announcing *Taller Mecánico*, *Taller Automotriz* or for groups of obviously disabled cars, patiently waiting their turn for repairs. Flat tires are restored to life at a *Vulcanizadora*, *Llantería* or *Desponchador* (a 'depuncturer').

Unless you're driving an oddball vehicle or one too complicated for a shade tree genius, repairs and servicing will be relatively easy to find. The farther you travel from highways and cities, the fewer and farther between any services will be, but with good maintenance and common sense you should have no trouble.

Rough Roads: Maintenance & Driving Tips

We have covered an incredible number of miles in the back country of Mexico and Guatemala, often in vehicles that were not particularly suited to the conditions. Our breakdowns, however, have been few and fortunately far between. Luck may have had a hand in this, but I prefer to rely on careful preparations and caution. Here are some suggestions for tackling tougher roads. The idea is not only to get there, but to get back, happy and in one piece.
• Pay special attention to routine maintenance. Even if you don't do your own work, early detection of a potential problem will save you both cash and lost time.
• Manufacturer's recommendations for various fluid and filter changes are based on highway driving, not on Mexican back roads. Cut them in half. I change the oil in our VW van every 1,500 miles rather than every 3,000. If it looks dirty even sooner, I gnash my teeth, but go ahead and change it. The same goes for gas filters, air cleaners, oil filters and whatever else is vital to your machine's long life.
• Rough roads can play hell with ignition timing, valve settings, distributor point gap, hose connections and so on. I halve the suggested times between tune-ups and valve adjustments. Checking the points more often gives me a chance to clean dust from the distributor and to wipe down the engine. After a really bad stretch of road I check the battery; half the time it's managed to fall over. It also goes dry when I least expect it.
• Check your tires often, especially on rocky roads. Gashes and bubbles are potential blowouts. I either change a damaged tire right away or let some air out (down to 15-20 pounds on the VW) and continue with great caution. If the damage isn't too bad, I'll leave the tire on until we get to a repair shop. Don't risk highway driving on a bad tire, however; the consequences of a blowout are just too awful.
• Carry at least five spare gallons of gas when exploring back roads and top off your tank whenever possible. It may be a hassle to get out the siphon hose and filter for just six liters, but you'll be glad you did, later.
• Drive slowly! Speed combined with unexpected and unmarked rocks and holes, will lead to breakdowns and blowouts. Put it in first or second, hang your arm out the window and enjoy the scenery.
• Stop for frequent rests, both for the driver, passengers and the engine. Overheating can be a problem on bad roads, and driver fatigue is dangerous. When you can't go on without great suffering and squabbling, it's past time to stop. Find a reasonable campsite and rest for the night.
• Don't drive at night. You're not only exposing yourself to additional driving hazards, but undoubtedly missing some nice scenery. Nighttime is for campfires, tall tales and the Bogeyman. If you must drive at night, use extreme caution. Watch for livestock, deer and well-concealed chuckholes. You'll probably see them all.
• The lower your vehicle's clearance, the slower you must go to avoid problems. A busted oil pan is a disaster anywhere, but a hundred miles into the Mexican boondocks, it's a downright depressing development. One impatient *gringo* spent ten days camped next to his car, waiting for parts. Low slung vehicles can make it over very lousy roads but only with extra care.
• When facing a very steep grade, up or down, that gives you a case of the sure-hope-we-can-do-its, stop and survey the prospects on foot. Downgrades *going in* are upgrades *coming out*. We've run into upgrades that took every spare shoulder to push us over the top. If you can't make a grade, try unloading and/or backing up the grade. Giving up, of course, is the safest choice. I let the decision rest on my burning

desire to continue, balanced by my dread of getting badly stuck. If I smell good skin diving or fishing over the next ridge, we usually hang on and go for it.

• Extremely tight switchbacks can be impossible to get around in less than two tries. Have someone block the rear wheels with a large rock or piece of wood before you make the second try. On very steep roads have as many people as possible walking alongside and behind the vehicle, prepared to block the wheel on quick notice. Tell them to watch out for flying gravel and rocks.

This type of road is usually found deep in the mountains. Drive with great care. Extra ballast in the rear, either rocks or passengers, may improve traction.

• Driving on sand is an interesting and often tense experience. Once you're moving along on top of the sand, it's best to hold the speed steady; don't overreact if you can avoid it. Hitting the brakes or swerving may sink you right down to the frame. Damage is unlikely but you are definitely stuck.

Driving on sand is much like driving on snow. Lug the engine slightly rather than shifting to a lower gear. This prevents spinning the tires, a sure way to bury them into the sand. When you must downshift, do it very gently.

• Don't drive on beaches unless you are very confident and have full insurance coverage. We came within minutes of losing a brand new Volvo to the tide. One second we were flying down the beach, laughing and honking at the seagulls; the next we were in sand up to the frame, fifty miles from the nearest tow truck. By one of those miracles familiar to Mexico travellers, a nearby rancher produced a World War II vintage Dodge Power Wagon and plucked us out, just as waves were lapping at the wheels. Anyone who camps on the beach will certainly spend at least one afternoon helping some foolish motorist dig out of the sand.

• Unimproved dirt roads quickly become unimproved mud slides during the rainy season. Though they may dry quickly and be passable most of the time, even during *las aguas* (the rains, rainy season), extra caution should be used. Slides, falling rocks, washouts and deep unmarked fords are common hazards. This is especially true in the deserts and mountains, where runoff really *runs*. I always thought Hollywood movies that included monster flash floods were a joke — until I saw one.

When it starts to rain, find a place to wait it out. A delay is better than getting stuck; once you're stuck, you'll be waiting anyway. If you're driving in an arroyo or canyon and can't get out or are definitely stuck, abandon the vehicle and run to high ground.

• Never attempt to ford a stream during a rainstorm unless your chances are one hundred percent that you'll get safely across. Water that is a foot deep now can easily be three feet or more within *minutes*. I know of one case where a passenger bus was swept away by a flash flood. Your car or pickup would be a chip in comparison.

Once your trip is about over, consider a front-end alignment. Not all shops have the necessary tools or experience to do this job, so ask a large car dealer or tire dealer for advice. Aligning the front end and balancing the tires can save a great deal of wear on the trip home.

We once ventured over a road so awful that it barely qualified as a burro trail. After seventy-five bone-cracking miles our VW van developed a severe tendency to go wherever it pleased, rather than where it was pointed. One look under the front end was enough; a steering arm was bent almost double. We wobbled into a typical Mexican auto *taller* (repair shop) and explained the situation to the *maestro* (master mechanic, boss).

"Do you have a chain?" he asked. I dug it out.

"Park it right there," he said, pointing to a huge post that supported the entire roof of his shop. Several assistants stood under the roof, taking advantage of the shade. The *maestro* quickly wrapped the chain around the post and hooked the other end to the steering rod.

"Put it in reverse and back up," he ordered, joining the others in the shade.

I shrugged. Fate had evidently decreed that I pull this shop down on their heads. At the first tentative pressure the post groaned, then a heavy shudder rattled the roof and walls. The mechanic and his friends looked up apprehensively.

"*¡Otra vez, mas recio!*" the *maestro* called ("Again, harder!"). I obediently popped the clutch. Mouths gaped open as the entire shop leaned drunkenly toward the van. "Harder! Harder!" he urged. Just as the roof rafters began to pop and splinter, showering many years' accumulation of bird droppings into the shop below, he yelled, "Okay!" The job was done.

Total cost: fifty cents. "It was your chain," the *maestro* explained. "I just supervised." As we drove away I avoided looking at the new angle of his shop.

Peccary   *Javelina*

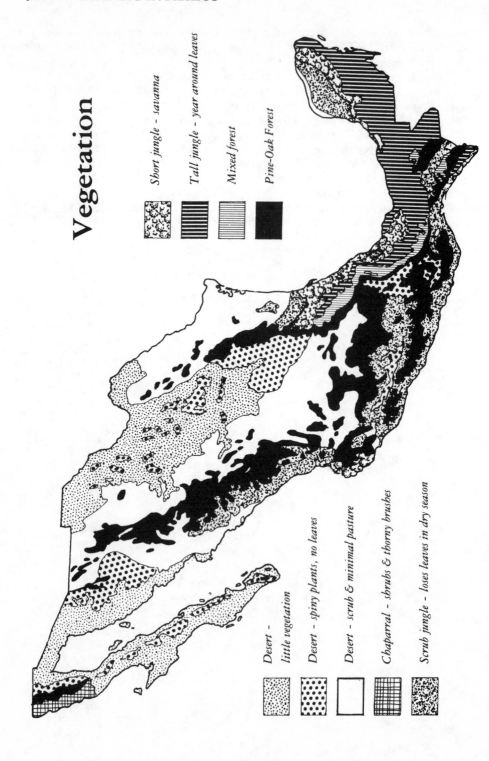

Vegetation

Short jungle - savanna

Tall jungle - year around leaves

Mixed forest

Pine-Oak Forest

Desert -
little vegetation

Desert - spiny plants, no leaves

Desert - scrub & minimal pasture

Chaparral - shrubs & thorny brushes

Scrub jungle - loses leaves in dry season

11. Red Tape

Tourist Card

American and Canadian citizens visiting Mexico need just one simple document to cross the border: a Tourist Card. This card, actually a slip of paper, can be obtained free of charge at the border, at Mexican consulate and Tourism offices in large American and Canadian cities, at travel agencies or from the airline office if you are flying. Tourist Cards will be issued upon presentation of proof of citizenship: passport, birth certificate, voter's registration card, military discharge papers or notarized proof of citizenship. Naturalized citizens must have a passport or naturalization papers. *A driver's license is not proof of citizenship* and will not be accepted.

Tourists under 18 years of age must have their parents' notarized consent if travelling alone or with just one parent. For example, a father and son must have the mother's notarized consent in order for the boy to enter Mexico. This rule is not always enforced but it *may be*.

Children under 15 may be included on their parent's Tourist Card, but the child cannot leave Mexico without the parent or the parent without the child. It's easier to have a separate Tourist Card for everyone.

Your Tourist Card must be validated by Mexican Immigration authorities at the border or at the airport when you land in Mexico. The length of your stay is determined at this time. Some Tourist Cards, especially those issued by airlines and tourist agencies, may have 30, 60 or 90 days in the space preceded by the words *Authorized To Remain In Mexico* _____ Days From Date of Entry. If you want to spend more time in Mexico (up to a legal limit of 180 days) ask the Immigration official to change the number. If the space is blank they'll ask how long you intend to be in Mexico. Give yourself a wide margin; once the number of days is written down you're stuck with it.

The best way to convince a skeptical official that you should be given the amount of time you want in Mexico is to be very polite, as respectable looking as possible and have enough money on hand to prove that you aren't a bum. When nothing else works (see *Bribes* in this chapter), you'll have to take what you get or try crossing into Mexico at another border point. Tourist Cards can be extended, but it usually isn't easy. The paperwork can take several weeks and may not be worth the trouble. The best procedure is to visit an office of *Migración* (Immigration) or *Turismo* (Tourism) inside Mexico well before your tourist papers expire. They'll tell you what to do next, but if you don't have proof of solvency (money) you may be out of luck. It all depends on the mood of the official you talk to and your gift of gab.

Car Permits

If you are driving into Mexico (beyond the border zone where casual visits do not require Tourist Cards) you will be issued, free of charge, a combination Tourist Card and Temporary Vehicle Importation Permit. This permit is issued on presentation of proof of citizenship (see *Tourist Cards* in this chapter), valid driver's license, car title or registration (or notarized affidavit if the car is not in your name, authorizing you to take the car into Mexico), and current license plates. If your plates are about to expire, don't worry about it; the Mexican police are supposed to overlook this.

Your combination Tourist Card/Car Permit will also have noted on it any large accessories: air conditioners, radios, tape decks, small trailers, etc. All these accessories must leave Mexico with you and the car or you are liable for a very stiff duty. This isn't always checked when you leave Mexico but you never know. Along with the Car Papers you'll be given a Tourist Sticker: this decal is pasted onto your windshield and rear or side window and identifies the vehicle as belonging to a tourist. If you don't get a Tourist Sticker, don't worry; they sometimes run out of them.

Note: Car Permits are not required for the Baja states but if you intend to cross to the mainland from Baja you'll need to visit the Immigration office in La Paz. I prefer to go through the paperwork at the border; it seems to go quicker there. 'Tipping' can often speed up the paperwork and I suggest you view these few dollars as valuable grease to lubricate the bureaucratic machinery.

You must leave Mexico, with the vehicle and all of its accessories, within the period of time noted as your authorized stay. If for any reason you can't do this, the vehicle can be temporarily impounded at a large airport or with a customs office (Oficina Federal de Haciende). A storage fee will be charged.

Immunizations

There are no immunizations required for tourists visiting Mexico, but campers should have a recent tetanus shot. Some doctors also recommend para-typhoid immunizations but others say it isn't worth it. Consult your family doctor. Some states and city health offices give free immunizations of all types. They'll also advise you of the latest regulations and recommendations given out by the State Department for travellers who visit really unhealthy areas of the world.

Car & Boat Insurance

Very few insurance policies issued in the U.S. and Canada are valid in Mexico. There are a bewildering variety of insurance offices on both sides of the border who will quickly write up a policy to cover you and your vehicle (and boat). Basic insurance rates are government controlled but most companies tack on additional clauses — and charges — that send the price much higher than the legal minimum. Read over the policy carefully; the most basic cover only liability (no payment to you, for example for body work, medical expenses or theft). Rates decrease significantly for long-term policies.

It is important to understand that in Mexico, insurance isn't just a way to pay off damages, it's also *'stay out of jail'* protection. In the event of an accident, especially one that involves injuries, all parties may be locked up until claims have been settled. Innocent or guilty, you could find yourself behind bars. Your insurance agent will deal with the cops for you. This puts a whole new light on insurance and for this reason I heartily recommend that you buy at least minimum liability coverage.

Larger companies (Sanborn's, AAA and others) give away free guidebooks, road maps and other information with their policies.

Boats and trailers are insured in addition to cars and other vehicles. Most car policies are not valid if the car is used to tow an uninsured boat or trailer.

Does your policy cover anyone who drives your car? Check it carefully to be certain. You also won't be covered (in most policies) if you have an accident while driving another vehicle.

Boats, Trailers, Motorcycles & Towed Cars

A monthly fee and a registration fee based on weight are charged for sport boats taken into Mexico. Depending on the official who issues your papers, this fee may be applied to car top boats or it may not. Boats over 22 feet in length must be bonded.

Boats, trailers and towed vehicles are usually treated separately, though they may be included on your Car Permit if the official at the border decides that would be easier. In other words, your motorbike might have its own papers or your boat, bike, trailer and hang glider might all be lumped together as 'accessories'. The more things you take into Mexico the more patient you must be while the *papaleo* (red tape) is being unraveled. Be helpful, patient, calm and understanding. You have nothing to gain by losing your temper. Tourists who 'fly off the handle' may find themselves refused entry into Mexico. As a visitor it is your responsibility to be cooperative.

CB Radios

CB radios were once banned in Mexico but the government has now authorized their use by tourists and private citizens. CB groups are becoming popular in Mexico but your use is restricted to Channel 11 (emergencies), 13 (caravans) and 14 (general chatter).

Yachts & Private Aircraft

Clearance papers may be obtained at Mexican Consulate offices or from marine customs brokers. These must be shown at ports of entry and departure. Boats under 5 tons are exempt from entry charges (theoretically anyway). If you or your crew intend to go ashore you should obtain Tourist Cards in advance.

The regulations for aircraft are basically the same as for cars. You must also send a written report of your flight plan to authorities of the international airport closest to where you intend to cross the border. There are other requirements and I suggest that you visit the nearest Mexican Consulate or write to Departmento de Transporte Aéreo Internacional, Dirección General de Aeronáutica Civil, Secretaría de

Comunicaciones y Transportes, Avenida Universidad y Xola, 2º Piso, Mexico 12, D.F. (phone 5-19-81-83 or 5-19-76-25). Or, easier yet, write to Aircraft Owners and Pilots Association, 4644 East-West Highway, Washington D.C. 20015.

Pets

To take a dog or cat into Mexico, you must present a veterinarian's certificate stating that the animal is in good health and has been innoculated against rabies within the past six months. This certificate must be visaed (stamped) by a Mexican consul for a fee. Go to the nearest Consul before you leave for Mexico; each Consul may certify pets only within the immediate area.

The regulations on returning to the U.S. with pet birds have become so strict that I highly advise against taking them with you to Mexico. For details write to: United States Department of Agriculture, Animal and Plant Health Inspection Service, Veterinary Services, Federal Center Building, Hyattsville, Maryland, 20782.

Pets are often a problem while travelling in Mexico, mainly because few hotels, motels and even trailer parks will allow them on the premises. Tourists are frequently shocked to find how rigid these rules are. Don't take your pet unless you're willing to put up with this. Keep a close eye on your animal, especially if it bites.

Mexican Customs Inspections, Bribes

Tourists are given a customs check when entering Mexico. This is done at the point where your Car Papers are issued or Tourist Card validated and occasionally at 'flying checkpoints' on major highways in northern Mexico.

The customs check is usually quite quick and casual, but if you're travelling with a vehicle and a great deal of camping gear you might find youself subjected to a more detailed inspection. Firearms are the main point of these searches, but in reality some customs inspectors use the opportunity to coax a bribe out of tourists who are eager to be on their way. Stay calm and pay the bribe; it probably won't be very much, but if you argue and complain the price will go up fast. The official policy is that bribes are absolutely prohibited and the reality is that they are often sought out and accepted. Any minor discrepancies in your paperwork or imagined violations (too many cameras, too much whiskey in the cupboard, etc.) can usually be straightened out with a few dollar bills.

Tourists of Hispanic extraction often complain that Mexican customs officials hit them especially hard for bribes and 'gifts'. This is probably because the officials also lean heavily on Mexican citizens returning from the U.S. and border zones. 'Contraband' can mean anything from too many new pairs of socks to a portable t.v. that looks like it just came off the shelf of a discount store. Once again, stay very calm and cool. If you speak Spanish it might be better not to until you've determined how rough they'll be in their search.

Keep your Tourist Card, Car Papers and other official documents close at hand and in a neat, clean condition. Fast checks go even faster when you're prepared for them.

Fishing & Spearfishing Licenses

The rules covering sport fishing and spearfishing seem to change about every two months in Mexico. At the present time I have 'official' information stating that children under 12 do not need a license and information stating that children under 16 do not need a license. Local officials often don't know what the rules are and sort of play it by ear. Your best bet is to buy a fishing license (which covers spearfishing and seafood foraging) and not worry too much about details unless someone questions what you're doing. Some popular bass fishing lakes, for example, fall under local management and such things as closed seasons and license fees may be changed at any moment.

Fishing licenses, fortunately, are very inexpensive and I suggest that you get one before you enter Mexico, especially if you have a boat. Licenses are sold within the country but it is often difficult to find out exactly where and when they are available. If you fish for bass, take special care to have a license; game wardens seem to concentrate their efforts around popular bass lakes.

Although enforcement of game laws, especially concerning fishing and diving, is both lax and erratic, tourists shouldn't take advantage by neglecting to buy a license. This will only bring stricter enforcement in the future (and a higher fee for licenses to pay the costs). Tourists comprise the greatest number of sport fishermen and women in Mexico; set a good example by complying with the law.

Some main points of the fishing laws are listed here but I suggest that you send for a full copy and buy

Parrotfish   *Loro*

a fishing license by mail at the same time. Write to Mexican Department of Fisheries, 1010 Second Avenue, Suite 1605, San Diego, California, 92101 or the same office, 395 West 6th Street, Suite 3, San Pedro, California, 90731.

Fishing Laws

• Sport license holders may not take abalone, pismo clams, shrimp, lobster, cabrilla (rock bass), oysters, totuava, turtles, coral, gorgonians (sea fans) or sea shells (within natural parks and reserves). These are reserved for Mexican commercial fishermen and they definitely resent it if tourists take what they consider to be their livelihood.
• No fishing of any type is allowed in natural parks and special reserves. Most of these are found in Baja, Quintana Roo and a few areas of the Pacific Coast. Look for signs that begin with *Prohibido* . . . A recent government directive declared all islands within the Gulf Of California as official fish and game reserves and sanctuaries, though it only bans hunting, plant collecting and general misuse rather than fishing.
• Spearfishing is allowed only with 'muscle powered' equipment, not explosive-propelled spears or 'bang sticks'. The use of spearfishing gear with scuba equipment is absolutely prohibited. I know of one case where a customs official refused to allow a diver to bring an air compressor into Mexico because he also had a trunk load of spearguns with him.
• Bag limits: (major species only): per day or trip (if it's longer than a day): one marlin, sailfish, swordfish and sawfish. (Once again the information is conflicting; some official handouts say that two sailfish a day can be taken.) Two of a kind: tarpon, roosterfish and dorado. Others: 5 of a kind. In brackish and fresh water the

limits vary a lot, from 5 of a kind to 20, depending on which 'official' bulletin you happen to read. Use restraint not only for the law's sake but for conservation.

Closed seasons are usually enforced on major lakes. Ask a local person when you get there: "*¿Está en veda la pesca?*" (Is the fishing closed?) or "*¿Se puede pescar sin problemas con la ley?*" (Can one fish without problems with the law?) This question is obviously loaded, since most Mexican fishermen only observe the law when they absolutely have to.

Hunting & Guns

The Mexican government has a very definite attitude toward firearms — they don't want to have them in Mexico. The rules, regulations and fees required for legal hunting are so stiff that I won't bother to detail them here. If you are a very serious hunter write to Wildlife Advisory Services, P.O. Box 76132, Los Angeles, California, 90076 or call them at 213-385-9311. They'll explain everything and help you through the mass of paperwork involved.

Illegally importing a gun into Mexico is extremely stupid. If you are caught with a gun while travelling in Mexico the *least* that will happen will be a stiff fine, the loss of the weapon and a long hassle with the cops or Army. Mexicans often ask tourists to bring them guns but nothing will ruin your vacation faster than getting caught.

Mexico: It's The Law

Tourists enjoy almost all of the rights of full Mexican citizens. When tourists do run afoul of the law it is usually the result of drugs, auto accidents or immoral behavior.

For full details I suggest you read *The People's Guide To Mexico: Tourists and The Law.* Briefly, it is illegal to possess and use drugs (the usual types, from marijuana to pills and heroin) and dangerous to be around anyone who does. The Mexican police operate on the principle that it's easier to arrest everyone at the scene of a suspected crime and then sort out the guilty from the innocent later (sometimes a lot later).

Cougar   *Puma*

Uninsured motorists involved in an accident are almost assured of a visit to the local jail, especially if there is an injury. An insurance agent is much cheaper than a lawyer and works a good deal faster to get you out on the street again.

Immoral behavior almost always means public nudity, which is absolutely illegal and very offensive to most Mexicans. This is a constant problem for the Mexican authorities, especially with sun-loving European tourists who think nudity is natural rather than offensive. I don't like to involve myself in other people's affairs but when campers start stripping, I consider it self-protection to ask them to go elsewhere. If they won't, we consider moving.

Returning To the United States: The Border

Travellers returning from Mexico are allowed to bring $300 worth of gifts and souvenirs (each), duty free. If you go beyond the limit you might be charged duty at a flat rate of 10%.

As we approach the border we always jot down a list of the things we've bought in Mexico, from medicines to food and souvenirs. It's better to declare everything you have from Mexico. If something is prohibited you aren't liable to legal action or fines *if* you declare the item. I read of an unfortunate tourist who was convicted of smuggling coffee from Mexico into the U.S. It is not illegal to import coffee; his crime was in hiding the coffee (a hundred pounds) and not declaring that he had it.

Adults may bring in a quart of booze, any number of cigarettes but only 100 cigars, medicines accompanied by a U.S. prescription (or good excuse), peanuts, garlic, coffee beans, papayas and almost any food not grown in the United States. The list of restricted foods and souvenirs is long and complicated, but in general don't take citrus fruits, birds, anything of bone or hair or feather, ivory, meat, switch-blades, narcotics or hallucinogens, potted plants or pornography. What does this leave? For endless lists of approved and prohibited items write to: Superintendent of Documents, U.S. Government Printing Office, Washington, D.C. 20402. Ask for a copy of "Customs Hints for Returning U.S. Residents." If you want to return with a pet monkey or bird write: Commissioner of Customs, Washington, D.C. 20226. For importing plants write Import and Permit Section, Plant Quarantine Division, 209 River Street, Hoboken, NJ, 07030.

Appendices

Services

Banks

Banks are very common and easy to locate. The two largest are *Banco de Mexico* and *Banco de Comercio*. Exchange rates vary slightly from one bank to another but the bank rate is always better than that given by other businesses. I like to keep at least one to two hundred dollars in cash on hand at all times. By using a Hidden Pocket (see *Clothing:* Chapter 9) and reasonable precautions, we've never felt too nervous carrying cash.

A bank officer's initial is usually required to cash a traveller's check; just show your checks to any employee and they'll direct you to the proper desk or cashier. A charge for cashing traveller's checks, or for converting foreign currency to pesos, is normal.

Bank hours are 9 a.m. to 1:30 p.m., Monday through Friday. Checks may not be cashed after 1:00 p.m. in most banks.

Credit cards are widely accepted in Mexico.

U.S. dollars are commonly used in Baja, though it's best to have some pesos too.

Post Office

Postal service in Mexico is notoriously erratic and in small towns and villages it can be downright ridiculous. In one village near our camp the postmistress was illiterate; she relied on neighbors to decipher addresses and to complete postal forms.

Normal post office hours are 9 a.m. to 1 p.m., then a break for siesta, and open again from 3 p.m. to 6 p.m. on weekdays. Saturdays are 8 a.m. to 12 noon for mailing letters only. These hours vary, so don't be shocked if the P.O. is open on Sunday — or closed on a Monday.

Send all letters and post cards by airmail: *por avión*. Ask anyone writing to you from outside of Mexico to write the same on the envelope; it doesn't matter what postage they use as long as the Mexican postal people think it's airmail.

Most travellers receive mail at General Delivery (*Lista de Correos*). Tell your friends to write the address and name very clearly. It should look like this:

Abe Lincoln
Lista de Correos
Rebalcitos, Jalisco (city and state)
Mexico

Go to the post office and ask to see the *Lista* or just say "*¿Hay una carta para Abe Lincoln, por favor?*" Write the name on a slip of paper to avoid confusion.

For information on packages, certified mail, change of address and other postal mysteries see *The People's Guide to Mexico*.

Telegraph

The *Telégrafos* may be close to the Post Office — or it may be across town. Working hours are often longer than the post office. The fastest service is *urgente*.

Telegrams can be received at a specific address, at the telegraph office *Lista de Telégrafos* (most common) or at *Lista de Correos*.

Money can be wired to Mexico as a *giro* (money order) and will be paid at the office in pesos. *Giros* are reasonably fast but don't hold your breath, delays of ten days are not unusual.

Telephones

If you must call home by all means call collect or it will cost an arm and a leg. Look for *Larga Distancia* signs. Small businesses, especially restaurants, serve as Long Distance sub-offices. The best time to call the U.S. and Canada is early or late in the day. Write out the following information:

> *Por cobrar* (collect) or *Pago aquí* (I'll pay here)
> *A quien contesta* (station-to-station)
> City
> State
> Country
> Area code and number
> *De* (from): your name

A charge for services rendered is normal and if the call isn't completed and the operator tried very hard, this charge can be fairly high (a few dollars). Credit cards may or may not be accepted.

Recommended Reading

The following include my personal favorites on camping, travel and Mexico. For more suggestions, see *The People's Guide To Mexico*. Finding some of these books may not be easy, so I have included a few good sources to help you out.

Mexico Desconocido Magazine by Harry Moller. Editorial Novaro, S.A. Apartado Postal 6-751, Mexico 6 D.F. I list "Unknown Mexico" magazine first for the simple reason that it is *the best* camping publication on Mexico I've ever seen. Articles include boating, caving, fishing, hiking, back road driving, Mexican history and culture, archaeology, folk art, herbal medicine . . . you name it, one of their contributors has written about it. The Spanish is rather flowery but lots of information can be gleaned with a dictionary (or the Vocabulary in this book) and a little patience. Students of Spanish will find the magazine a refreshing way to improve their language abilities. The current price is 40 pesos an issue (monthly) or about two dollars. Write for subscription prices, in English if you wish, and a price list of their maps.

Where There Is No Doctor by David Werner, The Hesperian Foundation, Box 1692, Palo Alto, CA 94302. A truly great book: readable, practical advice designed to keep you healthy with a minimum of treatment and expense. Used extensively in the Third World and originally written on the basis of the author's extensive experience in Mexico's back country. A non-profit publication, also available in Spanish. Take at least one extra copy in Spanish to give away to someone who needs it.

Kayaks Down The Nile by John Goddard, Brigham Young University Press, Provo, UT 84602. I know, I know; the Nile River isn't even close to Mexico. This is such an enjoyable adventure story, however, that I just had to tell you about it.

Mexican Wilderness and Wildlife by Ben Tinker, University of Texas Press, Austin, TX. Ben Tinker was appointed Game Guardian of Sonora by President Obregon in 1923. This book, beautifully illustrated by Doris Tischler, draws on many years of travel, by foot and horseback, in remote regions of northwestern Mexico. Mr. Tinker was a rancher and hunter; his love and knowledge of Mexican wildlife made him unusually well suited to act as its protector. I especially enjoy the short chapter entitled *Desert Water*. He includes brief tips on how and where to observe big game. A fine book.

Trails of the Sierra Madre by Eugene Boudreau, Capra Press and Pleasant Hill Press, 2600 Pleasant Hill Road, Sebastopol, CA 95472. This is a short book but full of information and well worth reading. Eugene Boudreau knows a lot about northwestern Mexico, its people and their way of life. Specific suggestions for two walking or pack animal trips are given. The book is not new (1973) but like most well-thought-out books on Mexico's back country, the information is almost timeless. Boudreau's other books on the area are also good: *Ways of the Sierra Madre, R. F. Grigsby's Sierra Madre Journal: 1864* and *Move Over Don Porfirio: Tales from the Sierra Madre.*

Backpacking in Mexico and Central America by Hilary and George Bradt. Short (134 pages) but informative, though the Bradt Enterprises (409 Beacon Street, Boston, MA 02115) title is rather misleading: most of the book is about Central America, with the emphasis on hiking in parks. Nonetheless, the book should be valuable if you're heading south of Mexico.

Roughing It Easy by Dian Thomas, Brigham Young University Press and Warner Books. Basically an 'idea book', with suggestions on everything from selecting a campsite to baking pineapple upsidedown cake on an open fire. A very good book, one that appeals to people who like to improvise gear. Many of the cooking hints involve homemade utensils from tin cans. With this book and a pair of sharp tin snips, you can become a self-trained metalsmith. Volume Two has more ideas but repeats much of Volume One.

Packrat Papers edited by Betty Mueller, Signpost Books, 8912 192nd SW, Edmonds, WA 98020. Subtitled *Tips on food (and other stuff) for campers, backpackers, and those who travel lightly.* There are two volumes, each about 90 pages, absolutely loaded with interesting tips and information. This collection was gleaned from issues of *Signpost Magazine,* one of the oldest and best camping publications to be found.

Make It and Take It: Homemade Gear For Camp and Trail by Russ Mohney, Pacific Search Press, 715 Harrison St., Seattle, WA 98109. Covers do-it-yourself cookware, fishing gear, seafood traps, packs, self-inflating mattresses, tents, camera hitches, utility bags and more, including a turkey call. Very clearly written and illustrated. A book that can obviously save you money. Note: the publisher also does nice cookbooks; ask for a catalog.

Backpacking One Step At A Time by Harvey Manning, Vintage Books/Random House. Outdoor 'how to' books tend to be as dry and flavorless as a two-year-old freeze dried breakfast. Manning is a fine exception to what I call the All Is Sacred In Nature school of writing; his book treats the subject with humor, warmth and feeling. Look at this book first; the man is obviously an expert.

Walking Softly In The Wilderness by John Hart. This is the Sierra Club's guide to backpacking: comprehensive, well illustrated and obviously authoritative.

Camping and Climbing in Baja by John W. Robinson, La Siesta Press, Box 406, Glendale, CA. Another oldie (1967) but goodie; I keep running across copies in used book stores. Detailed information, including trail directions, maps and nice photos.

Wild Rivers of North America by Michael Jenkinson, E. P. Dutton & Co., New York. Mostly about rivers in the U.S. but also includes the Rio Coco in Nicaragua, the Rio Patuca in Honduras and the Usumacinta and Santiago in Mexico. A good book, one that should be available in paperback — but isn't. The same author has done *Land of Clear Light* (Dutton), a very nice descriptive work that covers the American Southwest, the Sierra Madre of Mexico and Baja. Well written, with many excellent photos by Karl Kernberger.

A Field Guide to the Gems and Minerals of Mexico by Paul W. Johnson, Gembooks, Mentone, CA (1965). A detailed guide to mineral and gem collecting, one that we use not for 'rock hounding' but to locate interesting hiking and camping areas. Mining is usually done in places that are rugged and scenic. This book, unfortunately, is hard to find; I got one copy at a jeweler's supply shop, another at a flea market.

To Hell On Wheels: The Illustrated Manual of Desert Survival, by Alan H. Siebert, Brown Burro Press, P.O. Box 2863-D, Pasadena, CA 91105. Short and to the point: desert survival for the driver and hiker, with good information on snakebites, water, exposure, getting lost, foraging food and more. Well worth studying.

Foraging Along The California Coast by Peter Howorth, Capra Press, 631 State St., Santa Barbara, CA 93101. How to find and collect everything from clams to striped bass, with good clear tips on equipment, cleaning and preparation and recipes. Nice illustrations by Jane Jolley Howorth. The book applies to much of Mexico as well as California; I recommend it highly.

Guía Campista Paradores de México, Apdo Postal 177, Tlalnepantla, Edo. de México, México. This is a very basic guide to Mexican trailer parks and campgrounds. The Spanish is simple to translate, though the maps tend to be blurred and difficult to read. I have not used this book but it seems fairly complete. One of its nicest features is in the back: addresses for natural gas stations, ice plants, pure water plants and much more. It costs about four dollars and is sold in Mexico at bookstores and sidewalk book stalls.

The Baja Book II by Tom Miller and Elmar Baxter. Baja Trail Publications, Huntington Beach, CA. $8.95. They also publish *Mexico West,* an informal newsletter and *The World of the California Gray Whale* (by Tom Miller, $4.). All nicely done.

Offbeat Baja by Jim Hunter. Chronicle Books, 870 Market St., San Francisco 94102. $4.95. I'll take this the next time we drive to Baja.

How To Keep Your Volkswagen Alive by John Muir. $11.00, John Muir Publications, Box 613, Santa Fe, NM 87501. If you don't have this book in your VW, get one; you'll certainly need it, if only to check what that mechanic is doing. Now in Spanish ($8.00). A great gift for a Spanish-speaking friend or *mecánico.*

How To Keep Your VW Rabbit Alive by Richard Sealy. $13.00, John Muir Publications, Box 613, Santa Fe, NM 87501. This book covers the Rabbit & Scirocco, including carburetors, diesel and fuel injection. Spiral bound and profusely illustrated by Peter Aschwanden.

Field Guides: Field guides tend to be expensive and heavy. Some nice small exceptions are published by Minutiae Mexicana, S.A. de C.V., Insurgentes Centro 114-210, Mexico 4, D.F. These mini-guides in English include Birds, Mammals, Flowers and others. Sold in Mexican bookstores.

Book Sources

Don't overlook the local library; I often find out-of-print books on travel in Mexico in the stacks of the library that are truly fascinating. A true classic, for example, is *The Enchanted Vagabonds* by Lamb. One of the finest books ever written on life and travel in Mexico's back country is *Unknown Mexico* by Lumholtz. After more than 75 years his information is still quite useful.

If you can't find a book, ask your local bookstore to check for it in *Books In Print*. This massive reference book has everything you need to locate a publication.

The San Diego Map Centre: A fine collection of books on Mexico, with a strong emphasis on Baja. See *Maps and Sources*.

Tolliver's Books, 1634 S. Stearns Drive, Los Angeles, CA 90035. New, used and out-of-print books on "Life and Earth Sciences," a broad term, since they carry everything from guidebooks to scientific monographs. Tell them your interest and they'll send you a specific catalog that will drive you wild with temptation. Book lovers beware: they've got something for everyone.

The Rio Grande Press, Inc., Glorieta, NM 87535. Fine reprints of classic works on the Southwest and Mexico. These are the kind of books you won't loan out casually.

Maps and Sources

In the late 1950's the Mexican Society Of History And Geography estimated that 75% of Mexico was essentially unmapped and unknown, except in a general sense. In 1968 a program of detailed mapping was begun, relying heavily on aerial photography. This project is still incomplete, though a great deal of progress has been made. This means that detailed and *accurate* maps of Mexico are hard to come by and for some areas, next to impossible. What's the solution, especially if you plan to travel into a remote area? Gather as many different maps as you can and compare them constantly. This leads to unexpected discoveries and revelations: if a river is shown on two out of three maps, there's a reasonable chance that it actually exists. Do your maps agree on the location of a huge canyon in a relatively rainy area but show no river at the bottom? Logic tells you, even if the maps don't, that there's water there and perhaps a lot of it, especially during the late summer rains.

Learning to read maps doesn't require special skills, just a good dose of imagination. Can you identify a maguey plant from a fuzzy photo in a field guide? I couldn't; it takes more than one view or angle and time to compare the suspected maguey with other, similar plants. The same is true of maps; once you're familiar with each map's idiosyncrasies and shortcomings your mind will combine these images to form a clearer, overall picture of the countryside.

The following types and sources of maps are the best and most obvious I could find. Keep an eye open, however, for unexpected sources of maps. *The Handbook of American Indians*, for example, publishes hundreds of very small and very detailed maps in its scholarly works. These maps are for the use of archaeologists and anthropologists but by carefully comparing them to larger-scale maps, you can find details that are otherwise unavailable. Don't overlook old maps from outdated guidebooks, magazines and scholarly works. Many are still accurate, especially for the back country, and may even have been used as the basis for a supposedly 'new' map.

Road Maps: I call these gas station maps since that's where most people will find them. Unless you plan a trip into remote country or have the urge to travel little-known roads and waterways, a basic selection of tourist-oriented road maps should be sufficient. The absolute best of these are included in a series of maps I wouldn't go to Mexico without, the *Carta Turística* (described later).

Unfortunately, road maps are not handed out as liberally in Mexico as they are in the United States. In fact, it's easier to get a road map of Mexico in the U.S. Ask at gas stations near the border, tourist agencies, large hotels, insurance offices, bookstores and Mexican Consulate and National Tourism offices. Get two maps; you'll lose or absentmindedly start a campfire with one.

Members of AAA (American Automobile Association) will be given free Mexican road maps and driving logs upon request. Sanborn's Insurance Company also gives away free road logs. Most insurance companies offer some type of map, though they are rarely up-to-date or as good as the *Carta Turística*.

Carta Turística: There are six maps in this series, each covering a different region of Mexico. You just can't beat these maps; they are inexpensive, fairly detailed (much more detailed than any gas station map), accurate, entertaining to read and educational. There's just one hitch: the maps are relatively large and relatively hard to find (see *Sources*). Each map is a guidebook in itself, with a great deal of information on points of special interest, from waterfalls to historic sites. They are available in English (though I've yet to see one), but the Spanish version is easy to translate and the road map side is almost identical on both.

Serie Patria: These road maps are commonly known as the Blue Series or Serie Azul because of their bright blue cover. Each map covers one state and gives a brief history of the state and a chart indicating tourist facilities and attractions, in relatively simple Spanish. The back of each map has good city maps for the state. The Serie Azul is reasonably accurate but not much good for hikers or back country travellers, except for general orientation. Available in Mexican bookstores and not expensive. Issued also by Libería Patria, S.A., Cinco de Mayo 43, Mexico, D.F.

Atlases: The word "atlas" tends to conjure up an image of a huge book the size of a hatch cover. Fortunately, a good atlas of road maps, state by state, is available in magazine format from *Mexico Desconocido* magazine (see *Sources*). These maps are basic, with no frills, but that's often what you want when you're barrelling down the highway, madly trying to decide "left or right" with a second class bus on your tail.

A much more detailed atlas is published by Editorial Porrua (Argentina 15, Mexico 1, D.F.). It is called the *Nuevo Atlas Porrúa de la República Mexicana* and costs less than ten dollars. Like most standard atlases it has more details than you can absorb in a year, including such fascinating information as the amount of refined zinc exported in 1974.

Topographic Maps: Only a portion of Mexico (mainly the central region) has been mapped topographically and not all of those maps are always in print. Your best bet, by far, is to write or call the San Diego Map Centre (see *Sources*). I also recommend a visit to the central offices of CGNSI in Mexico City (see *Sources*). This is the agency that produces the topo maps. You can see what they have and if it meets your requirements. In general, our experience has been that topo maps aren't nearly as accurate as those in the U.S. They are also relatively expensive, especially if you need several to cover a proposed trip or an area of interest. Major foot trails may not be shown, rivers are missing, villages misplaced and so on. This doesn't make them useless; just keep on your toes and orient yourself with major ridges and mountains.

Aeronautical Charts: Large scale aeronautical charts are published by the U.S. Department of Commerce, National Oceanic and Atmospheric Administration, National Ocean Survey C-44, Riverdale, MD 20840. Four big charts cover all of Mexico, Guatemala and Belize. These charts are cheap and surprisingly accurate. We prefer them, mainly because of cost, over topo maps, and use them for boating as well as backpacking or back road exploring.

Sea Charts: Charts of Mexican waters (including those used by the Mexican Navy) are published by the U.S. Defense Mapping Agency, 5801 Tabor Avenue, Philadelphia, PA 19120. Ask for their catalog. They are slow in responding so do it early.

These charts are designed for ship navigation; if you are going by small boat or kayak an appropriate aeronautical chart or *Carta Turística* is just about as good, though it never hurts to have another view.

Mountain Climbing: Photo maps/charts showing climbing routes up three mountains near Mexico City (Iztaccihuatl, Citlaltepetl and Popocatepetl) are available from *Mexico Desconocido* magazine (see *Sources*). The reproduction is not of the best quality but the maps would obviously be useful to a climber.

Guatemala: Road maps of Guatemala are hard to find, especially in Guatemalan gas stations. Topo maps are even worse; because of the military situation most of Guatemala is "classified" and maps are not sold to the public. Ironically, you can buy Guatemalan topo maps in the U.S. from Guatemala. Write to Instituto Geográfico Nacional, Avenida Las Americas 5-76, Zona 13, Guatemala, C.A.

Map Sources

San Diego Map Centre: If you're feeling slightly confused and discouraged by now about Mexican maps, I really can't blame you. Collecting a good set of maps takes time, patience and a little money. Fortunately the San Diego Map Centre can relieve a great deal of the burden. They stock the *Carta Turística*, Serie Azul, Mexican topo maps, aeronautical charts and who-knows-what-else? Their service is good, prices fair and what more do you need? I love the place (especially their book selection on Mexico and particularly Baja). They have no main catalog but will give information based on your particular needs or interest. Write them at 2611 University Avenue, San Diego, CA 92104 or call 714-291-3830.

Mexico Desconocido Magazine: You can write to the office of Unknown Mexico magazine in English if you wish. They stock the *Carta Turística* (25 pesos; about $1.15 as of this writing) and the Atlas de Carreteras (50 pesos or $2.30). Because their costs will undoubtedly go up by the time you read this I suggest that you add at least 20% to these prices to cover inflation and postage.

The mountain-climbing maps of Iztaccihuatl, Citlaltepetl and Popocatepetl are 50 pesos each ($2.30), from *Mexico Desconocido*.

Coordinación General Nacional del Sistema de Información: CGNSI used to be known as Detenal, which used to be known as Cetenal. Fortunately their office doesn't change as often as their name. It is at Balderas 71 in Mexico City and easily reached by Metro (subway). Their showroom is a great place to browse and includes topo maps, climate maps and many others. Maps and books are sold in the mezzanine and I found the staff to be very helpful. They assured me that visitors who do not speak Spanish would be accommodated — in sign language if necessary. If you are planning an ambitious trip into a remote region I suggest that you check their stock of maps. Maps can also be ordered by mail. Write to Agencia CGNSI Balderas, Balderas No. 71, México 6, D.F., attn/Ing. Martin Galindo, Oficina de Ventas. Orders must be paid by certified check or money order. Their catalog is free upon request.

Other offices have a smaller stock of maps but are definitely worth visiting. They include:

San Antonio Abad No. 124, México 8, D.F.
Balderas No. 71, México, D.F. (one block from Hidalgo Metro station).
Centro Civico Comercial, 16 Septiembre 734, Guadalajara, Jalisco.
Cuauhtémoc 734, Monterrey, N.L.
M. de Cervantes S. 201-F, León, Gto.

Equipment Sources

Trial and error is an effective teacher but when it comes to buying camping equipment the errors can be both costly and frustrating. Over the years we have developed a list of hints that I suggest you take seriously.

• Quality, prices and service can vary dramatically from one company to another; your only assurance of getting what you want, when you want it — and at a good price — is to start requesting catalogs months in advance. Look them over carefully, comparing not only item prices but also shipping charges, guarantees and special deals. REI, for example, gives a yearly rebate to members. They also offer a toll free ordering number. When I want to order from them, I make a free call to inquire if the item is in stock. This avoids delays and misunderstandings. You can also take advantage of toll free ordering numbers to ask technical questions that may not be explained in the catalog.

• Don't order anything until you've got all the catalogs you need to make a detailed cost comparison. List everything you need on a sheet of paper, then write down the prices from each company. A quick look will tell you which company gives the best bargains.

• If you don't want substitutions, say so on your order form. Think this over; do you really care if your tent pegs are red or yellow? If not, mark "no substitutions" only on items that you really care about. After all, the tent model is important but the pegs aren't so critical.

• When time is limited don't accept back orders. They'll hold your money (if you send a check) until the item is back in stock. This can take lots of time.

• Before spending large amounts of money, make an initial small order to test quality and service. This is time consuming but it can save a lot of headaches in the long run. A good mail order supplier will fill your order fast. Any order that is delayed more than three weeks is too slow, no matter what excuse you may be given.

Recreational Equipment, Inc. (REI Coop), P.O. Box C-88125, Seattle, WA 98188. REI is *big* and handles everything from ski equipment to mountaineering and backpacking gear. Prices and service are good; they have a toll free ordering number.

Indiana Camp Supply Inc., P.O. Box 344, Pittsboro, IN 46167. Indiana's catalog costs $1.00. It is done on cheap newsprint and looks fairly funky. On the other hand, they have good prices and gave us the best service of any large mail order house. Their selection of first-aid items and books is outstanding.

Eastern Mountain Sports, Inc., Vose Farm Road, Peterborough, NH 03458. A big company, with a catalog similar to REI's.

The Ski Hut, P.O. Box 309, Berkeley, CA 94701. Disregard their name; this company has a wide assortment of outdoor gear.

Early Winters, 110 Prefontaine Place South, Seattle, WA 98104. Unusual and interesting (and often rather expensive) outdoor equipment, though not as broad a selection as the companies listed above.

The North Face, 4560 University Way NE, Seattle, WA 98105. Tents, bags, clothing and some general camping gear.

Stephenson's, RFD 4, Box 398, Gilford, NH 03246. Tents, packs, bags, etc. of their own design and manufacture. The catalog costs $3 but they swear that it's worth it if you're serious about equipment. *Note:* ignore nude models if they offend you.

Mountain Safety Research, 631 S. 96th St., Seattle, WA 98108. A small catalog with one big feature: the MSR stove. Model GK burns (they say) everything from Coleman fuel and unleaded auto and aviation gasoline to kerosene, solvent and No. 1 diesel. This stove is expensive but it would obviously be ideal for world travellers and campers who cannot depend on reliable fuel replenishment.

Campmor, 205 West Shore Ave., Bogota, NJ 07603. General camping gear.

Northwest River Supplies, 214 N. Main, P.O. Box 9186, Moscow, ID 83843. In dealing with this company we have found their quality, prices, service and good humor to be far better than most other mail order houses'. Highly recommended; they carry everything from rafts and wet suits to whitewater hardware, books and miscellaneous camping gear.

Klepper America, 35 Union Square West, N.Y., NY 10003, phone 212-CH3-3428. The best folding kayaks made, expensive but worth the money. Also rigid kayaks and accessories.

Eddyline Kayaks, 8423 Mukilteo Speedway, Everett, WA 98204, phone 206-743-9252. High quality, advanced design whitewater and touring kayaks. We will be testing an Eddyline ocean touring kayak on a long trip in the Sea of Cortez. Few kayak manufacturers put the kind of thought into ocean-going boats that we see in Eddyline's.

Sevylor, 213 Louisville Air Park, Louisville, KY 40213. Inflatable runabouts, kayaks and rafts. Sevylor boats are handled by some K Mart, Penney's and Montgomery Wards stores.

Old Town Canoe Company, Old Town, ME 04468. High quality canoes.

Easy Rider Kayaks, P.O. Box 88108, Tukwila Branch, 15666 West Valley Highway, Seattle, WA 98188, phone 206-228-3633. Good quality kayaks, including large capacity touring models.

Moor & Mountain, 63 Park St., Andover, MA 01810. A wide selection, from kayaks and canoes to a long list of books.

Nippenose, 330 Government Place, Williamsport, PA 17701. Canoes, kayaks and accessories.

Seda Products, P.O. Box 997, Chula Vista, CA 92012. Canoes, kayaks and accessories.

Voyageur's, Ltd., P.O. Box 409, Gardner, KS 66030, phone 913-764-7755. Waterproof gear bags, flotation bags and other boating accessories.

Chicagoland Canoe Base, Inc., 4019 N. Narragansett, Chicago, IL 60634, phone 312-777-1489. Canoes, kayaks and accessories.

Fishing Gear

Cabela's, 812 13th Ave., Sidney, NE 69162. An extensive catalog of fishing tackle and camping gear. Their prices are very good but we found their service to be awful; less than half of our order was filled. Refunds are given, of course, but unfulfilled orders are terribly inconvenient.

Robinson & Son, Ltd., 321 Central Ave., White Plains, NY 10606. As with Cabela's, this company puts out a very large catalog but doesn't seem to deliver the goods. I hope these two suppliers get on the stick and fulfill their obligation to their customers.

Bass Pro Shops, P.O. Box 4046, Springfield, MO 65804. Their complete catalog is $2.00 and it is huge and beautiful. Even if you aren't a bass fanatic you'll find good buys on fishing tackle. They also carry clothing and miscellaneous camping gear, with a heavy emphasis on gift items. We found their service to be good.

Netcraft Fishing Tackle Co., 2800 Tremainsville Rd., Toledo, OH 43613. Lots of tackle, nets and miscellaneous boating stuff. I haven't used this company but their catalog is quite interesting.

Diving Gear

I prefer to buy my diving gear in person, to avoid costly mistakes and disappointments. Although I have not dealt with the companies listed, their prices look good and their gear is high quality. When in doubt about diving gear, give the company a call and ask questions; it could save you money in the long run.

Danny's Dive Shop, 1579 Grand Ave., Baldwin, NY 11510.

M & E Marine Supply, Box 601, Camden, NJ 08101. Their catalog of diving gear costs $2.00 and covers just about everything you can think of. A catalog of boating gear is also $2.00.

Sub Aqua Specialties, 206 East Hill Ave., Valdosta, GA 31601. Good prices and a toll free ordering number.

Offroad Vehicle Gear

Dick Cepek, Inc., 5302 Tweedy Blvd., South Gate, CA 90280. All sorts of equipment for offroad vehicles, plus books and some camping gear.

Kits: Make It & Save $

Frostline Kits, Frostline Circle, Denver, CO 80241. The usual routine is to put off ordering a kit until it's too late and you are forced to pay full price for your gear. Send for a catalog now, even if you aren't sure you want to do-it-yourself.

Holubar Kits, 3650 S. Bristol St., Santa Ana, CA 92704.

Note: See *Recommended Reading* earlier in the *Appendices* for a good book on do-it-yourself camping gear.

Guided Tours & Adventures

There is no doubt that a good tour guide can save you a great deal of time and frustration when planning a trip in Mexico. It pays, however, to contact such people well in advance. Trips often depend on the climate and the number of interested clients. Under-booked trips may be cancelled, leaving you in the lurch, or you may learn that Baja is just too hot in August for kayaking.

Tour operators sometimes offer more than they deliver. In preparing this section, for example, over a dozen organizations contacted did not respond at all to our queries. Several others responded very slowly. A careful review of brochures may also reveal that the tour isn't what you really want. Some groups have strict restrictions on minimum age, others advise that you be in excellent physical condition. Whatever your interests or limitations may be, I advise you to be clear and honest; five days into a jungle trek is no time to announce that your pacemaker has a dead battery.

Don't hesitate to ask for a list of references. A few phone calls to past clients might provide a clearer idea of what to expect — and not expect — than the promoter's gushing brochures.

Finally, if you have information on trips that are not listed here, please write to me c/o John Muir Publications with full particulars.

Sierra Club, 530 Bush St., San Francisco, CA 94108. Tours in southern Mexico; Usumacinta river rafting; Baja overland and whale watching; Sea of Cortez "leisure boat trip."

National Outdoor Leadership School, P.O. Box AA, Lander, WY 82520, phone 307-332-4381. Wilderness camping and boating in southern Baja.

Wilderness World, 1342 Jewell Ave., Pacific Grove, CA 93950, phone 408-373-5882. Some raft trips but emphasis on overland travel in Mexico, Baja and Guatemala.

Questers Tours and Travel, Inc., 257 Park Ave. S., NY, NY 10010. Trips in southern Mexico, Guatemala, Belize and Honduras.

Oceanic Expeditions, 240 Fort Mason, San Francisco, CA 94123. Cruising, sailing, diving and snorkelling in Belize.

Sacred Monkey Expeditions, Box 363, Jerome, AZ 86331. Rafting on the Usumacinta and Jataté (Chiapas) and jungle treks.

Pacific Adventures, P.O. Box 5041, Riverside, CA, phone 714-684-1227. Tours in Baja and the Yucatán; island hopping, sailing, diving, kayaking in the Sea of Cortez; climbing and horseback trips in Baja.

Baja's Frontier Tours, 4365 New Jersey, San Diego, CA 92116, phone 714-464-1998. Whale watching, mule trips, camping or specialized trips upon request.

Infinite Odyssey, 14A Union Park St., Boston, MA 02118. Hiking and mountain climbing in Mexico.

Nature Expeditions International, 599 College Ave., Palo Alto, CA 94306, phone 415-328-6752. Camping and boating tours in Mexico, Baja and Guatemala.

High Country Passage, P.O. Box 1100, Hamilton, MT 59840, phone 406-363-2555. Hiking and canoeing in Guatemala.

Lighthouse Reef Expeditions, Ltd., P.O. Box 1249, Turlock, CA 95380, phone 209-634-1133. Boating and diving in Belize.

Nantahala Outdoor Center, Star Route, Box 68, Bryson City, NC 28713, phone 704-488-2175. Rafting and kayaking in Mexico, Guatemala and Belize.

Expediciones Nautilus/Mexamerica S.A., Paseo de la Reforma No. 92, Mezz., Mexico, D.F. Raft trips on Mezcala, Moctezuma, Usumacinta and Lower Amacuzac rivers. Short and inexpensive. Ask a travel agent in Mexico for details.

Nature Expeditions International, P.O. Box 1173, Los Altos, CA 94022. A variety of trips in Mexico, Baja and Guatemala.

The Educational Cooperative, Suite 2129, 176 W. Adams, Chicago, IL 60603. Minibus and camping trips in Mexico, Guatemala and Belize.

The Wilderness Institute, 333 Fairfax St., Denver, CO 80220. Mountain climbing in Mexico.

REI Adventure Travel, 1525 11th Ave., Seattle, WA 98122, phone 206-323-8333. Mountain climbing in Mexico.

Tracks To Mexico, P.O. Box 10200, El Paso, TX 79993, phone 915-779-3002. RV tours "piggyback" by train and ferry.

Point South Caravan Tours, 5309 Garden Grove Ave., Tarzana, CA 91356, phone 213-344-8687. RV caravan tours in Mexico and Central America.

The Mexican Peso

In 1976 the Mexican *peso* was devalued. What does this mean? Previous to 1976 each dollar was equivalent to 12.5 *pesos*. After devaluation each dollar was worth *more pesos*. Devaluation increases the number of *pesos* in each dollar and decreases the value, in dollars, of each *peso*. This means you pay even less for goods and services in Mexico. For example: a beer that cost 10 *pesos* in 1975 (equal at that time to 80 cents U.S.) and 10 *pesos* in 1977 has dropped in price to 44 cents U.S. If the *peso* is devalued while you are in Mexico, things will get even cheaper (see *Peso/Dollar Conversion Table*).

Dollars To Pesos

	Each *Peso* is worth (in cents)								
	4.66	4.4	4.35	4.2	4	3.85	3.6	3.3	2.9
	Pesos in each Dollar								
$ 1	21.5	22.5	23	24	25	26	28	30	35
$ 2	42	45.0	46	48	50	52	56	60	70
$ 3	63	67.5	69	72	75	78	84	90	115
$ 4	84	90	92	96	100	104	112	120	140
$ 5	105	112.5	115	120	125	130	140	150	175
$ 6	126	135	138	144	150	156	168	180	210
$ 7	147	157.5	161	168	175	182	196	210	245
$ 8	168	180	184	192	200	208	224	240	280
$ 9	189	202.5	207	216	225	234	252	270	315
$10	210	225	230	240	250	260	280	300	350
$20	420	450	460	480	500	520	560	600	700
$50	1050	1125	1150	1200	1250	1300	1400	1500	1750
$75	1575	1688	1725	1800	1875	1950	2100	2250	2625

Weights and Measures

1 quart . . . . .95 liters	1 inch . . . . .2.54 centimeters
1 gallon . . . . .3.875 liters	1 foot . . . . .30.5 centimeters
5 gallons . . . . .19.4 liters	1 yard . . . . .91.5 centimeters
10 gallons . . . . .38.75 liters	or .915 meters
15 gallons . . . . .58.1 liters	
20 gallons . . . . .77.5 liters	centimeter . . . . .39 inches
25 gallons . . . . .96.9 liters	meter . . . . .3.28 feet
	kilometer . . . . .62 miles
2.2 pounds . . . . . . .1000 grams (1 kilo)	1 mile . . . . .1.61 kilometers
1 pound . . . . .454 grams	
1/2 pound . . . . .227 grams	
1/4 pound . . . . .113.5 grams	
1 ounce . . . . .28.35 grams	

To Convert:

- Temperature in degrees F to Centigrade: $°F - 32 \times 5.5 = °C$.
- Temperature in degrees C to Fahrenheit: $°C + 17.8 \times 1.8 = °F$.
- Multiply *liters* by .26 to get *gallons*.
- Multiply *gallons* by 3.8 to get *liters*.
- Multiply *kilometers* by .62 to get *miles*.
- Divide *miles* by .62 to get *kilometers*.

Temperatures °F-°C

65°F . . . . .18.3°C	103.0°F . . . . .39.4°C
70°F . . . . .21.1°C	104.0°F . . . . .40.0°C
75°F . . . . .23.9°C	105.0°F . . . . .40.6°C
80°F . . . . .26.7°C	106.0°F . . . . .41.1°C
85°F . . . . .29.4°C	
90°F . . . . .32.2°C	250°F . . . . .121°C
95°F . . . . .35.0°C	275°F . . . . .135°C
98.6°F . . . . .37.0°C	300°F . . . . .149°C
99.0°F . . . . .37.2°C	325°F . . . . .163°C
99.5°F . . . . .37.5°C	350°F . . . . .177°C
100.0°F . . . . .37.8°C	375°F . . . . .191°C
100.5°F . . . . .38.1°C	400°F . . . . .204°C
101.0°F . . . . .38.3°C	450°F . . . . .232°C
101.5°F . . . . .38.6°C	500°F . . . . .260°C
102.0°F . . . . .38.9°C	550°F . . . . .288°C

Vocabulary

Words are listed in English and Spanish by general topics. In cases where a word is not easily translated it will be listed in Spanish and a definition given in English. The term *mueble,* for example, means "furniture" in the dictionary but is used in northern and rural Mexico for "vehicle." It is listed under General.

The Spanish used in the back country tends to be much simpler than you might expect. The term *"feo,"* for example, not only means "ugly" but also means rough, harsh, unpleasant, uncomfortable (the weather is *"feo"*), uncooperative . . . Country people are close-mouthed; you'll soon learn how they manage to convey a great deal in few words.

Diminutives are very important in Mexican Spanish. *"Hace calor"* (It is hot out) becomes *"Hace un calorcito"* (It is a little hot out). The "little" in this case actually means hotter, not cooler. *"Esta lejicitos"* (It's a little far) is farther away than just *"lejos."*

Use your imagination when you are at a loss for a word. What's the common term for "barren country" in Mexico? In almost every case, *"No hay nada"* (There is nothing) will be used to describe such a place. *"Monte,"* the word for forest and jungle (often confused by gringos with "mountain") can be simply modified to mean "high jungle" or "thick forest" by saying *"monte alto"* or *"puro monte."*

A special note: in Mexico the words stupid (*estupido*), *idiota* and *payaso* (clown) are very insulting in most circumstances and are not used casually to describe a person or their actions. Insults of any kind are best kept out of your working vocabulary; their power is too often destructive.

In describing animals, such as a burro, do not say *"El burro de Juan"* to mean "John's burro." In Mexico, this is heard instead as John-the-burro. The correct form is *"El burro es de Juan"* (The burro is "of" John). It's one of those easily made mistakes that can be embarrassing to all concerned.

Camping Gear, Tools & Hardware, Odds & Ends

acetylene torch	*soplete oxiacetilenico,*	blade	*hoja*
	autógeno	blanket	*cobija, frazada,*
allen wrench	*llave de alán*		*cubierta*
aluminum	*aluminio*	bolt	*tornillo*
axe	*hacha*	bottle	*botella, pomo*
ayate	carrying net	5 gallon	*garrafón*
backpack	*mochila*	box	*caja, cartón*
bag	*bolsa, costal,*	box end wrench	*llave ástria*
	morral	blacksmith	*herrero*
barrel	*tambor, tambo,*	broken	*roto, quebrado*
	barril, tinaco	bucket	*cubeta, cubo, balde*
basket	*canasta, cesto*	cable	*cable*
battery	*pila, batería*	canteen	*cantimplora*
bent	*doblado, chueco*	carbide	*carburo*

Camping Gear, Tools & Hardware, Odds & Ends (Cont'd)

catalyst	*catalizador*	*huacal*	stick box
CB radio	*transceptor, CB*	ice chest	*hielera*
chain	*cadena*	inflatable	*inflable, . . . de aire*
charcoal	*carbón*	iron	*férreo*
charcoal stove	*avafre, brasero*	*jícara*	gourd
chingado	all screwed up	key	*llave*
	(impolite)	knife	*cuchillo, navaja*
chisel	*cincel*	knot	*nudo*
clamp	*abrazadera*	lamp chimney (glass)	*bombilla*
compass	*brújula*	lantern	*linterna*
cord	*cuerda*	lariat	*riata*
cot	*catre*	lightbulb	*foco*
cotter pin	*chaveta*	lighter	*encendedor*
crescent wrench	*perico*	Liquid Wrench	*Afloja Todo*
crowbar	*barra*	lock	*cerradura, retén*
dog cage, house	*perrera*	luggage	*equipaje*
drill & bits	*taladro y brocas*	mantle (lantern)	*camisa, capuchón,*
emery paper	*lija de esmeril*		*mecha*
enamelware	*peltre*	map	*mapa*
epoxy	*epoxy*	mat	*petate*
equipment	*equipo, trastos*	mattress	*colchón*
extension cord	*cuerda, cable de*	air	*colchón de aire*
	extensión	mosquito net	*pabellón, mosquitero*
fiberglass	*fibra de vidrio*	nail	*clavo*
file	*lima*	needle	*aguja*
film; 35mm	*rollo; rollo para*	needle-nosepliers	*alicates*
	transparencias,	nut	*tuerca*
	diapositiva (slide)	open end wrench	*llave española*
filter	*filtro*	padlock	*candado*
flare	*bengala*	patch	*parche*
flashlight	*foco, luz*	phillips screwdriver	*desarmador decruz*
flit gun	*rociador*	pin	*perno*
foam rubber	*espuma de ule*	pipe	*pipa, tubo*
folding	*plegable*	pipe wrench	*llave stillson*
fuel	*combustible*	plastic sheet	*plastíco, ule*
funnel	*embudo*	pliers	*pinzas*
gate	*puerta, portal*	plug	*tapón, tapadera*
gear, provisions	*menesteres*	pole	*palo*
glue	*pegamiento, Resistol*	portable	*portátil*
gourd	*jícara*	pump	*bomba*
grease	*grasa*	ratchet	*matraca, llave de*
grill	*parilla*		*trinquete*
hack saw	*cegeta*	razor	*navaja*
hammer	*martillo*	refrigerator	*refrigerador*
hammock	*hamaca*	rivet	*remache*
hardware store	*ferretería*	rope	*mecate, soga*
hatchet	*hacha, hachachica*	RV	VR (*vehículo*
helmet	*casco*		*recreativo*)
hose	*mangera, tubo*	saddle	*silla de montar*

Camping Gear, Tools & Hardware, Odds & Ends (Cont'd)

sandpaper	*papel de lija*	thread	*hilo*
scissors	*tijeras*	tin	*lámina, hoja de lata*
screw	*tornillo*	tin snips	*tijeras para lámina*
screwdriver	*desarmador*	tools	*herramientas, fierros*
sharpening stone	*afiladera*	top, plug	*tapón, tapadera*
sheet metal	*lámina*	torch	*antorcha, bengala, so-*
shovel	*pala*		*plete* (pressurized)
siphon	*sifón*	tow	*remolque*
sleeping bag	*bolsa de dormir*	tow truck	*grúa, remolque*
socket	*soquet, dado*	trailer	*trayler, remolque, casa*
socket extension	*extensión*		*rodante* (house)
socket wrench	*llave de dado*	transceiver	*transceptor*
solder	*soldadura*	trap	*trampa*
soldering iron	*soldador*	rodent	*ratonera*
sponge	*esponja*	truck	*camioneta, pickup*
sprayer	*rociador*		*troque, camión* (big)
spring	*resorte*	tub	*tina, tinaco*
stake	*estaca*	twine	*hilillo, hilo, cuerda*
stainless steel	*acero inoxidable*	*vado*	dip or ford
stirrup	*estribo*	van	*combi, camioneta*
stove	*estufa*	vehicle	*vehículo, mueble*
strap, belt	*cincho*	vise	*tornillo*
string	*cuerda, hilillo*	vise grip pliers	*pinzas depresión*
stuck	*pegado*	washer	*rondana*
swimming pool	*alberca, balneario,*	water pump pliers	*pinzas de extensión*
	piscina	wick	*mecha*
tank	*tanque, tinaja*	winch	*malacate, winch*
tape	*cinta*	wire	*alambre*
electrical	*cinta de plástico*	wrench	*llave*
tarp	*lona, carpa*	zipper	*cierre, zípper*
tent	*casita de campaña,*		
	tiendade campaña		

Boating, Fishing, Diving, Hunting

aboard	*a bordo*	bite (fishing)	*un tirón*
anchor	*ancla, arana*	boat, large	*barco*
anchor, to	*anclar, dar fondo*	small	*lancha, bote, chalupa*
anchorage	*fondeadero*	folding	*plegable*
aqualung	*acualón*	motor	*motonauta*
arrow	*flecha*	boatman	*lanchero*
arrowhead	*punta de flecha*	bottom (sea)	*fondo*
bait	*carnada*	bow (archery)	*arco*
bar	*barra*	brackish	*salobre*
barge	*chalana*	breeze, sea	*brisa de mar*
bay	*bahía*	land	*brisa de tierra*
beach	*playa, litoral*	brine	*salmuera*

Boating, Fishing, Diving, Hunting (Cont'd)

bufa	rock, pinnacle	freshwater	*agua dulce*
bullet	*bala*	gaffhook	*gancho, garfio*
shot	*balazo, tiro*	ground swell	*marejada*
calms (river)	*remansos*	gun	*arma*
canal	*canal*	.22	*veintidos*
canoe	*canoa*	hook	*anzuelo, gancho*
dugout	*cayuco, bongo, chalupa*	hunt, to	*cazar*
cape	*cabo*	hunting	*cacería*
captain	*capitán*	inflatable	*inflable*
cartridge	*cartucho*	kayak	*kayak*
cast (fishing)	*firo, lanzamiento*	lake	*lago, presa, laguna*
cast, to	*tirar, lanzar*	lagoon	*laguna, estero*
cataract	*catarata*	land a boat	*barrar*
catch, to	*sacar*	launch a boat	*embarcar, echar al*
channel	*canal*		*agua, botar*
river	*cauce*	launching	*botadura*
coral	*coral*	launch ramp	*rampa*
corrales	fish camp	leader, fishing	*fol*
coast	*costa*	life vest	*chaleco salvavidas*
to follow	*costear*	lighthouse	*faro*
coastal	*costera, costeña*	keeper	*farolero, guardafaros*
cove	*caleta, en-*	line, fishing	*cuerda (de pescar)*
	senada	lure	*curricán, carnada*
creek	*riachuelo,*		*artificial, señuelo*
	arroyuelo	*malecón*	seawall, dike
crew	*tripulación*	*mancha*	school of fish
crewmember	*tripulante*	mask, diving	*visor*
current	*corriente*	*moro*	rock, pinnacle,
deep	*profundo*		coral head
depth	*profundidad*	mouth, river	*boca, desagüe*
dive, to	*bucear*	net	*trasmayo, chinchorro*
diving	*buceo*	castnet	*tarraya, tataraya*
diver	*buzo*	oar	*remo*
dock	*muelle, embarcadero*	ocean	*mar;* see *Sea*
draft (boat)	*calado*	outboard motor	*motor fuera de borda*
drag (reel)	*embrague, clutch*	overboard, to throw	*tirar por laborda*
estuary	*estero, laguna*	Man overboard	*¡Hombre al agua!*
fathom	*braza*	paddle	*remo*
ferrule	*anilleta, anillo*	paddle, to	*remar*
ferry	*transbordador,*	*panga*	fiberglass launch,
	chalana		canoe
fins	*aletas*	pinnacle	*moro, bufa*
firearm	*arma de fuego*	pistol	*pistola, arma*
fish, to	*pescar*	point	*punta*
fishing	*pesca*	pond	*charca, represa*
fishing derby	*torneo de pesca*	port	*puerto*
fly, artificial	*mosca artificial*	port captain	*capitán del puerto*
flow	*flujo*	raft	*balsa*
flow into	*desaguar en*	rubber	*balsa de ule, inflable*

Boating, Fishing, Diving, Hunting (Cont'd)

rapids	*rápidos, raudas, raudales*	shore	*orilla, ribera, litoral*
reef	*arrecife, escollo*	to follow	*orillar*
reel	*carrete*	shotgun	*escopeta*
spinning	*carrete espinning*	shrimp boat	*camaronero*
closed face	*carrete de cara cerrada*	sink	*hundir, naufragar*
rifle	*rifle*	sinker	*plomo*
river	*río*	ski	*esquí*
river bank	*ribera, orilla*	snorkel	*esnorkel*
river bed	*cauce, lecho*	spear	*arpón*
river bend	*recodo, vuelta*	speargun	*pistola, arpón*
river ford	*vado*	spear (pole)	*arpón de liga,*
river source	*nacimiento*		*hawaiana*
river mouth	*boca, desagüe*	spearfish, to	*arponear, pescar*
river, to run	*recorrer el río*	spool	*bobina*
river volume	*caudal*	spoon (fishing)	*cuchara*
rod, fishing	*cana (de pescar)*	stream	*arroyo, arroyuelo*
row, to	*remar*	surf	*olas, tumbos, oleaje*
rowboat	*bote de remos*	swim, to	*nadar, bañar*
sail	*vela*	tide	*marea*
sail, to	*velar, navegar*	high tide	*marea alta, pleamar*
sailboat	*velero, barco de vela*	low	*marea baja, bajamar*
sailor	*marinero*	flood	*marea creciente,*
saltwater	*agua salada, del mar*		*entrante*
school (fish)	*cardumen, mancha*	ebb	*marea vaciante,*
scuba gear	*equipo deacualón*		*saliente*
sea	*mar*	tributary	*tributario, afluente*
high seas	*alta mar*	turbulent	*turbulento, turbio*
open sea	*mar abierta*	vado	*dip, ford*
rough sea	*mar alta, fea; oleaje*	veda	*closed season*
season (closed)	*veda*	vessel	*embarcación*
shallow	*bajo, bajito*	waterfall	*caída de agua, salto*
shallows	*los bajos*		*de agua*
ship	*buque, barco*	wave	*ola, tumbo*
shipwreck	*naufragio, barco hundido*	wetsuit	*traje de ule*
		whirlpool	*remolino*
		worm (earth)	*lombriz de tierra*
shoot, to	*tirar, disparar*	rubber	*lombriz de ule*
		yacht	*yate*

Food, Drink & Dry Goods

alcohol	*alcohol, alcol*	avocado	*aguacate*
almond	*almendra*	baby food	*alimento infantil*
aluminum foil	*papel aluminio*	bacon	*tocino*
apple	*manzana*	bakery	*panadería*
apricot	*chabacano, chavacano*	baking soda	*bicarbonato sódico, de*
assortment	*surtido*		*sodio, desosa*

Food, Drink & Dry Goods (Cont'd)

banana	*platano, banana*	chia seeds	*chía, semillas de . . .*
cooking type	*platano macho*	chicken	*pollo*
stalk	*racimo*	chick peas	*garbanzos*
bay leaves	*laurel*	chili	*chile*
beans, cooked	*frijoles*	chinese parsley	*cilantro*
raw, dry	*frijol*	chocolate	*chocolate*
bean sprouts	*nacidos*	*chorizo*	spiced sausage
beef	*carne de res*	cigarettes	*cigarros*
beer	*cerveza*	pack	*cajetilla*
beets	*betabeles, remolachas*	cinnamon	*canela*
bell pepper	*pimienta, pimienta*	cloves	*clavos de especia*
	dulce	cocktail	*coctel, copita (booze)*
berries	*frambuesas, fresas,*	cocoa	*chocolate*
	fresas del monte	coconut	*coco*
beverage	*bebida*	coffee	*café*
bitter	*amargo*	instant	*Nescafé*
black pepper	*pimienta negra*	cook, to	*cocinar, preparar*
bleach	*blanqueador,cloro*	cookies	*galletas*
boil, to	*hervir*	cooking oil	*aceite, aceite comestible*
bottle	*botella, pomo, frasco*	cooking pot	*olla*
	casco envase	corkscrew	*sacacorchos*
bottle opener	*destapador*	corn	*maíz*
bouillion; cubes	*Maggi; cubitos de*	ear	*mazorca*
	Maggi	on-the-cob	*elote*
bowl	*olla*	corn flour	*harina de maíz, masa*
bread	*pan, bolillo(roll)*		*harina*
breakfast	*desayuno*	cornstarch	*Maizena*
broth	*caldillo, caldo*	crackers,salted	*galletas saladas*
butter	*mantequilla*	cream	*crema*
buttermilk	*jocoque*	cream cheese	*queso crema*
cabbage	*col, repollo*	cream of wheat	*crema de trigo*
cake mix	*harina preparada*	cucumber	*pepino*
	para pastel	cumin	*comino*
caldo	soup, broth,stew	cup	*taza*
camomile	*manzanilla,te de . . .*	custard	*flan*
candle	*vela*	date	*dátil*
candy	*dulces*	dessert	*postre*
canned	*enlatada*	detergent	*detergente*
cantaloupe	*melón*	dinner	*cena*
carrot	*zanahoria*	dog food	*comida para perros*
carton, case	*cartón, caja*	dry, dried	*seco, secado*
cashew	*marañón*	eggs	*blanquillos, huevos,*
cat food	*comida para gatos*		*yemas (yolk)*
catsup	*salsa de tomate, catsup*	fig	*higo*
cecina	dry spiced meat	fish	*pescado*
cereal, breakfast	by English brand-	flyswatter	*matamoscas*
	names	flour	*harina*
cheese	*queso*	food	*alimentos,comida*
cherries	*cerezas, capulín*	fork	*tenedor*

Food, Drink & Dry Goods (Cont'd)

fruit	*fruta*	matches	*cerillos*
fry, to	*freír*	mayonnaise	*mayonesa*
frying pan	*sartén, olla*	meal	*comida*
garbanzo beans	*garbanzos*	meat market	*carnicería*
garlic	*ajo*	meat tenderizer	*suavizador, ablande-*
ginger	*jenjibre*		*dor de carne*
glass (utensil)	*vaso*	milk	*leche*
grapefruit	*toronja*	canned sweet	*La Lechera*
grapes	*uvas*	dry	*Nido, leche en polvo*
greens	*quelites, verdolagas*	condensed	*leche evaporada*
green beans	*ejotes*	mineral water	*agua mineral,*
groceries	*abarrotes*		*Tehuacán*
grocery store	*tienda de abarrotes*	mint	*menta, yerba buena*
ground meat	*carne molida, pulpa*	molasses	*melaza, miel de sorgo*
guava	*guayaba*		or *cana*
guisado	stew	mushrooms	*champiñones, hongos*
ham	*jamón*	mustard	*mostaza*
herbs	*hierbas, yerbas,*	napkins	*servilletas*
	especias, olores	*nixtamal*	tortilla dough
hibiscus	*jamaica*	noodles	*fideos*
honey	*miel de abeja*	nuts	*nueces*
ice; icecubes	*hielo; cubitos de hielo*	oatmeal	*avena*
ice cream	*helado, nieve*	olives	*aceitunas*
ice pick	*picahielos*	olive oil	*aceite de oliva*
instant	*instantáneo*	onion	*cebolla*
jam; jelly	*mermelada; jalea*	oranges	*naranjas*
juice	*jugo*	orange leaf tea	*hojas denaranjo*
kitchen	*cocina*	oregano	*orégano*
knife	*cuchillo*	package	*paquete*
lamb	*carnero*	*paleta*	flavored ice
lard	*manteca*	paper plates	*platos de cartón*
lemon	*lima*	paper towels	*toallas de papel*
lentils	*lentejas*	parsley	*perejil*
lettuce	*lechuga*	peach	*durazno*
light bulb	*foco*	peanuts	*cacahuates*
lima beans	*habas, habas verdes*	peanut butter	*crema de cacahuates*
lime	*limón*	pear	*pera*
liquor	*vino, licor*	pecan	*nuez*
longaniza	spiced sausage	peas	*chícharos*
lunch	*almuerzo, comida*	peppers	*pimientas* (see chili)
macaroni	*fideos, pasta,*	pickles, dill	*pepinos agrios*
	macarrones	sweet	*pepinos dulces*
machaca	dry shredded meat	relish	*picados aderezados*
margarine	*margarina*	pineapple	*piña*
market	*mercado, plaza*	plate	*plato*
	comercial, tianguis	plum	*ciruela*
	(Indian)	pomegranate	*granada*
masa	dough, tortilla	popcorn	*maíz palomero;*
	dough		*palomitas* (popped)

Food, Drink & Dry Goods (Cont'd)

pork	carne de puerco	steak	bistec, bistek, filete
potatoes	papas	stove	estufa
pressure cooker	olla de presión	strawberries	fresas
prunes	ciruela pasa	straw	popote
pudding	pudín	sugar	azúcar
pumpkin	calabaza	sugarcane	cana de azúcar
pumpkin seeds	pepitas	sunflower seeds	semillas de girasol
quince	membrillo	sweet	dulce, azucarada
radish	rábano	sweet potatoes	camotes
raisins	pasas	tangerine	mandarina
razor blades	hojas de afeitar	tax	impuesto
ribs	costillas	tea	té
rice	arroz	thyme	tomillo
brown	arroz moreno	tablespoonful	cucharada
roast, to	asar	teaspoonful	cucharadita
sage	salvia	tianguis	Indian market
salad	ensalada	toilet paper	papel sanitario, Petalo
salad dressing	aderezo para ensaladas		or Regio
salt	sal	tomato, red	jitomate
sandwich	sanwich, torta	small green	tomate, tomatillo
sandwich meats	carnes frias	tomato puree	puré de jitomate
sausage	salchicha	tortilla flour	masa harina, Maseca
seafood	mariscos	turnip	nabo
seeds	semillas, pepitas	ultramarinos	liquor/deli shop
sesame	ajonjolí	vanilla	vainilla
shampoo	shampoo, champú	vegetables	verduras, legumbres
shortening	manteca vegetal, Inca	vinegar	vinagre
snack	botana, antojito	walnut	nogal, nuezcastilla
soap	jabón	watercress	berro
soda pop	refresco, agua	watermelon	sandía
sopa de . . .	soup (not watery)	waxed paper	papel encerado
soup	caldo, caldillo(watery)	wheat germ	germen de trigo
sour	agrio	wine	vino de uva
sour cream	crema acida or agria	worcestershire sauce	salsa inglesa
soy sauce	salsa soya, japonesa,	worm seed	epazote
	china	yam	camote
spaghetti	espaghetti, spaghetti,	yeast, baking	levadura
	fideo largo	brewer's	levadura de cerveza
spices	especias, olores	yogurt	yogurt, bulgara, leche
spinach	espinacas		bulgara
spoon	cuchara	zucchinis	calabacitas
squash	calabaza		

Health

abortion	aborto	adrenalin	adrenalina
adhesive tape	tela or cinta adhesiva	alcohol	alcohol, alcol

Health (Cont'd)

aloe vera	*áloe, sabila*	constipation	*estreñimiento*
allergic reaction	*reacción alergico*	contagious	*contagioso, pegajoso*
allergy	*alergia*	contraceptive	*anticonceptiva*
ambulance	*ambulancia*	cotton	*algodón*
amoeba	*ameba*	cough	*tos*
analysis	*análisis*	cough syrup	*jarabe para tos*
anesthetic	*anestésico*	crabs	*ladillas*
antibiotic	*antibiótico*	cramps	*calambres*
antihistamine	*antihistamínico*	crutch	*muleta*
antiseptic	*antiséptico*	cut	*cortada, herida*
antivenin	*antitoxina*	dentist	*dentista*
scorpion	*antialacrón*	dentures	*dentaduras*
snake	*antiviperino*	diabetes	*diabetes*
arm	*brazo*	dilate	*dilatar*
arthritis	*artritis, reuma*	dizzy	*tarantas*
aspirin	*aspirina*	doctor	*doctor, médico*
band aids	*vendas, venditas*	dosage	*dosis*
bandage	*venda*	douche	*ducha*
elastic	*venda elástica*	drops	*gotas*
birth	*nacimiento*	drown	*ahogarse*
birth control pills	*pastillas* or *pildoras*	drug	*droga*
	anticonceptivas	drugstore	*farmacia*
foam	*espuma anticonceptiva*	dysentery	*disentería*
injection	*inyección anticonceptiva*	ear (outer)	*oreja*
jelly	*gelatina anticonceptiva*	inner, middle	*oído*
bite, sting	*mordida, picadura*	earache	*dolor del oído*
bleeding	*sangramiento*	emergency	*emergencia*
blister	*ampolla*	examination	*examen, examinación*
blood	*sangre*	extraction	*extracción*
blood poisoning	*mal* or *envenenamiento*	eye	*ojo*
	de sangre	eye glasses	*anteojos, gafas*
blow, injury	*golpe*	faint, to	*desmayarse*
bone	*hueso*	fatigue	*cansancio, fatiga*
boric acid	*ácido bórico*	fever	*fiebre, calentura*
broken	*quebrado*	filling	*empaste, relleno*
burn	*quemadura*	first aid	*primeros auxilios*
calcium	*calcio*	flu	*gripe, gripa*
camphoral	*alcanfor*	food poisoning	*intoxicación alimenticia*
capsule	*cápsula*	fracture	*quebradura*
chap stick	*pomada para labios*	gauze	*gasa*
childbirth	*parto*	grippe	*gripe, gripa*
chloral hydrate	*hidrato de cloral*	hangover	*cruda*
clinic	*clínica*	headache	*dolor de cabeza*
clove oil	*aceite de clavo*	health, healthy	*salud, saludable*
codeine	*codeína*	heart attack	*infarto, ataque al*
coil, contraceptive	*alambrito, aparatito*		*corazón*
cold (illness)	*catarro, resfriado*	hemorrhage	*hemorragia*
concussion	*concusión*	hemorrhoids	*almorranas*
condom	*condón*	hepatitis	*hepatitis*

Health (Cont'd)

hiccups	*hipos*	poison	*veneno*
home remedy	*remedio casero*	poisoning	*envenenado, intoxicado*
hydrogen peroxide	*agua oxigenada*	poison ivy	*yedra venenosa*
hypothermia	*hipotermia*	powder(ed)	*polvo, en polvo*
infection	*infección*	pregnant	*embarazada*
inflammation	*inflamación*	prescription	*receta*
inject	*inyectar, poner una*	pulse	*pulso*
	inyección	pure	*puro*
injection	*inyección*	purify	*purificar*
injury	*herida, golpe*	pus	*pus*
insomnia	*insomnio*	rabies	*rabia*
insulin	*insulina*	rash	*salpullido*
intravenous	*intravenoso*	reaction	*reacción*
intramuscular	*intramuscular*	Red Cross	*Cruz Roja*
iodine	*yodo*	remedy	*remedio*
itch, to; an itch	*picar; comezón*	repellent	*repelente*
jaundice	*ictericia*	rescue	*rescate*
kotex	*kotex*	salt tablets	*comprimidos de sal*
laboratory	*laboratorio*	salve	*pomada*
laxative	*laxante*	seasick	*mareado, mareo*
liquid	*líquido*	serum	*suero*
litter, stretcher	*litera, cama*	shepherd's purse	*bolsa de pastor*
louse (head)	*piojo*	shock	*susto, choque;*
lump	*bola*		*espanto (mental)*
malaria	*paludismo*	sick	*enfermo, malo*
massage	*sobar*	splint, to	*entablillar*
masseur	*sobador*	splinter	*astilla, espina*
masseuse	*sobadora*	sprain	*torcedura,*
medicine	*medicina*		*falseo*
midwife	*partera*	sterile	*estéril*
miscarriage	*malparto, aborto*	sting, to	*picar, escozor*
	natural	sting, a	*piquete, picada,*
morphine	*morfina*		*picadura*
motion sickness	*mareado*	stitch, suture	*puntada*
muscle	*músculo*	stomach	*estómago*
nausea	*náusea, mareado*	stomachache	*dolor de estómago*
needle	*aguja*	stool	*excremento,*
nervous, scared	*nervioso, espantado*		*caca* (impolite)
numb	*tener adormecido*	stroke	*ataque*
ointment	*pomada*	sulfa	*sulfa*
opiate	*narcótico*	sulfur	*azufre*
opium	*opio*	sunburn	*quemadura de sol*
pain	*dolor, dolor de . . .*	sunglasses	*gafas* or *anteojos*
parasite	*parásito*		*de sol*
paregoric	*paregórico*	sunstroke	*insolación, asoleada*
penicillin	*penicilina*	suntan lotion	*loción para broncearse*
pills	*pastillas, píldoras,*	suppository	*calillo, supositorio*
	comprimidos	suture	*puntada*
pneumonia	*pulmonía*	sweat	*sudor*

Health (Cont'd)

swelling	*hinchazón*	tourniquet	*torniquete*
symptom	*síntoma*	treatment	*tratamiento*
syringe	*jeringa*	tweezers	*pinzas*
tablets	*comprimidos, pastillas*	typhoid	*tifoidea*
talcum powder	*talco*	unhealthy	*malsano*
tampax	*tampax*	urine	*orina, orin*
tape	*cinta*	urinary infection	*mal de orin, infección de . . .*
temperature	*temperatura*	urinate	*orinar, mear*
test	*prueba, exa-men, análisis*	vagina	*vagina*
		vaginal suppository	*ovulos*
tetracycline	*tetraciclina*	vaseline	*vaselina*
thermometer	*termómetro*	venom	*veneno*
throat	*garganta*	venomous	*venenoso*
tooth	*diente, muela*	vitamin	*vitamina*
toothache	*dolor de muelas*	vomit, to	*vómito; vomitar*
toothbrush	*cepillo dental*, or *para dientes*	weak	*débil*
		worms	*lombrices, gusanos*
toothpaste	*pasta para dientes, pasta dental*	wound	*herida, golpe*
		x-rays	*rayos equis*

General Vocabulary

above; on top of	*arriba; encina de, sobre*	artesian	*artesiano*
abyss	*abismo, sima*	ascent	*ascenso, subida, ascención*
acá	here, hereabouts		
advance payment	*adelanto, avance*	ask for, request	*pedir*
		assistance	*ayuda, auxilio*
aguacero	downpour	atlas	*atlas*
afternoon	*tarde*	*atotonilco*	hot spring
aguada	sink, cenote	avalanche	*alud, derrumbe*
Aguas	watch out, be careful	*ayuntamiento*	town council
albergue	hostel, refuge, shelter	backpacker	*mochilero*
		bache	chuck hole
alguacil	Indian bailiff	badlands	*malpaís*
alley	*callejón*	*bajada*	descent
alongside, next to	*junto, junto a*	bargain, deal, agreement	*trato*
altitude	*altitud*		
alto	high	beard	*barba*
antiguo	ancient, old	begin	*empezar*
animalback, by	*a lomo de bestia*	behind	*detrás*
animal train	*recua*	below	*abajo*
arrival	*llegada*	bend (trail, river)	*recodo, vuelta, recoveco*
arrive, to	*llegar*	*bestia*	beast, packanimal
arroyo	gully, gulch	beyond	*adelante de*

General Vocabulary (Cont'd)

blocked off	*bloqueado, tapado, cerrado, cegada, ciego* (blind)	cave, cavern	*cueva, gruta, sótano, hoyo, pozo*
		cerca	close
box	*caja, cajón*	*cerrado*	closed
boxed in	*encajonado*	*chapoteadero*	wading pool
branch (trail, river)	*rama, ramal, bifurcación*	charge, to $	*cobrar*
		chart (nautical)	*carta*
brand, mark	*marca*	*chipichipi*	drizzling rain
bravo	brave, tough,mean	*chubasco*	storm, squall, downpour
break, to	*quebrar, romper*		
brecha	rough road, trail	*ciclón*	hurricane
breeze	*brisa*	cliff	*acantilado, despeña-dero, precipicio, derrumbe, farallón*
bridge	*puente*		
hanging	*puente colgante, hamaca*		
		climate	*clima*
bridle	*brida, freno* (bit)	climb, a	*subida, ascención*
broken	*roto, quebrado*	climber	*escalador*
burn, to	*quemar, encender*	climb, to	*escalar, subir*
burned	*quemado, encendido*	closed	*cerrado*
cabalgadura	mount, riding horse	cloud, cloudy	*nube, nublado*
cabecera	county seat	coals (fire)	*brasas*
caca	shit	cobblestoned	*empedrado*
cacique	chief, headman	coconut plantation	*cocal, coquero, huerta de cocos*
camp, to	*acampar*		
campers	*campistas*	coffee plantation	*cafetal, cafetalera*
camper vehicle	*camper, casa rodante*	cold	*frío, helado* (icy)
campesino	country person	comfortable	*cómodo*
campfire	*fogata, lumbre*	community	*comunidad, pueblo*
campground	*campamento*	cone	*cono*
camping	*campismo*	*conseguir*	to get, find
campo	countryside, field	cool	*fresco*
canyon	*cañón, barranca, cañada*	*cordonazo*	hurricane, storm (Baja)
box canyon	*cañón, cerrado, tapado*	*coromuel*	storm, squall
canícula	dog days	corral	*corral*
care for, guard	*cuidar, guardar, vigilar*	*corrales*	fish camp
		cortijo	farm house, ranch
Careful!	*¡Ojo!* (Eye!) or *¡Aguas!* (Waters!) *¡Cuidado!*	country	*tierra, campo, país*
		countryside	*campo, campiña*
		course, route	*rumbo, trayecto*
carga	a load, freight	cowboy	*vaquero*
carpa	tarp, tent show	crag	*risco*
carry, to	*cargar, llevar, acarrear*	creek	*arroyuelo, riachuelo*
cart	*carreta*	crest	*cresta*
caserío	hamlet, settlement	crevice, fissure	*grieta*
castellano	the Spanish language	*cristiano*	Christian, non-Indian (insult)
cattle	*ganado*		
caution, care	*cuidado*	cross, crucifix	*cruz, crucifijo*
		crossroad	*cruce, crucero*

General Vocabulary (Cont'd)

cross, to	*cruzar*	fell, knock down, to	*tumbar*
cuenca	river basin	fence	*cerca, barda*
cueva	cave, cavern	*feo*	ugly, rough, unpleasant
cyclone	*ciclón*		
danger, dangerous	*peligro, peligroso*	*finca*	property, ranch
dark, darkness	*oscuro, oscuridad*	*finquero*	rancher, landowner
date palm grove	*palmera datilera, datilera*	fire	*lumbre, fuego, fogata*
		firewood	*leña*
dawn	*madrugada*	flat, level	*parejo, plano*
day, daytime	*día, de día*	flood	*inundación*
deep	*hondo, profundo*	fodder	*foraje, pasto*
dehydrated	*deshidratado, secado*	fog	*neblina*
delay, to	*dilatarse*	foothills	*faldas*
depart, to	*salir, irse*	footprint, track	*nuella*
departure	*salida*	forest; forested	*bosque, monte; boscoso*
derrumbe	avalanche	fork (trail)	*ramal, horcajo, bifurcación*
desert	*desierto, yermo*		
detour	*desviación*	freeway	*autopista, cuota* (toll road)
ditch	*zanja*		
don, doña	title of respect used before a person's name	freshwater	*agua dulce*
		friendly	*amable*
		front; in front of	*frente; delante, en frente de*
downpour	*aguacero, chubasco de agua*		
		gabacho	foreigner, gringo
downstream	*aguas abajo, río abajo*	garden	*huerta*
dressing room	*vestidor*	gate	*puerta, portal*
dried	*seco, secado*	geography	*geografía*
drink; to drink	*bebida; beber, tomar*	ghost	*fantasma*
dry season	*tiempo de secas, secas*	governor	*gobernador*
dunes	*médanos, dunas*	grotto	*gruta*
dust; dusty	*polvo; polvoroso*	grove	*arboleda*
dust devil	*polvareda*	guard, to, watch over	*guardar*
earth	*tierra*		
earthquake	*terremoto, temblor*	guest	*huésped, invitado, visita*
east, eastern	*este, oriental*		
eat, to	*comer, tomar*	guide	*guía*
ejido	rural cooperative	guide, acompany	*guiar, acompañar*
end; to end	*fin, límite; terminar*	gully, gulch	*cañada, arroyo*
encargado	person in charge, agent	gypsy	*húngaro*
		hail	*granizo*
encargo	favor, request	hanging	*colgante*
enramada	branch shelter	hanging bridge	*puente colgante, hamaca*
entrance, opening	*entrada*		
entronque	junction	hang, to	*colgar*
exit	*salida*	happy; to be	*contento, feliz; estar contento*
fall, a	*caída*		
fall, to	*caerse*	hazardous	*azaroso*
far	*lejos*	headland	*farallón*
favor	*favor, encargo, gallada*	heat, hot	*calor, caliente*

General Vocabulary (Cont'd)

heavy	*pesado*	*juzgado*	court (legal)
hedge	*cerca viva*	kill, to	*matar*
hembra	female (animal)	knot	*nudo*
herd, flock	*manada*	landing (plane)	*aterrizaje*
hermit	*ermitaño*	land (plane), to	*aterrizar*
hide, hidden	*esconderse, escondido*	landslide, cave-in	*derrumbe*
highway	*carretera, camino*	league	*legua*
hike	*caminata, marcha*	level	*nivel*
hiker	*caminante*	level, to	*anivelar*
hike, to	*caminar, marchar, andar a pie*	light	*luz*
		light, to	*encender*
hill	*colina, loma, lomita, cerro*	lightweight	*ligero*
		lluvias	rains
hire, to	*contratar, alquilar*	load, a	*carga*
hole	*hueco, ollo, hoyo, bache, pozo*	load, to	*cargar*
		loaded	*cargado*
horse	*caballo*	locate, find	*encontrar, hallar*
horseman	*jinete*	lodging	*alojamiento*
on horseback	*a lomo de caballo, a caballo*	long	*largo*
		lookout point	*mirador*
pack horse	*bestia, remuda, cabalgadura, caballo*	loose, loosen	*suelto, soltar*
		lost	*perdido*
to ride	*montar a caballo*	to get	*perderse*
horseshoe	*herradura*	*macizo*	ripe, stout, tough, strong
host	*anfitrión*		
hostel	*albergue*	*macho*	male animal, brave, tough
hot	*caliente*		
house	*casa, casita*	*malpaís*	badlands, lava beds
huerta	garden, orchard	map	*mapa*
humble	*humilde*	*mar*	sea
hunger; hungry, to be	*hambre; tener hambre*	meet, to	*encontrarse con, reunirse con*
hurricane	*ciclón, huracán, cordonazo*	meeting	*reunión, encuentro*
		message	*mensaje, recado*
hut	*palapa, choza, jacal*	microwave tower	*torre de microondas*
ingenio	sugar cane mill, refinery	*milpa*	corn, bean field
		mine	*mina*
inside; inside of	*interior; dentro de, a dentro*	miner	*minero*
		mineral	*mineral*
irrigation	*riego*	monsoon	*monzón*
jaula	cage, jail	*monte*	forest, jungle, wilderness
jefe	chief, boss		
journey, trek	*jornada*	mountain	*montaña, sierra, cerro*
judge	*juez*	mountain climber	*alpinista*
jump, leap	*brinco, salto*	mountainous	*montañoso, serranía (en plena sierra)*
jump, leap, to	*brincar*		
junction	*entronque, bifurcación*	mountain range	*sierra, cordillera (sierra brava)*
jungle	*monte, selva, jungla*		
just, fair	*justo*	mountain rescue	*socorro alpino*

General Vocabulary (Cont'd)

mud, mudhole	*lodo; lodazal, ciénaga*	plain	*llano, pradera, vega,*
mueble	vehicle, (furniture)		*plano, planicie,*
mule	*mula, bestia*		*llanura*
muleskinner	*arriero*	plane (small)	*avioneta; avión* (large)
narrow	*estrecho*	playing field, court	*cancha*
naturales	natives, Indians	pool (water)	*estanque, tanque,*
neighbor	*vecino*		*pileta, ojo de agua*
next, the	*próximo*	pool, swimming	*alberca, piscina,*
night; nighttime	*noche; de noche, por la*		*balneario*
	noche	portable	*portátil*
norte (weather)	norther, storm	*potable*	drinkable
north, northern	*norte; norteño,*	pothole	*bache*
	septentrional	pretty, nice	*bonito*
northeast	*nordeste*	priest	*padre*
northwest	*noroeste (vamos hacia,*	private property	*propiedad privada*
	al . . .)	prohibited entry	*prohibido el paso*
nun	*monja*	provinces, boondocks	*provincias*
nube	cloud	provisions	*bastimento*
one way	*de ida solo*	puddle, pond	*charco, tanque de agua*
onward	*adelante*	*puente*	bridge
outside; outside of	*afuera; fuera de*	*quebradas*	ravines, rough
owner	*dueño*		country
pack	*mochila, morral*	rain	*lluvia*
pack up, to	*empaquetar*	rain, to	*llover*
pack animal	*bestia de carga*	rainbow	*arco iris*
palenque	moonshine still,	rainy season	*temporada, temporal,*
	cockfight pit		*tiempo de lluvias, las*
palm grove	*palmera*		*lluvias, las aguas*
park	*parque*	*ramada*	branch shelter
park, to	*estacionarse*	*ranchería*	small settlement,
pass; to pass	*paso, desfiladero; pasar*		ranch
pasture	*pasto, pastura*	*rancho*	settlement, ranch,
path, trail	*vereda, camino, sendero,*		farm
	senda, camino real	reins	*riendas*
patrón	boss, leader, person	remote	*retirado, aislado*
	of respect	*remuda*	horse, mule,
pay for, to	*pagar*		pack animal
payment	*pago*	rent, to	*rentar, alquilar,*
peak	*picacho*		*contratar*
peligro	danger	rest; to rest	*descanso; descansar*
permission, permit	*permiso*	reward	*recompensa*
pet	*mascota*	ride (horse), to	*montar a (caballo)*
photograph; to	*foto, fotografía,*	ride (hitch)	*aventón, ride*
	retrado; retratar	risk	*riesgo*
pillar	*pilar*	rock	*piedra, roca*
pinnacle	*peñasco*	rock chimney	*mitra*
piss, to	*orinar, miar (impolite)*	rock climber	*escalador de rocas*
place, spot	*lugar, sitio*	rock painting	*pintura rupestre*
		rocky	*pedregoso*

General Vocabulary (Cont'd)

rough, harsh	*áspero, feo, picado, escabroso, fragoso*
round trip	*viaje redondo, viaje de ida y vuelta*
route	*rumbo, trayecto*
ruin	*ruina*
rumbo	route
rústico	rustic, crude, simple
sad, to be	*estar triste*
salary, daily wage	*sueldo, salario; pago diario, jornal*
salón (cave)	room
saltwater	*agua salada, agua del mar*
saltwater lagoon	*albufera, laguna*
sand, sandy	*arena, arenoso*
savannah	*sabana*
sawmill	*aserradero*
scarce, scarcity	*escaso, escasez*
sea	*mar*
sea level	*nivel del mar*
season	*temporada, temporal, tiempo de*
secas	dry season
sembrado	field, planted field
shade	*sombra*
sheer drop	*tiro vertical*
shelf, cliff	*cantil*
shelter	*abrigo, cubierto, albergue*
shepherd	*pastor*
shit, to	*caca; cagar* (impolite)
short (distance)	*corto*
short cut	*atajo*
signal, to	*señal; señalar*
slab	*laja*
sleep, to; to be sleepy	*dormirse; tener sueño*
slippery	*resbaloso*
slope, hillside	*ladero*
smoke, to	*humo, fumar*
snow, to	*nieve, nevar*
solar	lot, piece of land
sótano	cave, grotto, cellar
south; southern	*sur; meridional*
spillway	*vertedor*
spine	*espina*
spring (water)	*manantial, nacimiento, ojo de agua*
spring (season)	*primavera*

sprinkle (rain)	*llovizna, chipichipi*
spurs	*espuelas*
spur (mountain)	*contrafuerte*
stalactite	*estalactita*
stalagmite	*estalagmita*
stay, remain, to	*quedarse*
steal, to; stolen	*robar; robado*
steep	*parado, empinado*
step, rung	*escalón*
stingy, (to be)	*(ser) codo*
stone	*piedra, roca*
stop, a	*parada*
stop, to	*pararse, detenerse*
storm	*tempestad, chubasco, norte*
storeroom	*bodega*
strange; stranger	*extraño; extranjero, forastero*
stream	*arroyo, chorro*
stubborn	*terco*
subida	ascent
subterranean	*subterráneo*
summer	*verano*
summit	*cima, cumbre*
sun	*sol*
sunrise; dawn	*salida del sol; madrugada*
sunset; late afternoon	*puesta del sol, ocaso; atardecer*
swamp	*pantano, marisma, ciénaga*
tame	*manso, mansito*
teacher	*profesor(a), profe*
temblor	earthquake
terreno	lot, plot, acreage
tienda	store, awning, tarp, tent
tie up	*amarrar*
tierra caliente	hot country, lowlands
fría	cold country, highlands
templada	temperate country
toll	*cuota, peaje, cobro*
topil	Indian official
topography	*topografía*
tornado	*ciclón, tornado*
torrent	*chorro, torrente*
tourist	*turista*

General Vocabulary (Cont'd)

toward	*hacia, al*	*vereda*	trail
tower	*torre*	view	*vista, paisaje*
track, footprint	*huella*	village	*pueblo, rancho, villa*
trail	*vereda, camino, sendero,*	visitor	*visitante*
	senda, camino real	volcano	*volcán*
trail, to break	*abrirse paso*	wake up, to	*despertar*
trailer park	*parque de traylers,*	walk; to walk	*caminata; caminar,*
	campamento		*andar a pie*
trapiche	sugar cane press	walker	*caminante*
travel	*viajar*	water	*agua, agua dulce*
traveller	*viajero*		(fresh)
tributary	*tributario, afluente*	water hole	*tinaja, tina, ojo de*
trip	*viaje*		*agua*
trouble	*trabajo*	water level, at	*a flor de agua*
troublesome	*travieso*	weather	*tiempo*
tumpline	*mecapal*	weight	*peso*
turf, lawn	*césped*	well	*pozo, pozo de agua*
turn over	*volcar*	wild	*silvestre*
turn, to	*vuelta; voltear*	wilderness	*yermo, desierto*
twisted; twist, to	*torcido; torcer*	wind	*viento, aire*
ugly, rough, bad	*feo*	windy, it is	*hace viento*
underbrush	*maleza, matorral*	wind, against the	*contra el viento*
underground	*bajo tierra, subterráneo*	wind, with the	*con el viento*
unload	*descargar, desempacar*	winter	*invierno*
upstream	*aguas arribas, río*	witch; witchcraft	*bruja; brujería*
	arriba	work; to work	*trabajo; trabajar*
valley	*valle*	*zacate*	grass, straw
varón	man, respected man		

Fish & Sealife

abalone	*abulón*	chiton	*quitón, cucaracha*
albacore	*albacora, atún*	clam	*almeja*
amberjack	*atún, coronado*	claws (sealife)	*pinzas*
anchovy	*anchoa, sardina,*	cod	*bacalao*
	anchoveta	corvina	*corvina, corbina,*
barnacle	*percebe*		*curbina*
barracuda	*picuda, barracuda*	crab	*jaiba, cangrejo*
bass	*lobina, lisa, trucha*	crawfish	*langostino, camarón*
black bass	*lobina negra*		*del río, cucaracha*
blacktip shark	*gambuso, galano*	croaker	*boca dulce, gurrubata,*
bonefish	*macabi*		*corvina*
bonito, skipjack	*barrilete*	dolfinfish	*dorado*
bonito, mackerel		dolphin, porpoise	*marsopa, delfín*
shark	*mako, paloma*	drum	*corvina, roncador*
carp	*carpa, matalote*	eagle ray	*águila*
catfish	*gato, bagre*	eel	*anguila*

Fish & Sealife (Cont'd)

fins	*aletas*	rock bass	*cabrilla, garropa, mero*
fish	*pez, pescado* (caught)	roosterfish	*pez gallo*
flounder, sole	*lenguado, medio*	sailfish	*pez vela*
goatfish	*chivalo*	sardine	*sardina*
grouper	*mero, garropa*	scales	*escamas*
grunt	*ronco, sargo, mojarron,*	scallop	*concha*
	burrito	scorpionfish	*sapo, pez alacrán*
guts	*tripas*	sea bass	*mero, cabrilla, ribera*
halibut	*medio*	seal	*foca, lobomarino*
hammerhead shark	*cornuda*	sea lion	*león marino*
herring	*sardina, arenque*	sea snail	*concha, caracol del mar*
jack	*jurel, toro, cocinero*	sea trout	*trucha, corvina*
jack crevalle	*toro*	sea urchin	*erizo*
jellyfish	*malagua, aguamar,*	seaweed	*alga marina, hierba*
	medusa		*del mar*
jewfish	*cherna, mero*	school (fish)	*cardumen, mancha*
kelp	*quelpo*	shark	*tiburón*
killer whale	*orca*	skipjack tuna	*barilete*
ladyfish	*sabalo*	shrimp	*camarón*
lapa	giant limpet	*sierra*	Spanish mackerel
largemouth bass	*lobina*	smallmouth bass	*lobina, lisa, trucha*
lobster	*langosta*	snapper	*pargo*
lookdown	*joroba*	snook	*robalo*
mackerel	*macarela, sierra, atún*	Spanish mackerel	*sierra*
mackerel shark	*mako, paloma*	soapfish	*pez jabón*
mahi mahi	*dorado*	sole	*lenguado, medio*
manta ray	*manta raya*	spine	*espina*
marlin	*agujón, espadón,*	squid	*calamar*
	marlin	sting ray	*raya*
mojarra	perch, perch-like	swordfish	*espadón, pez espada*
moray eel	*morena*	tarpon	*sabalo, tarpón*
mullet	*lisa*	totuava	*totuava, corvina*
mussel	*mejillón*		*blanca*
needlefish	*agujón*	triggerfish	*bota, puerco, cochino*
octopus	*pulpo*	trout	*trucha*
oyster	*ostión*	tuna	*atún*
parrotfish	*loro, perico*	turtle; sea turtle	*tortuga; tortuga,*
perch	*mojarra, corvina*		*caguama, carey*
pompano	*pompano, palometa,*	wahoo	*sierra prieto, peto*
	pampanera	whale; killer	*ballena; orca*
porpoise	*marsopa, delfín*	white sea bass	*corvina blanca,*
rainbow trout	*trucha arco iris*		*trucha, totuava*
ray	*raya*		
red snapper	*huachinango*		

Animals, Birds, Reptiles, Insects

animal	animal, criatura	flamingo	flamenco
antelope	antílope, berrendo	flea	pulga
armadillo	armadillo	flock (birds)	bandada
bat	murciélago	fly (insect)	mosca
beak	pico	fox	zorra, zorro, gato
bear	oso		de monte
beaver	castor, nutria	frog	rana
bee	abeja	fur	piel
bighorn sheep	borrego, cimarrón,	gnat	jején
	carnero	goat	cabra
bird	ave, pájaro	goose	ganso
black widow	viuda, viuda negra	grouse	urogallo
boa constrictor	boa	hawk, falcon	halcón, gavilán
bobcat	lince, gato montes	herd	manada, rebaño, hato
brant (black)	ganso de collar	heron	garza
bugs	bichos, chinches,	hoof	pata
	insectos	horns	cuernos
bull	toro	horsefly	tábano
buzzard, vulture	zopilote, buitre	iguana	iguana
cacomixtle	ring-tailed cat	insect	insecto
calf	becerro	jackrabbit	liebre
cat; wildcat	gato; gato montes,	jaguar	tigre, jaguar,
	gato de noche,		yaguar, leopardo
	gato silvestre	lion	león, puma
cattle	ganado, ganado vacuno	livestock	ganadería, ganado
chachalaca	chachalaca	lizard	lagartija
chicken	pollo, gallina or gallo	macaw	guacamaya, papagayo
chukar	chukar	mallard	pato de collar
claws	garras, uñas,	man o' war bird	tijereta, rabihorcado,
	pinzas (sealife)		frigata
coatimundi	tejón	merganser	mergo
conch	caracol, concha	monkey	mono, chango
coral snake	coralillo	mosquito	mosco, mosquito,
false coral	falso coralillo		zancudo
cormorant	cormorán, cuervo	mouse	ratón
	marino	mule	mula
cougar	puma, león	mule deer	venado mula, bura
cow	vaca	nest	nido
coyote	coyote	no see'ums	jejenes
crane	grulla	ocelot	tigrillo, ocelote
crocodile	cocodrilo, lagarto	otter	nutria, perro de agua
crow	cuervo	owl	buho, tecolote
currason	faisán, real	parrot	loro, cotorra, papa-
deer	venado		gayo, perico
dog	perro	peccary	javalina, jabalí
eagle	águila	pelican	pelícan
egret	garceta	pet	mascota
feather	pluma	petrel	petrel

Animals, Birds, Reptiles, Insects (Cont'd)

pheasant	*faisán, faisán chino*	squirrel	*ardilla*
pig	*puerco, cochino, cerdo,*	swan	*cisne*
	marrano	tail	*cola*
pigeon	*palmona*	tarantula	*tarántula*
porcupine	*puerco espín*	teal	*zarceta, cerceta*
possum	*tlacuache, zorro*	*tejón*	badger, raccoon,
puppy	*cachorro*		coatimundi,
python	*pitón*		ring-tailed cat
quail	*codorniz, gallinácea*	tepesquintle	*paca, agouti*
rabbit	*conejo*	tick	*garrapata*
raccoon	*mapache, lavador, tejón*	*tlacuache*	possum
rat	*rata*	toad	*sapo, zapo, rana*
rattlesnake	*cascabel*	toucan	*tucán*
raven	*cuervo*	turkey	*guajolote, cócono, pavo,*
reptile	*reptil*		*pavo de monte*
scorpion	*alacrán, escorpión*		
seagull	*gaviota*	vampire bat	*murciélago vampiro*
shell, sea	*concha*	viper	*víbora*
skin	*piel, cuero*	vulture	*zopilote, buitre*
skunk	*zorillo*	wasp	*avispa*
snake	*culebra* (nonpoi-	weasel	*comadreja*
	sonous), *víbora*	wild	*silvestre, bravo*
	(poisonous)	wolf	*lobo*
		worm (earth)	*lombriz de tierra*
spider	*araña*	worm, grub	*gusano*

Plants & Trees

aloe	*sabila, áloe*	grass	*zacate, hierba*
bamboo	*bambú, caña*	grove	*arboleda*
bark	*cáscara, corteza*	jungle	*selva, monte, jungla*
branch; frond	*rama; palapa*	leaf	*oja, hoja*
bush, shrub	*arbusto*	madrona	*madroño*
cane	*carrizo, caña*	mahogany	*caoba*
canebrake	*cañar, cañaveral,*	mangrove	*mangle*
	cañal	mangrove swamp	*manglar*
cactus	*cacto*	*mata*	bunch, clump
organpipe	*organo*	mushroom(magic)	*hongo alucinante*
barrel	*visnaga*	oak	*roble*
cedar	*cedro*	palm	*palma*
century plant	*agave, maguey*	*penca*	cactus leaf
eucalyptus	*eucalipto*	pine	*pino*
fern	*helecho*	plant	*planta*
fir	*abeto, oyamel*	poppy	*amapola*
flower	*flor*	reed	*carrizo*
forest	*bosque, monte*	root	*raíz*
frond	*palapa, fronda*	seed	*semilla*

Plants & Trees (Cont'd)

stem	*tallo*	trunk	*tronco*
thicket	*matorral*	vine	*bejuco*
tree	*palo, árbol*	willow	*sauce*

Post Office, Telegraph, Telephone, Bank

address	*dirección*	post card	*tarjeta*
airgram	*aereogramo*	post office	*correo*
airmail	*correo aéreo*	postal money order	*giro*
certified	*certificado*	registered	*registrado*
change of address	*tarjeta de cambiar*	regular mail	*ordinario*
card	*dirección*	return address	*dirección del remitente*
duty, tax	*impuesto*	return to...*	*remite a...*
envelope	*sobre*	special handling	*entrega inmediata*
general delivery	*lista de correos*	stamp	*estampilla, timbre*
glue	*pegamento*	string	*cuerda*
letter	*carta*	weight	*peso*
package, box	*paquete, caja*	wrapped	*envuelto*

Is there any mail in General Delivery for Joe Blow? — *¿Hay algo en la lista para Joe Blow?*
Weigh it, please. — *Péselo, por favor.*
Does it need more postage? — *¿Necesita más estampillas?*
Three airmail envelopes, please. — *Tres sobres aéreos, por favor.*

money order	*giro*	telegram	*telegrama*
night letter	*carta nocturna,*	telegraph office	*telégrafos*
	carta de noche	urgent	*urgente*
regular	*ordinario*		

I would like to send a telegram to... — *Quiero mandar una telegrama a...*

call, a	*una llamada*	number	*número*
call, to	*llamar*	operator	*operador*
collect	*al cobrar*	person to person	*persona a persona*
credit card	*tarjeta de crédito*	station to station	*a quien contesta*
Hello!	*¡Ola!, ¡Bueno!*	telephone	*teléfono*
long distance	*larga distancia*	telephone office	*oficina de teléfonos*

I want to call the United States, please. The number is... — *Quiero llamar a los Estados Unidos, por favor. El número es...*

bank	*banco*	Mexican currency	*moneda nacional (MN)*
bank draft	*cheque del banco*	money	*dinero, lana*
bill	*billete*	personal check	*cheque personal*
cash, to; change	*cambiar*	signature	*firma*
change	*cambio, feria, suelto*	teller's window	*caja*
check	*cheque*	traveler's check	*cheque de viajero*
dollar	*dólar*	50 *centavos*, 20	*tostón, viente*

Can you cash a traveler's check? — *¿Se puede cambiar un cheque de viajero?*

Red Tape

age	*edad*	married	*casado (a)*
baggage	*equipaje*	minor	*menor de edad*
border	*frontera*	passport	*pasaporte*
car permit	*permiso de auto-*	profession or	*profesión* or
	móvil	occupation	*ocupación*
customs	*aduana*	registration	*registración*
divorced	*divorciado (a)*	single	*soltero (a)*
driver's license	*licencia de manejar*	suitcase	*maleta*
immigration	*migración*	tourist card	*tarjeta de turista*
inspection	*revisión*	widowed	*viudo (a)*
insurance	*seguros*	vaccination cer-	*certificado de*
license plates	*placas*	tificate	*vacunación*
marital status	*estado civil*		

Getting Around

airplane	*avión*	line or company	*linea* or *companía*
airport	*aeropuerto*	on the hour	*cada hora*
arrivals & departures		pack animal	*bestia*
(posted on 24		passenger	*pasajero*
hour time system)	*llegadas y salidas*	reservation	*reservación*
boat	*lancha*	reserved seat	*asiento reservado*
bus	*autobús, camión*	ride	*aventón, ride*
bus station	*terminal* or *estación*	second class	*segunda clase*
	de autobuses	taxi	*taxi, libre, coche*
bus stop	*parada*	taxi stand	*sitio*
canoe	*canoa*	ticket	*boleto*
city bus	*servicio urbano*	ticket window	*caja, taquilla*
daily	*diario*	train	*ferrocarril, tren*
driver	*chófer*	train station	*estación de ferrocarril*
every half hour	*cada media hora*	to get aboard	*subir*
first class	*primera clase*	to get off	*bajar*
get in	*sube*		

Where are you going? — *¿Dónde va?*   I'm going to . . . — *Me voy a . . .*
I want a ticket to . . . —*Quiero un boleta a . . .*
How much is a ticket to . . .? — *¿Cuánto cuesta un boleto a . . .?*
What bus line goes to . . .? — *¿Qué linea tiene servicio a . . .?*
What is the number of the bus? — *¿Qué es el número del autobús?*
What time does the bus leave for . . .? — *¿A qué hora sale el camión a . . .?*
Where does it leave from? — *¿De dónde sale?*
Where does this bus go? — *¿Dónde va este autobús?*
How many hours is it to . . .? — *¿Cuántas horas a . . .?*
I lost my baggage. — *Se me perdió me equipaje.*
How much time do we have here? — *¿Cuánto tiempo tenemos aquí?*
Let me off at the corner (off here). — *Quiero bajar en la esquina (aquí).*
Will you give me a ride to . . .? — *¿Me da un aventón a . . .?*
I'm travelling by thumb. — *Viajo por aventón.*
What will you charge to take me to . . .? — *¿Cuánto me cobra llevarme a . . .?*

Hotels

Air conditioned	*aire acondicionado*	guest house	*pensión*
bar	*bar*	inn	*posada*
bath	*baño*	hammock	*hamaca*
bathroom	*baño*	hot water	*agua caliente*
bed	*cama*	hotel	*hotel*
blanket	*cobija, cubierta*	key	*llave*
boarding house	*casa de huespedes*	manager	*gerente, dueño*
cot	*catre*	motel	*motel*
dining room	*comedor*	noise	*ruido*
double bed	*cama matrimonial*	room, double	*cuarto doble*
extra bed	*cama extra*	shower	*regador, regadera*
fan	*ventilador, abanico*	swimming pool	*alberca, piscina*

Do you know of a cheap hotel? — *¿Conoce usted un hotel económico?*
Do you have a room for two? — *¿Hay un cuarto para dos personas?*
Do you have a room with bath? — *¿Hay un cuarto con baño?*
with meals — *con comidas*
without meals — *sin comidas*
Is the car safe? — *¿Está seguro el coche?*
Is there a night watchman at the parking lot? — *¿Hay un velador en el estacionamiento?*
Do you have ice? — *¿Hay hielo?*
Please put in a cot for the child. — *Favor de poner un catre para el niño.*
The toilet is stopped up. — *Está tapada la taza.*

Houses

bedroom	*recámara*	landlord, owner	*dueño(a)*
by the week, month	*por la semana, el mes*	living room	*sala*
electricity	*electricidad*	maid	*criada*
for rent	*se renta, se alquila*	refrigerator	*refrigerador*
for sale	*se vende*	room	*cuarto*
furnished	*amueblada*	stove	*estufa*
house	*casa*	to sell	*vender*
kitchen	*cocina*	to rent	*alquilar, rentar*

Is this house for rent? — *¿Está de renta la casa?*
Who owns this house? — *¿Quién es el dueño de esta casa?*
Where does s/he live? — *¿Dónde vive?*
How much is it per month? — *¿Cuánto es por mes?*

Gas Stations

Gas cap	*tapón, tapa*	grease job	*lubricación, grasa*
gas station	*gasolinera*	oil	*aceite*
gasoline	*gasolina*	oil change	*cambio de aceite*
grease	*grasa*	pump	*bomba*
to grease	*engrasar*	tank	*tanque*

Gas Stations (Cont'd)

Fill it up, please. — *Lleno, por favor.*
Check the oil and water, please. — *Vea el aceite y agua, por favor.*
I want an oil change and grease job. — *Quiero un cambio de aceite y lubricación.*
Check the oil in the transmission and differential. — *Vea el aceite en la caja y diferencial.*
Put in a liter of 30 weight oil, please. — *Eche un litre de aceite número treinta, por favor.*
Put 30 pounds of air in the tires. — *Ponga treinta libras de aire en las llantas.*
Where is the restroom? — *¿Dónde está el baño?*
Do you have a map of Mexico? — *¿Hay un mapa de la republica?*

accelerator	*acelerador*	carburetor	*carburador*
adjust	*adjustar*	carburetor float	*flotador*
adjusting stars		carburetor jet	*esprea*
(brakes)	*ajustadores de frenos*	choke	*ahogador*
a-frame	*horguilla*	clutch	*clutch*
air filter	*filtro de aire*	clutch disc	*disco de clutch*
air filter cartridge	*cartucho del filtro de aire*	clutch pedal	*pedal de clutch*
		coil	*bobina*
alternator	*alternador*	coil springs	*resortes*
armature	*rotor*	condenser	*condensador*
assemble	*armar*	crankcase	*monoblock*
auto electric shop	*taller auto-eléctrico*	crankshaft	*cigüeñal*
auto parts	*refacciones*	cylinder	*cilindro*
auto parts store	*refaccionería*	cylinder sleeve	*camisa*
axle	*eje*	differential	*diferencial*
brake shoe	*zapata*	dismantle	*desarmar*
ball bearings	*baleros*	distributor	*distribuidor*
ball joints	*rótulas*	distributor cap	*tapa de distribuidor*
batteria	*acumulador, batería*	drive	*manejar*
battery cable	*cable de acumulador*	drive shaft	*flecha cardán*
block	*monoblock*	electrical system	*sistema eléctrica*
body and paint shop	*hojalatería y pintura*	fan	*ventilador*
boot (tire)	*huarache*	fan belt	*banda de ventilador*
brakes	*frenos*	fender	*guardabarros*
brake drum	*tambor*	fields	*campos*
brake fluid	*líquido de frenos*	fly wheel	*engrane volante*
brake line	*mangera de frenos*	frame	*bastidor*
brake lining	*balata*	front wheel	
brake pedal	*pedal de frenos*	alignment	*alineación*
brake plate	*plato de frenos*	front wheel bearings	*baleros de las ruedas adelantes*
gas tank	*tanque de gasolina*		
brushes	*carbones*	front wheel spindle	*mango*
bumper	*defensa*	fuel pump	*bomba de gasolina*
bus	*autobús, camión*	fuse	*fusible*
bushing	*bushing, buje*	garage (repair)	*taller mecánico, taller automotriz*
cable	*cable*		
camshaft	*árbol de levas*	gas cap	*tapón de gasolina*
camshaft bearings	*metales de árbol de levas*	gas line	*tubo, mangera de gasolina*
car	*coche, automóvil, carro*	gas tank	*tanque de gasolina*

Gas Stations (Cont'd)

gasket	*empaque, junta*	rocker arm	*balancín*
gasket set	*juego de empaques*	rod	*biela*
gear	*engrane*	rod bearing (insert)	*metales de bielas*
gear shift lever	*palanca de cambios*	rotor	*rotor*
generator	*generador*	seal	*retén*
ground	*tierra*	shaft	*flecha*
hand brake	*freno de mano*	shock absorber	*amortiguador*
head	*cabeza*	solenoid	*solenoide*
head gasket	*empaque de cabeza*	spark plug	*bujía (candela* in
headlights	*focos*		Guatemala*)*
horn	*klaxón, bocina*	spark plug wire	*cable de bujía*
hose	*mangera*	starter	*marcha*
hose clamp	*abrazadera*	starter ring gear	*cremallera*
ignition switch	*switch*	steering gear	*caja de dirección*
jack	*gato*	steering wheel	*volante*
kingpin	*perno, pivote de*	stop light	*luz de stop*
	dirección	stud	*birlo, perno prisionero*
kingpin carrier	*portamango*	tail pipe	*tubo de escape*
leaf springs	*muelles*	thermostat	*toma de agua, termósi*
lever	*palanca*	throw out bearing	*cojarín*
main bearings	*metales de bancada*	tie rod	*barrilla de dirección*
manifold	*múltiple*	tie rod end	*terminal de barrilla de*
exhaust	*múltiple de escape*		*dirección*
intake	*múltiple de admisión*	tighten	*apretar*
master cylinder	*cilindro maestro de*	timing gear	*engrange de árbol de*
	frenos		*levas*
mechanic	*mecánico, maestro*	tire	*llanta*
motor	*motor, máquina*	tire balancing	*balanceo*
muffler	*mofle*	tire gauge	*calibrador*
oil	*aceite*	tire repair shop	*vulcanízadora*
oil filter	*filtro de aceite*	tire tube	*cámara* or *tubo*
oil pump	*bomba de aceite*	tire, tubeless	*llanta sin cámara*
panel truck	*camioneta, panel*	tire valve	*válvula*
patch	*parche*	tow truck	*grúa*
pickup truck	*camioneta*	torsion bar	*barra de torsión*
piston	*pistón*	transmission	*transmisión, caja*
Pitman arm	*brazo Pitman*		(box)
points	*platinos*	truck	*camión*
pressure plate	*plato de presión*	tune	*afinar*
pulley	*polea*	tune up	*afinación*
push rod	*levador, puntería*	turn signals	*direccionales*
radiator	*radiador*	turn signal flasher	*destallador*
radiator cap	*tapón de radiador*	universal joint	*cruceta y yugo, cardán*
radiator hose	*mangera de radiador*	upholstery shop	
re-cap (tire)	*recubierta*	(auto)	*cubreasientos*
relay	*relais*	vacuum advance	*avance*
rings	*anillos*	valves	*válvulas*
compression ring	*anillo de compresión*	exhaust	*válvula de escape*
oil ring	*anillo de aceite*	intake	*válvula de admisión*

Gas Stations (Cont'd)

valve cover	*tapa de pulerias*	wheel	*rueda*
valve guide	*guía de válvula*	wheel cylinder	*cilindro de frenos*
valve lifter	*buso, levanta-válvulas*	windshield	*parabrisas*
valve springs	*resorte de válvula*	windshield wiper	*limpia parabrisas* or
valve spring keeper	*cazuela de válvula*		*limpiadores*
valve stem	*vastigo de válvula*	windshield wiper	
van	*camioneta*	blade	*pluma*
voltage regulator	*regulador de voltage*	wire	*alambre*
water pump	*bomba de agua*	wrist pin	*perno, pasador de*
weld	*soldar*		*émbolo*

It's bent. — *Está doblado.*
Adjust the clutch. — *Ajuste el clutch.*
Adjust the brakes. — *Ajuste los frenos.*
To bleed the brakes — *Purgar los frenos*
To rebuild the wheel cylinders — *Cambiar las gomas*
To turn the brake drums — *Rectificar los tambores*
Adjust the valves. — *Ajuste las válvulas.*
To grind the valves — *Asentar las válvulas*
Engine overhaul — *Ajuste general*
To turn the crankshaft — *Rectificar la cigüeñal*
To charge the battery — *Cargar la acumulador*
The engine is knocking. — *Suena la máquina.*
The engine is overheating. — *El motor se calienta.*
The engine is throwing oil. — *La máquina está tirando aceite.*
The engine is burning oil. — *La máquina está quemando aceite.*
The radiator is leaking. — *Está tirando la radiador.*
I want a major tune-up. — *Quiero una afinación mayor.*
Pack the front wheel bearings. — *Engrace los baleros de las ruedas adelantes.*
The tire is punctured. — *Está ponchada la llanta.*
The tire has a slow leak. — *La llanta está bajando poco a poco.*
Put a boot in the tire. — *Vucanice la llanta.*
Put 30 pounds of air in the tires. — *Ponga treinta libras de aire en las llantas.*

Tools, Hardware & Odds and Ends

acetylene torch	*soplete oxiacetilenico,*	compression	
	equipo de autógeno	gauge	*compresión metro*
allen wrench	*llave de alán*	cotter pin	*chaveta*
axe	*hacha*	crescent wrench	*perico*
bag	*bolsa*	crowbar	*barra*
chisel	*cincel*		

Indian Languages

This list was compiled with the generous assistance of language experts at the Instituto Nacional Indigenista. In several instances I have used phonetic spelling to simplify difficult pronunciations. Be aware that regional variations are more than common; they are the rule. Spanish translations are approximate, not literal. *Buenos días*, for example, might translate as in Mixteco: We give thanks to God that the sun appeared!

Alta Mixteca (Oaxaca)

Buenos días.	Taondí.	*Sí.*	Bahani; Baha
Buenas tardes.	Taoñini.		(bueno).
Buenas noches.	Taongua.	*No.*	Ñatuna (addressing
Por favor.	Sahani ja mani-ini.		women).
Gracias.	Ngutahabisa naa		Ñatutaa (addressing
	(feminine).		men).
	Ngutahabisa taa	*Adiós.*	Na cahao.
	(masculine).		

Zapoteco

Buenos días.	Sausuhel.	*Por favor.*	Ben guclen.
Buenas tardes.	Sausuhel.	*Gracias.*	Ursh clentgu.
Buenas noches.	Ursh clente chu	*Sí.*	Ya'gue.
	(arrival).	*No.*	Bi.
	Arture (departure).	*Adiós.*	Na ye llagchu.

Purépecha (Tarascan)

Buenos días.	Natz eranzk.	*Gracias.*	Iosi meiamu.
Buenas tardes.	Na chusk.	*Sí.*	Jo.
Buenas noches.	Na chirikua.	*No.*	No.
Por favor.	Char ses jimbo.	*Adiós.*	Nipa.

Maya

Buenos días.	Malo' kin anactech.	*Por favor.*	Anteni'.
	(The apostrophe	*Gracias.*	Dios bótic.
	means a high	*Sí.*	Jelé.
	intonation.)	*No.*	Ma'.
Buenas tardes.	Malo' kin anactech.	*Adiós.*	Jey lie'.
Buenas noches.	Malo' aka' anactech.		

Tarahumara (Lower)

Buenos(as) días,		*Sí.*	Ju.
tardes, noches.	Cuira or cuiraba.	*No.*	Table.
Por favor.	Pee'anachga.	*Adiós.*	Adisiba.
Gracias.	Chelierva.		

Indian Languages (Cont'd)

Nahuatl (from the sierra Huasteca)

Buenos(as) dias, tardes.	Tlaneski.	*Gracias.*	Tlaskamati.
		Sí.	Kena.
Buenas noches.	Youaltij.	*No.*	Amo.
Por favor.	Xinech chiuili se favor.	*Adiós.*	Asta mostla.

Important Abbreviations

Av.	*Avenida*	Avenue
C.	*Calle*	Street
Calz.	*Calzada*	Boulevard
CNEP	National Commission to Eradicate Malaria	
DDT	Transit Department (traffic cops)	
D.F.	*Distrito Federal*	Federal District
E., Ote.	*Este*	East
EUM	*Estados Unidos Mexicanos*	
Gral.	*General*	General
EE. UU. or E.U.A.	*Estados Unidos de America*	U.S.A.
Hnos.	*Hermanos*	Brothers
Ing.	*Ingeniero*	Engineer
INI	National Indian Institute	
KM.	*Kilómetro*	Kilometer
Kg.	*Kilogramo*	Kilogram
Kph.	Kilometers per hour	
Lic.	*Licenciado*	Lawyer, Degree holder
MN	*Moneda Nacional*	Mexican Currency (pesos)
N, Nte.	*Norte*	North
NO	*Noroeste*	Northwest
No.	*Número*	Number
NE	*Noreste*	Northeast
O., Pte.	*Oeste, Poniente*	West
Ote., E.	*Oriente*	East
P.B.	*Piso Bajo*	Main Floor
Pte.	*Poniente*	West
S.	*Sur*	South
SE	*Sureste*	Southeast
SO	*Suroeste*	Southwest
SAG	Department of Agriculture and Livestock	
s.n.m.	*sobre nivel del mar*	above sea level
Sr., Sra., Srta.	*Señor, Señora, Señorita*	Sir, Madam, Miss
SRH	Department of Water Resources	

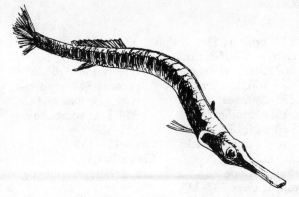

Index

Please send me _____ copies of Carl's great Camping Book at $10.00 /copy.

I'd like _____ set(s) of The People's Guide To Camping in Mexico and the People's Guide to Mexico for the discount price of $18.00/set.

I've enclosed $ _____ for _____ copies of the People's Guide To Camping in Mexico or $ _____ for _____ set(s) of both Carl's books, plus $1.25 postage for the first book and $.50 for each additional book.

NAME _____

ADDRESS _____

_____ ZIP _____

Send your order with a check or money order to:
John Muir Publications • P.O. Box 613-B • Santa Fe, NM 87501

Complete your set of Carl Franz's guides to Mexico — and save a buck using the order form below . . .

THE PEOPLE'S GUIDE TO MEXICO

Harper's Magazine called it "The best guidebook to adventure in the whole world . . . outrageous."

I'd like to save a buck so send me _____ copies of *The People's Guide To Mexico* (at $8.00 each with this coupon ONLY), plus $1.25 postage and handling for the first copy and $.50 for each additional copy.

NAME _____

ADDRESS _____

_____ ZIP _____

Send your order with a check or money order to:
John Muir Publications • P.O. Box 613-B • Santa Fe, NM 87501

More useful

& entertaining books

from

John Muir Publications

How to Keep Your Volkswagen Alive by John Muir (11.00)

Como Mantener Tu Volkswagen Vivo by John Muir (9.00)

Es Lebe Mein Volkswagen by John Muir (10.00)

Cassette of VW Sounds for the Compleat Idiot
narrated by John Muir (6.50)

How to Keep Your VW Rabbit Alive
by Richard Sealey (13.00)

The People's Guide to Mexico (Revised) by Carl Franz (9.00)

A Guide to Midwifery: Heart and Hands
by Elizabeth Davis (9.00)

The Food and Heat Producing Solar Greenhouse (Revised)
by Bill Yanda and Rick Fisher (9.00)

Training to Run the Perfect Marathon
by Michael Schreiber (7.50)

The Velvet Monkeywrench by John Muir (6.00)

Gardening for People by Douglas Moon (6.00)

Self Defense for Gentle People by Rolf Cahn (6.00)

La Vida de Dos Novios by Martin Vinaver (4.00)

Hammocks! The real thing! All cotton Matrimonial hammocks from the Yucatan. Sixteen feet long, these hammocks weigh 4 1/2 to 5 1/2 pounds and stretch out to 10
to 16 feet wide. (55.00)

Postage: send $1.25 for the first book and $.50 for each
additional book; $2.50 for hammocks.

John Muir Publications
P.O. Box 613
Santa Fe, NM 87501